Uruguay

the Bradt Travel Guide

Tim Burford

edition
2

www.bradtguides.com

Bradt Travel Guides Ltd, UK
The Globe Pequot Press Inc, USA

Relax at the Termas de Daymán – Uruguay's largest hot baths
page 330

San Javier is an ideal base for bird-watching trips along the Río Uruguay
page 314

Visit Fray Bentos and discover the history of the town's former meat-packing plant
page 304

Ride with gauchos & spend time on a traditional estancia like La Sirena
page 303

Take a tour of the Canelones department wineries
page 149

ARGENTINA

Embalse de Salto Grande

Cuchilla del Belén

Cuchilla del Daymán

Cuchilla San José

Cuchilla de Haedo

Queguay Grande

Cuchilla San Salvador

Embalse de Rincón del Bonete

Río de la Plata

ARGENTINA

Barra do Quarai
Monte Caseros
Bella Unión
Quaraí
R30
Artigas
Santana Livrame
Rivera
R4
R30
Tranqueras
R5
Concordia
Salto
Termas de Daymán
Daymán
R31
Minas d Corrale
R3
Tacuarembó
R26
Ansi
R26
R26
R5
Colón
Paysandú
R90
Guichón
San Gregorio de Polanco
San Javier
Young
R3
Gualeguaychú
Nuevo Berlín
Negro
Villa del Carmen
R6
Fray Bentos
La Sirena
R14
Mercedes
R5
Sarandí del Yi
R14
Soriano
Durazno
Dolores
R2
Rodó
Trinidad
R14
R21
R23
Cardona
R5
R7
Nueva Palmira
R3
Carmelo
R21
Florida
R7
Tigre
Colonia
San José
R11
Santa Lucía
Canelones
R8
BUENOS AIRES
R1
Las Piedras
Pando
Solís Mata
R1
Atlántida
MONTEVIDEO
Piriápe
Uruguay
Cuaró

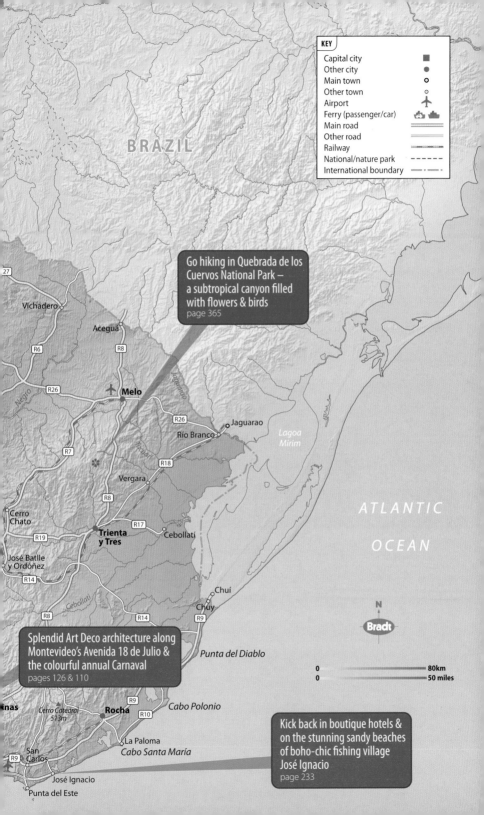

KEY
Capital city ■
Other city ●
Main town ○
Other town ○
Airport ✈
Ferry (passenger/car) 🚢 🛳
Main road
Other road
Railway
National/nature park
International boundary

BRAZIL

Go hiking in Quebrada de los Cuervos National Park – a subtropical canyon filled with flowers & birds
page 365

Vichadero

Aceguá

Melo

Jaguarao

Río Branco

Lagoa Mirim

Vergara

Cerro Chato

Trienta y Tres

Cebollatí

José Batlle y Ordóñez

Cebollatí

ATLANTIC

OCEAN

Chuí
Chuy

Splendid Art Deco architecture along Montevideo's Avenida 18 de Julio & the colourful annual Carnaval
pages 126 & 110

Punta del Diablo

N

Bradt

0   80km
0   50 miles

nas

Cerro Catedral 513m

Rochá

Cabo Polonio

Kick back in boutique hotels & on the stunning sandy beaches of boho-chic fishing village José Ignacio
page 233

San Carlos

La Paloma

Cabo Santa María

José Ignacio

Punta del Este

Uruguay
Don't
miss...

Montevideo
Grand buildings (like
the Palacio Legislativo,
pictured here), a friendly
atmosphere, 13km of
beaches and an 80-day
carnaval are just some
of the reasons to visit
Uruguay's laid-back capital
(SS) pages 79–142

Ride with *gauchos*
Visit a traditional *estancia* to
experience old-style hospitality
and even help round up cattle (JB)
page 42

Visit Uruguay's wineries

Tour the vineyards and cavernous cellars of the Canelones wineries (such as the historic Bodega Santa Rosa, pictured here — pages 151–2) and sample some of the finest South American wine (BSR) pages 149–66

Beaches

From the fashionable resorts of Punta del Este (pages 200–17) and José Ignacio (pages 233–8), to the isolation and tranquillity of Cabo Polonio (pictured here; pages 260–3), Uruguay is home to some of the best beaches on the continent (MTSU)

Fray Bentos

With its fascinating heritage museum, El Anglo meat-packing factory is well worth a visit to learn more about the country's industrial past (JB/ Alamy) pages 304–11

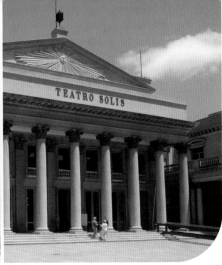

Uruguay in colour

above left   Old-fashioned façades line the streets of Montevideo's Ciudad Vieja (MM) pages 121–25

above right   Illustrating the city's relationship with the Belle Époque style, the Teatro Solis is one of Montevideo's most impressive landmarks (SS) page 125

left   Montevideo's most recognisable landmark, the Palacio Salvo was built on the site of Uruguay's very first tango performance (S/P) page 126

below   José Belloni's sculpture, *La Diligencia* (*The Stagecoach*), can be viewed in Parque del Prado (S/I) page 131

above   Hidden behind the old town lies one of South America's finest natural harbours, which was once the main port of the Río de la Plata (JB) page 79

right   The Edifico Pablo Ferrando is just one example of the many beautiful Art Nouveau buildings found across the capital (SS) page 125

below left   A chef grills different meats on his traditional *parrilla* inside the Mercado del Puerto (HL/Corbis) page 121

below right   A musician entertains those around him on a street in Montevideo (JB)

above left and left   The father of independent Uruguay, José Artigas is a remembered figure across the country – from wall art in Carmelo, to the equine statue above his mausoleum in Montevideo (SS) pages 16–17

above right   With its 18th-century cobbles, the Calle de los Suspiros in Colonia is the most photographed street in Uruguay (S/AT) page 284

below   Named after the saint's day on which its construction began, the Fortaleza Santa Teresa in Rocha has been captured by both the Spanish and Brazilians in its lifetime, showing that the country has always had cause to defend itself (MTSU) page 269

AUTHOR

Tim Burford studied languages at Oxford University. In 1991, after a brief career as a publisher, he began writing for Bradt, first covering hiking in eastern-central Europe and then backpacking and ecotourism in Latin America. He has now written nine books for Bradt and also leads hiking trips in Europe's mountains. He lives in Cambridge, loves train travel in Europe and flies only across oceans and as rarely as possible.

AUTHOR'S STORY

I knew before coming to Uruguay that its name meant 'River of Birds', but I had no idea how apt a name this was – except that maybe it should be 'Country of Birds'. I knew that there was a lot of empty pampas in Uruguay, inhabited by plenty of cattle and not many people, but I had no idea what this would mean in terms of wildlife, or that there were extensive wetlands along the Río Uruguay (the country's western border) and that the Atlantic coast is home to an amazing variety of birds.

I also found that the empty countryside, and the small towns hidden in it, had its own very special charm, due to the sense of space in the land and the sense of 'time to spare' in the people – nothing is rushed. Even the capital, Montevideo, is laidback; in fact, many people pop over to rest between wild weekends in Buenos Aires, the Argentine capital.

Compared with the hordes now visiting Argentina, very few tourists reach Uruguay, especially the interior, where there's still a real sense of being off the beaten track.

FEEDBACK REQUEST AND UPDATES WEBSITE

At Bradt Travel Guides we're aware that guidebooks start to go out of date on the day they're published – and that you, our readers, are out there in the field doing research of your own. You'll find out before us when a fine new family-run hotel opens or a favourite restaurant changes hands and goes downhill. So why not write and tell us about your experiences? Contact us on ☎ 01753 893444 or e info@bradtguides.com. We will forward emails to the author who may post 'one-off updates' on the Bradt website at www.bradtupdates.com/uruguay. Alternatively you can add a review of the book to www.bradtguides.com or Amazon.

Second edition published January 2014
First published 2010

Bradt Travel Guides Ltd
IDC House, The Vale, Chalfont St Peter, Bucks SL9 9RZ, England
www.bradtguides.com
Print edition published in the USA by The Globe Pequot Press Inc,
PO Box 480, Guilford, Connecticut 06437-0480

Text copyright © 2014 Tim Burford
Maps copyright © 2014 Bradt Travel Guides Ltd
Includes map data © OpenStreet Map contributors
Photographs copyright © 2014 Individual photographers (see below)
Project Managers: Anna Moores, Laura Pidgley and Claire Strange
Cover research: Pepi Bluck, Perfect Picture

ISBN: 978 1 84162 477 8 (print)
e-ISBN: 978 1 84162 779 3 (e-pub)
e-ISBN: 978 1 84162 680 2 (mobi)
British Library Cataloguing in Publication Data
A catalogue record for this book is available from the British Library

Photographers Alamy: Jack Barker/Alamy (JB/Alamy), Yaacov Dagan/Alamy (YD/Alamy); Ana Raquel S Hernandes (AH); Bodega Santa Rosa (BSR); Corbis: Holger Leue/Corbis (HL/Corbis); FLPA: Frans Lanting/FLPA (FL/FLPA), Jurgen & Christine Sohns/FLPA (J&CS/FLPA), Mike Lane/FLPA (ML/FLPA), Neil Bowman/FLPA (NB/FLPA), Robin Chittenden (RC/FLPA), Terry Whittaker/FLPA (TW/FLPA); Joerg Boethling (JB); Marco Muscarà (MM); Ministry of Tourism and Sport in Uruguay (MTSU); Shutterstock: Anibal Trejo (S/AT), Ivalin (S/I), Joel Blit (S/JB), Kobby Dagan (S/KD), photosil (S/P), Toniflap (S/T); SuperStock (SS)
Front cover Fiesta de la Patria Gaucha, Tacuarembó (YD/Alamy)
Back cover Fishing boat in boho-chic José Ignacio (SS), imposing skyline of Montevideo (SS)
Title page Candombé drummers have marched in Montevideo's *Carnaval* since 1870 (S/KD), red-breasted blackbird (RC/FLPA), traditional *maté* gourds (SS)

Maps David McCutcheon FBCart.S; colour map base by Nick Rowland FRGS

Typeset from the author's disc by Wakewing, High Wycombe
Production managed by Jellyfish Print Solutions; printed in India
Digital conversion by the Firsty Group

Acknowledgements

Thanks to Enrique Facelli and all at the Uruguayan embassy in London, Amy Ucar and all at the Ministry of Tourism in Montevideo, Matias Lasarte, Anne Greenhalgh, Chris Chandler, Adrián Stagi (Eco Tours), Ana Inés Motta (Los Caminos del Vino), Karen Vandergrift (Estancia Tierra Santa), Brian Meissner (El Diablo Tranquilo), Ricardo Hein (Apart-Hotel Bremen), Lucia and Rodney Bruce (Estancia La Sirena), Santiago (La Posada del Faro), Javier and Ximena (La Posta del Vinyet), Sandrine Pont-Nourat (Estancia Finca Piedra), Luis (Planet Montevideo Hostel), Andrea Bresso (Vida Silvestre/Posada al Sur), Melissa Gutiérrez (Retos al Sur/Posada al Sur), Agustín Carriquiry (Aves Uruguay), Juan Andrés Marichal (Bodega Marichal) and Nicolás Villagrán (Museo de la Diáspora Rusa).

For the second edition, special thanks to Daniel Traverso and Benjamin Liberoff, Adrián Stagi, John Kupiec, Tim Robertson, Alvaro and Paula Pivel, Ryan Hamilton (The Wine Experience), Fabiana Bracco (Narbona), Tom and Kelli Bardner (El Capullo), Lucie Cibulka (Caballos de Luz), Miguel and Monica (El Galope), Eduardo and Carla Santos (Una Noche Mas), Mauricio and Graciela Albacete (Destino26 Hostel), Pablo Duvós (Hotel Eldorado, Salto), Ansleigh Westfall and all at Playa Vik and Estancia Vik, Carla Bertellotti, Diego Pérez and Wilson Torres (Bodega Juanicó), Alessandro Taddei (Hostel El Nagual), Marco Guerrini (Hotel Oriental, Santa Lucía), Maria Clara Duvos (Hotel Español), Ana (Posada del Navegante, Carmelo), Carlos Marquez (Montevideo Hostel), Alfredo (Cabo Polonio), Ignacio Carrera (L'Auberge), Valentina, Amalia and Leslie (Artesana Winery), Fabiana Bracco (Finca Narbona), Laura Jauregui (Brisas de La Pedrera), Gustavo Magariños and all at Wines of Uruguay, Cecilia (Unplugged Hostels), Maria Silvia Bianchi (Viñedos Irurtia), Diego Vigano (Campotinto) and Cristina Santoto (Bodega Bouza).

Thank you also to those who took the time to write in with useful feedback on the first edition, namely Carlos Gaviola, Ron Korevaar, Michelle Switzer, Bart Hulsbosch and Andreas Speck.

DEDICATION

To Katy – you inspire me.

Contents

Introduction   VI

PART ONE   GENERAL INFORMATION   1

Chapter 1   **Background Information**   3
Geography 3, Climate 5, Natural history 5, Conservation 12,
History 12, Government and politics 22, Economy 23,
People 25, Language 26, Religion 26, Culture 26

Chapter 2   **Practical Information**   45
When to visit 45, Highlights 45, Suggested itineraries 46,
Tour operators 46, Red tape 48, Embassies 48, Getting
there and away 51, Health 56, Safety 59, What to take 61,
Maps 61, Money and budgeting 61, Getting around 63,
Accommodation 66, Eating and drinking 67, Public
holidays and festivals 71, Shopping 72, Opening
hours 73, Media and communications 73, Cultural and
business etiquette 75, Buying a property and moving to
Uruguay 75, Travelling positively 76

PART TWO   THE GUIDE   77

Chapter 3   **Montevideo**   79
History 79, Climate 83, Getting there and away 83, Getting
around 88, Orientation 91, Tourist information 92,
Where to stay 93, Where to eat and drink 100,
Nightlife 108, Entertainment 112, Shopping 115, Sport
and activities 118, Other practicalities 118, City tour 121,
Museums 134

Chapter 4   **Southern Uruguay**   143
Canelones department: West 143, Wineries of Uruguay 149,
Florida department 166, San José department 170,
Canelones department: East 176, Lavalleja department 180

Chapter 5   **Eastern Uruguay**   189
Maldonado department 189, Rocha department 242

Chapter 6	**Western Uruguay**	**275**
	Colonia department 275, Soriano department 296, Río Negro department 304, Paysandú department 315, Salto department 323	

Chapter 7	**The Interior**	**333**
	Artigas department 333, Rivera department 341, Tacuarembó department 346, Durazno department 354, Flores department 359, Treinta y Tres department 362, Cerro Largo department 367	

Appendix 1	**Language**	**375**
Appendix 2	**Further Information**	**378**

Index		**382**

LIST OF MAPS

Artigas	338	Montevideo Buceo	109
Atlántida	178	Montevideo city centre	94–5
Canelones	146	Montevideo Ciudad Vieja	
Carmelo	291	& Centro	122
Colonia Barrio Histórico	286	Montevideo overview	78
Colonia New Town	278	Paysandú	318
Durazno	355	Piriápolis	192
Eastern Uruguay	190–1	Punta del Diablo	266
Florida	168	Punta del Este	206–7
Florida department	167	Rivera	343
Fray Bentos	307	Rocha	247
Interior, The	334–5	Salto	326
José Ignacio	235	San José	172
La Barra	227	Santa Lucía	148
La Paloma	250	Southern Uruguay	144
La Pedrera	254	Tacuarembó	347
Lavalleja department	181	Treinta y Tres	363
Maldonado	222	Trinidad	360
Melo	368	Uruguay colour section ii–iii	
Mercedes	301	Western Uruguay	274
Minas	183		

NOTE ABOUT MAPS

Some maps use grid lines to allow easy location of sites. Map grid references are listed in square brackets after listings in the text, with page number followed by grid number, eg: [94 C3]. Please note, in order to keep the maps legible, not all sites have been pinpointed on the maps. However, grid references have been nonetheless supplied to highlight their general location.

Introduction

They won the first soccer World Cup; there are places called Fray Bentos and 33; and there are a lot more cattle than people. That's all most people know of Uruguay. Others may have seen a film about the sinking of the *Graf Spee*.

However, it has far more to offer the visitor, from the finest beaches and resorts in the region to traditional *estancias* (ranches) where you can ride with the gauchos towards the endless horizons, wetlands and lagoons with a fantastic array of birdlife and, in Montevideo, a capital that is fascinating yet laidback, with a totally different vibe from Buenos Aires, just across the water.

Interestingly, Uruguay has a similar relationship to Argentina (and Brazil too) as Canada has to the United States, Ireland to the United Kingdom, or Belgium to France – a permanent sense of being overshadowed by a larger, louder neighbour, while feeling deep inside that they are in fact the smarter, wittier, more creative ones. Indeed, the Uruguayan people are less party-loving than their neighbours in Argentina and Brazil, but more reliable and genuine, with a deep and innate sense of hospitality that delights all who take the time to get to know them. Having said that, come high summer resorts such as Punta del Este are packed with Argentines who ensure non-stop partying for a couple of months at least. And let's not forget the world's longest *carnaval* season, mainly in Montevideo but in other towns too, when Uruguayans show that they really can let their hair down.

Known in full as the República Oriental del Uruguay (the Oriental Republic of Uruguay), the country takes its name from the River Uruguay, which probably derives from the Guaraní for 'River of Birds'. The term 'Oriental' comes from 'Banda Oriental' (Eastern Shore), the name of the Spanish colonial province that eventually achieved independence from Argentina, its neighbour on the western shore of the Río Uruguay. It is not, as some might think, due to a mistaken notion among early explorers that Uruguay was in the Orient, close to China, Japan or India.

Uruguay continues to be an independent country, culturally distinct from its neighbours, and it is well worth proper exploration rather than a flying visit, or a week spent solely on the – admittedly superb – beaches.

Part One

GENERAL INFORMATION

Location South America – on the northeastern shore of the Río de la Plata (River Plate), between Brazil, Argentina and the Atlantic Ocean. Uruguay shares borders with Brazil to the north (1,068km) and Argentina to the west (580km).

Size 176,215km² (68,037 square miles)

Climate Warm-temperate

Time Uruguay is three hours behind UTC (GMT –3), thus four hours behind France and Germany, two hours ahead of Washington and New York and five hours ahead of California. Daylight Saving Time is generally in effect from the first Sunday of October until the second Sunday in March.

Electricity 220V, 50Hz. Plugs have either two European-style round pins (sometimes with an earth pin between them) or three (sometimes two) angled flat pins

International telephone code +598

Status Presidential republic

Currency Peso (UYU)

Population 3,397,514 (2013 estimate)

Population growth per year 0.466% (2009 estimate)

Life expectancy at birth 76.41 years (male 73.27, female 79.99; 2012 estimate)

Economy Dominated by agriculture, forestry and tourism. GDP US$49.7 billion at the official exchange rate, or US$53.55 billion at purchasing power parity, and US$15,800 per capita (2012).

Capital Montevideo (population 1.31m (2011))

Main cities Punta del Este, Colonia, Paysandú, Salto

Language Spanish (Español or Castellano)

Religion Roman Catholic 56% (nominally), Protestant 11%, Jewish 0.3%, atheist or agnostic 17%, other 16%

Flag The *pabellón nacional* (national flag) bears five horizontal white stripes alternating with four blue stripes, with a white square in the upper hoist corner with a yellow sun bearing a human face. The flag of Artigas (a white stripe between two blue stripes, with a diagonal red stripe, used mainly by the military) and the flag of the Treinta y Tres Orientales (a white stripe bearing the words 'Libertad o Muerte' – Liberty or Death – between a blue stripe and a red stripe) are also official national symbols.

Public holidays 1 January (New Year's Day), 6 January (Epiphany; Día de los Reyes), February/March (Carnaval; the two days before Ash Wednesday), February/March (five days for Holy Week; dates vary from year to year), 19 April (Day of the Landing of the 33 Orientales), 1 May (Labour Day), 18 May (Battle of Las Piedras), 19 June (Birthday of Artigas; also marking the end of the dictatorship), 18 July (Constitution Day), 25 August (Independence Day), 12 October (Columbus Day; Dia de la Raza), 2 November (All Saints), 25 December (Christmas)

1

Background Information

A small country sandwiched between two large and powerful ones, Uruguay can seem like Luxembourg or Canada, dominated by – and defined in contrast to – its neighbours. Where Argentina and Brazil are large and boisterous, Uruguay is small and quiet; where they have crazy drivers and less than wholly clean politicians, Uruguay has smoothly flowing traffic and boring technocrats. Nevertheless, Uruguay needs its neighbours, who take most of its exports and supply bodies to lie on its fantastic beaches and keep its tourism industry busy.

With near-total literacy and minimal corruption, Uruguay ranks with Chile as one of the two most peaceful countries in Latin America (according to the Global Peace Index), and in 2008 Montevideo was named by the Economist Intelligence Unit as the most liveable city in Latin America (it's now rated third).

GEOGRAPHY

With an area of 176,215km² (68,037 square miles), Uruguay is about 35% larger than England, marginally smaller than Oklahoma and barely half the size of Buenos Aires province. It's the second-smallest country in South America, after Suriname. Its population is much the same as Oklahoma's too. Its coastline (east of Punta del Este) is 220km long, with 450km of estuary shore to the west of Punta del Este; two-thirds of the population, and of the economy, is along these shores.

The most populated parts of Uruguay are the relatively small level areas along the Atlantic Ocean, the Río de la Plata (River Plate) and the Río Uruguay; the interior of the country is a rolling peneplain (an area almost levelled by erosion) intersected by rivers and by some ranges of hills, mainly in the southeast of the country. The highest and most rugged area of the country is the Cuchilla Grande (literally 'Big Knife'), which contains Uruguay's highest peak, Cerro Catedral (Cathedral Peak, 513.7m), although this does not rise much above the remarkable uniform ridges around it. Indeed, it was only in 1973 that it was found to be higher than the Sierra de las Ánimas (see page 199).

Geologically, Uruguay consists of a basement of Precambrian crystalline rocks (more than 542 million years old) that emerges in the centre-south of the country and is elsewhere covered by younger sediments and volcanic rocks. These consist of Early Jurassic basalts (200–176 million years old) in the northwest of the country and Permian sediments (290–251 million years old) in the north-centre, the two separated by the Piriápolis Fraile Muerto fracture zone that runs north–south from Brazil into Argentina. Relatively small areas of Tertiary and Cretaceous sediments (145–1.8 million years old) cover the southern half of the Río Uruguay littoral, together with Cenozoic sands (less than 65 million years old) along the coast.

Until the break-up of the Gondwanan super-continent and the opening of the South Atlantic Ocean (130–110 million years ago), present-day Uruguay abutted what is now Namibia; as Namibia and Brazil are two of the world's major sources of diamonds, there's a possibility that Uruguay also holds large reserves of diamonds, and prospecting is now beginning. The crystalline base may also contain silver, nickel, copper, lead, zinc and other metals; there is already limited gold-mining in Rivera department, and exports of amethysts from Artigas department are worth US$4 million per annum.

The most fertile land is in the west, along the Río Uruguay in the departments of Colonia and Soriano; the rest of the country is largely used for raising livestock (cattle above all), with some rice-growing in the east. The littoral of the Río Uruguay is low-lying, with a considerable risk of flooding. The northern half of the country is stonier and less productive, other than of large birds of prey. In the southeast, the Atlantic coastal plain is sandy, with marshy areas surrounding shallow lagoons.

In socio-geographical terms, the country can be divided into four regions (used as the basis for the chapter divisions of this book's *Guide* section): Montevideo and its hinterland; the coast to the east of the capital; the littoral (of the Río de la Plata and Río Uruguay) to the west; and the interior, by far the largest in size.

Uruguay has two research bases in Antarctica, one on the Antarctic Peninsula and one nearby on Isla Rey Jorge (King George Island), but has no territorial claim there.

There's no shortage of water, used both for farming and for hydro-electric power generation; to the south and west the country is bordered by the Río de la Plata and the Río Uruguay, while the Río Negro, flowing from east to west, almost cuts the country in half; in the centre of the country it has been dammed to form the Embalse del Río Negro, the largest artificial lake in South America. In addition, the **Guaraní Aquifer** is a huge underground reservoir that lies below Uruguay, Paraguay and parts of Brazil and Argentina, containing fresh water that's around 20,000 years old and is now seen as one of the world's most valuable water resources for the future.

About 90% of the country's area is suitable for growing crops, although only 12% is used in this way. Pasture covers 77% of the country, and forest and woods cover 6%, of which 3½% is natural and the rest planted, mainly with eucalyptus to feed pulp mills. The area planted with trees is growing fast and may soon cover 1.5 million hectares (9% of the country), quite a transformation from 0.3 million hectares in 1987.

Uruguay is heavily urbanised and rural areas are very lightly populated (although there are over ten million cows). More than 90% of the population lives in towns and cities, 43% of them in Montevideo (almost 1.7 million or 47% in the greater Montevideo area). Similarly, the chief town of each department is usually home to at least half its population. The average population density is 20 persons per km^2 (52 per square mile).

The country is named after the Río Uruguay, rather than the other way round. The name, derived from the Guaraní language, means roughly 'river of birds' – still a very apt description. The poet Juan Zorrilla de San Martín came up with a more colourful but less accurate translation, 'the river of painted birds'. The full official name of the country is República Oriental del Uruguay (Oriental Republic of Uruguay), a consequence of its early identity as the Spanish colony to the east of the Río Uruguay; thus Uruguayans are known as *Orientales*, despite not being in the least Asian. It's worth noting that the Río de la Plata, which people tend to assume flows from west to east, actually flows to the southeast, so much so that Montevideo lies to the south of Buenos Aires, and is in fact the southernmost capital city of South America.

CLIMATE

Uruguay has a warm-temperate (or subtropical) climate – in fact it's the only South American country to be wholly within the temperate zone. The sun shines for most of the year and temperatures hardly ever drop below freezing point. Nevertheless, the weather can be unstable, owing to the lack of hills to act as barriers, and it can be windy, especially in winter and spring, with storms blowing up on the Plata estuary. In winter, a warm spell is liable to be ended by the *pampero*, a chilly wind that can howl in from the southwest, while the warmer *sudestada* brings rain from the southeast when a high-pressure system south of Buenos Aires combines with low pressure over northeastern Argentina. In summer, ocean breezes can bring welcome relief on hot days, while winds from the north only bring heat and humidity.

The seasons are clearly defined, but without great extremes of heat or cold. Spring is usually cool, damp and breezy; summer is hot, autumn is milder, and winter is relatively chilly and wet. The northwest of Uruguay, however, being further from the sea and the River Plate, is hotter in summer and drier and warmer in winter, but it does get more rain than the rest of the country.

Average temperatures range from 12°C in winter (June–September) to 25°C in summer (December–March). Rainfall (1m per annum) is evenly distributed year-round, although the wettest months are July and August, when cold fronts bring grey, drizzly weather; in summer thunderstorms are common (tornados are possible but very rare). Droughts can occur in summer and are likely to become more common with global climate change, even though average rainfall may be increasing – Uruguay is becoming more tropical, with species already extending their range southwards from Brazil. A drought in 2008–09 cost the country US$500–900 million as a result of lost agricultural production and of oil imports needed to replace normally plentiful hydro-electricity. There was another drought in 2011–12, but 2012–13 was very wet, and then very hot – in February 2013 the country recorded summer demand for both electricity and water. However, natural gas deposits have recently been located offshore, and by 2015 wind power should cover 25% of demand.

A 2008 report by Maplecroft (*www.maplecroft.com*) showed that Uruguay was the ninth-best-placed country to adapt to climate change, owing to its combination of geography, low population density, agricultural capacity, education level and infrastructure provision. Increased rainfall will bring more flooding, but Uruguay should cope reasonably well.

NATURAL HISTORY

FLORA While not the flat pampas of popular imagination, most of Uruguay is nevertheless grassland, and remarkably unforested – despite plentiful water resources and seemingly suitable sheltered locations, natural forest covers only 3½% of the country's area. About 3% more has been planted with trees, most noticeably eucalyptus in the west of the country to feed pulp mills, but also pine, especially around Rivera. In addition large areas along the coasts were planted with pines around a century ago to control the sand dunes and make the area fit for development.

The plantations are not quite monocultures but there aren't many other plant species there, and parakeets and pigeons are more or less the only birds that choose to nest in eucalyptus. Eucalyptus also causes neighbouring farmland to dry out. However, the forestry industry has to be environmentally certified, which usually involves setting up nature reserves (where the first step is to exclude cattle). The area planted with soya is also growing fast, which likewise leads to a drop in biodiversity, with no food available for native birds.

In fact, conservationists are now realising that *pastizales* (undeveloped grasslands) are the main problem area for bird conservation – cattle ranching has become much more intensive in the last five years, as beef prices were rising fast (until the current global crisis). Over-grazing and use of fertiliser has led to a loss of native grasses (and thus of native birds), while the area planted with introduced grass species grew by 32% in the 1980s alone. In particular there's no winter feed for native bird species so conservation projects are replanting native grasses such as *Bromus auleticus*.

The largest natural area of Uruguay is tall-grass savanna, originally covered with around 400 species of grasses (notably *Andropogon, Bromus, Paspallum* and *Stipa* spp), and interrupted by marshy areas (*humedales*) and watercourses lined with gallery forest (*monte ribereño*), the most common form of woodland, dominated by native willow (*sauce criollo; Salix humboldtiana*) and viraró (*Ruprechtia salicifolia*), as well as *ceibo* (coral tree; *Erythrina crista-galli*), the bright red bloom of which is the national flower.

There are three other main groups of woodland types. First, **bosque parque** (park woodland), *algarrobal* (named after the algarrobo, misnamed the carob tree) and *bosque espinoso del litoral* (spiney coastal woodland), mainly in the west of the country and also in parts of Treinta y Tres and Cerro Largo departments. These range from open land with well-separated trees with plenty of room for grazing cattle, to denser woodland in the transition zones with *espinal* and *chaco* (in Argentina and Brazil). These are mainly composed of deciduous spiny trees such as *algarrobo* (*Prosopis nigra*), ñandubay (*P. affinis*), espinillo (*Acacia caven*), cina-cina (*Parkinsonia aculeata*), quebracho blanco (*Aspidosperma quebracho-blanco*) and chañar (*Geoffroea decorticans*) as well as palms such as *palma caranday* (*Trithrinax campestris*).

Second, **bosque serrano** (mountain woodland), made up of shorter shrubby trees such as coronilla (*Scutia buxifolia*), aruera (*Lithraea brasiliensis*), tala (*Celtis tala, C. spinosa*) and arazá (*Psidium cattleyanum, P. littorale*) is found mainly in the hills of southern and eastern Uruguay. Related to this is *monte de quebrada* (ravine forest), specific to the moist gorges of the north, and dominated by the very spiky *espina de la cruz* (*Colletia paradoxa*), with coronilla, canelon (*Myrsine lactevirens*) and the holly-like *congorosa* (*Maytenus ilicifolius*) as well. Lastly, the tail-end of the **mata Atlántica** (Atlantic rainforest) of southeastern Brazil (the most biodiverse in the world, with perhaps 25,000 plant species, but now almost wiped out) sneaks across the border in the extreme northeast of Uruguay.

There's also palm savanna, in the southeast and in valleys – grassland dotted with native butia palms, mainly *pindo* (*Butia capitata*), mostly in Maldonado, and *yatay* (*B. yatay*) in the wetter lowlands of Rocha and the northwest. You'll also see introduced canary palms (*Phoenix canariensis*) and tall *Washingtonia* palms along roads and in public spaces. The area of palm savanna is shrinking, a result of over-grazing, with young shoots being eaten by cattle.

Uruguay's *monte nativo* (native woodland) is all very low; any tall trees are exotics. The quintessential exotic tree is eucalyptus, first planted in Uruguay by Antonio Lussich (see page 201) in about 1896, to stabilise the sand dunes of Maldonado department (with pines and acacias); it was then planted nationwide for shade and timber, and more recently to feed pulp mills for the paper industry (see page 308). European poplars (*alamo; Populus alba*) are common around farms.

The national tree is the **arbol de Artigas** or ibirá-pitá (*Peltophorum dubium*), a large tree up to 25m in height, that grows in gallery forest in northern Uruguay and has also been widely planted along the streets of Montevideo; however, it should perhaps be the iconic but rare *ombú* (*Phytolacca dioica*), an evergreen up to 18m in height often found growing in a ring around where the parent tree used to be. Its soft wood can be cut with a knife but the sap is poisonous (and the leaves can be used to make a laxative tea), so that cattle and insects leave it alone. Large groups of ombú are found in only two places in Uruguay, by the Laguna de Castillos in Rocha and in the Cerro Arequita in Lavalleja.

FAUNA

Mammals It has to be said that native mammals are not exactly thick on the ground – sometimes it seems as if the European boar (*Sus scrofa*) and hare (*Lepus europaeus*) are the most common animals, together with the introduced axis deer (*Axis axis*) and fallow deer (*Dama dama*). However, you may see skunks (*Conepatus chinga*) and the weasel-like lesser grisón (*Galictis cuja*).

Deer The **marsh deer** (*Blastocerus dichotomus*), the largest South American deer, is probably extinct in Uruguay, although it survives to the north. Thus the principal surviving large mammals are the *guazuvirá* or **grey brocket deer** (*Mazama gouazoubira*), a small deer found over much of South America, and the *venado de campo* or **pampas deer** (*Ozotoceros bezoarticus*), which survives in two isolated groups, of 100–200 in the Sierra de Ajos (Rocha) and 1,000–1,300 near Arerunguá (Salto), as well as in Argentina; although protected, it is still hunted, as well as being accused of carrying the cattle disease brucellosis. Darwin recorded it as being tame, inquisitive, 'exceedingly abundant' and so indescribably foul-smelling that 'several times whilst skinning the specimen … I was almost overcome by nausea'.

Foxes There are two reasonably common species of fox, the *zorro de campo* or **pampas fox** (*Pseudalopex gymnocercus*) and the *zorro de monte* or **crab-eating fox** (*Cerdocyon thous*), both at the southern end of their range; the crab-eating fox is found more in wooded areas while the pampas fox more in grassland. There's also the *mano pelada* or **crab-eating raccoon** (*Procyon cancrivorus*), which, like the crab-eating fox, is an omnivore that happens to live in humid areas. The *aguaré guazú* or **maned wolf** (*Chrysocyon brachyurus*), a long-legged fox, was thought to be extinct in Uruguay, but in 2007 one specimen was shot near the Brazilian border in Cerro Largo.

Cats With the jaguar and puma no longer found in Uruguay, the largest cat is the **margay** (*Leopardus wiedii*), which weighs just 7kg but is still larger than the *gato montés* or **Geoffrey's cat** (*Oncifelis geoffroyi*) at 5kg or the *gato pajero* or *gato de pajonal* **pampas cat** (*Lynchailurus braccatus*) at 4kg, much the same as a domestic cat. The margay is the most arboreal of all the cats, while the others' habits are largely unknown but largely terrestrial and nocturnal.

Armadillos The *tatú* or **nine-banded armadillo** (*Dasypus novemcinctus*) is the same species found over much of the southeastern United States; it's not rare and is sometimes hunted and eaten. There's also the similar *mulita* or **southern long-nosed armadillo** (*D. hybridus*), and the *tatouay* or *tatú de rabo blondo*, the **greater naked-tailed armadillo** (*Cabassous gymnurus*), which is rare, being found only in

Nine-banded armadillo

1

Cerro Largo, Lavalleja and Treinta y Tres departments. The *peludo* or **yellow/six-banded armadillo** (*Euphractus sexcinctus*) is diurnal and thus the easiest to see of Uruguay's armadillos. The giant anteater is no longer found in Uruguay, but the smaller **tamandua** or *oso hormiguero chico* (*Tamandua tetradactyla*) can be seen in Tacuarembó, Artigas and Cerro Largo departments.

Rodents Rodents are relatively common, notably the **carpincho** (better known elsewhere as the capybara; *Hydrochoeris hydrochaeris uruguayensis*), the world's largest rodent at up to 70kg in weight – although archaeologists have found the skull of a four-million-year-old rodent west of Montevideo that they calculate would have weighed around a tonne, or 'more than a car' in newspaper-speak. The world's second-largest rodent is the **paca** (*Agouti paca*), found in the small enclave of mata Atlántica that crosses the border in the northeast. Seven of the approximately 50 species of **tuco-tuco** (the exact total is still under debate) are found in Uruguay, including at least two that are found only there and in Entre Ríos province, Argentina, *Ctenomys rionegrensis* and *C. pearsoni*. These are gopher-like rodents that spend much of their life underground, largely living alone; its name comes from its throaty call. Fortunately perhaps, the *viscacha* – a rodent closely related to chinchillas – has never crossed to the east side of the Río Uruguay.

Capybara

Marsupials The *cuica de agua* or **water opossum** (*Chironectes minimus*) is a small aquatic marsupial with a waterproof pouch (otherwise found only in the presumably extinct Tasmanian tiger); it's found only in the patch of mata Atlántica that crosses the border in the northeast.

Bats There are 17 species of bats in Uruguay, most excitingly the **vampire bat** (*Desmodus rotundus*), although for some unknown reason this does not generally carry rabies in Uruguay, apart from occasional incursions from Brazil to Rivera department.

Reptiles and amphibians There are over 100 reptiles and amphibians, including around 35 species of snakes, notably the **crossed pit viper** (*crucero*, *víbora de la cruz* or *yarará*; *Bothrops alternatus*), up to 1.4m in length, regarded as the most dangerous snake in Uruguay, although its bite rarely kills (and it plays an important role in controlling rodents). A smaller relative is the *yara* (*B. pubescens*). The **cascabel** (*vibora de cascabel*; *Crotalus durissus terrificus*) is almost as long at 1.3m, and is very rare, only being found in northeastern Uruguay. The **coral snake** (*vibora de coral*; *Micrurus altirostris*) is smaller and has its fangs set at the rear of its jaw, so that it's virtually incapable of poisoning a human. There are other smaller snakes, especially on the islands of the Río Uruguay, where the **yellow anaconda** (*Eunectes notaeus*) may also be found. This is also where the **broad-snouted caiman** (*yacaré*; *Caiman latirostris*), a small alligator, thrives.

The Argentine **black-and-white tegu** (*lagarto overa*; *Tupinambis merianae*) is a large lizard, over 1m long when mature, that you're likely to see scuttling away into the undergrowth; they make good pets and can apparently even be trained to use litter trays. There are also six species of freshwater turtles (*tortuga*) as well as a variety of frogs and toads, notably **Darwin's redbelly toad** (*sapito de Darwin*;

Melanophryniscus montevidensis). Sea turtles, which you might just see on boat trips, include **loggerhead** (*tortuga boba* or *tortuga careta*; *Caretta caretta*), **leatherback** (*tortuga laúd*; *Dermochelys coriacea*) and **green** (*tortuga verde*; *Chelonia mydas*) turtles.

Fish There are over 400 species of fish in Uruguay – saltwater, freshwater and those in the Río de la Plata which can't quite make up their minds, such as sharks, sea bass (*corvina*) and rays, including the catchily named Plate skate (*Atlantoraja platana*), fanskates (*Sympterygia* spp) and sandskates (*Psammobatis*

Green sea turtles

spp). There are over 20 species of *pejerrey* (silverside or silvermelt) of several genera, including the freshwater silverside (*Odontesthes bonariensis*) and the Río Negro basin silverside (*O. humensis*). Sharks in particular, such as the **hammerhead shark** (*tiburón martillo*; *Sphyrna* spp) and the vitamin or **glass-snouted shark** (*tiburón vitamínico* or *trompa de cristal*; *Galeorhinus galeus*), come to breed in the estuary of the Plate, where the Brazil and Malvinas/Falklands currents meet rivers bearing silt from the interior of the continent, stirring up a very nutritious soup. Other sea fish that you may at least find in restaurants include the *brótola* (*Urophycis brasiliensis*) and **sea bream** (*sargo*; *Diplodus argenteus*).

In the huge rivers that feed into the Plate estuary are fish that grow even bigger than those at sea, most notably the *surubí* (*Pseudoplatystoma coruscans*), a type of catfish that is the biggest freshwater fish of Argentina and Uruguay, the related *manguruyú* (*Microglanis cottoides*) and the *dorado* (*Salminus brasiliensis*), all eagerly sought out by sport fishers in the Río Uruguay. Likewise, the **tigerfish** (*tararira*; *Hoplias malabaricus*) is a large, almost salmon-like beast in the Río Negro and Río Yí. New species of catfish (eg: *Pimelodus* and *Rineloricaria* spp) are still being identified. The *pacú* (*Piaractus mesopotamicus*) is native to the Uruguay/Paraná system but now widely used for fish-farming elsewhere in the continent. It's known by various names, including: *patí, boga, bagre, sábalo, mojarra*.

Marine mammals There are large colonies of both sea lions and fur seals on Uruguay's Atlantic coast, and you're very likely to see them, especially the sea lions that breed on the Isla de Lobos and come into the harbour of Punta del Este in search of fish scraps. **Elephant seals** (*Mirounga leonina*) can also turn up on Uruguayan beaches in winter.

Southern sea lions (*lobo común* or *lobo marino de un pelo*; *Otaria flavescens*) are seals with small, clearly visible external ears. They are much more mobile on land than true seals, being able to rotate their rear flippers sideways to propel their bodies forward. Sea lions can move quite fast in this manner: something to remember if you meet an angry bull. A fully grown southern sea lion bull is much larger and more impressive than his northern cousin, the California sea lion. This massive animal measures well over 2m long, and weighs up to half a tonne. His enormous neck is adorned with a shaggy mane, hence the name 'sea lion', which also refers to his roar. The elegant limpid-eyed females that make up his harem weigh only a quarter of his great bulk, but then they expend less energy. From the time he comes ashore in December to when he leaves in March, the bull sea lion neither eats nor sleeps for more than a few minutes at a time. Guarding his harem is a full-time job.

The black, furry pups are born in January. They are not fully weaned for six months, but the females return to the sea for feeding before this time, leaving a nursery or 'pod' of pups to gain safety in numbers. In fact they have few land predators, and the high juvenile mortality rate is largely due to the clumsiness of fighting males.

Only their golden brown fur and upturned noses distinguish **southern fur seals** (*lobo fino austral* or *lobo marino de dos pelos*; *Arctocephalus australis*) from sea lions. This luxurious coat almost led to their extinction through hunting, but now they are fully protected and their numbers are increasing. The fur seal has two layers of fur: a soft, dense undercoat, and an outer layer of coarse hair which traps bubbles of air to increase insulation. In fact, fur seals often seem to get too hot, and you will see them wave their flippers around in an attempt to cool off. Their colonies are most active in January, when you'll hardly be able to tear yourself away.

Fourteen species of whales can be seen in Uruguayan waters, of which the **sperm whale** (*cachalote*; *Physeter macrocephalus*), **pygmy sperm whale** (*cachalote pigmeo*; *Kogia breviceps*), **humpbacked whale** (*ballena yubarta*; *Megaptera novoangliae*) and **southern right whale** (*ballena franca austral*; *Eubalaena australis*) pass very close to the coast on their migrations. There are 13 species of porpoise and dolphin (including the orca and the false and pygmy killer whales), of which the easiest to spot are the **Burmeister's porpoise** (*marsopa espinosa*; *Phocoena spinipinnis*), **River Plate dolphin** (*delfín del Plata* or *franciscana*; *Pontoporia blainvillei*) and **bottlenose dolphin** (*tonina* or *delfín nariz de botella*; *Turciops truncatus*).

Birds
Uruguay is home to a huge variety of birds relative to its area, with 459 species, a quarter of the total in Brazil (whose area is 48 times larger) and 40% of those in Argentina (16 times larger). The greatest number of species (311) are found in the Bañados del Este, the wetlands along the Atlantic coast.

In some ways the most obvious bird is the **greater rhea** (*ñandú*; *Rhea americana intermedia*), the ostrich-like bird that's easily visible in fields, especially in northern Uruguay; globally it's threatened by intensive farming, but numbers in Uruguay are holding up well enough. Also in pastureland you'll see the **spotted tinamou** (*Nothura maculosa*), popularly known as *perdiz* or partridge; despite hunting it's very common and easily spotted, running away ahead of you. The *hornero* or **ovenbird** (*Furnarius rufus rufus*) is emblematic, because of the rounded mud nests it places on fence-posts and trees (hence its name); it's pretty common, being very happy living close to humans. Endangered birds found in the savanna grasslands include the **yellow cardinal** (*cardenal amarillo*; *Gubernatrix cristata*), **saffron-cowled blackbird** (*dragón*; *Xanthopsar flavus*) and **bearded tachuri** (*Polystictus pectoralis*). The **firewood-gatherer** (*espinero común*; *Anumbius annumbi*) is a relative of the ovenbird, found in grassland (dry or wet), but rather than a mud nest it builds one of twigs, a smaller version of the monk parakeet's (see page 12).

There are nine woodpeckers and flickers, mostly of course in woodland, but the most common in fact feeds on open grassland. This is the **yellowy-green field flicker** (*carpintero de campo*; *Colaptes campestris*) – a flicker being a woodpecker that doesn't peck wood. There are nine species of hummingbirds (in summer).

You'll see large numbers of **turkey vultures** (*buitre cabo roja*; *Cathartes aura*) circling overhead; the **Andean black vulture** (*buitre de cabeza negra*; *Coragyps atratus foetens*) was more common but has been overtaken in recent decades. A third species, the **yellow-headed vulture** (*buitre de cabeza amarilla*; *Cathartes burrovianus*) is rare in Uruguay. There are no fewer than 36 other raptors, including 17 hawks, buzzards and eagles, ten owls, and three caracaras, which are common scavengers of carrion. Swainson's hawk (*busardo chapulinero; Buteo swainsoni*), which has the second-longest migration of any raptor, over 20,000km, feeds mainly on insects and is being badly affected by pesticide use.

The national bird is the *tero* or **southern lapwing** (*Vanellus chilensis*), a crested wader which seems omnipresent, having taken to nesting in fields, parks and gardens. It defends its nest by squawking and then flying at you, although it stops short of actual contact. When not breeding, it lives in wetlands and seasonally flooded grassland, where the attractive **black-and-white monjita** (*viudita blanca grande; Heteroxolmis dominicana*) and **red-breasted blackbird** (*pecho colorado grande; Sturnella militaris*), actually a meadowlark, are also fairly common. Indeed, most Uruguayan birds (perhaps 400 species) are found in wetlands, both on the coast and in the littoral of the Río Uruguay, including 11 species of egret, heron and night-heron, up to 22 ducks, four grebes, three kingfishers, three storks, the **American darter** or snakebird (*Anhinga anhinga*), one spoonbill (*Ajaja ajaja*) and one flamingo (*Phoenicopterus chilensis*). Smaller and less easily seen birds include nine types of rail and crake, three types of moorhen and three types of coot.

The seedeaters (tiny passerines, related to tanagers and Darwin's finches) are a focus of conservation interest at the moment, because of trapping for the caged bird trade, loss of habitat, and problems actually categorising the separate species. The **chestnut seedeater** (*capuchino corona gris; Sporophila cinnamomea*) is found in grassland, while others, such as the **dark-throated seedeater** (*capuchino garganta café; S. ruficollis*) and **rufous-rumped seedeater** (*capuchino castaño; S. hypochroma*), are found more in marshes and damper pastures. The white-collared or **Entre Ríos seedeater** (*capuchino de collar; Sporophila zelichi*) and **marsh seedeater** (*capuchino pecho blanco; S. palustris*) are found in marshes and also in gallery forest. The Southern Cone Grasslands Alliance aims to restore the mix of short grass and tussocky long grass formed by traditional cattle ranching to restore populations of seedeaters and the ochre-breasted pipit (*bisbita ocre; Anthus natereri*).

In tidal areas and elsewhere there are seven species of sandpipers, two dotterels, two snipe, the Hudsonian godwit and other waders – many of these migrate from the northern hemisphere and thus are familiar to North Americans, who are happy to fund conservation initiatives to protect them in Uruguay. Marine birds include five gulls, six albatrosses, 12 terns, 17 petrels, the **snowy sheathbill** (*paloma antártica; Chionis albus*), the **frigatebird** (*fregata; Fregata magnificens*), and even two penguins, the **rockhopper** (*Eudyptes chrysocome*) and **Magellanic penguin** (*Spheniscus magellanicus*).

Characteristic birds of mountain woodland (*bosque serrano*) include the **diademed tanager** (*cardenal azul; Stephanophorus diadematus*), **rufous-browed peppershrike** (*Juan Chiviro; Cyclarhis gujanensis*), **long-tailed reed-finch** (*pajonalera cabeza gris; Donacospiza albifrons*) and **chopi blackbird** (*mirlo charrúa; Gnorimopsar chopi*). In the *monte de quebrada* of the north, you may also see the **buff-necked ibis** (*bandurria baya; Theristicus caudatus*), **crested-black tyrant** (*viudita copetona; Knipolegus lophotes*), **cliff flycatcher** (*viudita colorada; Hirundinea bellicosa*), **yellow-rumped marshbird** (*canario de la sierras; Pseudoleistes guirahuro*) and (red-legged) **seriema** (*Cariama cristata*), like a secretary bird with its silly crest.

In the mata Atlántica you may find some subtropical species such as **brown tinamou** (*perdiz marrón; Crypturellus obsoletus*), **red-winged tinamou** (*martineta del monte; Rhynchotus rufescens*), **rufous gnat-eater** (*chupadientes castaño; Conopophaga lineata*), **scaled woodcreeper** (*trepador escamado; Lepidocolaptes squamatus*) and the **blue jay** (*urraca azul; Cyanocorax caeruleus*).

There are seven members of the parrot family in Uruguay, of which the most ubiquitous is the **monk parakeet** (*cotorra común*; *Myiopsitta monachus*), which is very talkative (captive birds develop large vocabularies) and makes huge communal nests of twigs. It has taken to nesting in eucalyptus trees, and so its numbers have increased greatly along with the area of eucalyptus plantations; unfortunately it does considerable damage to crops. Otherwise there are various species of attractive Aratinga parakeets in the northwest of the country.

Of the seven introduced bird species, the only common ones are the **European sparrow** (*gorrión*; *Passer domesticus*) and the **rock pigeon** (*paloma doméstica*; *Columba livia*), which you'll see in every town but not outside; however, there are eight species of attractive native doves.

CONSERVATION

In Montevideo at least, people seem always to be carrying bags of rubbish to big wheelie-bins, which are constantly visited by scavenging *hergaderos* with horse carts, mainly taking cardboard. Proper recycling is only just getting off the ground, with a few bins for glass, tins and batteries appearing from 2008.

A report in 2008 by the United Nations Environment Programme criticised many aspects of Uruguay's environmental situation, notably problems linked to increasing affluence, such as over-consumption, excessive packaging, poorly organised waste disposal and limited recycling. There's a great lack of monitoring and information and of joined-up government policy, but DINAMA, the National Environment Bureau (*www.dinama.gub.uy*) is now monitoring the emissions of 395 companies.

The UNEP report did note positive new developments such as environmental education initiatives, a new law on returnable bottles and the new Sistema Nacional de Areas Protegidas or National Protected Area System (*SNAP; www.snap.gub.uy*); there are now plenty of low-energy bulbs in use.

The SNAP was set up in 2005 (under a law passed in 2000), and will cover 20 state, NGO and private protected areas. The oldest, dating from 1916, is the Parque Roosevelt on the outskirts of Montevideo, which is totally planted with eucalyptus and of no conservation value whatsoever; later additions are more worthwhile, and SNAP's two priority areas are hybrids of various categories of reserve, to be managed holistically. These are Lunarejo, in the north (see page 342) and the Esteros de Farrapos y Islas del Río Uruguay, in the west (see page 312). The latter is the country's second Ramsar wetland site, following the Bañados del Este (on the Atlantic coast), which also combines various separate protected areas (including a couple of colonial forts) and became Uruguay's first Coastal-Marine Protected Area in 2007.

HISTORY

It seems that humans first crossed into the Americas from Asia over the Bering land-bridge about 60,000 years ago, and headed south, crossing into South America around 15,000 years ago and reaching Tierra del Fuego approximately 4,000 years later. The oldest human artefacts (arrowheads and spearheads) yet found in Uruguay (in Maldonado department) have been dated to 12,900 years ago; at this time small family bands of nomadic hunter-gatherers were probably moving south from present-day Brazil. Remains dating from around 10,000 years ago have also been found in the northwest of the country.

Around 9,000 years ago larger groups formed, eating a wider range of foods and with more advanced methods of shaping stones for blades, scrapers and bolas (throwing) stones. As the climate warmed, about 8,000 years ago, the megafauna (such as giant sloths and sabre-toothed tigers) died out.

In the centre and west of the country, **rock carvings** (*grabados rupestres*) began to appear c4,000 years ago, to the north of the Río Negro, followed around 2,000 years ago by rock paintings (*pinturas rupestres*, in a range of reds), to the south of the river. In the east of the country, from approximately 4,000 years ago, large mounds known as **cerritos** (up to 40m in diameter and 7m in height) were constructed; detailed investigation is only now beginning, but it seems that they were not, as assumed, burial mounds, but the sites of villages created as the climate changed and marshlands dried out. Traces of squash, maize and beans (as well as butia palm fruit) indicate that agriculture began far earlier than had been thought in this part of the continent. Strange bird-shaped stones known as *ornitholithos*, carved around 3,300 years ago, have been found mainly in the nearby coastal parts of Rocha and Maldonado departments; ceramics also appeared about 3,000 years ago.

From about 4,000 years ago, the people loosely known as the **Charrúa** were driven south into what is now Uruguay by the Guaraní. Although their population only numbered between 5,000 and 10,000, they were the best documented of the peoples encountered by Europeans after their first arrival here in 1516 (at latest), and the last to die out. Other peoples included the Chaná, Guenoa and Yaro.

EUROPEAN COLONISATION Amerigo Vespucci may have reached present-day Uruguay in 1502, but the first certain contact came in 1516 when a Spanish expedition led by **Juan Díaz de Solís** followed the coast south from Brazil, reaching the Río de la Plata (River Plate, which he named the Río Dulce or Sweet River, having found fresh water out at sea) and the confluence of the Río Uruguay and Río Paraná. He and most of his fellows were killed (and allegedly eaten) by the native people, and for the next century the region was left largely undisturbed, due mainly to its presumed lack of gold or silver. Magellan also visited the Plate on his way to the Pacific in 1520.

Sebastián Gaboto was the son of the explorer known to the British as John Cabot, and may have sailed with him to eastern Canada. He entered the service of Spain and in 1526 led a fleet to the Plate and on up the Paraná and Uruguay rivers, establishing the fort of San Salvador at the confluence of the Río Uruguay and the Río San Salvador, west of Dolores – the first European settlement in what is now Uruguay. He also founded the first European settlement in what is now Argentina at Espíritu Santo on the Río Paraná, which was soon wiped out by the indigenous peoples. In 1529 San Salvador was abandoned and the expedition returned to Spain.

In 1580 the city of Buenos Aires was founded (after a failed attempt in 1536) on the Argentine side of the Plate, and in about 1611 cattle were released on the Uruguayan side of the estuary by the legendary Hernandarias (Hernando Arias de Saavedra, 1561–1634, Governor of Asunción), with expeditions coming to slaughter some from time to time (for leather more than for meat). The first permanent European settlement in Uruguay came in 1624, when the Jesuits founded the mission of Santo Domingo de Soriano, on Isla Vizcaino (later moved to the mainland; see page 296).

The Portuguese, already established in Brazil, sought to expand their territory to the Plate and the Río Uruguay, establishing a fort at Colonia del Sacramento, across the Plate from Buenos Aires, in 1680. This was resisted by the Spanish, and Colonia was under attack or blockade for much of its early history. The Spanish also established a fort and settlement at Montevideo in 1724.

British involvement was limited in this period to the regular passage of buccaneers and privateers such as Francis Drake (1578), his cousin John Drake (1581), Robert Withrington (1587), John Childley (1589), Thomas Cavendish (1592) and Edward Davis (1683). A little later, in 1768, Captain Cook stopped in Uruguay with the scientists Sir Joseph Banks and Daniel Carl Solander; likewise in 1832 Charles Darwin spent a considerable time in Uruguay, travelling from Maldonado inland to Minas and from Montevideo to Colonia and near Mercedes, and writing perceptively and entertainingly about his experiences.

As the colonisation of the Banda Oriental (the Eastern Shore of the River Plate) became established, further towns were founded, notably Paysandú (in 1749), Maldonado (1755), Salto (1756), San Carlos (1763), San José (1783), Minas (1784), Rocha (1794) and Melo (1795). In addition, forts were built near the Brazilian border, at San Miguel (1734) and Santa Teresa (1762–76).

The War of the Spanish Succession (fought mainly in Europe) ended in 1715 with Colonia confirmed as a Portuguese possession, but from 1737 it was again blockaded by Spain. The Treaty of Tordesillas, in 1494, had set a north–south line 370 leagues (about 1,770km) west of the Cape Verde Islands as the boundary between Portugal and Spain. Portugal's colony in Brazil quickly overran this boundary, and it was soon ignored. However, it was only in 1750 that the treaty was officially superseded by the Treaty of Madrid, which settled the southwestern border of Brazil and gave Colonia to Spain, although it was not actually handed over until 1777. Similarly, Spain was required to cede to Portugal the territory of seven Jesuit reductions or missions on the upper Río Uruguay (to the north of present-day Uruguay). This reckoned without their Guaraní inhabitants, who were to be relocated in Spanish territory – when they refused to go, the Spanish and Portuguese armies joined forces to drive them out in the brutal Guaraní War of 1754–56.

This effort was rendered worthless in 1761 when, because of the difficulties of implementing it, the Treaty of Madrid was abrogated by Spain, which now kept the area of the missions; the Treaty of Paris (1763) ending the Seven Years War, which had set Spain against Portugal in a largely European conflict, returned Colonia to Portugal while Spain held the province of Río Grande do Sul, now the southernmost part of Brazil.

The Portuguese saw the Jesuits as backing the Guaraní in their refusal to be uprooted and, when the Pope died in 1758, moved quickly to dispossess the order of all their possessions in Portuguese territory. Likewise, the Spanish saw the huge and largely autonomous Jesuit estate of Yapeyú, covering the present departments of Paysandú, Salto and Artigas and parts of Río Negro and Tacuarembó, as well as Entre Ríos and Corrientes in Argentina, as a power within the state, and in 1767 the order was expelled from all Spanish domains.

Another Spanish–Portuguese War in 1776–77 was settled by the treaties of San Ildefonso (1777) and El Pardo (1778), reaffirming the Treaty of Madrid and confirming Portuguese control of Brazil (in particular Río Grande do Sul) and Spanish control of the Banda Oriental (Uruguay), including Colonia.

Also in 1776, the Spanish government created the Viceroyalty of the Río de la Plata, with control of present-day Argentina, Uruguay, Paraguay and southern Bolivia passing from Lima to Buenos Aires, with the aim of better countering the growth of Brazil. The port of Buenos Aires was opened to transatlantic shipping for the first time, leading to a rapid increase in trade, as well as smuggling, in which Montevideo and Colonia played important roles. The original one bull and seven cows released in the Banda Oriental prospered and bred like crazy (as did seven stallions and seven mares); increasingly they were rounded up, branded and kept on huge estancias (rural estates), of which there were 102 by 1757, with over 133,000 cattle, 124,000 horses and 71,000 sheep. These were almost all killed or stolen by the Portuguese in the wars of the mid 18th century, and only repopulated after 1819 (with merino sheep introduced from 1832). Nevertheless, the number of cowhides exported increased ten-fold between 1760 and 1780, as the (human) population grew and trade increased. By the end of the 18th century the population of the Banda Oriental was just over 30,000, of whom two-thirds were in the Montevideo area.

THE WARS OF INDEPENDENCE Spain's colonies were never allowed to develop, other than as sources of raw materials, but a *criollo* (native-born) middle class did grow up and was increasingly able to run its own affairs. Spain allied itself with Napoleon's France, and in June 1806 British forces captured Buenos Aires; the royalist forces proved to be useless, but the British were driven out in August by the naval officer Santiago Liniers, who landed with troops and militia forces from Montevideo. The British, once reinforced, crossed the Plate, capturing Maldonado and then Montevideo after a fierce battle on 3 February 1807. In July they again attacked Buenos Aires, defeated Liniers but failed to occupy the city at once; when they did attack they met fierce resistance in which half the British forces were either killed or wounded. The British withdrew to Montevideo, abandoning that as well in September 1807 after a peaceful occupation.

In 1808 Napoleon invaded Spain and forced King Carlos IV to abdicate, putting his brother on the throne instead. The Governor of Montevideo, Francisco Javier de Elío, pressured Liniers (now Viceroy of the Plate, but French-born) to declare his loyalty to the Spanish crown, but Liniers issued an ambiguous statement. Accused of complicity with Napoleon by Elío and the *cabildo* (council) of Buenos Aires, he summoned Elío to Buenos Aires, replacing him with Juan Ángel de Michelena. The citizens of Montevideo backed Elío and called for a *cabildo abierto* (open council), held on 21 September 1808; Michelena fled and a royalist *Junta* (ruling council) was set up, a crucial phase in the Banda Oriental's development of an identity separate to Buenos Aires. Only in May 1810 did the criollo people of Buenos Aires set up an autonomous Junta, forcing the viceroy to move to Montevideo.

A certain José Gervasio Artigas (see the box on pages 16–17), who had fought under Liniers in Buenos Aires and then in the defence of Montevideo where he was wounded and captured, went in the opposite direction, deserting from the army and heading for Buenos Aires in February 1811 to join the movement for independence of the Banda Oriental from Spanish rule, which had begun with the Grito de Asencio (the 'Cry of Asencio') (27 February 1811), and the capture of Mercedes and Santo Domingo de Soriano the next day. He returned in April with around 180 men, defeating Spanish forces at the Battle of Las Piedras in May and besieging Montevideo. Threatened by armies from both Buenos Aires and Brazil, he led perhaps 10,000 soldiers and civilians across the Río Uruguay from Salto in the so-called Exodo del Pueblo Oriental (Exodus of the Eastern People); having regrouped, he returned in 1812 to beat the Spanish at El Cerrito and was acclaimed as leader of the Orientales in December. In January 1813 a congress in Buenos Aires claimed independence for the whole of the Spanish viceroyalty; in April a meeting of the Orientales (presided over by Artigas) at Tres Cruces accepted this but with conditions (known as the 'Instrucciones del Año XIII') specifying autonomy for the provinces within a federation and the separation of the three branches of government. In 1814 an army from Buenos Aires drove the Spanish from Montevideo, and was in turn driven out in 1815 by Oriental forces under Fructuoso Rivera, securing the autonomy of the Provincia Oriental at the Battle of Guayabos. Artigas attended the congress in Concepción del Uruguay (in present-day Argentina) at which the provinces of the Banda Oriental, Córdoba, Corrientes, Entre Ríos, Misiones and Santa Fe declared their independence from Spain and formed the Liga Federal (Federal League), in opposition above all to Buenos Aires, which saw itself as capital of the United Provinces of the Plate. With the tacit backing of Buenos Aires, a Portuguese army invaded, capturing Montevideo in January 1817; Artigas held the interior of the country for the next three years, but his federalist allies, the Governors of Santa Fe and Entre Ríos, came to an agreement with Buenos Aires and abandoned him. In 1820 he was defeated by the Portuguese at Tacuarembó and went into exile in Paraguay, staying there until his death in 1850.

The Brazilians were welcomed as protection from the domination of Buenos Aires; in 1821 the Congreso Cisplatina in Montevideo voted for the incorporation of the province within the Portuguese Empire (and thus from 1822 the independent Brazil). However, the United Provinces of the River Plate now backed the Orientals (led by Rivera and Juan Antonio Lavalleja) in an independence struggle; the Cruzada Libertadora (Crusade of Liberation) began on 19 April 1825 when 33 Orientals (the famous Treinta y Tres Orientales or 33 Easterners) led by Juan Antonio Lavalleja landed at the Playa de la Agraciada; the next day they joined up with Rivera (although accounts vary as to how willing Rivera was to ally himself

EL PROCER – JOSÉ GERVASIO ARTIGAS

Although the Artigas family settled in Montevideo in as early as 1726, and José Gervasio Artigas was born there in 1764, he spent his youth in the country, northeast of the city near Sauce, gaining the outdoor skills that fitted him for military success. Living as a gaucho (and even dabbling in a bit of smuggling), he came to see the indigenous people as equals, an attitude which marked his later career. In 1797 he joined the Blandengues, a cavalry regiment newly created to guard the Banda Oriental's borders, and rose to the rank of captain. Inspired by the movement for independence from Spain, he fled to Buenos Aires and returned in April 1811 with a small amount of men and money to lead an uprising against Spain in the Banda Oriental, laying siege to Montevideo, together with troops from Buenos Aires. However he was disgusted by the truce of October 1811 between the Spanish viceroy and the Junta of Buenos Aires and took his troops and many more people across the Río Uruguay to regroup, returning in 1812 once the truce had collapsed to continue the struggle. His delegates to the Asamblea General Constituyente in Buenos Aires in 1813 demanded a liberal republican and federalist constitution based on that of the United States of America; this was rejected, and Artigas abandoned the siege of Montevideo. His rivals in Buenos Aires declared him a traitor, but he was able to take control of the rest of the country and then capture Montevideo in 1815, ensuring the independence of the Banda Oriental from Buenos Aires.

Artigas continued to resist the centralising ambition of Buenos Aires, organising the Liga Federal of the Banda Oriental and five provinces on the western side of the Río Uruguay (all now part of Argentina), with free trade between them and land redistributed to his supporters, including native and mixed-race people. Artigas based himself at Purificación, about 100km north of Paysandú, and in June 1815 called a Congreso de los Pueblos Libres in Concepción del Uruguay (on what is now the Argentine side of the Río Uruguay) where he was named Protector de los Pueblos Libres (Protector of the Free Peoples). The other provinces of the former Viceroyalty of the River Plate were invited to join the Liga Federal, provoking with Lavalleja – one version has him being captured and forced to sign on pain of death). In June 1825 a provisional government was formed in Florida, where on 25 August a congress of deputies of the Provincia Oriental voted this time for independence within the United Provinces. Brazil went to war with the United Provinces, blockading the ports of Montevideo and Buenos Aires, but was hampered by internal revolts in raising a decent army. After Lavalleja's victory at Sarandí in October 1825 the Argentines joined the war against Brazil and eventually peace and **Uruguayan independence** were mediated by the British diplomat Lord John Ponsonby, Britain being anxious to create a buffer state between Argentina and Brazil to secure its trade interests in the region. The war ended in August 1828 and an Asamblea Constituyente y Legislativa (constituent and legislative assembly) met to draw up a constitution, approved in September 1829 and sworn nationwide on 18 July 1830. It created a democratic republic now known as the República Oriental del Uruguay (Oriental Republic of Uruguay).

INDEPENDENCE AND CIVIL WAR Uruguay had finally achieved independence from both Brazil and Argentina, although its borders were still not fixed. Lavalleja became interim head of state, with Rivera elected the country's **first president** in 1830.

Buenos Aires to take control of the other provinces and to connive with Portugal to invade the Banda Oriental and depose Artigas. Montevideo was captured in 1817 but resistance continued until 1820 when Artigas fled into exile in Paraguay.

Not allowed to communicate with anyone abroad, he lived here for another 30 years, with only his trusted companion Joaquín Lenzina, known as 'el negro Ansina', an Afro-Uruguayan who had been enslaved by the Portuguese and whose freedom he had bought at the turn of the 19th century. Like San Martín and O'Higgins, the liberators of Argentina and Chile, he was to die in exile. Portraits show him looking increasingly like a Greek philosopher, and he was soon revered as *el procer* or father of the nation (as opposed to the liberator, which title belongs to Juan Antonio Lavalleja); nowadays there's an Avenida (or Plaza) Artigas in almost every town. In 1855, five years after his death, his remains were brought back to Montevideo and buried in the Central Cemetery; in 1950 they were moved to the Tres Cruces obelisk, and in 1977 to the mausoleum on Plaza Independencia. In 2009 it was announced that he was to be moved again, to the Casa de Gobierno across the road, due to the mausoleum's association with the military dictatorship, but this plan was abandoned after protests.

Artigas's heroic stature is enhanced by the fact that he had 14 children by eight mothers (including indigenous women); he was married to Isabel Sánchez from 1791 until her death in 1804, then to his cousin Rosalía Rafaela Villagrán. This marriage was annulled due to her mental illness, and in 1815, in his base of Purificación, he took as his third wife Melchora Cuenca, a Paraguayan lancer, no less, and much younger than him; when he went into exile she stayed in Uruguay, putting up with many difficulties due to being his wife.

His first son Juan Manuel, born in 1791, became colonel of a cavalry regiment, and also married in 1815, in his father's camp at Purificación; from 1821 until his death in 1851 he lived in Entre Ríos, now a province of Argentina. José María, born in 1806, also rose to the rank of lieutenant-colonel.

The young country got off to an appalling start by massacring its few remaining indigenous people on 11 April 1831 – Rivera's nephew Bernabé Rivera invited the Charrúa (whose numbers had fallen to about 500) to a meeting in the ravine of **Salsipuedes** (aptly named 'Get out if you can') and then ambushed them, killing almost all the men. The women and children were spared and distributed as virtual slaves, but effectively there was no indigenous culture left in Uruguay (although a few hundred mixed-blood Charrúa remain in Argentina). Four Uruguayan Charrúa captured at Salsipuedes – Vaimaca-Piru (who had fought with Artigas and Rivera), the medicine-man Senaca and a younger couple, Tacuabe and Guyunusa – were taken in 1833 to be exhibited in France (where a baby was born and they all died). A print of *Los Últimós Charrúas* (The Last Charrúas) was produced as publicity (and served as the basis for the statue of the same name in Montevideo's Prado Park in 1939, by which time attitudes were changing and Uruguayans increasingly deplored the genocide and the loss of part of their heritage). In addition, a group of Guaraní came from the Jesuit missions when these were finally incorporated into Brazil, living from 1833 to 1862 in San Francisco de Borja del Yí (10km from Durazno), until this was forcibly closed down and the remaining Guaraní assimilated into the local population.

In 1834 Manuel Oribe, one of the 33, was elected the country's second president, but the next year Rivera rose in revolt, starting the **Guerra Grande** or Great War, a civil war that polarised the country for the rest of the century. Rivera's party, known as Colorados from their red armbands (torn from the lining of their ponchos), were unitarists, standing for a fully independent Uruguay, while Oribe's Blancos (whose white armbands were torn from a flag) stood for a federal solution – Artigas's dream – and were backed by the landowners and the Argentine dictator Rosas. In October 1838 Oribe fled to Argentina and Rivera became president again, but within days Rosas declared war; Rivera beat his forces at Cagancha in 1839 but fled to Brazil in 1845; Blanco forces (and Argentine ships) blockaded Montevideo from 1843 to 1851, but the war ended as a draw in 1851 (followed by Rosas's overthrow) and Rivera returned in 1853 to rule as part of a triumvirate with Lavalleja and the Colorado Venancio Flores. However, Lavalleja died that year and Rivera in 1854, leaving Flores as interim president until 1855, when he stepped down and went to Argentina.

When the Blanco government of Bernardo Berro supposedly discriminated against Brazilian-born landowners, Brazil and Argentina invaded Uruguay to put Flores and the Colorados into power in 1865. Later that year Berro's ally, the tinpot dictator of Paraguay, Francisco Solano López, declared war on Uruguay, launching the War of the Triple Alliance in which Uruguay, Brazil and Argentina blockaded Paraguay's access to the sea and still managed to take five years and lose huge numbers of troops before winning. Flores ruled as a virtual dictator until February 1868; four days after stepping down, both he and Berro were assassinated.

The Paraguayan war finally ended in March 1870; in September the Blanco leader Timoteo Aparicio launched the so-called Revolución de las Lanzas (Revolution of the Lances, named after the makeshift weapons of knives tied to sugarcanes), which ended in April 1872 with a power-sharing agreement that was to last until the early 20th century. Although this marked the end of Uruguay's civil war, the political scenery continued to be dominated by the division between conservative, rural Blancos (aka the Partido Nacional) and the liberal, urban Colorados; both were aligned with similar factions in Argentina. The two parties now agreed not to interfere in one another's spheres of influence, but the mindset of *caudillismo* (the dominance of local party bosses who became virtual warlords in their own patch) was difficult to erase, ending only with the death of Aparicio Saravia in 1904 in a failed uprising.

MODERNISATION Industrial development began to take off in the 1860s, with the introduction of railways, barbed wire and Hereford cattle – there was a massive shift from cowhides to huge quantities of beef, processed by the Fray Bentos meat-packing plant and shipped worldwide (in cans until 1905, then also in freezer ships). From the 1870s there was mass immigration, mainly from Spain and Italy, the population growing from 450,000 in 1873 to one million in 1900, 1.3 million in 1914 and 1.9 million in 1930. There was also a massive inflow of European investment, with 27 banks and over a hundred financial societies founded by 1900 (in addition to the Banco Nacional, created in 1887).

The election of the Colorado **José Batlle y Ordóñez** (1856–1929) as president in 1903 was a major turning point for Uruguay, the start of a period of economic prosperity, social reform and widening democracy which lasted until the Great Depression. From the defeat of Aparicio Saravia in 1904 until 1907 he concentrated on consolidating democracy after the period of caudillismo; Church and State were also separated, divorce introduced and education expanded. Re-elected for a second term from 1911 to 1915, Batlle (pronounced 'badge-eh') abolished the death penalty and moved on to the economy, seeking to replace foreign dominance with state control. Unemployment pay was introduced in 1914 and the eight-hour working day in 1915, followed by proportional representation and secret ballots in 1916; in 1917 the country was decared a secular state. Similar policies were pursued by Claudio Williman (1863–1934), hand-picked to be president between Batlle's two terms, and by Baltasar Brum (1883–1933), president from 1919 to 1923, who continued reforms of the educational and welfare systems.

This golden age of progress and prosperity came to a sudden end with the arrival of the Great Depression and the collapse of prices for Uruguay's exports, as well as the imposition of tariffs by the developed nations. Gabriel Terra (1873–1942; also a Colorado) became president in 1931 and suspended congress in 1933, introducing a new constitution in 1934 and establishing himself as president with dictatorial powers. Brum was so outraged by the coup and the way that Uruguayans seemed to be accepting it that he killed himself in a dramatic protest; there was a revolt in 1935 but it was swiftly suppressed.

Terra stood down in 1938 and his successors kept Uruguay neutral but aligned with the anti-fascist Allies; in 1949 the British-owned railways and water companies were nationalised (actually in payment for meat supplied to Britain during World War II), as the state tightened its control of the economy. Exports of food for the allied armies fighting in Korea helped boost the economy under President Luis Batlle Berres (nephew of José; 1897–1964). Then in 1952 a new constitution established a ruling college like Switzerland's (as originally proposed by José Batlle y Ordóñez); the Consejo Nacional de Gobierno (National Council of Government) had six members from the majority party and three from the minority party, but because the majority was rarely united and the president had no real power it was ineffective, and in 1967 Uruguay returned to the presidential system. Nevertheless, from 1959 to 1966 the Blancos did have a rare chance to run the country; they tried to implement economic reforms but were blocked by the unions.

MILITARY DICTATORSHIP AND AFTER In 1971 the left-wing Movimiento de Liberación Nacional (National Liberation Movement, known as the Tupamaros) opted for armed struggle; at the same time the legitimate left-wing parties at last formed a united platform, the Frente Amplio (Broad Front). The elections at the end of 1971 were won (with the help of some CIA interference) by Juan María Bordaberry (1928–2011) who in 1973 'invited' the military to take power. In fact the Tupamaros urban guerrillas had been effectively wiped out by 1972, but a period of brutal repression followed (with some 200 of around 7,000 political prisoners being killed), coupled with neoliberal economic policies that caused real wages to fall to less than half their 1968 levels. Around 10% of the population emigrated for political or economic reasons, and in 1980 the military failed to persuade the electorate to endorse an authoritarian new constitution. In the face of the worst economic crisis since the 1930s, they were increasingly keen to hand back power, and the return of democracy in Argentina after the Falklands/Malvinas War encouraged the opposition, as did the 1983 visit of King Juan Carlos of Spain, seen (ironically) as a symbol of democracy and liberty. Negotiations led to elections in 1984 and the moderate Colorado Julio María Sanguinetti (b1936) became president in February 1985, with an amnesty granted to protect those who committed human rights abuses under the dictatorship. The economy continued to struggle, with inflation reaching 130% by the end of 1990; however, Uruguay played a key role in negotiations leading to the foundation of Mercosur, the South American common market, in 1991. Sanguinetti was succeeded in 1991 by the moderate conservative Luis Alberto Lacalle (b1941), whose free-market policies and budget cuts were unpopular; he lost the 1994 elections to Sanguinetti, who held the presidency again from 1995 to 2000. He worked with the Blancos to reform social security, ending the state monopoly of insurance and pensions; the Frente Amplio, now holding a third of seats in the legislature, won support by backing the welfare state, although it was increasingly unaffordable.

In fact Sanguinetti had won only 24.7% of the vote in the 1994 elections, but was elected as the leading candidate of the party with the most votes in total, although the Frente Amplio's Tabaré Vásquez (named after the half-Charrúa hero of the national poem *Tabaré*) won 30.6% of the vote. In 1996 a referendum approved changes, including a run-off vote for the presidency, but in 1999 Vásquez was again kept from the presidency by an alliance of the Blancos and Colorados, taking 46% of the vote in the run-off against the centrist Colorado Jorge Batlle (b1927, son of Luis). Batlle pushed through controversial reforms, including privatisations and the outsourcing of some public services to the private sector. Although he inherited a strong economy (with GDP growth of around 5% per annum in 1996–98), it was dragged down by the economic problems of Brazil and Argentina, coupled with drought and high oil prices. In 2001 the collapse of the Argentine economy led to bank deposits there being frozen and Argentines making huge withdrawals of US dollars stashed in Uruguayan banks; about a third of the country's deposits were taken out of the financial system and five financial institutions became insolvent, largely the result of a failure of regulation (sound familiar?). In July 2002 the Uruguayan peso plunged, and GDP fell close to 20% in the next four years, while inflation and unemployment soared. Loans from the IMF allowed Uruguay to restructure its external debt (with virtually all foreign creditors accepting a 20% loss), and the country did not default on its debt, unlike Argentina.

As a result of the economic crisis, at the end of 2004 **Tabaré Vásquez** finally managed to get elected, and was remarkably successful and popular, continuing to work part-time at his cancer clinic and taking camping and fishing holidays near Mercedes. One of his first moves was to restore diplomatic ties with Cuba, a declaration of independence from the United States after 170 years of right-wing rule; but in 2007 he signed a trade and investment 'framework agreement' with the US. However, the left wing of the coalition kept him from moving further towards a full free-trade deal. This would also be resisted by Uruguay's partners in the Mercosur trade group; Argentina already tends to be less than neighbourly, doing little to counter the blockades set up at the border bridge to protest against

JOSÉ MUJICA

Inaugurated as President of Uruguay at the age of 74 in March 2010, José 'Pepe' Mujica is the most colourful politician the country has seen in half a century. Routinely described in the foreign media as 'a former guerrilla leader', he fought with the Tupamaros in the 1970s, and was jailed from 1972 to 1985 (including two years spent at the bottom of a well). A more ruthless dictatorship would have killed him, but he was eventually released and has stuck to non-violent political action ever since. He founded the Movimiento de Participación Popular (the Movement of Popular Participation), despite the refusal of some former guerrillas to participate in 'bourgeois politics', and was elected to congress in 1994. The MPP is now the largest faction of the Frente Amplio coalition.

Known for his colourful, even profane, way of speaking, and for addressing people as *compañero* (ie: comrade), he's anathema to many on the right and even to those on the more centrist side of the Frente Amplio coalition. He has little interest in economics (or in speaking English), and so it was essential for his defeated rival Danilo Astori to accept the vice-presidential slot and give his campaign a broader appeal. Generally a scruffy-looking believer in the simple vegetarian life, he was tidied up and put into a good suit for meetings with foreign heads of state in the later stages of the campaign, and began speaking from prepared texts. President Vásquez finally embraced him publicly, although he had wanted Mujica as vice- president to Astori. Mujica has stressed that he represents continuity with the highly popular Vásquez government (Uruguay's first elected leftist administration) but in truth the continuity is provided by Astori, rather than Mujica, the agriculture minister who just sat back and benefited from the worldwide boom in commodity prices.

Even so, he has a strong connection with the young, as well as with the widely mocked dinosaurs of the 'Jurassic left'. He admits he doesn't believe in working too hard, and travelled by bus to public meetings throughout his presidential campaign.

Mujica still has a tendency to speak his mind in a way that often gets him into trouble; Uruguay's intelligentsia feared he'd adopt the same sort of populist policies as the Kirchners in Argentina, but in fact he's also offended them by speaking too freely. Nevertheless he had enough of an understanding with them to find a way out of the impasse over the Botnia pulp mill.

He and his wife, Lucía Topolansky, whom he met during the urban guerrilla period and finally married in 2005, live on a simple farm near Montevideo where they grew flowers after the return of democracy. Lucía is a senator too, and in fact received more votes than any other in the 2009 election, so that she became president of the Senate and thus next in line to become president herself if both her husband and Astori (neither very young) die or become too ill to stay in office.

After two years in office Mujica was fairly unpopular at home (weakened by arguments over the expiry of the 1986 amnesty law and a proposed land tax), but had become famous abroad for giving away 90% of his salary to charity.

the Botnia pulp mill (see pages 308–9), imposing import restrictions; and delaying dredging of a vital shared channel.

Uruguayans seem happy with their mixed economy, with the state controlling most utilities; some are tempted by the more dynamic capitalism of Chile, but they are reluctant to become less egalitarian. With tax breaks and legal safeguards for investors, and an educated workforce, there are hopes that call centres and outsourced back-offices will be established in Uruguay.

MUJICA AND THE FUTURE With the very popular Vásquez unable to run for a second consecutive term as president, the ruling Frente Amplio ignored his preferred successor, his former finance minister, Danilo Astori, a technocrat who finds it hard to smile for the cameras, and chose the rather more charismatic José Mujica. A former Tupamaros guerrilla, later agriculture minister and then senator, he had the support of the trade unions; the intelligentsia is wary of him, less because of his guerrilla past than because they see him adopting the same sort of populist policies as the Kirchners in Argentina, as well as Venezuela's late president Hugo Chávez and Bolivia's Evo Morales. To gain wider acceptability he was forced to select Astori, seen as the architect of Uruguay's steady economic growth over the previous four years, as his running mate.

His main rival was the former president Luis Lacalle of the Partido Nacional (with Jorge Larrañaga as his running mate), followed by Pedro Bordaberry of the Colorados (whose father invited the military to take over in 1973). In the elections of October 2009, Mujica won 48% of the vote, followed by Lacalle with 29% and Bordaberry with 18%, so that a second round was required in November. In this, Lacalle took 44% of the vote while Mujica won 52%; the Frente Amplio also kept its parliamentary majority. The Colorados received less than 17% of the vote, but that was enough for them to be delighted, given how they have been totally eclipsed by the Partido Nacional. In any case, after the elections all the candidates were very conciliatory, stressing that Mujica was the president of all Uruguayans, not just one party. Indeed there has been a consensus on socially progressive legislation, permitting same-sex marriage, abortion and marijuana use. There's a very good chance that Tabaré Vásquez will be elected president again at the end of 2014.

GOVERNMENT AND POLITICS

Uruguayans love politics and are always talking about it (and football) – sometimes it seems that campaigning never ends, as parties choose pre-candidates and then one or more candidates proper before the actual election campaign gets under way. This means that people generally vote for serious politicians, rather than the charlatans who are usually the only choice in neighbouring Argentina, and thus the standard of governance is generally much higher. This was true even in the 1830s, when Darwin noted:

> There are many [retired generals] always on the watch to create disturbance and to overturn a government which as yet had never rested on any stable foundation. I noticed, however, … a very general interest in the ensuing election for the President; and this appears a good sign for the prosperity of this little country.

Uruguay is a presidential republic with independent legislative, judicial and executive branches. There is a two-chamber legislature composed of the House of Representatives (Camera de Representants) and the Senate (Camera de

Senadores). National elections, for president and vice president, 30 senators and 99 deputies, are held in October every five years (next in 2014), with compulsory voting for all those over 18 years of age; the president and vice president may not serve consecutive terms, but may stand again at later elections. The vice president chairs the Senate (and occasionally the General Assembly of senators and representatives together); the representatives elect a new speaker every year. Supreme Court judges serve ten-year terms and are nominated by the president and confirmed by the General Assembly.

The country is divided into 19 departments, each governed by an elected *intendant* (mayor). The departments are presently more or less synonymous with their principal city, and in the May 2010 local elections local councils were introduced in 89 municipalities. Most of these cities (other than Minas, San José and Tacuarembó) are right on the edge of their departments, along the rivers that form the departmental (and national) boundaries, but rural populations are so low that this hardly matters.

ECONOMY

Uruguay's economy is far smaller than those of its neighbours, but it's open and well managed, with very little corruption. With a well-educated labour force and a sizeable middle class, Uruguay's economy is marked by a high level of state involvement, with utilities still publicly owned and government stakes in companies such as PLUNA, the national airline. There's a high level of social spending, funded by a hefty payroll tax, meaning that it can be hard for small businesses to recruit staff, given the more than comfortable welfare payments.

Whereas Argentina and Brazil, with their large domestic markets, would seem to be better placed to withstand a global recession, in fact Uruguay is likely to suffer less, because of its historical avoidance of populist policies that can lead to economic overheating and subsequent collapse. Although the tourism industry is still largely dependent on Argentine beach-lovers, the economy as a whole is much less tightly coupled to Argentina than it was. In 2007 Brazil replaced Argentina as Uruguay's main trading partner, taking over US$1 billion in exports (17% of Uruguay's total exports – more than to the US and now twice as much as goes to Argentina). Uruguay also now imports more from Brazil than from Argentina. Mercosur, the common market of South America, is dominated by Brazil and Argentina; despite being host to Mercosur's headquarters, Uruguay often finds itself arguing to avert some of their more populist policies, and in particular an Argentine urge to protectionism.

In fact, Uruguay benefits from Argentine misgovernment, as Argentines traditionally move their money abroad, sometimes depositing it in Uruguayan banks or buying farmland in Uruguay. What's more, the government's firm support for the Botnia pulp mill, in the face of Argentine blockades (see pages 308–9), has boosted the confidence of foreign investors. Botnia alone has already boosted Uruguay's GDP by 1%, plus another 1% in indirect gains, since its opening in late 2007. The Aratiri iron-ore mining project (see page 363), which will cover 120,000ha in central Uruguay, is expected to add another 1.5% to GDP.

Uruguay established diplomatic relations with China in 1988, and was one of the few countries not to condemn the Tiananmen Square killings the following year. Bilateral trade between China and Uruguay shot up from US$125 million in 1998 to US$1.6 billion in 2008, and 2009 saw the first exports of live dairy cattle from Latin America to China. In 2007, Chery, the largest Chinese independent car-maker, opened a factory in Montevideo, producing Tiggo compact SUVs and QQ compact cars, mainly for export to Argentina and Brazil.

Services are now the largest sector of the economy, accounting in 2008 for 57% of GDP and 76% of jobs; this includes banking, retail and **tourism**, which contributes nearly US$2 billion per year to the economy, with close to three million visitors annually. Half of these come from Argentina (contributing 2.8% of Uruguayan GDP), followed by 300,000 from Brazil; the number of visitors from Britain in 2007 and 2008 was around 15,000, double the level of 2002.

Despite the global recession, the number of tourists coming to Punta del Este has remained high, but they are staying for less time, with an average stay of ten days, compared with three or four weeks a decade or so ago. The Argentines are less likely to stay in hotels and eat in restaurants, shifting to renting apartments and villas and cooking for themselves. Cruise tourism is booming, with the number of ships visiting Punta del Este and Montevideo rising from 83 in 2007–08 to 240 in 2012–13, over a season that now lasts six months.

The service sector now also includes outsourced technology services, with engineers in Montevideo working while their colleagues in India sleep.

The industrial sector, including food and wood-pulp processing and leatherworking, accounts for 32.8% of GDP and 15% of jobs; its share of GDP is falling, although the construction sector is growing. Finally, **agriculture** dominates much of the country's area; it's relatively unimportant in terms of revenue and employment, accounting for just 8.2% of GDP and 13% of jobs in 2006, but is very export-oriented. Beef alone accounted for 37% of exports, now worth about US$1.5 billion a year. Traditionally, beef cattle have been raised in the north and east of the country, with dairy farming concentrated on the greener fields of Colonia department, and sheep in the south and west of the country. Uruguayan wool is of relatively poor quality and mostly exported to China; mutton and lamb account for just 6% of meat exports, although this does not include sales of live sheep for halal slaughter in the Middle East. In addition to wineries (see page 149) and forestry (see pages 308–9), there's a well-established citrus-growing industry around Paysandú, in the west of the country, and a newer rice-growing industry around the lagoons of eastern Uruguay; soya is also becoming an important crop, covering a million hectares and producing export sales worth US$1.1 billion.

Economic growth averaged 8% annually from 2004 to 2008; GDP growth plunged to 2.9% in 2010, thanks to global recession, but soon recovered to 6½% in 2011 and 3.9% in 2012; GDP growth for 2013 is expected to be about the same.

CASINOS

There are 36 casinos in Uruguay (34 run by the state, plus two run by the city of Montevideo – see page 112), with a turnover of over US$150 million per year. Over 90% of that revenue comes from *tragamonedas* (slot machines); in most cases an Uruguayan casino is simply a *sala de esparcimiento*, a tawdry hall full of these machines. Most casinos are in tourist resorts and near border crossings, as the main clients are visitors from Brazil, where gambling is banned, although Argentines are also keen on a flutter. Since 1996 the government has been moving from state control to a mixed system in which the state runs the actual gambling but private companies provide the premises and marketing; this has been very successful and places like the Conrad in Punta del Este can rival Las Vegas's biggest operations.

GDP for 2012 was US$49.7 billion at the official exchange rate, or US$53.55 billion at purchasing power parity (PPP); GDP per capita at PPP was US$15,800. Uruguay has weathered the global recession remarkably well. Exports were expected to fall by a third in 2009 but actually fell by less than 9%, while imports fell almost 18%, mainly due to reduced demand for oil. Exports rose no less than 23% in 2010, to US$6.7 billion, and in 2012 they rose 9% to a record US$8.7 billion (with soya, beef and rice the most important); Foreign Direct Investment was also a record US$2.35 billion (nearly double the 2005 level).

Inflation was 5.9% at the end of 2009, and rose to almost 7% in 2010, 8% in 2011 and 7.5% in 2012 and probably 8.8% in 2013; this is seen as the Uruguayan economy's main problem, and is widely blamed on Argentine contagion. Public debt is also growing – in 2012 the fiscal deficit was US$1.35 billion (2.8% of GDP, against a target of 2.2%), the highest since 2003, but the government has announced plans to keep it under control. Unemployment is consistently about 7%.

PEOPLE

Uruguay's population is close to 3.5 million, almost all on the coast and littoral and overwhelmingly urban, with 43% of the population living in Montevideo. As a largely secular urbanised society, it's no surprise that population growth is low (the lowest in South America, at 0.466%) but that life expectancy is high, at 76½ years.

The indigenous population has been essentially wiped out (see page 18), although 8% of the population are *mestizo* (of mixed European and native descent). African slaves were brought in in considerable numbers but have now been largely assimilated – just 4% of Uruguayans are black, but 10% of Uruguayans (over 13% of those under 20) claim to be *afrodescendiente*, although many are broadly indistinguishable from the bulk of the populace. The Afro-Uruguayan cultural influence is, however, far stronger than this would lead you to expect, with *candombé* drumming (see page 28) and carnaval in general a key part of Uruguayan identity throughout the population. However, 56% of Afro-Uruguayan children live below the poverty line, and the average black wage is 70% of the average white wage; in Montevideo, the Afro-Uruguayan areas of Barrio Sur and Palermo are clearly deprived and run-down, if with pockets of trendiness.

Most Uruguayans are in fact of Spanish and Italian stock – the first mass immigration, from c1824, was of French Basques, followed by their Spanish relatives. In the late 19th and early 20th centuries there was an exodus from southern Italy to Uruguay (as well as to Argentina and the United States) which has left pizza and pasta as omnipresent menu items and Italian words (and gestures) as distinctively Uruguayan aspects of the Spanish language. More Spaniards (especially Basques) arrived after 1936, fleeing Franco's fascists.

You might think there is also a substantial population of Chinese and Koreans in Montevideo, but the groups of men you see hanging around are mainly crew from fishing and cruise ships. Nevertheless there are a few Chinese and Korean restaurants in the city.

Around 45,000 Uruguayans live in the United States, mostly working in professional jobs; many also work in Europe, though mostly in less well-paid jobs. Over 15,000 Uruguayans apply every year for Italian citizenship (granted to all male descendants of Italian immigrants, and some female); some apply for Spanish citizenship, but this is open only to children of Spanish citizens and to grandchildren of victims of Franco's dictatorship.

LANGUAGE

The national language is Spanish (see page 377 for local peculiarities), but a Spanish–Portuguese hybrid called Portunol or Brazilero is also spoken on the Brazilian frontier.

RELIGION

Uruguay is one of the most secular countries in Latin America, although 56% of the population claims to be Roman Catholic and 11% Protestant. Those claiming to be atheist or agnostic total 17% of the populace, with 16% classified as 'other', which presumably includes followers of the animist African Umbanda religion. Just 0.3% are Jewish (and the Simon Wiesenthal Centre says there is virtually no anti-Semitism in Uruguay), while Muslims, Buddhists and Hindus are too few to be recorded.

Since the economic crisis of 2002 the Iglesia Universal del Reino de Dios (Universal Church of the Kingdom of God), a dynamic Brazilian Pentecostalist Church, has erupted all over Uruguay, often taking over former cinemas and theatres which can be recognised by banners proclaiming Pare de Sufrir (Stop Suffering). Smaller evangelical groups often meet in private homes, and make a surprising amount of noise.

ORIXA Although Umbanda priests and priestesses are available for consultation all year round, they only really emerge in public on 2 February, when the festival of the *orixa* Iemanjá is celebrated in Montevideo and Punta del Este. The seven orixas (or orishas) are intermediate gods, providing contact between humanity and the supreme creator Olodumare. Lemanjá, a river goddess in Yorubá Africa, has here become the *orixa* of the ocean and the patron of fishermen and shipwreck survivors, as well as representing the feminine aspects of creation and motherhood. In Porto Alegre in Brazil, 2 February (the feast of the Virgin of Candelaria) is also celebrated by the Roman Catholic Church as the festival of Nossa Senhora dos Navegantes (Our Lady of the Seafarers), while a similar celebration is held in Salvador da Bahia on 8 December, as in Rio de Janeiro on New Year's Eve. In the voodoo religion of Cuba and the southern USA she is known as Yemaja or Yemalla.

From around sunset devotees clad in white or pale blue gather on the beaches, setting candles in holes in the sand and piling up offerings of fruit and flowers. Some load these on to sand models of boats, while many more bring paper boats that are launched to sea bearing candles, flowers and money. Drums play and men in white and pale blue and women in white 19th-century dresses dance themselves into a trance; others line up for priests to lay on hands and purify them; in addition Iemanjá is said to grant wishes (though not for love, as she keeps the best-looking men for herself).

Meanwhile, on the *rambla* (esplanade) above Montevideo's Playa Ramírez more and more spectators gather every year, significantly whiter-skinned than the devotees below and not in white, but respectful enough nevertheless. The rites continue to around 03.00 or even dawn, leaving a remarkable quantity of trash on the beaches.

CULTURE

As a small country, Uruguay has one iconic national painter (Joaquín Torres García), one national composer (Eduardo Fabini), one national novelist (Juan

Carlos Onetti) and even one national philosopher (Carlos Vaz Ferreira) – but in fact this belies the range and quantity of cultural activity. There's a profusion of artists, writers and musicians, some living and working abroad, and architecture in particular is currently bringing the country worldwide recognition (see page 34).

MUSIC

Leading musical figures Uruguayan classical music became established in colonial times, with the four-part Misa para día de Difuntos (Mass for the Day of the Dead) written in 1802 by José Manuel Ubeda. The leading figure in Uruguayan musical history is **Eduardo Fabini** (1882–1950), born in Lavalleja (see page 184), who studied in Montevideo and at the Brussels Conservatoire (where he won first prize for violin in 1902). He returned to live in Montevideo, but spent much time in Lavalleja, in touch with nature and folk traditions, which were at the heart of his music. His international breakthrough came with the choral symphony *Campo* in 1922, followed by his *Tristes* (1925) for piano and guitar. In 1927, he was appointed artistic attaché at the Uruguayan Embassy in the United States. Back in Uruguay, he became the leader of a small group of nationalist composers, including Alfonso Broqua (1876–1946) and Luis Cluzeau-Mortet (1889–1957); in 1946 he became director of the Conservatorio Nacional de Música, which he had co-founded in 1907, and the state paid him a pension for life in exchange for the rights to his music.

The leading contemporary Uruguayan musical figure is **José Serebrier**, best known as a conductor but also a composer, who has been based in the United States for most of his career. One of the most recorded conductors of his generation, his recordings have received 32 Grammy nominations thus far, and eight have won Grammies. He was the first to record Charles Ives's *Fourth Symphony*, previously regarded as almost unplayable and generally performed with three conductors working together. He has not conducted with a baton since stabbing himself in the hand in a moment of over-excitement in an Easter Day concert in 1975. Hailed by the great Leopold Stokowski as 'the greatest master of orchestral balance' when he was just 22, he worked as Stokowski's assistant for five years and as music director of the Cleveland Philharmonic before leaving to work as a guest conductor with any number of orchestras and director of various festivals, leaving time for his composing. More recently he has gained praise for his recorded cycle of the Glazunov symphonies with the Royal Scottish National Orchestra.

As a composer he has been awarded two Guggenheim Fellowships (the first at 19, the youngest person ever to be granted one), as well as other awards. His *First Symphony* was premiered, by Stokowski, when he was just 17 and was followed two years later by his *Second Symphony*, which he conducted himself with America's National Symphony Orchestra. Perhaps his best work, in his characteristically lively, colourful and tuneful style, is the *Carmen Symphony* of 2004.

Jorge Drexler, born in Montevideo in 1964, gave up a medical career to be a singer-songwriter, also working as a lifeguard and a synagogue singer, and released his first album in 1992. He's best known for his soundtrack to the film of *The Motorcycle Diaries*, the theme song winning him an Academy Award in 2005 – the first Oscar won by an Uruguayan, and the first for a Spanish-language song. Although Drexler wrote both the words and the music, and sang the song himself on the soundtrack, he was snubbed by the organisers of the Oscars, who chose the actor Antonio Banderas to sing it at the ceremony; nevertheless when collecting his award he sang a couple of verses unaccompanied – the scandal and his dignified response largely overshadowing the inauguration on the same day of Uruguay's first leftist government. Based in Spain since 1995, his songs are routinely covered by many Hispanic singers and his live album *Cara B* was nominated for a Grammy as Best Latin Pop Album in 2009.

Tango The tango is almost as important to Uruguayans as it is to Argentines (see page 350 for Carlos Gardel's Uruguayan background). One of the most famous tangos is 'La Cumparsita' or The Little Parade (of Endless Miseries), written by Gerardo Matos 'Becho' Rodríguez (1897–1948) and first performed in 1917 where Montevideo's Palacio Salvo now stands. It remains very popular and is commonly played as the last dance of the night at Uruguayan *milongas* (dancehalls); thus there was outrage when the Argentine team at the 2000 Olympics in Sydney marched in to 'La Cumparsita'.

The first tango recorded by Gardel, indeed the first tango to be recorded with lyrics, was 'Mi Noche Triste' (My Sad Night), written in 1915 by the Argentine Samuel Castriota; lyrics were added without the composer's knowledge by Pascual Contursi (1888–1932) in Montevideo. Gardel recorded it in 1917 and later brought about an agreement between the two writers over the song's copyright.

Tango was born in the port cities of Buenos Aires and Montevideo when the folk music of the poor Italian and Spanish immigrants blended with the rhythms of the African slaves and their descendants (the word *tango* originally meant a social gathering of the slaves, and was then extended to the music they played). In essence it's a simple eight-step dance but with variation and ornamentation (kicks, turns, leaps and lunges); the mournful lyrics are a 20th-century addition. Its most characteristic instrument, the *bandoneón* (button accordion) was introduced by German immigrants after 1870. Originally men danced with men, as if in a duel, and then with prostitutes; gestures and eye contact remain minimal, but charged with meaning. The dancers entangle themselves intimately and yet resist each other, the music straining between tragedy and ecstasy; the eroticism and constrained violence led the upper classes to spurn it as scandalous until it had established itself in Paris and the Old World and made its way back to the New World. Nowadays tango is popular even in the interior where it never existed before, but without the searing (some would say ludicrously over-the-top) intensity of its Argentine form. It's easy enough to find tango in Montevideo (see page 108) but there's little tango tourism, unlike in Buenos Aires. In September 2009, a joint bid by Argentina and Uruguay for tango to be listed as part of the Intangible Cultural Heritage of Humanity was accepted by UNESCO.

Murga Murga is a key element of the Uruguayan carnival, a type of musical theatre derived from the *chirigota* of Cádiz in Spain. It's usually performed by a group of up to 17 men in fantastical costumes who sing opening and closing songs (*saludo* and *despedida*) together, along with a series of satirical pieces accompanied by bass drum, snare drum and cymbals. Performed on stages around Montevideo throughout Carnaval (and in competition at the Teatro del Verano), the musical style also finds its way into Uruguayan popular music.

Candombé Candombé (or *candomblé*) is the style of drumming that developed in Montevideo's Afro-Uruguayan barrios and has become an emblematic part of Carnaval and of Uruguayan culture in general. The thunderous rhythms pounded out by a *cuerda* of scores of drummers marching in a dense block through the city streets can be positively intimidating, leading to the white élite banning candombé in 1808; however, it proved impossible to enforce and Afro-Uruguayan culture has made its way to the heart of Uruguayan identity. In 1870 candombé was officially incorporated into Montevideo's Carnaval, and by 1900 the participants were largely white.

The barrel-like drums (*tamboriles*) come in three main sizes: *chico* (small and relatively high-pitched, marking the tempo), *repique* (mid-sized, used for syncopation and improvisation) and *piano* (large and relatively low-pitched, playing a melody). All are carried on shoulder straps and played with one stick and one bare hand – a key rhythmic figure is the *clave*, a 3/2 figure played by striking the side of the drum (*hacer madera* or making wood). Before performing, the leather tops are tuned by holding them over a fire.

The great set-piece of candombé is the Las Llamadas procession ('The Calls') at the start of the carnaval season in Montevideo, usually in February. Close to 100 *comparsas* (groups of drummers) march through the Barrio Sur and Palermo, the bloc of drummers (in some kind of costume, often with straw hats and blackened faces, to show the music's slave origins) preceded by female dancers (known as *mulatas*), often in scanty samba-style costumes with sequins and feathers, and stock characters such as the *la mama vieja* (the old mother) with fan and parasol, *el gramillero* (the medicine man) with his white cotton-wool beard, top hat, frock coat, glasses and a briefcase of medicinal herbs, and *el escobero* (the stick-holder) juggling a long magical staff – originally a tasselled cane, this now looks exactly like a broomstick. The comparsas also compete during Carnaval in the Teatro del Verano, the open-air theatre near Parque Rodó.

Milonga Milonga is a term for a tango dancehall, and also a type of music that derived from Spanish folk forms in the 1870s and was a predecessor of the tango. Originally it was a folk song, partly improvised and set to a lively 2/4 tempo, accompanied by guitar. With time, this came to be accompanied by a syncopated dance, like tango but faster, simpler and with limbs and body held less rigidly. In fact it's like a jerky rhythmic walking, to which *traspiés* or *contrapasos* can be added, a sort of shuffle transferring weight from one foot to the other and back again in double time or three steps in two beats.

The best-known Uruguayan singer of milongas and other folk songs was **Alfredo Zitarossa** (1936–89), one of the great voices of Latin America, whose lyrics and poetry were strongly rooted in the Uruguayan countryside and in leftist politics. He lived in exile during the dictatorship, when his music was banned in Uruguay, Argentina and Chile.

Music festivals Uruguay's main popular music festivals are Pilsen Rock in Durazno in October (which attracts 120,000) and jazz festivals in Mercedes and Punte del Este, both held in January.

LITERATURE The earliest noteworthy Uruguayan literature is the gaucho-flavoured poetry of **Bartolomé Hidalgo** (1788–1822). The leading Romantic poet in Uruguay was **Juan Zorrilla de San Martín** (1855–1931; see page 141), whose epic poem *Tabaré* (1886) describes the clash between Spanish colonists and native people that led to the extinction of the aboriginal culture.

José Enrique Rodó (1871–1917) is best known for his essay *Ariel* (1900), based on Shakespeare's *The Tempest*, with Prospero as narrator championing Western classical culture, Caliban standing for utilitarian materialistic North America and Ariel for the rebellious youth of Latin America. Rodó was opposed to democracy, which he saw as entailing mediocrity and vulgarity; nevertheless he remains revered as a theorist of Modernist thought and a champion of Latin America's identity.

Florencio Sánchez (1875–1910) is still Uruguay's best-known playwright; having dropped out of school in Minas, he became an anarchist and a self-taught journalist before turning to plays, which mostly depict life in working-class tenements, including poor immigrant families. Although very successful, he blew it all on bohemian nightlife and died young of tuberculosis.

Julio Herrera y Reissig (1875–1910), nephew of President Julio Herrera y Obes, was a somewhat Proustian figure who was unable to travel much because of a heart defect but hosted a literary salon, and as a poet moved from late Romanticism to avant-garde Modernism, his subtle works finding fame only after his early death. **Juana de Ibarbourou** (1892–1979) remains highly popular (and is still on the thousand-peso banknote), an early feminist whose poetry is largely defined by nature imagery and eroticism.

The philosopher **Carlos Vaz Ferreira** (1872–1958) was particularly influenced by Henri Bergson and William James, and introduced liberal, pluralistic political values and a pragmatic but emotional rationalism to South America. His most important works, such as *Problemas de la Libertad* (Problems of Liberty), *Conocimiento y Acción* (Knowledge and Action), *Moral para Intelectuales* (Morals for Intellectuals), *El Pragmatismo* (Pragmatism) and *Lógica Viva* (Living Logic), were published between 1907 and 1910. There's a locally famous photo of him sitting on a park bench with Einstein, who was visiting a cousin in Uruguay, in 1925. Vaz served as Vice Chancellor of the University of the Republic in 1928–31 and 1935–41, taking a break because of ill-health, when he produced other books such as *Sobre el Feminismo* (On Feminism, 1933), one of the earliest discussions of the topic in Latin America.

Horacio Quiroga (1878–1937) was a very popular and influential writer of short stories, many set in the 'jungles' of Argentina's Misiones province and prefiguring Magical Realism. He had a tragic life, his father shooting himself in a hunting accident, then himself shooting a friend while explaining how a gun worked; his first wife killed herself with cyanide as he himself did when diagnosed with cancer; and their two children also later killed themselves.

Felisberto Hernández (1902–64) was a fine short-story writer who had little success, working as a pianist in cinemas and cafés, and remains little known. His deranged first-person narrators produce an off-kilter version of reality that influenced writers such as Gabriel García Márquez, Italo Calvino and Julio Cortázar.

Uruguay's leading 20th-century novelist was **Juan Carlos Onetti** (1909–94), who was born and grew up in Montevideo, dropping out of school to be a journalist, film critic and short-story writer. His first novel, *El Pozo*, was privately published and largely ignored in 1939 but is now seen as the first truly modern Spanish American novel, with its Modernist technique and an alienated protagonist who leads a futile life in a city where he fails to communicate with others. His second novel, *Tierra de Nadie* (No-man's Land, 1941), consisting of brief scenes and conversations, marked the first appearance of the former brothel-keeper Larsen, while the 1950s Santa María trilogy was set in the fictional town of that name on the Plate; perhaps his greatest work is *El Astillero* (The Shipyard, 1961), also set in Santa Maria, where Larsen takes a job as manager of a bankrupt shipyard, which increasingly comes to resemble his own hopeless interior life.

Having worked as an editor for Reuters in Montevideo and Buenos Aires and as manager of an advertising agency, Onetti became director of Montevideo's municipal libraries in 1957. After being briefly held in a mental hospital in 1974 by the dictatorship, he moved to Madrid and lived there until his death; in *Dejemos Hablar al Viento* (Let the Wind Speak, 1979), his first novel written in Spain, he had

Santa María, always a seedy dump, burnt down at the close, reflecting his despair. Nevertheless in 1980 he won the Spanish-speaking world's most prestigious literary prize, the Premio Cervantes, and in 1985 the President of Uruguay flew to Spain to present him with the National Literary Award.

His isolated urban characters, in their existential alienation, are a million miles from the gauchos of earlier Latin American literature, and also have little to do with the fantastical characters and plots of the Magical Realists. In fact there's very little clear narrative, but the portrayal of mood and setting is unparalleled – the use of language owes much to the French novelist Louis-Ferdinand Céline, while the alienation foreshadows Beckett and Camus.

Mario Benedetti (1920–2009) was a prolific poet, novelist and journalist, not well known in the English-speaking world but considered one of the major contemporary writers of Latin America. He came to prominence in 1959 with the publication of *Montevideanos* (Montevideans), a set of short stories hinting at James Joyce's *Dubliners*. The most visible member of the political wing of the Tupamaros guerrillas, he also went into exile under the dictatorship and afterwards continued to divide his time between Montevideo and Madrid.

More controversial is **Eduardo Galeano** (b1940), whose writing mixes fiction, journalism, political analysis and history. His best-known work, *Las Venas Abiertas de América Latina* (The Open Veins of Latin America, 1971), is an analysis of Latin American history from European colonisation to the present, arguing against the northern hemisphere's economic and political domination, and especially against globalisation and the IMF. At the April 2009 Summit of the Americas, Venezuela's then-president, Hugo Chávez gave a copy to US President Barack Obama, pushing both the English- and Spanish-language versions high up the bestseller lists. After editing the weekly journal *Marcha* (previously edited by Onetti) and running the University of Uruguay Press, he too went into exile under the dictatorship, ending up in Spain where he wrote the widely praised trilogy, *Memoria del Fuego* (Memory of Fire, 1982–86), a fictionalisation of the history of the Americas, involving the figures actually involved, from pre-Columbian times to the 1980s. In 1985 he returned to Montevideo, and wrote perhaps his most daring work, *El Libro de los Abrazos* (The Book of Embraces, 1989), a collection of stories giving his views on art, emotion and values, as well as another scathing critique of modern capitalism. Then he relaxed a bit, producing *El Fútbol a Sol y Sombra* (Football in Sun and Shadow, 1995), a history of the game that naturally inveighs against its unholy alliance with global capitalism.

Most recently, *Espejos: Una Historia Casi Universal* (Mirrors: Stories of Almost Everyone, 2008) is another broad mosaic of history told through hundreds of kaleidoscopic vignettes, the voices of the unseen, unheard and forgotten, free of the restrictions of chronology.

It's worth mentioning the great Argentine writer **Jorge Luis Borges** (1899–1986), whose mother was Uruguayan; he spent childhood summers near Fray Bentos and in Montevideo and was a perceptive commentator on Uruguayan history and culture; some of his characters are realistically Uruguayan, above all the great Funes the Memorious, who came from Fray Bentos.

Finally, **Isabel Fonseca**, whose father was the Uruguayan sculptor Gonzalo Fonseca, was born in the United States (her mother was the daughter of a grape-juice tycoon) and studied at Columbia and Oxford universities before joining the *Times Literary Supplement*. Writing in English, her first book was *Bury Me Standing* (1995), a very successful non-fiction account of Europe's Roma or Gypsies, followed by a memoir about her brother's death from AIDS. The novelist Martin Amis left his wife and family for her in 1993, and from 2003 to 2006 they lived in Uruguay, building a house in José Ignacio (see pages 233–4), where she began work on a fictional account of her family's experiences during the dictatorship. Instead she ended up writing a novel (*Attachment*, 2008) about an American–British couple taking a sabbatical in the tropics, before returning to the original idea.

ART Uruguay's museums are virtually all free and chronically underfunded; however, this matters less in art museums than in others, at least on the surface. The annual Museos en la Noche (Museums at Night) event, usually on the first Friday of December, is the peg for a variety of free activities in museums across the country. The website (*www.mnav.gub.uy/artistas.htm*) is the best source of information on Uruguayan artists.

Painters The leading Uruguayan painter of the 19th century was **Juan Manuel Blanes** (1830–1901), after whom the country's main art gallery is named. Born in Montevideo, his education was disrupted by civil war and family break-up, but he was able to train himself as an artist while working as a newspaper typographer. In 1855 he moved to Salto, where he established himself as a portrait painter, and in 1857 to Concepción del Uruguay (in Argentina); in 1861 a government grant took him to Italy, which he revisited several times, the last occasion being in 1899 to search for his son who had gone missing there. He painted in a pretty academic style but, thanks to his Italian neoclassical training, created some iconic images of Artigas.

Pedro Blanes Viale (1878–1926) was born in Mercedes but in 1893 the family moved back to his father's native Mallorca; nevertheless Blanes Viale returned regularly to Uruguay and indeed died in Montevideo. Although he preferred to paint landscapes (in a Fauvist style in his last years) he is best known for his portraits.

Rafael Barradas (1890–1929) worked as a magazine illustrator and founded his own magazine satirising the Montevideo cultural scene; he moved to Spain in 1914, where he knew Dalí, Bunuel and Lorca, as well as Torres García (see opposite), and developed his own distinctive style, derived from Cubism and Futurism, which he called *Vibracionismo* (Vibrationism). After moving to the Catalan countryside he started painting in a more Realist style; seriously ill, he returned to Montevideo to die.

Pedro Figari (1861–1938) had a successful legal career while painting as an amateur. He played a key part in the abolition of the death penalty in 1907, and in 1915–17 he was interim director of the Escuela Nacional de Artes, reorganising it thoroughly. From 1917 (with his *Piedras*, or troglodyte, paintings) his style changed radically from Realism to a more Expressionist style, and in 1921 he moved to Buenos Aires to dedicate himself to painting full-time, moving on to Europe for nine years from 1925. In 1927 he was appointed ambassador to Britain, also publishing poems and short stories. His paintings seem not just naïve but amateurish, but he is still highly regarded in Uruguay, partly for his role in portraying Afro-Uruguayan culture and bringing it towards the mainstream.

José Cúneo (1887–1977) studied in Montevideo, Italy and France, absorbing the work of Cézanne, Matisse, Soutine and Van Dongen. He returned to Uruguay in 1917 and the next year held a very successful exhibition in Montevideo which launched the Planismo style, dominant in Uruguay until the 1930s. Derived from Fauvism and Cubism, it was marked by strong colours in flat-seeming planes with no sense of depth or volume (mainly in landscapes, and also some portraits). Although never a school or group as such, it was widely taken up by the generation born between 1875 and 1895 (many marked by their travels to Europe thanks to government scholarships), notably Barradas, Figari, Carlos Federico Sáez (1878–1901), Carlos Roberto Rúfalo (1880–1975), Carmelo de Arzadun (1888–1968), Alfredo de Simone (1898–1950) and Petrona Viera (1895–1960), who had to work especially hard to overcome prejudice against her as the daughter of President Feliciano Viera.

Later, living in rural Florida department, Cúneo developed a freer style, becoming known for his paintings of farms and of the moon. He revisited Europe in 1954, discovering abstraction, and in the 1960s began to be well known abroad as well as at home. He returned to Europe in 1976, and died in Bonn the following year.

The best-known Uruguayan artist remains **Joaquín Torres García** (1874–1949), who moved with his family to Spain in 1891, where he studied at the Academia de Bellas Artes in Barcelona and joined the young artists such as Picasso who met at the El Quatre Gats café. From 1904 he worked with Gaudí on stained glass for the cathedral of Palma de Mallorca and the church of the Sagrada Familia in Barcelona. He painted the Uruguayan pavilion for the 1910 World Fair in Brussels, then after 1915 moved from a neoclassical style to Modernism, and from 1920 developed a sideline in educational wooden toys (having grown up in the family carpentry shop). From 1926, living in Paris, and influenced by Theo van Doesburg, Piet Mondrian and primitive and African art, he developed his own Constructivismo Universal (Universal Constructivism), a form of abstraction combining a grid-like structure (based on the Golden Section) with symbolic images such as fish, clocks, a ladder, a man and a woman, and even a steam locomotive.

In 1932 he moved to Madrid, developing an interest in pre-Columbian art from the Americas, and in 1934 (feeling that Europe was artistically dead and that there was a need for new approaches) returned to Uruguay where he became an energetic teacher and propagandist. He founded the Taller Torres García (the Torres García Studio), which influenced a generation of Uruguayan painters including José Gurvich, Gonzalo Fonseca, Manuel Pailós, Julio Alpuy and his sons Augusto and Horacio Torres; these are known as the Escuela del Sur (Southern School) after Torres García's saying, 'our north is their south', illustrated with an upside-down map, referring to pre-Columbian culture. Alfredo Testoni (1919–2003) was a painter and also perhaps the best Uruguayan photographer of the 20th century, recording the Taller Torres García and working for *Time* and *Life* magazines.

José Gurvich (1927–74) was born Zusmanas Gurvicius in Lithuania, and came to Uruguay at the age of five. He studied under Cúneo at the Escuela Nacional de Bellas Artes and from 1945 at the Taller Torres García, becoming a teacher there and exhibiting in the studio's collaborative shows. He travelled in Europe and lived on a kibbutz in Israel, returning to Uruguay between 1965 and 1969 and then living from 1970 in New York, where he died of a heart attack at just 47. His paintings, influenced by Bosch, Brueghel and Chagall with their fusion of the fantastic and the everyday, often show scenes of shtetl and kibbutz life as well as Old Testament themes such as Adam and Eve, and included works on leather, plaster casts and ceramics.

Carmelo Arden Quin (1913–2010) studied with Torres García and moved in 1938 to Buenos Aires, where he was bowled over by abstract art. In 1946 he launched the MADI movement, whose playful, even mad, art sought to liberate painting from the constraints of the frame, with irregularly shaped works, sometimes pierced or articulated, that blurred the distinctions between painting and sculpture. Using brightly coloured circles, spirals, stripes and other shapes, MADI art (and architecture, poetry and dance) is abstract and free of symbolic meaning, focused on form rather than content. The movement's name, with its overtones of Dada, is probably nonsense, although all sorts of theories exist explaining its origin (such

1

as from carMelo ArDen quIn, Movimiento Artístico de Invención or the English 'mad-eye'). By late 1946 he was in Paris, working furiously and leading a chaotic bohemian life. He died in France in 2010.

Two of the leading followers of the MADI movement are the Uruguayans Rhod Rothfuss (1920–69) and Volf Roitman (1930–2010), a painter, poet and architect best known for designing the MADI Museum in Dallas, Texas. Roitman also studied in Buenos Aires but only met Arden Quin after moving to Paris in 1951.

Carlos Páez Vilaró (b1923) is the highest-profile figure in contemporary Uruguayan art, thanks to his successful marketing of himself and his presence in Punta del Este, where his fantastical studio-cum-hotel Casapueblo can be visited (see page 217). He travelled to Europe and visited Picasso in 1957 (recorded in a much-used photo), but the influence of Picasso and Matisse on his art, although obvious, was relatively shallow. Back in Montevideo, he lived in the Mediomundo *conventillo* (tenement) in the Barrio Sur, where he became deeply involved in candombé and played a major role in opening up Afro-Uruguayan culture to the middle classes. His brother Jorge (1922–95) was an abstract painter who returned to figurative art in the 1960s, aiming for a universal art rooted in primitive art and folk traditions.

Sculptors As for sculpture, **José Belloni** (1882–1965) spent much of his career in Europe but was also based in Uruguay, where he's remembered for major sculptures in Montevideo such as *La Carreta* and *La Diligencia* in the Prado (see pages 128 and 131) and *El Entrevero* in Plaza Fabini (see page 126). His son Stelio (1920–89) was also a successful sculptor, together with Federico Escalada (1888–1960). **Germán Cabrera** (1903–90), who worked as assistant to José Belloni from 1918 to 1925, then went on a scholarship to France, where he met Despiau and Bourdelle. He spent the years from 1938 to 1951 in Venezuela, then returned to Montevideo, although he made many more trips to Europe as well as to New York City; until World War II he produced mainly stone figures, then moved to a more abstract style, working also in steel.

Like José Belloni, **José Luis Zorrilla de San Martín** (1891–1975) left a significant legacy on the streets of Montevideo, including the statue of the *Gaucho* (see page 127), and the Monument to the Constituents (the *Obelisco*; see page 128).

Octavio Podestá (b1929) studied in Europe and then based himself in Montevideo; he was the first Uruguayan sculptor to make hinged and moving pieces, using pieces of steel and other industrial scrap. **Wifredo Diaz Valdez** (b1932) worked along similar lines, producing articulated wooden sculptures from the 1980s, partly by disassembling violins, guitars and the like. **Pablo Atchugarry** (b1954) works in marble, producing amazingly delicate abstract sculptures; he lives mainly in Italy but has a gallery just east of Punta del Este (see pages 232–3).

ARCHITECTURE After independence, the Baroque style of colonial architecture was soon abandoned for a neoclassical style that drew on French and Italian – rather than Spanish – roots, while French-style boulevards were superimposed on the Spanish grid of equal-sized streets. Most of Uruguay's churches are neoclassical in style, with porticos, rounded arches, barrel vaults and domes, while in the late 19th century many public buildings were built in a style known as Belle Époque or Beaux Arts eclectic historicism, notably the Teatro Solís (1842–56), Casa de Gobierno (1873), Estación Central (1897) and Palacio Taranco (1908) in Montevideo.

The first individual architect to have a widespread impact in Uruguay was **Giovanni (Juan) Veltroni** (1880–1942), who was born in Florence and came to Montevideo in 1908; he built many public buildings including the port administration building (1910), the Banco de la República (1926–38), the Ministerio de Salud Pública (Ministry of Public Health, 1928) and the *liceos* (high schools) of Canelones and Durazno. Similarly, **Mario Palanti** (1885–1979) trained in Milan and settled in Buenos Aires in 1909, designing many fine buildings on both shores of the Plate, notably the Palacio Salvo (1928, and still Montevideo's main landmark), with fine Moderne (similar to Art Deco) decoration.

Only a few buildings were constructed in the Art Nouveau style, such as the Edificio Pablo Ferrando (1917) and the Centro Cultural de España (1932) in Montevideo, although it had a greater influence on decorative detailing. In the 1920s and 1930s economic prosperity coupled with an open liberal climate and an educated population led to the construction of many modern buildings, notably schools designed by Juan Antonio Scasso from 1926, the Aduana (Customs House, 1929) and the Palacio Municipal (City Hall, 1930). Art Deco towers and apartment blocks include the Palacio Rinaldi (1929) and Palacio Díaz (1929), and many very successful Art Deco houses, in Montevideo and nationwide. There followed a seamless move into Bauhaus-style Modernism, with buildings such as the Edificio Lapido (1930), Estadio Centenario (1930; see page 128) by Scasso and José Domato, and the Bolsa de Comercio (Stock Exchange, 1936).

Le Corbusier gave a very influential series of lectures in Buenos Aires in 1929, and even drew up a plan for the redevelopment of Montevideo (thanks to the aviation pioneers Jean Mermoz and Antoine de Saint-Exupéry, he was able to fly over Montevideo and other cities), but relatively few buildings were built in Corbusieresque style, other than a large block near Montevideo's yacht club (see page 133) and a few buildings in Punta del Este and Punta Ballena. The leading architect of the 1930s was **Julio Vilamajó** (1894–1948), who taught at the University of the Republic and built its Faculty of Engineering (1937) and many other buildings (including all their fittings in some cases), as well as laying out Villa Serrana in Minas (see page 187).

Eladio Dieste (1917–2000) was an engineer who almost accidentally became one of Uruguay's best-loved architects. Inspired by the Taller Torres García's functional approach to the arts, he devised a structural system to allow double-curved tiled or brick vaults, held by just a thin layer of concrete. After designing a couple of factories and warehouses, in 1957–58 he designed the Iglesia del Cristo Obrero (Church of Christ the Worker), 4km north of Atlántida (see page 179), where undulating brick walls magically meet an undulating roof while hidden openings direct light to the altar. To achieve this the construction had to be accurate to within 5mm. He later rebuilt the church of San Pedro in Durazno (see page 357), but his main speciality was daringly wide and thin arched roofs for bus stations, gymnasia and the like, as in Salto (see page 328).

Uruguay currently boasts two world-class architects who have done much of their work abroad but have recently returned to design prestigious projects at home. **Rafael Viñoly** (b1944) studied in Buenos Aires and practised there before moving to New York in 1978; he built many major buildings across the world, such as the Princeton University Stadium, the Kimmel Arts Center in Philadelphia, the University of Chicago's Graduate School of Business, The Curve in Leicester (a theatre, which cost double its budget at £61 million) and the US$1.5 billion Tokyo International Forum. He has built a considerable reputation for his great curving shapes in glass and steel; future projects include a couple in London, the so-called 'Walkie-Talkie' (like a squeezed-in tower block, next to the 'Gherkin') and Battersea Power Station.

His first building in Uruguay, finished in 2008, was the Acqua building in Punta del Este, a luxury apartment block (so called because of its tiers of swimming pools) where the penthouse sold for US\$7.3 million. He followed this with the new terminal at Montevideo's Carrasco airport, opened in 2009, where a huge curved roof arches over the approach roads, entry atrium and separate arrival and departure levels, with glazed walls on all four sides allowing plenty of natural light in.

Carlos Ott (b1946), mainly based in Toronto, has designed the new Bastille Opera in Paris, various theatres in China, and the Ushuaia and Calafate airports in Argentina; he returned in 1992 to design Uruguay's 'other' airport, at Punta del Este, as well as the Punta shopping centre and the Torre de las Communicaciones (Antel's headquarters), by far the tallest building in Montevideo (see page 129).

CINEMA Uruguay has a tiny film industry, producing around five features a year, but there is considerable interest in cinema, with film festivals in Montevideo, Piriápolis and Punta del Este. Cinema actually has quite a long history here, the first film being shown in 1896, and the second film made anywhere in Latin America, *Una Carrera de Ciclismo en el Velódromo de Arroyo Seco* (A Cycling Race at the Arroyo Seco Velodrome), being made in 1898. However, Uruguayans only saw foreign (mainly Argentine) films until Juan Antonio Borges's *Almas de la Costa* (Souls of the Coast), the first full-length Uruguayan film, was released in 1923 (although the studio only made one more film before closing). Documentaries were made of the 1930 World Cup in Montevideo, but the Depression again killed off the Uruguayan industry. Even after World War II only a few documentaries and comedies had any success, and the first viable full-length dramas, the gaucho story *Guri* and *Mataron a Venancio Flores* (The Murder of Venancio Flores), came only in 1980 and 1982, respectively. In the 1980s the return of democracy and the growth of the video industry led to the making of some politically controversial films, and in the 1990s both the city of Montevideo and the national government set up funds to boost the industry, finally allowing it to achieve a degree of stability.

The Memory of Blas Quadra (2000) and *The Southern Star* (2002), both directed by Luis Nieto, did well, as did the slacker comedy *25 Watts* (2002) by Pablo Stoll and Juan Pablo Rebella, whose *Whisky* (2003) won the Un Certain Regard Prize at the Cannes Film Festival. A dark comedy about the owner of a sock factory who sets up a fake relationship with an employee to show his expatriate brother that he has a full life, it's subtle, sad and very smart. Alas, Rebella died in 2006 at just 32.

More recently, *El Baño del Papa* (The Pope's Toilet, 2007), by Enrique Fernandez and César Charlone (who lives in Brazil and was nominated for a Best Cinematography Oscar for *City of God*), is an excellent comedy about the build-up to a papal visit to the small town of Melo. In 2009 both *Gigante* (Giant) by Adrián Biniez and *Mal Día Para Pescar* (Bad Day to Go Fishing; from an Onetti short story) by Álvaro Brechner were well received. *La Casa Muda* (The Silent House, 2010) is a horror film telling, supposedly in a single take, the story of a father and daughter visiting a deserted, ill-lit cottage they once lived in; in 2013 its director Gustavo Hernández was making another horror film, *Dios Local* (Local God).

In fact most people, asked about Uruguayan film, would first think of Costa-Gavras's *State of Siege* (1972), a French classic about the kidnapping and murder of the undercover US agent Dan Mitrione by the Tupamaros guerrillas. It's also worth mentioning the Uruguayan director Israel Adrián Caetano, who works in Argentina, co-directing films such as *Pizza, Beer and Smokes* (1997).

Uruguay's best-known actor is **China Zorrilla** (b1922), daughter of the sculptor Jose Luis Zorrilla de San Martin and granddaughter of the poet Juan Zorrilla de San

Martin, who studied at RADA in London, starred on stage and in film in Madrid, Paris and Buenos Aires, won the Best Actress award at the Moscow Film Festival in 2004, and was awarded France's *Légion d'honneur* in 2008.

SPECTATOR SPORTS Most people know two things about Uruguayan sport – that they won the first World Cup, and that a college rugby team crashed in the Andes on the way to a tour in Chile, with cannibalism ensuing (a story well told by Piers Paul Read in his book *Alive*; see page 379).

Soccer The national sport is, of course, soccer (*fútbol*) and even if Uruguay had not won two World Cups that would still be the case. Uruguay's golden age was the 1920s and 1930s, when they won Olympic gold in 1924 and 1928 and then the inaugural World Cup of 1930. However, they may have had a better team in 1950 when they won their second World Cup, including Juan Alberto 'Pepe' Schiaffino (1925–2002), who moved to Italy after the 1954 World Cup (when Uruguay finished fourth), playing for AC Milan and Roma, and indeed for the Italian national team. Ladislao Mazurkiewicz (1945–2013) was only 5ft 10in tall but was one of the great goalkeepers, playing in three consecutive World Cups.

Uruguay's legendary captain Obdulio Varela (1917–96) inspired the team to beat Brazil in the 1950 final in Rio's Maracanã stadium before a crowd of almost 200,000, perhaps the largest ever at a sporting event; it's commonly held that if Varela had not been injured in the 1954 quarter-final against England, Uruguay could have gone on to win the cup again. Instead, their first-ever World Cup defeat came in the semi-final against Hungary's legendary 'Golden Team'. Since then they have done less well, but the 2010 World Cup marked a return to form, with Uruguay finishing in fourth place. However there was outrage when Luis Suárez handled the ball to block a certain goal by Ghana, allowing Uruguay to win a penalty shoot-out and reach the semi-final.

To mark the 50th anniversary of the first World Cup, Uruguay hosted the so-called Mundialito (Little World Cup) between the former winners of the cup (with the Netherlands replacing England, who declined their invitation). In the 1980 final (actually in January 1981) Uruguay defeated Brazil 2–1, as they did in the 1950 final; Uruguay's coach, Roque Máspoli, had been Uruguay's goalkeeper in the 1950 game.

It's generally felt that the game is in decline in Uruguay now, with talented youngsters making their names abroad and one agent, Paco Casal, having a stranglehold on all the transfer *pases*. Many players build their careers in Argentina and with luck move on to Europe – the Uruguayan season is the same as Europe's to aid transfers. There are problems with hooligan fans, but nowhere near as bad as in Argentina, where there are half a dozen murders every year. Fans still stand on the terraces, gathering especially behind the goals, but the stadiums are often only a third full – the huge Estadio Centenario is even emptier except for *clásicos* or derbies between the capital's two main teams, Peñarol and Nacional.

When reading the sports pages, *celeste* (sky blue) refers to the Uruguayan national team and *tricolor* refers to Nacional, who play in red, white and blue; Peñarol play in yellow and black and are known as the *carboneros* or *mirasoles*.

One of the most successful – and popular – players of recent years has been **Gustavo Poyet** (b1967), a powerful midfielder who played in Europe for Zaragoza (captaining the team that won the 1995 Cup Winners' Cup), Chelsea (scoring the winner in the 1998 UEFA Super Cup final) and Spurs, as well as playing for Uruguay. He then became a coach with Swindon Town, Leeds United and Spurs, leaving with manager Juande Ramos when he was sacked in 2008. He was manager

1

of Brighton and Hove Albion from 2009 to 2013 when he took over at Sunderland, and is likely to end up coaching the Uruguayan team at some point.

The star of the next generation was **Diego Forlán** (b1979), whose father Pablo played for Uruguay in the 1966 and 1974 World Cups. Diego made his reputation as a striker in Argentina, then transferred to Manchester United in 2002 and failed to score for eight months, becoming nicknamed 'Diego Forlorn' (and when he did score it was from a penalty). Although things did improve for him, he was always inconsistent, and when Wayne Rooney joined the club Forlán moved to Villarreal and then in 2007 to Atlético Madrid. He found form in Spain, prompting talk of a return to Britain, perhaps with Spurs, Aston Villa or Sunderland; however, he chose to move to Inter Milan and then to Internacional of Porto Alegre, nearer to home. He holds the Uruguayan records for both international caps and goals.

Álvaro Recoba (b1976) played for Internazionale for ten seasons, and 69 times for the Uruguayan national team, and is now seeing out his career with Nacional, as is **Sebastián Abreu**, born the same year and with 70 caps. The current crop of players include striker **Marcelo Zalayeta** (b1978), now back at Peñarol, Real Sociedad winger **Gonzalo Castro** (b1984), **Cristian Rodriguez** (b1985) of Atlético Madrid, **Maxi Pereira** (b1984) of Benfica, defensive midfielder **Alvaro Pereira** (b1985), now with Inter Milan, **Juan Ángel Albín** (b1986), an attacking midfielder with Nacional, Juventus centre-half **Martín Cáceres**, Paris Saint-Germain striker **Edinson Cavani**, striker **Bruno Fornaroli**, on loan from Sampdoria to Nacional, and Liverpool

LUIS SUÁREZ

Easily the most controversial player (and one of the most gifted) to come out of South America since Diego Maradona is Uruguay's Luis Suárez. Born in Salto in 1987, he showed early promise as a striker but was sent off at the age of 15 for headbutting a referee, no less. He made his name with Nacional in Montevideo (scoring ten goals in 27 games to take them to the league title), and was sent off in his first international in 2007. Later that year he moved to Ajax in Amsterdam for €7.5m and before the year was out had been banned for seven matches for biting another player. By 2010 he seemed to have settled down, becoming captain of Ajax and Dutch Player of the Year, scoring 33 goals in 35 matches.

In the 2010 World Cup, his goal against Mexico allowed Uruguay to claim top spot in their group, then a spectacular strike against South Korea took Uruguay through to a quarter-final against Ghana. In the last minute of extra time Suárez handled the ball on the goal line to stop a certain winner – he was sent off (and thus banned for the semi-final) and a penalty was awarded to Ghana. Amazingly, Asamoah Gyan missed and the game ended with a penalty shoot-out, which Uruguay won, triggering worldwide shock. When things had calmed down, most people agreed that Suárez did what most professional players would have done, but his refusal to apologise, his shameless celebrations when Ghana failed to score from the penalty, and his boasting of 'the hand of God' (Maradona's old excuse) alienated many.

Uruguay were knocked out in the semi-final, but the runners-up play-off against Germany, which Uruguay lost 3–2, was a far better game than the final. In 2011 Suárez moved to Liverpool for £22.8 million (nearly double their original bid of £12.7 million), and scored on his debut. In July Suárez's two goals against Peru took Uruguay to the final of the Copa América; it was Diego Forlán's goals that won them their record 15th South American championship, but no-one matched Suárez's international performances overall in 2011.

striker **Luis Suárez** (all four born in 1987), and **Tabaré Viudez** (b1989), an attacking midfielder now playing at Kasımpaşa in Turkey. Cavani, who is just as famous as Suárez outside Britain (both come from Salto, as it happens), signed for Paris Saint-Germain in 2013, while there are also rumours of Suárez leaving Britain.

The fast-rising midfielder **Nicolás Lodeiro** (b1989) produced a fine display in the 2009 South American U21 championships and moved from Montevideo's Nacional to Ajax early the next year, and to Botafogo in 2012. His agent is **Daniel Fonseca** (b1969) who also played for Nacional as a forward before moving to Napoli, Roma and Juventus, while also scoring 11 goals in 30 games for Uruguay. **Abel Hernández** (b1990) of Palermo and **Nicolás López** (b1993) of Udinese are probably the strikers who will replace Forlán, Suárez and Cavani in the future.

It's been calculated that in the first decade of this century Uruguay 'exported' 1,414 players: 95 from Nacional, with 238 going to Argentina, 113 to Mexico and 102 to Spain; in 2010 alone 111 players and 14 coaches left the country.

Interestingly, five-a-side football (known as *fútsal* or indoor football) was created for a Montevideo YMCA in 1930 by a local teacher, Juan Carlos Ceriani.

Rugby Rugby was introduced to Uruguay in the 1860s but remains a minority interest, mainly in the wealthier Anglophile suburbs such as Carrasco. Clubs have names like Old Boys, Old Christians and Montevideo Cricket, and all but one are in Montevideo – the exception is Paysandú, half of whose players are students in

In October 2011 Manchester United's Patrice Evra accused Suárez of using racist language against him, and he was also accused of diving against West Bromwich Albion and of giving a one-fingered salute when a goal against Fulham was disallowed as offside. Fellow Uruguayan Gus Poyet (then manager of Brighton) insisted he wasn't racist, explaining cultural differences that make it just as acceptable to call someone 'Blacky' as 'Shorty', and Viv Anderson, the first black player to represent England, thought the FA should make allowances – but they imposed an eight-match ban and a £40,000 fine, causing outrage on the Kop and in Uruguay.

Inevitably, Suárez's comeback was against Manchester United; having promised to shake Evra's hand before the game he then failed to do so, but did at least apologise fully afterwards.

Captain of the Uruguayan team for the 2012 Olympics, he was upset to be booed when his face appeared on screens during the Uruguayan anthem; he failed to score, and Uruguay were knocked out by Team GB. He has continued to perform brilliantly for Liverpool, where he is a firm favourite, and hates to be rested. Although there have been multiple instances of shocking behaviour, it's clear that they come from his almost excessively competitive nature, and in some ways he is the model modern professional, and far more committed than some of his equally well-paid colleagues. When in January 2013 he scored with a handball against Mansfield, it was ruled not deliberate and soon forgotten about. In April 2013 he punched Chile's Gonzálo Jara and then bit Chelsea defender Branislav Ivanovic resulting in a fine, a ten-match ban and an offer of anger management therapy. He may choose to move abroad for a fresh start, but at Liverpool he's seen as so valuable he'd be worth double his estimated pay of £100,000 a week.

Montevideo and train there. After a slow start, the international team (known as Los Teros or southern lapwings) now usually beats other South American nations with the inevitable exception of

For information on cycling, see pages 65 and 90.

Argentina. Qualifying for the 1999 and 2003 rugby World Cups (but not 2007's) boosted the game's popularity, although it's still behind soccer and basketball. At the time of the 2003 World Cup ten players were playing professionally abroad, three in France's top league, which is boosting skill levels. They narrowly failed to qualify for the 2011 World Cup.

Tennis Uruguay's leading tennis player is **Pablo Cuevas** (b1986, across the river in Argentina), who won the men's doubles (with Peru's Luis Horna) at the 2008 French Open, and reached an ATP world singles ranking of No 88 in the same year. In 2009 he won the men's doubles (with Argentina's Brian Dabul) at the Chilean Open, taking him to a world doubles ranking of No 17. Uruguay's No 2 player is **Marcel Felder** (b1984), who was suspended for two months in 2008 for marijuana use.

The only previous Uruguayan to win a Grand Slam event was **Fiorella Bonicelli** (b1951), who won the mixed doubles at the 1975 French Open and the women's doubles at the 1976 French Open.

Boxing It's worth mentioning the female boxer **Chris Namús** (b1987), who is very popular and seen as an excellent role model; she trains with the Uruguayan commandos.

SURFING

Just as Argentines flock to Uruguay's beaches in summer (because there are no decent beaches near Buenos Aires), so too do their surfers. Although there's no truly demanding surf here, there's plenty of it and you'll usually manage to have fun. The bars and the babes in bikinis are also said to add to the experience.

Surfing is feasible all year, thanks to the reliable Atlantic swell from the southeast. Waves range from 1–1.5m (3–5ft) in January and February (when water temperatures are up to 17°C/68°F) to 2–2.5m (6–8ft) in July and August (when the water is only 13°C/54°F, and a full wetsuit is definitely required, with gloves and booties). Conversely in summer you'll need to protect yourself against the sun. In fact the best surfing is in November, December, March and April when the weather is kind and the beaches are not too busy.

Some airlines classify surfboards as sporting equipment and transport them without charge. Likewise, it's easy to bring boards from Buenos Aires as the ferry and bus companies carry them free. You'll probably want to rent a car (perhaps even a 4x4) if you plan to visit the remoter, emptier beaches; be sure to bring straps to tie the boards to the car.

Punta del Este is the big centre for all beach-related activities: it's often windy, which can spoil surfing proper, but makes this a good site for kite-surfing or windsurfing. Just east of downtown Punta del Este is La Barra, where the young people like to hang out and show off to each other; surfing is good here but it can get very crowded (and with not very skilful surfers at that). There are good breaks on either side of the river mouth, although you need to beware rocks and a strong rip on the right-hand side. Montoya, Bikini and Mantantiales beaches are also very popular, partly because of their trendy bars and nightlife.

OUTDOOR ACTIVITIES The favourite outdoor activity of most Uruguayans is, of course, simply going to the beach, and even towns in the interior have beaches on rivers or lakes which are packed out on sunny weekends. There's not actually much activity involved (exemplified by the fact that most Uruguayans take a folding chair and *matero* (see page 70) to the beach, rather than a towel), but the young bucks will show off by playing *fulbito* (mini soccer) on the beach. In Punta del Este the beachfront condominiums and hotels stake out a stretch of beach and provide chairs and umbrellas in their own particular colour scheme for their guests – all beaches in Uruguay are public, so it can be contentious if they try to keep non-guests away.

Hiking
There's limited scope for hiking, which is best combined with birdwatching in the Bañados del Este or the wetlands of the Río Uruguay *litoral* (see pages 244 and 312). However, there is some attractive hillier terrain in the southeast of the country, including its highest peak, Cerro Catedral (see page 240), as well as the areas of Villa Serrana and the Salto del Penitente, and the Cerro Arequita and Quebrada de los Cuervos protected areas.

Golf
There are just 11 golf courses in Uruguay, but four of those have been built since 1994, with more doubtless on the way. Golf brings in US$55 million a year in the Punta del Este area alone, with four clubs all busy with tournaments in January. Two courses, in Montevideo and Fray Bentos, are historical delights, designed in 1928–30 by Dr Alister MacKenzie, a Scottish surgeon who laid out many of the classic American courses, including the Augusta National. Seeing how the Boers

Continuing eastwards, surfing is possible more or less everywhere, depending on weather and tides, and the beaches get emptier and emptier as you go. You can also try dune-surfing here with snowboards. José Ignacio, like Punta del Este, has a *mansa* (sheltered) beach as well as the *brava* (exposed) one, giving better conditions for novices with fewer cross-currents.

La Paloma is a surfing town, also on a headland with good conditions likely on at least one side; waves of up to 4m have been ridden here. Neighbouring La Pedrera is quieter in terms of nightlife but just as good for surfing. The bohemian enclave of Cabo Polonio, with no road access, apparently has a legendary point break. Punta del Diablo has long empty beaches and good surf; immediately beyond, Santa Teresa occasionally has waves up to 4m high and is popular with Brazilian surfers.

To the west of Punta del Este the surf loses its power as it enters the shallow waters of the River Plate; in Canelones and San José waves are rarely over 1m in height. The water is also an alarming brown colour here, although that's actually nothing to worry about.

It's estimated that there are around 12,000 surfers in Uruguay, of whom just a few hundred are members of the Union de Surf del Uruguay, which runs competitive surfing. The only professional surfer is Marco Giorgi, sponsored by a Brazilian surfwear company and generally assumed to be Brazilian himself. Similarly, most of the boards and other equipment you'll see are Brazilian-made, although some accessories are made in Uruguay. There are surf shops and schools in the main resorts, and a well-established bi-monthly magazine, *Mareas*.

Websites with information on surfing in Uruguay include: www.wannasurf. com, www.olasyvientos.com, www.oceanmind.net and www.paipo.com.uy.

used the lie of the land to hide themselves led him to work on camouflage in World War I, and then to become the first great golf course designer who wasn't actually a good golfer himself.

The season lasts for ten months a year; see the Asociación Uruguaya de Golf website (*www.aug.com.uy*) for more information.

Horseriding With 14 million hectares of prairie grassland, it's no surprise that horses are one of the iconic features of the Uruguayan landscape and lifestyle,

THE URUGUAYAN GAUCHO

Uruguayan gauchos have their origins in the *reducciones* (missions) set up by the Jesuits to protect and 'civilise' the native Guaraní people; here they planted *maté*, herded cattle and learnt leatherworking. After the closure of the missions their mestizo descendants adopted a semi-nomadic lifestyle, and as the cattle industry developed from simply rounding up wild cattle to more organised ranching, they became the most sought-after workers, thanks to their skills on horseback and their ability to survive happily in the *campo* with almost nothing but a large knife and an unrelieved meat diet.

Darwin observed Uruguayan gauchos in 1832 and wrote in detail about their use of the *lazo* (lasso), made of plaited leather strips, to catch cattle, and the *bolas*, two or three stone balls wrapped in leather and linked by a leather rope, to catch rheas. When he tried to use the *bolas* himself, he got one ball caught on a bush and another around his horse's leg, causing general hilarity but fortunately no injuries to man or beast. He strongly approved of the gauchos' character, finding excuses for their faults:

The gauchos, or countrymen, are very superior to those who reside in the towns. The gaucho is invariably most obliging, polite, and hospitable: I did not meet with even one instance of rudeness or inhospitability. He is modest, both respecting himself and country, but at the same time a spirited, bold fellow. On the other hand, many robberies are committed, and there is much bloodshed: the habit of constantly wearing the knife is the chief cause of the latter. It is lamentable to hear how many lives are lost in trifling quarrels. In fighting, each party tries to mark the face of his adversary by slashing his nose or eyes; as is often attested by deep and horrid-looking scars. Robberies are a natural consequence of universal gambling, much drinking, and extreme indolence.

Even now, *gauchada* refers to an act of kindness or a good deed.

In Montevideo it's well worth visiting the Museo del Gaucho (see page 138) with its displays of silverware and leatherware. Holy Week sees the Semana Criolla in the Prado Park, with rodeos and *asados* (barbecues) But to see gaucho culture at its best you should head for Tacuarembó during the second week of March, for the Fiesta de la Patria Gaucha (*Gaucho Homeland Festival*; http://patriagaucha.com.uy), with perhaps 3,000 horsemen (and maybe a few women) competing in rodeo events, and many more people in gaucho garb applauding, shopping for crafts and more practical rural bits and pieces. In the evenings there's *asado con cuero* (a cow barbecued with the skin still attached) and performances of dance, song and poetry. If you happen to be here in winter, you'll find horse races held on Sundays in many villages.

and riding is a key element of many people's visits to the country. This can range from helping gauchos round up cattle on a working farm to polo courses at luxury estancias (ranches). In fact horse riding is increasingly popular in the tourism industry, with rides of a few hours or a day available on and near the beaches (where full-moon rides are the new thing), as well as in grassland and the hills. Equitherapy for the disabled is also developing.

The classic Uruguayan breed of horse (designated by UNESCO as part of the country's Intangible Cultural Heritage) is the *criollo* (native), descended from horses brought from Spain in the 17th century, which are loose-gaited, docile and willing, and combine speed and stamina. There are also quarter-horses, bred in the United States from the 17th century for quarter-mile sprint races, and introduced to Uruguay from 1980. Polo ponies are mostly crosses of thoroughbreds with criollo horses.

A local speciality is endurance riding (*www.uruguayendurance.com*), with a pan-American series (held every two years) of 80km and 120km races, in which Uruguay won gold in 2005 and silver in 2007.

Uruguayans ride with both reins held loosely in one hand, using neck-reining to guide the horse (rather than pulling on the bridle). Whereas you may be used to pulling the right rein to turn right, here you lay the left rein against the horse's neck – a subtle difference, but important. Gaucho saddles are flat and wide and have a much bigger pommel than British ones; they are covered with a sheepskin, with two separate girths to hold them in place. They also use longer stirrups than you may be used to, although that's easy to change.

Almost any estancia listed in this book will offer riding; see also page 47 for companies offering riding tours, and page 114 for horse racing in Montevideo.

2

Practical Information

WHEN TO VISIT

Uruguay can be visited all year round, but the high season is summer, from late December to February, when it's hot and sunny and perfect for hanging out on the beach. It's never really cold or wet at other times, but it certainly can be chilly in winter. Carnaval (carnival) is also a high point, culminating on Shrove Tuesday but starting (in Uruguay) long before then – see pages 110–11.

HIGHLIGHTS

MONTEVIDEO In Montevideo you should enjoy the grand buildings along the main Avenida 18 de Julio, as well as candombé drumming groups rehearsing on Sundays for the Las Llamadas procession. Montevideo's Carnaval is also spectacular (see pages 110–11), and at Easter there are impressive rodeos here. Montevideo is also a good base for visiting the wineries of Canelones department and nearby.

BEACHES Some of the best and most popular beaches in South America lie east of the capital, near the over-developed resort of Punta del Este and also the fashionable little villages of La Pedrera and José Ignacio, with their boutique hotels and restaurants. See pages 200, 233 and 253.

HIKING AND HORSERIDING Inland there is attractive hill country with opportunities for hiking and horseriding; the country's most dramatic scenery is the Quebrada de los Cuervos, a gorge sheltering subtropical flora and fauna. See pages 365–6.

BIRDWATCHING In the west of the country, there's great birdwatching (and spectacular sunsets) by the Río Uruguay. See page 312.

HOT SPRINGS Further north there are many hot-springs resorts, such as the Termas de Daymán, near Salto. See page 330.

TRADITIONAL ESTANCIAS Spend time on an *estancia* (ranch) such as La Sirena, near Mercedes, riding with gauchos, boating, birdwatching, and enjoying the relaxed old-style hospitality. See pages 170, 303–4 and 352.

FRAY BENTOS The *El Anglo* meat-processing plant at Fray Bentos is being restored as a wonderful museum of industrial heritage. See pages 310 and 311.

SUGGESTED ITINERARIES

Almost all visits to Uruguay start in **Montevideo**, home of half of the country's population, hub of its transport system and a place to enjoy architecture, markets, street life, beaches and museums. From there most visitors follow the coast, either west to **Colonia** or east to **beach resorts**, lagoons and wetlands. There's less to see in the interior, with good roads linking a few towns that make good bases for visiting **estancias** – ideal locations to sample horseriding and country life. To the west **larger cities** lie along the Río Uruguay, which forms the border with Argentina, and make good bases for more riding and as well as **birdwatching** in the wetlands.

Many people visit **from Argentina**, often just for a short side trip. A basic triangular route would go by ferry from Buenos Aires to Colonia, by bus to Montevideo and back to Buenos Aires by ferry, but it's worth taking a side trip up to **Carmelo**, and if possible visiting the **wineries** near Montevideo. With a couple of extra days you could also go east to a beach.

Others are **passing through from Buenos Aires to Brazil** – most follow the coast, maybe bypassing Punta for **La Pedrera**, **Cabo Polonio** or **José Ignacio** – but it's also possible to go through the interior to Rivera (which offers the best onward connections) or other border points. It's also possible to travel up the litoral of western Uruguay and through Argentina (entering from Fray Bentos, Paysandú or Salto) to reach Iguazú Falls and the pantanal.

SAMPLE ITINERARIES These are feasible by bus or with a rental car.

One week From Montevideo, head east along the coast, perhaps going to La Pedrera, La Paloma, Cabo Polonio or José Igancio (depending on taste and budget) rather than Punta del Este; then head inland to Minas and back to Montevideo via the Canelones wineries, and possibly add on an extension westwards to Colonia.

Two weeks From Montevideo go west to Colonia, Carmelo and Fray Bentos, follow the litoral north to Paysandú or Salto, then head east to Tacuarembó. From here either go south to Montevideo via the Canelones wineries, or via Minas to the beaches of eastern Uruguay and then back to Montevideo, maybe with a day trip to some wineries from there.

Three or more weeks From Montevideo go west to Colonia, Carmelo and Fray Bentos, follow the litoral north to Paysandú or Salto, then head on to Artigas and Rivera, then south to Tacuarembó. Next head east to Melo and Treinta y Tres, then down to Rocha and the beaches of eastern Uruguay before heading back to Montevideo, maybe with a day trip to some wineries from there.

TOUR OPERATORS

Uruguay is ignored by many operators, or features only as a one-day side trip from Buenos Aires to Colonia; overland truck tours pass through pretty quickly between Rio de Janeiro and Buenos Aires (usually via Iguazú Falls). The one exception is horse-riding tours, many of which come to Uruguay, especially the coast of Rocha.

TOURS

Adventure Center 1311 63rd St, Suite 200, Emeryville, CA 94608, USA; \ +1 510 654 1879; tf +1 866 338 8735; www.adventurecenter.com. Overland trip from Buenos Aires to Rio via Uruguay & Iguazú.

Chimu Adventures 1st Floor, 16 Winchester Walk, London SE1 9AQ; ☎ 020 7403 8265; www. chimuadventures.com. Pro-sustainability operator with excellent website.

Discover Uruguay 30 Woodland St, Suite 11-JK, Hartford, CT 06105, USA; ☎ +1 860 246 7777; tf +1 877 987 8482; www.discoveruruguay.com

Dragoman Camp Green, Debenham, Suffolk IP14 6LA, UK; ☎ 01728 861133; www.dragoman.co.uk. Overland trip from Buenos Aires to Rio via Uruguay & Iguazú.

G Adventures (formerly GAP) UK: 40 Star St, London W2 1QB; ☎ 0844 272 0000; Canada: 19 Charlotte St, Toronto, Ontario M5V 2H5; ☎ +1 416 260 0999; tf +1 888 800 4100; Australia: 172 Bridge Rd, Richmond, VIC 3121; ☎ +61 300 796 618; www.gadventures.com. Uruguay is a stopover on a variety of South American tours.

Intrepid Travel UK: Cross & Pillory Hse, 1 Cross & Pillory Lane, Alton, Hants GU34 1HL; ☎ 01373 828303; tf 0800 781 1660; e uk@intrepidtravel. com; Australia: Level 3, 380 Lonsdale St, Melbourne, VIC 3000; ☎ +61 394 732 626; www. intrepidtravel.com. Uruguay is a stopover on a variety of overland tours.

Journey Latin America 12 Heathfield Terrace, London W4 4JE, UK; ☎ 020 3432 1554; www. journeylatinamerica.co.uk. The leading Latin America specialists, superb for custom-made trips, but their only organised tour to Uruguay is a 4-day trip from Buenos Aires.

Last Frontiers The Mill, Quainton Rd, Waddesdon, Bucks HP18 0LP, UK; ☎ 01296 653000; www.lastfrontiers.com. Offers 3 9-day tours: Montevideo, Punta del Este, Colonia & an estancia; horseriding in Maldonado & Rocha; chic destinations of José Ignacio & Colonia. Also tailor-made trips.

Tucan Travel UK: 316 Uxbridge Rd, London W3 9QP; ☎ 020 8896 1600; tf 0800 804 8435; Australia: 217 Alison Rd, Randwick, NSW 2031; tf +61 1 300 769 249; New Zealand: tf +64 800 444 352; South Africa: tf +27 800 983 999; Canada: tf +1 855 566 8660; USA: ☎ +1 855 444 9110; www.tucantravel.com. Overland trips from Buenos Aires to Rio via Uruguay & Iguazú.

TAILOR-MADE TRIPS

Austral Tours 20 Upper Tachbrook St, London SW1V 1SH, UK; ☎ 020 7233 5384; www. latinamerica.co.uk

Cazenove & Loyd Imperial Studios, 3–11 Imperial Rd, London SW6 2AG, UK; ☎ 020 7384 2332; www.cazloyd.com. 10 days in Uruguay from £3,500.

Exsus Travel 118–119 Fenchurch St, London EC3M 5BA, UK; ☎ 020 7337 9000; USA: ☎ +1 347 809 3426; www.exsus.com. Tailor-made luxury tours.

Mila Tours 100 S Greenleaf, Gurnee, IL 60031, USA; ☎ +1 847 249 2111; tf +1 800 367 7378; e milalatin@aol.com; www.milatours.com. Deluxe & tailor-made packages, eg: 4-day tour from Buenos Aires.

Steppes Latin America 51 Castle St, Cirencester, Glos GL7 1QD, UK; ☎ 01285 880980; www. steppestravel.co.uk; USA: tf +1 855 352 7606. Tailor-made luxury holidays in Montevideo, Colonia & Punta del Este.

The Ultimate Travel Company 25–27 Vanston Pl, London SW6 1AZ, UK; ☎ 020 3582 2515; www. theultimatetravelcompany.co.uk

HORSERIDING

Boojum Expeditions 14543 Kelly Canyon Rd, Bozeman, MT 59715, USA; ☎ +1 406 587 0125; tf +1 800 287 0125; www.boojum.com

Equitours PO Box 807, 10 Stalnaker St, Dubois, WY 82513, USA; ☎ +1 307 455 3363; tf +1 800 545 0019; www.ridingtours.com

Hidden Trails 659A Moberly Rd, Vancouver, BC V5Z 4B3, Canada; ☎ +1 604 323 1141; tf +1 888 987 2457; www.hiddentrails.com

In The Saddle Reaside, Neen Savage, Cleobury Mortimer, Shropshire DY14 8ES, UK; ☎ 01299 272997; Canada/US: tf +1 888 732 7505; www. inthesaddle.com

Ride World Wide Staddon Farm, North Tawton, Devon EX20 2BX, UK; ☎ 01837 82544; www. rideworldwide.co.uk

WINE TOURS

Arblaster & Clarke Wine Tours Cedar Court, 5 College St, Petersfield, Hants GU31 4AE, UK; ☎ 01730 263111; USA: ☎ +1 415 906 5165; www. winetours.co.uk

DuVine Adventures 667 Somerville Av, Somerville, MA 02143, USA; ☎ +1 617 776 4441; tf +1 888 396 5383; www.duvine.com. Divine cycling/wine tours.

Lares Tours Wilson Ferreira Aldunate 1341, Montevideo; ☎ 2901 9120; m 099 592009; e info@lares.com.uy; www.larestours.com

Robertson Wine Tours Argentina: ☎+54 911 4093 7738; USA: ☎+1 707 927 4167; Skype: Robertson Wine Tours; www.robertsonwinetours.com

ADVENTURE AND NATURE TOURISM

Cecilia Regules Viajes Bacacay 1334, Galeria Ciudadela, Local C, Montevideo; ☎2916 3011/2; www.ceciliaregulesviajes.com. The longest-established agency for visits to estancias.

Eco Tours Avda Rivera 2088, office 601, 11200 Montevideo; ☎2400 6245; www.ecotours.com.uy. Founded in 2005, this co-op of experts from NGOs & academia offers tours focusing on birds, mammals, amphibians & reptiles, butterflies, mushrooms, geology & palaeontology, the gaucho experience, plus cycling, canoeing & health tourism w/ends.

Expedición Uruguay m 098 664226; www.expedicionuruguay.com.uy. Working with the NGO Vida Silvestre & LMG Turismo (*Cerro Largo 1078 & Río Negro, Montevideo;* ☎2902 3395/6), offering 1- & 2-day trips to places of natural interest, such as the Quebrada de los Cuervos & the Sierra de las Ánimas.

Guyrapytâ ☎2400 6245; m 094 427409, Spain: ☎+34 639 333 831; e info@guyrapyta.com; www.guyrapyta.com. Excellent birdwatching tours (see advert on page 44).

Lares Aldunate 1322, Montevideo; ☎2901 9120; m 099 592009; www.lares.com.uy. Organises estancia, birdwatching, fishing & hunting trips.

Recorriendo Uruguay m 094 276194; e recorriendo.uruguay@gmail.com; www.recorriendouruguay.com.uy. Estancia stays, horseriding & other rural tourism activities.

TransHotel Acevedo Díaz 1671, Montevideo; ☎2402 9935; www.transhotel.com.uy. City tours & transfers in Montevideo, Colonia & Punta del Este; birdwatching & other tours.

CRUISES

All the usual suspects have ships that call in at either Montevideo or Punta del Este on their way to or from Buenos Aires:

Costa Cruises www.costacruises.co.uk
Crystal Cruises www.crystalcruises.com
Holland America Line www.hollandamerica.com
Princess Cruises www.princess.com
Regent Seven Seas Cruises www.rssc.com
Silversea Cruises www.silversea.com
Swan Hellenic www.swanhellenic.com

RED TAPE

Citizens of most countries (except China, India, Russia and a few smaller countries) require only a passport for visits of up to three months to Uruguay. The same usually applies to Australians (although there was a hiatus in mid-2007 when an agreement lapsed and visas were required for a while).

If you wish to extend your stay for a further three months, contact the Dirección Nacional de Migración (*National Office of Migration; Montevideo; www.dnm. minterior.gub.uy – in Spanish only;* see page 120) or in departmental capitals – but it's generally easier to leave the country for a night and return. If you wish to settle in Uruguay, contact the Inspectoría de Migración (e *dnm-residencias@minterior. gub.uy*), although it's really better to discuss this first with the Uruguayan embassy in your home country.

Arriving by plane, you'll be given two forms, for Immigration and Customs; they are currently in Spanish only but are not difficult to fill in (just remember that your *apellido* is your family name). You'll be given a white form to keep with your passport, but if this gets lost it shouldn't be a problem as long as you have the correct stamp in your passport. Immigration queues are dealt with pretty fast, and there are special desks for the disabled and pregnant and those with babies.

EMBASSIES

OVERSEAS EMBASSIES IN MONTEVIDEO

🇦🇷 Argentina Cuareim 1470; ☎2902 8166; e eurug@mrecic.gov.ar; http://eurug.cancilleria.gov. ar; ⏰ 10.00–15.00 Mon–Fri. Consulate: Wilson

Ferreira Aldunate 1281; ☎2902 8623–5;
e cmdeo@mrecic.gov.ar; ⏰ 13.00–18.30 Mon–Fri
🇪 **Australia** Honorary Consulate: Cerro Largo
1000; ☎2901 0743; e ausconur@adinet.com.uy
🇪 **Bolivia** Dr Prudencio de Peña 2469; ☎2708
3573; e repbol@adinet.com.uy; www.aladi.org/
bolivia
🇪 **Brazil** Bvar Artigas 1394; ☎2707 2119;
e montevideu@brasil.org.uy; http://montevideu.
itamaraty.gov.br; ⏰ 10.00–13.00, 15.00–18.00
Mon–Fri. Consulate: Convención 1343 & 18 de
Julio, 6th Flr; ☎2901 2024; e cg.montevideu@
itamaraty.gov.br; http://cgmontevideu.itamaraty.
gov.br
🇪 **Canada** Plaza Independencia 749, office 102;
☎2902 2030; e mvdeo@international.gc.ca; www.
canadainternational.gc.ca/uruguay; ⏰ 08.30–
12.30, 13.00–17.00 Mon–Thu, 08.30–14.00 Fri
🇪 **Chile** 25 de Mayo 575; ☎2916 4090;
e echileuy@netgate.com.uy; ⏰ 09.00–17.30
Mon–Thu, 09.00–17.00 Fri. Consulate: ☎2916
2346; e cgideouy@netgate.com.uy; http://
chileabroad.gov.cl/montevideo; ⏰ 09.00–14.00
Mon–Fri
🇪 **France** Uruguay 853 & Andes; ☎2902 0077,
217050 000; e ambafranceuruguay@gmail.com;
www.ambafranceuruguay.org. Consulate: ☎2170
50000; ⏰ 09.00–12.00 Mon–Fri
🇪 **Germany** La Cumparsita 1435; ☎2902 5222;
e info@montevideo.diplo.de; www.montevideo.
diplo.de; ⏰ 09.00–11.30 Mon, Wed, Thu & Fri,
13.00–15.30 Tue
🇪 **Israel** Bvar Artigas 1585; ☎2400 4164-6;
e info@montevideo.mfa.gov.il; http://montevideo.
mfa.gov.il; ⏰ 09.30–12.30 Mon–Fri
🇪 **Italy** J Benito Lamas 2857; ☎2708 0542/5316;
e ambasciata.montevideo@esteri.it; www.
ambmontevideo.esteri.it. Consulate: Canning 2535;
☎2480 7080; e consolato.montevideo@esteri.it;
www.consmontevideo.esteri.it
🇪 **Netherlands** Consulate: Costa Rica 1661;
☎2600 2539; e info@honorair-consul-uruguay.
com
Paraguay Bvar Artigas 1256; ☎2707 2138;
e embapur@netgate.com.uy; ⏰ 09.30–16.00
Mon–Fri. Consulate: Bvar Artigas 1191; ☎2400 2215
🇪 **Peru** Calle Obligado 1384 & Rivera, Carrasco;
☎2707 7208/1420; e emba8@easymail.com.uy;
www.embaperu.org.uy
🇪 **South Africa** C Echevarriarza 3335; ☎2623
0161; e safem@netgate.com.uy

🇪 **Spain** Libertad 2738; ☎2708 6010;
e embespuy@correo.mae.es; ⏰ 08.00–13.30
Mon–Fri
🇪 **Sweden** Consulate: Rambla 25 de Agosto de
1825, No 508, 5th Flr; ☎2917 0289; e suecia@
consulado.schandy.com; ⏰ 11.00–13.00 Mon–Fri
🇪 **UK** Marco Bruto 1073 (Buceo), CP 16024,
11300 Montevideo; ☎2622 3630/50;
e ukinuruguay@adinet.com.uy; www.gov.uk/
government/world/uruguay; ⏰ 09.00–13.00,
14.00–17.30 Mon–Thu, 09.00–14.00 Fri (Jan
08.30–14.30 Mon–Fri). Consulate: e consular.
enquiriesmontevideo@fco.gov.uk; ⏰ 09.00–13.00
Mon–Fri
🇪 **US** Lauro Müller 1776, 11100 Montevideo;
☎2177 02000; http://uruguay.usembassy.gov;
⏰ 08.30–17.30 Mon–Fri. American Citizen Services
☎2177 02222; e MontevideoACS@state.gov

URUGUAYAN EMBASSIES AND CONSULATES ABROAD

🇪 **Argentina** Avda Las Heras 1907, 15th Flr,
Buenos Aires 1127; ☎11 4807 3040/60/61;
e urubaires@embajadadeluruguay.com.ar; www.
embajadadeluruguay.com.ar; ⏰ 09.00–16.00
Mon–Fri. Main consulate: Avda Las Heras 1907,
Ground Flr; ☎11 4807 3051 ext 269 or 241;
e conurubaires@embajadadeluruguay.com.ar;
⏰ 09.30–15.30 Mon–Fri. Other consulates: San
Martín 417, 3280 *Colón*; ☎344 742 1999;
e consulado@grouarnetbyz.com.ar; ⏰ 08.00–
14.00 Mon–Fri; Asunción 131, 3200 *Concordia*;
☎345 422 1426, 421 0380; e conurucon@arnet.
com.ar; ⏰ 07.00–13.00 Mon–Fri; Edificio St
Michel, San Jerónimo 167, 20th Floor, 5000
Córdoba; ☎351 424 1028; e cgcordoba@mrree.
gub.uy; ⏰ 09.00–14.00 Mon–Fri; Rivadavia 510,
2820 *Gualeguaychú*; ☎344 642 6168;
e conuruguale@entrerios.net; ⏰ 08.00–14.00
Mon–Fri; San Luis 441 (between Alem & 1º de
Mayo), 2000 *Rosario*; ☎341 424 6860, 421 9077;
e cdrosario@consuladodeluruguay.com.ar;
⏰ 08.00–14.00 Mon–Fri
🇪 **Australia** Suite 2, Level 4, Commerce Hse, 24
Brisbane Av, Barton, ACT 2600; ☎02 6273 9100;
e urucan@iimetro.com.au; ⏰ 09.00–15.00 Mon–
Fri. Consulates: Level 20, 44 Market St, *Sydney*,
NSW 2000; ☎2 9290 2896; e curuguay@bigpond.
net.au; ⏰ 10.00–14.00 Mon–Fri; Level 1, 107
Puckle St, Moonee Ponds, *Melbourne*, VIC 3039;
☎3 9370 6621; e consulurumelb@gmail.com

❸ **Austria** Naglergasse 9, 3rd Flr, door 17, Vienna; ✆1 535 6657/6636; e uruvien@embuy.at. Consulate: Alpenstrasse 75, 5033 *Salzburg*; ✆662 205 1625
❸ **Belgium** 22 B Franklin Roosevelt Av, 1050 Brussels; ✆2 640 1169; e uruemb@skynet.be; ⏲ 09.00–17.00 Mon–Fri
❸ **Bolivia** Calle 21 Calacoto (San Miguel) 8350, Edifício Monroy Velez, 7th Flr, La Paz; ✆2 279 1482/1465; e urulivia@acelerate.com; ⏲ 09.00–15.30 Mon–Fri. Consulate: Avda Cristobal de Mendoza 214, 12th Flr, office 12C, Edificio Castelo Branco, *Santa Cruz*; ✆3 333 5665; e conurucruz@acelerate.com, conurucruz@scbbs-bo.com
❸ **Brazil** Avda das Naçoes, lote 14, Quadra 803 Sul, CEP 70450-900 Brasilia; ✆61 3322 1200/4528/4533; e urubras@emburuguai.org.br; www.emburuguai.org.br; ⏲ 09.30–13.00, 14.00–17.30 Mon–Fri. Consulates: Avda do Contorno 6777, Sala 1301/2, CEP 30110-935 *Belo Horizonte*; ✆31 3296 7527/7873; e conrubelo@terra.com.br; ⏲ 10.00–16.00 Mon–Fri; Rua Venezuela 311, CEP 96255-000 *Chuí*; ✆53 3265 1151; e cdchui@mrree.gub.uy; ⏲ 09.00–15.00 Mon–Fri; Alameda Carlos de Carvalho 417, 31st Flr, office 3101A, Edificio Curitiba Trade Center, CEP 80410-180 *Curitiba*; ✆41 3225 5550; e conurucur@terra.com.br; ⏲ 10.00–16.00 Mon–Fri; Avda Rio Branco 387, 5th Flr, CEP 88015-210 *Florianopolis*; ✆48 3222 3718; e conuruflop@yahoo.com.br; ⏲ 09.00–15.00 Mon–Fri; Avda Dom Luis 500, sala 1925, Shopping Aldeota-Expansão, CEP 60160-230 *Fortaleza*; ✆85 4006 5880; e conuruceara@gmail.com; ⏲ 08.00–12.00, 13.00–17.00 Mon–Fri; Rua 27 de Janeiro, CEP 96300-000 *Jaguarão*; ✆53 3261 1411; e cdyaguaron@mrree.gub.uy; ⏲ 08.00–14.00 Mon–Fri; Rua Prudente de Morais 281, CEP 53020-140 *Olinda*; ✆81 3439 8849; e conurupe@terra.com.br; ⏲ 10.00–14.00 Mon–Fri; Avda Gabriela de Lara 1040, CEP 83203-550 *Paranaguá*; ✆41 3420 7513; ⏲ 08.30–11.30, 14.30–17.30 Mon–Fri; Avda Ferreira Viana 1635, Salas 404 y 405, Barrio Areal, CEP 96085-000 *Pelotas*; ✆53 3229 1901/1843; e cdpelotas@mrree.gub.uy; ⏲ 09.00–12.00, 13.30–16.30 Mon–Fri; Avda Cristovão Colombo 2999, Higienópolis, CEP 90560-005 *Porto Alegre*; ✆51 3325 6197/94; e cgportoalegre@mrree.gub.uy; ⏲ 09.00–15.00 Mon–Fri; Rua Bento Gonçalves 180, apt 23, CEP 97560-000 *Quaraí*; ✆55 3423 1802; e cdquaray@mrree.gub.uy; ⏲ 09.00–15.00 Mon–Fri; Praia de Botafogo 242, 6th Flr, CEP 22250-040

Rio de Janeiro; ✆21 2553 6030/15; e conuruguana@consulado-uruguay-rio.org.br; ⏲ 09.00–14.00 Mon–Fri; Rua Gregorio de Matos 20, 1st Flr, Pelourihno, CEP 40025-060 *Salvador*; ✆71 322 7096; e conurubahia@terra.com.br; ⏲ 09.30–16.00 Mon–Fri; Rua Estados Unidos 1284, Jardins, CEP 01427-001 *San Pablo* (São Paulo); ✆11 2879 6600–08, 3085 5941; e conurupa@osite.com.br; ⏲ 11.00–16.00 Mon–Fri; Avda Tamandaré 2080, 5th Flr, CEP 97573-531 *Santa Ana do Livramento*; ✆55 3242 1416; e cdlivramento@mrree.gub.uy; ⏲ 08.00–14.00 Mon–Fri; Rua Venancio Aires 1761, CEP 97010-003 *Santa María*; ✆55 3221 1180; ⏲ 13.30–18.00 Mon–Fri; Rua Alexandre Fleming 437 apt 31, CEP 11040-010 *Santos*; ✆13 3238 1886; ⏲ 07.00–13.00 Mon–Fri; Rua 15 de Novembro 554, CEP 96300-000 *Jaguarão*; ✆3261 1411; e conuruya@brturbo.com.br; ⏲ 08.00–14.00 Mon–Fri
❸ **Canada** 130 Albert St, Suite 1905, Ottawa, Ontario KIP 5G4; ✆613 234 2937; e embassy@embassyofuruguay.ca; www.embassyofuruguay.ca; ⏲ 09.30–16.30 Mon–Fri. Consulates: 1411 rue Peel, Bureau 603, *Montreal*, Quebec H3A 1S5; ✆514 288 0990; e conurumont@gmail.com; ⏲ 09.00–15.00 Mon–Fri; 300 Sheppard Av W, Suite 302, *Toronto*, Ontario M2N 1N5; ✆416 730 1289; e conurutor@on.aibn.com; ⏲ 09.00–15.00 Mon–Fri; 3 Bentall Centre, Suite 833, 595 Burrard St, PO Box 49058, *Vancouver* BC, V7X 1C4; ✆778 329 0433; e uruguay@northstar.ca; ⏲ 08.30–17.00 Mon–Fri
Chile Avda Pedro de Valdivia 711, Providencia, Santiago; ✆2 204 7988, 274 4066; e urusgo@uruguay.cl; www.uruguay.cl. Main consulate: ✆2 223 8398; e courusgo@uruguay.cl; ⏲ 10.00–16.00 Mon–Fri, 10.00–12.00 Sat. Other consulates: Copiapó 1071, 5th Flr, office 10, *Antofagasta*; ✆55 250138; e consuluruguay2@hotmail.com; ⏲ 09.30–13.30 Mon–Fri; 21 de Mayo 345, offices 31–32, *Arica*; ✆58 2231536; Talca 119, office 206, *Puerto Montt*; ✆65 253155; e nitzalacoa@telsur.cl; Pasaje El Ovejero 0530, *Punta Arenas*; ✆61 215671, 311123; e pipa.ma@gmail.com; Plaza Sotomayor 50, *Valparaíso*; ✆32 2203570; e jaldunate@vtr.net
❸ **France** 15 rue Le Sueur, 1st Flr, 75116 Paris; ✆01 45 00 81 37; e amburuguay.urugalia@fr.oleane.com. Main consulate: ✆01 45 00 53 32; ⏲ 11.00–15.00 Mon–Fri. Other consulates in Bordeaux, Marseilles & Toulouse
❸ **Germany** Budapesterstrasse 39, 3rd Flr, 10787 Berlin; ✆030 263 90160; e urubrande@

t-online.de; ⏰ 09.00–16.30 Mon–Fri. Consulates in Bremen, Düsseldorf, Frankfurt, Hamburg, München, Potsdam & Stuttgart
e Ireland Consulate: Tullycushlin, Bailieborough, Co Cavan; ✆ 429 665392; e peadarreynolds@ hotmail.com
e Italy Via Vittorio Veneto 183, 5th Flr, 00187 Roma; ✆ 06 482 1776/77, 482 1001; e uruit@ ambasciatauruguay.it; ⏰ 09.00–14.00 Mon–Fri. Consulates in Bologna, Livorno, Milano, Napoli & Padova
e New Zealand Consulate: 39 Yardley St, Christchurch 0842; ✆ 3 342 5520; e consulurunz@ gmail.com
e Paraguay Avda Guido Boggiani 5832, 3rd Flr, Asunción; ✆ 021 664244/6; e uruasun@embajadauruguay.com.py; www. embajadauruguay.com.py. Consulate: Ground Flr; ✆ 021 610595; e conrupar@embajadauruguay. com.py; ⏰ 09.00–15.00 Mon–Fri
e Peru José D Anchorena 084, San Isidro, Lima 27; ✆ 01 719 2550/2552/2865; e uruinca@ americatelnet.com.pe; ⏰ 09.30–13.30 Mon–Fri. Consulate: Calle Quezada 110B, Yanahuara, Arequipa; ✆ 51 5425 9364; e consuladoagp-uruguay@speedy.com.pe
e South Africa 1119 Burnett St, MIB Hse, office 301, Hatfield 0028, POB 14818, Pretoria; ✆ 12 362 6522; e urusud@pixie.co.za; www. embassyofuruguay.co.za; ⏰ 08.30–15.30 Mon–Fri
e Spain Paseo del Pintor Rosales 32, 1st Flr, 28008 Madrid; ✆ 91 758 0475; e urumatri@ urumatri.com; www.urumatri.com;

⏰ 09.00–15.00 Mon–Fri. Main consulate: 8th Flr; ✆ 91 548 2282; e coruespa@terra.es; ⏰ summer 09.00–15.00; winter 09.00–18.00 Mon–Fri. Other consulates: Passeig de Gracia 55, 5th Flr, 08007 Barcelona; ✆ 935 514 984, 285 566/68; e couruguay@consuladouy-bcn.es, conurubar@ consuladouy-bcn.org; ⏰ 09.30–15.30 Mon–Fri; & in Bilbao, Las Palmas (Gran Canaria), Palma (Mallorca), Pamplona, Santa Cruz (Tenerife), Santiago de Compostela, Sevilla, Valencia & Vigo
e UK 125 High St Kensington, 1st Flr, London W8 5SF; ✆ 020 7937 4170; e emburuguay@ emburuguay.org.uk; http://uruguay. embassyhomepage.com; ⏰ 10.00–16.00 Mon–Fri
e US 1913 I St NW, Washington, DC 20006; ✆ 202 331 1313–6; e uruwashi@uruwashi.org; www. uruwashi.org. Main consulate: ✆ 202 331 4219; e conuruwashi@uruwashi.org; ⏰ 09.00–13.00, 14.00–16.00 Mon–Fri. Other consulates: 875 North Michigan Av, Suite 1318, Chicago, IL 60611; ✆ 312 642 3430; e consulado@uruguaychicago. org; ⏰ 10.00–16.00 Mon–Fri; 2103 Coral Way, Suite 600, Miami, FL 33145; ✆ 305 443 9764, 443 7253, 443 7453; e cgmiami@mrree.gub.uy; ⏰ 09.00–15.00 Mon–Fri; 420 Madison Av, 6th Flr, New York, NY; ✆ 212 753 8581/2; e conuruyork@ consuladouruguaynewyork.com; ⏰ 09.30–15.30 Mon–Fri; 429 Santa Monica Bd, Suite 400, Santa Monica, CA 90401; ✆ 310 394 5777; e conurula@ conurula.org, consulado@conurula.org; ⏰ 09.00–15.00 Mon–Fri; also honorary consulates in Boston, Honolulu, Houston, New Orleans, Sandy UT, San Francisco & San Juan PR

GETTING THERE AND AWAY

BY AIR From the northern hemisphere, most people will naturally arrive by air. From Madrid, for a long time Iberia flew direct every night to Montevideo, code-sharing with the Uruguayan flag-carrier Pluna and British Airways; Pluna closed down in 2012 and Iberia announced early in 2013 that they were giving up the route. The new **BQB** local airline (*www.flybqb.com*) announced plans to take over the route (Uruguay's key link to Europe), flying six times a week with leased Boeing 777s, code-sharing with Iberia. In addition **Air France–KLM** (*www.airfrance.co.uk*) announced plans for their Paris–Buenos Aires flights (also with 777s) to stop five times a week in Montevideo. **Air Europa** (*www.aireuropa.com*) also flies three times a week from Madrid.

Alternatives are to fly to Buenos Aires and then cross the River Plate by air (to Montevideo or Punta del Este) or ferry (to Montevideo or Colonia), or to change planes in Brazil.

From North America, **American Airlines** (*www.aa.com*) flies non-stop from Miami to Montevideo daily. From 2014 Brazil's **TAM** (*www.tam.com.br*)will be a

Oneworld partner of American Airlines and BA, giving connections from New York, Miami, London and elsewhere via São Paulo or Rio de Janeiro. **LAN** (*www.lan.com*) flies from Santiago to Montevideo twice a day; **COPA** (*www.copaair.com*) flies daily from Panama City and **TACA** (*www.taca.com*) has three flights a week from Lima, with connections from the United States in conjunction with United Airlines. **GOL** (*www.voegol.com*) has around four flights a day from Montevideo to São Paulo, some calling at Porto Alegre, southern Brazil's main transport hub.

Montevideo has far fewer long-distance connections than Buenos Aires, in particular, and it may prove cheaper to fly to Buenos Aires and take either the short flight across the River Plate to Montevideo or Punta del Este, or the ferry or bus (see below and page 54). However, this almost always requires transferring from the Ezeiza long-distance airport (EZE) to the Aeroparque (AEP), the airport in the city's northern suburbs that handles flights within Argentina and to neighbouring countries. This is fairly easy and well organised, either by Aerolíneas Argentinas if flying both legs with them or with the Manuel Tienda León shuttle company (*www.tiendaleon.com.ar*). This route is flown by Aerolíneas, BQB and the small Argentine company Sol (*www.sol.com.ar*), which began operating in 2006 and flies to Montevideo Monday to Friday only. In all there are around ten flights each way daily (the last at about 21.00), taking just 40 minutes. Be aware that Aerolíneas in particular is notorious for changing schedules and if you don't check you may turn up to find that your flight has already left.

In addition there's at least one flight a day from Buenos Aires (Aeroparque) to Punta del Este (PDP), with four or five on winter weekends and up to a dozen per day in summer, operated by Aerolíneas Argentinas, BQB and Sol. The new BQB airline (*www.flybqb.com*), set up by the owner of the Buquebus ferry company, flies from Montevideo to Salto and Rivera, and internationally to Buenos Aires, Porto Alegre, Florianopolis, Iguazú and Asunción, and from Buenos Aires to Punta del Este. It is asking for rights to serve the Montevideo–Madrid route, although it remains to be seen whether this is practical for a small regional airline.

Alternatives are to change planes in São Paulo or Rio de Janeiro, continuing with TAM or GOL. GOL is allied with Air France–KLM and Delta, and TAM with LAN, BA, American Airlines and Iberia. TAM flies direct from London (Heathrow), Paris, Frankfurt, Milan, Madrid, New York and Miami to São Paulo, with connections to Montevideo.

BY FERRY Several companies operate ferries between Argentina and Uruguay. The best known is **Buquebus** (*www.buquebus.com*), which runs both fast ferries and traditional slower ships from Buenos Aires; these no longer go directly to Punta del Este, but connecting buses go there from both Colonia and Montevideo. Fast ferries reach Colonia in an hour from Buenos Aires or Montevideo in three hours, while slower ships are scheduled to take three hours to Colonia. Both types of vessel carry cars. The fast ferries are quick enough but rather cramped, with lots of over-excited children running around, no access to the deck and a disproportionate amount of space set aside for first-class and *primera especial* accommodation – totally unnecessary on a one-hour crossing, but an easy way to part Argentines from their money.

Fares from Buenos Aires to Colonia start at US$44 by ship (US$55 first class, or US$62 primera especial) and US$65 by fast ferry (US$84 first class, US$90 primera especial); from Buenos Aires to Montevideo costs from US$91 by fast ferry (US$145 first class). Taking a bus from Montevideo to Colonia and then a ship brings the cost down to US$66 (US$77 first class) or US$78 by fast ferry (US$90 first class, US$97 primera especial). Taking a car from Buenos Aires to Colonia costs from US$70 by ship or US$87 by fast ferry, or US$114 from Buenos Aires to Montevideo. It's also possible to book bus connections to Piriápolis, La Paloma, Carmelo and the Termas de Arapey, as well as packages including accommodation. There are discounts for children and senior citizens (formerly only for Argentines and Uruguayans, but now available to all); regular passengers can get every fifth trip free.

Sailings are often fully booked, especially at weekends and peak holiday times, so you should book in advance (particularly with a vehicle), although reservations are only available 90 days ahead. The Buquebus website (*www.buquebus.com*), which used to be notoriously poor, now works well, although it's best to use the Internet Explorer browser. If you can use the Spanish-language site, you'll find it more straightforward than the English version. You'll get an e-ticket, and be told to check in an hour before departure (thus turning a one-hour journey into a two-hour one), giving plenty of time to linger in the departure lounge. Allow plenty of time if buying tickets in person at Buquebus's terminal in Buenos Aires: the counters are unsigned, but you'll book at one counter then queue again to pay at another, in a typically Argentine job-creation scheme. Baggage (and bicycles) can be checked in, but you are free to carry rucksacks on board. There's no ATM at the Buenos Aires terminal, but Uruguay's Banco de la República has an exchange kiosk here. Argentine and Uruguayan immigration procedures are carried out together at the departure port, so you're free to leave rapidly on arrival. At Colonia, a new terminal offers a café, ATMs, car rental and other facilities. There are duty-free shops on board the ships, with cheap alcohol, but the restaurants are overpriced. There's free Wi-Fi between Buenos Aires and Montevideo, which also allows the use of mobile phones at sea.

Two smaller, cheaper competitors are snapping at Buquebus's heels. **Colonia Express** (*www.coloniaexpress.com*) offers web fares as low as US$18 each way from Buenos Aires to Colonia, booking at least 21 days in advance; the fare leaps to US$27.50 each way if booked 16–20 days ahead, US$31 eight to 15 days ahead, and US$36 after that. They offer three crossings a day with fast ferries taking an hour from Buenos Aires to Colonia; from here buses connect to Montevideo (US$8–13 extra). Passengers for Punta del Este transfer to a COPSA bus at Montevideo's Tres Cruces bus terminal. **SeaCat Colonia** (*www.seacatcolonia.com*) operates fast ferries from Buenos Aires to Colonia twice a day (four times on Saturdays). Fares start at US$30, with connecting buses costing US$13 to Montevideo and US$19 to Punta del Este. First-class accommodation is also available on the ferries.

It's also possible to take the far smaller, simpler boats (which don't carry cars) from the pleasant resort of Tigre through the Paraná Delta, full of birdlife. In Tigre the international boats leave from Lavalle 520, across a bridge from the main Terminal Fluvial (where the tourist office is) at Mitre 319.

Cacciola Viajes (*www.cacciolaviajes.com*) operate a service twice a day from Tigre to Carmelo, with a minibus from downtown Buenos Aires to Tigre, and others from Carmelo to Colonia and Montevideo (a total of eight hours from capital to capital). Fares are US$30 each way Tigre–Carmelo or US$45 each way Buenos Aires–Montevideo.

Similarly, **Líneas Delta Argentinas** (*www.lineasdelta.com.ar*) sail once daily from Tigre to Nuevo Palmira, north of Carmelo, leaving early in the morning and returning from Uruguay in the afternoon. The fare is US$30 single/US$50 return, plus US$10 for a connecting bus to Colonia (*1¼hrs*).

Ferry offices

In Argentina

Buquebus Terminal Fluvial, Avda Antártida Argentina 821, Dársena Norte, Buenos Aires; ☎4316 6500; ⏰ 06.30–midnight Sun–Fri, 06.30–21.00 Sat (call centre); ⏰ 08.00–21.00 Mon–Fri, 09.00–14.00 Sat. Others include: Avda Córdoba 867, Microcentro, Buenos Aires; Posadas 1452, Recoleta, Buenos Aires; Retiro bus terminal, offices 20–22, Buenos Aires; all ⏰ 09.00–19.00 Mon–Fri, 09.00–14.00 Sat (*call centre:* ☎*4316 6500;* ⏰ *08.00–21.00 Mon–Fri, 09.00–14.00 Sat*); www.buquebus.com

Cacciola Viajes Florida 520 casi Lavalle, 1st Flr, Buenos Aires; ☎4393 6100, 4394 5520; Terminal Fluvial, Lavalle 520, Tigre; ☎4749 2369/0931/0329; www.cacciolaviajes.com

Colonia Express Avda Córdoba 753, Buenos Aires; ☎4317 4100; ⏰ 10.00–19.00 Mon–Fri; terminal: Avda Pedro de Mendoza 330, Darsena Sur, Buenos Aires; ⏰ 10.00–19.00 Mon–Fri, 10.00–12.00 Sat, 10.00–16.00 Sun; www.coloniaexpress.com

Lineas Delta Argentinas Terminal Fluvial, Mitre 305, Tigre, office 6; ☎4731 1236, 4749 0537; www.lineasdelta.com.ar

SeaCat Colonia Avda Córdoba 772 & Esmeralda, Buenos Aires; ☎4322 9551/3–6; ℮ agencias@ferrylineas.com.ar; ⏰ 09.00–19.00 Mon–Fri, 09.00–13.00 Sat (*call centre:* ☎*4314 5100;* ⏰ *07.00–20.00 daily*); www.seacatcolonia.com

In Uruguay

Buquebus Port, Montevideo; Hotel Radisson Victoria Plaza, Colonia 751 & Florida, Montevideo Centro; ⏰ 10.00–18.00 Mon–Fri, 09.00–13.00 Sat; Tres Cruces bus terminal, office B28/9, Montevideo; ⏰ 06.30–02.00 daily; Shopping Punta Carretas, No 219, Montevideo; ⏰ 10.00–

22.00 daily; Hectór Miranda 2443 near Ellauri, Punta Carretas, Montevideo; ⏰ 10.00–19.00 Mon–Fri, 09.00–13.00 Sat; Carrasco airport; ☎2604 9015; bus terminal, Colonia; ⏰ 08.00–20.00 Mon–Sat, 12.00–20.00 Sun; bus terminal, Piriápolis; ⏰ 10.00–19.00 daily; bus terminal, office 09, Punta del Este; ⏰ 09.00–17.00 daily; Punta Shopping, No 104, Punta del Este; ⏰ mid-Dec–mid-Mar 10.00–22.00 daily; rest of the year 11.00–20.00 daily; Avda Solari & Calle de la Virgén, La Paloma; ⏰ 10.00–19.00 Mon–Fri, 09.00–14.00 Sat (*telephone sales:* ☎*2-130* ⏰ *08.00–21.00 Mon–Fri, 09.00–14.00 Sat*); Sarandí 541, Rivera; ⏰ 10.00–19.00 Mon–Fri, 09.00–14.00 Sat; Salto Shopping Local 8; ⏰ 10.00–19.00 Mon–Fri, 10.00–14.00 Sat; www.buquebus.com.uy

Cacciola Tres Cruces bus terminal, Montevideo, office B32; ☎2401 9350/5721; ⏰ 09.00–21.00 Mon–Sat; Calle del Puerto 263, Carmelo; ☎4542 7551

Colonia Express Tres Cruces bus terminal, Montevideo, offices B17/18; ☎2400 3939; ferry terminal, Colonia; ☎4522 9677/8; ⏰ 10.00–19.00 Mon–Fri, 10.00–16.00 Sat, 10.00–12.00 Sun; & at COPSA bus company offices in Piriápolis, Maldonado, Punta del Este & Solanas (Portezuelo) bus terminals; www.coloniaexpress.com

Lineas Delta Argentinas Nueva Palmira; ☎4544 7589; ℮ ldapalmi@adinet.com.uy; www.lineasdelta.com.ar

SeaCat Colonia Río Negro 1400 & Colonia, Montevideo; ☎2900 6617, 2901 3835; ℮ ventas@ferryturismo.com.uy; ⏰ 09.00–19.00 Mon–Fri, 09.00–12.00 Sat; Tres Cruces bus terminal, offices B28/29, Montevideo; ⏰ 07.00–23.00 daily; port, Colonia; ☎4522 2919; ⏰ 07.30–19.00 daily; bus terminal, office 9, Punta del Este; ☎4249 3892; (*call centre:* ☎*2915 0202;* ⏰ *08.00–21.00 Mon–Fri, 09.00–14.00 Sat*); www.ferryturismo.com.uy

BY BUS Although it's a long way around, buses do run from Buenos Aires to Montevideo and Punta del Este, offering an overnight journey at a far lower cost than Buquebus. Leaving between 21.30 and 23.30, they take eight hours and charge US$55 each way (US$40 between Buenos Aires and Fray Bentos or Mercedes) or US$70 for a *cama* (a seat that reclines to form a bed). **Bus de la Carrera**, **Cauvi** and **General Belgrano** all run to and from the Tres Cruces terminal in Montevideo (see opposite and page 88 for contact details), and General Belgrano also serves Punta del Este. Bus de la Carrera also has a daytime service, leaving at 10.00 in each direction.

There are also regular *leito* (bed) and *executivo* (or *semi-leito*) buses from Montevideo and Punta del Este to southern Brazil, via the Chuy border crossing.

TTL (Transporte Turismo Limitada) runs an executivo bus from Porto Alegre to Montevideo (*US$80*) five nights a week, via Pelotas, Chuí, San Carlos and Punta del Este; and a *leito* on Friday nights (*returning on Sun; US$110*). Similarly, **EGA** runs from Porto Alegre to Montevideo (*Sun–Fri*), and on Fridays (*plus Sun & Tue at busy times*) from São Paulo (*US$210 semi-cama, US$268 cama*), Curitiba and Florianopolis.

You can also cross the border on foot or by taxi and catch an internal bus from the *rodoviaria* (bus station) on the Brazilian side, giving a much greater choice of destinations and departure times. From Chuí there are two buses daily (one overnight) to Porto Alegre (*US$33–40; 7¾hrs*) as well as five to Pelotas, and three a week to Florianopolis, Curitiba and São Paulo; from Jaguarão there are three buses a day to Porto Alegre (*US$35; 6hrs*), and seven to Pelotas (five on Sundays). From Santana do Livramento five **Ouro e Prata** buses daily go to Porto Alegre (*convencional US$40, executivo US$53, leito US$68; 7hrs*); **NS da Penha** has a daily service to Curitiba (*US$85; 19hrs*). From Uruguaiana there are two buses daily to Curitiba (*US$67; 19hrs*) and six to Porto Alegre (*US$39–88; 8½hrs*), plus one on Saturdays and Sundays only to Santana do Livramento.

There are also services from Brazil to Argentina passing through Uruguay but avoiding Montevideo: in summer **Ouro e Prata** runs (on Sunday night, returning on Fridays) from Porto Alegre to Rivera, Tacuarembó, Salto and Paysandú, for onward connections into Argentina with **FlechaBus** (*www.flechabus.com.ar*). (FlechaBus also provides more convenient services from Brazil to Argentina via Iguazú.) At its hub in Montevideo, EGA's buses from Brazil connect to Asunción (Paraguay) and Foz de Iguaçu (Brazil), to Paraná, Santa Fé, Rosario, Córdoba, San Luis and Mendoza (Argentina) and to Santiago (Chile).

International bus companies

In Argentina

Bus de la Carrera Retiro bus terminal, office 194, Buenos Aires; 4315 8796, 4313 1700

Cauvi Retiro bus terminal, office 198, Buenos Aires; 4314 6999

EGA Terminal NETOC, office 27, Córdoba; 0351 425 4765; Terminal del Sol, office E7, Mendoza; 0261 431 2140; Terminal M Moreno, Local 32, Rosario; 0341 438 0065; bus terminal, office 18/9, Paraná; 0343 421 9699; bus terminal, office 22, Santa Fé; 0342 455 7013

IGUAZÚ FALLS

Visitors to Uruguay often want to continue to Iguazú Falls, on the border of Argentina and Brazil. There are no direct buses, but the journey can be made relatively simply. From Salto, take the ferry to Concordia (Argentina), then go to the bus terminal at Juan B Justo and Hipólito Yrigoyen and book a ticket to Iguazú with **Expreso Tigre-Iguazú** (*office 7;* 0345 423 0842, 0810 333 7575; *www.tigreiguazu.com.ar*). There's a good choice of buses, mostly overnight – you'll be told to return to the terminal about 40 minutes before your scheduled departure to be taken by taxi (no extra charge) to a police checkpoint on the bypass, where the bus will collect you. It's another ten or so hours to Iguazú, with reasonable service and meals, and less good films. From eastern Uruguay you might prefer to go to Florianopólis in Brazil, and take the **Catarinense** bus from there to Foz de Iguaçu, leaving daily at 16.00 (*www.catarinense.net*) (*US$62; 15hrs*). Alternatively there are now flights with BQB from Montevideo and Salto to Foz de Iguaçu (from US$125).

FlechaBus Retiro bus terminal, offices 141–146; ☎011 4000 5200
Pullman General Belgrano Retiro bus terminal, office 204, Buenos Aires; ☎4315 1226/6522; www.gralbelgrano.com.ar

In Brazil
EGA Gonçalves Chávez 659, office 12, Pelotas; ☎0532 223817; Rodoviaria, offices 6 & 18, Porto Alegre; ☎051 3211 4977; e egapoa@terra.com.br; Rodoviaria Rita María Sector D, Florianópolis; ☎048 3222 5061/5012; e egafloventas@hotmail.com; Rodoviaria, Local 29, Curitiba; ☎041 323 4221; Rodoviaria Tieté, office 386, São Paulo (San Pablo); ☎011 2221 1100; e egasao@terra.com.br
Ouro e Prata Rodoviaria, Porto Alegre; ☎051 3225 8771; e alaint@ouroeprata.com; www.viacaoouroeprata.com.br
TTL Rua Dona Teodora 1643, Navegantes, Porto Alegre; ☎051 3224 7690; e ttl@ttl.com. br; BR 471, km651, Chuí; ☎053 3265 1226; c/o Horizonte Azul Passagens, Estaciao Rodoferroviária, office B 23F, Curitiba; ☎041 3233 2192; e josmar. francisco@terra.com.br; Rodoviária, international wing, office 03, Florianópolis; ☎048 3324 1416; e ttlflo@ttl.com.br; c/o Unesul de Transporte Ltda, Rodoviaria, Avda Brasil 99, Foz do Iguaçu; ☎045 3522 2070; Avda Presidente João Goulart 4605, office 35, Pelotas; ☎053 3281 1990; e agpel@ unesul.com.br; Rodoviaria, Rio Grande; ☎053 3232 6220; e rdvriog@vetorialnet.com.br; Rodoviaria, international wing, Largo Julio Veppo, Porto Alegre; ☎051 3224 7557/7690; e ttlrod@ttl.com.

br; Rodoviaria Tieté, office 385, São Paulo; ☎011 2221 3811/3531; e ttlrosao@ttl.com.br; www.ttl. com.br

In Chile
EGA Terminal Sur, office 50, Alameda O'Higgins 3850, Santiago; ☎2779 3536; e egachile@hotmail.com

In Paraguay
EGA Eligio Ayala 693, Asunción; ☎021 492 473; terminal, offices 105/6; ☎021 559 795; e clotyegatoa@hotmail.com

In Uruguay
Bus de la Carrera Tres Cruces terminal, office B25/26, Montevideo; ☎2402 1313
Cauvi Tres Cruces terminal, office B31, Montevideo; ☎2401 9196
EGA Tres Cruces terminal, office B30, Montevideo; ☎2402 5164–7; e reservas@ega. com.uy; Punta del Este bus terminal, c/o El Maragato Turismo, office 7; ☎4249 2380; e maragatoturismo2009@hotmail.com; Melo bus terminal, office 7; ☎4642 0505; e agenciamelo@ hotmail.com; Treinta y Tres, Avda Meléndez 163; ☎4452 0783; e egatyt@hotmail.com; www. egakeguay.com/index.php
General Belgrano Tres Cruces terminal, office B27, Montevideo; ☎2401 4764
TTL Tres Cruces terminal, office B27, Montevideo; ☎2401 1410

HEALTH *with Dr Felicity Nicholson*

Uruguay is a clean temperate country with very few nasty diseases or health risks, and a good standard of healthcare. There is a low risk of rabies and no malaria, and a very low risk of dengue fever, although in early 2009 Argentina's health ministry belatedly admitted an outbreak affecting up to 15,000 people in Chaco and other northern states. Cities such as Paysandú are working hard to eliminate the *Aedes aegypti* mosquito, which carries the dengue virus; you should in any case take precautions against mosquito bites in the daytime. Similarly, yellow fever is found in Argentina's Misiones and Corrientes states and in adjacent parts of Brazil, but not as yet in Uruguay. It is recommended to have a yellow fever vaccination at least ten days before visiting the subtropical forests of Argentina and Brazil. The vaccine is not suitable for everyone, so ensure that you seek medical advice before booking your trip if you wish to stray outside of Uruguay. If you are coming from a yellow fever endemic zone into Uruguay then they will ask for a certificate. If you cannot have the vaccine for medical reasons then ensure that you obtain an exemption certificate from your GP or a travel clinic.

Apart from yellow fever, as described above, no other vaccinations are required, but make sure you're up to date with tetanus and diphtheria (which now come together with polio as the all-in-one Revaxis) and hepatitis A jabs. Entry requirements can be checked with the **Ministry of Public Health** (📞 *0800 4444;* e *sanidadfronteras@msp.gub.uy;* ⏰ *09.00–13.00 Mon–Fri*). Further information is available from NHS Scotland's **Fit for Travel** website (*www.fitfortravel.scot.nhs.uk*), the **National Travel Health Network and Centre** (*www.nathnac.org/ds/c_pages/country_page_uy.htm*) or the **Centers for Disease Control and Prevention** (*www.cdc.gov/travel/destinations/uruguay.aspx*).

In general, your best health protection is to be fit and well before you set off. Have your teeth checked and carry your prescription if you wear glasses (or leave it as an email message to yourself).

TRAVEL CLINICS AND HEALTH INFORMATION A full list of current travel clinic websites worldwide is available on www.istm.org. For other journey preparation information, consult www.nathnac.org/ds/map_world.aspx (UK) or http://wwwnc.cdc.gov/travel/ (US). Information about various medications may be found on www.netdoctor.co.uk/travel. All advice found online should be used in conjunction with expert advice received prior to or during travel.

HEALTHCARE Uruguay's healthcare system is a mixture of private and socialised provision, with 48 non-profit healthcare bodies providing care to almost half the population through an insurance system. The rest of the population relies on facilities provided by the Ministry of Public Health and the University of the Republic, which also provide free emergency treatment to all. The Ministry of Public Health also provides an effective system of care for mothers and babies, and for tackling outbreaks of diseases such as dengue fever.

Medical care is good but can be expensive; foreigners will usually be expected to pay cash, and arrange reimbursement from their insurer later. Travel insurance is essential, more so that you can be flown out if necessary. Pharmacies supply most internationally available medications, and the well-trained staff are able to supply most drugs, except for narcotics, without a doctor's prescription.

Expat residents can join a Uruguayan insurance scheme, paying US$150–200 a month for coverage including a private room (with visitor's bed); co-payments are just US$5 to see a doctor or for lab tests, from US$15 for an ambulance, or US$70 for an MRI.

FOOD AND WATER HYGIENE Standards of hygiene are generally high throughout Uruguay, but if in doubt bottled water is widely available.

RABIES Whilst rabies is not usually present in Uruguay, it is in the neighbouring countries of Argentina and Brazil. Any bite, scratch or lick from any warm-blooded mammal should be treated as suspicious. Scrub the wound with soap and water, apply antiseptic and get medical care as soon as possible. If you have not had rabies vaccine before you travel then you would need treatment with Rabies Immunoglobulin (RIG) and a full course of rabies vaccine (usually five doses over a month).

SUN EXPOSURE People say that the ozone layer in Uruguay is thin, leading to increased risk of sunburn, but the problem is (ironically) more the lack of pollution in the air. In any case, you should wear a hat, keep your arms covered in the middle of the day, and use plenty of sunblock.

HIV/AIDS The HIV rate in Uruguay is double that of the UK, with around 0.3% of the population having HIV or AIDS. If you must indulge in sex, use condoms or femidoms, which help reduce the risk of transmission. If you notice any genital ulcers or discharge, get treatment promptly since these increase the risk of acquiring HIV. If you do have unprotected sex, visit a clinic as soon as possible; this should be within 24 hours, or no later than 72 hours, for post-exposure prophylaxis.

OTHER MEDICAL MATTERS There's a high rate of oesophageal cancer in Uruguay and neighbouring regions, which has been linked to drinking *maté* – research suggests that the problem is not the tea itself but the high temperatures at which some people drink it.

Other problems associated with the beaches are jellyfish, especially Portuguese men-of-war (*fragata portuguesa; Physalia physalis*), increasingly common in 2009 owing to the drought which reduced the water flow in the River Plate and allowed

LONG-HAUL FLIGHTS, CLOTS AND DVT

Any prolonged immobility, including travel by land or air, can result in deep-vein thrombosis (DVT) with the risk of embolus to the lungs. Certain factors can increase the risk and these include:

- Having a previous clot or a close relative with a history
- Being over 40, with increased risk in over 80s
- Recent major operation or varicose-veins surgery
- Cancer
- Stroke
- Heart disease
- Obesity
- Pregnancy
- Hormone therapy
- Heavy smoking
- Severe varicose veins
- Being tall (over 6ft/1.8m) or short (under 5ft/1½m).

A deep-vein thrombosis causes painful swelling and redness of the calf or sometimes the thigh. It is only dangerous if a clot travels to the lungs (pulmonary embolus). Symptoms of a pulmonary embolus (PE) – which commonly start three to ten days after a long flight – include chest pain, shortness of breath, and sometimes coughing up small amounts of blood. Anyone who thinks that they might have a DVT needs to see a doctor immediately.

PREVENTION OF DVT
- Keep mobile before and during the flight; move around every couple of hours
- Drink plenty of fluids during the flight
- Avoid taking sleeping pills and excessive tea, coffee and alcohol
- Consider wearing flight socks or support stockings (see *www.legshealth. com*).

If you think you are at increased risk of a clot, ask your doctor if it is safe to travel.

other currents to carry them in to the beaches. If stung, wash the contact zone with seawater (not drinking water), remove any remaining parts of the tentacles with gloves or tweezers (not a bare hand!), apply ice in a plastic bag for ten minutes or more, and take painkillers. Do not rub the area with a towel or sand.

SMOKING Not surprisingly with a doctor as president, and a cancer specialist at that, Uruguay led the way in introducing some of the world's most effective controls on tobacco use. In 2006, smoking was banned in all enclosed public spaces, from shopping malls to restaurants, offices and buses. Coupled with an advertising ban and measures to educate and persuade, this caused the number of smokers to drop from a third of the population to less than a quarter, and President Tabaré Vásquez was awarded the World Health Organisation's Director-General's Award for his achievements. In 2009 he raised taxes on cigarettes by 29%, and in February 2010, a week before leaving office, Vázquez raised tobacco taxes to 70% of the cost of a pack, nearly doubling the price of an average pack of cigarettes, and required health warnings to cover 80% of the pack; Philip Morris (makers of Marlboro, whose revenues are double Uruguay's GDP) responded by suing for US$2 billion, and in late 2011 closed its plant in Montevideo, cutting 62 jobs.

SAFETY

There's little casual crime in Uruguay, generally seen as an oasis of personal security in South America. Even so, you should take sensible precautions, especially in Montevideo. Avoid looking like a wealthy tourist: leave jewellery and other such valuables at home. If you carry a bag in addition to your pack, never put it down: keep it under your arm or over your shoulder. Do not keep valuables in it: not only can it be snatched, but it can also be picked, slit or slashed open. The same applies to a 'bum bag', although this is a handy way to carry a compact camera.

Divide your money and travellers' cheques between at least two different places, in your baggage and on your body. For your passport and cash reserves, use a money-belt, neck pouch or secret inside pocket. Alternatively, you can sew a hidden pocket into the front of your trousers or shorts. If your passport is too bulky to carry comfortably and safely, take some other form of identification, such as a driving licence or photocopies of the key pages of your passport. Keep the numbers of your travellers' cheques, passport, credit cards and flight itineraries separate from other valuables, so that if they are lost you can replace them more easily; it's also smart to leave them as an email message to yourself. You can even scan or take digital photos of passports and flight itineraries and attach them to your email.

If you are robbed and wish to claim on insurance, ask the police for a copy of the official report (*la denuncia*); similarly in the case of a road accident ask for the *constancia*. Even though you presumably won't be around for the official ratification of the complaint in court, explain that you need it for insurance purposes; you may just be given a slip with a reference number and a few lines of explanation, which should be enough for your insurance company.

There were 109,000 reported thefts in 2007, making it the most common crime in Uruguay; but there's little violence and it's not something you're likely to notice at all. Where people in Argentina fear kidnappings, in Uruguay the worst that happens is petnapping.

See the box on page 73 for emergency telephone numbers.

WOMEN TRAVELLERS In some ways Uruguay is a conservative country, but it's not ridiculously macho and religion has relatively little sway. Although gender roles are traditional, with women largely identified with child-rearing, especially outside Montevideo, female travellers can relax as this is one of the safest and most hassle-free Latin American countries. Men may shout and whistle, but as a rule that's as far as it goes. There certainly are bars where women should not go alone, but they're pretty obvious. Dressing and behaving reasonably modestly is simply good manners in a conservative society, but this is less necessary in the main beach resorts.

TRAVELLING WITH CHILDREN Uruguayans love children but facilities may not always be what you're accustomed to. In Montevideo and the major coastal resorts, you should be able to buy the supplies you're used to at home; however there will be a more limited choice of baby food in particular. Elsewhere, there's less choice, and English is less likely to be spoken if you need to explain your specific needs.

Uruguay has wide expanses of empty beaches where children can frolic freely, as well as busier resorts with family-friendly beach clubs and restaurants. Staying on a rural estancia may well also be a good choice, with plenty of animal-related activities in a largely traffic-free environment. However, in Colonia there are many cobbled streets, and in Montevideo the pavements can be rough – buggies, push-chairs and strollers are not very practical here.

DISABLED TRAVELLERS Facilities for the disabled are very limited in Uruguay, although you'll find that in Montevideo bus routes CA1 and 125 are fully accessible to wheelchairs, as is Plaza Independencia, according to signs posted there. Modern Antel phone centres are built to a standard design with ramped access. It has now been decreed that Uruguay is to be accessible by 2018, and wheelchair ramps and accessible taxis are appearing fast in Montevideo (*www. discapacidaduruguay.org*).

There are special immigration desks for disabled travellers at the new Carrasco airport terminal, where there are good facilities for wheelchair users and others. Spa hotels (including those at the hot springs of the northwest) are more likely to have accessible rooms and facilities than other hotels.

GAY AND LESBIAN TRAVELLERS Montevideo doesn't have the kind of gay tourism scene now found in Buenos Aires, but it's a relaxed place, and there are various gay-only and gay-friendly clubs. A Plaza de Diversidad Sexual was created in 2005 (at Sarandí & Mitre, in Montevideo), and in 2008 Uruguay banned and punished discrimination against gay couples, and allowed transsexuals to change their registered gender. In 2009, gays were allowed to join the military and gay couples to adopt children and in 2013 same-sex marriage was legalised. According to the 2013 Spartacus Gay Travel Index, Uruguay is the most gay-friendly country in Latin America – and the tenth worldwide.

Some gays are of course still in the closet, but many, especially the young, are out, as Uruguay is a tolerant, laid-back country where religion has little power. For more information see the blog http://uruguaydiverso.blogspot.com. A map of gay Montevideo is available, along with a list of gay-friendly hotels, restaurants, bookshops and clubs (*La Lupa Libros, Bacacay 1318, Ciudad Vieja; www.friendlymap.com.uy*). Viajes Sunlight in Montevideo (\ *2355 3400; www. viajessunlight.com*) specialise in gay travel.

WHAT TO TAKE

Travelling in Uruguay requires pretty much whatever you'd take on a trip in Europe or North America, the only real proviso being to take plenty of sunblock and some long-sleeved clothing.

It's very useful to bring a small daypack, to use as a carry-on for long bus trips, or to leave things in a hotel while you're backpacking; in any case you invariably end up coming home with more luggage than you started with. A lightweight nylon bag with a lockable zip is ideal, or a stuff-sack for your sleeping bag can double up if need be.

Other useful items include pencils or ballpoint pens, a notebook and paper, travel alarm clock, penknife (preferably a Swiss Army type), a few Ziploc plastic bags, a universal bath plug (or punctured squash-ball), a sewing kit (with heavy thread and needles for tent repairs), safety pins, clothes pegs, dental floss (excellent for repairs, as well as teeth), toilet paper and a Latin-American Spanish dictionary or phrasebook.

MAPS

The best map of Uruguay is that published by ITMB in Vancouver (Canada), at a scale of 1:800,000, with detailed insets of Montevideo, Colonia and Punta del Este (£7.99). Nelles publish a map of Argentina North and Uruguay at 1:2.5m (with an inset of central Montevideo), as well as one of Argentina South and Uruguay (£7.95 each).

For regional tours, ITMB has a good map of Southern South America at 1:2.8m (£7.99); Marco Polo and GeoCenter World Map both have maps of Brazil, Bolivia, Paraguay and Uruguay at 1:4m. Firestone have both a map of Chile, Southern Brazil, Paraguay and Uruguay at 1:2.75m (£9.95), and a road atlas of Argentina, Bolivia, Chile, Southern Brazil, Paraguay and Uruguay (£27.50).

There are rather clunky searchable townplans at http://200.55.6.87/es/a2.asp?vista=MDCA&pais=Uruguay and www.pueblos20.net/uruguay/index.php, as well as the more familiar https://maps.google.com.uy.

MONEY AND BUDGETING

The Uruguayan peso (P in this book, though the usual symbol in Uruguay is $) is a stable currency, trading at about P23 to the US dollar, P36 to the pound sterling and P32 to the euro at the time of going to print; for the latest exchange rates, see www.xe.com. The US dollar and Argentine peso are widely accepted in summer in resorts such as Punta del Este. The cheapest and easiest way to obtain pesos (or US dollars) is from the ATMs (*bancomats*) found in virtually every town and airport. The major private banks all belong to the BanRed consortium (*www.banred.com. uy*), whose machines accept virtually all foreign cards; you can also pay with a debit card in shops through the BanRed system. ATMs with a Red Link label, in particular, work with cards bearing the international Plus and Cirrus logos.

The bank with most branches is the state-owned Banco del República Oriental del Uruguay (*BROU; www.bancorepublica.com.uy*). Spain's BBVA and Santander are also widespread, along with Britain's HSBC and Lloyds TSB, and the American Citibank.

Credit cards (Visa above all) are widely accepted, in better hotels and restaurants and by car-rental companies and the better bus companies.

To change travellers' cheques you'll have to pay a commission of about 3%, or accept a differential rate which comes to the same thing. A few exchange offices (*casas de cambio*), mainly in Montevideo, will oblige, but as a rule you'll need a bank (see 73 for bank opening hours). If you go to an American Express agent you can change your Amex cheques to US dollars without commission, then exchange the cash at a cambio as required. Exchange offices will take US dollars and Argentine pesos, and as a rule euros, sterling and Canadian dollars too. Other currencies may prove more difficult, especially outside Montevideo.

Unlike many of its neighbours, whose money bears the images of generals and presidents, Uruguay's banknotes perpetuate the memory of artistic and cultural luminaries. The lowest-denomination note, P20 (now being withdrawn), shows the poet and diplomat Juan Zorrilla de San Martín (1855–1931). On the P50 note is the educational reformer José Pedro Varela (1845–79), on the P100 note the composer Eduardo Fabini (1882–1950), on the P200 note the painter Pedro Figari (1861–1938), on the P500 note Alfredo Vásquez Acevedo (1844–1923), lawyer, academic and politician, and on the P1,000 note the poet Juana de Ibarbourou (1892–1979). There's also the rare P2,000 note, bearing the image of the priest and public figure Dámaso Antonio Larrañaga (1771–1848). At Montevideo's Numismatic Museum (see page 137) you can see all these and many other banknotes.

There are also coins worth P1, P2, P5, P10 and P50; until 2010 a peso consisted of 100 centésimos, but these have now been phased out. There's no lack of change, unlike in Argentina.

Lost American Express travellers' cheques should be reported to Turisport (*San José 930, Montevideo;* \2902 0829; *or Benito Blanco 837, Local 1, Pocitos, Montevideo;* \ *2712 4797*), and lost Thomas Cook travellers' cheques to \ *000 413 598 2388.* Following are contact details for a lost credit card: Visa (\ *2140 1800; www.visa.com*); MasterCard (\ *2902 6800; www.mastercard.com*); American Express (\ *2140 1800; www.americanexpress.com*); Diners Club (\ *2915 0000; www.dinersclub.com*).

BUDGETING In the last few years Uruguay's currency has strengthened, so the country has become more expensive for foreign visitors. It does remain cheaper than Chile, though pricier than Argentina or Brazil, in general.

The cheapest hostel beds cost around US$12, but you can easily pay over US$100 a night for a good hotel. For food, you can shop in markets and supermarkets and use hostel kitchens, or you can plunge right in and enjoy great steaks every night. Thus it's possible to travel on a budget of just US$20 a day, or you can max out your credit cards. Buses cost about US$10 from Montevideo to Punta del Este or US$22 to Chuy. City buses cost about US$0.60.

A simple restaurant lunch should cost US$10–15, while dinner for two in a posh restaurant could run to US$50–70. A cinema ticket at the weekend costs US$7 (more in Montevideo). A 750ml bottle of beer is about US$4, and a loaf of bread or a litre of milk, or half a litre of petrol, will cost you about US$1.

Prices in resorts like Punta del Este fall sharply from April to December. Haggling is not part of the culture, although there may be some leeway in craft markets.

TIPPING In restaurants and hotels a tip (*propina*) of 10% is usual; taxi fares should be rounded up to the nearest peso, and a tip of about P10 is reasonable at filling stations and for tour guides. This is in addition to the IVA or *impuesto de valor agregado* (value-added tax), a levy of 22% on shopping and restaurant meals (10% on some basic goods and medicines). This is usually included in bills where relevant, although it's always sensible to check (*¿IVA incluido?*).

GETTING AROUND

BY CAR Uruguay has excellent infrastructure, with modern main roads (*rutas nacionales*) and bus stations; many minor roads (*caminos*) are unsurfaced but decently maintained. The main roads from Montevideo to Colonia and Punta del Este (Ruta 1 and the Ruta Interbalnearia, abbreviated to IB) are toll roads, and there are tolls on other main roads, often at departmental boundaries; these are fairly inexpensive at about US$3. Payment is accepted in Uruguayan or Argentine pesos, Brazilian reals or US dollars, but change is given only in Uruguayan pesos.

The major highways fan out from Montevideo and are numbered from west to east with single digits. The main route north from Montevideo (dual carriageway as far as Canelones) is Ruta 5; Ruta 6 is pretty minor, Ruta 7 and 8 cross at Melo and are the wrong way around to the north, ie: Ruta 7 runs to the east and Ruta 8 runs to the west. Along the coast, Ruta 10 only exists in isolated sections. The only routes to cross the country are Ruta 14 and Ruta 26, together with Ruta 11 which bypasses Montevideo. The Anillo Perimetral, a new bypass of Montevideo, closer to the city, has recently been completed. Kilometre markers are placed alternately on the left and the right side of most roads. As in much of South America, there's an obsession with speed bumps (*lomadas*), which are often fierce and should be taken very slowly (if you're following a bus, in particular, expect it to almost stop).

Since 2007 it's been obligatory for all drivers and passengers to wear seatbelts, and dipped headlights are required on main roads. The national speed limit is 110km/h (68mph), although this is only permitted on a few main roads; elsewhere the maximum is 90km/h (56mph). The blood alcohol limit is zero, so don't even think of drinking and driving. Driving is on the right, and there's no right turn at red lights. Traffic gives way to vehicles on the LEFT – thus vehicles on roundabouts have priority. There are lots of scooters and small motorbikes on the roads, which tend to move surprisingly slowly; take care after dark in particular.

Uruguayan drivers are relaxed and patient, and driving standards are far higher than in Argentina – but in summer there are plenty of Argentine drivers, especially

---

CACHILAS AND CHERYS

Uruguayans once drove on the left-hand side of the road; this changed in 1946, as a near-bankrupt Britain lost its influence. Cars were not built in Uruguay and imports were heavily taxed. Thus drivers rarely replaced their vehicles and an amazing number of classic cars, known as *cachilas*, have survived, generally in pretty poor condition but kept working with ingenuity and persistence. In recent years, these have been sought after by foreign collectors and enthusiasts, and many have been exported; this has also had the effect of making Uruguayans appreciate their highway heritage, and many are now being restored and used for Sunday best or displayed in museums. Television advertisements (especially in the US) purportedly set in Cuba are in fact often filmed in Uruguay, especially in Montevideo's Ciudad Vieja, thanks to the availability of these cars.

However, in 2007 cachilas ceased to be the only cars exported from Uruguay when Chery, the largest Chinese independent car-maker, opened a factory in Montevideo, producing Tiggo compact SUVs and QQ compact cars, mainly for export to Argentina and Brazil (they also produce bullet-proof cars here and plan to make cars that run on alternative fuels).

along the coast, some performing testosterone-charged stunts (overtaking on the inside, not stopping at crossings) and others just slightly lost.

Petrol (gasoline) is known as *nafta* and diesel as *gasoil*; the fuel alcohol that so many Brazilian cars run on is not available here.

Car crime is minimal, but you should take the usual precautions, at least in Montevideo – lock your car and don't leave valuables or documents visible. Parking is generally free except in the centre of Montevideo (see page 89); even cheap hotels tend to have some kind of secure parking available nearby.

Car rental The major international car-rental chains are easily found, especially in Montevideo and Punta del Este, as well as good local companies which may well be cheaper. You'll need only a valid driving licence from your home country. A compact car with manual transmission will probably cost about US$40 a day or US$300 a week outside peak season, with unlimited mileage included, and also child seats if required. Automatics are rarer and much more expensive. Most companies offer a good range of vehicles from compacts to minibuses.

There are no one-way rentals except occasionally between Montevideo, Colonia and Punta del Este. Details of rental companies are given on page 90 for Montevideo (and at Carrasco airport), and in the accounts of other towns.

See page 89 for details of taxis.

BY TRAIN There are very limited passenger train services, on just two lines in the Montevideo hinterland. Passenger services have been suspended altogether at various times in the past, and there are currently no Sunday trains. Fares are very low, but the service is too infrequent to be very useful, especially if you want to head out from Montevideo in the morning and back in the evening. However, special trains are put on for passengers from cruise ships visiting the Juanicó winery.

After decades of underinvestment, by 2000 the national freight network was in such poor condition that a maximum speed of 25km/h was imposed, making it even harder to compete for business. In 2003 the state railway company AFE (*www.afe.com. uy*) was restructured into separate infrastructure and operating divisions, to allow private investment and 'open-access' operators. The government was seeking US$56 million of private finance to upgrade the 1,114km core network from Montevideo to Rivera, Río Branco and Minas, as well as branches to Fray Bentos and Salto, to be paid back by payments from freight operators. The rationale was that booming timber production would increase freight traffic from 0.9 million to 1.2 million tonnes within two years, and that it would be cheaper to use the railways than to maintain the roads to cope with that level of traffic. Nevertheless the government continued slowly with upgrading the main line to Brazil via Rivera, using rail supplied by Russia to pay its debts; the Mercosur trade bloc is funding improvements on the line to Argentina via Salto. In 2013 AFE was restructured to allow for privatisation.

In Montevideo there are two railway heritage organisations that struggle to preserve old steam locomotives and carriages. The Círculo de Estudios Ferroviarios del Uruguay (*Railway Studies Circle of Uruguay;* e *cefu@adinet.com.uy; www.cefu. com.uy*), at the Peñarol railway works in the northern suburbs, has two British-built Hawthorne-Leslie and Beyer-Peacock locomotives as well as a narrow-gauge German O&K locomotive. The Asociación Uruguaya Amigos del Riel (*Uruguayan Railfans Association; www.trenesavapor.com*) at the Bella Vista yard (nearer the centre, at Lorenzo Carnelli station) has a beautifully preserved Beyer-Peacock 2-6-0, built in Britain in 1910, plus two Dutch coaches from the 1950s, used for excursions for private groups.

BY BUS Being a relatively small country, Uruguay does not generally have separate systems of local and long-distance buses; most interurban buses will stop to pick up passengers who flag them down by the roadside. Standing passengers are allowed, but a point may come at which no more will be picked up. However, at busy times one departure will in fact consist of several buses leaving at the same time, some of which will omit stops at certain towns, as well as roadside pickups (check your ticket carefully to see which one you should be on). The bus number and destination are displayed in the front windscreen, often on a dot-matrix screen; middle-distance buses headed for Montevideo may show 'XXX' to represent Montevideo's Tres Cruces terminal, but longer-distance ones simply show 'Montevideo'. There are virtually no buses across the middle of the country – you'll almost always have to pass through Tres Cruces.

Buses are comfortable vehicles with reclining seats (Uruguayans do love to recline their seats at once, and as far back as possible) and good ventilation or air conditioning. There are a few *cama* (bed) buses from Montevideo to the far north of the country. They stick to a maximum of 90km/h, but given the country's straight open roads they manage pretty creditable average speeds.

It's often worth booking in advance, especially if you want to go to Punta del Este on a Friday afternoon. If the bus terminal is on the outskirts of town, bus companies will usually have a ticket office downtown. You'll be offered a choice of seats, or perhaps standing space (no cheaper) if the departure is full. Some companies have decent websites, but there's no online booking.

The driver's assistant handles money, tickets and baggage; he (never she) will usually tag your bags – keep the counterfoil to be checked when you get off. At larger terminals a baggage handler may load your bags – if you offer a tip it'll be assumed you're an Argentine tourist. A small departure fee is charged only at shared municipal terminals, as in Montevideo, Punta del Este and Mercedes; elsewhere buses usually leave from the company's own offices. These offices usually have basic toilets (take your own paper) and let you leave baggage for an hour or two; at larger terminals toilets will be better, and usually free, but you will have to pay to leave baggage.

The **SummerBus Uruguay** backpackers' hop-on-hop-off service (❧ 4277 5781; *www.summerbus.com*) was introduced in 2010, running five days a week along the coast from Punta del Este to Montevideo, from there to Punta del Diablo and then back to Punta del Diablo, calling at many hostels along the way. Tickets (from a minimum of US$10 to US$35 from Montevideo to Punta del Diablo) can be bought online, by phone or at associated hostels.

BY BICYCLE There's quite a lot of cycling in Uruguay but (apart from a few clubs of lycra-clad road racers with high-tech gear) it's very much of the popping-around-the-corner variety, almost always without panniers or lights. Many bikes are of the 'beach cruiser' type, with curved double top tubes designed to look a bit like a motorbike – some even have fake fuel tanks, to appeal to boys. There are a few mountain-bike-style machines, but they're really pretty cheap and not much use for serious cycling.

Cycle parking is limited, but given the low crime rate that's probably not a big issue; there are cycle lanes in places, mostly alongside main roads leading out of towns, but these are intermittent, generally unsigned and often with concrete blocks across half the lane at junctions. Touring cyclists looking to maintain a reasonable average speed will probably choose to ride on the main carriageway, which is generally safe given the courteous, laid-back attitude of Uruguayan drivers. The main highways have good shoulders – it's normal to see cyclists even alongside Ruta 5, the busy dual carriageway north from Montevideo to Canelones. Perhaps the most enjoyable touring is in Maldonado department, on Ruta 39 and Ruta 109 north from San Carlos and Rocha towards Aiguá, and the dirt road linking them that passes Cerro Catedral, the country's highest point (see page 240). Just west, in Rocha department, there's also good touring on Ruta 15 from Rocha to Velázquez and Lascano, returning to La Coronilla on the coast by Ruta 14. The coastal Ruta 10 in Maldonado and Rocha can also be pleasant if windy cycling (heading west is advisable), but it's not a continuous route.

Buses will carry bikes, but it's very much dependent on what else needs loading and on the mood of the driver – mention the bike as soon as you ask for your ticket. Trains also carry bikes, although this is only useful as a means of getting out of the greater Montevideo area.

Cycle racing was introduced to Uruguay by the Montevideo Cricket Club in 1888. The country's premium cycle race (the oldest stage race in the continent, founded in 1939) is the Vuelta Ciclista del Uruguay. Held annually during Semana Santa (Easter Week), this covers a circuit of roughly 1,500km from Montevideo, returning there for a grand finish along Avenida 18 de Julio. Over 150 of the leading North and South American cyclists compete, some in national teams and some in sponsored commercial teams.

In 2013, a new road 'safety' law allowed police to confiscate the bikes of cyclists without helmets; it remains to be seen whether this absurdly regressive measure will be enforced or quietly forgotten.

ACCOMMODATION

There's a good range of places to sleep in Uruguay, although the country does not have *residencials* (cheap guesthouses) found in neighbouring countries (in fact *residencial* here refers to a home for senior citizens). In Montevideo there's a very wide choice, from international-class luxury hotels to real dives, as well as several hostels.

HOTELS Cheap hotels often have a choice of rooms with private (en-suite) bathrooms or with shared bathrooms down the corridor; in the latter case you'll probably have a basin in the bedroom, but the hot tap won't work. The showers, however, always produce very hot water, and are far better than the useless Brazilian showerhead heaters. Check-out is usually at 10.00, with check-in from noon.

Better hotels usually claim at least one more star than they'd qualify for in the northern hemisphere – thus the many four-star hotels in Montevideo's Centro are really worth three stars at best. However, the luxury hotels around Punta del Este really are world class.

Moves to stimulate the economy in 2009 included exempting foreigners paying hotel bills by credit or debit card from IVA (value added tax), as well as a 9% reduction on restaurant bills and car rental if paid by card. Whether these measures will be extended in future years remains to be seen.

HOSTEL VERSUS HOSTAL

A *hostel* has the same meaning as in English, a place for backpackers to sleep in shared dorms or private rooms, with shared or private bathrooms; a *hostal* is something rather better than this, and indeed better than a *hospedaje*, which is a fairly basic family-run guesthouse.

Accommodation listings are laid out in decreasing price order, under the following categories: 'Luxury', 'Mid-range' and 'Budget'. The following key (also on the inside front cover) gives an indication of prices. Prices are based on a double room (including tax) per night. Prices are usually quoted in dollars, except in the very cheapest of places.

$$$$$	P3,000+	£105+	US$160+
$$$$	P2,201–3,000	£81–105	US$121–160
$$$	P1,501–2,200	£54–80	US$81–120
$$	P1,000–1,500	£33–53	US50–80
$	<P1,000	<£33	<US$50

MOTELS In a few small towns that are yet to see much tourism, municipal motels in fact consist of a few very simple rooms, perhaps on a campsite, with no additional services.

HOSTELS Some hostels are affiliated to Hostelling International (*national office, Paraguay 1212 & Canelones;* \ *2900 5749;* e *albergues@hosteluruguay.org; www. hosteluruguay.org*); there's also the looser HoLa grouping of green-minded hostels (*Hostels Latinoamérica; www.holahostels.com*). There are many other backpackers' hostels in Colonia, Punta del Este and elsewhere, plus a delightful old-fashioned rural hostel in Villa Serrana. You should bring your own towel if you plan to stay in hostels, plus a padlock for the lockers provided in most of them.

CAMPSITES Many Uruguayans use campsites for day use only (although they bring enough gear for a week's stay), but you should be able to camp overnight – there are 44 major campsites, all along the coast of the Atlantic and the Río Uruguay, that offer pretty decent facilities, although not luxury. These have chalets or *cabañas* for two to eight people, the larger ones with private bathrooms, that provide more comfort than a tent. In the smaller beach resorts there are many cabañas and cottages to rent – most Uruguayans just turn up and wing it, looking for *alquila* (for rent) signs, or they just call the number they call every year, but foreigners may need to use an agency.

EATING AND DRINKING

Although Uruguay is famed for its steak and other meat products (even better than Argentina's, at least according to the Uruguayans), there's also a great range of Italian dishes in almost all restaurants, which makes the country surprisingly welcoming to vegetarians (restaurants and bars are also now smoke-free). There's also a strong Spanish influence (especially in seafood, where the Basques excel), as well as Slav and Jewish influences.

The beef is of course grass-fed, with no corn or soya involved, and a year older than in the US – and you can taste the difference. Traditionally it's cooked on an *asado* grill, which is fuelled with wood, rather than charcoal as in Argentina.

In a bid to establish its carnivorous credentials, Uruguay staged the world's biggest barbecue in 2008, when 1,250 *asadors* cooked 12 tonnes (26,400lb – 50% more than the previous record) of meat on 1,500 separate *parrillas* (grills), and fed it to 20,000 hungry people. In 2010 it was reported that Uruguayans eat an average of 58.2kg of beef per year, making them the world's leading consumers per capita; they also have Latin America's highest per-capita consumption of milk, drinking 225 litres a year.

A meal should begin with offal – *mollejas* (sweetbreads), intestines, chorizo sausage – although strangely gringos often choose to skip this stage, or to have *provoleta* (grilled provolone cheese with herbs). Then comes the full asado or parrillada, a grilled selection of *lomo* (steak), chops, ribs and sausages (including *morcilla*, blood sausages), with some grilled chicken for light relief. Potatoes and bread are frowned upon as unnecessary distractions that just fill you up and distract you from the main mission of eating meat. A few peppers, yams and other vegetables are, however, grilled alongside the meat, and use of the ubiquitous and very tasty *chimichurri* sauce is also encouraged. Supposedly introduced by an Englishman called Jimmy Curry, this is like a spicy version of Italian pesto, made of finely chopped parsley, garlic, red pepper flakes, oil and vinegar, with other ingredients such as paprika (*pimentón dulce*), oregano, cumin and bay leaf (laurel) depending on the region. When you sit down in a restaurant you'll also usually be given a garlic mayonnaise dip with bread.

If this kind of assault course is not what you feel like, a lighter alternative is a **chivito**, which is really Uruguay's national dish, not found in the neighbouring countries. In Argentina a chivito is a young goat, as the name implies, but in Uruguay it's a sandwich of skirt steak, with lettuce, tomato, mozzarella, olives and mayonnaise, with possible extras such as fried egg, grilled peppers, beetroot, palm hearts, pickles and ham, served with chips (French fries). It can also be served *al plato* (often for two people), on a bed of green salad and fries rather than bread, and with Russian salad and other veggies on the side – etiquette requires you to slice through it all and get a bit of everything on your fork. A *chivito canadiense* is served with bacon too. At the La Pasiva chain, in and around Montevideo, Colonia and Punta del Este, you'll get excellent chivito, as well as a mystery sauce, in unlabelled plastic squeezy bottles on your table. It's supposedly a mixture of mustard, beer and flour, with an unknown secret ingredient.

Less iconic but still very popular is the **pancho** or hot dog, served in a Viennese roll with a choice of sauces; these are bought from *carritos*, the stainless-steel trailers semi-permanently parked at street corners all over Montevideo and elsewhere. Alternatively, a chorizo sausage served in a bread roll is called a *choripán*, as in *chorizo y pan* (sausage and bread).

Another Uruguayan speciality is **pamplona de cerdo** or stuffed rolled pork (although chicken and beef can also be used), with meat wrapped around cheese, chopped olives, peppers and whatever else the chef fancies. The cheese is often very bland, but with something more interesting this can be a delight.

Other meat dishes include *milanesa* (steak in breadcrumbs), stews known as *estofado* and *puchero*, and *emapanadas*, like small Cornish pasties or turnovers filled with beef or ham and cheese, or with cheese and onion. An *empanada gallega* or Galician empanada is filled with fish, onion and green peppers. *Caprese* refers to any cheese and tomato filling, especially in empanadas or sandwiches, while an *Olímpico* is with tomato, egg, ham, cheese and lettuce, often as a double or club sandwich. In fact almost any type of sandwich, with the exception of the caprese, comes with compulsory ham. A *pascualina* is a Genoese pie of spinach and hard-boiled egg, which is a reliable vegetarian alternative in cafés and bars; you may also find *tortilla a la española* (with or without chorizo) or *tortilla de papas*, a quiche or omelette with potatoes. Other vegetables include mushrooms, grilled or caramelised sweet potatoes (yams), *zapallo* (pumpkin), which can taste much like sweet potato and is often served as purée or *mermelada*, and a local speciality, the *zapallito*, a small spherical green squash that's often used in pies and quiches.

A local speciality in some of the Atlantic coastal resorts of Rocha is **lechuga de mar** (sea lettuce; *Ulva fasciata, U. lactuca*), a seaweed served in omelettes (and also pies and *buñuelos* or fritters) that is said to contain ten times as much vitamin C as oranges and twice as much vitamin A as cabbage; it needs to be eaten very fresh.

All these meat dishes should not overshadow Uruguay's marvellous **seafood**, with both freshwater and saltwater fish as well as shellfish; all naturally go well with the local white wines.

Virtually every restaurant has a choice of **pasta** dishes, and probably pizza too – usually there'll be vegetarian options, but if not they'll easily knock something up. You'll often have a choice of pastas, often including gnocchi (spelt *ñoqui* here), and then a choice of sauces, such as *tuco* (the tomato sauce known as *sugo* in Italy), *filetto* (also a tomato sauce), *rossini* (tomato sauce with Bechamel) or *caruso* (a Uruguayan speciality, made of cream, mushroom, ham and onion). *Sorrentinos* are an Argentine type of pasta, like large round ravioli filled with ham, mozzarella and perhaps ricotta and other cheeses too.

In better restaurants **pizza** is much as you'd expect, with a variety of toppings, but in snack-bars and take-aways it's rather different. It has a thicker, more bready crust, and is square, because of the shape of the *pala* or shovel used to take it in and out of the wood-fired oven – it's even available for sale by the metre in these places. It'll come with nothing but a tomato sauce, with garlic, onion, basil and oregano, that is sweeter than in Italy – if you want cheese, order a *muzarela* or *muza*, which costs twice as much and comes with a light stringy cheese that is less oily than real Italian mozzarella. In cheaper restaurants a 'pizza' is a snack based on a half-baguette; if you want real pizza, you'll need to order *pizzeta*.

It's also traditional to order *faina*, a very thin chickpea pancake, topped with white pepper, that's derived from the Genoese *farinata*. Muza topped with faina is known as *pizza a caballo* (pizza on horseback).

Uruguayan ice cream is superb, but other **dairy products** are not amazing (with a few exceptions – see page 219). The Swiss of Colonia Suiza are particularly associated with cheese-making, but it doesn't really live up to its reputation. *Dulce de leche*, the caramelised milk spread that's found across South America, is used in a range of typical pastries and desserts, such as *alfajores* (shortbread cookies with a filling of *dulce de leche*), or *chajá*, a dessert from Paysandú that consists of meringue, dulce de leche and peach. *Dulce de membrillo* is a quince jelly that's eaten with Colonia cheese in a dessert known as *Martín Fierro* after the gaucho hero.

The quintessential restaurant dessert is *flan* or crème caramel (usually *casero* or homemade), which can be served with dulce de leche on top. German strudel is popular, most often with an apple filling, while *budín inglés* (English pudding) is a fruit cake that's associated with Christmas and New Year's Eve.

2

DRINKS The best bottled soft drinks are the Paso de los Toros line, produced in the town of the same name (see page 352). Virtually all cafés and restaurants also offer native herbal teas such as *boldo* and *manzanilla*; you may also find other *yuyos medicinales*, infusions of herbs such as *malva* (mallow) and *marcela* (*Achyrocline satureoides, A. flaccida*), which is something like camomile, taken as a tea for

MATÉ

If you're wondering why so many people seem to be carrying an oversized leather binocular case, it's not because they're dedicated birdwatchers but because they are afficionados of maté, the infusion of the leaves of the *Ilex paraguianensis* shrub to which many inhabitants of Uruguay and the neighbouring countries seem to be almost addicted. The case is the *matero*, containing a *thermo* or vacuum flask of hot water, a supply of *yerba maté* leaves (pronounced 'zherba mat-ay', at least in Uruguay), a gourd also known as a *maté* (from the Quechua for 'cup'), a silver straw called a *bombilla*, and an *escobilla* with which to clean the bombilla. Maté can also be drunk from a *pezuña* (cow's hoof) or *guampa* (bull's horn), but this is generally seen as affected. Whoever is in charge of the thermo fills the gourd with maté and hot water, drinks the first cup himself, adds more water, and passes it to the person on his left. He or she drinks and returns it for recharging, and so it continues to circulate clockwise. It may continue to circulate for hours, as the group relax, chat and watch the world go by. Unlike tea, maté does not get bitter when left brewing and can be topped up multiple times. Do not say 'thank you' until you have drunk your fill and don't want another refill; and never wash the gourd with soap. If the gourd is filled to overflowing, or with cold water, or just not filled immediately, this can be taken as a sign that your presence is not welcome.

There's an indefinable difference between Argentina, where you may get the impression that people would happily drink maté for ever rather than risk going to work, and Uruguay, where maté-drinking seems more like a justified relaxation before or after getting on with the rest of one's life. The social rites of maté-drinking began with the Guaraní people and were then adopted and spread by the Jesuits; now you'll see people happily preparing maté on the beach in the hottest of weather, in bus stations, and whenever they're watching television or hanging out with friends.

The maté should not be too hot (there's a possible link between hot maté and oesophageal cancer); if it's too bitter (and for some of us, it's always too bitter), wait until the gourd has been around a couple of times. In some places it's normal to take maté with sugar (*dulce*) but in Uruguay it's usually without (*amargo*); however, herbs such as mint, or orange or lemon peel, are sometimes added. It can also be found nowadays in teabags and in cans (toasted and sweetened, and drunk cold). In southern Brazil the yerba is finer and the gourds are bigger; it can also be made with cold water there (and is called *tereré*).

Yerba maté contains an alkaloid called matteine, very similar to caffeine, which makes one feel more alert and less hungry, but doesn't lead to jitteriness and palpitations; it's also said to ease the digestion and reduce blood pressure. It also contains useful doses of vitamins B1, B6 and C, calcium, phosphate, magnesium, sodium, potassium and iron.

digestive, gastrointestinal or menstrual disorders and as a sedative. Marcela is also said to be rich in antioxidants, so is more popular than ever, also being used in handcreams, for instance.

Uruguay's national drink (even more so than Argentina's) is, of course *maté*, the infusion of the leaves of *Ilex paraguariensis*, a shrub of the holly family (see box opposite).

Uruguayan **wine** can be excellent (see page 149) and almost any restaurant will serve something decent. While it's red wine you need to go with steak, white wine is very popular, and is also served with orange juice (as *sangría*) and with apples, grapes and perhaps melon or pineapple (as *clericó*). Grappa (brandy) can be quite strong but is made much smoother with the addition of honey, the result being known as *grappamiel*.

Beer is of course widely available – *chopp* means draught, but generally refers to the basic lager-style beer, even if it comes in a bottle. Amber (or red) and dark beers may also be available. The most widely available beer is Pilsen (brewed in Montevideo since 1866), but it's usually possible to find the rather better Patricia (both are now owned by the global giant InBev), which comes in dark (*negra*) or light (*común*) varieties. Zillertal is another premium beer, harder to find and much more expensive than Patricia. The country's only real ale or craft brewers are Mastra (*www.mastra.com.uy*) and Davok (*www.davok.com.uy*), producing varieties such as Golden, Scotch Red Ale, IPA, Weizen and Stout; these are only found in a very few bars and upmarket supermarkets such as Tienda Inglesa.

PUBLIC HOLIDAYS AND FESTIVALS

1 January	New Year's Day
6 January	Epiphany (Día de los Reyes)
February/March	Carnival (the two days before Ash Wednesday)
February/March	Five days for Holy Week (Semana de Turismo; dates vary from year to year)
19 April	Day of the Landing of the 33 Orientales
1 May	Labour Day
18 May	Battle of Las Piedras
19 June	Birthday of Artigas (also marking the end of the dictatorship)
18 July	Constitution Day
25 August	Independence Day
12 October	Columbus Day (Dia de la Raza)
2 November	All Saints
25 December	Christmas (Día de la Familia)

A midweek holiday may be transferred to the preceding Monday or following Friday.

Christmas Eve (Nochebuena) and New Year's Eve are times for partying, with large amounts of fizzy cider and *medio y medio* ('half & half' – mixed dry white wine and sparkling wine) sprayed around at places like Montevideo's Mercado del Puerto. Fireworks are sold on the street, and let off at midnight; in addition water (to cool people down) and torn-up old calendars may be thrown from upper windows on New Year's Eve.

Christmas starts with fireworks at midnight on the 24th, followed by a family feast, ideally consisting of a whole lamb or piglet. Decorations appear just a week or so beforehand, and buses and shops operate fairly normally until early evening.

On Christmas Day nothing is open for most of the day except the main Antel call centres; some long-distance buses run from around 16.00, and by early evening some corner stores and petrol stations will be open.

Children get yet more presents for Epiphany (Día de los Reyes); the previous day shops are open as late as 02.00 for last-minute shopping, but there's only a Saturday bus service.

Easter Week (Semana Santa, or Semana de Turismo) marks the end of the holiday season, with one last rush to the beaches. There are fewer Europeans and North Americans sunning themselves at this season, and more Brazilians.

There are holidays more or less monthly through the autumn and winter. Since the 1970s the evening of 24 August has become known as La Noche de la Nostalgia (Nostalgia Night), when oldie records are played on the radio and in restaurants and bars, and people hold parties to dance to them regardless of age or usual tastes – it's remarkably popular. It's also an excuse to sleep through much of Independence Day (marking independence from Brazil in 1825) on 25 August. Resorts such as Punta del Este are pretty lively for the weekend nearest to Independence Day. The second Sunday of August is Children's Day, when kids get new toys, and events are laid on with music, clowns and bouncy castles.

September is the season of agricultural shows, other than the main one, La Rural, which is held in Montevideo's Prado Park over Easter Week.

The Día de la Raza (known as Columbus Day in North America), on 12 October, celebrates (somewhat controversially) the union of the Spanish colonisers with the indigenous population, and the continuing links between Spain and Latin America. See http://fiestasuruguayas.com.uy for more information.

SHOPPING

About 35–40% of food sales are in supermarkets, far less than in neighbouring countries where the level is over 70%; however, the rapid development of hypermarkets is likely to push this level upwards. Outside Montevideo in particular, food is largely bought in local private grocery stores.

Ta-Ta is a chain of high-street supermarkets, not to be confused with To To, a chain of shoe shops (or Si Si, selling women's swimwear and underwear, or the scarcely credible Tits, selling women's fashion). Equally misnamed is the Disco Group, which owns Disco supermarkets, Devoto and Géant hypermarkets, and the Fresh Market grocery supermarkets. Other supermarket chains include MultiAhorro and Tienda Inglesa ('English Shop', whose owners are indeed of English descent and have paid close attention to the methods of Tesco and Sainsbury's).

If you want to do something sensible like bringing a backpack to put your shopping in, you won't be allowed to – all bags have to be left in a locker, so you'll more or less have to use their plastic bags.

You'll find various craft markets and specialised shops in Montevideo (see page 115) and elsewhere – look out for leatherware, carved wood and bone, and knitting, in particular the *ruana*, a triangular shawl that opens at the front and is easier to take on and off indoors than a poncho. You might also want a pair of *alpargatas*, the espadrilles or canvas-topped shoes worn by the gauchos, which are also ideal for the beach. Another speciality is semi-precious stones, such as amethyst and agate, from Artigas, Rivera and Tacuarembó departments, which are sold mainly in their unfinished state as geodes or crystal stones, as well as cut and polished gems. They're believed in China to cleanse negative energy from a room, so a kilogram of stones, worth up to US$10 in Uruguay, can fetch as much as US$150 in China.

OPENING HOURS

Business hours are from 09.00 to 18.00 Monday to Friday; shops are generally open from 09.00 or 09.30 to 19.00 or 19.30, and from 09.00 to 13.00 on Saturdays. Malls and shopping centres are open from 10.00 to 22.00 daily, and supermarkets and hypermarkets from between 07.30 and 08.30 (some only at 09.00 on Sundays) to 22.00. Banks are open from 13.00 to 17.00 Monday to Friday (although some now open at 11.00).

Most restaurants open for lunch and dinner daily (although some close on Sunday evenings), whereas cheaper, more café-like places will open all day from breakfast onwards. Dinner often doesn't start until 21.00 (although there's no problem getting served in restaurants from about 19.00), so it may be wise to take an early evening nap, and not to schedule meetings before 10.00.

Museums are very poor at showing their opening hours, especially when they're closed, and there are no standard hours – some open Monday to Friday, some daily except Mondays, and they may be open quite late into the evening; they're usually free (or almost). On the Días del Patrimonio, the last weekend of September or the first of October, museums will stage special events and other historic buildings may open specially; on the Noche de los Museos in mid-December, museums stay open until midnight, again with special events.

MEDIA AND COMMUNICATIONS

POST Uruguayans don't seem to use the postal service much – there are no letter boxes except in Correo offices, and these can be hard to find, many having been relocated from prestigious town-centre properties to anonymous shopfronts. For all locations – including many *farmacías* (with a Correo sign outside) – where you can buy stamps, visit the Correo website (*www.correo.com.uy*) and follow the *locales comerciales* link. Postcards and aerogrammes are also hard to find, although the main post office in Montevideo does have some cards with postage included in the cost.

TELEPHONES The national telephone company, Antel, which still has a monopoly on landlines, provides cardphones on the streets and plazas, and call centres in many towns. These have very non-standard opening times: for these, go to the Antel

---

USEFUL TELEPHONE NUMBERS

EMERGENCY
Police ✆ 911
Fire ✆ 104
Montevideo port emergency ✆ 106
Ambulance ✆ 105
Highway police ✆ 108

OTHER USEFUL NUMBERS
Time ✆ 16
Long-distance operator ✆ 120
Directory information ✆ 122
International operator ✆ 0007 (Latin America) or 0008 (rest of the world)

website (*www.antel.com.uy*), then click on *telefónia pública* and then on *ubicación* (under *telecentros*). You can buy a *tarjeta telefónica* (a phonecard, worth P25, P50, P100 or P200) at news kiosks or other small shops – make sure you do get an *Antel* card (the assumption is always that you want credit for an *Ancel* mobile phone). The main call centres are open even on Christmas Day, and currently charge from US$0.10 per minute for calls to Uruguayan landlines to US$0.25 per minute to North America and US$0.80 per minute to much of the rest of the world; they also offer internet access, at a slightly higher cost than the private *cibercentros*. These are efficient and easy to find, although there are complaints about the maximum 3 Mbps speed, which limits the growth of teleworking and outsourcing. There are very few email providers; putting a company name in front of @adinet.com.uy will very often work.

MOBILE PHONES Antel provides mobile phone (cellphone) service through its Ancel brand, but it has been overtaken by Movistar (owned by the Spanish company Telefónica) which now has more customers, and slightly better coverage of the country. You can bring a tri-band GSM phone, or put your own SIM card into a local handset; if you bring in a phone you should register it with Customs (*Aduana*) on arrival, and if you pay a fee of US$6, you will then be able to buy an Uruguayan SIM card and credit.

INTERNET Uruguay is giga-streets ahead of its neighbours in providing wireless internet access – not only do virtually all hostels and many hotels offer free Wi-Fi (*inalámbrica* – but *Wi-Fi* is always understood), but there's also a national policy of providing it on the main plazas of most towns and, in theory, at every school. You'll see children with cute little green-and-white XO laptops, provided under the government's Plan Ceibal (an acronym for 'Basic informatic educative connectivity for online learning' in Spanish), which will soon have distributed 220,000 of these Linux machines (known as *ceibalitos*). In addition 58% of households now have a personal computer.

MEDIA There are more than 20 television channels (including the state-owned TV Nacional Uruguay), with many more available on cable, and over 100 radio stations (including the state-owned Radiodifusión Nacional SODRE). The main Montevideo daily newspapers are *El País*, *El Observador* and *La Republica*, all of which are a decent standard. Freedom of speech is well established and, although laws against 'insulting the state' are still on the statute book, they are effectively out of use.

CULTURAL AND BUSINESS ETIQUETTE

Uruguayans are rather warmer than most Europeans and North Americans and require less personal space – in conversation (whether personal or business, male or female) they stand close and may touch your arm or shoulder. It may be considered rude to back away. When meeting, whether male or female, it's normal to shake hands, with direct eye contact. Male friends will often share an *abrazo* or hug, with back-slapping; otherwise a light kiss on or near the right cheek is normal between friends or family.

If invited to a social event at, say, 21.00, you should probably expect people to turn up nearer 22.00. Buses, films, etc, will usually start on time; business meetings may not, and in any case tend to start with some light chat to break the ice, after which they become more formal. There's no need to bring presents to business contacts (and you should certainly not try to bribe anyone), but you should give business cards to all at a meeting. It's normal to discuss business over lunch, but not over dinner, which is meant to be more sociable; it's quite acceptable to talk about politics, as well as soccer, of course. Uruguayans are proud of their country and happy to discuss its attractions; but do not confuse it with Paraguay!

Taboos include using a toothpick in public and sitting or putting your feet on a ledge, desk or table; it's also rude to point at someone – you should usually just tilt your head in the direction of whoever you're talking about. A thumbs-up sign is positive (ok, thanks, good luck), and a thumbs-down is negative; flicking your fingers under your chin indicates not knowing or caring.

Dress is more sober than elsewhere in Latin America, but shorts are generally acceptable. For business meetings you should wear a suit, but it's increasingly acceptable to remove jackets and ties – take your cue from your local contacts.

BUYING A PROPERTY AND MOVING TO URUGUAY

Foreigners can buy property and engage in any other kind of business activity under the protection of the same laws as a Uruguayan citizen. Buying property is a two-stage process, as in Britain, with an initial agreement known as the *reserva* that subjects both buyer and seller to a penalty of 10% or more of the purchase price if they back out – the buyer is required to deposit this sum in an escrow account and the seller hands over the deeds. After this the lawyer carries out the normal searches, taking up to two months, and then the final contract is signed and the keys are formally handed over. You don't actually have to be present if you give power of attorney to an agent.

To be legally resident in Uruguay, you need to show a passport (valid for at least another six months), a notarized certificate of good conduct (certifying that you have a clear criminal record), your birth certificate and marriage and divorce

STUFF YOUR RUCKSACK

This simple idea, the brainchild of British television presenter Kate Humble, basically consists of a website (*www.stuffyourrucksack.com*) where travellers can look up schools, charities and other organisations which may need items that can easily be stuffed into your rucksack before you go. Those arriving back from a destination where schools need books, orphanages need toys or charities need cash can also register these on the website.

papers as relevant, and a notarised document showing that your family income is adequate to support you in Uruguay. Once in Uruguay you'll also have to undergo a medical examination. It's that easy.

TRAVELLING POSITIVELY

As a fairly prosperous and peaceful country with no massive inequality of income, Uruguay is not an obvious target for charities and volunteers. Nevertheless, there are things you can do if you want your stay in the country to be a positive exchange.

Academia Uruguay Juan Carlos Gómez 1408, CP 11000 Montevideo; ☎ 2915 2496; www. academiauruguay.com. This language school offers the possibility of doing voluntary work while studying Spanish in Montevideo, giving a full immersion in Uruguayan culture. You are asked to pay for a minimum of 3 weeks of classes (currently US$230/week for 20hrs' tuition), with at least 4 weeks on your voluntary project, & all payments to the charities or voluntary organisations will be made by the school. Possible tasks include working in a kitchen, bakery or radio station, teaching English, sports or computing skills, or childcare. The programme is also open to couples & families, & accommodation is available with families, groups of fellow volunteers, or in private apartments; there are also combined programmes with the academy's sister school in Buenos Aires.

Asociación Nacional de ONG de Uruguay (National Association of NGOs) Avda del Libertador 1985 esc 202; ☎ 2924 0812; www. anong.org.uy. This organisation can put you in touch with a relevant group if you have some specific interests or needs.

Cruz Roja Uruguaya (Uruguayan Red Cross) Avda 8 de Octubre 2990, 11600 Montevideo; ☎ 2480 2112; e cruzroja@adinet.com.uy; http:// cruzrojauruguaya.org. If you speak good Spanish, the Cruz accepts applications from volunteers 14.00–19.30 Mon–Fri (Jan–Feb 08.00–13.00).

El Abrojo Soriano 1153, Montevideo; ☎ 2903 0144; www.elabrojo.org.uy. Works with street children in Las Piedras, a suburb of Montevideo, & volunteers are welcome.

Karumbé Project D Murillo 6334, 11500 Montevideo; ☎ 2401 0101; m 098 614201, 099 917811; e volkarumbe@gmail.com; www. karumbe.org. The project helps to study & protect sea turtles, sea lions & dolphins in Rocha. You'll spend time in boats & the water, & with local villagers, studying fishery practices & helping with workshops & other educational activities. You may also find yourself tending sick turtles or your fellow volunteers, cooking or cleaning as required. Volunteers are needed for periods of 2 weeks to a month. There's a fee of US$100 for every 15 days, plus US$18/day for bed & board.

Posada al Sur Pérez Castillano 1424, Montevideo; ☎ 2916 5287; www.posadaalsur.com. uy, www.retosalsur.org. A self-styled B&B which focuses on sustainable & community tourism, working with local groups both in Montevideo (offering tours of the deprived but very colourful Barrio Sur & Palermo) & in Rocha, Río Negro & Tacuarembó. Taking these tours will support local tourism initiatives & suppliers of food & other services.

Un Techo para mi País (A Roof for My Country) Paysandú 824, Montevideo; ☎ 2908 8456; e info. uruguay@techo.org; www.techo.org/uruguay. This organisation, a partner of Habitat for Humanity, nearly always requires a steady supply of strapping young labourers to build houses for the poor.

You could also support two other conservation NGOs, to be found in Montevideo's Catholic Centre (*Canelones 1164 & Gutiérrez Ruiz*), although they don't have much need for foreign volunteers. **Vida Silvestre** (☎ 2902 5853; *http://vidasilvestre.org.uy;* ⊕ *15.00–20.00 Mon & Thu, 13.00–16.00 Wed*) puts on a monthly excursion open to all – a two/three-day hiking and camping trip, as a rule, with a guide and six to ten participants, to explore some wild area and observe nature. **Aves Uruguay** (*Birdlife Uruguay;* ☎ *2092 8642; www.avesuruguay.org.uy;* ⊕ *16.00–20.00 Mon–Fri*) also puts on a monthly trip, focused more on birdwatching, of course.

Part Two

THE GUIDE

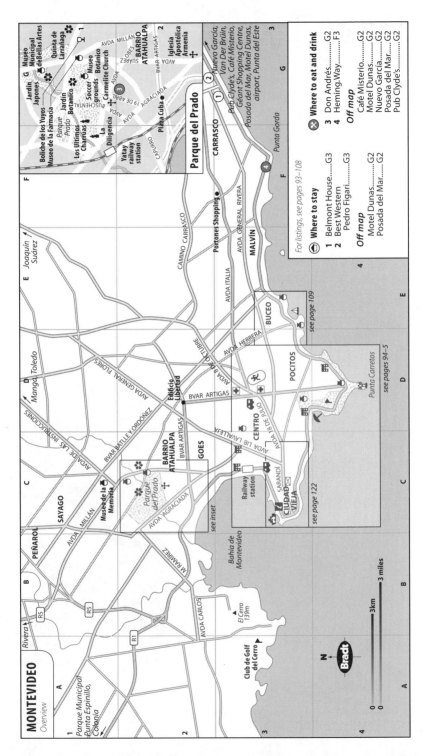

3

Montevideo

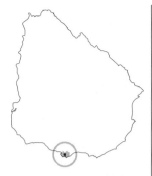

Uruguay's capital, indeed its only major city, sits on the estuary of the River Plate, with 13km of beaches linked by a waterfront boulevard known as the *rambla*. In fact one of South America's finest natural harbours is tucked away, half-forgotten, behind the old town. It's a delightfully laid-back, peaceful and friendly city where a normal working day seems like a sleepy Sunday morning in Buenos Aires, but it has all the services you'd expect plus a lively social and cultural scene. In 2009 *The Economist* ranked Montevideo as the city with the best quality of life (for expats) in Latin America, and third-best in terms of infrastructure. The great Argentine writer Jorge Luis Borges wrote nostalgically of Montevideo:

> You are the Buenos Aires we once had,
> That slipped away quietly over the years.
> False door in time,
> Your streets contemplate a lighter past.

In an area of 525.5km² there's a population of some 1.31 million, or 1.8 million in the wider metropolitan area (in 2011). In 2010 the city telephone numbers were changed from the original seven numbers (prefixed by '02' when called from outside the city) to eight numbers starting with 2 (from anywhere in Uruguay). There's useful information on the city council's website (*www.montevideo.gub.uy*).

HISTORY

In 1723 the Portuguese, already established in Colonia, decided to found a settlement at the equally fine natural harbour of Montevideo, but were driven away in January of 1724 by a Spanish force under the Governor of Buenos Aires, Bruno Zabala, who began to construct fortifications on the site of the present Plaza Zabala and Palacio Taranco. The city of San Felipe y Santiago de Montevideo was officially founded in November 1726 with the arrival of 96 settlers from the Canary Islands (in fact six families had already arrived from Buenos Aires), with a second group of Canariots arriving in 1729. In 1726 Pedro Millán distributed land to the settlers (including a certain Juan Antonio Artigas), but large sections of the original site on the tip of the peninsula were, as usual, reserved for a church and other official buildings on a plaza, plus a strong fortress. In January 1730 Zabala set up the first *cabildo* or council for the fast-growing town, the population of which reached around 7,000 by 1770 and close to 10,000 (perhaps a quarter black and mixed-race), although nowadays these are almost invisible) by 1800.

On 3 February 1807 the British attacked the city; after several days of bombardment of the weakest part of the city wall (close to the present Anglican church), soldiers broke through and seized the cathedral, from the tower of which they were able to use their new-fangled rifles to great effect against the *ciudadela* (citadel), which was soon captured. The British occupation of Montevideo was amicable until their departure in September 1807.

In 1808 Napoleon invaded Spain and forced King Carlos IV to abdicate, putting his brother on the throne instead. The Governor of Montevideo, Francisco Javier de Elío, pressured the French-born viceroy of the Plate, Santiago Liniers, to declare his loyalty to the Spanish crown, but he only issued an ambiguous statement. Accused of complicity with Napoleon by Elío and the cabildo of Buenos Aires, Liniers summoned Elío to Buenos Aires, replacing him with Juan Ángel de Michelena. The citizens of Montevideo backed Elío and called for a *cabildo abierto* or open council, which was held on 21 September 1808; Michelena fled and a

THE *GRAF SPEE*

At the start of World War II, the German navy sent the pocket battleship *Admiral Graf Spee* (one of the most modern ships built, with her electrically welded hull and diesel engines) to raid Allied merchant shipping in the South Atlantic, where she sank nine merchantmen, captured two and left one immobilised, while the Royal Navy scrambled desperately to find her. One of the merchant ships sunk off South Africa managed to get off a radio message first, and Commodore (later Admiral Sir) Henry Harwood correctly guessed the *Graf Spee* would head for the Plate estuary.

On 12 December 1939, 240km off the coast of southern Brazil, the *Graf Spee*'s lookouts saw what they thought was a cruiser and two destroyers escorting a convoy, and she moved in to attack. The 'destroyers' were actually the light cruisers HMS *Ajax* (with Harwood aboard) and HMNZS *Achilles* (loaned by Britain to New Zealand, although around 40% of the crew were British), with the heavy cruiser HMS *Exeter*, and no convoy.

The next day the so-called Battle of the River Plate (in fact well out into the Atlantic, 500km off Punta del Este), the first major naval battle of World War II, left 36 Germans and 72 British and New Zealanders dead. The *Graf Spee* had six 11-inch (280mm) guns against the *Exeter*'s six 8-inch (203mm) guns, which gave her a longer range and allowed her to do a lot of damage – but the *Ajax* and *Achilles*, each with eight 6-inch (152mm) guns, were able to come in on the other side and do enough damage to force the *Graf Spee* to break off and head for the temporary safety of Uruguayan waters. The *Exeter* was crippled (having taken three hits, destroying two of her three gun turrets), but the two light cruisers shadowed the *Graf Spee* to Montevideo.

Captain Hans Langsdorff of the *Graf Spee* knew that he'd used up too much fuel and ammunition to be able to fight his way back to Germany for repairs; in addition, the British minister in Montevideo, Sir Eugen Millington-Drake (also known as a playwright, and as father of Teddy Millington-Drake, artist and lover of Bruce Chatwin), was working hard spreading rumours about the British forces about to arrive. In fact HMS *Cumberland* had been refitting in the Falklands and had to steam flat-out to reach the Plate late on 14 December; and the aircraft-carrier *Ark Royal* was in Rio de Janeiro, 1,600km away. British skullduggery also slowed down the repairs to the *Graf Spee*; by international law she was only allowed to stay for 24 hours in a neutral port, although a presidential decree extended this to 72 hours. The German naval headquarters were pressing for Langsdorff to head out to sea and engage the British ships, but just before the deadline on the royalist Junta (ruling council) was set up, a crucial phase in the Banda Oriental's development of an identity separate from Buenos Aires. Only in May 1810 did the criollo people of Buenos Aires set up an autonomous Junta, forcing the viceroy to move to Montevideo, which remained loyal to the crown. A second siege started in 1813, with the Spanish being driven from Montevideo in 1814 by the forces of independent Buenos Aires, themselves driven out the next year by Rivera. Once Uruguay achieved independence in 1828, Montevideo became the national capital; its population was actually about one-third French and Basque at this point.

The British, who had helped bring about Uruguay's independence from Brazil, promoted Montevideo as an alternative port to Buenos Aires; in 1832 the *Beagle* was anchored there when a government minister was rowed out to the ship to plead for help against the mutinying black troops. Fitzroy, Darwin and 50 men landed,

evening of 17 December he scuttled the *Graf Spee* a couple of miles off Punta Yeguas, immediately west of Montevideo.

The crew of over 1,000 men was taken to Buenos Aires, as Argentina was more sympathetic to Germany than was Uruguay (indeed, if Langsdorff had headed for La Plata rather than Montevideo, the outcome might have been rather different); they were interned for the duration of the war, although a few escaped and made it back to Germany. Many of those who remained ended up marrying and staying in Argentina after 1945.

Langsdorff shot himself in his hotel room in Buenos Aires on 19 December; he remains widely respected as an honourable old-school officer who fought bravely but then refused to sacrifice the lives of his crew in a pointless battle – he also ensured that the crews of the merchantmen sunk by the *Graf Spee* were all taken off first, and that not one was killed. At the funeral – in Buenos Aires's Chacarita Cemetery – of some of the Germans killed in the battle, when everyone else including the priests gave the Nazi salute he pointedly gave the old naval salute. Other Germans were buried in Montevideo's Cementerio del Norte. Three sailors from the *Achilles* lie in the British Cemetery, while the *Exeter*'s dead were buried at sea.

The British merchant seamen held on the *Graf Spee* were released in Montevideo; her supply ship *Altmark*, with 299 others, set sail for Germany, passing through neutral Norwegian waters, where naval officers inspected her but failed to find the prisoners. Nevertheless, on 16 February 1940, the British destroyer HMS *Cossack* followed her in to the Jøssingfjord, where a boarding party seized the ship and rescued the prisoners. This incident may have brought forward the German invasion of Denmark and Norway, which took place on 9 April 1940.

The *Graf Spee* sank in shallow water, with most of her superstructure remaining above water; gradually she sank into the mud and sand until little more than her masthead was visible at low tide. Immediately after the battle British intelligence agents removed her radar equipment, and in 1997 one of the secondary gun mounts was removed and placed outside the naval museum (see page 142). In 2004 it was announced that the wreck was to be raised and moved to become a museum; the huge rangefinder was removed and is now at the entry to the port (see page 121) and in 2006 a bronze eagle was removed from the ship's stern (with its swastika wrapped in tarpaulin). It remains to be seen whether the ship herself can ever be moved.

armed with muskets and cutlasses, but the mutineers melted away. The British group spent the night in the ciudadela, cooking steaks, and returned to the ship in the morning with a sense of anticlimax.

The old city walls (with two gates north and south of the present Cabildo, historically open from dawn to sunset, with a wicket open until 20.00) gradually fell into disuse and were demolished. The city was blockaded throughout the Guerra Grande of 1843–51, but there was no actual assault. A rather more effective blockade of Buenos Aires was mounted by Uruguay's French and English allies, with the unexpected result that Montevideo flourished and became the major port of the Río de la Plata, boosted by the British-built railways after 1860. A new town (the present-day Centro) was laid out in 1829–33, but only actually built after 1861, with wide, tree-lined streets and the new plazas Independencia and Cagancha. By 1867 development had crept beyond the present Palacio Municipal into the Cordón area, and in 1868 the Barrio Atahualpa was laid out near the Prado, until then an area of weekend retreats for the city's affluent citizens. It was only at the start of the 20th century that Avenida 18 de Julio became the city's main thoroughfare.

By 1860 the city's population had grown to almost 58,000; 30 years later it was 215,000 (at least half foreign-born), owing to mass immigration from Europe. This process continued throughout the 20th century, with large numbers of Italians and Spaniards, then French (and Basques), Poles, Lebanese, Armenians and Jews from all over eastern Europe bringing the great cultural diversity that still marks the city today. The British community was small but affluent and influential, being involved in trade and investment; in 1861 the Montevideo Cricket Club was founded and the same year put on the first rugby[sic] match outside Europe; in 1868 a cricket game against Buenos Aires was the first international cricket match in South America.

An earthquake in 1888 led to many houses being rebuilt around their own central patios (often covered with a glass roof), and the development of *conventillos* or tenements, with rooms occupied by families. Economic prosperity brought large public buildings in the Belle-Époque style, such as the Teatro Solís, Estación Central and Palacio Taranco, as well as grand hotels such as the Parque (by the Parque Rodó) and Carrasco; these were followed in the 1920s by the Palacio Salvo (still Montevideo's main landmark) and many Art Deco towers and apartment blocks include the Palacio Rinaldi and Palacio Díaz, as well as many very successful Art Deco houses, which carried on being built into the 1950s. In the 1930s came Bauhaus-style Modernism, with buildings such as the Edificio Lapido and the Bolsa de Comercio (Stock Exchange).

The first horse-drawn trams appeared in 1917, and motor buses in 1926. Construction of the riverside *ramblas*, one of the city's iconic features, began in 1916 with the Playa Ramírez–Pocitos section, followed from 1926 by the section west from there past the Barrio Sur (considerable areas of estuary being cut off and reclaimed), and the Rambla Gran Bretaña, to the east, in 1935. Avenida Agraciada, to the north, was built in 1927–35, and the Estadio Centenario was built for the first soccer World Cup in 1930, with the surrounding Parque Batlle opened in 1934 and the Palacio Municipal in 1941.

The motor car was taking over at this time (and some of those original cars can still be seen); the first traffic lights appeared on Avenida 18 de Julio (outside the Palacio Municipal) in 1953, and the last electric tram ran in 1956 (the No 9 from Punta Carretas to Estación Goes, as it happens). The Avenida 8 de Octubre tunnel was built in 1961, under the present Tres Cruces bus terminal (itself dating from 1994; until then, bus companies had individual offices on Plaza Cagancha).

There was a construction boom in the late 1970s, when modern buildings (some quite attractive) began to intrude on the main avenues; however, the military dictatorship also led to an exodus, particularly of younger people, giving a sense of stagnation that took a long time to dissipate altogether. Suburban sprawl has now spread across the whole department; the waterfront suburbs to the east of the city centre, as far as Carrasco, developed as weekend resorts for the city's affluent residents, but now, thanks to the development of the road system, are now their permanent homes (with their holiday homes now much further east, in Maldonado and Rocha). Since the 1980s large shopping malls and hypermarkets have appeared as the economy has prospered again, and a progressive council has pushed ahead with improvement projects.

The headquarters of Mercosur, the South American common market, was established here (in the former Hotel Parque) in 1997, and in 1998 the Teatro Solís closed for refurbishment, a process that finally ended ten years later. Also in 2008 the city inaugurated the largest park created in half a century, the Parque Andalucía, north of the centre by the Arroyo Miguelete. Tabaré Vásquez was Mayor of Montevideo from 1990 to 1995, and as a cancer doctor soon began the process of banning smoking on municipal property, which he continued as President of Uruguay to 2010.

CLIMATE

Being on the estuary of the River Plate (referred to as *el mar* or 'the sea'), Montevideo has a more maritime version of the Uruguayan climate, ie: slightly warmer in winter and cooler in summer. In summer thunderstorms are common, and you may want a second layer of clothing in the evenings. Sea breezes bring relief from the daytime heat, but are less welcome in winter, when it can really get quite chilly (although there's really no need for the locals to wrap up as if they were in Siberia), and also foggy. There may be a couple of days with temperatures below 10°C (50°F), but they're usually followed by warm sunny days.

Average temperatures are 23°C in summer, 17°C in spring, 18°C in autumn and 12°C in winter (when high humidity makes it feel colder). The average high and low temperatures in January are 28°C and 17°C, with a highest recorded maximum of 43°C; and 14°C and 6°C in July, with a minimum recorded of –4°C. Rainfall averages 950mm annually.

The river is often mud-coloured due to dirt but is fine to swim in, although this is not recommended for 24 hours after rain.

GETTING THERE AND AWAY

Naturally the capital is where most visitors to the country will arrive, chiefly by air or by ferry from Buenos Aires.

BY AIR Passenger traffic at the Carrasco airport (see *Southern Uruguay* map, page 144) (*code MVD;* \ *2604 0272/0329; www.aic.com.uy*), 20km east of the centre, grew by 50% from 2003 to 2008, to 1.24 million passengers; fortunately a much larger new terminal (designed by the star architect Rafael Viñoly – see page 35) opened in 2009, although it still has only eight gates (on four airbridges). The sweeping curve of its roof seems to float above the departure level, with glazed walls on all four sides; above the departure level a terrace holds a restaurant and other commercial outlets. From the roof above this hang a plane, dating from 1913, and a glider, dating from 1945. Arriving passengers also enter on a mezzanine before descending to the Immigration and baggage halls. It has free Wi-Fi, ATMs, cafés, exchange offices and car-rental offices (Avis, Budget, Hertz and Europcar); the COT bus company has an office (✆ 2409 4949; *www.cot.com.uy*), with buses calling in on the way to Punta del Este and other places along the coast to the east. There's a helpful tourist office (✆ 2604 0329/86; ⊕ 08.00–20.00 daily).

Departing passengers have to pay an airport fee of US$40; it's usually included with your ticket, but otherwise you can pay at the Pago de Tasas (Tax Payment) counter, in dollars or Uruguayan pesos, by cash or credit card; for the Puente Aéreo shuttle to Buenos Aires it's only US$19. The new terminal cost US$134 million, so we'll be paying for a while. There's duty-free shopping (with plenty of Uruguayan wines) on both arrival and departure; online check-in, not possible at the old terminal, is available in the new one.

Airport transport White Airport Shuttle minibuses (e *info@taxisaeropuerto. com; www.taxisaeropuerto.com/transfer.html*) take you direct to destinations in the city for US$14 per person. A taxi costs US$60–65 to the Centro or Ciudad Vieja (US$50 to Pocitos); it's cheaper to book a *remise* (see page 89) for about US$50 to the Centro. Buses currently cost P36 (*US$1.60*), with suburban routes such as Nos 700, 701, 704, 710, 711 and 724 getting you into town pretty efficiently. These take about 30 minutes to the Tres Cruces bus terminal (US$1) and ten–15 minutes more to the Baltasar Brum terminal [122 E1] (*Galicia 911 & Río Branco*) on the north side of the Centro, where there's an ATM, Wi-Fi and empanada stalls. They all take the busy Avenida Italia to Tres Cruces, except for the DM1 which runs (every 15 minutes) nearer the coast to Buceo and Pocitos. Some long-distance buses operated by CUT and COPSA, mainly to Punta del Este, call at the airport.

Heading out to the airport, *suburbano* buses leave frequently from the Baltasar Brum terminal, and pick up on Paysandú at its junctions with Río Negro, Yaguarón and Fernández Crespo, and on Muñoz by the Tres Cruces bus terminal [95 F1] (at the junction of Haedo and Acevedo Díaz).

Airline offices in Montevideo

✈ **Aerolíneas Argentinas** Plaza Independencia 818; ✆ 2902 3691/0828; e mvdrcar@aerolineas. com.uy; www.aerolineas.com.ar; ⊕ 09.00–18.00 Mon–Fri (*call centre (English spoken):* ✆ *000 405 486527;* ⊕ *09.00–19.00 Mon–Sat*)

✈ **Air France–KLM** Río Negro 1354; ✆ 2902 5023/26; www.airfrance.com.uy; ⊕ 09.00–12.30, 13.30–17.00 Mon–Fri

✈ **American Airlines** Sarandí 699 bis, Plaza Independencia; ✆ 2916 3929; www.aa.com; ⊕ 09.00–18.00 Mon–Fri, 10.00–13.00 Sat; Montevideo Shopping, Local 2434 (2nd Flr); ⊕ 10.00–22.00 daily

✈ **BQB** Colonia 751 & Florida (Radisson Hotel); ✆ 2902 0526/9397; ⊕ 10.00–18.00 Mon–Fri, 09.00–13.00 Sat (*call centre:* ✆ *130;* ⊕ *08.00– 21.00 Mon–Fri, 09.00–14.00 Sat*). Tres Cruces bus terminal, office B28/9; Héctor Miranda 2443 (Punta Carretas); Carrasco airport; ✆ 2604 6711; www.flybqb.com.uy

✈ **Copa Airlines** World Trade Center, Herrera 1248, Local 28; ✆ 2707 2672 (*24hrs*), 2623 4903; www.copaair.com; ⊕ 08.00–18.00 Mon–Fri, 08.00–12.00 Sat

✈ **Delta** Colonia 981, office 201; ✆ 2900 7776; www.delta.com; ⊕ 09.00–13.00, 14.00–18.00 Mon–Fri

✈ **Gol** Wilson Ferreira Aldunate 1336 & Avda 18 de Julio; ⊕ 10.00–18.30 Mon–Fri; Carrasco airport; tf 2606 0901–3, 000 405 5127; www. voegol.com

✈ **Iberia** Colonia 975, near Herrera y Obes; ✆ 2908 1032/4343; www.iberia.com.uy; ⊕ 09.00–17.30 Mon–Fri

✈ **LAN** Ellauri 343; ✆ 2712 5555; Carrasco airport; ✆ 2604 0184/0268; ⊕ 10.00–18.30 Mon–Fri; www.lan.com

✈ **Sol** Carrasco airport; ✆ 2601 2072 (*call centre:* ✆ *000 405 210053;* ⊕ *09.00–18.30 Mon–Thu, 09.00–13.00 Fri*); www.sol.com.ar

✈ **TACA** Plaza Independencia 831, office 807 (*call centre:* ☎ *000 405 1004*); www.taca.com

✈ **TAM Mercosur** Plaza Cagancha 1335 (Torre Libertad) near Avda 18 de Julio, office 804; ☎ 2901 8451, 000 401 90223; www.tamairlines.com

BY SEA The direct ferry from Buenos Aires operated by **Buquebus** docks at the port on the north side of the Ciudad Vieja (Old Town), where you'll find an attractive terminal [122 A2] with an ATM, Wi-Fi, phones and a café. Unless you get straight on to Buquebus's own connecting bus, you'll walk out between the big *Aduana* (Customs) building and the Ministry of Tourism, across the road from the Mercado del Puerto, two blocks from city bus stops. Buquebus also offers the cheaper option of going via Colonia, with their own buses direct to and from the port (see page 52).

Two other companies, **Colonia Express** and **SeaCat Colonia**, operate fast ferries from Buenos Aires to Colonia, with bus connections from the port direct to Montevideo and Punta del Este. **Trans Uruguay** offers a twice-daily Buenos Aires service starting with a three-hour bus journey to Carmelo for the ferry to Tigre and Cacciola Viajes. For all contact details, see pages 52–4.

Cruise liners also dock in the port, by the Ciudad Vieja [122 A2], where you'll find the Isla de Información y Servicios (Cruise Service Island), with cafeteria, international phone and internet office, and another office renting mobile telephones and video and digital cameras. Cruise companies usually provide transfers from the dock to Plaza Independencia (between the old and new towns). Tourist police are stationed at the port exit, on the Peatonal Sarandí and in other popular areas (in the Ciudad Vieja and the Centro).

Yachts should head for the Yacht Club Uruguayo at Puerto Buceo, just east of the centre, where there are 238 berths and 24-hour showers (☎ *2622 1221;* e *info@ ycu.org.uy. Port administration:* ☎ *2623 3411;* e *puertobuceo@dnh.gub.uy;* ⏱ *09.00– 17.00 daily).*

Ferries to Argentina

🚢 **Buquebus** office B28/9; ☎ 130; e atcliente@ buquebus.com; www.buquebus.com.uy

🚢 **Cacciola** office B32; ☎ 2908 2244; e caccaiolacentro@ribertel.com.ar; http:// cacciolauruguay.com.ar

🚢 **Colonia Express** office B31; ☎ 2401 6666; www.coloniaexpress.com

🚢 **Seacat Colonia** office B28/9; ☎ 130, 2409 8198/9; e atcliente@seacatcolonia.com.uy; www. seacatcolonia.com

BY BUS Long-distance and international buses arrive in Montevideo at the modern Tres Cruces terminal [95 F1] (*Bvar Artigas 1825 at Dr Ferrer Serra, facing the end of Avda Italia;* ☎ *2401 8998; www.trescruces.com.uy*), about 3km east of the Centro and 4km east of the Ciudad Vieja. It has clean, free toilets; a bank (⏱ *13.00– 17.00 Mon–Fri*) and ATMs; luggage storage (*guardería de equipajes;* ☎ *2402 8195;* e *lebagage@adinet.com.uy;* ⏱ *24hrs; 2hrs free; with bus ticket, 24hrs free; without ticket, 4hrs US$2.50 to 12–24hrs US$6*); tourist information (*office T-12A;* ☎ *2409 7399;* ⏱ *08.00–22.00 Mon–Fri, 09.00–22.00 Sat–Sun*); currency exchange (*Cambio Indumex;* ⏱ *06.00–midnight daily*); post office (⏱ *09.00–22.00 Mon–Fri, 10.00– 22.00 Sat–Sun*), and 24-hour phone and internet centres. There's no free Wi-Fi except what you pick up from waiting buses. It's underneath a shopping mall with a Ta-Ta supermarket (⏱ *08.00–23.30 daily*) and a choice of fast-foody restaurants including a 24-hour McDonald's. The terminal's excellent website gives information on all services, matched by the arrival and departure screens. There are also ticket desks for all the ferry companies to Buenos Aires.

You'll find a boarding fee of P4–16 added to the cost of your ticket.

Transport to/from the city From the Tres Cruces terminal there are **buses** to all parts of the city. From a stop on Bulevar Artigas (by a statue of Rivera), route CA1 goes the length of Avenida 18 de Julio and the Ciudad Vieja (*every 6–10mins 07.30–21.20 Mon–Fri, 08.00–14.00 Sat, not Sun*); the modern, wheelchair-accessible buses cost just P8. From Ferrer Serra, on the south side of the terminal, Nos 121, 164, 180, 187, 188, 330 D9 and D10 run to the Ciudad Vieja via Avenida 18 de Julio and Plaza Independencia. Buses for Pocitos leave from the same stop as the CA1. Buses to and from the airport will also pick you up and set you down here.

A **taxi** to the Centro costs around US$10.

BUS COMPANIES OPERATING IN MONTEVIDEO

USING THE TRES CRUCES LONG-DISTANCE TERMINAL

🚌 **Agencia Central (including Magic, Chadre, Sabelin)** office B17/18; ☎ 1717; e agenciacentral@adinet.com.uy; www.agenciacentral.com.uy

🚌 **Bruno Hermanos** office B23B; ☎ 2402 8212; e brunoh@adinet.com.uy; www.brunohnos.com.uy

🚌 **CITA** office B11/12; ☎ 2402 5425; e cita@adinet.com.uy; www.cita.com.uy

🚌 **Copay** office B4; ☎ 2402 7290; e copay@adinet.com.uy

🚌 **COPSA** office B5; ☎ 1975; www.copsa.com.uy

🚌 **COPSA Este** office B9; ☎ 17120; www.copsa.com.uy

🚌 **Corporacion** office B19; ☎ 2402 1920; e cutcorp@adinet.com.uy

🚌 **COT (Compañía Oriental de Transporte)** office B15/16; ☎ 2409 4949; e info@cot.com.uy; www.cot.com.uy

🚌 **COTMI** office B5; ☎ 2401 7443; e cotmiturismo@adinet.com.uy

🚌 **Cromin** office B10; ☎ 2403 4657; e rutasdelsol@adinet.com.uy

🚌 **CTTM** office B17/18; ☎ 1717

🚌 **CUT** office B19/20; ☎ 2402 1920; www.cutcorporacion.com.uy

🚌 **Cynsa** office B13/14; ☎ 2402 5363, 2408 6670; e nunezcynsa@adinet.com.uy; www.cynsa.com.uy

🚌 **El Norteño** office B11; ☎ 2402 1042; e bus2676@adinet.com.uy

🚌 **Emdal** office B8; ☎ 2408 9738; http://grupocotar.com.uy

🚌 **Expreso Chago** office B23; ☎ 2409 0999/5699; http://grupocotar.com.uy

🚌 **Expreso Minuano** office B8; ☎ 2402 5075; e expresominuano@adinet.com.uy

🚌 **Intertür** office B23; ☎ 2401 7729, 2409 7098

🚌 **Nion** office B23; ☎ 2409 0547; e nionsrl@adinet.com.uy

🚌 **Nossar** office B7; ☎ 1880; www.nossar.com.uy

🚌 **Nuñez** office B13/14; ☎ 2402 5363, 2408 6670; e nunezcynsa@adinet.com.uy; www.nunez.com.uy, www.cynsa.com.uy

🚌 **Rutas del Plata** office B24; ☎ 2402 5129, 2409 7099; e corpla@adinet.com.uy; www.rutasdelplata.com.uy

🚌 **Rutas del Sol** office B10; ☎ 2403 4657, 2402 5451; e rutasdelsol@adinet.com.uy

🚌 **Turil** office B21/22; ☎ 1990; e ag3cruces@turil.com.uy; www.turil.com.uy

🚌 **Turismar** office B23A; ☎ 2409 0999/5699; e turismar@montevideo.com.uy; www.turismar.com.uy

USING THE REGIONAL TERMINAL BALTASAR BRUM (RÍO BRANCO)

🚌 **CITA** ☎ 2902 5466

🚌 **Cutcsa** ☎ 2204 0000; e cac@cutcsa.com.uy; www.cutcsa.com.uy

Buses from Montevideo On some routes there are fewer services at weekends, but on others there will actually be more on Sundays, especially heading back to Montevideo in the evening. In summer there may be extra departures, or more commonly multiple buses for each departure, some *directo* and others handling intermediate traffic – be sure to check your ticket for the number of your *coche*, printed along with your *asiento* (seat number) on your ticket.

The main companies have websites with timetables (see box opposite), but you can't yet book online. The Tres Cruces terminal's website (*www.trescruces.com.uy*) also includes a timetable. 'MDF' means 'not on Sundays or holidays'.

Major domestic departures from Montevideo

Fares are from mid-2013. Operators here will often accept debit cards, but outside Montevideo you'll usually have to pay cash. The following services all leave from the Tres Cruces terminal.

✈**Artigas** (*US$37; 7hr–7hrs 50mins*) Corporación/CUT 1–2/day; Turil 2–3/day (1 non-stop)

✈**Bella Unión** (*US$35; 8hrs*) Agencia Central (Chadre) 2/day via Colonia – 13hr; El Norteño 1–2/day (Sat–Sun/Mon–Fri)

✈**Canelones** (*US$2.30; 1hr–1hr 10mins*) CITA 26–29/day (w/end/Mon–Fri); Turil 5/day (to Rivera)

✈**Carmelo** (*US$14; 3hrs–3hrs 50mins*) Agencia Central (Chadre, Sabelin) 3–8/day (Sun/Mon–Fri); Intertur 3–5/day (Sun/Mon–Fri)

✈**Castillos** (*US$16.50; 3hrs 45mins*) COT 2/4/day (winter/summer); Cynsa 5/day; Rutas del Sol 6/day

✈**Chuy** (*US$21; 4hrs 45mins–5hrs*) COT 4/day; Cynsa 4/day; Rutas del Sol 6/day

✈**Colonia** (*US$11; 2hrs 20mins–2hrs 45mins*) Chadre 2/day; COT 9–21/day (winter/summer); Turil 7–9/day

✈**Dolores** (*US$18; 3hrs 30mins–5hrs*) Agencia Central (Chadre, Sabelin) 4–5/day (& 2/day via Colonia – 5hr 10min); Intertur 4–5/day

✈**Durazno** (*US$11.60; 2hrs 20mins–2hrs 50mins*) Agencia Central (Chadre/CTTM) 3/day; Bruno Hermanos 1–3/day; Nossar 7–10/day; Nuñez 2–3/day; Turil 3/day; Turismar 3–4/day

✈**Florida** (*US$7; 1hr 30mins–1hr 50mins*) Bruno Hermanos 1–3/day (to Durazno, Sarandí Grande); CITA 14–24/day (Sun/Mon–Fri); CTTM 2/day (to Durazno, San Gregorio de Polanco); Turismar 3/day (to Durazno)

✈**Fray Bentos** (*US$19; 4hrs–4hrs 40mins*) Agencia Central (Chadre, Sabelin) 1/day (& 2/day via Colonia – 6hr 45min); CUT 5–8/day

✈**José Ignacio** (*US$11; 3hrs 15mins*) COPSA 2–3/day (winter/summer); COT 3/day via airport

✈**La Paloma** (*US$14.70; 3hrs 20mins–3hrs 50mins*)/**La Pedrera** (*US$15.30; 3hrs 45mins–4hrs 15min*) COT 2–3/day (winter/summer); Cynsa 3–4/day (winter/summer); Rutas del Sol 4/day

✈**Maldonado** (*US$8.60; 1hr 50mins*) COPSA 17–26/day (winter/summer); COT 19/day

✈**Melo** (*US$25; 5hrs–6hrs 15min, also via Ruta 7, 6–7hrs*) Cynsa/Nuñez 7/day (Ruta 8), 2/day (Ruta 7); Turil 2–4/day; Turismar (Emdal, Expreso Chago, Posada) 2–3/day (Ruta 7), 1/day (Ruta 8)

✈**Mercedes** (*US$17; 3hrs 40mins*) Agencia Central (Chadre, Sabelin) 6–8/day (& 2/day via Colonia – 6hr); CUT 6–8/day

✈**Minas** (*US$10; 1hr 45mins–2hrs*) Corporación (CUT) 7–11/day; Cromin 5/day; Cynsa/Nuñez 5–6/day (Mon–Fri); EGA 1/day (Mon–Fri); Emdal/Expreso Chago 3/day; Expreso Minuano 8–11/day; Rutas del Plata 2–4/day; Turil 2–3/day

✈**Pan de Azucar** (*US$6; 1hr 25mins*) COT 5/day; Cynsa 6/day; Rutas del Sol 7/day

✈**Paso de los Toros** (*US$15; 3hrs–3hrs 45mins*) CTTM 2/day; Nuñez 2–3/day; Nossar 3–4/day; Turil 3–5/day

✈**Paysandú** (*US$23; 4hrs 30mins–5hrs*) Agencia Central (Chadre, Magic, Sabelin) 3/day via San José/Trinidad/Young, 2/day via Durazno/Trinidad/Young (& 2/day via Colonia 6hr); Copay 4/day; Nuñez 2/3/day

✈**Piriápolis** (*US$6; 1hr 35mins*) COPSA 12/day; COT 10/day

✈**Punta del Diablo** (*US$16; 4hrs 15mins*) COT 3/day; Cynsa 3–4/day; Rutas del Sol 3–5/day (winter/summer)

✈**Punta del Este** (*US$9; 2hrs*) COPSA 18–27/day (winter/summer); COT 22/day via airport

✈**Río Branco** (*US$25.50; 6hrs–6hrs 35mins*) Cynsa/Nuñez 2/day; Rutas del Plata 4/day

✈**Rivera** (*US$30; 6hrs–6hrs 45mins*) Agencia Central (Sabelin) 3–4/day; Nossar 1/day; Nuñez 2–3/day; Turil 6/day (2 non-stop)

Rocha (*US$13; 3hrs*) COT 5–6/day; Cynsa 7/day (8 Sun); Rutas del Sol 15/day

Salto (*US$30; 5hrs 30mins–6hrs 30mins*) Agencia Central (Chadre, Sabelin) 8/day (4 direct, 2 via Durazno; & 2 via Colonia – 7hrs 20mins); El Norteño 1/day; Nuñez 2–4/day (2 non-stop, 2 via Trinidad/Young/Paysandú)

San Carlos (*US$8.50; 2hrs*) COT 7/day; Cynsa 6–8/day (winter/summer); Rutas del Sol 8/day

San José (*US$5.70; 1hr 20mins–1hr 50mins*) Agencia Central 8/day (to Trinidad & Paysandú); CITA 17–34/day (Sun/Mon–Fri); Copay 4/day; COTMI 11–16/day (Sun/Mon–Fri)

Tacuarembó (*US$24; 4hrs 30mins–5hrs*) Agencia Central (Chadre) 4/day; Nuñez 2–3/day; Turil 6–8/day

Treinta y Tres (*US$18; 4–5hrs*) Cynsa/Nuñez 9–11/day; EGA 2–3/day; Expreso Minuano 1–2/day; Rutas del Plata 2–4/day; Turil 2–4/day

Trinidad (*US$11.60; 2hrs 20mins–3hrs*) Agencia Central (Chadre, ETA, Sabelin) 6/day; Copay 4/day (to Paysandú); El Norteño 1/day (to Salto/Bella Unión); Nossar 2/day; Nuñez 2–3/day (to Salto)

Valizas/Cabo Polonio (*US$17; 4hrs 40mins*) COT 1/day (summer only); Cynsa 1/day; Rutas del Sol 5–8/day (winter/summer)

Buses to Argentina

Bus de la Carrera office B25/6; ☎2402 1313; e bus@adinet.com.uy; www.busdelacarrera.com.uy

Cauvi office B31; ☎2401 9196/9198; e cauvi3x@hotmail.com

EGA office B30; ☎2402 5164–7; e egaxxx@hotmail.com, egakeguay@hotmail.com; www.ega.com.uy

El Cóndor office B25/6; ☎2401 4764; e bus@adinet.com.uy; www.condorestrella.com.ar

El Rápido office B27; ☎2400 8747, 2401 4764; e belgranouruguay@hotmail.com; www.elrapidoint.com.ar

Pullman General Belgrano office B27; ☎2401 4764; e belgranouruguay@hotmail.com; www.gralbelgrano.com.ar

TTL office B26; ☎2401 1410; e ttlrug@adinet.com.uy; www.ttlturismo.com

BY TRAIN Train travel is almost non-existent in Uruguay, with just a limited commuter service north from Montevideo. (A line along the coast east from the city would be very useful, but sadly doesn't exist.) Passenger services have been suspended altogether at various times in the past, and there are currently no Sunday trains. Fares are very low, but the service is too slow and infrequent to be very useful, especially if you want to head out from Montevideo in the morning and back in the evening.

Montevideo's Central Station was closed in 2004, when it was sold to a state-owned bank (at a low price) for a controversial development project which hasn't yet begun; a modern but much smaller station was provided 500m north. Frequent buses pass the new station, but many passengers declared they would not travel the extra distance to their workplaces, and train loadings may be as much as a third lower than before the closure.

From the fiercely air-conditioned modern station [94 C1] (☎ 2924 8080; e afepasajeros@adinet.com.uy; www.afe.com.uy) trains run four times a day Monday to Friday (*twice on Sat*) to Progreso, in the city's northern suburbs, with two continuing (Monday–Saturday) to Canelones, Santa Lucía and 25 de Agosto; there are no services on Sundays or holidays.

GETTING AROUND

BY BUS An efficient bus network (*www.montevideobus.com.uy*) reaches every corner of Montevideo, although there are no trams or metro. Smartcards have recently been introduced on city and suburban buses, although you can still pay cash to a conductor. The most useful innovation so far is the CA1 service, introduced in 2008, with modern, low-emission, wheelchair-accessible buses with large baggage racks shuttling every six–ten minutes (⊕ *07.30–21.10 Mon–Fri, 08.00–14.00 Sat*) between the Ciudad Vieja, the Centro and the Tres Cruces bus terminal [95 F1] . Drivers have no Formula One fantasies (and all wear seatbelts), unlike in neighbouring countries. Buses start running between 04.35 and 06.15, and finish between 22.30 and midnight, with some services running hourly through the night. Any bus for Aduana, Ciudad Vieja or Ciudadela will get you to the Ciudad Vieja. From January 2013 a standard ticket or *boleto común*, valid for an hour (with transfers to any operator's buses), costs P20 (US$1); a two-hour ticket costs P30 (US$1.50), and a short hop (*zona local*) costs P11 (US$0.55), and a *céntrico* ticket (valid in the Centro and Ciudad Vieja, and on bus CA1 from Tres Cruces) costs P13 (US$0.70); it's valid for one hour, with one transfer on a bus of the same company that sold you the ticket. *Diferencial* or *metropolitano* tickets, costing P20, are valid for express and longer-distance buses, or for two hours' unlimited travel; and it's P36 to the airport. Suburban buses use stops marked with a green 'S'.

The new **Bus Turístico Montevideo** (2908 6469; e *busturisticomontevideo@ coit.com.uy; www.busturisticomontevideo.com.uy;* ⊕ *09.00–17.00 daily; in winter from 10.00; US$25*) leaves hourly from the Mercado del Puerto (opposite the Yacaré gate to the port) to Plaza Independencia, the Municipal Palace, National Library, Legislative Palace, Botanic Garden, Tres Cruces bus terminal, Estadio Centenario (for the Museo del Fútbol), Montevideo Shopping, Shopping Punta Carretas, Parque Rodó, and back to the Mercado del Puerto after two hours. The modern buses have a shaded open upper deck and commentary in eight languages.

BY TAXI There are plenty of black-and-yellow taxis, either waiting at street corners or cruising, with reliable meters producing a figure that needs to be decoded from a laminated price sheet. Taxis are safe and affordable (though fares are higher late at night and at weekends); the only time you might want to agree the fare in advance is when heading for the airport. There's no need to tip, but rounding up a little bit is appreciated.

To call a taxi, phone Radio Taxi 141 (*141*), Radio Taxi Cooperativa (*2311 1030*), Radio Taxi Scot (*2208 0810*) or Fono Taxi (*2203 7000*).

It's also possible to book a remise (car with driver), for day tours or a cheaper transfer to the airport – companies include Remises Montevideo (*San José 1226 bis;* *2902 8844, 2900 0015; 24hr* m *099 628725;* e *remis@adinet.com.uy*), Independencia Remises (*Colonia 807;* *2902 6766, 2900 3448*), Remises Carrasco (*2606 1412; 24hr* m *9440 5473; www.remisescarrasco.com.uy*), Remises La Española (*Herrera 628;* *2622 2323; www.remiseslaespanola.com*), Remises Pocitos (*26 de Marzo 1269;* *2709 8175;* m *099 645541*) and Remisat (*Bvar Artigas 1919, Tres Cruces;* *2401 8241;* e *reservas@remisat.com.uy*). Remises charge around US$16 per hour, or a little more if booked through a hotel or if going outside Montevideo department.

BY CAR Driving in Montevideo is easy and relaxed by Latin American standards, with the usual grid of one-way streets. The ramblas are usually the easiest way to get to the east and north of the city, with a speed of 75km/h allowed in places. Parking in the Ciudad Vieja and the Centro must be paid for Monday to Friday (⊕ *10.00–18.00*), with tickets bought from shops using the Abitab and Redpagos systems (US$0.50/30min); there's a free day once a month, which causes a degree of chaos.

There are several 24-hour filling stations on Avenida Italia, one on Artigas at Echevería, and various others.

Car rental

Americar Cerro Largo 907 y Convención; **tf** 0800 8339, 2902 2949; 24hr **m** 099 704289; **e** americar@ebicarmotors.com; www. ebicarmotors.com

America Rentacar 21 de Setiembre 2784 bis; ✆ 2710 2886; **e** reserva@americarentacar. com.uy

Avis Yaguaron 1421; ✆ 1700, 2683 8383, 2900 9694; ⏰ 09.00–19.00 Mon–Fri, 09.00–13.00 Sat; Carrasco airport; ✆ 2604 0334; ⏰ 24hrs; **e** avis@avis.com.uy; www.avis.com.uy

Budget Soliño s/n facing the Sheraton Hotel); ✆ 2712 2020; ⏰ 09.00–19.00 daily; Carrasco airport; ✆ 2600 9986; ⏰ 24hrs; **e** budget@budget.com.uy; www.budget.com.uy

Dollar Durazno 1390 & Santiago de Chile, Palermo ✆ 2902 7540; **m** 093 990873; Ruta 101, Carrasco (near airport); ✆ 2682 8350; 24hr **m** 094 444706; **e** dollarpdp@adinet.com.uy; www.dollar. com.uy

Eleven Rentacar Avda de las Américas 7853; ✆ 2601 2701/59; **m** 094 264935; www. elevenrentacar.com

Europcar Bvar Artigas 1875, Tres Cruces; ✆ 2401 0575; 24hr **m** 9440 4570; ⏰ 09.00–19.00 Mon–Fri, 09.00–13.00 Sat; Carrasco airport; ✆ 2604 0350; port ⏰ for ferry arrivals; **m** 096 846447; ⏰ 07.00–22.00 Mon–Sat, 08.00–22.00 Sun; **e** reservas@europcar.com.uy; www.europcar. com.uy

Federal Car Rental Miguelete 2169; ✆ 2409 2737/2759; 24hr **m** 096 443688; **e** reservas@ federal.com.uy; Carrasco airport (Esso filling station); ✆ 2682 4772; 24hr **m** 096 183209; **e** aeropuerto@ federal.com.uy; www.federal.com.uy

Hertz Guipuzcoa 404 & Solano García; ✆ 2712 5000; 24hr **m** 094 640200; ⏰ 09.00–19.00 Mon–Fri, 09.00–13.00 Sat; Carrasco airport; ✆ 2604 0006, 2606 1137; 24hr **m** 094 640200;

⏰ 07.00–23.00 daily; **e** info@hertz.com.uy; www.hertz.com.uy

Multicar Colonia 1277, between Yí & Cuareim; ✆ 2902 2555; 24hr **m** 099 660959; Francisco Bonilla (200m from Carrasco airport/Ruta 101); ✆ 2682 2707; 24hr **m** 099 660959; Ascencio 1277 (Prado); ✆ 2204 0878; 24hr **m** 094 307048; ⏰ all 09.00–19.00 Mon–Fri, 09.00–13.00 Sat; www.redmulticar.com

Power Rentacar Avda Italia 3394; ✆ 2486 1350; **m** 094 360400; **e** franciscoperez@power-rent-a-car.com

Prado Rentacar Duvimiosio Terra 2341 & Avda Garibaldi; ✆ 2203 2463; www.pradorentacar. com

Punta Car Cerro Largo 1383-1401; ✆ 2900 2772; Avda de los Américas 8239 (km17); Avda de la Playa; ✆ 2604 1111; www.puntacar.com

Rally Rentacar Avda Brasil 2917 bis; ✆ 2707 3910; 24hr **m** 099 632262; **e** consultas@ rallyrentacar.com.uy; www.rallyrentacar.com.uy

Rentacar Del Río Germán Barbato 1431, between Mercedes & Colonia; ✆ 2908 4140

Rentautos Marcelino Sosa 2222; ✆ 2203 7080; **m** 099 416327; **e** rentautosmvd@hotmail. com

Snappy Car Rental Andes 1363, Local 17 & 18 de Julio; ✆ 2900 7728, 2901 6588; **m** 099 660660; **e** consultas@snappy.com.uy; www. snappy.com.uy

Sudancar Avda Italia 2665 & Avda Garibaldi; ✆ 2480 3855; **m** 24hr 099 627607; www.sudancar. com.uy

Thrifty Bvar Artigas 2966 & Martínez, Tres Cruces; ✆ 0800 8278 (**tf** 09.00–19.00 Mon–Fri, 09.00–13.00 Sat), 2481 8170; **e** montevideo@ thrifty.com.uy; Carrasco airport; ✆ 2682 4495; Montevideo port; ✆ 2916 8632; www.thrifty. com.uy

BY BICYCLE Cycling is relatively civilised in Montevideo, thanks to the courteous local drivers. In any case the best excursion is traffic-free, alongside the rambla, which stretches 22km along the seafront from the Escollera Sarandí to the Puente Carrasco. In its busier parts this has a segregated cycle track, while elsewhere cyclists and pedestrians (and a few rollerbladers) share the same space. There's a gravel track alongside the outer stretch of Avenida Italia; there are also quite a few cyclists on the shoulders of Ruta 5, the main dual carriageway north from Montevideo, both lycra-clad club riders and locals on shopper bikes.

If your hostel or hotel doesn't offer bikes, there are a few bike-rental outlets to call. Uruguay Rent A Bike (*San José 1230*; ✆ *2902 6677*; **m** *099 165213/473521*;

e *rentabikeuruguay@hotmail.com*) has a range of leisure, mountain and children's bikes and will deliver them to you, along with helmet and lock. They also offer tours. Enjoy Montevideo by Bike (m *099 187377;* e *BikeMontevideo@gmail.com*) is based at the Posada al Sur (see page 97) and shares its social concerns.

Tours are offered by Bike Tours Montevideo (*Chucarro 1286/102;* m *099 591519;* e *alicia@biketoursuruguay.com; www.biketoursuruguay.com*) and Biking Uruguay (*Avda Italia 2364, office 304;* ↘ *2480 2287; www.bikinguruguay.com/joomla/index. php;* ⊕ *10.00–19.00 Mon–Fri*).

The Centro de Investigación y Promoción de la Bicicleta en Uruguay (*www. urubike.com*) is a pressure group which organises some group rides; in 2009 they inaugurated a *bicipunto* at the Punta Carretas ANCAP station (*Rambla & Bvar Artigas*), a sort of DIY maintenance/repair facility.

Bicicletería Sur (*Aquiles Lanza 1100 & Durazno;* ↘ *2901 0792;* ⊕ *09.00–13.00, 15.00–19.00 Mon–Fri, 09.00–15.00 Sat*) mostly undertakes scooter repairs, but does also offer bike rental, although the bikes are not very sophisticated. La Clínica de Bicicletas (*Maldonado 1701 & Magellanes;* ⊕ *09.00–20.00 Mon–Sat*) is good for repairs, and GT Bicycles (*Barreiro 3225, Pocitos*) is a good modern bike shop.

ORIENTATION

The **Ciudad Vieja** or old city of Montevideo sits on a peninsula south of the port. The financial district is here, and is very lively in the daytime, but the rest of the old city is now somewhat run-down and not particularly safe at night, although regeneration projects aim to turn this around, especially along the pedestrianised route between the cathedral and the Mercado del Puerto, and the city's liveliest bars are also found here. Beyond Plaza Independencia [122 D2], and the landmark tower of the Palacio Salvo [122 D2], is the **Centro**, often described as 'downtown', a lively area of shops, offices and hotels on either side of Avenida 18 de Julio, the city's main axis. To the south are the residential districts of the **Barrio Sur** and **Palermo**, once home to the middle class (with some fine Art Deco houses) but now a poorer area with many Afro-Uruguayan residents. Beyond the Intendencia or Palacio Municipal (City Hall) [122 G2], 18 de Julio continues through Cordón, a mixed district of shops and apartments, to **Tres Cruces**, where the bus terminal [95 F1] sits opposite the start of Avenida Italia, the main highway east to the airport and the beach resorts. Just a few blocks east, this passes Parque Batlle [95 G1], site of the Estadio Centenario, the stadium built for the first soccer World Cup.

The bus terminal is also on Bulevar Artigas, leading north towards the north and west of the country and south to the headland of Punta Carretas, passing Parque Rodó [95 F4] and the even more luxuriant golf club [95 F5]. On the coast to the east of Punta Carretas is **Pocitos**, a very agreeable residential area with plenty of good restaurants, pubs and hostels and enjoyable streetlife. There's a fine beach here [95 H4], lined with a row of uniform, middle-class apartment blocks; property isn't as expensive as in the more exclusive suburbs along the coast to the east, but here people actually walk to local shops and restaurants rather than driving everywhere. To the east are Buceo, Malvín and Punta Gorda, desirable suburbs with bungalows and villas nearer the waterfront, and denser housing inland. The city ends with Carrasco, its wealthiest suburb, handy for the airport and with some fine restaurants.

A riverside boulevard known as the rambla runs for 22km along the shore of the River Plate, from the Escollera Sarandí, the breakwater that juts like a narwhal's horn from the end of the Ciudad Vieja peninsula, to the Puente Carrasco, the bridge that marks the end of the city (and of Montevideo department), although the coastline is built up for a long way further east, beyond the resort of Atlántida. In the other direction the rambla continues as a busy highway past the docks, brewery and oil refinery to the west and north of the country.

To the north of the centre, the Legislative Palace [94 D1] sits on a small hill in the **Aguada** district to the east of the modern railway station [94 C1] and the soaring modern Torre de las Communicaciones (Communications Tower) [94 C1]; beyond here are mainly poorer residential districts, surrounding the Prado, where the country's élite had first their weekend homes and then (once public transport was available) their permanent residences, in park-like gardens, many of which still exist. In addition, the Jardín Botánico (Botanic Garden), Parque del Prado (Prado Park) and Museo de Bellas Artes (Art Museum) are in this neighbourhood.

The city is not totally flat but it's still pretty easy to walk (or cycle) around, and there are no no-go areas (although a few places are less safe after dark – see page 119). The city's main squares all have two names, one official and one that is generally used because of a building or statue found there, eg: Plaza Constitución/Matriz, Plaza Independencia/Artigas, Plaza Fabini/Entrevero, Plaza Libertad/Cagancha and Plaza Treinta y Tres/Lavalleja (also known as Plaza Bomberos). The southern half of Calle Yaguarón is now Aquiles Lanza, but is still better known as 'Shaguarón'; and Cuareim is now Michelini. Building numbers are not matched to city blocks, ie: No 301 will probably not be on the corner of the third block up the street; *piso* means floor.

TOURIST INFORMATION

There's a tourist information office (✆ *2604 0329/86*), run by Canelones department, at the airport, and a Uruguay Natural (Ministry of Tourism) office (✆ *2409 7399;* ⊕ *08.00–22.00 Mon–Fri, 09.00–22.00 Sat–Sun*) at the Tres Cruces bus terminal.

In the Ciudad Vieja, there's a good municipal tourist information centre [122 B2] (*Piedras 252, near the Mercado del Puerto;* ✆ *2916 8434;* e *imminfotour@*

STREET NAMES

As in much of Latin America, many streets are named after dates; for example:

19 de Abril	The landing of the Treinta y Tres Orientales (33 Uruguayans) in 1825
18 de Mayo	The Battle of Las Piedras in 1811, a crucial battle in the struggle for independence
25 de Mayo	The overthrow of the viceroy in Buenos Aires in the Semana de Mayo, 1810
19 de Junio	The birth of Artigas in 1764
18 de Julio	The swearing of the constitution in 1830
25 de Agosto	The declaration of independence in 1825
21 de Setiembre	The *cabildo abierto* or open council of 1808

Other streets are named after places, mainly battlefields, such as **Ituzaingó** (an Argentine–Uruguayan victory over Brazil on 20 February 1827) and **Sarandí** (Lavalleja's victory over Brazil on 12 October 1825); the **Arenal Grande** was the stream on the north side of the Playa Agraciada (Lucky Beach) where Lavalleja (*El libertador*, as distinct from Artigas, *El procer*) landed with his 32 companions on 19 April 1825.

gmail.com; ⊕ *09.00–17.00 daily).* Across the rambla by the entry to the port, the Ministry of Tourism (✆ *2188 5100)* has an information desk [122 B2] (✆ *1885, 2188 5111;* ⊕ *09.00–18.30 Mon–Fri; www.turismo.gub.uy, www.uruguaynatural.com)* in the former Depósito Santos warehouse. Inside the port there's also the Isla de Información y Servicios (*Cruise Service Island;* ⊕ *when cruise ships are in port)*, with staff speaking English, Spanish and Portuguese.

In the Centro there's a municipal information kiosk [122 G2] (*18 de Julio at Ejido, in front of the Palacio Municipal;* ✆ *1950, 1830;* ⊕ *09.30–17.30 daily)*.

City maps can be bought for about US$5 at some news kiosks, but the standard free handout map will be fine for the area between the Ciudad Vieja, Pocitos and Tres Cruces (but not for the Prado).

⌂ WHERE TO STAY

Accommodation is mostly found in the Centro, wth some cheaper options in the Ciudad Vieja, Pocitos and elsewhere. A relatively new concept here, **bed and breakfasts** are a great way to engage with local residents (see page 98). For **longer stays**, perhaps on business or with a family, an apartment may be more convenient than a hotel. Rentahome (*www.rentahome.com.uy)* is an agency, while www. mvdapartments.com is a link to futher information; see page 98 for some options.

Montevideo has a good supply of **backpacker hostels** (see pages 99–100), mostly well located in the Centro and Pocitos. These are open all year, usually 24 hours a day, and are clean and safe, with lockers (bring a padlock) and English spoken. If you don't feel the need for networking with fellow travellers, free internet access and English-speaking staff, the cheapest hotels will give you a private room for the price of a dorm bed in a hostel. You'll get a simple breakfast in a hostel but not in a cheap hotel.

Of the **cheaper hotels** (pages 97–9), those in old family homes with rooms around a patio are far more pleasant than those in more modern multi-storey buildings, which are often airless and noisy.

Montevideo's **Centro** is home to many large 3- and 4-star hotels (similar to European 2- and 3-star establishments), all built in the 1960s & 1970s in the same monolithic style, and lightly refurbished as a rule.

Carrasco is handy for the airport, but most cheaper hotels are in fact motels, intended for couples trying to get away from the in-laws, or something a bit more illicit.

For those **camping** (see page 100), camper vans can stop at the ANCAP service station at Punta Carretas, where there's 24-hour security, or even on the sandy point immediately to the south, where there's much less traffic noise. There are two decent campsites in Atlántida, 45km east (an hour by bus) – see page 177 – and one nearer town near Santiago Vásquez (see page 170).

For a key to accommodation price codes, please see the inside-front cover of this guide.

All listings are included on one of the four city maps; accommodation in Ciudad Vieja and Centro is mapped on page 122, while the city-centre options can be found on pages 94–5 and accommodation east of the city centre is shown on a map on page 109. Page references for accommodation found in other areas are included below.

LUXURY
Ciudad Vieja
⌂ **Radisson Montevideo Victoria Plaza**
Plaza Independencia 759; ✆ 2902 0111;

e reservas@radisson.com.uy; www.radisson.com/ montevideouy. In a great location right between the old & new towns, this towering block of drab red brick is known for its fine restaurant on the

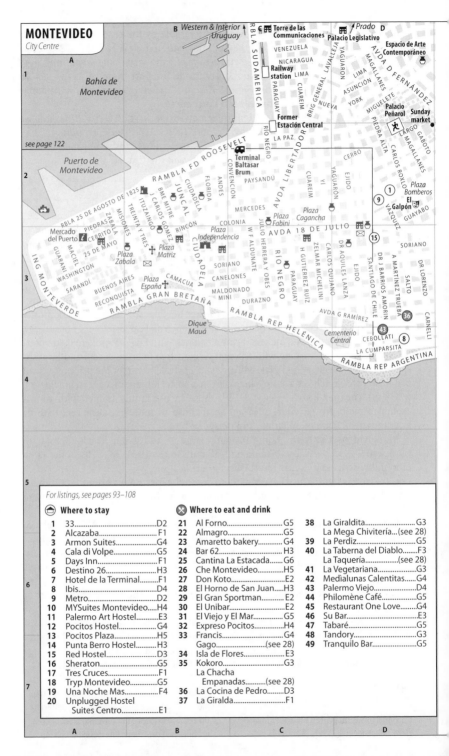

MONTEVIDEO
City Centre

Bahía de Montevideo

see page 122

Puerto de Montevideo

Western & Interior Uruguay

Torre de las Communicaciones
Palacio Legislativo
Prado

Espacio de Arte Contemporáneo

VENEZUELA
NICARAGUA
LIMA
Railway station
PARAGUAY
PAYSANDÚ
CUAREIM
NUEVA
YORK
Palacio Peñarol
Sunday market

Former Estación Central
LA PAZ

RIO NEGRO
CONVENCIÓN
FLORIDA
ANDES
CIUDADELA
JUNCAL
J CARLOS GÓMEZ
BME MITRE
ITUZAINGÓ
TREINTA Y TRES
RINCÓN
GUARANÍ
MACIEL
ZABALA
PIEDRAS
CERRITO
25 DE MAYO
WASHINGTON
SARANDÍ
BUENOS AIRES
RECONQUISTA

Terminal Baltasar Brum

Mercado del Puerto

Plaza Zabala

Plaza Matriz

Plaza Independencia

Plaza España

Plaza Fabini

Plaza Cagancha

Plaza Bomberos
El Galpón

Plaza Gran Bretaña

COLONIA
MERCEDES
SORIANO
CANELONES
MALDONADO
MINI
DURAZNO

CAMACUA

AVDA LIBERTADOR
CUAREIM
YAGUARÓN
EJIDO
YI
AVDA 18 DE JULIO
JULIO HERRERA Y OBES
W FALDUNATE
RIO NEGRO
PARAGUAY
H GUTIÉRREZ RUIZ
ZELMAR MICHELINI
CARLOS QUIJANO
DR AQUILES LANZA
SANTIAGO DE CHILE
EJIDO
DR J BARRIOS AMORÍN
A MARTÍNEZ TRUEBA
SALTO
DR LORENZO
CARNELLI

AVDA G RAMÍREZ
Cementerio Central
CEBOLLATI
LA CUMPARSITA

Dique Mauá

RAMBLA REP HELÉNICA
RAMBLA REP ARGENTINA

For listings, see pages 93–108

Where to stay

1	33	D2
2	Alcazaba	F1
3	Armon Suites	G4
4	Cala di Volpe	G5
5	Days Inn	F1
6	Destino 26	H3
7	Hotel de la Terminal	F1
8	Ibis	D4
9	Metro	D2
10	MYSuites Montevideo	H4
11	Palermo Art Hostel	E3
12	Pocitos Hostel	G4
13	Pocitos Plaza	H5
14	Punta Berro Hostel	H3
15	Red Hostel	D3
16	Sheraton	G5
17	Tres Cruces	F1
18	Tryp Montevideo	G5
19	Una Noche Mas	F4
20	Unplugged Hostel Suites Centro	E1

Where to eat and drink

21	Al Forno	G5
22	Almagro	G5
23	Amaretto bakery	G4
24	Bar 62	H3
25	Cantina La Estacada	G6
26	Che Montevideo	H5
27	Don Koto	E2
28	El Horno de San Juan	H3
29	El Gran Sportman	E2
30	El Unibar	E2
31	El Viejo y El Mar	G5
32	Expreso Pocitos	H4
33	Francis	G4
	Gago	(see 28)
34	Isla de Flores	E3
35	Kokoro	G3
	La Chacha Empanadas	(see 28)
36	La Cocina de Pedro	D3
37	La Giralda	F1
38	La Giraldita	G3
	La Mega Chivitería	(see 28)
39	La Perdiz	G5
40	La Taberna del Diablo	F3
	La Taquería	(see 28)
41	La Vegetariana	G3
42	Medialunas Calentitas	G4
43	Palermo Viejo	D4
44	Philomène Café	G5
45	Restaurant One Love	G4
46	Su Bar	E3
47	Tabaré	G5
48	Tandory	G3
49	Tranquilo Bar	G5

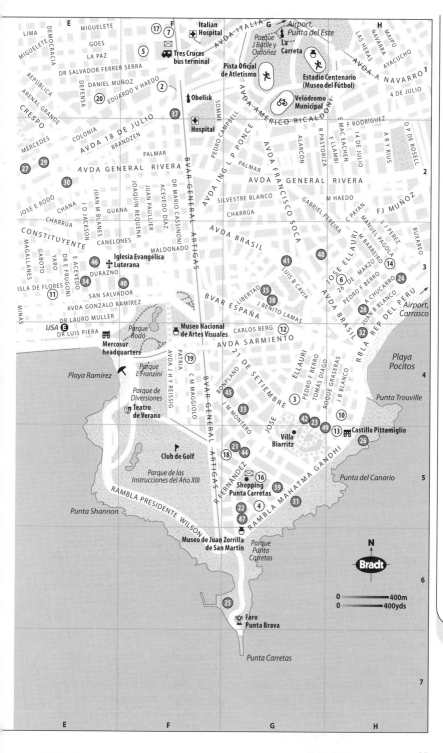

LIMA MIGUELETE
MIGUELETE E
DEMOCRACIA
GOES
REPÚBLICA LA PAZ
DR SALVADOR FERRER SERRA
ARENAL GRANDE DEFENSA DANIEL MUÑOZ
CRESPO ⑳ EDUARDO V HAEDO ②
MERCEDES COLONIA
AVDA 18 DE JULIO
㉗ ㉙ BRANDZEN
㉚ PALMAR
AVDA GENERAL RIVERA
JOSE E RODÓ CHANA J D JACKSON GUANA JOAQUIN REQUENA
CONSTITUYENTE CANELONES
MAGALLANES GABOTO E ACEVEDO DURAZNO
YARO DR E FRUGONI MALDONADO
ISLA DE FLORES ㊱ SAN SALVADOR
⑪ AVDA GONZALO RAMÍREZ
MINAS DR LAURO MULLER
USA ⒺDR LUIS PIERA
Mercosur headquarters

② F Italian Hospital
⑰ ⑦
⑤ Tres Cruces bus terminal
② Obelisk
㊲
Hospital

AVDA ITALIA G Airport, Punta del Este
Parque J Batlle y Ordóñez La Carreta
Pista Oficial de Atletismo
Estadio Centenario (Museo del Fútbol)
Velódromo Municipal

MIGUELETE E
Italian Hospital F
AVDA AMÉRICO RICALDONI
SOMME PEDRO CAMPBELL
AVDA ING L P PONCE
PALMAR SILVESTRE BLANCO
AVDA FRANCISCO SOCA ALARCÓN R PASTORIZA F LLAMBI E MAC EACHEN 14 DE JULIO R Y RIUS D P DE ROSELL
CHARRÚA GABRIEL PEREIRA M HAEDO C PAYAN FJ MUÑOZ
AVDA BRASIL JOSÉ ELLAURI MANUEL PAGOLA L J PEREZ BUXAREO
⑥ 26 DE MARZO PEDRO F BERRO ㉔
㊶ ㊸ A CHUCARRO
LUIS B CAVIA JUAN B BLANCO
BVAR ESPAÑA ㉟ J LIBERTAD ㉘
J BENITO LAMAS ㊳ ㉜ R BLA REP DEL PERU
Museo Nacional de Artes Visuales CARLOS BERG ⑫ Airport, Carrasco
AVDA SARMIENTO
Parque Rodó ⑲ Playa Pocitos
Parque L'Franzini
Playa Ramírez Parque de Diversiones
Teatro de Verano ㉝ ③
Club de Golf ⑱ ㉑ ㊹ Villa Biarritz ㊷ ㉓ ㊹ ⑬ Castillo Pittamiglio ㉖
Parque de las Instrucciones del Año XIII ⑯ Shopping Punta Carretas ㊴ ㉛
RAMBLA PRESIDENTE WILSON ㉒ ④
Punta Shannon ㊼
Museo de Juan Zorrilla de San Martín Parque Punta Carretas
㉕ Faro Punta Brava
Punta Carretas

AVDA GENERAL RIVERA
SILVESTRE BLANCO
CHARRÚA
LUIS B CAVIA
ELLAURI PEDRO J BERRO TOMAS DIAGO ROQUE GRASERAS J B BLANCO
Punta Trouville
Punta del Canario
Punta Carretas

N
Bradt

0 ——— 400m
0 ——— 400yds

E F G H

25th floor, with views over the harbour. It also has a huge foyer with pianist & original art, a fine ballroom, spa & a large casino. Rooms are spacious with all those 5-star fitments, & service is excellent. $$$$$

Centro

🏨 **Esplendor Montevideo** Soriano 868 (between Andes & Convención); ✆ 2900 1900; www.esplendormontevideo.com. To be at the heart of the new future Barrio de los Artes, this historic hotel (where intellectuals such as Borges once stayed) has been modernised to include a rooftop garden with a view to the Plate, swimming pool, spa & gym, as well as 84 boutique rooms. $$$$$

🏨 **Four Points by Sheraton** Ejido 1275 near San José; ✆ 2901 7000; www.fourpoints.com/montevideo. Next to the Palacio Municipal & by far the best hotel in the Centro; clean modern styling with non-smoking rooms, indoor swimming pool & attractive café-restaurant. $$$$$

Punta Carretas and Pocitos

[map, page 95]

🏨 **MYSuites Montevideo** Benito Blanco 674 & 21 de Setiembre; ✆ 2712 3434; www.mysuites.com.uy. A self-styled wine hotel, this glass-fronted modern block has 40 comfortable suites (with kitchenettes) hung with paintings by local artists & an 11th-floor swimming pool, sauna, gym, wine bar & restaurant; its speciality is its wine tastings (⏱ 20.00 Tue–Sat; US$15, free to guests), with a range of Uruguayan wines with warm bread, Uruguayan olive oils & tapenade. $$$$$

🏨 **Sheraton Montevideo** Victor Soliño 349; ✆ 2710 2121; e sheraton.montevideo@sheraton.com; www.sheraton.com. In a somewhat odd location near the pleasant residential district of Pocitos, this is your classic American luxury hotel with one of the city's best shopping malls attached. $$$$$

🏨 **Tryp Montevideo** Héctor Miranda 2361; ✆ 2710 3800, 0808 234 1953; e tryp.montevideo@melia.com; www.melia.com. On a quiet street near the golf club, this modern 4-star hotel is literally very cool, with chilly AC as well as black leather & brushed steel décor. Facilities include swimming pool, gym, sauna & hydromassage. Rates include breakfast, parking, internet access & business centre access; & there's an overrated restaurant & bar. $$$$$

Carrasco

[map, page 78]

🏨 **Belmont House** Avda Rivera 6512; ✆ 2600 0430; www.belmonthouse.com.uy. In a swanky area nearer the airport than the city centre, this is the city's only luxury hotel that isn't part of an international chain. It has spacious lawns with outdoor swimming pool, & gym, sauna & jacuzzi indoors, as well as a good restaurant, cocktail bar & salón de té. With only 24 rooms & 4 suites, as well as antique furniture & portraits by J M Blanes, this really does feel like a secluded retreat from city bustle. $$$$$

MID-RANGE

Ciudad Vieja

🏨 **Don Boutique Hotel** Piedras 234; ✆ 2915 9999; www.donhotel.com.uy. In a striking Art Deco building (built in 1938) facing the Mercado del Puerto, this new 'Design Hotel' has just 21 rooms, including 1 luxury suite. Perhaps the hippest place in town, with a medio y medio (a 'cocktail' of dry white wine & sparkling wine) to greet you on arrival, a swish contemporary interior & a terrace & rooftop swimming pool, it's handy for ferries to Buenos Aires but not in the best area at night. $$$$

🏨 **NH Columbia** Rambla Gran Bretaña 473; ✆ 2916 0001; e nhcolumbia@nh-hotels.com; www.nh-hotels.com. An excellent hotel, with views of the river & good restaurant, but not in the safest of areas – you may prefer taxis to walking. 3 computers in the lobby, Wi-Fi, 24hr room service, restaurant & 10 meeting rooms. $$$$

Palermo

[map, page 94]

🏨 **Ibis** La Cumparsita 1473; ✆ 2413 7000; e ibismontevideo@accor.com.uy; www.ibishotel.com. Not luxury but excellent value as you'd expect from this chain; handy for US & German embassies. Rooms are AC, there's Wi-Fi & a 24hr bar with snacks, & buffet restaurant. B/fast not inc. $$$$

Centro

🏨 **Balmoral Plaza** Plaza Cagancha 1126 & San José 1121; ✆ 2902 2393; e balmoral@netgate.com.uy; www.balmoral.com.uy. A good, professionally run place with comfortable rooms, terrace with panoramic view & BBQ, sauna, gym, secure parking, business centre & meeting rooms.

The restaurant does a good lunch & dinner. Buffet b/fast inc. **$$$$**

🏠 **Embajador** San José 1212; 📞2902 0012/0193; e reservas@hotelembajador.com; www.hotelembajador.com. Recently refurbished, this is still a typical 1970s block, although rooms now have magnetic keycards as well as minibar, TV & AC. 8 suites have terraces, & there's multi-storey parking across the road. **$$$**

🏠 **Lancaster** Plaza Cagancha 1334; 📞2902 1054; www.lancasterhotel.com.uy. Particularly well sited (with its sister, the Hotel Iguazú, nearby), well refurbished with AC, flat-screen cable TV, free Wi-Fi & hairdryers in all rooms. **$$$**

🏠 **Oxford** Paraguay 1286; 📞2902 0046; www.hoteloxford.com.uy. A friendly place with small & rather dated rooms & free but rather slow internet access. Good b/fast & teatime snack inc. **$$$**

Punta Carretas and Pocitos
[map, page 95]

🏠 **Cala di Volpe** Rambla Mahatma Gandhi 205 & Parva Domus; 📞2710 2000; e hotel@ hotelcaladivolpe.com.uy; www.hotelcaladivolpe.com.uy. A self-proclaimed boutique hotel (although a 12-storey tower doesn't really seem boutique-sized), this is a good modern hotel, worth 4 stars in most parts of the world. Good views of the Río de la Plata. **$$$$**

🏠 **Pocitos Plaza Hotel** Benito Blanco 640 & 21 de Setiembre; 📞2712 3939; www.pocitosplazahotel.com.uy. Remarkably good value in this relaxed residential area with beach, shopping & neighbourhood restaurants close at hand; the 50 rooms have AC, Wi-Fi, cable TV & hairdryer. Business centre & meeting rooms, gym & sauna, garage, friendly service & good food. **$$$**

Tres Cruces
[map, page 95]

🏠 **Days Inn** Acevedo Díaz 1821; 📞2400 4840; www.daysinn.com.uy. Friendly & decent but slightly impersonal 4-star place by the bus terminal; in addition to very effective AC it has electronic door locks, safes, Wi-Fi, garage, gym, jacuzzi & sauna. **$$$**

Carrasco
[map, page 78]

🏠 **Best Western Pedro Figari** Rambla República de Mexico 6535; 📞2600 8824;

e hfigari@hotelpedrofigari.com; www.hotelpedrofigari.com. A relatively small red-brick place on the waterfront, this is a very decent place to stay within reach of the airport. Rates include a welcome drink, buffet breakfast, Wi-Fi throughout the hotel & business centre; suites are available with kitchenette. **$$$$**

BUDGET
Ciudad Vieja

🏠 **Posada al Sur** Pérez Castillano 1424 between 25 de Mayo & Washington; 📞2916 5287; m 096 452889; e info@posadaalsur.uy; www.posadaalsur.com.uy. A self-styled B&B, this estimable place feels more like a large shared apartment. It exists to support sustainable & community tourism, working with local groups to offer tours of the deprived but very colourful Barrio Sur & Palermo districts of Montevideo, & in Rocha, Río Negro & Tacuarembó (see page 76). Big kitchen, laundry, internet access (including Wi-Fi), roof terrace, bike rental & common room for activities such as Spanish or tango classes. From US$16 pp (room for 6), US$50 (dbl with shared bathroom), US$70 (private bathroom), all include good organic breakfast (*until noon*) plus sheets & towels. There's also a very cute wooden rooftop cabin, with double bedroom, kitchen, bathroom & living room, from US$85 for 2. Rates are cheaper by the week. **$$**

🏠 **Splendido** Mitre 1314; 📞2916 4900; e splendidohotel@gmail.com; www.splendidohotel.com.uy. Once the Hotel Solís, this is now a 'Hotel & Hostel', offering beds in shared & private rooms, with a choice of shared & private bathrooms, right above some of the noisiest bars in Montevideo. Kitchen, internet access & cable TV. **$$–$**

Centro

🏠 **Campoamor** Rondeau 1446 1st Flr & Mercedes; 📞2902 2137; www.hotelcampoamor.com. The rooms have been renovated in fairly drab style, but the building is still an Art Nouveau treasure, with the original lift still in place. Rooms AC with cable TV; Wi-Fi. 'Artesanal' breakfast, sourced from local farms. **$$**

🏠 **Casablanca** San José 1039; 📞2901 0918; www.hotelcasablanca.com.uy. A traditional 2-star place built in 1900 (by a man from Casablanca, Morocco!) – splendid period reception rooms lead to 18 rooms modernised with lots of pine panelling, AC & free Wi-Fi. **$$**

⌂ **Iberia** Maldonado 1097 & Paraguay; ☏2901 3633; e hoiberia@hotmail.com; www.hoteliberia. com.uy. Stylish & affordable new 2-star hotel with immensely friendly & helpful staff. Free Wi-Fi but no lift or parking. Good b/fast US$7extra. **$$**

⌂ **Colonia** Colonia 1168; ☏2901 0390. A classic Belle-Époque building. Somewhat run-down & not very quiet; but prices are reasonable. Rooms with or without bathroom available. **$**

⌂ **Florida** Uruguay 808 & Florida; ☏2900 3667; www.hotelflorida.com.uy. A classic 2-star hotel dating from 1901, rooms with & without private bathroom. A cafeteria serves breakfast (not inc), lunch & dinner. **$**

⌂ **ITA** San José 1160; ☏2901 3363. Basic 1-star hotel with internal light-well – all rooms have private bathroom & fan, but cost more with TV. **$**

⌂ **Juncal** Durazno 1279; ☏2908 7997. Cheap but adequate 1-star place; rooms with private bathroom, cable TV, fans & towel. **$**

City centre

⌂ **33** Mercedes 1516; ☏2409 7154; e anabelmoo@hotmail.com. Very quiet budget hotel near Plaza de Bomberos; rooms, with private or shared bathrooms, come with fan, mirror & bedside light, though no TV. **$**

⌂ **Metro** Barrios Amorin 1440; ☏2401 3451. A fine old-style 1-star with Belle-Époque exterior & Art Deco interior, with several skylit lobbies on the 1st floor, this has small rooms with & without private bathroom, all with cable TV. No food available. **$**

Tres Cruces
[map, page 95]

⌂ **Hotel de la Terminal** Goës 2377; ☏2400 0264; www.hoteldelaterminal.com/english. html. On the north side of the bus terminal, this affordable little place has rooms with & without private bathroom. Some have jacuzzis, & there's internet access in the lobby. **$$**

⌂ **Hotel Tres Cruces** Miguelete 2356 & Acevedo Díaz; ☏2402 3474; www.hoteltrescruces. com.uy. Friendly, decent 3-star in a fairly modern tower just north of the bus terminal has coffeeshop/cafetería (⊕ until 23.00 daily) & free internet access in the lobby. **$$**

⌂ **Alcazaba** Cassinoni 1669; ☏2408 0701/0915. A decent enough little 2-star just south of the bus terminal that offers rooms with private

bath, AC & cable TV, with a sliding scale of charges: arriving after 18.00 (Sun–Thu) you'll pay US$27 for a double, after 13.00 US$40, & after 07.00 US$48 (or US$27 for day use until 21.00); on Fri–Sat & eves of holidays these rates are US$40/52/60. To just wash & freshen up after an overnight journey costs US$10; parking costs US$5. **$**

Carrasco
[off map, page 78]

⌂ **Motel Dunas** Rambla Costanera & Piriápolis; ☏2601 2209/2336. This makes a decent enough stopover near the airport; rooms have cable TV & jacuzzi, & there's an adequate cafeteria. **$$**

⌂ **Posada del Mar** Rambla Costanera & Tacuari; ☏2601 2539; www.posadadelmar.com. uy. This attractive red-brick motel, in well-kept gardens, is a perfectly civilised place with 24hr room service. **$$**

BED AND BREAKFAST
[map, page 95]

⌂ **Una Noche Mas** Patria 712 & Figueira, Punta Carretas; m 096 227406 e esantospasek@gmail. com; www.unanochemas.com.uy. A cosy & friendly place with 2 bedrooms sharing an attractive bathroom, & a lovely octagonal rooftop *glorieta* (a lookout for ships entering harbour), plus a good breakfast, Wi-Fi & a PC; you can have a massage from Clara, go to the market with Eduardo, & generally share their lives. **$$**

LONGER STAYS

⌂ **Armon Suites** [95 G4] 21 de Setiembre 2885, Punta Carretas; ☏2712 4120; www.armonsuites. com.uy. Much slicker & more businesslike than the Bremen, this has lift, sauna, tiny swimming pool, PCs & Wi-Fi (all included) together with buffet breakfast. Rates from US$108 for 2; w/end discounts. **$$$$$**

⌂ **Apart-Hotel Bremen** [122 G3] Aquiles Lanza 1168, Centro; ☏4622 9070; m 095 061448; e hotel@bremenmontevideo.com; www. bremenmontevideo.com. In several houses on the block next to the office/reception (English & German spoken) are 15 apartments of various sizes, nicely fitted out, decorated in pale blue & cream, with kitchen, CD player, TV in every bedroom, washing machine & internet cable. Prices from US$69/75 for 2/3 to US$95–120 for 2–5, or US$160 for a 5-person penthouse; there

are attractive monthly rates too. In the same block is the Bremen pub-restaurant (see page 107).
$$$

⌂ **Pensión Río** [122 B3] Alazibar 1333 & Sarandí; ☏ 2917 0643. Simple but perfectly decent, this pension takes guests for a min of 15 days (US$130), with use of a kitchen. **$**

HOSTELS
Ciudad Vieja

⌂ **Che Lagarto** Plaza Independencia 713; ☏ 2903 0175; e montevideo@chelagarto.com; www.chelagarto.com. Offshoot of an Argentine chain of party-oriented hostels, this one is easy to find your way back to late at night, but rather noisy with buses & other traffic. There's a good range of rooms (book early to get your choice) from singles, doubles, triples & quadruples to dorms (some women-only & with bathrooms en suite) & family rooms, from US$12 pp (US$9 for 3 or more nights) including breakfast, sheets & taxes. Common areas include non-smoking, games & TV rooms, a pub, & a secret backyard; there's also a computer room plus free Wi-Fi, & a guest kitchen. Laundry service, bike rental & bike & luggage storage available. **$**

Centro

⌂ **Planet Hostel** Canelones 1095 & Paraguay; ☏ 2900 0733; www.planetmontevideohostel.com. A friendly smaller hostel in the Centro. Dorms are fairly small, almost cramped, without enough power sockets, & segregated by gender – each is named after a planet, with appropriate décor. Beds are made daily, & a good breakfast is included, for US$14 pp, as well as free Wi-Fi, baggage storage, a small kitchen & terrace with BBQ. Private rooms are available (US$28 sgl/US$40 dbl/US$54 quad). **$$**

⌂ **El Viajero Down Town Hostel** Soriano 1073; ☏ 2908 2913; www.elviajerodowntown. com. The lively El Viajero chain has recently expanded from the Ciudad Vieja to take over a former hotel in the Centro, with 12 en-suite rooms (shared dorms US$13–18 pp, dbls US$65–71), patio & garden, kitchen, 24hr bar, TV/DVD room, PCs & Wi-Fi (parking & gym are available at extra cost). Bikes can be rented, & city tours, bus tickets, & Spanish & tango lessons can be arranged. **$**

⌂ **Montevideo Hostel** Canelones 935 & W Ferreira Aldunate; ☏ 2908 1324; e mvdhostel@montevideohostel.com.uy; www. montevideohostel.com.uy. Montevideo's original

Hostelling International outpost, now over 30 years old, this is still a friendly backpacker place but slightly tattier & less hip than some newer hostels. The main hall is a covered courtyard which can be noisy till midnight, although there is also a cellar bar with pool table, karaoke & musical instruments. A spiral iron staircase leads to a mezzanine with a free PC (free Wi-Fi too) & to a roof terrace with BBQ. There's a large kitchen, laundry service, & decent bikes can be rented (& stored) here. There are mixed & segregated dorms (US$14 pp including breakfast, sheets & taxes) plus a split-level family room, with a double bed & 3 singles above. **$**

East of the Centro
[map, pages 94–5]

⌂ **Unplugged Hostel Suites Centro** Colonia 2063 & Martínez; ☏ 2401 5787; e unpluggedhostelsuites@gmail.com; www. unpluggedhostel.com/centro. Actually in Cordón, not the Centro, this is the nearest hostel to the Tres Cruces terminal. It's a lively Hostelling International place with 2 en-suite dorms on each floor & a 5th-floor terrace & grill. Traffic can be noisy, but buses do stop right outside; there are PCs & Wi-Fi, & huge lockers (with flimsy hasps) under the beds. Dorm beds cost from US$18 (HI members US$15) & doubles US$65 (HI US$55) in season, & as little as US$11 & US$23 online in winter. B/fast inc. **$$$**

⌂ **Pocitos Hostel** Avda Sarmiento 2641 & Aguilar, Pocitos; ☏ 2711 8780; www.pocitos-hostel.com. In a nice old house in probably the most pleasant district of Montevideo, & run by a friendly gang of rugby-playing students, this hostel offers mixed-sex & women-only dorms with big cupboards & plenty of power sockets for US$16 pp (US$18 summer), plus private rooms (US$35/45 sgl, US$50/60 twin & dbl). A good breakfast & sheets are included, with towels & bikes for rent. There's free Wi-Fi, kitchen & a nice garden with BBQ, & a basement bar & DVD theatre for winter use – but mercifully there's no cable TV to take over the common spaces. From the airport, bus DM1 will drop you on the far side of Avda España; from the bus terminal, bus 183 leaves you just a block away, at España & Avda Sarmiento. **$$**

⌂ **Punta Berro Hostel** Berro 1320, Pocitos; ☏ 2707 7090; www.puntoberrohostel.com. A friendly, laid-back little hostel (although not always the cleanest) in an attractive period house;

AC shared rooms for 6, 4 or 2 cost US$13/18/22 pp (US$18/22/25 Jan–Feb & Easter), & AC private doubles (with TV but with shared bathroom) cost US$45/50 (US$55/60 peak) – all including breakfast & sheets, lockers & use of kitchen. There's free Wi-Fi & a PC. **$$**

⌂ **Red Hostel** San José 1406 & Santiago de Chile; ✆2908 8514/16; www.redhostel.com. This stylish & laidback hostel, in a family home built in 1912 with central light-well, fireplace, large rooftop terrace with hammocks. Nicely restored, it's definitely red in colour (rather than referring to a *red* or network); the rooms are fairly spacious, with small balconies over the street, but bathrooms are somewhat cramped. There's free internet access including Wi-Fi, plus smallish kitchen, bar & gym. US$18 pp in mixed dorm, including good breakfast, sheets & towels. **$$**

⌂ **Destino26** 26 de Marzo 1125 between Martí & Masini, Pocitos; ✆2707 6041; www.destino26hostel. com. In a lovely 1930s house painted bright orange, this is a friendly little place with an attractive garden & an unfurnished roof terrace, a kitchen & washing machine, plus cable TV, Wi-Fi & 1 PC; bikes can be rented. Dorms (mixed or women-only) cost US$18 including breakfast; 2 private rooms with bathroom, TV & towels US$60. **$$–$**

⌂ **Palermo Art Hostel** Gaboto 1010 & San Salvador, Palermo; ✆2410 6519; www. palermoarthostel.com. Seemingly more a party hostel than an art hostel, patronised more by boho South Americans than by tourists from the northern hemisphere. Stylishly designed, with 2 adjacent houses interconnecting in a mysterious manner, but there's not much real art in evidence, apart from live music at weekends. The location is a bit odd, although handy enough for Playa Ramírez beach. Dorm beds with bedding included (though not towels or breakfast), for US$15/20 pp, private rooms for US$50, & there's a guest kitchen, plus PCs & Wi-Fi. Bikes can be rented, & Spanish, tango & candombé drumming lessons are offered. **$**

CAMPING

⋏ **Parque Municipal Punta Espinillo** [off map 78 A1] ✆2312 0013; e campamentopuntaespinillo@gmail.com; ⏲ 1 Dec–15 Apr daily; all year w/ends & holidays. The nearest campsite to Montevideo & situated well to the west near Santiago Vásquez – it's 8km southwest on Camino General Basilio Muñoz from km20 of Ruta 1 (the exit for the Complejo Carcelario or prison). The campsite has space for 70 tents (with electric lighting & hot water – but no drinking water), 10 cabins, BBQs & a stony little beach; there's a *parador* with restaurant & shop at the gate. **$**

✗ WHERE TO EAT AND DRINK

The **Mercado del Puerto** [122 A3] (*www.mercadodelpuerto.com.uy*) is an unmissable market that shelters a variety of restaurants specialising in fish and, of course, *asado*. They are not cheap but are very popular with locals and tourists alike, especially at weekend lunchtimes. Inside, the market restaurants close early (around 17.30), while those outside have open-air terraces and a lively evening trade too; however, you should take a taxi home at night.

There's a very thin dividing line between bars and restaurants, so that you can eat at some of the places listed here, or go to many restaurants just to have a drink. There are two **chains** that are recommended, Cerveceria La Posita and La Cigale (see page 104). Both are ubiquitous and excellent value.

Note that some restaurants close for holidays in January. All listings in Ciudad Vieja and Centro are mapped on page 122 while those in the city centre can be found on pages 94–5. Page references for listings found in other areas are included below.

LUXURY
Ciudad Vieja
✗ **Estrecho** Sarandí 460; ✆2915 6107; ⏲ 11.00–17.00 Mon–Fri. The only seating at this cool contemporary place, open only for weekday lunches, is at the long bar; the food is simple French *cuisine moderne*, using fresh seasonal ingredients. No credit cards. **$$$$**

✖ **La Corte** Sarandí 586; ☎2916 0435; www.
lacorte.com.uy; ⏰ 12.00–15.30 Mon–Sat
(Jan–Feb Mon–Fri only). Near the cathedral with
tables on Plaza Constitución, this classy restaurant
specialises in regional cuisine with a nouvelle
touch. $$$$

Centro

✖ **Rara Avis** Buenos Aires 652 & Juncal; ☎2915
0330; www.raraavis.com.uy; ⏰ noon–02.00
Mon–Fri, 19.00–02.00 Sat. In a beautiful space in
the Teatro Solis, this is one of the classiest & most
interesting restaurants in town; some find the
service pretentious, others love the live piano &
interludes of song. The lunch menu costs US$25;
otherwise pastas & risottos cost US$20–28, & fish
& meats US$33–45. $$$$$

✖ **Walther's Restaurante & Gastro-pub**
Herrera y Obes 1222 & Canelones; ☎2903 9176;
www.walthershouse.com; ⏰ 20.00–23.30
Tue–Sat, 12.00–16.00 Sat–Sun. Run by a Swedish
woman in a classic old house, with fine stained
glass & occasional jazz, this has an excellent lunch
menu, great fish, & Mastra craft beers on draught.
There's bar food (US$10–16) & the restaurant
(US$10–16 for pasta, chivitos, etc, US$13.50–16
for fish or paella, US$13–27 for meats, or
US$7.50–11 for pizza). $$$$

City centre

✖ **Isla de Flores** Isla de Flores 1900 & Acevedo,
Palermo; ☎2410 5188; www.isladeflores1900.
com; ⏰ Apr–Dec evenings only Mon–Sat. True
'cocina de autor' in a former butcher's shop, with
fine meats (lamb, rabbit, beef, pork) & offal cooked
in a mix of European styles – the bone marrow
with coarse salt & toast is notable. There are just 6
tables & in summer the whole operation decamps
to José Ignacio (see page 237). $$$$

Punta Carretas

[map, page 95]

✖ **Francis** Luis de la Torre 502 & Montero;
☎2711 8603; www.francis.com.uy;
⏰ 12.00–15.00, 20.00–midnight daily (to 01.00
Fri–Sat; may close Jan–Feb. Although claiming
to be a *parrilla gourmet*, this is also a fine seafood
restaurant, serving, for instance, grilled *chipirones*
(grilled baby squid), stuffed pollock, seafood stew,
2 types of paella & sushi, as well as pasta & meats.
Main courses cost US$20–32. $$$$$

✖ **La Perdiz** Guipúzcoa 350 & Balinas; ☎2711
8963; e laperdiz2007@hotmail.com; www.
restaurantlaperdiz.com; ⏰ 12.00–16.00, 20.00–
midnight daily. Despite its name, 'The Partridge'
actually specialises in Basque fish dishes, as well
as the standard *parrilla*, *milanesa* & pasta. Good
choices include rack of lamb, *chipirones*, seafood
lasagne or *pescado a la bizkania* (pan-fried fish,
perhaps salmon, sea bass or sole, in a tomato sauce
with red peppers & parsley). Although handy for
the Sheraton, this feels like a neighbourhood bistro
(with a partially covered terrace) where everyone
is greeted like an old friend. $$$$$

Buceo

[map, page 122]

✖ **Gardenia Restaurant** Plaza Las Torres,
Herrera 1249 & 26 de Marzo; ☎2628 8838; www.
gardeniamvd.com; ⏰ 12.00–00.30 Mon–Fri,
13.00–16.00, 20.00–00.30 Sat, 13.00–16.00
Sun. In the heart of the World Trade Center,
this naturally has an upmarket clientele for
its fine international/Mediterranean cuisine
with a Brazilian flavour, but you might find the
After-Office tapas & cocktails on the deck more
affordable & relaxed. Mains US$25–30. $$$$$

Carrasco

[off map, page 78]

✖ **Café Misterio** Costa Rica 1700 & Rivera;
☎2601 8765; www.cafemisterio.com.uy;
⏰ 12.00–16.00, 20.00–01.00 Mon–Sat; closed
Easter Week. One of the trendiest places in town,
serving sushi as well as modern Mediterranean-
style cuisine, with an excellent wine list & desserts.
Service seems to be better at lunchtime, whereas
in the evening the see-&-be-seen element takes
over. Prices are high at all times. $$$$$

✖ **Nuevo García** Arocena 1587 & Otero; ☎2601
8681, 2602 2703; ⏰ 09.00–02.00 daily. Business
travellers who spurn airline food often come
here to eat before or after flights, although some
complain of bad service & the bar-like ambience.
The *parrilla* is generally excellent (the baby beef
is renowned) & there's also fish or pasta, with
mediocre deserts to follow. $$$$$

✖ **Pub Clyde's** Costa Rica 1690 & Rivera; ☎2600
4198; www.clydes.com.uy; ⏰ from 20.00 Mon–Sat.
A Carrasco classic, an American-style bar serving
classy burgers with excellent service & cocktails,
though prices match the neighbourhood. $$$$

MID-RANGE
Ciudad Vieja
✖ **Cabaña Verónica** Mercado del Puerto; ☎2915 1901; ⏰ 12.00–17.30 Tue–Sun. Sitting at one of only 2 remaining *mostradors* or bars left inside the market is much more fun than sitting in yet another AC tourist restaurant, & you'll pay half the regular cover charge for bread, *chimichurri* sauce, olive oil & maybe a free glass of *medio y medio*. With the grill just feet away from you, the range of meats (from chorizo at US$3 to filet at US$15) is obvious, but there's also good pasta & seafood. $$$

✖ **Cervecería Matriz** Sarandí 582; ☎2916 1582; ⏰ 08.00–midnight Mon–Thu, until 02.00 Fri–Sat. A very modern diner-style place with efficient service (including at tables on the plaza) & a wide range of dishes at pretty fair prices; try the *pizzetas* or the *revuelto gramajo* (scrambled egg with potato, onion & ham). $$$

✖ **El Palenque** Perez Castellanos 1597; ☎2917 0190, 2915 4704; www.elpalenque.com.uy; ⏰ 12.00–17.30 Tue–Sun. Founded in 1958, this is one of the classic Mercado del Puerto restaurants, serving the usual range of asado, fish & pasta. You can eat at the bar (with 100 seats), indoors or on an outdoor terrace & it's open into the evening. $$$

✖ **Rincón de Zabala** Rincón 787; ☎2915 1617; ⏰ 09.30–17.30 Mon–Fri. Known as RdZ ('erre-day-zayta'), this is a stylish place for lunch, aimed at financial types but very affordable for those working through the nearby museums. In addition to the inexpensive menu of the day there are sandwiches, & specialities such as *ternera* (veal), *zapallitos rellenos de ricota* (round squashes stuffed with ricotta cheese) & paella. Wi-Fi is available. $$$

✖ **Urbani** Durango 381; ☎2916 4229; m 093 808787; ⏰ 12.00–16.00 Mon–Fri. On Plaza Zabala, this serves 'business food', including salads, sandwiches & snacks, but it's notable for its pasta, such as sorrentinos with ham, ricotta & walnut, or with a 4-cheese sauce. $$$

✖ **Jacinto** Sarandí 349 & Alzáibar; ☎2915 2731; e jacintorestaurant@gmail.com; ⏰ 12.00–18.30 Mon–Fri, 12.00–17.00 Sat. This bright & airy place (with Wi-Fi) on the Peatonal has a limited lunch menu featuring soups, fine salads (eg: rucula, almond & goat's cheese), wholewheat quiches, pasta & desserts. $$$–$$

✖ **Samsara** Zabala 1316 between Sarandí & Buenos Aires; ☎2915 1949; www.espaciosamsara.com.uy; ⏰ 09.00–15.00 Mon–Fri. In a funky interior of tangerine walls, wooden tables & open kitchen, this offers vegetarian cooking with Middle Eastern, Latin American & Thai influences. There's a buffet by weight, breakfasts, soups, salads, empanadas, quiches, soya milanesas, spring rolls & veggie sushi, as well as homemade lemonades & juices. $$$–$$

✖ **Las Misiones** 25 de Mayo 449; ☎2915 4495; ⏰ 07.00–18.00 Mon–Fri. Behind a beautiful green-tiled shopfront, dating from 1907, is a café-bar-restaurant specialising in good straightforward business lunches. $$$–$$

Centro
✖ **El Fogón** San José 1080; ☎2900 0900; e elfogon@elfogon.com.uy; ⏰ 12.00–16.00, 19.00–01.00 daily. One of the most renowned *parrilladas* in town, & well placed for many mid-range hotels. It's well known to coach parties, but there are private rooms for them (or for you), with AC; it's also generally popular for late-night dinners. In addition to grilled beef, it offers seafood, pasta & salads, at very reasonable prices. There's covered parking nearby (*San José 1066*). $$$$

✖ **Los Leños Uruguayos** San José 909; ☎2900 2285; www.parrilla.com.uy; ⏰ 11.45–15.30, 19.30–midnight daily. Famed for its steaks, this is a typical Uruguayan *parrillada*, serving good seafood alongside the grilled meat & vegetables. The style is casual but efficient, with the quality remarkably consistent, & there's Wi-Fi. $$$$

✖ **Tannat** San José 1063; ☎2900 8127; www.tannatrestaurant.com; ⏰ 12.00–03.00 Tue–Sun. As the name implies, this is as much a wine bar as a restaurant, but unexpectedly it serves sushi, as well as boar, lamb, risotto & pasta. They also offer a vegetarian parrilla as well as the usual meaty version. It's a classy venue & one of the more expensive in this area. $$$$

✖ **Locos de Asar** San José 1065; ☎2903 2120; www.locosdeasar.com; ⏰ 11.30–00.30 Tue–Sat. This place is 'Crazy about Grilling' as its name implies – it's one of the leading venues for parrilla, with the usual alternatives of fish & pasta; service is excellent, with English-speaking staff & Wi-Fi. $$$$–$$$

✖ **Pacharán Taberna Vasca** San José 1168; ☎2902 3519; www.pacharan.com.uy; ⏰ 20.00–

00.30 Mon–Thu, 12.00–16.00, 20.00–01.30 Fri–Sat. Founded in 1912, the Basque Institute has a fine old-style restaurant, offering an excellent lunchtime *menú del día* with Basque-style garlic-heavy fish of the day (US$12.50), paella (inc a vegetarian version), pork or chicken, as well as picadas (snacks; US$6–12); next to the restaurant is a *frontón* (handball court), battered but still in use. $$$$–$$

✖ **El Lobizón** Michelini 1264; ☎2901 1334; ⏰ 20.00–03.00 daily. A cosy cellar-pub, 'The Werewolf' offers attentive service & very reasonable prices. The meat is hardly the best in town, but the *revuelto gramajo* (scrambled eggs with potato, onions & ham) is renowned. The *tortilla gallega* (potato tortilla) & *pollo al ajillo* (chicken with garlic) are also excellent. To drink, *sangría* & *clericó* are house specialities. $$$

✖ **Mesón Viejo Sancho** San José 1229; ☎2900 4063; ⏰ 12.00–15.00, 20.00–midnight Mon–Sat (until 01.00 Fri–Sat). One of the Centro's classic restaurants for 3 decades, & seemingly never redecorated, the very attentive staff serve huge portions of filling food such as *kassler* (pork chops smoked then grilled) with *papas a la suiza* (rösti), steak, *milanesa* or chicken, followed by amazing desserts, & all at prices that hardly seem to have gone up since they opened. $$$

✖ **Ruffino** San José 1166; ☎2908 3384; ⏰ 12.00–15.00, 20.00–midnight Mon–Fri (from 20.30 Sat), 12.00–15.30 Sun. A classic Italian restaurant, complete with red-&-white-chequered tablecloths & a good wine list, serving homemade pasta & pizza, as well as steak, followed by desserts such as *profiteroli* or ice cream. $$$

✖ **Clube Brasileiro** 18 de Julio 994, 2nd Flr; ☎2902 4344, 2908 7430; e comikrestaurante@ gmail.com; ⏰ 08.30–22.00 Mon–Sat. The 2nd-floor cafeteria serves a good *feijoada* (typically Brazilian bean stew with beef & pork) plus *chivitos*, pizzas, salads & other snacks; it makes a handy lunchtime stop, with a *menú ejecutivo* (executive menu) at US$10. $$$–$$

Barrio Sur
[map, page 122]

✖ **Jacinta** Carlos Gardel 1123; ☎2908 2192; e casajacinta@montevideo.com.uy; ⏰ lunch & evening Tue–Sat, lunch Sun. In a discreet but beautifully restored house dating from 1880, with a large central patio in which they put on musical

events & cabaret, as well as art shows; the food is a fine blend of traditional Uruguayan & modern Mexican cuisines. $$$

✖ **La Olla de Barro** Maldonado 1390 between Ejido & Santiago de Chile; ☎2900 6560; e laolladebarro@gmail.com; ⏰ 12.00–15.30 Mon–Fri. Montevideo's first organic vegetarian restaurant, founded in 2006, this serves delicious food with laid-back service & very moderate prices. They also deliver, & offer veggie cookery classes on the 1st Sat of the month; at the same site is the Ecotiendas health-food shop. $$$–$$

Pocitos and around
[map, page 95]

✖ **Al Forno** Solano García 2421 & Lagunillas, Punta Carretas; ☎2710 1518; m 099 375566; http://federicoamandola.com; ⏰ 12.00–16.00, 20.00–midnight daily. Perhaps the most imaginative cooking in Montevideo, inspired by Francis Mallmann (see page 242), for instance in their use of cast-iron boxes. Dishes such as wagyu beef, king crab lasagne, brótola, salmon ravioli or porcini risotto cost cUS$15–30. $$$$

✖ **Che Montevideo** Rambla Gandhi 630; ☎2710 6941; ⏰ 09.00–03.00 daily. Opposite the Castillo Pittamiglio (see page 141), with a great waterfront setting (& its own tiny beach), this is a place to come to for the view & atmosphere rather than the food, which is decent but slightly overpriced. They serve good-sized portions of fish, seafood & pizza, but it's probably best to come for lunch or an afternoon snack. $$$$

✖ **El Viejo y El Mar** Rambla Gandhi 400, Punta Carretas; ☎2710 5704; www.elviejoyelmar. uy; ⏰ 12.00–16.00, 20.00–01.00 daily. One of the best places in the area for fish, but there's good pasta & salads on offer too; service is poor, however. There's a nautical theme, with an old boat converted into the bar, a terrace looking out to sea, & Wi-Fi. $$$$

✖ **Tandory** Libertad 2855 & Massini, Pocitos; ☎2709 6616; e tandoryrestaurant@gmail.com; www.tandory.com; ⏰ 12.30–15.00 Tue–Fri & 20.00–midnight Mon–Sat. Definitely not your normal curry-house, this is an upmarket place offering superb 'global fusion' cooking influenced by the Slow Food movement, with Chinese & Thai dishes as well as tandoori. $$$$

✖ **Restaurant One Love** Montero 2683 (Plazoleta Manuel Azaña); ☎2710 1371; www.

onelove.com.uy; ⏱ 12.00–16.00 Wed–Sun & 20.00–midnight Tue–Thu, 20.00–01.00 Fri–Sat. A new restaurant with stylish décor & music, & better food than you might expect – mains cost US$14–25 & the set lunch (Wed–Fri) costs US$16. $$$$–$$$

✕ **Almagro** Zorrilla de San Martín 176, Punta Carretas; ☎2711 1900; ⏱ from 19.00 Tue–Sun, lunch Sat–Sun. A new parrilla, classical in style but with a modern twist, & a deck with a sea view. As well as grilled meats they serve pasta & excellent desserts. $$$

✕ **Cantina La Estacada** Camino El Faro, Punta Carretas (at the Club de Pesca behind the Punta Brava naval station); ☎2710 0576, 2712 1566; ⏱ lunch & dinner daily. Behind the deceptively hippyish front, this is a very good & popular seafood restaurant. $$$

✕ **Kokoro** Libertad 2592 & Viejo Pancho, Pocitos; ☎2706 9140; www.kokoro.com.uy; ⏱ 12.00–15.00 Tue–Sat (20.30–midnight Mon–Sat). Apart from a couple of overpriced places out in Carasco, this offers best the best sushi in town, with authentically minimalist décor & excellent service. $$$

City centre

✕ **Don Koto** Colonia 1758 & Gaboto; ☎2408 8430; ⏱ 12.00–15.30, 20.00–01.00 Mon–Sat, 12.00–16.00 Sun. Highly regarded traditional local parrilla, with friendly service & excellent meats at affordable prices. $$$

Prado

[map, page 78]

✕ **Don Andrés** Lucas Obes 1054 & 19 de Abril; ☎2336 6418; www.donandres.com.uy; ⏱ 20.00–00.30 Tue–Thu, 20.00–01.30 Fri, 12.00–15.45, 20.00–01.30 Sat, 12.00–15.45, 20.00–midnight Sun. Something of a hidden treasure, this is a local institution, a friendly parrilla that also serves fish, lasagne & classic desserts. $$$

Buceo and Punta Gorda

[map, pages 78 and 109]

✕ **Casa Violeta** Rambla Armenia 3667, Buceo; ☎2628 7626; e cvioleta@adinet.com.uy; www. lacasaviolleta.com; ⏱ from 12.30 & from 19.30 daily. A parrilla (actually inspired by Brazilian *churrascarias*) with a huge salad bar in the middle of the room, serving good grilled beef in cuts rarely

found in Uruguay, such as rib-eye & porterhouse, as well as fish, seafood & pasta, all served in a friendly, relaxed atmosphere, looking out over the rambla to the Plate. $$$$

✕ **El Italiano** Quivén, Puerto de Buceo; ☎2622 7930; ⏱ 12.00–01.00; closed Mon in winter. Just west of the Yacht Club, this is one of the best & most affordable seafood restaurants in town. $$$

✕ **Heming.Way** Rambla República de México 5535, Punta Gorda; ☎2600 0121; ⏱ 09.00–02.00 daily. The food is decent enough (a fairly standard choice of beef, fish & pasta), but people come here mainly for the view. Set on a hillside, with a non-smoking terrace giving views along the coast to the city centre, this is one of the best places in town to while away the sunset hour. $$$

BUDGET
Chains

✕ **Cervecería La Pasiva** This well-established chain has managed to acquire prime locations on every plaza in the city, including Plaza Constitución, Plaza Independencia (next to the Palacio Salvo), Plaza Fabini, Plaza Cagancha, the Montevideo & Punta Carretas shopping centres & at Benito Blanco 920 & Avenida Brasil in Pocitos. Calling itself a *cervecería* or beer-hall, it's known above all for its chivitos (steak sandwiches) & *panchos* (hot dogs), & more especially its mystery mustard sauce (see page 68). It also serves burgers, steaks, salads & a wide range of pastas, all very reasonably priced. Some branches have Wi-Fi. $$

⎔ **La Cigale** The ice-cream equivalent of La Pasiva, also found in the city's main squares & shopping centres. Its success is well deserved, as these really are the best ices around. $

Ciudad Vieja

✕ **El Copacabana** Sarandí 454 & Misiones; ☎2915 3205; www.elcopacabana.com.uy; ⏱ 06.00–22.00 Mon–Sat. A nice cafetería-restaurant, with a standard menu including good chivitos & well-presented special coffees, served with a glass of fresh orange juice, whipped cream & cake. There's Wi-Fi, though only from 15.00. $$

✕ **Empanadas El Rincón** Rincón 402 & Zabala; ☎2916 9367; also Gestido near Simón Bolivar, Pocitos; ☎2706 7525; www.empanadaselrincon. com; ⏱ Mon–Fri. Eat in or out, with upmarket empanadas at US$2 each (or US$1.40 for sweet ones). $

✗ **Empanadas La Barca** Reconquista 331 & Alzáibar; 2915 4454; www.empanadaslabarca. com; 11.00–15-00, 20.00–midnight Mon–Fri, 20.00–midnight Sat–Sun; also 21 de Setiembre & Scosería, Punta Carretas; 2711 1484; Herrera 1245, Buceo; 2628 8282, 2623 4495; Orinoco 4845 & Río de la Plata, Malvín; 2619 2230, 2613 0923. No fewer than 46 types of excellent empanadas, to eat here or take away, or delivered to homes & offices. $

Centro

✗ **Albahaca** Ferreira Aldunate 1311; 2900 6189; 08.00–20.00 Mon–Sat. A nice little café serving simple snacks including breakfast, a dish of the day (US$10), quiches, empanadas & afternoon tea, all at very reasonable prices. $$

✗ **El Candil** San José 1095; 2908 8246. 'The Lantern' is a simple neighbourhood café-bar that's handy for some of the Centro's hostels & *hospedajes*. It serves breakfasts, pizzas, tortillas & other standards, & is good value, even if the service is a bit sluggish. $$

✗ **La Vegetariana** Yí 1369; 2902 3178; 11.30–15.30, 19.30–midnight Mon–Sat (until 00.30 Fri–Sat), 12.00–16.00 Sun. A hot buffet of various overcooked veggies & pulses, this isn't the most welcoming of places, but if you're tired of pizza & pasta it's a healthy alternative. US$8 for all you can eat, or at lunchtimes you can pay US$10 per kilo. $$

✗ **Manchester** 18 de Julio 899 & Convención; 2900 4383. An old-school local diner that serves a Dagwoodesque chivito-with-everything for US$10, as well as a dish of the day & full afternoon tea (but the WCs can be grubby). $$

✗ **Madison** Andes 1403 & Colonia; 2900 4074. A simple neighbourhood café-restaurant, not easily confused with the Radisson, just around the corner – here you'll get pasta, *milanesa* & other simple dishes, with friendly service & an English-language menu. $

✗ **Pizzeria El Gaucho** 18 de Julio 1449 & Barrios Amorín; 2900 3914; www.elgaucho.com.uy; 08.00–01.00 daily. Despite the name, this really is an all-purpose eatery, open all day for everything from tea & toast to a full meal. But the small pizza really is small. There's free Wi-Fi. $

🍽 **La Catedral de los Sandwiches** Sarandí 502; 2915 7349; 07.30–21.00 Mon–Fri, 07.30–16.00 Sat. As it says, the Cathedral of

Sandwiches – not a London sandwich shop or a New York deli, but a classy café where you can have a sandwich plate or a salad, as well as a pastry, a soft drink or a beer. $$

Palermo
[map, page 89]

✗ **La Taberna del Diablo** Gonzalo Ramírez 2051 & Dr Pablo de María; 2413 7543; www. latabernadeldiablo.com; 11.00–02.00 daily. Despite the name, this is a pleasant family restaurant, known for its empanadas; it serves set lunches (11.00–16.00 Mon–Sat) & also has Wi-Fi. $$

Pocitos and around
[map, pages 94–5 and 122]

✗ **Amaretto Bakery Café** 21 de Setiembre 2998 & Roque Graseras, Villa Biarritz; 2711 9934; www.amaretto.com.uy; 08.00–23.00 daily. All kinds of coffee, plus muffins, pastries, soups, salads, sandwiches, indoors on the terrace, as well as live music on some weekend evenings. $$

✗ **La Negra Tomasa** Pedro Bustamente 1165 & Tomás de Lezanas, Puerto Buceo; 2622 2218; 12.00–midnight Mon–Sat, closed Sun. Excellent pizza & *faina* (if a bit pricey – & deliveries are unreliable) near the Montevideo Shopping. $$

✗ **Chivitos Marcos** Herrera 1186 & 26 de Marzo, Buceo; 2628 3512/6326; until 01.00 Sun–Thu, until 03.00 Fri–Sat. Also at Avda Italia 4675 & Troitiña, Malvín; 2613 5535; & Coimbra 5855 & General Paz, Punta Gorda; 2604 4562, 2606 2827. Serving reputedly the best chivitos in town for over 20 years, although the service & ambience can be poor. Also a good veggie version, & deliveries. $

🍽 **Medialunas Calentitas** 21 de Setiembre 2982, Pocitos; 2710 5045; 24hrs; also at 26 de Marzo 1161; 2709 5344, 2706 7354; & Zona América, Ruta 8 km17½; 2518 2972; www.medialunascalentitas.com. A chain of cafés specialising in *medialunas* or small croissants with a variety of great fillings, as well as breakfasts, sandwiches & cakes. $

City centre

✗ **La Vegetariana** Libertad 2729 & Avda Brasil; 2709 8272/4208; 11.30–15.30, 19.00– midnight Mon–Fri, 08.00–22.00 Sat–Sun. An offshoot of the long-established veggie place in closer to the Centro, with a hot buffet of various overcooked veggies & pulses. US$8 for all you can eat, or at lunchtimes you can pay US$10 per kilo. **$$**

📖 **Philomène Café** Solano García 2455 & Miñones; ☏ 2711 1770; www.philomenecafe. com; ⏰ 09.00–20.30 Mon–Fri, 11.00–20.30 Sat. A relaxing café (with AC & Wi-Fi) serving a good range of coffees, teas, licuados & shakes, & fresh healthy sandwiches, salads, quiches & wraps followed by delicious cakes. They also do a good cheese platter & *flammkuchen* (Alsatian 'pizza'). **$$**

BARS
Ciudad Vieja

✕ **Café Bacacay** Bacacay 1306 & Buenos Aires; ☏ 2916 6074; www.bacacay.com.uy; ⏰ 09.00 to at least 02.00 Mon–Fri, from 10.00 Sat, closed Sun. Home to the actors of the Teatro Solís for almost a century, this was bought by a German in 1995 & converted to a chic café-bistro. Its kitchen is now open non-stop, serving dishes such as steak, pasta, fish & chicken, as well as sandwiches, cappuccinos & other drinks.

🍷 **Café Brasileiro** Ituzaingó 1447. Opened in 1877, this remains perhaps the classic Montevideo bar (frequented by writer Eduardo Galeano), a spacious room with Art Nouveau features & big windows that fail to overcome the dark wood panelling. Come here for coffee (or perhaps a *carajillo*, with rum), tea or hot chocolate, with croissants, toast or a sandwich; or to hear the live music on Thu or Fri evening.

🍷 **Baar Fun-Fun** Ciudadela 1229; ☏ 2915 8005; www.barfunfun.com. Founded in 1895, this is known as Montevideo's historic tango-bar, where Gardel was inspired to sing unaccompanied in 1933 after sampling an *uvita*, a mixture of port & wine concocted by the bar's founder. Described as 'half Glasgow pub, half museum of life', it has moved several times, ending up in a faithful reconstruction in the former Mercado Central, with its original tin bar & an autographed photo of Gardel. There's live music Wed–Sat evenings (tango on Fri), & you can get snacks & pizzas.

🍷 **Corchos** 25 de Mayo 651 & Mitre ; ☏ 2917 2051; www.corchos.com.uy; ⏰ 11.00–17.00 Mon–Fri (20.00–midnight Thu–Fri); closed Sat–Sun. The best place in the country for tasting & buying Uruguayan wines, but the food is excellent

CHEAP EATS

There's a fascinating row of cheap restaurants (mainly ethnic take-aways) at the bottom of José Martí [95 H3], including **La Chacha Empanadas** (☏ *2706 8505*); **Gago** (☏ *2706 7876*), serving Armenian dishes such as shwarma, shish, hummus, falafel and borek; **La Taquería** (☏ *2709 3260*) for Mexican tacos and burritos; **La Mega Chivitería** (☏ *2706 9999*); and **El Horno de San Juan** (☏ *2707 8676*) for pizza. See map, pages 94–5 for locations.

too, including carpaccio, swordfish or spinach *bocconcini*. A glass of wine costs from US$5, tastings cost US$21 for 4 glasses & 4 snacks, or US$35 (min 6 persons) for 5 glasses of premium wine, food, a video & presentation in any of 4 languages.

🍷 **El Pony Pisador** Mitre 1323 & 1326; ☏ 2915 7470; ⏰ 17.00–08.00 Mon–Fri, 20.00–08.00 Sat–Sun. A hectic late-night pub, split on both sides of the street, with karaoke Wed & Sun, live music Sat, serving passable pizzas, calzones & other snacks.

🍷 **La Crêperie** Mitre 1332; ☏ 2915 9858; ⏰ from 11.00 Mon–Fri, 12.00–17.00 & from 20.00 Sat. Crêpes are available, but essentially this is one of a row of party-pubs, with tables on both sides of the Ciudad Vieja's liveliest street as well as in the wood-panelled interior.

🍷 **La Ronda** Ciudadela 1182; ☏ 2902 6962; ⏰ from 12.00 Mon–Fri, from 19.30 Sat–Sun. Less noisy than the bars on Mitre & Bacacay, this is nevertheless very popular with the cool kids; sharing its owner with the next-door Cheesecake Records, it has walls covered with record sleeves & classic LPs playing (except after 22.00 Thu when there may be a poetry slam). Soak up the drink with a *masticable*, a sort of Mexican wrap.

🍷 **Roldós** Mercado del Porto No 09; ☏ 2915 1520; www.roldos.com.uy. Founded in 1886 as a general store & converted into a proper bar in 1930, this Montevideo institution has always been associated with *medio y medio* ('half & half' – actually 3 parts dry white wine & 1 part sparkling wine) that makes a great aperitif before an asado (although you should drink a fuller, smoother wine with the meat). Past customers include Enrico Caruso, Jean-Louis Barrault & Carlos Fuentes. In addition to the stand-up bar there's also a small seating area.

✖ **Tasende** Ciudadela 1300 & San José. Founded in 1931, this is one of Montevideo's classic *boliches* – legend has it that one president used to bring his cabinet here to relax tense meetings. It's a straightforward bar-restaurant, serving its unique style of pizza for over 75 years.

♀ **The Shannon** Mitre 1318; ✆2916 9585; ⊕ 18.30–04.30 Mon–Fri, 19.00–05.00 Sat–Sun. An Irish pub on Montevideo's liveliest pub street, with a wide range of beers (although Uruguayans find it hard to understand why an Irish pub doesn't serve Irish coffee), with decent snacks available & live music, often semi-Celtic.

Centro

✖ **Bar Iberia** Uruguay & Florida. In the 1980s this place sold more beer than any other Montevideo bar, thanks to some very thirsty Polish & Russian fishing crews; now it's a pleasant traditional café-bar, serving empanadas, pizzettas & panchos as well as all the usual drinks.

♀ **Bremen** Aquiles Lanza 1150 & Maldonado; ✆2903 2094; ⊕ from 19.00 Mon–Sat. Montevideo's German pub, with good beer, well-loaded plates of German food, a very cheery atmosphere & a roof terrace.

♀ **Montevideo Sur** Paraguay 1150 & Maldonado. An authentic pre-war shop/bar, still with its Art Deco furnishings & *azulejo* tiles, & lots of empty whisky bottles. Cold pies & *milanesas* are available,

but it's probably best to stop for a drink & move on to eat.

♀ **Su Bar** Jackson 1151 & Maldonado; ✆2419 8827; ⊕ 08.00–20.00 Mon–Fri, 12.00–15.30 Sat. A traditional Spanish bar near the Parque Rodó (with a great range of whiskies) & also a good place for weekday lunch, serving dishes such as spinach canelones & milanesas.

City centre

✖ **El Gran Sportman** 18 de Julio 1803 & Tristán Narvaja. Opposite the university, this bar (founded in 1892 & supposedly named after an English gentleman) has always attracted intellectuals such as Borges, as well as the Argentine rocker Charly García; but it's not really a drinking bar, more a place for a quiet coffee or a quick chivito or pizza (although the lunchtime *menú ejecutivo* does offer more choices).

♀ **El Unibar** Eduardo Acevedo 1450 & Guayabos. To the rear of the university, this little place is a student bar par excellence; there's a small street-side terrace.

✖ **La Giralda** Bvar Artigas 1598 & Francisco Canaro; ⊕ 24hrs. Founded in 1943 (& claiming to have sold the first Coke in Montevideo), this has always been popular with staff from the nearby hospitals, also serving lots of pies & pizzas to eat in or take away.

Barrio Sur
[map, pages 94 and 122]

✖ **La Cocina de Pedro** Gonzalo Ramírez 1483 & Morales; ✆2411 0909, 2413 7453; ⊕ 12.00–15.30, 20.00–midnight Mon–Sat, 12.00–16.00 Sun. A friendly Uruguayan pub-parrilla (also serving pizza, pasta, risotto & salads) with semi-industrial décor, a nice little garden at the rear &

BOLICHE MONTEVIDEANO

The *boliche Montevideano* or Montevideo pub developed out of the 18th-century *almacénes de ramos generales* (general shops) that also sold drinks, much as happened in small Irish villages, and became a bar that also sold foodstuffs, and nowadays meals. In many you'll still see glass-fronted display cases. Many of the most traditional *boliches* have gone, including the legendary Tupí Nambá, where Gardel had his own table facing Solís Street. A project to boost interest in the remaining ones has produced a fine coffee-table book (see page 378), and a leaflet promoting two dozen of the best ones.

live music at weekends. There's a weekday lunch menu (from US$11) & Wi-Fi.

✗ **Palermo Viejo** Barrios Amorín 949 & Gonzalo Ramírez; ☎2902 8269/6132; ⏲ 09.00–01.30 daily (to 02.30 Fri–Sun). A trendy café-bar gourmet with a good pavement terrace, serving pizza & a lunchtime fixed menu.

♀ **Recoleta** Santiago de Chile 951 & Gonzalo Ramírez; ☎2901 5325, 2908 5366; ⏲ from 11.30. A lively local pub with Wi-Fi that also serves parrilla, pizza & pasta, fish & chicken stroganoff.

Pocitos and Punta Carretas
[map, page 95]

✗ **Bar 62** Barreiro 3301 & Chucarro; ☎2707 3022; www.62bar.com; ⏲ 10.00–02.00 Mon–Sat, 10.00–16.00 Sun. In the former terminal of the city's first trolley-bus line (route 62, in 1951), this is a lively bar (especially Sat nights) that also does good, if slightly pricey, food, including parrilla & fish (such as seared tuna with sesame, salmon teriyaki or sushi) & desserts that include a fine pear *tarte tatin*.

✗ **Expreso Pocitos** Benito Blanco 956 & Brasil. In the Edificio El Mastil, one of the city's finest Art Deco buildings, this is a good, largeish café-restaurant (& *cocktelería-cafetería-sandwichería*) that's still at the heart of the local community.

♀ **La Giraldita** Benito Lamas 2745 & E Muñoz. Opened in the early 20th century, this is one of the city's most attractive & best-preserved shop/bars, with its brown wood bar, glass-fronted display cases & walls cluttered with posters, as well as lots of outside seating.

♀ **Tabaré** Zorrilla de San Martín 152 & Tabaré, Punta Carretas; ☎2712 3242; http://bartabare.com; ⏲ 20.00–01.00 Mon–Sat. Founded in 1919 as a shop & fishermen's bar, this survived to be listed in the 1990s by *Time* magazine as one of the world's 100 best bars, with pasta & bottles displayed in glass-fronted wooden cases; in 2003 it was refurbished & reopened

with a restaurant upstairs. There are 2 small pavement terraces, & tango on Wed.

♀ **Tranquilo Bar** 21 de Setiembre 3000 & Roque Graseras, Punta Carretas; ☎2711 2127; www.tranquilobar.com. Although only a few decades old, this is a typical Galician bar, favoured by actors & writers. With a small interior bar, the best place to be is on the largish terrace, where you can eat sandwiches or simple meals, including a dish of the day or plates of cheeses or cold meats, each costing US$10. There's Wi-Fi.

Buceo
[map, page 122]

♀ **El Pony Pisador** José Iturriaga 3497 & Herrera; ☎2622 1885; www.elponypisador.com.uy; ⏲ from 20.00 Thu–Sat & eves of holidays. A branch of the Ciudad Vieja disco-pub (see page 106), with karaoke Thu, live music Fri–Sat.

✗ **La Fonda del Puertito** Herrera 1132; ☎2628 7362; www.facebook.com/lafonda.mvd; ⏲ 12.00–16.00, 20.00–late daily. A grill & seafood restaurant, this aims to be a cut above the pubs on this lively strip; food & service are good, & it also has a very decent wine list.

✗ **La Vaca** 26 de Marzo 3572 between Herrera & the rambla; ☎2622 5077; www.lavaca.com.uy; ⏲ 12.00–15.30, 20.00–late Mon–Fri, 12.00–16.00 Sat–Sun. A self-styled parrilla *gourmet* (with salad bar & garden) that shares the energy of the nearby pubs.

✗ **Sacame El Maleficio** Herrera 1184 & 26 de Marzo; ☎2628 8800; m 097 418246; www.sacameelmaleficio.com; ⏲ 19.30–01.00 Mon–Wed, 19.30–02.00 Thu–Fri, 19.30–03.00 Sat. A pub-restaurant (serving pizza, pasta & snacks), & wine bar, with Wi-Fi & a choice of terrace or AC, decorated with all kinds of wacky bric-a-brac. Prices are a bit high, aiming to indicate that it's classier than its neighbours.

NIGHTLIFE

TANGO Uruguayans are proud of their tango tradition (see page 350 on Carlos Gardel's roots), but in a quieter, less intense way than in Buenos Aires. The city of Montevideo is attempting to cash in a bit more, with tango festivals and other events (see *http://ciudaddetango.blogspot.co.uk*).

There's more information at www.montevideo-tango.com/mvdt/info.htm and www.montevideo.gub.uy/ciudad/cultura/tango; tango kit is for sale at **La Botica de Tango** in the Mercado de los Artesanos (see page 115) [122 G2] (*San José 1312*; m 094 206990; e boticadetango@gmail.com).

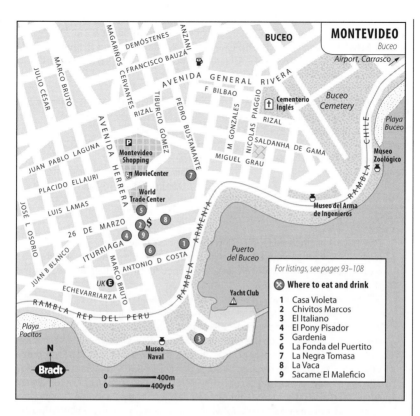

For listings, see pages 93–108

⊗ Where to eat and drink

1 Casa Violeta
2 Chivitos Marcos
3 El Italiano
4 El Pony Pisador
5 Gardenia
6 La Fonda del Puertito
7 La Negra Tomasa
8 La Vaca
9 Sacame El Maleficio

If you can tango a bit already, there's free open-air tango most evenings (from 19.30) on Plaza Fabini. The dancing seems pretty poor to Buenos Aires tango snobs, but it's friendly and relaxed.

Dance lessons

Academia Azúcar Para Ti [122 F2] Soriano 1068 & Río Negro; m 094 594628; e nando5982@ hotmail.com; ⊕ until 21.30 Mon–Sat. Salsa.
La Crêperie [122 D2] Mitre 1332; ☏2915 9858; ⊕ 18.30–20.00 Tue; summer 19.30–21.00. Tango.
Tanguería Salú [95 G5] García Cortinas 2398, Punta Carretas; ☏2711 2896; ⊕ Sat from 21.00 evenings. Tango.

For the more experienced

Baar Fun-Fun [122 D3] Ciudadela 1229; ☏2915 8005; ⊕ Wed–Sun
Joven Tango [122 G2] At the Centro Cultural Mercado de la Abundancia; Aquiles Lanza 1290 & San José; ☏2901 5561; www.joventango.org; ⊕ Fri–Sun

Lo de Margot [95 E3] Upstairs at Constituyente 1812 & Yaro; ☏2413 6694, 4160 6230; ⊕ Tue & Thu
Café Literario Las Musas [122 E2] San José 885 & Andes; m 094 221307; e lasmusas@adinet.com. uy; ⊕ Wed & Sun
Vieja Viola [94 D2] Paysandú 1639 near Minas; ☏2403 6230, 2924 3109; ⊕ Sat.

Dinner shows

El Milongón [94 D1] Gaboto 1810 & La Paz; ☏2929 0594; e elmilongon@adinet.com.uy; www.elmilongon.com.uy; ⊕ 20.30 Mon–Sat
La Casa de Becho [94 C1] Nueva York 1415; ☏2400 2717; ⊕ 22.30 Fri–Sat
Tangombe [95 E2] Rivera 1989 & Jackson; ☏2403 5682; ⊕ 22.00 Fri–Sat

DISCOS The liveliest pubs or boliches are on Mitre in the Ciudad Vieja; there's a selection of discos nearby on Rincón [122 D2], including **Almodóbar** at No 626

(℡ *2916 6665*); **La Rinco** at No 734 (℡ *2902 6492*); **Puerto Barra** at No 735 (℡ *2901 0139*); **MK 1 Dance** at No 740 and Ciudadela (℡ *2908 5696*) and **Evolución** at No 746 (m *094 381581, 099 623364*). All tend to open from c22.30 Friday–Saturday. Other clubs and discos include:

☆ **Café-Dance Azabeche** [95 G1] Avda Dr Lorenzo Merola, Parque Batlle; ℡ 2487 2405; www.azabachecafe.com; ⏰ from 21.30 Wed–Sun, with dancing from midnight; salsa Wed.

☆ **Código** [78 F3] Rambla Rep de México, Punta Gorda ℡ 2600 8913

☆ **Mariachi** [95 H3] Uruguay 1136 & Rondeau; ℡ 2901 6264; www.discomariachi.com.uy; ⏰ 22.00 Fri–Sun

☆ **New York** [78 F3] Mar Artico 1227, Punta Gorda; ℡ 2600 0444

☆ **Saideíra** [95 E3] Gonzalo Ramírez 1963; ⏰ 23.00 Thu, midnight Fri–Sat)

CARNAVAL

Uruguay takes great pride in having the longest carnival season of any country, over 80 days long, although it has to be said that between the opening and closing parades the activities are largely confined to various open-air theatres and stages across Montevideo.

The prelude to carnaval season, usually on the last Thursday of January, is a grand parade, when huge floats, giant puppets and groups of *murga* (see pages 28 and 111) performers proceed for five hours along Avenida 18 de Julio, the city's main axis. A week later (on the first Thursday and Friday of February) Las Llamadas ('The Calls') is a procession of 40 different *comparsas* or *cuerdas* (candombé drumming groups) each night through the Barrio Sur and Palermo (see page 29). The 40 days of Lent are occupied by performances on *tablados* or temporary stages in the various quarters of Montevideo and in the Teatro del Verano, the open-air theatre near Parque Rodó, where a competition is held to choose the very best acts. The climax comes the weekend before Shrove Tuesday and the start of Lent, but it may not finally wind up until the following weekend, especially if rain has caused delays. For exact dates, contact the city council's culture department on ℡ 1950 or http://cultura.montevideo.gub.uy.

Uruguay's Carnaval has various sources: in classical antiquity, the Church calendar, Venetian carnival, the commedia dell'arte, and in the Bantu and Angolan Benguela cultures brought by African slaves. Candombé remains specially associated with the Afro-Uruguayan community, although the majority of drummers nowadays are of European descent (there are increasing numbers of female drummers, too).

Many slaves were brought from Africa to Montevideo after 1750, developing the habit of meeting to dance on the shore at weekends, gatherings known as *tambos* or *tangos*. These were restricted after 1808 by a fearful white population, but continued in a more discreet form. Candombé was first recorded in 1834 and then 1839, and was banned, although the Afro-Uruguayan population was in any case declining, due to assimilation and civil wars. The first drumming comparsas were founded in the 1860s by Afro-Uruguayans, and in 1876 a black-face comparsa, Los Negros Lubolos, was founded by a group of upper-class young white men. Imitating the Afro-Uruguayan groups, they were a great success at that year's Carnaval and paved the way for candombé to enter the mainstream of white Uruguayan culture. Even now, a white drummer is known as a *negro lubolo*.

In the 20th century there was massive European immigration to Montevideo, with many poor immigrants living in the crowded *conventillo* tenements of Barrio

☆ **W Lounge** [95 F4] Rambla Wilson & Requena, Parque Rodó; ☎ 2712 1177; ⏱ 00.30–07.00   Thu–Sat. V trendy – playing techno downstairs & rock upstairs.

LIVE MUSIC Live bands can be heard in the various pubs and at **BJ** [122 E3] (*Banda Joven; Soriano 820 near Convención;* ☎ *2908 5703;* e *gramonproducciones@gmail.com; www.bandajoven.com;* ⏱ *22.00–05.00 daily*), **Espacio Guambia** [122 C2] (*25 de Mayo 591 & Gómez;* ☎ *2916 3800; www.guambia.com.uy*) and **La Barraca** [95 E1] (*Muñoz 2049 & Defensa, Tres Cruces;* ☎ *2402 9704*). There's pub-rock and metal at **La Comuna** [94 D3] (*Santiago de Chile 1508 & Soriano;* ☎ *2908 6607;* m *096 718961;* e *oktubreproducciones@hotmail.com*), while the **Amarcord Pub** [122 E3] (*Herrera y Obes 1231 & Soriano;* ☎ *2901 9381*) hosts rock jams.

Sur and Palermo, learning candombé drumming from their Afro-Uruguayan neighbours. Meanwhile the banner-twirling which has also become a major feature of Las Llamadas seems to have Basque origins. The most important comparsas (many of which survive today) were racially mixed, and blacks and whites contributed together to creating a wholly Uruguayan art form, which has seen its popularity grow steadily since the 1950s. The drummers are preceded by scantily clad dancers (mostly female …) and costumed characters such as *la mama vieja* and the *gramillero* (see page 29).

At the start of the 20th century the festivities were extended to over a month, and the carnival parade, which used to wind through the Ciudad Vieja, was moved to Avenida 18 de Julio. In 1958 the Las Llamadas procession was created as a separate event – the painter Ruben Galloza had wanted to revive the traditional Afro-Uruguayan celebrations between Christmas and Epiphany (a time when slaves were given more freedom) but an all-white municipal commission decided to add it to carnaval. In the 1990s the drumming became even more popular, spreading into the middle-class suburbs of Pocitos, Buceo, and Malvín.

The other distinctive form of carnaval is murga, a kind of musical theatre with bass drum, snare drum and cymbals backing up to 17 male singers with painted faces, colourful costumes and unique harmonies. Each neighbourhood has its own troupe (known as *parodistas*), developing a new show each year and performing on temporary stages across the city. With its roots in Cádiz, Spain, murgas had appeared in Montevideo by 1910 and soon became a central part of carnaval, lampooning public figures and satirising current society and politics, while also appealing to children. Women and the young are now increasingly involved, and latex and polyurethane have opened up new possibilities for masks and costumes, with more and more outlandish punk and SM features. The best troupes are now full-time, spending much of the year visiting schools and village halls across the country.

Montevideo's Carnaval is typically Uruguayan and has relatively little in common with the slick dance performances by the perfectly honed athletes of the Brazilian samba schools (although these can be seen in the carnival of Artigas, on the Brazilian border) – despite the satire of the murga shows, the carnival as a whole has a sort of small-town innocence about it.

Even if you can't be in Montevideo for Las Llamadas or Carnaval, you'll learn a lot from visiting the Museo del Carnaval, near the Mercado del Puerto in Montevideo's old town (see page 134).

International touring bands are likely to play at the **Sala Zitarossa** [122 E2] (*Plaza Fabini, Avda 18 de Julio 1012;* ☎ *2901 7303; www.salazitarrosa.com.uy; box office* ⏰ *15.00–21.00 daily*), the open-air **Teatro de Verano** [95 F4] (*Rambla Wilson s/n south of Parque Rodó;* ☎ *2712 4972; www.teatrodeverano.org.uy*) or the **Gran Teatro Metro** [122 F2] (*San José 1211 & Zelmar Michelini;* ☎ *2902 2017; www.teatrometro. com; box office* ⏰ *15.00–21.00 daily*), in addition to playing in pubs and bars (see page 106). There's no real listings magazine, but you'll get an idea of what's on from the *Busca* newspaper's weekly *Galeria* supplement or at www.rockdeluruguay.com.

CASINOS The best of the state casinos (*www.casinos.gub.uy*) in Montevideo is the **Plaza Victoria Casino** [122 D2] (*Radisson Hotel, Plaza Independencia 759;* ☎ *2902 2155;* ⏰ *from 14.00 daily*), which offers baccarat, blackjack, bingo, roulette (mainly for European visitors) and the ubiquitous slot machines. The **Sala 18 de Julio** [122 G2] (*Avda 18 de Julio 1297 & Yaguarón;* ☎ *2902 3065;* ⏰ *09.00–05.00 Mon–Thu, non-stop Fri–Sun*) is similar to the Radisson but smaller. There are more slot machines at Sarandí 533 (☎ *4622 6671*), the Montevideo Shopping mall [map page 109] (*Avda Hererra;* ☎ *2628 5965*) and the Géant hypermarket [off map, 78 G2] (*Avda Giannattasio;* ☎ *2600 9282*). The city of Montevideo owns two historic casinos, in the Hotel Sofitel Carrasco (reopened in 2013 after a US$80 million investment) and the former Hotel Parque (*Pablo de María & Rambla Pte Wilson;* ☎ *2418 2365, 2410 6058; www.casinoparquehotel.com.uy*), small and very run-down but which should soon be moved to new premises in the Parque Rodó.

GAY MONTEVIDEO A map of gay (or 'friendly') Montevideo is available at La Lupa Libros (*Bacacay 1318, Ciudad Vieja; www.lalupalibros.com.uy*) and online (*www. friendlymap.com.uy*). There's the gay-friendly 'love hotel' **Hotel Marivent** [78 D2] (*Cipriano Miró 2969 between Apóstoles & Agaces;* ☎ *2507 0725; www.marivent.com. uy; $$*).

Cruising spots include Plaza Libertad, the Mercado del Puerto, the Carreta statue in Parque Batlle y Ordóñez, the Rose Garden in the Prado Park, the Parque de Los Aliados near the Obelisco, and the Playa Turisferia beach just over the Arroyo de Carrasco into Canelones department.

☆ **Cain Dance Club** [95 E1] Cerro Largo 1833 & Fernández Crespo; m 099 600427; www. caindance.com; ⏰ midnight–07.00 Fri–Sat. Montevideo's largest club, with 2 dance floors (techno & Latin), shows & a dark room.

☆ **Chains Disco-Pub** [122 E3] Soriano 827 & Andes; m 094 020468; www.chainspub.com; ⏰ from midnight Thu–Sat

☆ **Ibiza** [122 F1] Rondeau 1493 & Uruguay; ☎ 2901 7643; www.ibizamegadisco.com.uy; ⏰ 01.30–09.00 Wed–Sun & eves of holidays. Cruisey bar with dark room & drag queens. Strippers Thu, live bands Fri–Sun.

☆ **Il Tempo** [95 F3] Gonzalo Ramírez 2121 bis & Salterain, Parque Rodó; m 098 582300/736589; e iltempopub@gmail.com; www.iltempodisco. com; ⏰ midnight–08.00 Wed–Sun. Gay-friendly disco with live shows & strippers.

☆ **Sauna Horus** [122 E3] Herrera y Obes 1240 & Soriano; http://saunahorus.com; ⏰ 15.00– midnight Mon–Thu, 15.00–08.00 Fri–Sat. Men-only sauna.

☆ **Small Club** [95 F1] Brandzen 2172 bis & Acevedo Díaz, Tres Cruces; ☎ 2402 5473; e infosmallclub@gmail.com; ⏰ 21.30–02.00 Wed–Sun. A lounge-bar with drag shows Thu & Sun.

ENTERTAINMENT

TICKETS Ticket agencies include Cartelera (*www.cartelera.com.uy*) and Palacio de la Música (*www.palaciodelamusica.com.uy*) at Punta Carretas Shopping Centre

(*Local 136/137;* ☎ *2711 1242*), Tres Cruces bus terminal (*Local 35;* ☎ *2408 6925*), Avenida 18 de Julio 1112 & Paraguay (☎ *2902 1958*) and Portones Shopping Centre (*Avda Italia 5775, Local 262;* ☎ *2601 7843*).

THEATRE

☺ **Gran Teatro Metro** [122 F2] San José 1211 & Michelini; ☎ 2902 2017; www.teatrometro.com

☺ **Teatro Agadu** [122 F3] Canelones 1122; ☎ 2901 1855; www.agadu.org. Home to the Uruguayan Authors' Association.

☺ **Teatro Alianza Cultural Uruguay-Estados Unidos** [122 F3] Paraguay 1217; ☎ 2908 1953; www.alianza.edu.uy. The Uruguay–US cultural centre, often putting on English-language plays.

☺ **Teatro Anglo** [122 G2] San José 1426; ☎ 2901 8819; www.italiafausta.com.uy. A centre for English-language culture, with 2 auditoria.

☺ **Teatro Circular** [122 F2] Avda Rondeau 1388, Plaza Cagancha; ☎ 2901 5952; e tcircular@adinet. com.uy; box office ⊕ 18.00–22.00 Tue–Thu, 18.00–midnight Fri–Sat, 18.00–21.00 Sun. At the side below the Ateneo, this was the first theatre in the round in Latin America, founded in 1954.

☺ **Teatro del Centro** [122 F2] Plaza Cagancha 1168; ☎ 2902 8915; e teatrodelcentro@elpais. com.uy

☺ **Teatro del Círculo** [94 D3] Soriano 1710–24 & Minas; ☎ 2411 9719, 2401 9719

☺ **Teatro del Notariado** [95 E2] Guayabo 1729; ☎ 2408 3669. An outpost of the Comedia Nacional.

☺ **Teatro El Galpón** [94 D2] Avda 18 de Julio 1618; ☎ 2408 3366; www.teatroelgalpon.org.uy; box office ⊕ 17.00–21.00 Mon–Sat, 17.00–20.00 Sun. Perhaps the city's leading independent theatre, & recently refurbished.

☺ **Teatro El Tinglado** [95 E2] Colonia 2035; ☎ 2408 5362. The city's oldest independent theatre, founded in 1947.

☺ **Teatro La Candela** [95 G5] Ellauri 308 (Shopping Punta Carretas); ☎ 2712 3227; www. teatrodelacandela.com.uy

☺ **Teatro La Casa de los Siete Vientos** [95 E3] Gonzalo Ramírez 1595, Palermo; ☎ 2419 2598; www.7vientos.com/el_espacio.htm

☺ **Teatro Sala Verdi** [122 E3] Soriano 914; ☎ 2901 7453. This recently refurbished Belle-Époque theatre houses an outpost of the Comedia Nacional.

☺ **Teatro Solís** [122 D3] Buenos Aires 652; ☎ 2916 0908; www.teatrosolis.org.uy; box office ☎ 1950 3323/5; ⊕ 11.00–20.00 Tue–Sat, 15.00–20.00 Sun–Mon. Montevideo's main theatre, home of the Comedia Nacional & of opera, ballet & orchestral music. In the west wing are a shop (⊕ 15.00–20.00 Mon, 10.00–20.00 Tue–Sun) & the Allegro café (*www.allegrocafe.com.uy;* ⊕ 10.00–19.00 daily, or until the start of performances).

☺ **Teatro Stella d'Italia** [95 E2] Mercedes 1805 & Tristán Narvaja; ☎ 2408 2649; box office ⊕ 16.00–20.00 Tue–Sun. Founded in 1895 & now housing the La Gaviota (Seagull) company, this is a National Historic Monument.

☺ **Teatro Victoria** [122 E1/2] Río Negro 1479 between Mercedes & Uruguay; ☎ 2901 9971; www.teatrovictoria.net. In a National Historic Monument over 100 years old.

Other cultural centres

Alliance Française Bvar Artigas 1271; ☎ 2400 0505; www.alliancefrancaise.edu.uy. The French cultural centre, with frequent events & films (& the Café-Bistro Sucré-Salé).

Ateneo de Montevideo Plaza Cagancha 1157; ☎ 2900 0987; www.ateneodemontevideo.com. Montevideo's Atheneum, with art exhibits, free concerts & other events.

Centro Cultural de España Rincón 629; ☎ 2915 2250; www.cce.org.uy; ⊕ 11.00–19.00 Mon–Fri, 11.00–17.00 Sat. A strikingly refurbished building with free avant-garde art exhibits & films.

Centro Cultural Lapid (Unión Latina) Avda 18 de Julio 948, 1st Flr; ☎ 2307 4318

Goethe Institut Santiago de Chile 874; ☎ 2908 0234; e info@montevideo.goethe.de; www. goethe.de/montevideo. The very active German cultural centre.

Punto de Encuentro MEC San José 1116 & Paraguay; ☎ 2902 3941; ⊕ 10.00–19.00 Mon–Fri. Run by the culture ministry, this puts on good shows of contemporary art.

MUSIC Uruguay's leading **orchestra** is the Filarmónica de Montevideo (*www. filarmonica.org.uy*), founded by the city in 1958 and based at the Teatro Solís. The state broadcasting body SODRE (*www.sodre.gub.uy*) also has an orchestra, although it's plagued by labour problems; they perform in the modern Teatro Sodre [122 D2] (*at Mercedes & Andes*) and the fantastic Deco Auditorio Nelly Goitiño [122 E2] (*formerly Sala Brunet; Avda 18 de Julio 930 & Río Branco;* ☏ 2901 2850; box office ⊕ 15.30–21.30 Mon–Sat, 10.00–12.00, 15.00–20.00 Sun).

CINEMA The first film was shown in Montevideo in 1896, and the first three cinemas opened in 1908. Since 1999 multiplexes have opened in the modern shopping centres, so that the cinema-going experience is now just the same as anywhere else in the world. Tickets start at about US$6.50, or US$12 in the multiplexes; they cost slightly more from Friday to Sunday and on holidays, and there are discounts for children and senior citizens in most cinemas. In March and April 2013 the 31st Uruguayan International Film Festival (*www.cinemateca.org.uy/festivales.html*) was held at the four Cinemateca screens, with over 100 films of various kinds shown; there's also a winter film festival, in August.

🎬 **Cine Casablanca** 21 de Setiembre 2838, Pocitos; ☏ 2712 3795

🎬 **Cinemateca** Lorenzo Carnell 1311 & Soriano; ☏ 2418 2460, 2419 5795; http://cinemateca.org.uy

🎬 **Cinemateca 18** Avda 18 de Julio 1280; ☏ 2900 9056

🎬 **Cinemateca Sala Pocitos** Chucarro 1036; ☏ 2707 4718

🎬 **Cine Opera** Avda 18 de Julio 1710 & Magallanes; ☏ 2403 1415

🎬 **Cine Universitaria** Canelones 1280; ☏ 2901 6768; e cuniver2010@gmail.com; www.cineuniversitariodeluruguay.org.uy. With a video store too.

🎬 **Grupocine** Ejido 1377; Colonia 1297 & Yaguarón; both ☏ 2900 4730; Shopping Punta Carretas, Ellauri 350; ☏ 2711 5288; Avda Arocena 1660, Carrasco; ☏ 2601 7992; www.grupocine. com.uy

🎬 **Life Cinemas** Barreiro 3231 & Berro, Pocitos; Punta Carretas Shopping Centre, Ellauri 350; both ☏ 2707 3037; Avda Giannattasio km20.2 Shopping Costa Urbana Level 2; ☏ 2682 0522; www. lifecinemas.com.uy

🎬 **Maturana** Avda Agraciada 3178; ☏ 2203 3244

🎬 **MovieCenter** Luis A de Herrera 1290, Buceo (Montevideo Shopping); Shopping Punta Carretas, Ellauri 350; Portones Avenida Italia 5775; all ☏ 2900 3900; www.movie.com.uy

HORSERACING AND BETTING The **casino** at Avenida 18 de Julio 1297 is shared with Maroñas (☏ 2900 8149; *www.maronas.com.uy*; ⊕ 24hrs), which runs **horseracing**, held at the Hipódromo Nacional (*Maroñas district*). Maroñas has other betting shops (with slot machines) in the Montevideo Shopping [map page 109] (*Herrera 1290;* ☏ 2622 5055; ⊕ 24hrs), the Géant Shopping Centre [78 G2] (*Avda Giannattasio & Avda La Playa;* ☏ 2600 9282; ⊕ 10.00–03.00 Sun–Thu, 10.00–05.00 Fri–Sat) and the Sala Las Piedras [95 E2] (*Rivera 613;* ☏ 2365 8700; ⊕ 10.00–02.00 Sun–Thu, 10.00–04.00 Fri–Sat). Races are held every Sunday and most Saturdays throughout the year, and on 6 January, whichever day of the week it is, when the country's premium race, the Gran Premio José Pedro Ramírez, is run.

SPECIAL EVENTS Summer starts on the first Friday of December (as a rule) with the annual **Museos en la Noche (Museums at Night)** event, the peg for a variety of free activities in museums, most of which stay open until midnight.

The **Noche de las Luces (Night of Lights)** is a massive firework display over the Pocitos rambla at 22.00 on the second Saturday of December (as a rule), preceded by a Disneyfied parade of Santa, the Three Kings and other figures. All traffic is halted from late afternoon and most of the 600,000 or so spectators walk in along the rambla.

In December or January the **Carrera de San Felipe y Santiago** (San Felipe y Santiago was the original name of the city of Montevideo) is a 10km race along the rambla from Carrasco to Pocitos. Students return to Montevideo in March or April, and the city gets livelier after the summer torpor.

Holy Week (Semana Santa or **Semana del Turismo)**, the week leading up to Easter Sunday, is a time for many people to take a last few days on the beach, but it's also a busy time in the city, with the finish of the Vuelta Ciclista del Uruguay along Avenida 18 de Julio and the **Semana Criolla** (Countryside Week, more or less), hosted by the Sociedad Rural in the Parque del Prado. There are rodeos and asados, arts and crafts for sale and live music, and hordes of people, more from the countryside than the city, with special trains and buses coming in from all around. There's also a rodeo in Parque Roosevelt the same week, but the Rural show in the Prado is the main event, with quite staggering levels of horsemanship on display.

SHOPPING

Uruguay is unusual in that most food, at least, is still bought from local grocery stores, but even so there are huge suburban malls and hypermarkets, and the city-centre shops have felt the need to attract customers. So on the second Saturday of each month (*10.00–22.00*) the Encuentros Felipe y Santiago in the Ciudad Vieja offer tango shows, choirs and military bands. On the Día del Centro y Cordón, on two Thursdays a month, shops along Avenida 18 de Julio and nearby charge no IVA (ie: give an 18% discount). The Día de la Ciudad Vieja, on the second Thursday of the month, is similar. Avenida 18 de Julio is the traditional shopping district, although tourists are more likely to find what they want elsewhere.

There's a wide range of crafts for sale in the **Mercado de los Artesanos**, on the ground floor of the former Mercado de la Abundancia [122 G2] (*San José 1312;* ⊕ *12.00–16.00 Mon–Sat*), including knitting and woodcarvings; upstairs there's a choice of cheap eateries. The Mercado de los Artesanos also has an outlet in an arcade at Plaza Cagancha 1365 [122 F2], where there are also some craft kiosks on the plaza. At San José 1029 Arte y Tradición [122 F2] (⏴ *2908 2241;* ⊕ *09.30–19.30 Mon–Fri, 09.30–14.00 Sat*) sells gaucho leatherwork, knives, etc.

For more edible gifts, Esencia Uruguay [122 B3] (*Sarandí 359 & Alzáibar; www. esenciauruguay.com*) offers wine tasting with cheese, sweets, biscuits and liquors of dulce de leche and walnut or butía palm.

LEATHERWARE The most obvious purchase for tourists, and transfers are provided from cruise ships to the main stores, Casa Mario [122 C1] (*Piedras 641 & Mitre;* ⏴ *2916 2356; www.casamarioleather.com*) and Leather Factory [122 D2] (*Plaza Independencia 832;* ⏴ *2908 9541; www.montevideoleatherfactory.com*). They sell a great variety of men's and women's jackets, coats, trousers, belts and other items, in suede and sheepskin too. There's also Montevideo Leather in Punta Carretas [95 G5] (*Solano García 2492 & Ellauri;* ⏴ *2710 3075; www.mvdleather. com*). More upmarket products are available at Pecarí [122 C2] (*J C Gómez 1412;* ⏴ *2915 6696);* [78 F3] (*Arocena 1552, Carrasco;* ⏴ *2601 7037; www.pecari.com.uy;* ⊕ *10.00–19.00 Mon–Fri, 10.20–13.30 Sat*); Giuliana Masilotti [122 D2] (*Sarandí 645;* ⏴ *2916 8114; www.giulianamasilotti.com*); and La Escondida [122 B3] (*Durango 375, Plaza Zabala;* ⏴ *2916 3525; www.laescondida.com.uy;* ⊕ *10.00–18.00 Mon–Fri, 10.00–14.00 Sat*), which also sells fine woollens, hats and other gifts. The Talabartaría [122 E1] (*Paysandú 1033*) is an authentic saddlery shop, selling tack for horses and boots, ponchos, *bombachas* and sombreros for their riders.

FASHION Fashion in Montevideo is classical in style and beautifully made; some designer boutiques are on Calle Ellauri, near the Sheraton in Punta Carretas, while some younger, more cutting-edge designers can be found in the Ciudad Vieja, such as Imaginario Sur [122 B2] (*25 de Mayo 263;* ✆ *2916 0383*) and Ana Livni [122 B2] (*25 de Mayo 280;* ✆ *2916 5076; www.analivni.com;* ⊕ *11.00–18.00 Mon–Fri*), which claims to deal in Slow Fashion. Imaginario Sur also has a stylish café, selling Segafredo coffee, *licuados* (fruit drinks) and so on. Bandolera [122 D2] (*Bacacay 1331;* ⊕ *10.30–20.00 Mon–Sat*) is a trendy boutique selling designer clothes and accessories.

Manos del Uruguay [122 F2] San José 1111; ✆ 2900 4910; www.manos.com.uy. A women's co-operative producing fine knitwear (& yarns & wools for the likes of Ralph Lauren & Benetton). You'll pay about a third of what you'd pay abroad for their knitwear.

Hecho Aca [122 B2] Edificio Santos, by the port entrance on Rambla 25 de Agosto; ✆ 2915 4341; www.hechoaca.com.uy. 'Made Here' is a non-profit body also encouraging high-quality contemporary artisans. They have a shop in the Tourism Ministry, as well as in the Montevideo Shopping & Portones Shopping malls.

SEMI-PRECIOUS STONES Semi-precious stones such as agate and amethyst from the north of Uruguay are also popular, the main outlets being Van Der Brüin [off map, 78 G2] (*Saez 6442;* ✆ *2600 3589;* e *bdv@gmail.com; www.vanderbruin.com. uy*), Mundo Mineral [122 C3] (*Sarandí 672;* ✆ *2915 0194;* ⊕ *09.30–19.00 Mon–Fri*) and Amatistas Uruguayas [122 C3] (*Sarandí 604;* ✆ *2916 6456*).

MARKETS It's well worth being in Montevideo for the **Sunday market** [94 D2] (*Calle Tristán Narvaja, opposite the university;* ⊕ *roughly 09.00–15.00*), where you can find fishing tackle, shoes, DVDs, posters, bookstalls, caged birds, kittens, rabbits, guinea pigs, hamsters and almost anything else, including cheese, fruit and vegetables. This is also a great place to see *cachila* trucks, which look as if they've struggled in from rural farms and probably won't make it back again. There's an antique market on Saturdays on Plaza Matriz [122 C2] (which spills over on to Sarandí, and also takes place on weekdays in the tourist season), with old postcards, photos and frames, gaucho trappings, watches, jewellery, maté gourds and lots of silver. There's a smaller clothes market in the Parque Juan Zorrilla de San Martín [95 G5] in the Villa Biarritz area of Punta Carretas until 15.00 on Saturdays, reappearing by the Parque Rodó castle [95 F3] on Sundays.

BOOKSHOPS Tristán Narvaja [95 E2] is also the main area for secondhand **bookshops** (which also open on Sundays, from around 09.00), such as Neruda Libros (*No 1506*), Afrodita Libros (*No 1528*), Librería Horizonte (*No 1585*), Babilonia Libros (*No 1591/1601*), Librería Montevideanos (*No 1617*), Finisterre Libros (*No 1635*), Areté Libros Usados (*No 1641*), Librería Latina (*No 1645*), Librería del Cordón (*No 1728*), Librería Rubén (*No 1736*) and Tertulia (*Colonia 1802*). In the Ciudad Vieja there are a couple of fine old-style bookshops, Librería Oriente-Occidente [122 D2] (*Rincón 609 & J C Gómez; www.mosesbks.com*) and Librería Linardi y Risso [122 C2] (*J C Gómez 1435 & Rincón; www.linardiyrisso.com*). Also in the old town, Mas Puro Verso [122 D2] (*Sarandí 675; www.libreriapuroverso. com*) is in a beautiful building next to the Museo Torres García. On the other side of the Ciudad Vieja, between the Teatro Solís and the Anglican church, La Pasionaría [122 D3] (*Reconquista 587*) is a stylish new design shop and bookshop with the excellent El Beso café (✆ *2915 6852;* ⊕ *10.00–19.00 Mon–Fri, 12.00–18.00 Sat*).

Next to the Palacio Salvo, the Librería Palace [122 D2] (*Plaza Independencia 842*) is a good general bookshop, and there are similar places nearby on Avenida 18 de Julio, such as MVD Books (*No 1261*) and Librería América Latina (*No 2089*). At the Teatro El Galpón [94 D2] (*Avda 18 de Julio 1618*), Libros Banda Oriental publishes and sells books on Uruguayan culture, and in the same place Auídiscos sells mainly folk and traditional Uruguayan music. Tamborilarte [95 E2] (*Rodó 1994 & Jackson; www.tamborilearte.com.uy*) sells candombé drums and carnival costumes.

FOOD SHOPPING In the city centre there are Disco, Ta-Ta, Micro-Macro and MultiAhorro **supermarkets**, with larger outlets such as Fresh Market, Devoto and Tienda Inglesa hypermarkets on suburban arteries such as Avenida Italia; there's one Géant hypermarket (*Avda Giannattasio, Carrasco*). There are also the **malls** or Shoppings, which usually contain a supermarket or hypermarket (and a food court and cinemas): the main ones are Montevideo Shopping [map page 109] (*Luis A de Herrera 1290, Buceo*), Portones [78 F3] (*Avda Italia & Bolivia*), Punta Carretas [95 G5] (*Ellauri 350*) and above the Tres Cruces bus terminal [95 F1]. All are easily accessible, with Portones serving as a terminal for many buses out on Avenida Italia.

For other types of food shopping, one Montevideo speciality is the fresh **pasta shops**, which sell ready meals and are particularly busy on Sunday mornings (and close on Mondays to recover) – for some reason there are a lot of these in Pocitos, such as La Spezia [95 G3] (*Libertad & España*), Santa Paula [95 G3] (*Brasil 2897 & Ellauri*) and La Doménica [95 G3] (*Libertad 2935*), as well as Pastas Blanes [95 F3] in Parque Rodó (*Blanes 1000 & Salvador; www.pastasblanes.com*) and Los Dos Leones [122 G3] (*Aquiles Lanza 1327*) in the Centro.

In the Centro, however, there are some small **health-food shops**, such as Primer Centro de Ecología [95 E2] (*Tristán Narvaja 1612*), El Naranjo [122 G2] (*18 de Julio 2164*), Ecotiendas [122 G3] (*Maldonado 1390 between Ejido & Santiago de Chile; www.ecotiendas.com.uy*), which also has a lunchtime restaurant (see page 103), and in the Ciudad Vieja Ecosol [111 D2] (*25 de Mayo 687 & Juncal*), which sells food and also clothes, presents and crafts. The Madre Tierra chain (*www.madretierra.com.uy*) has outlets at 18 de Julio 2086 and Requena; Treinta y Tres 1381 and Sarandí; Colonia 1327 and Ejido; Colonia 1753 and Gaboto; and Scosería 2645 and Aguilar.

There are some specialised **wine shops**, selling both Uruguayan and imported wines (some now sell Uruguayan olive oil as well). These include Cachi [122 E2] (*Herrera y Obes 1397 & Colonia*), Iberpark at Avenida 18 de Julio 1852 and 2033, Soriano 1249 and the Tres Cruces and Costa Urbana malls, La Cava 306 [95 G3] (*Avda Brasil 2557 & Brito del Pino; www.lacava306.com.uy*), Las Croabas [95 G2] (*Rivera 2666 & Brito del Pino*), Vinos del Mundo [95 G4] (*Montero 2177 & Williman, Punta Carretas;* \ *2712 0341; www.vinosdelmundo.com.uy*), Las Duelas [95 G3] (*Bvar España 2511 & Obligado*) and Los Dominguez [122 F2] (*Paraguay 1400 & Colonia, & in Montevideo Shopping; www.losdominguez.com*). There are also the online retailers (*www.vinoacasa.com, www.vinosuy.com*). The Museo del Vino [122 F3] (*Maldonado 1150 & Gutierrez Ruíz;* \ *2908 3430; www.museodelvino. com.uy*) is not a museum, but acts as a shop in the daytime and hosts classical, jazz, chanson and tango evenings as well as wine-tasting classes.

MISCELLANEOUS Montevideo is, naturally, not the best place in South America for **camping and hiking gear**, but the Doite chain ([95 E2] *Avda 18 de Julio 1743 & Gaboto;* [122 G2] *Avda 18 de Julio 1237 & Yí; Montevideo Shopping* [map page 109], *Portones* [78 F3], *Punta Carretas & Tres Cruces shopping centres; www.doitestore.com*) is decent enough. Martín Pescador (*Kingfisher;* [95 E3] *Gonzalo Ramírez 1358 & Ejido,*

& [122 A3] *Cuestas 1400 & Washington; www.martinpescador.com.uy*) has fishing and camping gear. The place for **car parts** (*repuestos*) is on Galicia east of Libertad. The best **photography** shop is the Fuji Center [122 G2] (*18 de Julio & Yaguarón*); there are other Fuji shops, which will all have black-and-white and slide film.

SPORT AND ACTIVITIES

The capital's, indeed the nation's, two leading **soccer** teams are Peñarol and Nacional (see page 37), both founded in the 1890s and based respectively at the Estadio Parque Central (in La Blanqueada) and the Estadio Centenario [95 G1] (in the Parque Batlle). Matches between the two, known as *clásicos*, are always at the Estadio Centenario, the stadium built for the 1930 World Cup (although the Estadio Parque Central was also used in that competition). Other Montevideo clubs include Liverpool, Danubio, Defensor Sporting, River Plate, Bella Vista, Central Español, Wanderers and Rampla Juniors, their names revealing both British origins and some influence from Buenos Aires. Peñarol is a suburb in northern Montevideo, home to the railway works where the club was founded, but their headquarters are now in the bright yellow Palacio Peñarol [94 D2] (*Cerro Largo 1411, between Minas & Magallanes, Centro*), with a covered arena that's used for boxing and other sports. A good alternative is to watch Defensores (the *violetas; www.defensorsporting.com.uy*) play at their intimate stadium in Parque Franzini, Punta Carretas. Fanaticos Futbol Tours (m *099 862325/968115; www.futboltours.com.uy*) can arrange tickets and logistics.

There are two **golf** clubs in the city, the better-known being the Club de Golf del Uruguay [95 F5], which occupies a large area of prime real estate in Punta Carretas (*Bvar Artigas 379;* ↘ *2710 1721–5;* e *cgu@cgu.com.uy; www.cgu.com.uy*); laid out by the Scottish designer Alister MacKenzie in 1930, this seems like an exclusive private club but is technically a municipal course where guests are welcome and visitors can wander around on Sunday afternoons. It has an excellent restaurant, open to non-members except for Sunday lunch. The alternative is the Club de Golf del Cerro [78 A3] (*west of the centre at Punta de Lobos;* ↘ *2311 1305;* e *cgcerro@adinet.com.uy, www.cgcerro.com.uy*). Established in 1905–10 by the owners of the Frigorífico Swift, it has a vintage clubhouse and a delightful course, lined with old native trees and with two of its 18 holes by the Plate, vaguely like a Scottish links. There's also one suburban course, the La Tahona Golf Club (*Ruta Interbalnearia km23.9, Camino de los Horneros 220, Lomas de Carrasco;* ↘ *2684 0004;* e *latahona@latahona.com.uy*), founded in 1996 in Canelones department.

Also on the Canelones coast just east of the city is the Montevideo Cricket Club (*Ruta Interbalnearia km23½, Solymar;* ↘ *2696 4762; www.montevideocricketclub.com*), founded as the Victoria Cricket Club in 1842 and known for **rugby** as much as for **cricket**; in fact the MCC is the eighth-oldest rugby club in the world, and the first to be founded outside Europe. In 1878 it also introduced soccer to Uruguay (bizarrely, one of its leading players was called Henry Stanley Bowles).

In 1874 some members also formed the **Montevideo Rowing Club**, and in 1894 others formed the Club de Golf del Uruguay in Punta Carretas.

OTHER PRACTICALITIES

BANKS There are plenty of ATMs (*bancomats*) all over town, especially along Avenida 18 de Julio and in the airport, port and bus terminal. The financial district, with the national headquarters of Uruguayan and international banks, is in the

Ciudad Vieja, in the area of Cerrito and Misiones. Exchange offices (*cambios*), including Abitab, Gales, Indumex, etc, are located in this area, especially on the 450s block of Rincón (⊕ *Mon–Fri only*), in Pocitos and Buceo, and in places like the bus terminal (*also* ⊕ *Sat or Sat–Sun*).

COMMUNICATIONS The **main post office** (Correo) [122 C3] is at Sarandí 468 and Misiones, Ciudad Vieja; the main branch in the Centro is in the side of the Palacio Municipal [122 G1] on Ejido; and the Pocitos branch [95 H4] is at Benito Blanco 992 (⊕ all *09.00–18.00 Mon–Fri*). There are useful branches with extended hours in the Tres Cruces bus terminal [95 F1] (⊕ *09.00–22.00 Mon–Sat, 10.00–22.00 Sun*) and Montevideo Shopping (*Plaza de Servicios, Local 7;* ⊕ *10.00–22.00 daily*). There are also many *farmacías* in which you can buy stamps, although the Correo signs aren't obvious.

For international **courier service**, try Federal Express [122 D2] (*Juncal 1321, Plaza Independencia;* ✆ *2628 0100;* ⊕ *10.00–13.00, 14.00–19.00 Mon–Fri; Avda Rivera 3528;* ⊕ *10.00–20.00 Mon–Fri*), DHL (*Zabala 1377;* ⊕ *10.00–19.00 Mon–Fri; Montevideo Shopping, Local 8;* ⊕ *10.00–22.00 daily; Tres Cruces bus terminal, Local KT31;* ⊕ *09.00–22.00 daily; & Avda De Las Americas 7777 bis, Carrasco;* ⊕ *09.00–19.00 Mon–Fri*), or TNT (*J C Gómez 1390;* ✆ *2916 2080, & Herrera 1248, 14th Flr, World Trade Center;* e tnt@tnt.com.uy) or UPS (*Treinta y Tres 1590;* ✆ *2916 1638*).

The telephone company Antel has **call centres** at Rincón 501 and Treinta y Tres, Ciudad Vieja (⊕ *09.00–18.00 Mon–Fri*); Yaguaron 1344 and 18 de Julio (⊕ *08.00–22.30 Mon–Fri, 08.30–22.00 Sat, 10.00–22.00 Sun*); García Cortinas 2408 and Ellauri (*near Punta Carretas Shopping;* ⊕ *09.00–19.00 Mon–Sat*); and the Tres Cruces bus terminal (⊕ *24hrs*). Antel's telecentros are marked on the standard city map handed out at tourist information offices.

Internet access is available at numerous cybercafés, particularly in the Centro, eg: Cyber [122 E3] (*Soriano 1083*), Cyber Centro [122 E2] (*Mercedes 866*), Cybercafé El Navegante [122 F2] (*San José & Gutierrez Ruiz*), International Calls and Internet [122 D2] (*Florida 1475*) and Maico Computers Cybercafé [122 F2] (*Paraguay 1331*); and in Cordón, eg: Beltron [95 F1] (*18 de Julio 2226, Tres Cruces*), Café Internet @ Del Sur [94 D2] (*Guayabo 1858*), Cyber Montevideo [94 D2] (*Mercedes 1650*), Cybernet [94 D2] (*Gaboto 1478*), Cyberspace [95 E2] (*Jackson 1412 & Rodó*), and 3w Cibercafe [94 D2] (*Roxlo 1359 bis*). In the Ciudad Vieja there's UroBrasNet [122 B3] (*Alzáibar 1314*), and in the eastern suburbs Jugador X [95 G3] (*Ellauri 982, Punta Carretas*) and Cyberzone [map page 109] (*Herrera 3525, Buceo*). There's no free Wi-Fi in the plazas, unlike the rest of the country, but it is available in Punta Carretas Shopping [95 G5], the Buquebus ferry terminal [94 A2], the airport, most decent hotels and quite few pubs and restaurants.

CRIME, SAFETY AND POLICE Generally, Montevideo is a safe friendly city, and you'll find it a relaxing place to explore on foot. Throughout the evening and even after midnight you'll see local women happily walking home from shops or friends' homes without worry. That said, there's a risk of mugging after dark in the further reaches of the Ciudad Vieja, beyond Calle Ituzaingó. Sarandí, where most of the pubs are, has a police presence all night and is safe; the Mercado del Puerto is busy and lively, but you should probably take a taxi home. The Barrio Sur and Palermo have a similar reputation but are now much better; on the rambla in particular you'll find many families happily strolling well into the night. The one area that you should definitely avoid at night is El Cerro, known for drug-related violence.

In the main tourist areas, such as the Peatonal Sarandí and Avenida 18 de Julio, you'll see Tourist Police in bright yellow tabards, whose main qualification is that they speak some English; they can be called on ☎ 0800 8226. Police headquarters are at Carlos Quijano 1310 [122 G2], in the Centro. In the Ciudad Vieja the Primera Comisaria de Policía is at 25 de Mayo 238 [122 B3], immediately west of Pérez Castellano. For immigration issues and residence permits, the Dirección Nacional de Migraciones is at Misiones 1513 [122 C2] (☎ 2916 0471, 2915 4742; e dnm-visas@minterior.gub.uy, dnm-residencias@ minterior.gub.uy; www.dnm.minterior.gub.uy; ⊕ 09.15–14.00 Mon–Fri), at the airport (☎ 2604 0322/0161; e dnm-carrasco@minterior.gub.uy) and the port (☎ 2915 4253; e dnm-montevideopuerto@minterior.gub.uy).

HEALTH The main hospitals are on Bulevar Artigas [95 F2] and on Avenida Italia [95 F1], near the Tres Cruces bus terminal. The best, private ones are the Hospital Británico [95 F1] (*Avda Italia 2420;* ☎ *2487 1020; www.hospitalbritanico.org.uy*) and the Hospital Italiano [95 F1] (*Ospedale Italiano Umberto I; Bvar Artigas 1632;* ☎ *2487 9717*). Nearby are the public Hospital Pereira Rossell [95 F1] (*Bvar Artigas 1550;* ☎ *2708 7741; www. pereirarossell.gub.uy*), the Hospital Española [95 F2] (*Bvar Artigas 1515;* ☎ *1920, 1920 5050/52; www.espanola.com.uy*) and the University of the Republic's Hospital de Clínicas [95 G1] (*Avda Italia s/n;* ☎ *2487 1515/2922; www.hc.edu.uy*), all more than adequate. The main children's hospital is the Hospital Pereira Rossell.

Ambulance services

➕ **SEMM** Bvar Artigas 870; ☎ 2711 2121, emergency ☎ 159; www.semm.com.uy
➕ **SUAT** Avda Sarmiento 2570; ☎ 2711 0711,

emergency ☎ 133; www.suat.com.uy
➕ **UCM** Bvar Artigas 1958; ☎ 2487 3333, emergency ☎ 147

WORSHIP

✝ **Iglesia Matriz (Roman Catholic Cathedral)** [122 C2] Plaza Constitución; ☎ 2915 7018. Masses 12.00 & 17.00 Mon–Sat, 11.00 Sun.
✝ **Iglesia Anglicana (Church of England)** [122 C3] Reconquista 522; ☎ 2915 9627; http:// uruguay.anglican.org. Eucharist Sun 10.00 English/11.30 Spanish.
✝ **Iglesia Evangélica Luterana (German Lutheran Church)** [95 E3] Blanes 1116 & Durazno; ☎ 2418 3066; [95 E3] Venancio Benavides 3616, Prado; ☎ 2336 1115; & [122 G2] Yi 1447 & Mercedes; ☎ 2908 2003; e luteranos@adinet. com.uy. Services in German 10.00 Sun & 11.30 in Spanish at Blanes 1116.
✝ **Iglesia Metodista (Methodist Church)** [122 G2] Constituyente 1460 & Barrios Amorín; ☎ 2413 6552/4; http://imu.org.uy. 11.00 Sun.
✝ **Iglesia Apostólica Armenia (Armenian Apostolic Church)** [78 G2] Church of St Nerces Shnorhali, Avda Agraciada 2842; ☎ 2209 0165. 10.00 Sun. Cathedral of Nuestra Señora de Bzonmar, Avda 19 de Abril 3325, Prado. 16.00 Mon–Sat, 11.00 Sun.

✝ **Comunidad Israelita del Uruguay (Jewish Community of Uruguay)** [122 F3] Canelones 1084; ☎ 2902 5750; www.kehila.org.uy
✝ **Comunidad Sefaradí (Sephardic Community)** [122 B3] Buenos Aires 234; ☎ 2915 4751, 2916 1136; e comsefar@adinet.com.uy
✝ **Nueva Comunidad Israelita (New Jewish Community)** [122 E3] Payán 3030; ☎ 2709 0709; www.nci.org.uy
✝ **Vaad-Hair synagogue** [122 F3] Canelones 828; ☎ 2900 6106
✝ **Yavne synagogue** [95 G3] Cavia 2729/2800, Pocitos; m 094 221474; e shayfro@hotmail.com
✝ **Centro Islámico Egipcio de Cultura (Egyptian Islamic Cultural Centre)** [95 G3] Baltasar Vargas 1178, Pocitos; ☎ 2708 5637; ⊕ 17.00–21.00 Mon–Fri
✝ **Centro Islámico del Uruguay (Muslim Centre of Uruguay)** [122 F2] Ejido 1233/101 & Soriano; ☎ 2902 2578; e jaiumi@adinet.com.uy

CITY TOUR

CIUDAD VIEJA The obvious place to begin a tour of the city is the **Mercado del Puerto** [122 B2], across the road from where ferry and cruise passengers emerge from the port. Although it's widely believed that this cast-iron structure, opened in 1868, was intended to be a railway station in Chile, this is an urban myth, as it was always planned to be a market here. The metalwork was, however, cast in the Union Foundry of Liverpool. In 1897 an iron fountain was added in the centre of the market, and a clock that was restarted in 1996 and is still going strong.

The 3,500m^2 market is now one of the city's prime tourist attractions, and a hub for *montevideanos* too, especially at weekends, when the many restaurants inside (see page 102) are buzzing. There's no smoking inside, of course, but thanks to all the parrillas grilling away inside, the cloudy vaults could almost belong to a steam-era railway station after all. There are also restaurants outside, which remain open into the evening when the market itself is closed, and there are buskers and other entertainment, especially at weekends.

Alongside the Mercado is the **Museo del Carnaval** [122 A2] (see page 134); across the road is the massive **Customs building** [122 A2] (*Aduana*, 1923), and on its north side (passing a plaque put up by the Customs men in honour of the 1928 Olympic soccer team) the entry to the port. Show your ID here and you can go in to see an anchor of the battleship *Admiral Graf Spee* (see the box on pages 80–1) and her 27-tonne rangefinder, salvaged in 2004, as well as a small dockside steam crane and other bits and pieces.

The area around the Mercado has now been pedestrianised, including the stretch of Pérez Castellano south to Sarandí; there are some decent shops at the northern end, but little but fast-food joints up the hill to the south. Just to the east, at 25 de Mayo 279, the new **Museo de Arte Precolombino y Indígena** [122 B2] (MAPI; see page 134) has taken over the former Defence Ministry building. Another two blocks brings you into the heart of a very poor residential district where you have the classic Ciudad Vieja sight of roads sloping down to the sea on three sides. To the west, Sarandí leads past the **Cuartel de Dragones** [122 A3] (the Dragoon Barracks, rebuilt in 1831 and now run-down but in use as part of the Maciel hospital) and down to the Escollera Sarandí, a long breakwater that's very popular for fishing; the views of the harbour are a bit too industrial to be attractive. Nearby a very anonymous building (usually closed) houses the **Almacén del Hacha** [122 B3] (*Buenos Aires 202 & Maciel*), the oldest commercial building in the city; in 1794 a barman was killed with an axe by an Italian seaman, giving it its name, the Shop of the Axe.

In the other direction, the pedestrianised Sarandí leads to Plaza Matriz (see page 123) and the cathedral, passing immediately south of **Plaza Zabala** [122 B3], a pleasant open space set at 45° to the road grid; there's a sizeable colony of *cotorras* (monk parakeets) here to entertain you, and a very grand bronze statue (1931) of Bruno Mauricio de Zabala, the founder of Montevideo. This was the site of the original Spanish fort, then of the Casa de Gobierno (Government House), which became a public library in 1816 and was demolished in 1880; the plaza was inaugurated in 1890. On the north side of the square is the splendid **Palacio Taranco** [122 B2], now the **Museo de Artes Decorativas** (see page 134), on the site of the city's first theatre, and a block further north is the church of **San Francisco** [122 B2], built in 1864 in Eclectic style (with a rather unusual steeple, finished in 1895) and now closed for conversion to a cultural centre.

Just west of the Palacio Taranco, at 25 de Mayo 314, is the **Casa Garibaldi** [122 B2], now in the care of the Museo Histórico Nacional (see page 136). Rincón leads

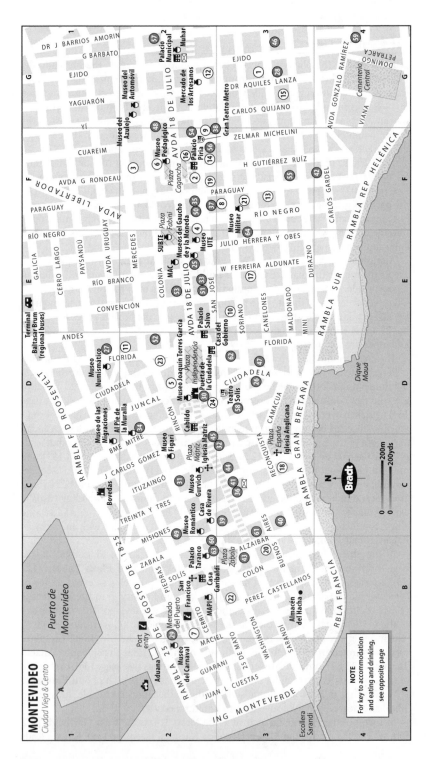

MONTEVIDEO
Ciudad Vieja & Centro

DR J BARRIOS AMORIN
G BARBATO
EJIDO
YAGUARÓN
YÍ
CUAREIM
AVDA G RONDEAU
PARAGUAY
RÍO NEGRO
GALICIA
PAYSANDÚ
CERRO LARGO
RÍO BRANCO
CONVENCIÓN
ANDES
FLORIDA
CIUDADELA
JUNCAL
RINCÓN
BME MITRE
J CARLOS GÓMEZ
ITUZAINGÓ
TREINTA Y TRES
MISIONES
ZABALA
PIEDRAS
SOLÍS
CERRITO
MACIEL
GUARANÍ
JUAN L CUESTAS
25 DE MAYO
WASHINGTON
SARANDÍ
ING MONTEVERDE
PEREZ CASTELLANOS
COLÓN
BUENOS AIRES
ALZAIBAR
RECONQUISTA
CAMACUA
GRAN BRETAÑA
RBLA FRANCIA
RAMBLA GRAN BRETAÑA
RAMBLA SUR
DURAZNO
MINI
MALDONADO
CANELONES
SORIANO
FLORIDA
SAN JOSÉ
SAN JOSÉ
JULIO HERRERA Y OBES
W FERREIRA ALDUNATE
RÍO NEGRO
PARAGUAY
H GUTIÉRREZ RUÍZ
ZELMAR MICHELINI
CARLOS QUIJANO
DR AQUILES LANZA
EJIDO

AVDA LIBERTADOR
RAMBLA F D ROOSEVELT
AVDA 18 DE JULIO
AVDA 18 DE JULIO
AVDA 18 DE JULIO

Puerto de Montevideo

Port entry
Aduana
Mercado del Puerto
Museo del Carnaval
Terminal Baltasar Brum (regional buses)
Museo de las Migraciones
Al Pie de la Muralla
Bóvedas
Museo Figari
Plaza Matriz
Iglesia Matriz
Museo Gurvich
Casa de Rivera
Museo Romántico
Palacio Taranco
Casa Garibaldi
San Francisco
MAPI
Plaza Zabala
Plaza España
Iglesia Anglicana
Almacén del Hacha
Museo Joaquín Torres García
Museo Numismático
Cabildo
Plaza Independencia
Puerta de la Ciudadela
Teatro Solís
CIUDADELA
Casa del Gobierno
Palacio Salvo
Palacio de Gobierno
MAC
SUBTE
Museos del Gaucho y de la Moneda
Museo UTE
Plaza Fabini
Museo Militar
Plaza Cagancha
Palacio Piria
Museo Pedagógico
Museo del Azulejo
Museo del Automóvil
Palacio Municipal
Mercado de los Artesanos
Gran Teatro Metro
Muhar
Cementerio Central
DOMINGO PETRARCA
AVDA GONZALO RAMÍREZ
VIANA
CARLOS GARDEL
RAMBLA REP HELÉNICA
Dique Maud
Escollera Sarandí

N
Bradt
0   200m
0   200yds

NOTE
For key to accommodation and eating and drinking, see opposite page

122

east from Plaza Zabala, passing the Montevideo Waterworks Company's neoclassical former offices on the corner of Zabala, and the main branch of the Museo Histórico Nacional in the **Casa de Rivera** [122 C2] at Rincón 437. A fairly simple two-storey building with a distinctive lighthouse-like tower in the centre (added in the 1850s), this was the home of Uruguay's first president, Fructuoso Rivera, from 1834 (he bought it from the family of a widow killed by her own slaves). Opposite it at Misiones 1399 is the former headquarters of the Banco de Montevideo (1929), and across the road from that the Bolsa de Comercio [122 C2] (*Stock Exchange; Misiones 1400*), a fine Modernist block built in 1936. To the rear (north) of the Casa de Rivera is the **Casa Montero** [122 C2] (*25 de Mayo 428*), a two-storey neoclassical house that now houses the **Museo Romántico** (see page 135), another branch of the Museo Histórico Nacional. A block away at 25 de Mayo 500 the **Caja Obrera** [122 C2] (Workers' Bank; 1941) displays some fine reliefs by Edmundo Prati.

Another block east along Rincón from the Bolsa de Comercio is **Plaza Constitución** [122 C2], also known as **Plaza Matriz** because of the **cathedral** (*Iglesia Matriz;* ⊕ *09.00–18.00 Mon–Sat, 10.00–12.30 Sun*) on its west side. This is not an especially grand basilica (it was built by a military engineer in 1790–1804 as the Baroque style was going out of fashion), but does have some nice tombs, including those of Juan Antonio Lavalleja, Dámaso Antonio Larrañaga and presidents Rivera and Suárez. There's a splendid neorenaissance baptistry, with marble walls and plaster ceiling, just inside the main doors to the right – it's usually closed but you can look through the glass doors (it's always lit).

Around the fine fountain in the centre of the plaza there's an antiques market on Saturdays and often on other days too. On the south side of the plaza is a row of

---

MONTEVIDEO Ciudad Vieja & Centro
For listings, see pages 93–108

⊕ **Where to stay**

1	Apart-Hotel Bremen.....G3
2	Balmoral Plaza.................F2
3	Campoamor....................F2
4	Casablanca.....................F2
5	Che Legarto....................D2
6	Colonia............................F2
7	Don Boutique.................B2
8	El Viajero Down Town Hostel.................F3
9	Embajador......................F2
10	Esplendor Montevideo.................E3
11	Florida............................D2
12	Four Points by Sheraton....................G2
13	Iberia..............................F3
14	ITA..................................F2
15	Juncal.............................G3
16	Lancaster........................F2
17	Montevideo Hostel......E3
18	NH Columbia.................C3
19	Oxford.............................F2
20	Pensión Río....................B3
21	Planet Hostel.................F3
22	Posada al Sur....................B3
23	Radisson Montevideo Victoria Plaza.................D2
24	Splendido........................D2

⊗ **Where to eat and drink**

25	Albahaca........................E2
26	Baar Fun-Fun.................D3
27	Bar Iberia.......................D1
28	Bremen...........................G3
29	Cabaña Verónica...........B2
30	Café Bacacay..................D2
31	Café Brasileiro................C2
32	Cervecería Matriz..........C3
33	Clube Brasileiro.............E2
34	Corchos..........................D2
35	El Candíl.........................F2
36	El Copacabana...............C3
37	El Fogón.........................F2
38	El Lobizón.......................F2
	El Palenque...........(see 29)
	El Pony Pisador....(see 30)
39	Empanadas El Rincón...C3
40	Empanadas La Barca.....C3
41	Estrecho.........................C3
42	Jacinta............................F4
43	Jacinto............................B3
44	La Catedral de los Sandwiches.................C3
45	La Corte..........................C2
	La Crêperie.............(see 30)
46	La Olla de Barro.............G3
47	La Ronda.........................D3
48	La Vegetariano...............G2
49	Las Misiones..................C2
50	Locos de Asar.................F2
51	Los Leños Uruguayos.....E2
52	Madison..........................D2
53	Manchester.....................E2
54	Méson Viejo Sancho.......F2
55	Montevideo Sur..............F3
56	Pacharán Taberna Vasca..........................F2
57	Pizzería El Gaucho.........G2
58	Rara Avis........................D3
59	Recoleta.........................G4
60	Rincón de Zabala............B2
	Roldós....................(see 29)
	Ruffino...................(see 56)
61	Samsara..........................C3
	Tannat....................(see 16)
62	Tasende..........................D3
	The Shannon........(see 30)
63	Urbani.............................B2
64	Walther's........................E3

imposing buildings, notably the Club Uruguay, built in 1885–88 in the Historical Eclectic style; on the west side is the **Cabildo** or former City Hall [122 D2], a fine neoclassical palace built in 1804. One of the city's few unaltered colonial buildings, it housed courts and a prison and is now a museum (see page 137). Just to its north, at Gómez 1390, is a striking Art Deco apartment block. On the north side of the cathedral is the **Museo Gurvich** [122 C2] (see page 136); on the north side of the plaza at Rincón 575 is an ugly government block housing on its ground floor the **Sala de Arte Carlos Federico Sáez** [122 C2] (*www.mtop.gub.uy/salasaez;* ⊕ *09.30– 18.00 Mon–Fri*), which puts on free shows of art and photography. Just north at J C Gómez 1427 is the new **Museo Figari** [122 C2] (see page 136).

Two blocks south of the cathedral is **Holy Trinity Church** [122 C3], the Anglican cathedral (Templo Inglés), a fine neoclassical edifice (with no steeple) that's now very tatty and in a run-down area. Built in 1844 close to the shore, it was moved inland in 1935 when the Rambla Gran Bretaña was built.

To the north of Plaza Matriz lies the financial district, the busiest part of the Ciudad Vieja in the daytime, and home to some good restaurants (mostly lunchtime only) as well as bank headquarters. A block north of the plaza at the junction of Gómez and 25 de Mayo is a spiky 'flamboyant neogothic' confection that was built as the Casa Gómez in 1870–85 but was never lived in; it now houses the Junta Departamental de Montevideo, the seat of the council for the department of Montevideo (not just the city). A block west of this, at 25 de Mayo 555, a striking Expressionist tower [122 C2] marks the Edificio Centenario (1930). Continuing three blocks north to the main road on the south side of the docks (*Rambla 25 de Agosto*), where the historic shoreline was, you'll reach the Parque Portuario, a new plaza of bare sun-baked white stone, and at its west end the **Bovedas** (Vaults) [122 C1], the remains of a series of 34 shellproof powder stores built in 1794–1807; one blew up in 1815, killing over 100 people. Most were demolished in 1926, but those that survived have recently been restored, along with the neoclassical Casa de los Ximénez (1817), facing them at Rambla 25 de Agosto 580–86.

Just east of here, at Mitre 1550 and Piedras, is the new **Museo de las Migraciones** [122 C1] (see page 136), and just south of that, **Al Pie de la Muralla** cultural centre [122 C2] (see page 136) – the two linked by a recently discovered stretch of the colonial city wall where the future Museo de la Ciudad (City Museum) is planned.

If you choose to loop back to the Mercado del Puerto from here on Cerrito, you'll pass the former Banco de Londres (now the National Stage School) at Zabala 1486, a neoclassical pediment (1890) attached to the modern Lloyds TSB bank on Cerrito, the site of the Artigas family home at Zabala 1500, then the Banco de la República Oriental at Cerrito 351, a neoclassical pile (built by Giovanni Veltroni in 1926–38) that occupies the entire block. At Zabala 1469 the **Casa Lavalleja** [122 B2] is a plain two-storey colonial house, built in 1783 by Manuel Cipriano de Melo; bought in 1830 by Juan Antonio Lavalleja (then interim head of state), it was his home until his death in 1853. It's now owned by the Museo Histórico Nacional but is not open to the public. Across the rambla at the north end of Zabala you'll glimpse a warehouse by Eladio Dieste (see page 35), not very special architecture but recognisably in his style of undulating brickwork.

If you prefer to continue from Plaza Matriz towards the Centro, you can go along Rincón, passing the **Palacio Gandos** [122 D2] (now the Consorcio del Uruguay) at No 649 and the Centro Cultural de España [122 D2] at No 629 (see page 113). Built as an ironmongers in 1870, this has been beautifully refurbished around the original steel columns and covered atrium. The rear of the first floor is a *mediateca*, with free use of books, newspapers and films, and the front is a *café literaria*, very relaxing as the clients are all quietly browsing arty magazines.

Alternatively you can follow **Sarandí** from the Cabildo – this stretch was pedestrianised in 1995 and is busy with hippies selling the handmade jewellery that Uruguayans seem to need so much of, as well as art galleries and antique shops. To the right, Mitre and Bacacay, lined with restaurants and bars, are the city's busiest area at night. Opposite Bacacay, the **Edifico Pablo Ferrando** [122 D2] (*Sarandí 675*) is a beautiful Art Nouveau building (1917) with a huge area of window; it's now a bookshop. Next to it is the **Museo Joaquín Torres García** [122 D2] (see page 137), dedicated to Uruguay's national painter and well worth a visit.

Just west, the **Puerta de la Ciudadela** [122 D2], dating from 1746, is all that remains of the citadel of Montevideo; it now marks the entry point from the Ciudad Vieja to **Plaza Independencia** [122 D2] and the Centro or New Town. A line of orange paint on the Plaza marks the outline of the Ciudadela, which was demolished in 1829–33, except for a few bits of wall still visible at the northwest corner of the plaza. (At the junction of Buenos Aires and Mitre, just west of the Teatro Solís, you can also see the remains of the Batería San Sebastían.) A public market grew up on the site of the citadel, which was known as Plaza Independencia by 1843; by the 1860s there was an even Doric colonnade (based on the rue de Rivoli in Paris) all the way around the square, but this was largely lost when the square was expanded in 1877.

The **Teatro Solís** [122 D3], to the southwest of Plaza Independencia, is one of the city's chief landmarks and its cultural heart. Built in 1842–56, with lateral wings added in 1868–74 (originally housing the national museum and public library), it was very well refurbished in 1998–2008. The lyre-shaped hall has superb acoustics, and a new set of stairs connects all the floors, doing away with the original set-up that kept the rich patrons apart from those in the cheaper seats. The basement exhibition hall (☉ *15.00–20.00 Tue–Sun*) shows varying displays of costumes, set designs and the like (there are also very nice toilets). Backstage tours (*16.00 Tue & Thu, 11.00, 12.00 & 16.00 Wed, Fri & Sun, 11.00, 12.00, 13.00 & 16.00 Sat*) cost US$1 in Spanish or US$2.50 in other languages (*book on ☎ 1950 3323/5*); they are free on Wednesdays (in Spanish only).

In the centre of Plaza Independencia is the great bronze equestrian **statue of Artigas** [122 D2], the father of independent Uruguay, by the Italian sculptor Angelo Zanelli, erected in 1923. Beneath it (on the west side) the ashes of Artigas were installed in 1977 in a dramatically lit mausoleum, where two guards from the ceremonial Regimiento Blandengues flank the urn and the walls are inscribed with the key dates of his career. The arcaded building on the south side of the plaza is the **Casa de Gobierno** [122 D2] (1873–74; also known as the Palacio Estévez after its builder, and as the Edificio Independencia), which served as the seat of government from 1880 to 1985; it's now the *presidencia*, used only for protocol receptions and as a museum of the presidents (see page 137).

The ugly block between the Edificio Independencia and the Teatro Solís is the Torre Ejecutiva (Executive Tower – formerly the Palacio de Justicia), which was started in 1965, left as a steel frame for several decades, and finally completed in 2008. The presidency, moved at the end of the dictatorship into the Ministry of Defence (now known as the Edificio Libertad), out in the northern suburbs, returned here in 2009.

THE CENTRO The Centro (New Town or midtown) is the commercial heart of the city, and to many Uruguayans and tourists it *is* the city. It was laid out after

1861, and by 1867 development had spread beyond the present Palacio Municipal into the Cordón area. The main axis is **Avenida 18 de Julio**, running from Plaza Independencia via Plaza Fabini (aka Plaza Entrevero) and Plaza Libertad (aka Plaza Cagancha) to the **Palacio Municipal** [122 G2] (aka the Intendencia) at Ejido. It's a busy shopping street and bus artery, and is also lined with superb Eclectic and Art Deco buildings.

The city's most recognisable landmark is the **Palacio Salvo** [122 D2], built in 1922–28 on the site of the Confitería la Giralda, the café where the very first tango, 'La Cumparsita', was performed in 1917. Originally a hotel, with a theatre in the basement (now a car park) in which Josephine Baker performed, it was converted into apartments in the 1960s. When it opened it was the tallest building in Latin America and the highest reinforced-concrete building in the world; another tower, the Palacio Barolo, was built in Buenos Aires at the same time, and the plan was to signal between the two with lights (as if radio had not been invented). In any case, the curvature of the earth meant that the distance was just a bit too great for the scheme to work. Something like a gigantic space rocket dreamt up by Jules Verne, with four booster-rocket turrets strapped to the main tower, it should be ugly but manages to be loveable. There's a small display in the foyer, which is drab but lively, with residents coming and going.

On the other side of Avenida 18 de Julio, the **Palacio Rinaldi** [122 D2] (*Plaza Independencia 1356–58*) is a fine Art Deco apartment block (built in 1929) with beautiful reliefs on the façade. Buildings to look out for along the avenida include the Jockey Club at No 857 (built in 1920 in Historical Eclectic style), the Edifico Lapido at No 948–50 (a splendid Expressionist apartment block, built in 1930), the Palacio Brasil at No 984–94 (built in 1919 in Historical Eclectic style) and the Palacio Uriarte de Heber at No 998–1000 (built in 1896–97 in Historical Eclectic style), now housing the museums of the Gaucho and of the Mint (see page 138). Across the road from this, on the south side of Plaza Fabini, is the Edificio Cine Rex, built as a cinema (but now a theatre) in 1928, in Historical Eclectic style.

Plaza Fabini [122 E2] was remodelled in 1964, with the sculpture of *El Entrevero* (The Brawl) by José Belloni installed in 1967; with its curving path, continuous benches and combined café-bus stop, it's regarded as one of the most successful pieces of urban design worldwide. Just north of the plaza at Herrera y Obes 1431 is the church of the **Immaculate Conception** [122 E2], established in 1858 after the Bishop of Bayonne sent priests to tend to the Basque community; a slightly odd neoclassical building, with the organ behind the altar, it's still the centre of the city's Basque community.

Continuing up Avenida 18 de Julio, it's just two blocks (passing the Edificio del London-Paris, built in 1908 in Historical Eclectic style) to **Plaza Cagancha** [122 F2], also known as Plaza Libertad after the statue of Liberty (1866) atop a column in the centre of the avenue. On the south side of the plaza chocolate-box soldiers stand guard outside the **Supreme Court** [122 F2], in the **Palacio Piria** at Gutiérrez Ruiz 1310 (actually on the pedestrianised Pasaje de los Derechos Humanos or Human Rights Passage); built in 1910 in Historical Eclectic style, this was the town house of the property developer and alchemist Francisco Piria (see page 189). On the north side of the plaza is the Ateneo or **Athenaeum** [122 F2], built in 1900 in Historical Eclectic style as an arts centre; immediately on its east side is the Museo Pedagógico (see page 138), a neoclassical mansion built in 1889.

Avenida 18 de Julio continues out of the square past the Edificio Sorocabana, built in 1925 in Historical Eclectic style, with a prominent tower on its leading corner. A block further east, the **Palacio Santos** [122 F2], a single-storey villa built in 1881–86 by President Maximo Santos, now houses the Ministry of Foreign Affairs (although most of the work is done in a modern block at the rear, well disguised by the slope of the street). Opposite is the former Confitería La Americana (*18 de Julio 1216–20*), a pleasantly asymmetrical Art Deco block built in 1937. On the next block to the east, the former building of the *El Día* newspaper, with its huge portico, faces the Edificio Café Montevideo, both built in the 1920s in Historical Eclectic style. On the next block, at Avenida 18 de Julio 1333, the **Palacio Díaz** [122 G2] (1929) is a spectacular Art Deco apartment block that tapers upwards into a tower like a miniature Empire State Building.

On the next block east, the **Palacio Municipal** [122 G2] or Intendencia (the City Hall) rises behind a small plaza at 18 de Julio 1352–60; built in 1936–41 (but not finally completed until 1968), it's an otherwise plain brick Modernist building with a grand loggia. In front stands what is supposedly one of only three good copies of Michelangelo's *David* in the world. In the spacious entry hall there are usually interesting exhibitions; the doors to the Sala Aquiles Lanza are early 20th-century replicas of the Puerta del Paraíso, Ghiberti's doors to the Baptistry of the Duomo in Florence, and there are also replicas of 13th- and 15th-century carvings from Chartres and Amiens cathedrals. In fact the Muhar collection (see page 138), below the Palacio, largely consists of replicas of great artworks from all around the world. On the floor of the entry hall is a satellite view of Montevideo, but you can see the real thing from the 22nd-floor viewing platform, 77m above (with telescopes). Admission is free, but you'll need to pick up a ticket from the tourist office on the plaza in front of the palacio (⊕ *10.00–12.00, 13.30–15.30 Mon–Fri*) and then make your way to the rear of the building (*Soriano 1375 & Ejido;* ✆ *2902 0666*).

Below the palacio, the **Centro Municipal de Fotografía** (*http://cdf.montevideo. gub.uy;* ⊕ *10.00–19.00 Mon–Fri, 09.30–14.30 Sat; free*) puts on very good photography shows in a small exhibition space off the tunnel at San José 1360; they have another space at 18 de Julio 885 (*between Andes & Convención;* ⊕ *15.00– 21.00 daily*), and open-air exhibits (*24hrs*) in the Prado (*Pasaje Clara Silva & Avda Delmira Agustini*), Parque Rodó (*Pablo de María & Rambla*) and the Ciudad Vieja (*Piedras, at the rear of the Museo del Carnaval*).

CORDÓN Immediately east of the Palacio Municipal the main avenue splits on either side of the *Gaucho* **statue** [122 G2] (1927, by José Luis Zorrilla de San Martín), with Avenida 18 de Julio swinging slightly to the left and Constituyentes heading to the right towards Palermo and Parque Rodó. To the south of the statue at Constituyente 1460 is the city's **Methodist church** [94 D2] (1909), much like a Catholic church but with a style of steeple that's only possible with concrete.

Five blocks up Avenida 18 de Julio you'll pass **Plaza de los Treinta y Tres Orientales** [94 D2], better known as Plaza Lavalleja (because of a statue) or Plaza Bomberos (because of the imposing 1920s fire station on its north side, known as the Cuartel Centenario de Bomberos). It's two blocks further to the Lycée Français (1937) at Avenida 18 de Julio 1772 and the **Biblioteca Nacional** (National Library; 1937–55) at No 1790, their neoclassical porticos echoing each other. Immediately beyond (opposite Tristán Narvaja, site of the Sunday market) is the main building of the Universidad de la República (now the Law Faculty; 1911); there are a few student bars and bookshops in this area, but not as many as you might expect.

Just to the east, the Ministerio de Salud Pública (Public Health Ministry) stands across the avenue from a bright neoclassical portico at Avenida 18 de Julio 1865, home to the Institut Nacional de la Juventud; just beyond, at the crossroads of Avenida Crespo, stand the modern Banco Hipotecario del Uruguay (Mortgage

Bank of Uruguay) and the Dirección General Impositiva (Tax Office), beyond which it's another eight blocks of apartment blocks (with some nice Art Deco buildings) before the busy Bulevar Artigas and the **Obelisco** [89 F1], erected in 1938 in homage to the Constituyentes, those who drew up the country's constitution in 1830. The sculptures of Law, Liberty and Strength around the base of the 40m-high obelisk are by José Luis Zorrilla de San Martín. Just to the northeast of the obelisk, the **Hospital Italiano** [95 F1] is a beautiful arcaded building, built in 1890 by Luis Andreoni (also responsible for the Estación Central and the Club Uruguay).

Back on the west side of Artigas (beyond a crucifix and monument to John Paul II, the first Pope to visit Uruguay) is the **Tres Cruces bus terminal** [95 F1] (see page 85). The name comes from the wooden crosses commemorating three travellers killed by robbers here in the early 18th century; it's also where Artigas's 'Instrucciones del Año XIII' were debated (see page 15). Just north of the terminal, what looks like a mission church is actually the church of San Expedito, the chapel of the women's prison (*Acevedo Díaz 1923 & Miguelete;* ⏲ *14.00–17.00 Tue & Thu, 08.30–11.00 Sun, & 07.00–19.30 on 19th of each month*) – over 10,000 pilgrims come here on 19 April each year.

On the south side of the Hospital Italiano, Canning and Lord Ponsonby (named after the British diplomats who brought about Uruguayan independence) lead east to **Parque Batlle y Ordóñez** [95 G1], passing the residences of the British and American ambassadors, fine villas set in spacious gardens. Space for a park was allocated in 1907, and the French landscape designer Charles Thays started work in 1911; after World War I it was known as Parque de los Aliados, after the victorious allies, but was then named after Uruguay's greatest president. The park was only opened in 1934, after the first soccer World Cup. On the far side of the park is the **Estadio Centenario** (Centenary Stadium) [95 G1], built in a rush by Juan Scasso in 1929–30, and not actually ready for the opening matches of the World Cup. The world's first stadium built specifically for soccer, it was declared an International Historical Football Monument in 1980 and now houses the Museum of Football (see page 139). Built to mark the centenary of the adoption of the constitution, it accommodated 100,000 spectators (now 70,000) and had a 100m-high Homage Tower, built to display the spotlit winners' flag, which gives panoramic views. There are other sports facilities, such as a velodrome and an athletics track, in the park, and immediately beyond it on Avenida Italia the Hospital de Clínicas [95 G1], the country's largest public hospital. José Belloni's life-size sculpture *La Carreta* (The Oxcart; 1934), in honour of the country's rural pioneers, is visible in the park from Avenida Italia, along with other sculptures nearby.

NORTH TO THE PRADO From Plaza Fabini the broad Avenida del Libertador General Lavalleja runs northeast through the Aguada district to the massive Palacio Legislativo; it passes the historic **Estación Central** [94 C2], two blocks west of La Paz. Opened in 1897, this was controversially closed in 2003 when a much smaller modern terminal was opened about 500m to the north – passenger numbers on the already attenuated suburban service were far too low for the cavernous train shed of the Estación Central, but the remoter location of the new station was predicted to drive loadings down even further. The property developer bought the site at a low price on condition of converting the original station into a cultural centre, but this has not happened, and the building has fallen into a distressing state of decay, with homeless people sleeping behind the statues of George Stephenson, Volta, Papin and Watt in front of the building. In 2009 it was agreed that the tracks would be reconnected so that the port could handle containers on the station approaches.

Heading north from the Estación Central on Paraguay, you'll come to the modern station, and immediately north, the dramatic **Torre de las Communicaciones** [94 C1], the tallest building in the country at 158m, recently renamed the Torre Joaquín Torres García. Built for the national phone company Antel in 2002 by Carlos Ott, it has a *mirador* (viewing area) on the 26th floor (❧ *2928 4417;* e *visitasguiadas@ antel.com.uy;* ① *15.30–17.00 Mon, Wed & Fri, 10.30–12.00 Tue–Thu*); it's best to call ahead as the *mirador* is often closed for private events. There's also a small museum of telecommunications (see page 139), a multi-purpose hall and amphitheatre, and outdoor sculptures by Nelsón Ramos and Águeda Dicancro.

Three blocks south of the Palacio Legislativo at Avenida Libertador 1960 is the **Iglesia Sagrado Corazón (Sacred Heart Church)** [94 C1], a fairly grand but tatty neoclassical structure with a new façade added in 1837 – this is where the Asamblea General Constituyente y Legislativa (the General Constituent and Legislative Assembly) met from February to April of 1829 to draft the new country's constitution. Half a dozen blocks to the east at Arenal Grande 1930, the former Miguelete prison (1888) has been converted into the **Espacio de Arte Contemporáneo** (see page 140).

The **Palacio Legislativo** (Legislative Palace) [94 D1], also known as the Congreso, sits on a small hill and makes a fine sight along Avenida Libertador, even if it can't really be seen from the heart of the city. It was designed by Vittorio Meano, who died a mysterious death before he knew he'd won the competition, leaving Cayetano Moretti and others to oversee construction, from 1908 to 1925. It's a massive neoclassical pile with ornate decorations (largely by Italian artists) in white marble, granite, porphyry and basalt. On the lawns on the north and south sides are two matching pairs of Rodinesque sculptures (representing Law, Justice, the Sciences and Labour) by Giannino Castiglioni, who also designed the façades along with José Belloni and Gervasio Furest. Guided tours (❧ *2924 1783;* e *protocolo@ parlamento.gub.uy;* ① *10.30 & 15.00 Mon–Fri; US$3*) take up to 1½ hours, and start on the north side (Avda Flores). You'll begin by being led up into the huge Salón de los Pasos Perdidos (Hall of Lost Steps), where two guards in 19th-century uniforms flank the text of Uruguay's Declaration of Independence in the centre of the hall, beneath allegorical stained-glass windows and Venetian mosaics of the arts and the sciences (by Giovanni Buffa), four plaster reliefs by Edmundo Prati showing key scenes of Uruguayan history, from the Grito de Asencio to Independence, and four reliefs of the national symbols by José Belloni on the ceiling. The floor and walls are composed of 52 types of Uruguayan marble, as well as granite and porphyry, with light fittings of bronze and Murano glass.

At the south end is the small Reception Hall, with two big and slightly lurid paintings by Manuel Rosé (on canvas, although they look like murals) and an almost photorealist depiction by Pedro Blanes Viale of the Swearing of the Constitution of 1830 (behind the text of the constitution itself, flanked by two more guards). At the other end of the central hall is the Fiesta Hall, with a Byzantine-style ceiling of wood and gold leaf by the Venetian Enrico Albertazzi. Here there are portraits of Lavalleja and Rivera by José Luis Zorrilla de San Martín, portraits of Rivera and Oribe and a Battle of Las Piedras by Rosé, and *Las Instrucciones del Año XIII* by Pedro Blanes Viale.

On one side of the central Salón de los Pasos Perdidos is the chamber of the Diputados, panelled in Italian walnut, and on the other that of the Senadores, in Paraguayan mahogany; tours are taken upstairs to view them from galleries. The 99 deputies sit facing a painting of Artigas meeting Rondeau during the second siege of Montevideo in 1813, by the French artist Fernand Laroche. The Senate chamber (with just 30 members) is a rather smaller semicircle, with a bust of Pallas Athena (goddess of wisdom) above the national shield.

Going up another flight (you'll also see the white marble caryatids around the exterior of the central lantern, and the sgraffito decoration of the four internal courts around it) is the Pompeiian-style library. Also panelled in very dark wood, it has very tempting leather armchairs and bookcases with stained-glass doors, a copy of the *Venus de Milo* and in the centre of the room a maquette of the statue of Artigas by Angelo Zanelli now in the Plaza Independencia. A copy of every book by an Uruguayan author has to be deposited here, along with one at the Biblioteca Nacional, and it now contains close to 300,000 books. It's open to the public in the mornings, and in the afternoon to legislators only.

Four blocks north at José L Terra 2220 and J J de Amézaga [78 C3], the classic Mercado Agrícola de Montevideo opened in 1913 (✆ *2200 8879; www.mam.com. uy*) is being restored as a modern market and gastronomic centre with performance and exhibition spaces.

From the Palacio Legislativo, Avenida Agraciada heads northwest, roughly parallel to the shoreline, eventually crossing Bulevar Artigas, the main road to the west, and coming to the west side of the Prado, once an area of *quintas*, weekend homes for the city's most affluent citizens, and still an upmarket residential district. You'll pass the Armenian Apostolic church of St Nerces Shnorhali [78 G2] (*Avda Agraciada 2842*), with a miraculous relief of St Gregory the Illuminator and, outside, a monument raised in 1975 to the victims of the 1915 genocide of the Armenians in Turkey. Typically, it has an altar raised on a proscenium stage (in the apse) but otherwise has a fairly anonymous interior.

Just north of the Armenian church, a statue of Joaquín Suárez stands in a road junction, from where Avenida Suárez runs north to the east side of the Prado Park; at No 3765 is the remarkably low-key presidential residence, next to the Castillo Soneira at No 3781, a mock castle incongruously set opposite McDonald's. Continuing north (now on Avenida Millán), you'll pass some fine villas, and at Avenida Millán 4015 reach the Museo de Bellas Artes (Museum of Fine Arts; see page 140), a typical large quinta with behind it the **Jardín Japones** [78 G1] (⊕ *12.00–18.00 Wed–Mon; free*), an authentically Japanese garden fitted around the existing trees in 2001, including an *ishi-doro* stone lantern, a zigzag bridge, a tea house and a stone garden. Immediately to the north is the Arroyo del Miguelete, the only river flowing through Montevideo, alongside which a new park has been created.

Just south of the Museum of Fine Arts, Avenida Luis Alberto de Herrera leads west to the Prado via the Botanic Garden (see page 140) and east to the **Barrio Atahualpa** [78 C2], Montevideo's best-known garden suburb, laid out in 1868. Three blocks east (at Cubo del Norte) you'll come to the **Boliche de los Yuyos** [78 G1] (the Pub of the Herbs, founded in 1906 and so called because of the herb-flavoured grappas it specialised in), with a fine Art Deco house opposite it, and then the neogothic Capilla Jackson, built in 1870 for the same family that built the present Museo del Gaucho. Just to the east is the former **Quinta de Larrañaga** [78 G1], built in 1830 by Dámaso Antonio Larrañaga (1771–1848), a priest who was very active in public and scientific life; its attractive grounds are now used by a youth sports organisation, but you're free to walk around. To the south of Herrera is the dull Plaza Atahualpa and the Quinta de Vaz Ferreira (1918), now hemmed in by suburban houses but once a larger estate where the philosopher Carlos Vaz Ferreira grew up as seemingly the only normal one among nine dysfunctional siblings. At the rear of the modern Farmacía Atahualpa (*Avda Millán 3701*) is the Pharmacy Museum (see page 141), founded in 1908 on the other side of the road.

To the west of Avenida Millán, Avenida Herrera leads swiftly to the northern gate of the Jardín Botánico (Botanic Garden; see page 140), although the main gate is to the south at Avenida 19 de Abril 1181; the River Plate, Montevideo Wanderers and Bella Vista soccer grounds are in this area too. Immediately beyond, you'll reach the Arroyo Miguelete and the Parque del Prado proper, famed for its Easter Week rodeo and cattle show, and for the Rosedal (Rose Garden), laid out in 1912 by the French garden designer Charles Racine. Turning left on to Avenida Delmira Agustín, on the south side of the arroyo, you'll pass the sculptural group of *Los Últimos Charrúas* [78 G1] by Edmundo Prati, Gervasio Furest Muñoz and Enrique Lussich (1938), commemorating the four sad Charrúa *indigenas* (plus a baby born in France) who were shipped off to Paris to be exhibited and never returned (see page 18). Beyond it at the Plaza del Policía (on Avenida Agraciada) is *La Diligencia* (The Stagecoach) [78 F1], another sculpture by José Belloni (1952). This is the Paso del Molino, once the only crossing of the Miguelete and a prestigious resort in the 19th century. There are plenty of buses back to the city centre on Avenida Agraciada, but it's also interesting to walk some way south, past the Mauresque ex-cinema at Agraciada 3759 and the very grand quintas at No 3567 (now a Salvation Army retirement home), Capurro 980 and Agraciada (now the naval hydrographic and meteorological service), Agraciada 3451 (headquarters of the army's First Division), No 3423, and No 3397–3401 (formerly the Argentine embassy).

EL CERRO On the far side of the harbour, west of the Prado and across Highway 1 to Colonia, rises the distinctive Cerro de Montevideo, the 139m-high mount that gave Montevideo its name. Uruguay's oldest lighthouse was built here by Spain in 1802, surrounded in 1809–11 (after the British invasions) by a fort, from which the flag of the United Provinces was first flown, in defiance of Spain. In the Battle of El Cerro in 1826, Uruguayan troops, led by Manuel Oribe, drove off Brazilian forces. In 1860–64 it was used to quarantine victims of yellow fever, and then decayed until it was restored in 1931–39 to become a military museum. Turning off Ruta 1 and then following Gracia parallel to the shore, turn right up Viacara through the run-down residential area and then left at a small Che Guevara monument to the *castillo*. It's possible to take a bus (line 76, 125, 128 or 195) and then walk up from Gracia, but most people prefer to take a taxi, which will wait while you admire the museum and the view. Known since 1882 as the Fortaleza General Artigas, it's staffed by friendly soldiers who will point out where the *Graf Spee* was scuttled, off Punta Yeguas.

Below the fortress to the southwest (beyond a newly refurbished stretch of rambla and the Playa Cerro bus terminal) lies the delightful Club de Golf del Cerro [78 A3], with its vintage clubhouse, founded in 1905 as the Chimont (Chicago–Montevideo), a nod to the home of the owners of the Frigórifico Montevideo. The Frigórifico Montevideo, known as the Frigórifico Swift from 1916, is the meat-packing plant immediately to the south on Punta de Lobos. Just to the west is the Frigórifico Nacional, also American-owned; both were closed by 1978. El Cerro grew up as a settlement of immigrants attracted by the jobs in the *frigórificos*, and the streets are named after their countries of origin, such as Poland, Portugal, France, England, Bulgaria and China.

THE EASTERN SUBURBS To the south of the Centro is the **Barrio Sur**, a poor residential district with many run-down Belle-Époque houses and a few Art Deco ones; this is the heart of the candombé culture, with comparsas often drumming in the streets on evenings and Sunday mornings (c11.00). The only tourist sight in the area, other than the stroll along the rambla past the formerly British gasworks, is the **Cementerio Central** [122 G4] (*Central Cemetery; Gonzalo Ramírez 1302;* ☼ *10.00–16.45 daily*), laid out in 1835. Its alleys are lined with grand tombs including those of the Pittamiglio family (on the way to the central chapel), Dr Washington Beltrán, a journalist and statesman (just inside the gate to the right) and President Claudio Williman (in a large grey tomb on the diagonal alley to the left from the gate). The Panteón Nacional (National Pantheon) holds the remains of major cultural figures such as Rodó, Figari, Benedetti et al (see pages 29–32). The cemetery is also enlivened by its population of parakeets.

To the east of Ejido, running south from the Palacio Municipal, is **Palermo**, similar but with patches of gentrification, and a few bars and restaurants along Avenida Gonzálo Ramírez; No 1497 (at Martínez Trueba; now the Edificio Montserrat) was the home of the novelist Juan Carlos Onetti (see page 30). On the rambla is the **US embassy** [95 E4], an early Brutalist design by I M Pei (1959–68), but not too fortress-like. Two streets were closed by bollards in the 1990s, but after constant complaints they were opened up again in 2007, although it's still not possible to pass through and underneath the building as Pei intended. To the east is the **Parque Rodó** district, around the 43ha of the same name, opened in 1901 and now named after the writer José Enrique Rodó, who died in 1917; there's a large monument to him (as well as statues of Confucius, Einstein and the playwright Florencio Sánchez), and a small castle by a lake that houses a children's library and is a venue for storytelling and puppet shows. On the east side of the park is the excellent **Museo Nacional de Artes Visuales** [95 F4] (see page 141). To the south is a funfair, and across the rambla is Playa Ramírez, the nearest beach to the city centre, popular for beach volleyball and soccer. Heading south, the rambla splits and passes either side of the open-air **Teatro del Verano (Summer Theatre)** [95 F4], venue of candombé and murga competitions during Carnaval.

The rambla swings around the Club de Golf del Uruguay, with various fishing clubs on the seaward side, as well as the Holocaust Memorial, to **Punta Carretas** [95 G6], the southernmost point of the city, jutting out into the River Plate. A dusty track leads south to the *faro* [95 G6] (*lighthouse; Punta Brava;* ☼ *24hrs; US$1*), built in 1876. The final steps are steep and awkward and not at all Health and Safety-compliant. It's not very high (20m), but gives nice views east and west. The whole headland is pleasantly informal, with people driving out to fish and drink maté. Not far north of the rambla, the Punta Carretas prison, which was notorious during the dictatorship for its treatment of political prisoners (over 100 of whom broke out in 1971) reopened in 1995 after a very successful conversion into the Punta Carretas Shopping mall. The surrounding area of Punta Carretas has also been transformed, from a somewhat gloomy area to a desirable suburb with fine bars and restaurants. It's also home to the Juan Zorrilla de San Martín Museum (see page 141), in the poet/diplomat's lovely Andalusian-style home, and the truly eccentric Castillo Pittamiglio (see page 141).

The upmarket Villa Biarritz and Punta Trouville residential areas lie along the rambla as it leads back northwards to **Pocitos**, a livelier district with plenty of shops, bars and restaurants (a block or three inland from the rambla), and plenty of streetlife in and around them. Apartments here are not cheap, but it's not an exclusive area, so it's popular with young professionals and families; it also has a decent beach, longer but less sheltered than Playa Ramírez. This is lined with an almost unbroken line of eight- to ten-storey apartment blocks, leading some to describe this as Montevideo's Copacabana. The main arteries leading inland (to Bulevar Artigas) are Bulevar España and Avenida Brasil, with some fine Art

Nouveau and Art Deco villas; the two blocks of Santiago Vásquez east of Brasil also have some fine old buildings, but otherwise Pocitos has been almost entirely rebuilt since the 1950s. At the junction of Avenida Brasil and Benito Blanco, the Edificio El Mástil is one of the city's major Art Deco buildings.

To the east of Pocitos (beyond the Naval Museum – see page 142) is the **Buceo** district [map page 109], with the World Trade Center, Yacht Club Uruguayo and the Puerto del Buceo, a small harbour for yachts, sport-fishing boats and tours out to the **Isla de Flores**, 30km to the east (and 12km offshore), a quarantine island for slaves and later for immigrants and for mail (which was sterilised in an autoclave), and in the 1930s a prison for intellectuals and others opposed to the dictatorship of Gabriel Terra. On the highest point of the island stands a stumpy, Portuguese-style lighthouse – many ships were wrecked on the Banco Ingles (English Bank, once known as the *tragabarcos* or ship-eater), just to the east, but the authorities in Buenos Aires refused to allow the construction of a lighthouse because it would have attracted trade to the rival port of Montevideo; eventually a cunning treaty recognised Brazilian ownership of Rio Grande do Sul state in exchange for Brazil building a lighthouse here in 1828. There are still the remains of the first- and second-class hotels (reminiscent of the opening of *Little Dorrit*), through which passed almost 58,000 immigrants between 1871 and 1891; later a narrow-gauge railway was built to reach the isolation unit at the end of the island. The lighthouse is closed, but the island can be visited, mainly by birdwatchers (in about October some areas are closed in deference to nesting gulls).

Buceo owes its name ('Diving') to the many colonial wrecks along this shore which are still being discovered by divers; just east of the harbour (above the mosque-like Zoological Museum – see page 142) is the Buceo cemetery, opened in 1835, and now stuffed with ornate marble tombs decorated with allegorical angels and many more sculptures by Belloni, José Luis de San Martín, and many leading Italian sculptors. Perhaps the most famous resident is the *blanco* warlord Aparicio Saravia, buried in 1904. Alongside is the British Cemetery, where many merchants and engineers lie, as well as victims of the world wars, including some killed in the Battle of the River Plate.

There's a succession of beaches, interspersed with rocky areas where cormorants and other birds feed, along the seafront of the quiet residential district of Malvín, before the Playa de los Ingleses and the minor protrusion of **Punta Gorda**, a more expensive suburb where people actually used to come for beach holidays from Montevideo. There's a pleasant viewpoint at the Plaza de la Armada (Navy Plaza, also known as Plaza Vergilio), with a monument to those lost at sea on naval duty (representing man struggling against the sea), which may have a *hornero* (ovenbird) nest inside it. Immediately to the east, at Mar Antártico 1227, is the house of the engineer–architect Eladio Dieste (see page 35), a typically modest structure built in 1961–63 and largely hidden behind a brick screen wall. Not far to the east (at Podesta 1421 and Larghero) is the house where Carlos Gardel planned to spend his retirement; it's now a centre for the disabled.

From here the rambla continues past more beaches and fishing clubs (with cheap fried-fish restaurants) to **Carrasco**, the most upmarket of Montevideo's suburbs long before the presence of the airport made it even more desirable. Its focal point is the massive Belle-Époque Hotel-Casino Carrasco, opened in 1922 (having been left half-built throughout World War I) and now awaiting a major refurbishment from Hyatt or some similar chain. Immediately west of it is a squash club, while a few blocks north on Avenida Arocena is the Carrasco Lawn Tennis Club, where Davis Cup matches are held. There's a 'villagey' feel to this section of Arocena,

Montevideo CITY TOUR

although restaurants such as Nuevo García and Dackel are very expensive. The most recent developments along the rambla are in the minimalist white-cube style of José Ignacio (not otherwise seen in Montevideo), but one of the finest Art Deco buildings in the city is the peach-coloured **Hotel Riviera**, eight blocks west of the casino at Rambla México 6095 and 6 de Abril, sadly now only a *centro de eventos* and tea room.

Just east of the casino, where Cartagena and Otero meet the rambla, the Carrasco Kite Center (*www.ckc.com.uy*) offers windsurfing and kite-surfing and has a nice bar over the beach, serving sushi, fish and pasta; another few blocks east the rambla passes the Escuela de Guerra Naval (Naval War School), with anti-aircraft guns and propellers mounted in front, facing the Playa Miramar. Immediately beyond is the Puente Carrasco, where the rambla crosses the Arroyo de Carrasco and leaves the city for Canelones department. Just north, Avenida Italia crosses the arroyo and splits, with Avenida Giannattasio continuing towards Punta del Este and Avenida de las Américas swinging left to the airport and Minas; both pass through the Parque Nacional Roosevelt, which is wholly planted with eucalyptus and of no conservation value. Nearby are the Bañados de Carrasco, wetlands with many waterbirds, though these are not currently safe to visit without a guide because of a number of illegal settlements.

MUSEUMS

CIUDAD VIEJA
Museo del Carnaval [122 A2] (*Carnival Museum; Rambla 25 de Agosto 218 & Maciel;* \ *2915 0807; www.museodelcarnaval.org;* ⊕ *11.00–17.00 Tue–Sun, closed 22–25 Dec, 29 Dec–1 Jan, 6 Jan; US$3.50, free Tue*) Expanded in 2010, this is one of the best-presented museums in Uruguay, with great examples of carnival costumes, masks and drums, coupled with detailed information on the origins and history of the event.

Museo de Arte Precolombino y Indígena (MAPI) [122 B2] (*Museum of pre-Colombian and Indigenous Art; 25 de Mayo 279;* \ *2916 9360; www.mapi.org. uy;* ⊕ *11.30–17.30 Mon–Fri, 10.00–16.00 Sat; US$3.50*) One of the most exciting museum projects now under way in Montevideo, this opened in 2004 to show the refurbishment work in progress and a small portion of its collection. A palace built for the hugely ambitious Emilio Reus, director of the Banco Nacional, it was intended to be the Establicimiento Médico Hidro Termo Terápico. However, Reus died in 1891 at just 33, impoverished and broken by the banking crisis of 1890, and the building was used by a bank, then various government ministries, before being handed to the city in 2003. To the rear of the atrium, the main hall was a hot pool (with a proscenium stage). Currently the ground-floor exhibition is not huge, with *rompacabezas* (clubs) and spear- and arrowheads from the Cuenca del Plata (River Plate basin), *zoolitos* (animal-shaped carved stones) from Rocha, and other archaeological pieces from the Diaguita and Condorhuasi cultures of northwestern Argentina, and the Maya, Moche and Inca cultures. Upstairs there's a collection of Latin American musical instruments, a photography room, and temporary shows provided by other institutions. On the top floor you can walk around the gallery but nothing else is open.

Museo de Artes Decorativas (Palacio Taranco) [122 B2] (*Museum of Decorative Arts; 25 de Mayo 376;* \ *2915 6080;* ⊕ *12.30–18.00 Mon–Fri; free*) On

the site of the city's first theatre, La Casa de Comedias (1793), the mansion of the Ortiz de Taranco family was built in 1908–10 in the Historical Eclectic style by the French architects Charles Louis Girault and Jules León Chifflot, also responsible for the Petit Palais in Paris and the French embassy in Vienna. The Prince of Wales (later King Edward VIII) stayed here in 1925; the Acta de Montevideo, a treaty between Argentina, Chile and the Vatican to settle Argentine–Chilean frontier disputes, was signed here in 1979 and ratified in 1987 in the presence of Pope John Paul II. Beautifully kept, its fine furnishings and paintings now form the Museum of Decorative Arts.

The grand entrance leads to a Louis XV interior with Palladian loggias opening on to a small garden (sometimes open). There are paintings by the Spanish painters Sorolla y Bastida (1863–1923), Mariano Barbasán (1864–1924) – who worked, appropriately enough, in the Barbizon style – and Narciso Díaz de la Peña (1807–90), while Uruguayan art is represented by Juan Manuel Blanes. There are three pianos on the ground floor (one a Pleyel, transferred from the presidential residence in 2005). In the dining room are seven specially woven Aubusson tapestries and two lovely Art Nouveau vases.

At the top of the stairs (with their Art Nouveau banisters) is a painting of San Roque by José Ribera (1588–1656) and a portrait by Sorolla y Bastida of Señora de Signorini (1887); otherwise the upper floor is much less ornate than the ground floor, with a pair of Edmundo Prati busts in the library, some fine marble fireplaces and parquet flooring. Staff tend to keep the upper floor closed, but it's worth a look if you can persuade them to allow you upstairs. In the basement is a classical collection of Greek (and Iranian) pots, glass and bronzes.

Museo Histórico Nacional (Casa de Rivera) [122 C2] (*National Historical Museum; Rincón 437 & Misiones;* \ *2915 1051; www.museohn.org.uy;* ⊕ *11.00–16.45 Mon–Fri; free*) Once the home of Uruguay's first president, this is now the museum's main branch, with a collection ranging from pre-Columbian stone weapons and ceramics to portraits of colonial and independence-era figures, as well as Lavalleja's armchair, Admiral William Brown's (creator of the Argentine navy; 1777–1857) bureau and barometer, and a leather chair owned by both Artigas and Juan Zorrilla de San Martín. You'll learn something of the country's history, but it's best to have some previous knowledge, or to refer regularly to this book's history section.

Museo Romántico [122 C2] (*25 de Mayo 428;* \ *2915 5361; www.mhn.gub.uy;* ⊕ *11.30–16.45 Tue–Fri; free*) A two-storey patrician home known as the Casa Montero, this was built in 1782 for Bernardo de la Torre (who had his shop on the ground floor) and taken over in 1831 by Antonio Montero, who made it one of the most luxurious homes in the city. In 1896 the first cinema in Uruguay was set up here in the Salón Rouge. In 1962 it became part of the National Historical Museum, displaying patrician living quarters of the second half of the 19th century.

The rooms open to the public are upstairs, around the attractive patio with its unusual octagonal balcony and classical marble statues and basin. There are portraits by Juan Manuel Blanes and the little-known but very decent Cayetano Gallino; the dining room has late 19th-century furnishings including the table and chairs of Alfredo Vásquez Acevedo (1844–1923), politician and Rector of the University of the Republic, and the silverware used by his son Jacobo Varela Acevedo (1876–1962) when he was ambassador to the USA. Elsewhere are six portraits by the French-born Amadeo Gras (1805–71), with fans and other accessories, the dress worn by Ninon Vallin (1886–1961) as Massenet's Manon (on tour with Caruso), an

Egyptian-style desk and bureau owned by two presidents, the bedroom furniture of President Maximo Santos (1847–89) and other furniture owned by his bitter rival Julio Herrera y Obes (1841–1912). This museum may be temporarily closed.

Casa Garibaldi [122 B2] (*25 de Mayo 314;* ⊕ *11.00–17.00 Mon–Fri; free*) Giuseppe Garibaldi (1807–82), exiled from Italy because of his revolutionary activities, lived in this house from 1841; the following year he married his Brazilian lover Anita Ribeiro da Silva, and they had four children by 1847. Initially working as a maths teacher and commercial agent, in 1842 he was placed in command of the Uruguayan fleet and raised an 'Italian Legion' to support Rivera's Colorado government against Oribe's Blancos, backed by the Argentina dictator Juan Manuel de Rosas. He and his men wore gaucho ponchos and sombreros, with the red shirts that later became their trademark when they fought for Italian independence. Developing guerrilla tactics on land and sea, he was very successful in harrying the Oribist forces; his capture of Colonia, Isla Martín García and Gualeguaychú in 1845 opened up the Río Uruguay, and in 1846 he defeated Oribe twice near Salto. However, in 1848, the year of revolutions in Europe, he led his Italian Legion to fight for the freedom of their homeland.

The house was built in 1830 around two patios hung with vines; the Garibaldis lived to the right of the entry to the first patio, with a small kitchen to the rear (opening on to the second patio). It became a museum in 1957. There's a display of documents, garments, medals and engravings evoking Garibaldi's heroic career. This museum may be temporarily closed.

Museo Figari [122 C2] (*J C Gómez 1427;* ☎ *2915 7065/7265;* e *museofigari@mec. gub.uy; www.museofigari.blogspot.com;* ⊕ *13.00–18.00 Tue–Fri, 10.00–14.00 Sat; free*) In a 1914 Belle-Époque structure, this new museum currently displays 14 of Pedro Figari's deceptively amateurish paintings (see page 32) and temporary shows of contemporary art on the ground floor only; the two upper floors are still being renovated.

Museo de las Migraciones (MUMI) [122 C1] (*Museum of Migrations; Mitre 1550 & Piedras;* ☎ *1950 1777;* e *museomigraciones@gmail.com; http://mumi.montevideo. gub.uy;* ⊕ *12.00–18.00 Mon–Fri; free*) Part of the Open Wall Cultural Centre, you'll see temporary art exhibits before passing through a post-industrial basement and out to an 80m-long stretch of the old city wall, only excavated in 2008.

Espacio Cultural Al Pie de la Muralla [122 C2] (*'At the Foot of the Wall' Cultural Space; Mitre 1464;* ☎ *2915 9343; www.alpiedelamuralla.com;* ⊕ *09.00– 17.00 Mon–Fri, 11.00–16.00 Sat; free*) Also backing onto the old city wall, this is a cultural centre, putting on educational and artistic events; on the first Saturday of the month, their De Cubo a Cubo walking tour tracing the lost fortifications, with actors, is recommended (*1½hrs; US$25; book on* ☎ *2915 9343;* e *alpiedelamuralla@ adinet.com.uy*).

Museo Gurvich [122 C2] (*Ituzaingó 1377;* ☎ *2915 7826; www.museogurvich.org;* ⊕ *10.00–18.00 Mon–Fri, 11.00–15.00 Sat; US$3.50, free Tue*) Next to the cathedral on Plaza Constitución, this building has seen a good modern internal conversion to house a small art shop and coffee shop as well as display space for José Gurvich's paintings (see page 33). Upstairs there's also a changing display of works by his teacher Joaquín Torres García and other pupils.

Cabildo [122 D2] (*Old City Hall; J C Gómez 1362, Plaza Constitución;* ✆ 2915 9685; e *museocabildo@correo.imm.gub.uy;* ⏰ *12.30–17.30 Tue–Fri & Sun, 11.30– 16.30 Sat; free*) In the two courtyards of this fine colonial edifice are displays on colonial shipbuilding and the like; upstairs (passing a statue of Artigas by José Luis Zorrilla de San Martín halfway up), you'll find a great display of historical maps and prints (some by English artists William Heath and Edward Burney, and by Conrad Martens, who came here to join the *Beagle* as official artist) to the right, together with pistols and rifles and replicas of *peinetones*, the elaborate 18th-century women's headdresses. There's also a *Mater Dolorosa* brought from the Canary Islands with the first settlers. On the other side are the Assembly Room (with fairly antique furniture) and a long tiled gallery with furniture, chandeliers and some very miscellaneous paintings.

Museo Joaquín Torres García [122 D2] (*Sarandí 683;* ✆ *2916 2663; www. torresgarcia.org.uy;* ⏰ *09.30–19.30 Mon–Fri, 10.00–18.00 Sat; US$3*) Another good modern conversion, preserving the fine staircase. There's an art shop and bookshop downstairs (with some of Torres García's wooden toys, and a colour catalogue in English for just US$10). On the first floor there's a good video and biographical information, and some of his works up to the 1930s (similar to Mondrian and van Doesburg but never quite as good). The second floor shows the development of Universal Constructivism, in works that are more individual and more interesting. Outside, high above the junction of Sarandí and Bacacay, is a reproduction of his mural, *Pax in Lucem*.

THE CENTRO

Museo Numismático [122 D1] (*Numismatic Museum; Florida & 25 de Mayo;* ⏰ *10.00–16.00 Mon–Fri; free*) In the ugly Banco Central tower (sign in and leave ID at the downstairs entry) there's a display of Uruguayan money (from the first coins, issued in 1840), with banknotes from before and after the reform of 1975, when P1,000 became P1. There's also a collection of notes from Africa and elsewhere, and on the mezzanine an amusing collection of piggybanks and a display on the destruction of old notes.

Museo de la Casa de Gobierno [122 D2] (*Museum of the House of Government; Edificio Independencia, Plaza Independencia;* ⏰ *10.00–17.00 Mon–Fri; free*) In the former seat of government (to 1985), there's now a display on the nation's presidents. It's well presented, starting with Fructuoso Rivera's coach on the first-floor landing, and continuing with lots of swords, medals, busts, portraits and death masks, not forgetting Venancio Flores's stuffed dog, but it doesn't provide much historical narrative. There's no need for ID, but you will have to leave any bags at the entrance.

Museo Militar [122 F3] (*Military Museum; Soriano 1090 & Paraguay;* ⏰ *10.00–16.00 Tue–Fri; free*) The former Italian hospital was built in 1858, to an Italian Renaissance design, but when the money ran out it was given to the army, serving as a military hospital (1865–70) and then offering university courses for women; it became the Military Museum in 1981. The main patio is now the Sala de Uniformología, displaying figures in historic uniforms; other rooms show prehistoric arrowheads, displays on Artigas and his campaigns, the Guerra Grande of 1843–51, the War of the Triple Alliance of 1865–69, and finally a room on peace-keeping – Uruguay had around 2,000 troops each in Mozambique and Angola in the 1990s, and more recently 1,000 or so in the Democratic Republic of Congo and in Haiti. Uruguay contributes more troops to the UN per head of population than any other country.

There are also military museums at El Cerro (see page 131) and in the forts of Santa Teresa and San Miguel in Rocha (see pages 269 and 272).

Museo Pedagógico [122 F2] (*Museum of Education; Plaza Cagancha 1175;* \ *2902 0915; www.crnti.edu.uy/museo;* ⊕ *16 Dec–14 Mar 08.30–13.30 Mon–Fri, English group visits 17.30 Thu; rest of the year 09.00–19.00 Mon–Fri; free*) Bigger and (slightly) better than you might expect, this museum displays lots of old teaching aids, especially for the sciences, as well as a *gorro de burro* (dunce's hat with donkey ears). It also looks at the history of education in Uruguay from the opening of the first free school in Montevideo in 1809, with emphasis on the reforms of José Pedro Varela in the 1870s and 1880s, when teacher training was introduced for the first time, and compulsory, free and secular primary education laid the foundations for a democratic modern society.

Museos del Gaucho y de la Moneda [122 E2] (*Museums of the Gaucho and the Mint; 18 de Julio 998 & Herrera y Obes;* \ *2900 8764; www.brounet.com.uy;* ⊕ *10.00–17.00 Mon–Fri; free*) In the Palacio Heber, built in 1896–97 by the French architect Alfred Massüe and now owned by the Banco de la República, these two museums share a delight in silver – the Museo de la Moneda has a very dated display (in Spanish only) of money, including ancient Chinese bronze 'coins', colonial gold pieces, the first Uruguayan coins from 1840 (in copper, then later silver) and notes from 1887, as well as commemorative medals. Upstairs, the Gaucho Museum displays silver maté gourds and *cuchillos* (knives), massive carved bulls' horns, stone bolas wrapped in leather (a small one held in the hand and two larger ones), lassos, branding irons, pistols, spurs and stirrups, men's and women's costumes, and a row of five full-size model horses in harness – a pretty good collection, although not very well displayed. In addition, the Espacio Cultural Banco República shows temporary art exhibitions.

SUBTE – Centro Municipal de Exposiciones [122 E2] (*Municipal Exhibition Centre; under Plaza Fabini;* \ *2908 7643; www.subte.montevideo.gub.uy;* ⊕ *11.00–21.00 Tue–Sun; free*) A municipal space for changing art exhibitions, often with a political or avant-garde tinge.

Museo del Azulejo [122 G2] (*Museum of Decorative Tiles; Yí 1444;* \ *2709 6352;* e *museodelazulejo@adinet.com.uy;* ⊕ *12.00–18.00 Tue–Sun; free*) A collection of over 4,000 tiles, the great majority made in Desvres in northern France between 1840 and 1900. There are also a few colonial Spanish tiles, some very basic hand-painted 19th-century tiles from Maldonado, and 20th-century European tiles, as well as many photos of church domes and bars – almost every major Uruguayan church has a tiled dome.

Museo de Historía del Arte (Muhar) [122 G2] (*Museum of the History of Art; Ejido 1326;* \ *2908 9252;* ⊕ *12.00–17.30 Tue–Sun (mid-Dec–mid-Mar 13.30–19.00 Tue–Sun); free*) In the corner of the City Hall, this large collection contains a few original pieces but is mostly plaster replicas of great works of art (mainly sculptures, as well as ceramics and jewellery) from all the world's ancient cultures, a very refreshing antidote to a Eurocentric view of culture. Near the entrance you'll see copies of the *Winged Victory of Samothrace*, Donatello's *St George* and *David* and a Della Robbia majolica, among others; one floor below you'll see copies of Greek sculptures such as the *Apollo Belvedere*, rather fewer Roman ones, a Khmer Buddha, Persian, Hittite, Assyrian and Egyptian carvings, and an authentic 3rd-century Gandhara Buddha. In the lower level are replicas from Meso-American cultures, such as a basalt Aztec calendar; ceramics, gold and crystal heads from pre-Columbian Mexico; original 8th- to 12th-century pieces from Costa Rica including a jaguar *metate* and gold votive jewellery; Mayan ceramics and jade; ceramics and stone from pre-Incan Peru, Bolivia, Ecuador and northwestern Argentina, authentic Uruguayan shaped stones, 12,000–9,000 years old (and bird-shaped ones 3,300–2,200 years old), as well as pottery from the litoral of the Río Uruguay that's 4,500–2,500 years old. It's all well displayed, with quite a bit of information, all in Spanish.

Museo de Arte Contempóraneo (MAC) [122 E2] (*Museum of Contemporary Art; 18 de Julio 965, 2nd Flr;* ✎ *2900 6662;* ⏲ *14.00–18.30 Mon, 14.00–20.00 Tue–Sat; free*) A small space, putting on temporary shows with a few pieces of contemporary Uruguayan art on permanent display at the rear.

Museo del Automóvil Club del Uruguay [122 G2] (*Museum of the Automobile Club of Uruguay; Colonia 1251 & Yí, 6th Flr;* ✎ *2902 4792; www.acu.com.uy/museo;* ⏲ *14.00–19.00 Tue–Sun; free*) At the rear of the ACU petrol station, take the lift by the offices to the sixth floor, where you'll see a fine collection of vintage cars, starting with a Belgian Delin manufactured in 1899, the oldest car in Uruguay, and a pair of Clement Bayard and De Dion Boutons from 1904, and others including a 1923 Model T Ford, three Model A Fords, Armstrong Siddeleys from 1948 and 1950, a 1955 Renault Frégate, various Packards, Cadillacs and Chevrolets from the 1950s and 1960s (with jet fighters on the bonnet), a Ferrari and an E-Type Jaguar. You'll also see the trophies won by Hector Suppici Sedes, the Uruguayan racing driver killed in a crash in Chile in 1948.

Museo UTE [122 E2] (*Museum of the State Electrical Company; Herrera y Obes 1322, just south of Plaza Fabini;* ✎ *2908 5262;* ⏲ *09.00–15.00 Mon–Fri; free*) The museum of Usinas y Transmisiones Electricos (formerly Usinas y Telefonos del Estado, State Power Stations and Telephones) has a small but well-displayed collection of vintage ammeters and other gear, as well as information on the first electric lighting in Montevideo (in 1886) and later hydro-electric schemes. There's not much to it, but it's something to see on a Monday.

NORTHERN MONTEVIDEO
Museo de las Telecomunicaciones [94 C1] (*Museum of Telecommunications; Guatemala 2097 & Paraguay;* ✎ *2928 4124;* ⏲ *09.00–18.00 Mon–Fri; free*) If you're visiting the viewpoint in Montevideo's highest building you might as well pop in to this small collection of old phones, including the first magnetic cardphones in Uruguay (1988) and the first mobile telephone (cellphone; 1991). A couple of rescued murals by Joaquín Torres García (done in 1944 for the Hospital St-Bois in Colón, in Montevideo's northern suburbs) are also here, with another in the reception area of the main tower.

Museo del Fútbol [95 G1] (*Museum of Football; Avda Ricaldoni s/n, Parque Batlle y Ordóñez;* ✎ *2480 1258; www.estadiocentenario.com.uy;* ⏲ *10.00–17.00 Mon–Fri; US$4*) This museum, in the Estadio Centenario, by the tower opposite the Medical

Faculty, is a couple of minutes' walk from the bus stops on Avenida Italia (and even closer to the Bus Turístico).

A fine film (made for FIFA by a British team in 2004, with a good tango soundtrack) covers the achievements of the Uruguayan soccer team at the Olympics (their matches in the 1928 Amsterdam games were relayed by telegram and loudspeakers to huge crowds in Plaza Independencia) and then the first World Cup in 1930 (with clips of very bad colour film). The architect Juan Scasso only had eight months to build this stadium, the first built specifically for soccer, and in fact the first game of the first World Cup had to be played at the Pocitos stadium.

There's a display on José Leandro Andrade, the 'black marvel' of the 1930 team, the only Uruguayan player in FIFA's Hall of Champions of the greatest players of the 20th century (announced in 2000), on the basis that he was the game's first iconic figure (he also led a comparsa of candombé drummers, although that's not mentioned here). There's also material on Obdulio Varela of Albion FC, captain of the 1950 team; general Olympic mementoes, a photo of Westminster School cloisters (the 'cradle of football'!), Maradona's shirt, and new exhibits on Uruguay's *anni mirabili* 2010/11, when they made a huge impact in both the World Cup and the Copa América; in addition to the permanent museum there are also temporary exhibits.

Espacio de Arte Contemporáneo [94 D1] (*Contemporary Art Space; Arenal Grande 1930;* \ *2929 2066; www.eac.gub.uy;* ⊕ *14.00–20.00 Wed–Sat; Dec–Feb 15.00–21.00 Wed–Sat, 11.00–17.00 Sun, not hols; free*) This abandoned prison is gradually being opened up as exhibition space, although a glass wall offers a view onto an unrenovated area; there's a guided visit at 17.00 on Saturdays. It will eventually contain a cinema, restaurant and artist spaces; there's already a great variety of exhibitions, many from Spanish regional museums.

Museo Municipal de Bellas Artes Juan Manuel Blanes [78 G1] (*Juan Manuel Blanes Municipal Museum of Fine Arts; Avda Millán 4015, Prado;* \ *2336 2248; www.museoblanes.org.uy;* ⊕ *12.15–17.45 Tue–Sun; free*) A typical quinta with beautiful gardens (as well as the Japanese Garden to the rear – see page 130), this doesn't contain a great deal of art, taking at most half an hour to visit. There's one gallery dedicated to the pretty academic paintings of Juan Manuel Blanes, some of them enormous, including a ceiling mural of the *Eternal Father and Four Evangelists* (c1884). The collection also includes oils and drawings by Pedro Figari and works by Pedro Blanes Viale, Rafael Barradas, Raúl Cabrera and other Uruguayan artists, which may not be on display, depending on what temporary shows are on.

Jardín y Museo Botánico [78 G1] (*Botanic Garden & Museum; Avda 19 de Abril 1181, Prado;* \ *2336 4005; www.montevideo.gub.uy/ciudad/paseos/jardin-botanico;* ⊕ *07.00–19.00 daily; free*) The Botanic Garden was founded in 1902 and is laid out on either side of an imaginary Equator, with northern hemisphere flora to the north, and southern to the south, in theory – there are actually eucalyptus trees to the north, and a nice avenue of oaks to the south. In any case it's a delightful, well-tended garden, with over 1,000 species planted in its 13ha, and most plants are decently labelled; there are also plenty of parakeets and other birds. Opposite the south gate is the Botanic Museum (⊕ *09.00–17.00 Mon–Fri; free*), with samples of rocks and minerals, slices of tree trunks and displays on recognising seeds and basic flower parts.

Museo de la Farmacia [78 G1] (*Pharmacy Museum; Avda Millán 3701, Barrio Atahualpa;* ↘ *2336 3534;* ⏱ *08.00–21.00 Mon–Fri, 08.00–14.00 Sat; free*) At the rear of the modern Farmacia Atahualpa are the cabinets, bottles, emulsifier, autoclave and mortars of the original pharmacy, as well as old advertisements and photos, and an interactive multi-lingual touch-screen.

Museo de la Memoria (MUME) [78 C1] (*Museum of Memory; Avda de las Instrucciones 1057;* ↘ *2355 5449/50; http://museodelamemoria.org.uy;* ⏱ *12.00–18.00 Mon–Sat; mid-Dec–mid-Mar 13.00–19.00 Mon–Sat; free*) The Quinta de Santos, the country house of the 19th-century dictator Máximo Santos, is a fitting home for this memorial to the victims of the military dictatorship of 1973–85; the permanent collection is in six sections covering Assassinations and Forced Disappearances, The Installation of the Dictatorship, Popular Resistance, The Cells, Return to Democracy, and Exile. There are also a variety of temporary exhibitions, usually artistic, and events. The guided visit at 16.00 Monday–Saturday (free) is well worthwhile.

And finally On your way out to the wineries, it's worth mentioning the project to create a museum in the **Peñarol railway works**, founded in 1890 by a British company, and by 1910 the largest industrial site in Uruguay. At the moment it's only open 14.00–19.00 on Saturdays, or by reservation on m 099 038219.

EASTERN MONTEVIDEO
Museo Nacional de Artes Visuales [95 F4] (*National Museum of Visual Arts; Julio Herrera y Reissig s/n;* ↘ *2711 6054/6124; www.mnav.gub.uy;* ⏱ *14.00–19.00 Tue–Sun; free*) It's always worth checking out the shows at this museum, also known as the Museo Parque Rodó. The first room houses 11 portraits by Juan Manuel Blanes, not especially good but he does at least show ugly people without prettification. The main spaces house temporary shows which may include works by Joaquín Torres García, Cúneo, Sáez, the brothers Nerses and Ohannes Ounanian, and Europeans such as Delaunay, Arp, Chagall, Klee, Balla, Picasso, Braque, Léger, Gris, Cézanne, Manet, Delacroix and Daumier – although these are usually in store. Modern sculptures stand in the gardens (including one by Joaquín Torres García) and in the central strip of the road outside.

Museo de Juan Zorrilla de San Martín [95 G6] (*J L Zorrilla de San Martín 96;* ↘ *2710 1818;* ⏱ *14.00–19.00 Tue–Sun; free*) The poet and diplomat Juan Zorrilla de San Martín had this white Andalusian-style villa built in 1904, set in peaceful gardens with fountains, and expanded in 1921. Now there's also a café, a shop and an air-conditioned modern display room. The ground floor is open as a museum, with his personal effects and furnishings, including the contents of the room in the Ciudad Vieja in which he died. You'll also see his private oratory – he was strongly Roman Catholic, fathering 13 children and negotiating with Rome to have an archbishopric in Montevideo. Zorrilla de San Martín was a traditional patrician, filling his house with Spanish paintings, but as a poet he created Uruguay's 'national myth' and established the country's Latin American identity.

Castillo Pittamiglio [95 H5] (*Rambla Gandhi 633, Pocitos;* ↘ *2710 1089;* e *espaciocultural.pittamiglio@gmail.com; www.castillopittamiglio.com;* ⏱ *only for guided visits 17.00 Tue & Thu, 17.30 (summer 19.00) Sat–Sun; US$4*) The most eccentric building in Montevideo, built in 1933 by the architect and alchemist

Humberto Pittamiglio (1887–1976), is now occupied by the Uruguayan Association of Private Property Developers, who allow tours and events after working hours. Pittamiglio left the Castillo to the city when he died, but his 150,000 books, Murano chandeliers and mirrors, and other furnishings had all vanished by the time the city took possession.

Entering from the rambla (which didn't exist when the house was built – the original entry is now part of the Montecristo Restaurant, to the north at Francisco Vidal 638), you go upstairs to a reception room, then up a narrow staircase to the reading room, with a fireplace of walnut (the alchemist's wood) and a mandala; around it are claustrophobic passages, offering alternative routes through the house. The décor is mostly wood, with elements of Art Nouveau and Arts and Crafts styles; but you'll see various symbols portraying aspects of man's journey to understanding and the transformation of metals and of society. The original unrestored bathroom is worth a look before you go out to the internal terrace, below the Tuscan-style tower, where you'll see a beautiful relief of the goddess Diana with a hound. Overlooking the entrance and the beach is a circular room below the ship's prow and replica of the *Winged Victory of Samothrace* that will have caught your attention from the rambla. Beneath is a circular room with a square in a circle in the ceiling, and a Templar cross hidden under the table, the room with the most energy in the building.

Museo del Arma de Ingenieros [map page 109] (*Museum of Military Engineering; Aduana de Oribe, Rambla Armenia 3975 & Riveros;* \ *2622 1480; www. ingenierosmilitares.org.uy;* ⊕ *14.00–17.00 Sat–Sun; free*) In an old brick building on the rambla west of the Zoological Museum, this displays the usual rifles and so on plus tools and models of fortifications, and also more contemporary displays on de-mining, for instance.

Museo Zoológico [map page 109] (*Zoological Museum; Rambla República de Chile 4215;* \ *2622 0258;* ⊕ *10.00–16.00 Tue–Sun; free*) This mosque-like building was constructed in 1930–33 as the Café Morisco, but this soon failed and the building was used as an oceanographic station, and then from 1956 as the Zoological Museum. It's in good condition, but the tower (or minaret) is not open. The left-hand side of the building is full of stuffed birds, almost all Uruguayan and reasonably well labelled; to the right are mammals and other types of animals.

Museo Naval [map page 109] (*Naval Museum; Rambla Charles de Gaulle & Avda Herrera;* \ *2622 1084;* e *museonaval@adinet.com.uy;* ⊕ *08.00–12.00, 14.00–18.00 Fri–Wed; US$3*) At the terminal of bus routes 116 and 185 (to Pocitos), the naval museum has dated displays of which only those on the Battle of the River Plate are likely to interest tourists. There are maps and photos, a uniform from the *Graf Spee* and the dress uniform of Admiral Sir Henry Harwood, then a commodore in command of the British ships. One of the *Graf Spee's* secondary 150mm guns was placed outside the museum in 1997, along with torpedos, anchors and other guns. Inside there's a 24-pounder cannon from HMS *Agammenon*, which sank off Punta del Este in 1812. There are also displays on the *Capitán Miranda*, a three-masted schooner that sails around the world with naval cadets and samples of Uruguayan foodstuffs and wines, and on the 1993–94 Around the World race which stopped in Punta del Este both outbound and inbound.

4

Southern Uruguay

The area around Montevideo is densely populated by Uruguayan standards, but will seem fairly empty to most tourists, apart from the semi-continuous strip of resorts along the coast, especially to the east of Montevideo. Closest to Montevideo is Canelones department, with fairly small mixed farms (producing vegetables for the capital), rather than the huge estancias further into the country's interior, and with small vineyards that produce the bulk of the country's wine. To the north and west are Florida and San José departments, largely given over to dairy farming, and to the northeast (inland from Maldonado department, covered in *Chapter 5*) is Lavalleja department, whose capital, Minas, is an easy excursion from Montevideo, although the further parts of the department are clearly part of the interior.

CANELONES DEPARTMENT: WEST

The department of Canelones (named not after a type of Italian pasta but after the *canelon* tree) is also known as the *comuna canaria*, many of its earliest settlers having come from the Canary Islands. Later it attracted Spanish and Italian immigrants, very religious by Uruguayan standards, especially to the area known as El Santoral in the centre of the department, where many of the villages are named after saints. The department has 65km of coastline, most of it east of the capital, and over 160 vineyards and wineries. The main road through the department is Ruta 5, heading north from Montevideo to Durazno, Tacuarembó and Rivera; starting at the port as Rambla 25 de Agosto, it's a good dual carriageway that passes El Cerro, splits from Ruta 1 (which leads west to Colonia) at km7, meets the new Ruta 102 to the airport at km17, and passes junctions to the small towns of Las Piedras, La Paz and Progreso at km19½, km20 and km26½. The new Museo de la Uva y del Vino (*Grape and Wine Museum;* \ *2365 7633;* e *museo.uvavino@imcanelones.gub.uy;* ⏰ *10.30– 17.00 Mon–Fri, w/ends by appointment*) – is in the Parque Tecnológico Canario, on Ruta 67 at Elías Regules in Las Piedras, and is bypassed by almost all tourists. At km37½ you'll pass the Bodega Juanicó, perhaps the country's best-known winery (see page 160), and at km43 the dual carriageway ends at the junction to the town of Canelones, 45km from Montevideo.

CANELONES The town of Canelones is fairly nondescript but pleasant enough to visit. It was founded in 1774 as Villa Nuestra Señora de Guadalupe. Here the first independent government of the Banda Oriental was set up in 1813, and the Uruguayan flag was unfurled for the first time in 1829 (with more stripes than the current version). There's nowhere to stay, although this would make a logical base for winery tours.

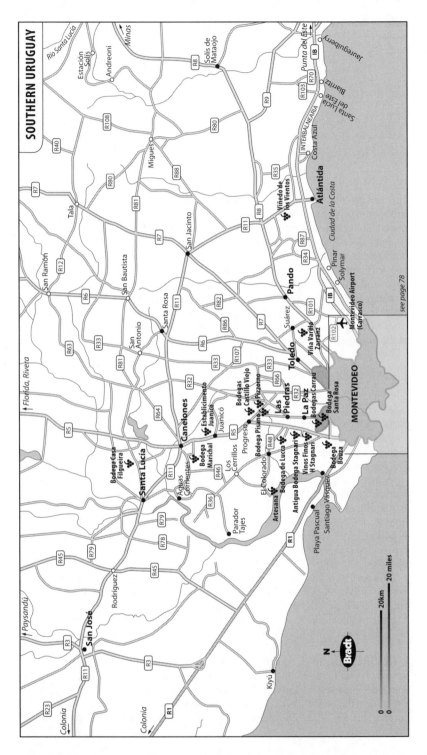

SOUTHERN URUGUAY

Río Santa Lucía
Estación Solís
Solís
Andreoni
Minas
R8
Solís de Mataojo
R40
R108
R80
R9
Punta del Este
R70
R103
Santa Lucía del Este
Biarritz
Jaureguiberry
IB
Costa Azul
INTERBALNEARIA
R88
Atlántida
Ciudad de la Costa
Migues
R7
R81
R80
R35
Viñedo de los Vientos
Tala
R8
R11
Pinar
R87
Solymar
R12
San Ramón
San Bautista
San Jacinto
R34
IB
Montevideo Airport (Carrasco)
R6
Santa Rosa
R11
R82
Pando
R7
Suárez
R101
R102
San Antonio
R63
R33
R81
R6
R86
R107
R33
Toledo
Viña Varela Zárraz
Florida, Rivera
R5
R64
R32
R33
R66
Bodegas Castillo Viejo
Pizzorno
R32
Las Piedras
La Paz
Bodegas Carrau
Bodega Santa Rosa
Establecimiento Juanicó
Canelones
Juanicó
Progreso
Bodega Pisano
MONTEVIDEO
Bodega Casa Filgueira
Bodega Marichal
R5
Cerrillos
El Colorado
R48
Vinos Finos H Stagnari
Bodega Bouza
Santa Lucía
Aguas Corrientes
R11
Los Cerrillos
R46
Bodega de Lucca
Bodega Stagnari
see page 78
R36
Parador Tajes
Artesana
Antigua Bodega Stagnari
Santiago Vázquez
Paysandú
R79
Playa Pascual
R45
R79
R78
Rodríguez
R45
R1
San José
R3
R11
R3
Kiyú
Colonia
R23
R3
R1
Colonia

N
Bradt

0 ____ 20km
0 ____ 20 miles

144

Getting there and away Frequent **buses** from Montevideo (Tres Cruces) and elsewhere leave you at the Plaza 18 de Julio, where the cathedral stands on the south side, a standard neoclassical building with blue and white *azulejos* on the exterior of its dome, and a clean blue and white interior too. You'll also notice the bishopric on the west side of the plaza, and the huge Monument to the Flag in the centre.

The COPSA bus company (for Montevideo, Santa Lucía, Atlántida and Costa Azul) has an office a block south of the plaza (*Batlle y Ordóñez;* \ *4332 2379;* ⊕ *06.00–20.30 Mon–Fri, 06.00–13.00 Sat*), although you should buy tickets on the bus. CITA (for Montevideo, Santa Lucía, San José and Florida) has an office on the west side of the plaza (*Batlle y Ordóñez 559;* \ *4332 3001;* ⊕ *06.45–21.00 Mon–Fri, 06.45–14.15, 15.30–21.00 Sat, 17.30–21.00 Sun*). Both companies have buses roughly every half-hour to Montevideo (both Tres Cruces and Baltasar Brum terminals); three Turil buses a day to Durazno, Tacuarembó and Rivera also call here (*Rodó 373;* \ *4332 3001*). Zeballos Hermanos (*6 blocks north of the plaza at Batlle y Ordóñez 913;* \ *4332 3318*) go to Aguas Corrientes (direct or via Los Cerrillos) a dozen times a day (seven on Sunday), and to Atlántida five times a day (*3 on Sun*).

Tourist information The tourist information centre (*Avda Martínez Monegal & Héctor Miranda;* \ *4332 3457/2286; www.canelonesturismo.gub.uy;* ⊕ *08.00–19.00 daily*) is five blocks east of the plaza at Monegal and Ruta 11, just west of the junction with Ruta 5.

✗ Where to eat Perhaps the best places to eat are the **Old Cat Pizzería-Chivitería** (**$$**), opposite the COPSA office at Batlle y Ordóñez 499, and the **Preta pub-restaurant** (**$$**), on the east side of the plaza at Treinta y Tres 222, serving pizza, parrilla, chivitos and quesadillas.

Other practicalities On the north side of the plaza you'll find the post office, Antel and the Banco República; there are other ATMs on the west side and the southeast corner of the plaza. The new Comeca (Co-operativa Medica de Canelones) hospital is south of the centre at Treinta y Tres 127 (\ *4332 2250*). The public hospital is on a small plaza seven blocks north of the centre at Calle Cendan, just north of the Ta-Ta supermarket at Batlle y Ordóñez 960 (⊕ *08.00–22.00*); the La Casona supermarket is at the rear of the cathedral at Batlle y Ordóñez 529 (⊕ *08.30–12.30, 15.00–21.00 Mon–Fri, 08.30–13.00, 16.00–21.00 Sat*).

What to see and do There are a couple of less than exciting museums in the town. The **Museo Arqueológico Taddei** (*east end of Joaquín Suárez;* ⊕ *10.00–18.00 daily; free*) – named after Professor Antonio Taddei (1908–95), who played first-division soccer before turning to archaeology in 1940 – has a pretty poor display of relics of Uruguay's earliest cultures. The **Casa Juan Spikerman** (*Treinta y Tres & Juan Zorrilla de San Martín;* ⊕ *09.00–16.00 Tue–Fri; free*), three blocks south of the plaza, has very fancy neogothic décor on an otherwise ordinary house, and a garden with a cart and a printing press parked in it. Named after one of the Treinta y Tres (now buried in the cathedral), it's the departmental history museum, with a very missable one-room collections of items such as 19th-century pistols, swords and portraits.

Immediately north of the archaeological museum there's a small **zoo** (⊕ *12.00–18.00 Tue–Fri, 10.00–18.00 Sat–Sun & holidays; free*) with domestic and introduced species and few interesting wild animals.

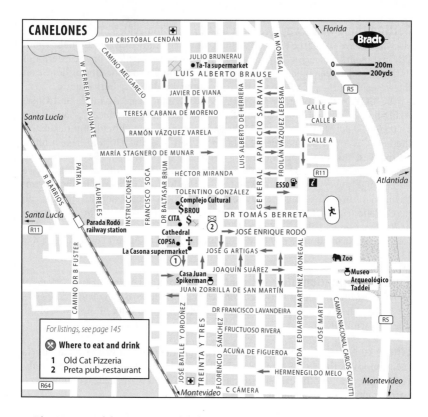

For listings, see page 145

❌ **Where to eat and drink**
1   Old Cat Pizzeria
2   Preta pub-restaurant

The Teatro Eslabón, just south of the plaza on Batlle y Ordóñez, the Teatro Politeama, just east of the plaza at Berreta 312, and the Complejo Cultural Lumiere, a striking Art Deco former cinema immediately north of the plaza at Batlle y Ordóñez 621, may offer distraction.

At km53½ on Ruta 5, 7km north of town, the Represa Canelon Grande is an artificial lake with a campsite that's a popular spot for local people to come for a swim on hot days. At km64 a very long bridge over the Río Santa Lucía marks the boundary with Florida department, a good birdwatching location with plenty of *monte* (native woodland).

WESTERN CANELONES

Santa Lucía To the northwest of Canelones, 61km from Montevideo where Ruta 11 crosses the Río Santa Lucía into San José department, is Santa Lucía, a quiet historic town founded in 1782 as Villa San Juan Bautista. It's best known for the **Quinta Capurro** (☏ *4334 6137;* ⏱ *10.30–19.00 daily; free*), a country house built in 1870–73 that has preserved its historic charm. The 9ha walled park is delightful, with plants brought from Europe and Asia, including magnolia, camellia, wisteria, bamboo and a 120-year-old *Agathis robusta* (Queensland kauri). The quinta is on Bulevar Capurro at the northern end of Calle Roosevelt, five blocks from Plaza Berreta, also well planted with palms and camellias.

Five blocks west of the plaza on Rivera is the **Casa de Cultura 'Casa de Rodó'**, the slightly Moorish house (built in 1871) in which the writer José Enrique Rodó (see page 29) spent his first nine years, and which now houses a small museum of local history (⏰ *07.00–21.00 Mon–Fri, 08.00–20.00 Sat–Sun; free*). It's another five blocks to the municipal park by the river, beyond the railway station (which has a few slow trains a day to Montevideo via Canelones); the riverside beaches here are very popular for swimming.

Getting there and away Frequent **buses** to Montevideo are operated by CITA (*Roosevelt 551*; to Tres Cruces) and Copsa (*Rivera 496*; to Baltasar Brum), mostly via Canelones although ten per day run via Aguas Corrientes; Zeballos Hermanos run via Canelones to Atlántida. From Artigas 716 and the northwestern corner of the plaza, Comsa run at least hourly to San José, also served by CITA. Cars can be rented from V&O Rentacar at Sarandí 30, just east of the river on Ruta 11 (☎ *4334 5122;* **m** *099 710662*).

Tourist information On the south side of Ruta 11 at km83 there is a tourist information centre (☎ *4334 9803*).

🏠 **Where to stay** Facing the station at Batlle y Ordóñez 99 are the Oriental and Biltmore hotels, opened in 1872 as Uruguay's first tourist hotel, and now split in two. Many distinguished people took holidays here, including José Enrique Rodó, José Pedro Varela, Carlos Gardel and Argentine presidents Domingo Sarmiento and Juárez Celman, and President Máximo Santos actually took it over and ruled Uruguay from here for the summer of 1885–86. All listings are included on the map, page 148.

🏠 **Biltmore** ☎ 4334 6276. Now somewhat run-down, the Biltmore does offer AC rooms with Wi-Fi & parking. **$$**

🏠 **Hotel Lamas** Diego Lamas & Herrera; ☎ 4334 7130; www.hotellamas.com.uy. On the eastern edge of town is this single-storey motel-style establishment, which has modern rooms

with cable TV, AC, Wi-Fi, parking & a swimming pool. **$$**

🏠 **Oriental** ☎ 4334 6276; **e** hoteloriental@gmail.com; www.hotel-oriental.com. Now beautifully restored, with antique furniture but modern comforts & large bathrooms, & a good breakfast. **$$**

RURAL TOURISM IN CANELONES

The Dirección de Desarrollo Turistico (Tourism Development Office) of Canelones has some interesting projects to develop rural tourism. On the second Sunday of each month they put on a tour (*bookings* ☎ *4332 2288;* **m** *095 331157;* **e** *paseoporelrincon@hotmail.com, turismo@imcanelones.gub.uy*) of vine-, fruit- and flower-growers in the southwestern corner of the department, known as the Rincón del Colorado. One family produces fruit and flowers such as fuchsias, another makes wine and grows lemons and mushrooms. Lunch is provided by a rural women's group. The trip leaves from the Sociedad de Fomento Rural de Rincón del Colorado at Ruta 48 km8½, where there's also a bar and shop (at km7.8 you can buy homemade Mamboretá jams and liquors, at km8 La Cueva del Art sells artworks and at km10 there's horse riding at Cabaña El Viraro – ☎ *4367 7788*). A tourist information centre is under construction at the junction of Ruta 36 and Ruta 48, on the edge of El Colorado.

On the third Sunday of each month they also have a tour (*bookings* ☎ *4334 7412;* **m** *099 475515;* **e** *senderosantalucia@hotmail.com*) of similar places to the northeast of Santa Lucía, starting with the Filgueira winery (see page 162).

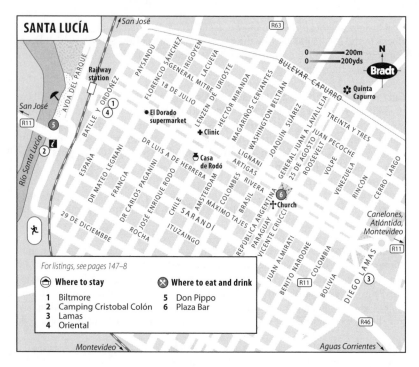

SANTA LUCÍA

San José

R63

Railway station

San José
R11

Río Santa Lucía

0 ————— 200m   N
0 ————— 200yds

Bradt

Quinta
Capurro

PAYSANDÚ
FLORENCIO SANCHEZ
GENERAL MITRE
IRIGOYEN
LACUEVA
18 DE JULIO
LENZEN DE URIOSTE
HECTOR MIRANDA
MAGARIÑOS CERVANTES
WASHINGTON BELTRAN
JOAQUIN SUAREZ
GENERAL JUAN A LAVALLEJA
25 DE AGOSTO
JUAN PECOCHE
ROOSEVELT
TREINTA Y TRES
VOLPE
VENEZUELA
RINCON
CERRO LARGO

● El Dorado
supermarket

✚ Clinic

DR LUIS A DE HERRERA

DR MATEO LEGNANI

FRANCIA

ESPAÑA

DR CARLOS PAGANINI

JOSÉ ENRIQUE RODO

CHILE

AMSTERDAM

SARANDÍ

MÁXIMO TAJES

COLOMBES

BRASIL

RIVERA

ARTIGAS

LIGNANI

🏛 Casa
de Rodó

BULEVAR CAPURRO

AVDA DEL PARQUE

BATLLE Y ORDOÑEZ

29 DE DICIEMBRE

ROCHA

ITUZAINGO

REPUBLICA ARGENTINA

PARAGUAY

VICENTE CRUCCI

JUAN ALMIRATI

BENITO NARDONE

COLOMBIA

BOLIVIA

DIEGO LAMAS

6 ✚ Church

Canelones,
Atlántida,
Montevideo

R11

R11

③

R46

For listings, see pages 147–8

⌂ Where to stay   ✕ Where to eat and drink

1 Biltmore   5 Don Pippo
2 Camping Cristobal Colón   6 Plaza Bar
3 Lamas
4 Oriental

Montevideo ↘   Aguas Corrientes ↘

🅐 **Camping Cristóbal Colón** ✆4334 5472. On the south side of Ruta 11 at km83, just west of

the bridge over the Río Santa Lucía, with electric lighting & hot water. **$**

🍴 *Where to eat* Facing the campsite, by the river at the Club Nautico, **Don Pippo** (✆ 4334 5253) is a standard parrilla that also serves pizza; on the western corner of the plaza, the **Plaza Bar** is good for a beer only.

Other practicalities There's an ATM on the north side of the plaza, and the El Dorado supermarket (⊕ 08.00–23.00 daily) is on Rivera east of Legnani. The Comeca emergency clinic is at Artigas 287 and Miranda, opposite the Antel call centre (⊕ 09.00–17.00 Mon–Fri).

Aguas Corrientes One of the most interesting sights in western Canelones is the **Museo del Agua** (*Museum of Water;* ✆ 1952 1601; www.ose.com.uy; ⊕ *by appointment & some w/ends; free*) in Aguas Corrientes, 7km south of Santa Lucía on Ruta 46 (served by ten buses a day (seven at weekends) between Montevideo and Santa Lucía), where a British-built purification plant, opened in 1871, took water from the Río Santa Lucía and fed it into Montevideo's drinking water supply. It's perfectly preserved, with its Babcock and Wilcox boilers and Worthington pumps still in place. You'll visit **Casa Uno** (House No 1) on Avenida del Parque in the centre of the village, and also the inlet valves near the river, beyond the filtration beds. There is a **campsite**, at the riverside Club Náutico, at the west end of Ramón López (✆ 4337 3102), where you can rent canoes; paddling down the river from Aguas Corrientes or Santa Lucía to the Parador Tajes makes a delightful day out, a distance of 11km or 32km in total. There's also the **Natura Costa Hermosa campsite** at km54½ of Ruta 46 (✆ 4330 3547).

Also on the east bank of the Río Santa Lucía, 21km south as the canoe follows the river, is the **Parador Tajes**, the Italian-style mansion that Máximo Tajes built when he became President of Uruguay in 1886. It's maintained by the army and houses a **Museum of Arms and Uniforms** (✎ *4330 3641;* ⊕ *10.00–18.00 Sat–Sun; free*), mainly displaying flags and uniforms of the Artiguista period. There's also a viewpoint with views of the river and wetlands, and paths through 60ha of woodland. There's also a campsite (with electric lighting and wash-blocks), a restaurant, and the Puerto Jackson beach and canoe rental. The army currently levies a charge of US$1 per car to enter the whole site, but this is controversial and may be removed. COPSA's bus 803, from Montevideo to Santa Lucía, comes this way twice a day.

Below here the Río Santa Lucía, swollen by the waters of the Río San José, becomes much wider and is navigable by larger boats, although there are increasing numbers of islands; fishing is very popular here.

WINERIES OF URUGUAY

The first vines in Uruguay (probably Muscat table grapes) were planted near Colonia by 1688, and wine was soon being produced for domestic consumption, as well as for Communion. In the 1870s, after the Guerra Grande, the country was stable and both agricultural investment and immigrants began to flood in. From 1880 the government began to offer incentives to the wine industry. New varieties of grape, such as Tannat (see box, pages 156–7), Folie Noire and Gamay Noire began to be planted, and in 1883 the first vintage was produced of what might be called 'fine wine', ie: something better than rough table wine made of *uvas tintas* or mixed red grapes. The pioneers of fine winemaking in Uruguay were the Basque Pascual Harriague, who established a vineyard near Salto in 1870, and Francisco Vidiella, a Catalan who set up a winery in Colón (now in Montevideo's northern suburbs) in 1874, as well as Francisco Piría (see page 189). In fact the Tannat grape was initially known in Uruguay as Harriague, and Folie Noire as Vidiella or Peñarol, while Gamay Noire, planted in the Carrasco area of Montevideo from 1880, was known as Borgoña.

In 1903 the Viticulture Law (still largely in force) gave the state considerable powers over the industry, which continued mass-producing rough table wines for much of the 20th century. These were semi-sweet whites and rosés and rough reds, largely produced from hybrid grapes giving high yields per hectare.

The process of 'conversion' to a modern, higher-quality industry began in the early 1970s, with consultants brought from France and California, and the start of a programme of replanting with cloned, virus-free rootstocks. In 1988 the government set up the National Institute of Winemaking (INAVI), which works to improve the industry, for instance by researching which grape varieties are most suited to Uruguay's soils and microclimates, and through marketing and training. A 1991 study by Californian experts decided that Uruguay should concentrate on Tannat, and with government help most vineyards started growing it. The area planted with vines has shrunk from 120,000ha to 9,000ha but is now producing far better wines, at higher prices than bulk table wines. Production is around 95 million litres per year, with ten million litres exported (40% to Brazil, 10% to the USA, 8% to Canada, 5% to Switzerland, 4% to the UK and 3% each to Germany, Benelux, Poland, Russia and Mexico). Most of the exports are of fine wines, while most domestic consumption (25 litres per year, the 13th-highest level in the world) is of bulk table wines, often sold in *demijuanas* (demijohns) of five litres.

Most of Uruguay's wineries being near the sea, their weather is changeable and winemaking is challenging, with varying results (2002, 2004 and 2007 were particularly good years). The main problem is that humidity brings disease. Cabernet grapes, which ripen late (perhaps after the autumn rains have come), can struggle, with skill and care required. White wine grapes and Merlot do well but Malbec, so common in Argentina, is virtually unknown here. Similarly, the Rioja grape Tempranillo likes drier climates, but does well enough in Uruguay. Pinot Noir is not common in Uruguay, but with cool nights it can produce delicate complex wines. In the last 40 years, the average alcohol level of Uruguayan grapes has risen from 10% to 12% (though still slightly lower than French and Californian grapes); hotter weather should benefit Merlot in particular (and Tannat–Merlot blends may become very successful). Winemakers are also experimenting with less traditional varieties such as Petit Verdot and Albariño (which is proving very well suited to Uruguayan conditions).

Increasingly, as harvest draws near, the grapes are not just checked daily for polyphenol and tannin levels, but are tasted and the colour of the pips examined, in a move from purely chemical analysis to an 'organoleptic' approach. It's expensive, but given the family-sized scale of the industry the boutique approach is the only way for Uruguay's industry to go – the entire country produces less wine than Chile's giant Concha y Toro. These very different vintages and the small size of the wineries mean that there will never be many Uruguayan wines in northern hemisphere supermarkets (although production levels are sufficient for the more specialist wine shops) – although Colinas de Garzón may be a game-changer in this respect. This small scale also works in favour of wine tourism, as tastings are often accompanied by the winemaker or a member of the immediate family, giving special personal insights.

Each winemaker works in his own way with the local environment, and each vineyard has its own character. Pesticides are not widely used but spraying of some is compulsory, so there is no certified organic wine production. Grapes are generally picked by hand and efforts are increasingly made to reduce the amount of handling, using gravity rather than pumping where possible to move the wine. In most vineyards cement tanks have been fitted with epoxy linings, but for white wine in particular chilled stainless steel tanks are becoming more important. Most fine wine is stored in oak barrels for six months or more, although some white wines are unoaked.

Virtually all of Uruguay's 270 or so wineries are small, family-run private businesses, and five or ten go out of business every year, having failed to change with the times; however, those that have adapted are doing very well. Fourteen of the most export-oriented wineries have formed an association called Los Caminos del Vino – Bodegas Familiares del Uruguay (*Wine Roads – Family Wineries of Uruguay;* m *099 149662; www.uruguaywinetours.com*), and visits can be arranged to these (they have good websites and can easily be contacted by phone or email). Almost all are in Montevideo and Canelones departments (though two have outposts in Salto and Rivera), but new wineries are appearing in Colonia and in particular Maldonado. The wineries near Montevideo are mostly close to Ruta 5 and it's easy to visit three or more in a day by car; the welcome is warm and an English-speaking guide can usually be provided. A tasting of three or four wines, with snacks and a tour of the winery, costs US$15; with a barbecue lunch it costs US$50–70. A few of the larger wineries have restaurants, but most tastings will be accompanied by cold meats and cheese or homemade empanadas. The larger wineries, close to Ruta 5, host groups from cruise ships in Montevideo harbour, and are also popular for weddings and other events.

The Wine Experience (m *097 348445; http://thewine-experience.com*), **Robertson Wine Tours** (*The Penthouse 1202, Vázquez Ledesma 2865, CP 11200, Villa Biarritz, Montevideo;* ↘ *2711 3032;* m *094 345144; www.robertsonwinetours.com; from US$575 pp including everything except accommodation*) and **Daniel Reyes** (*Colonia 892, office 601, Montevideo;* ↘ *2902 2054;* e *reservas@danielreyes.com.uy*) offer upmarket and very well-informed tours of Argentine and Uruguayan wineries.

Private custom tours can be arranged with Lares Tours (*W Ferreira Aldunate 1341, Montevideo;* ↘ *2901 9120;* m *099 592009;* e *info@lares.com.uy; www. larestours.com*) who offer the Tannat Experience day-tour as well as two- and three-day tours combining the Colonia and Montevideo areas, with visits to wineries and cheese-makers.

In addition to tours and tastings, wineries are increasingly putting on **harvest festivals** (February/March for red wine, and to a lesser extent in January for white) and **pruning festivals** (Festival de la Poda) in mid-August. The members of Los Caminos del Vino open to the public for El Día de la Vendimia, probably on the first Saturday of March.

THE WINERIES There are two fine wineries in Montevideo's northern suburb of Villa Colón. On the Plaza Colón (best reached by bus G from the Ciudad Vieja) is a statue of Francisco Vidiella (see page 149), as well as a branch of La Pasiva. Just north is a church by Eladio Dieste (see page 35) and then on the left of the main road north to La Paz and Las Piedras, the Bodega Santa Rosa.

Bodega Santa Rosa (*Avda César Mayo Gutiérrez 2211;* ↘ *2320 9921;* e *export@ bodegasantarosa.com.uy; www.bodegasantarosa.com.uy*) One of the country's larger and more historic wineries, Santa Rosa was founded in 1898 by Juan Passadore, who was responsible for introducing European grape varieties such as Cabernet Sauvignon, Merlot, Sauvignon Blanc and Pinot Blanc to Uruguay, and was important in the mid 20th century, exporting to the United States, and also producing grappa until the government set up a monopoly. It also made the sparkling white wine for Roldós medio y medio (see page 107) for 40 years before parting company with them. The bodega is now run by the founder's great-grandson (who speaks good English and handles tours for foreigners). Sparkling white wine is still a speciality (with around 80% of the domestic market), and they still produce a tiny amount of table wine, supplied in three-litre bottles to a few favoured restaurants, as well as cider for New Year's Eve. However, this is now a thoroughly modern producer of fine wines, with grapes grown in Las Violetas, 17km away in Canelones department, and processed here largely by gravity rather than pumping, and using ozone rather than chlorine for cleaning; they've used screw tops for many years.

Below the winery, the cellars are cavernous, with massive 19th-century oak tanks from Nancy, two of which are still in use (though most of the wine is made in epoxy-lined concrete tanks). There's a museo where old machines and bottles are displayed, with a nice small tasting area. You can also see the Champenoise process for making sparkling wines, including an old German cooling machine. For up to 100 people, tastings can be organised with an asado and a live tango and candombé show.

Chardonnay, Pinot Noir and Pinot Blanc grapes for sparkling whites are harvested a couple of weeks early for greater acidity, sugar and yeast are added and the wine is bottled with a crown cap and kept in the cellar for up to 16 months, where 30,000 bottles are riddled (rotated a quarter-turn) in eight hours and then turned back the other way for a period of 30 days. This gathers the sediment of dead yeast in the neck; this is placed in ice water and opened, and the frozen plug of sediment is blown out by the pressure inside the bottle, after which it is topped up with some sugared Chardonnay and corked and sealed. Their best sparkling white is Le Fond de Cave (known as Le Chef de Cave for export), with 60% Pinot Noir and 40% Chardonnay kept for 16 months to produce the smallest of bubbles. The Brut Sauvage is all Chardonnay (10% of it spending a year in a French oak *barrique*), with a surprising amount of fruit colour and aroma, something like a Veuve Cliquot but only costing US$10! The (non-sparkling) Sauvignon Blanc Reserva, made in traditional Sancerre style by a visiting French oenologist, is also excellent, with no wood taste, moderate acidity and excellent structure.

The red wines are also excellent, including the fruity Cabernet Sauvignon and Merlot Reservas and the Cabernet Clásico, which is one of Uruguay's best-selling wines (a blend of Cabernet Sauvignon and Cabernet Franc, with a touch of Tannat). The Tannat Reserva is smooth and clean and not too tannic (with just 30% aged for a year in French oak), while the Tannat del Museo Gran Reserva (in fact 20% Merlot) is much softer, with plenty of fruit and subtlety. It is great with cheese and pasta but a tad light for rich meat like game. The Merlot del Museo Reserva is smooth and fruity, while the Juan Bautista Gran Reserva (60% Tannat, with Merlot and Cabernet Sauvignon) is young and wooded.

Bodegas Carrau (*Avda César Mayo Gutiérrez 2556;* \ *2320 0238, 4620 2279;* e *info@bodegascarrau.com; www.bodegascarrau.com*) Across the road just to the north, Bodegas Carrau is one of the country's largest and most progressive winemakers, although like Santa Rosa they grow their grapes elsewhere. Juan Carrau Sust arrived in Uruguay in 1930 (his family having made wine in Catalunya since 1752) and helped Santa Rosa boom in the 1930s and 1940s (introducing champenoise-style sparkling wines to Uruguay). His son Juan Carrau Pujol ran Santa Rosa for 25 years before going independent, setting up a vineyard in Brazil and then in 1975 Vinos Finos Juan Carrau, using an old winery here in Colón and growing grapes on 24ha (now 35ha) at the Castel Pujol vineyard in Las Violetas.

In 1972, following a study by the University of California at Davis that identified the Brazilian–Uruguayan border area as ideal for growing grapes for fine wines, he planted vines in Cerro Chapeu, near Rivera, the highest vineyards in Uruguay at over 300m. Initially the grapes were trucked south to Colón overnight, but in 1998 a striking modern winery was opened at Cerro Chapeu, built into the hill to allow the wine to be moved by gravity rather than pumping. With well-drained sandy soils and a stable continental climate, their best grapes are grown here, with low yields to produce a more concentrated taste, the wine still being moved south for blending and bottling.

The aim has always been to produce fine wines for export. Today Carrau produces a million bottles a year, with around 40% exported to 30 countries (roughly a quarter of Uruguay's exports).

Carrau marketed the first 100% Tannat Reserva in 1979. In the last decade, with government support, they began a project to study Tannat's genetic variations (as part of Uruguay's cultural heritage) and produce a more authentic standardised stock; you'll be shown a small test plot of century-old Tannat clones. The Amat line is judged by experts as Uruguay's best Tannat; in fact it's the only Uruguayan wine in Hugh Johnson's *1001 Wines You Must Try Before You Die*. It's hand-picked at Cerro Chapeu, kept in new oak barrels for 20 months, bottled without filtering and kept for another year in the cellar; it's well worth laying down for many years. The Bodegas Carrau Tannat de Reserva, which spends a year in French oak and a year in the bottle, is also excellent, with lovely soft tannins. The Ysern Tannat is a blend of wines from Las Violetas and Cerro Chapeu, aged in oak for 20 months, fantastic value for money. There's also an Ysern Cabernet Sauvignon (60% from Cerro Chapeu) that's aged for 12 months in year-old French oak. The Tannat Rosé Saigné is made with hand-picked grapes from Las Violetas, and the Vivent fortified Tannat, with rich raspberry and sultana flavours, is soon to be added to the range.

The 1752 Gran Tradición Juan Carrau Pujol range is made from the best Tannat, Cabernet Sauvignon and Cabernet Franc grapes of each vintage, kept in new French oak barrels for 18–20 months and then aged in the bottle for a year; the Tannat is a 50–50 mix of grapes from Cerro Chapeu and Castel Pujol, with a complexity and maturity that make it worth keeping for up to 20 years. The Tannat Juan Carrau is, unusually, made with grapes from Las Violetas only and is very good, with earthy soft tannins. There are also plenty of younger wines, mostly aged in oak for about six months, that won't keep for so long but offer a more affordable taste of what can be done.

On the white side, the Bodegas Carrau Sauvignon Blanc Sur Lie has been produced specifically for North American tastes; fermented in temperature-controlled stainless-steel tanks, it's aged for six months with the lees, or yeast sediments, and is soft and juicy with lightly spicy flavours. Castel Pujol is Carrau's most popular brand in the domestic market – the Sauvignon Blanc, kept in steel tanks for six months, is more conventionally smooth but more citric than the usual Sauvignon Blanc – excellent with fish or desserts. One of the more interesting wines is the single vineyard Vilasar; some of the Nebbiolo vines planted at the start of the 20th century were identified at the end of the century as Marzemino, one of the best red varieties from the Trentino in northern Italy, and this is now produced as a blend of 90% Nebbiolo and 10% Marzemino. The Sust (named after Juan Carrau Sust, who introduced the champenoise method to Uruguay in 1930) sparkling wines are 75–80% Chardonnay blended with Pinot Noir, and fermented in the bottle at 12°C for 18 months; it's dry and indeed rather austere in taste.

Guided tours and tastings are available from Monday to Friday (⏲ *09.30–15.00; about 90mins*), when a wine shop is also open. Groups of four or more can also arrange to have tastings with cold meats and cheeses (*2½hrs, also possible Sat mornings*), or a full meal (*Mon–Fri*). Tuesdays may be busy with school groups (sampling grape juice rather than wine). In an extension to the 1887 house you'll see some nice historical photographs and documents relating to the family's history.

Bodega Bouza (*Camino de la Redención 7658 bis;* ☎ *2323 4030;* e *visitas@bodegabouza.com; www.bodegabouza.com*) Turning west off Ruta 5 at km13½, it's 1,300m to Bodegas Bouza, one of the best organised wineries for visits. Bus G11 from Colón passes roughly hourly. Despite being in a Montevideo department it's delightfully rural, at the headwaters of the Arroyo de Melilla, with paperbark, cork and Brazilian araucaria trees on the lawns. In 2001 Montevideo businessman Juan Luis Bouza bought the run-down winery (built in 1942) here, and a vineyard just north in the Las Violetas region of Canelones, installed state-of-the-art equipment and now produces a modest 100,000 bottles a year, mostly for restaurants and wine shops, and half exported. Using parcel vinification (hand-picking and processing of just one small plot at a time, with very detailed record-keeping), and small tanks, remarkably good results are produced.

In addition to the inherited Tannat, Merlot and Chardonnay, Bouza has planted the rarer Tempranillo and Albariño (a Galician white-wine grape planted for the first time in Uruguay in 2001).

4

The product range includes standard and premium lines of Tannat, Merlot, Tempranillo, Chardonnay and Albariño. There's an unoaked Chardonnay (produced only for export and for blending) as well as a delightfully complex blend produced 60% in stainless-steel tanks and 40% in French oak, for the domestic and export markets. The Albariño (partly oaked) is lovely, with subtle floral aromas, good acidity and a long finish. In 2010 they introduced the Cocó premium blend of the best Chardonnay, aged for over nine months, with Albariño kept in stainless steel for the same period. Riesling and Pinot Noir have recently been planted in a new vineyard near Pan de Azúcar – watch this space.

Other unique blends are the Tempranillo–Tannat, the elegance of the Tempranillo (60%) given strength and acidity by the Tannat (40%), and the top-of-the-range Monte Vide Eu, a blend of 50–60% Tannat with Tempranillo and Merlot, all kept in oak for 14 months and benefiting from further time in the cellar. Although the superb Tannat Parcela Única wines are unblended, kept for just six months in new French oak barrels, and bottled without filtering, with mature fruits and spices, the tannin gives structure but no more. Bouza's other Tannats may in fact contain a large proportion of Merlot, kept in oak for nine to 14 months. They also now have a Merlot Parcela Única, full of dark fruit with smoky, spicy touches.

Since 2008, Bouza has made a Tempranillo Rosé, macerated for 12 hours and kept for three months over the vine leaves before being put into oak barrels. There are also grappas of Tempranillo, Tannat, Chardonnay and Albariño, made in very small batches with an old French still.

The winery is **open** from 09.00 to 18.00 daily, in summer to 19.00 (*tours 11.00, 13.00, 16.00 daily; US$19, US$36 or US$52 inc tasting*). There's a very good restaurant (\ *2323 4030*; ① *12.00–15.30 daily, booking essential at w/ends*), serving vegetables and Hampshire Down sheep raised at the bodega. About once a month on average, this serves a cruise group of 80–100 people, but usually it's peaceful enough except at Sunday lunchtime. In 2010 the winery and restaurant were extended, and a shop added, selling woollen wear and Galician-style cheese as well as their wines (which range between US$16 and US$130).

An old railway carriage is to be restored to provide two bedrooms, and more accommodation is planned (a simple dinner and breakfast will be provided).

Another of Bouza's interests is *cachilas* or classic cars – a barn houses a growing collection of superbly restored models such as six Model T Fords (one red, with metal spokes, as opposed to the near-compulsory black, with wooden spokes), a Willy's Jeep, Škodas and Alfa Romeos, BMW and Raleigh motorbikes, a Messerschmidt three-wheeler, and a Uruguayan-made Rago. There are tours of the collection at 11.00 and 16.00 daily, and some are driven around outside on Saturdays.

Antigua Bodega Stagnari and Vinos Finos H Stagnari Continuing north up Ruta 5 to km20 (3km beyond the Anillo Perimetral, Montevideo's new bypass) and heading west for 1.6km (on a fairly rough road), you'll come to the two Stagnari vineyards, originally all one but now split between the older and younger generations of the Stagnari family, which has been making wine since 1880 in Italy, and since 1928 in Uruguay. First is the **Antigua Bodega Stagnari** (*Santos Lugares, La Paz;* \ *2362 2137;* e *info@antiguabodegastagnari.com.uy; www.antiguabodegastagnari. com.uy*), where Merlot is grown on a soil of decomposed pink granite; Syrah, Tannat, Sangiovese, Cabernet Sauvignon, Sauvignon Blanc and Chardonnay are all grown nearby at Riberas de Santa Lucía.

The standard wines are the Del Pedregal range (aged in oak barrels for six months), with the better Prima Donna wines (in oak for around eight months) and then the new Osiris Reserva Tannat and Merlot at the top, their only 100% single varietals. These are aged in American oak barrels for 12–15 months to give complexity and a balance of fruit and wood. In the Del Pedregal range there's a Tannat, a Merlot, a Cabernet Sauvignon, a Tannat–Merlot (60%–40%, full and fruity for those who find Tannat too strong alone) and even a Tannat–Merlot–Cabernet blend. There's also a Del Pedregal Rosé, which is pure Merlot (a relatively common choice in Chile, if not elsewhere). As for white wines, there's the Del Pedregal Chardonnay (aged in oak for just three months), and the Prima Donna Sauvignon Blanc, both fresh and easy-drinking wines.

Tastings cost US$20 (for three or four wines), or US$38 with lunch – there's no restaurant as yet, but a good meal can be laid on. The philosophy is to connect personally with visitors and show the winery as a family business, and questions are welcomed.

More or less across the road is **Vinos Finos H Stagnari** (*Santos Lugares;* ☎ *2362 2940;* m *096 109604;* e *turismo@stagnari.com; www.stagnari.com*), set up by Héctor Stagnari in 2000. All the vines were planted by him, the first in Uruguay to be planted at a density of 10,000 vines per hectare, thus producing under 1kg per plant, but with more concentrated sugar. Héctor also set up microplantations all over Uruguay, trying to determine the best place to grow the Tannat grape, ending up at Nueva Hesperides, just outside Salto and very close to where Pascual Harriague first planted Tannat in Uruguay – daytime temperatures reach 40°C, falling to 20°C at night, ideal conditions for developing sugars and alcohol. The wine is all made here, in a high-tech new winery with temperature-controlled 10,000-litre stainless steel tanks. Volumes are relatively low, and only 20% is exported, with most of the wine sold through hotels, restaurants and the more upmarket supermarkets such as Tienda Inglesa. Although no table wines are made here, since 2002 fine wine has been sold to restaurants in two-litre bottles with plastic corks at a similar price to table wine.

The Daymán 'Castel La Puebla' Tannat, with grapes from Salto aged for a year in French oak and then two months in American oak, was voted world champion red in Ljubljana in 2006. However, the Tannat Viejo is even better (well balanced, with a big nose, soft tannins and a chocolatey finish), and the Dinastía (90% Tannat, aged in French oak for 14 months, and only made in small quantities) was the 2007 world champion. The Premier Tannat is younger and a bit heavy on tannins but is remarkably good value if you can lay it down for a couple of years. There are also some good Cabernet Sauvignons, and a Syrah, with grapes from Salto, young and moderately light.

Grapes for white wines (Chardonnay, Viognier, Gewurztraminer and Moscatel d'Alejandria) are grown at La Puebla in Canelones department. They're distinctive for Uruguayan whites, very aromatic and with well-balanced acidity (like white Burgundy). The Chardonnay de Virginia (created for Héctor's wife) is full and fruity, especially compared with other Uruguayan Chardonnays, and doesn't seem as young as it is, with a good body. Their only oaked white wine is the Dinastía Blanco (90% Chardonnay). The Blush Moscatel d'Alejandria (pink from a touch of Tannat) is sweet and very perfumed, with good balance and fruit.

Since around 2007, tourists have been welcomed. For **tours in English** (*US$22, with 4 wines, cold meats & cheese*) you should call at least a day ahead; an excellent parrilla is available for groups. There's a choice of an air-conditioned tasting room (decorated with award certificates) or a larger room with a view over the vineyards (nicely lit up at night). The style is more modern and technological than at Antiguo Stagnari, with oenologists who will happily talk chemistry with you.

Bodega De Lucca (*Ruta 48 km13.1, El Colorado;* ✆ *2367 8076;* e *reideluc@adinet. com.uy, deluccawines@adinet.com.uy; www.deluccawines.com*) Turning west off Ruta 5 at km32, you'll come in 13km to the Bodega De Lucca, where the mercurial Reinaldo De Lucca has been growing grapes (first planted by his grandfather in 1906) for a long time, starting to replant his vines and modernise his business around 1990. While very proud of his degrees from Montevideo, Penn State and Montepellier and his experience abroad, he also feels very much in touch with this land and climate, where no irrigation, fertilisers or insecticides are needed (though minimal use of fungicide can't be avoided). In a hilly area on either side of the Arroyo El Colorado, his four vineyards have shallow, well-drained soils that still store enough water for the dry growing season, and the relatively humid climate is similar to Burgundy without producing the overripe fruit of Argentine vines. Speaking of fruit, you'll be given melon with your Marsanne, as well as peaches, plums, strawberries or whatever else he sees as the right match, rather than meats and cheeses.

For red wines, Reinaldo grows mainly Merlot, Tannat, Syrah, Cabernet Sauvignon, Cabernet Franc and Sangiovese; and for whites, Sauvignon Blanc, Chardonnay, Marsanne and Rousanne. His best wine may be the Syrah, produced mainly for export, with 20% Tannat and Marsanne; it's well structured and balanced, with elegant tannins, and subtle, complex floral aromas with a bit of spice. The Merlot is well structured and full-bodied with round tannins and a complex aroma of nuts, toasted almonds and hints of tobacco. The Cabernet Sauvignon is very elegant, with

TANNAT

The grape that is, rightly or wrongly, always associated with Uruguay is Tannat, originally from the Madiran region of southwestern France, near the Pyrenees, and therefore known to the Basques who came to Uruguay in the 19th century and played a major role in starting its winemaking industry. In 1870 one of them, Pascual Harriague, planted Tannat vines near Salto in the northwest of the country, and in 1876 Francisco Vidiela planted them in Colón, now in Montevideo's northern suburbs. As early as 1877 Tannat (then called Harriague) was known as the 'Uruguayan grape', and in the late 20th century it became associated with the country's resurgent wine industry. Winemakers have used Tannat as Uruguay's calling card, even more than Chilean winemakers have used Carménère, and most visitors to Uruguay will want to try it. In fact it is quite hard to avoid as it's used a lot, being very productive, ripening late and coping well with frost. It produces large, tight bunches of smallish grapes which are easy to pick, an important consideration as harvesting in Uruguay is almost always done by hand (unusually, its leaves begin with three lobes and then develop two more). It produces a full-bodied, deep red-black wine that's fruity and a bit smoky.

However, there is a problem. Tannat is known for its very high tannin levels (the name is no coincidence), a consequence of the grape's thick skin, and on its own Tannat can be just too much for many people. Historically this has happened when the summer has been wet or the grapes have not ripened fully, or when it's been aged for too long in poor barrels; good management is vital. In France it has always been used mainly as a blending grape, and the rules of the Madiran *appellation* require Tannat to be blended with Cabernet Sauvignon, Cabernet Franc or Fer. It is also blended with Manseng and Courbu Noir, but blending Tannat with Merlot has been particularly successful in giving softer, fruitier wines. Tannat's high acidity ripe fruit on the nose, notes of liquorice and aromatic hints of ripe red peppers. The Tannat is a bit heavy, with very ripe concentrated fruit and velvety tannins. The Río Colorado is a blend of the best Cabernet Sauvignon, Tannat and Merlot.

On the white side, the Marsanne (probably the only Uruguayan Marsanne is exotic, with an elegant structure and long finish. The Sauvignon Blanc is well balanced, with lots of ripe fruit and good acidity. A Viognier will soon be released too.

Tastings are usually conducted by Reinaldo himself, who will tell you everything about pairing wine and fruit, particularly to bring out the wine's erotic potential. He's highly entertaining, but also very knowledgeable and serious about his craft.

Artesana (*Ruta 48 km3.6, Las Brujas;* m *095 780629, 098 231711;* e *turismo@ artesanawinery.com; https://artesanawinery.com*) American-owned, and with two female winemakers, this is an exciting new winery that is the first in Uruguay to use the Zinfandel grape, although most of their area is planted with Tannat. Having planted 8½ha in 2007, they started making wine in 2010. Their ruling principle is to work in very small batches from specific parcels of vines, handling the grapes as gently as possible, with no fining or filtration. The juice is fermented seperately in small temperature-controlled tanks, allowing maximum flexibility in blending; wines are then aged in best-quality oak barrels for 12–18 months, followed by six–eight months in the bottle – even then they are expected to continue maturing for up to ten years after purchase. Artesana aim to give all their wines fruity depth,

allows it to be aged in oak barrels for up to 20 months to soften the tannins and bring out its flavour, and it benefits further from bottle ageing (up to six years) and from decanting before serving. French rosés made with Tannat are allowed to macerate or steep for only a short time, to stop the wine becoming too tannic. The technique of micro-oxygenation was introduced in Madiran in 1990, with oxygen being bubbled through fermenting Tannat, to soften the wine's tannins.

In Uruguay, Tannat has been bred to be less acidic and tannic but with higher alcohol levels and more complex fruit tones. Some winemakers blend these modern clones with grapes from the 'old vines' descended from the original French cuttings; both types of Tannat are often blended with fruitier grapes such as Merlot or Cabernet Sauvignon. Some of these blends work immensely well; in addition fortified and distilled Tannats (like port or brandy) are now appearing and seem to be very successful. With luck, the days of people having to add ice or soda to their Tannat to make it drinkable are over. Indeed, *Financial Times* wine writer Jancis Robinson chose a 2006 Uruguayan Tannat as one of her 30 choices for Christmas, perhaps because it goes so well with chocolate.

Tannat has now spread from Uruguay to Argentina, Chile, California and Australia; in the last five years most vineyards in Mendoza, Argentina, have taken to adding 5–10% Tannat to their Malbec, an amount that doesn't have to be shown on the label. In California it's used in Meritage (or Bordeaux-style) wines and also blended with Cabernet Franc, Sangiovese and Syrah grapes.

Around 25% of Uruguay's vineyard area is now planted with Tannat, mostly in Canelones and elsewhere in the south. However, in recent years it's been found to do even better in the north, and new vineyards are being established near Salto (where Tannat was first planted in Uruguay) and Rivera.

complex structure but also elegance. The Tannat and Tannat–Merlot (60%–40%) spend a year in French oak barrels and are rich and fruity. They are still learning how to handle Zinfandel, not an easy grape at the best of times, in Uruguayan conditions not far from the Río de la Plata. The 2011 vintage spent a year in oak (and the Reserva spent 16 months), while the 2012 was aged in stainless steel for six months; in 2013 they will release what must be the world's only Tannat–Zinfandel–Merlot Reserva.

A **tour and a tasting** of Tannat, Tannat–Merlot and Zinfandel (with meats, cheeses and coffee) costs US$25 (US$20 for 8 or more); with a Reserva as well as lunch it costs US$50.

Bodegas Castillo Viejo (*Ruta 68 km24½, Las Piedras;* \2368 9606; e *directorio@ castilloviejo.com; www.castilloviejo.com*) On the less hilly eastern side of Ruta 5, Bodegas Castillo Viejo is 3km north of Las Piedras off Ruta 67. Founded in 1927 on a very small scale, another 150ha were bought in the cooler terrain of San José department in the 1960s, although purely for the production of table wines. Since 1982 the winery has been run by the third generation of the Etcheverry family, who started to modernise from 1986, with classic French grape varieties grown on V-shaped Open Lyre trellises (then almost unknown in South America), to expose the grapes to light and air. They benefited from the skills of a New Zealand consultant who subsequently married into the family, helping them to produce clean tangy Sauvignons Blancs. They're also known for their old-vine Cabernet Franc, including a rosé. They produce over a million litres a year, half of it bulk table wine; of the fine wine, 75% (especially white wine) is exported, with sales to 22 countries including less obvious ones such as Poland and Iceland.

The Catamayor ('Good Tasting') brand includes the entry-level Clásico range, with young (unoaked) Sauvignon Blanc, Chardonnay, Cabernet Franc, Merlot and blends of both of these last two reds with Tannat, as well as a Tannat that's aged in oak for ten months and in the bottle for six months; these are all full of fruit and colour but well balanced. The Catamayor Reserva range, aged in oak for six–ten months, includes Tannat, Tannat–Cabernet Franc, Merlot and a lovely Viognier; and the Vieja Parcela Reserva de la Familia line includes Tannat and Cabernet Franc, both oaked for ten months (but needing to be aged in the bottle for a year or so after purchase), and a Sauvignon Blanc of which 5% is aged in oak barrels for concentration and persistence. In 2005 the El Preciado Primer Gran Reserva wines were released – they're generic blends of red (largely Cabernet Franc) and white (mainly Viognier), but top quality, with 8% of the red and 65% of the white aged in oak for a full 15 months. There's also the Hasparren Brut sparkling wine.

Tourism is important to them – there's no charge for **tastings**, but these tend to end in people buying their better wines (though at lower prices than in the shops). It's well set up, starting with a video in the old cellar, and one of the three siblings who run the business is usually present. It's possible to have lunch, the usual asado, with grilled vegetables and a dessert. You can also arrange to visit the San José vineyard for a relaxing day in the country, with bikes or a tractor and trailer to take you to a viewpoint and then at 19.30 an asado, before watching (or helping with) the grape-picking, which – perhaps uniquely in the world – takes place only at night.

Pizzorno Wines (*Ruta 32 km23, Canelón Chico;* \2368 9601; *www.pizzornowines. com*) Just south of Castillo Viejo (and employing the same New Zealand consultant), Pizzorno Wines was founded in 1910 and is now run by the founder's grandson, Carlos Pizzorno. His wife Ana is a doctor who's researching the benefits of moderate red wine consumption in preventing cancer of the colon (linked to Uruguay's meat-rich diet). Like most wineries in this area it has moved successfully from mass-production table wine to crafting fine wines. They've done so well that they are the only Uruguayans to get a wine into a British supermarket (the Merlot–Tannat, described as well structured, supple and smooth in the mouth, soft but full of flavour and deliciously smoky, underpinned by soft tannins, and available at Waitrose, admittedly hidden among the Argentine wines). The Tannat Reserva is superb, if a bit 'international' in style, with complexity and concentration, and smoky plum and ripe blackberry fruits. There's also an unoaked Tannat, a little rougher but still fine, and a Tannat–Merlot, also unoaked, which works well. They are also the only Uruguayan vineyard to have adopted carbonic maceration, fermenting the grapes in CO_2 before gently pressing them and continuing a cool fermentation, as for a rosé, producing a light young wine with plenty of fruit and little tannin – a Tannat for those who do not like Tannat. It can be served as an aperitif or with fish, and should not be kept for long.

There's also Cabernet Sauvignon, and the Primo Reserva red (at least half Tannat, with Cabernet Sauvignon, Merlot and perhaps a bit of Petit Verdot) that in a good year is well integrated, with smoky fruits and soft tannins, but may need time to mature in other years. There's a sparkling Chardonnay, with 10% Sauvignon Blanc, that's light and refreshing but without much depth, and an excellent Sauvignon Blanc, with touches of citrus and vanilla and good acidity (and a Sauvignon Blanc Reserva launched in 2009). The Sauvignon Blanc is almost all for export, and now has screwtops and English-language labels.

Visitors are welcome with 48 hours' notice, and a new cellar, tasting room and shop are under construction.

Bodega Pisano (*Ruta 68 km29, Progreso;* ☎ *2368 9077;* e *pisano@adinet.com.uy;* *www.pisanowines.com*) To the north of Las Piedras, just short of Progreso, Bodega Pisano is Uruguay's leading exporter of fine wines by value, selling to 38 countries. Their wines are in fact pretty pricey, but that's not a problem as every bottle of their deliberately limited production (about 350,000 bottles) is soon sold. Founded in 1924, the winery is now run by the fifth generation, three brothers who all believe in small-scale production, with hand-picking of high-density/low-yielding vines and simple equipment with limited chilling and use of new oak barrels. Tastings, with cold meats and cheeses, are in a funky sampling room.

Tannat is a speciality, the headliner being the Axis Mundi Premium Tannat, which costs no less than £70 a bottle in Britain but may actually be worth it; having spent a massive 30 months in French oak it has huge power and concentration. The Arretxea blend of Tannat and Cabernet Sauvignon (40% each) with Merlot, aged in French oak for a year, has complexity, elegance and well-defined spices; there's also an Arretxea Tannat–Petit Verdot. The core range of reserve varietals is called Reserva Personal Familiar (RPF; The Family's Personal Reserve); the Tannat has intense colour and complex concentrated tannins with long robust fruit and spice. The RPF line also includes Merlot, Cabernet Sauvignon, Petit Verdot and Pinot Noir, and the white Chardonnay.

At the budget end of the range, the Cisplatina Tannat–Merlot (60%–40%) is a good everyday blend; the Río de los Pájaros Tannat and Merlot–Tannat are a bit more complex. There's also a Río de los Pájaros Tannat–Syrah–Viognier, very purple with spicy aromas and toasty fruits. They also produce the light, fresh Brut Negro sparkling Tannat, and the extraordinary Etxe Oneko fortified dessert wine, something between a port and an amarone, made from late-harvested Tannat.

They've also planted Syrah and Moscato Giallo, although these are not yet in production; Sangiovese has been tried but wasn't a success here.

On the white side, there's superb Torrontés (which usually does best in arid high-altitude parts of Argentina, rather than in relatively humid Uruguay) in the affordable Río de los Pájaros and Cisplatino lines, and the Fabula Late Harvest Viognier–Torrontes, a sweet dessert wine full of soft peach and honey flavours. The Arretxea Lyrios is a white blend to match the red Arretxea, with Chardonnay, Viognier and Riesling all aged separately for 18 months before blending and bottling.

Establicimiento Juanicó (*Ruta 5 km37½, Juanicó;* \ *4335 9725;* m *094 847482;* e *visita@juanico.com; www.juanico.com*) The biggest and most successful of Uruguay's family wineries is right on Ruta 5 (and the 34th parallel), 6km south of the town of Canelones. The Establicimiento Juanicó was built in 1755 as a farm. In 1820 it was bought by Francisco Juanicó, who began planting vines and about 1840 built some fine brick cellars, declared a national historical monument in 2009 – it's claimed that this is the oldest continuously operating winery in South America.

The winery ended up in the hands of the state, which supplied the Free French forces with beef during World War II. Unable to repay the debt in cash, in 1946 the French government built a modern winery like a concrete flying saucer, a state-of-the-art complex with gravity-fed processing, although now run from a 21st-century computerised control room. In 1979 the winery was bought from the government by the Deicas family, who set about transforming it with new techniques and new grapes (especially the 'noble' Bordeaux varieties), and a change from quantity to quality, cutting yields from 25,000kg/ha to between 2,000 and 12,000. Relaunched as a producer of fine wines in 1984, it began exporting and winning medals in the 1990s. The Don Pascual brand (named in honour of Pascual Harriague, who introduced the Tannat grape to Uruguay and founded the country's wine industry) was launched in 1996, and is now found in most of the country's restaurants. Indeed the brand is so omnipresent that a careless guidebook writer might assume that many restaurants are named Don Pascual.

In 1999 Juanicó set up the first Uruguayan joint venture with a French winery, Château Pape Clement (owned by the Magrez family of Bordeaux) to produce a high-quality Tannat called Casa Magrez; these vines are on a separate, far smaller vineyard nearby, and the intention is to set up a separate winery here too. It's a strong, complex wine, smooth and intense in the mouth and with a very long finish.

Juanicó now produces over five million litres of wine a year and supplies 30% of the domestic market; in fact 70% of the production is still table wine (mostly made from grapes bought in from other growers). It's immensely impressive that so much wine is mass-produced here at the same time as small batches of genuinely world-class wines. With around 10,000 visitors a year, Juanicó has the most professional tourist operation in Uruguay – more so than Bouza, which gets the majority of the cruise-ship business. **Tastings** cost US$5–25, including a tour of the vineyard, the winery and the cellars, and of course ends in the shop.

The vines at Juanicó are managed 'semi-organically', being sprayed against Botrytis fungus but otherwise managed naturally, encouraging natural predators to control insects, and with all seeds and stalks being composted. They're planted at a high density, with up to 8,000 vines per hectare, but with only two bunches per plant, to give highly concentrated sugars. Laboratory analysis and tasting show the precise moment for picking (by hand, naturally). Although the vineyard is at only 45m altitude, temperatures can range between 35°C by day and 18°C by night, ideal for boosting sugar and alcohol levels.

The Don Pascual range (exported under the name Bodegones del Sur, with labels showing Uruguayan Constructivist art) includes the single varietal reds Tannat, Merlot, Petit Verdot, Cabernet Sauvignon, Cabernet Franc and Pinot Noir and Marselan; Tannat–Merlot and Shiraz–Tannat blends; and the whites Chardonnay, Sauvignon Blanc, Viognier and Tempranillo. Marselan (a cross between Cabernet Sauvignon and Grenache) was developed in France in 1961 and has been used here since 2002; it's partly oaked, but displays less tannin and less fruit than you might expect, and goes well with heavy pasta, meat and cheese. Tempranillo is the only non-French grape grown here, used mainly in a rosé.

The Don Pascual Tannat Reserva is young but excellent, with fruit, spice and leather shining through the sharp complex tannins, and a long finish. There's also the Tannat Roble, aged for a year in American oak, with softer tannins and better structure. The Pinot Noir Reserva is not bad, with sweetish fruit and a slightly thin finish; likewise, the Cabernet Sauvignon Reserva, partly aged in oak for balance and structure, has plenty of acidity and alcohol but can be a bit cloying and needs time to open up. The Petit Verdot Roble, also aged in oak, is a fine Bordeaux-style wine that goes well with game, duck and pheasant.

Among the more limited range of whites, the Sauvignon Gris, Marselan and Viognier Reservas are fine, but the Viognier works better as an oak-aged blend with Chardonnay, with good acidity and light fruits plus hints of ginger. There are also two sparkling whites, the Cuvée Castelar Extra Brut and Brut Reserva, also blends of Chardonnay with just 10% of Viognier, light, acidic and very dry.

The premium wines, under the Familia Deicas name, include the Cru Garage Tannat (*garage* being a Bordeaux term for a small winery) – one of the best Tannats you could hope for, with intense inky-black fruit with toffee and chocolate, and superb structure – and the Preludio blends. The red blend is composed of Tannat (40%), Cabernet Sauvignon, Cabernet Franc, Merlot, Petit Verdot and, since 2002, precisely 2% of Marselan, all from the best plots of old vines, aged in oak for 22 months. It's quite superb, as is vouched for by its presence on the wine list of the very prestigious Fat Duck run by Heston Blumenthal in Bray, and the many prizes it has won. The Preludio Blanco, almost as good, is 95% Chardonnay, with Sauvignon Blanc and Viognier, also aged in oak for length and structure, with luscious, buttery fruit and good acidity. The small amounts of varietal wines made for blending in Preludio, but not used, are bottled as Single Barrel Limited Editions.

Also in the Familia Deicas range is the Botrytis Noble Cosecha Tarde, the late harvest dessert wine (like a Sauternes) that's blended from Sauvignon Blanc, Sauvignon Gris, Gewurztraminer, Petit Grain and Rossesse grapes, picked right at the end of the season when the 'noble rot' fungus has taken hold.

Finally, also in the Familia Deicas range, the licor de Tannat is a port-style fortified wine that's full of fruit and almost syrupy-sweet, and excellent with Stilton-type cheeses (not easily found in Uruguay). Historically, cognac was also produced at Juanicó, and there are still Ugni Blanc vines here, but none is made now.

Turning off Ruta 5, a dirt track winds through the beautifully tended vineyards and past the railway station (used by occasional charter trains for cruise groups) to the winery. **Tastings** are held in a lovely red-brick hall (built by the British in the 1860s). Below this are the original cellars, built in about 1840 and still in use, where you'll see some Art Nouveau stained glass rescued from Montevideo's legendary Tupi Namba bar; there's also plenty of contemporary art on show. Visits are very professionally managed, with a tour of the vineyard, winery, cellar and historic buildings. There are three cachilas (vintage cars) under a thatched roof, and you might see a *lagarto overa* (tegu lizard) on the lawn, or some of the 120 species of birds recorded here (a large part of the estate is still woodland). Tastings start at US$15 with four wines; you can try up to eight wines, or choose cold meats and cheeses, empanadas or a full lunch, usually the classic asado with a huge salad and dessert. Naturally you can buy wines in their shop too.

Bodega Marichal (*Ruta 64 km48½, Etchevarría;* \ *4332 1949;* e *visitas@ marichalwines.com; www.marichalwines.com*) Turning west from Ruta 5 at km39, it's almost 7km to Bodega Marichal, a relatively small winery founded in 1910 and now run by the third and fourth generations of the family. It's one of the nicest to visit, thanks to the charming Juan Andrés Marichal, who handles all English-speaking visits, as well as to the food laid on by 'Granny Teresita'. They have 50ha of vines here, on gentle slopes with semi-permeable soils that almost never need irrigation. White grapes (Chardonnay, Semillon and Sauvignon Blanc) account for 30% of production and Tannat for about half of the remainder; there's also Merlot, Pinot Noir, Cabernet Franc and some experimental varieties. No less than 70% of their fine wines are exported, to Europe, Brazil and Barbados.

The Pinot Noir, grown on a hill enjoying cool breezes at night, has done well on its own (with 70% kept in oak for 11 months) and also in a very unconventional blend with Tannat that has the delicacy of Pinot but the body and colour of Tannat. Pinot Noir is even blended with Chardonnay to give a delightful, buttery, light-red wine with good cherry fruit. The Reserve Collection Tannat (with 65% kept in oak for 11 months and then aged in the bottle for a year) needs to be decanted or given time to open up, but then works very well, with some spice on the nose and a long finish; a Grand Reserve Tannat was launched in 2009, after a full 18 months in oak.

The Cabernet Franc is used for a young unoaked rosé, and there's an excellent fresh Chardonnay, made without malolactic fermentation. The Blanc de Noir, made of Pinot Noir with 35% Chardonnay and kept in oak for just three months, is very creamy, and excellent with food.

Tastings cost from US$20 (for three wines with cold meats and cheese) to US$33 (five wines with cold meats, cheeses and homemade empanadas), or US$55 with an asado. Booking is essential, except for the Día de la Vendimia (Harvest Festival) in early March and the Dia del Patrimonio (Heritage Day) in October.

Bodega Casa Filgueira (*Ruta 81 km7, Cuchilla Verde;* \ *4334 6438, 2711 3521;* e *info@bodegafilgueira.com; www.bodegafilgueira.com*) Turning off Ruta 5 at km47, north of Canelones town, and going to the end of Ruta 62 and a little bit to the left, you'll come to Bodega Casa Filgueira. A little out of the tourist mainstream, this is a friendly and modern winery that only started making fine wines in 1998 (although the family has been making wine here since 1927). Vines are trained on Open Lyre stands and replaced every eight years; the grapes are hand-picked early in the morning, and processed in chilled stainless steel tanks. Tannat vines cover 40% of the 45ha area, followed by Cabernet Sauvignon, Cabernet Franc, Merlot, Pinot Noir and, most recently, Sauvignon Gris.

The Clásico range of young wines (to be drunk within a year) is aged only in the bottle, for between two and eight months. The Reserva and Reserva de la Familía ranges include Tannat, Merlot, Cabernet Sauvignon and Chardonnay, all aged in French oak barrels for between eight and 15 months to give structure and complexity to go with their intense fresh aromas. At the top end are the Premiun Merlot (oaked for 15 months) and Sauvignon Gris (aged in the bottle only, for eight months); Casa Filgueira is the first winery in Uruguay to tackle the rare Sauvignon Gris (or Grigio) variety, and claims to account for 5% of world production already.

Visits are welcome with 48 hours' notice (🕐 *10.00–15.00 Mon–Sat*). You'll see the vines, winery and cellar, and **taste** the wines either with cheese and snacks or with an asado lunch and salad.

Viña Varela Zarranz (*Ruta 74 km29, Suárez;* 📞 *2364 4587;* e *info@varelazarranz.com; www.varelazarranz.com*) Between Ruta 7 and Ruta 8, to the northeast of Montevideo, Viña Varela Zarranz is a historic estate entered along an avenue of century-old olive trees; grand araucarias, casuarinas, eucalyptus and other trees stand in the park.

Diego Pons – banker, senator and ambassador to Italy – bought this estate in 1888 and entertained politicians including Julio Herrera y Obes, José Batlle y Ordóñez, Claudio Williman and Baltasar Brum in his Italianate mansion. He planted French vines here and in 1892 built the winery and cellar, with winemaking equipment from Italy and massive oak vats from Nancy in France. In 1944 the estate was bought by brothers Ramón and Antonio Varela, who had founded the Viticultores Unidos del Uruguay (VUDU) co-operative winery in 1933. Ramón married María Zarranz, and their four sons in time took over the business. Since 1986 the third generation has been in charge, bringing in new investors to set up Viña Varela Zarranz as fine-winemakers alongside VUDU, which continues to produce table wines.

With 60ha of vines here and another 50ha at Cuatro Piedras on the far side of Ruta 5, they've steadily replaced old vines with healthy new French stock, now growing on Open Lyre stands, for greater exposure to light and air. In addition to the traditional Tannat (20% of the total), Merlot, Cabernet Franc, Cabernet Sauvignon, Chardonnay and Sauvignon Blanc, they've added unusual varieties such as Muscat de Frontignan, Muscat de Ottonel, Bourboulenc, Marsanne and Viognier. New technology includes machines to gently remove the grapes from the stalks, low-pressure pneumatic presses, chilled stainless steel tanks and bottling with inert gas. Table wine, which accounts for about 94% of production (c2½ million litres a year), is made in far bigger tanks than the fine wine, without chilling, and is bottled (with plastic corks) in 1.5- or two-litre bottles, demijohns of up to ten litres, or even Tetrapaks.

White wines, all unoaked, include a delicate Sauvignon Blanc, Chardonnay and the only Muscat Petit Grain made in Uruguay – this is dry (despite first impressions on the nose) and smooth, with citric aromas and good fruit. There's also an unoaked Cabernet Sauvignon rosé. The María Zarranz sparkling champenoise (a blend of Viognier, Marsanne, Bourboulenc and Chardonnay) was introduced in 2008; young, fresh and fruity, it's aimed at the domestic market.

Among the red wines, there's an unoaked Cabernet Franc–Tannat (young and plummy, although it will age well); the others are all aged in oak barrels, although the Cabernet Sauvignon only gets a month and 40% of the regular Tannat gets two months. The Tannat Reserva is aged in oak for six months, and there are three premium Tannats, the Roble (aged for ten months) and the Crianza and 150 Años Teatro Solís, which spend a year in French and American oak, giving lots of concentrated fruit with smoky notes, and good structure with smooth tannins. The Guidaí Detí (Charrúa for 'Three Moons') is a premium blend of Tannat (55%) Cabernet Sauvignon (25%) and Cabernet Franc (20%), all fermented separately, then blended and kept in oak for 14 months; it's full of black fruits and rounded tannins, with good structure and complexity.

Visits are available, mostly for small groups (it's a bit far from the port for cruise groups, although it is the handiest winery for the airport). **Tastings** for up to 30 are held in the atmospheric original cellars, although a barn is being converted for bigger events. Regular tastings cost US$25, or around US$60 for lunch (for groups of ten or more; smaller groups can have empanadas); with luck the impressive sommelier Magdalena Américo will lead you through the sampling. You'll see French oak barrels dating from 1903, holding about 10,200 and 16,900 litres, now used only for storing table wine rather than ageing.

Viñedo de los Vientos (*Ruta 11 km162, Atlántida;* ⤷ *4372 1622;* m *099 372723;* e *info@vinedodelosvientos.com; www.vinedodelosvientos.com; see advert on page 188*) Finally, at the eastern end of Canelones department, Viñedo de los Vientos is a delightfully offbeat place that is, however, totally serious about winemaking. Pablo Fallabrino is a surfer dude whose family has been growing grapes here since 1947. He loves the land, and its 150 bird species, managing it as sustainably as possible, with only low-impact fungicides and minimal amounts of organic fertiliser. You'll see plenty of flickers and horned beetles busy controlling insect pests. He also goes with his instincts as a winemaker, with some very interesting choices of grapes and blends; he tends to blend during the fermentation process, rather than making varietal wines and then blending them.

Most of the original vines have been replaced by virus-free stock from France and South Africa (there's still some Ugni Blanc, which is sold for table wine). Now there's Tannat, Cabernet Sauvignon, Ruby Cabernet, Trebbiano, Gewurztraminer, Moscato Blanco and Chardonnay, and Pablo is planting Nebbiolo and Dolcetto, which should work well as a blend with Tannat. Just 4km from the sea, there's plenty of wind and humidity, so the vines are trained high above the ground for ventilation. Pablo built the winery in 1998, before which the grapes were sold for blending as table wine; even now, about 40% goes for blending.

The standard white wine is Estival (60% Gewurztraminer, 30% Chardonnay, 10% Moscato Blanco), which is very quaffable with or without food. There's also the fine Blanc de Bianco (80% Chardonnay, 10% Trebbiano, 10% Viognier), aged for six months in French oak over the spent yeast (*sur lie*); it has lots of rounded, light fruit flavours. The standard Tannat is young and light but very approachable, with more fruit than you'd expect and hints of oak and smoke. The Eolo Gran Reserva is 80% Tannat (with Ruby Cabernet), aged for a year in French oak, and very good. Pablo also makes a Ripasso di Tannat, fermenting Tannat for a second time over leftover Tannat skins, producing a rich, dry, raisiny wine a little lighter than an Amarone. Alcyone is a Tannat dessert wine (sold by the half-bottle), fortified with brandy and full of velvety fruit, chocolate, honey and vanilla.

Midway between Montevideo and Punta del Este (and under half an hour from Carrasco airport), the winery sees a certain number of tourists, as well as locals calling in to fill up their jugs. **Tastings**, costing US$12 with four wines, should be booked 24 hours ahead. You can also book the Antipasto Special (US$30 for two), with fine snacks accompanying the four wines, or a four-course meal with four matching wines (US$50 each, with a minimum of four people) – Pablo's partner Mariana is a superb cook!

Other wineries Other wineries worth visiting include **Alto de la Ballena** in Maldonado (see page 219), **Los Cerros de San Juan** in Colonia (see page 289), **Irurtia** and others in Carmelo (see page 294), and those below.

Granja Aripuca (*Ruta 103 s/n, Canelones, north off the Interbalnearia at km55½;* ⤷ *4373 7024;* m *094 410108;* e *aripuca@adinet.com.uy; www.aripuca.com.uy*) Aripuca is somewhat tourist-oriented, with horse riding available and a country restaurant, but also makes some decent Tannat, Pinot Noir, Cabernet Sauvignon and Gewurztraminer, as well as a fortified *licor de Tannat*.

La Cruz (*Ruta 5 km117, La Cruz, Florida;* ☎ *4350 2115*) La Cruz is the only certified organic winery in Uruguay and is probably also the country's oldest winery, founded in 1887. Some Tannat vines and French oak vats, brought here in 1903, are still in use. Of the 60ha of vineyards, 20ha are organic, producing a dry velvety Malbec; it's also certified sugar-free and thus suitable for diabetics. They also grow Nebbiolo, Merlot, Tannat, Pinot Noir, Muscat d'Hamburg and Sauvignon Blanc. There's a Pinot Noir–Folie Noir sparkler, and in 2009 they released a white wine made from Arriloba grapes (a cross of Sauvignon Blanc and Raffiat de Moncade). They have a small museum and tasting room; call a day ahead.

Ariano Hermanos (*Ruta 48 km15, El Colorado;* ☎ *2364 5290, 2365 2066;* e *arianohnos@cs.com.uy; www.arianohermanos.com*) Just beyond the Bodega De Lucca, Hermanos is one of the larger, established family wineries, but doesn't offer tastings and visits. Founded in 1929, it has vineyards in Canelones and Paysandú departments and produces 1.5 million litres of wine a year, 60% of it table wine. They produce good Merlot, Cabernet Franc, Tannat, Muscat Ottonel (an Alsace-style white that's ideal with desserts) and Chardonnay, and blends of Tannat with Cabernet Franc, Merlot, Syrah and Cabernet Sauvignon, mostly aged in oak barrels for around six months. Tannatino is a port-like licor de Tannat, matured in oak barrels for six months.

Viñedos y Bodegas Bartora (*Ruta 5 km39, Las Violetas, Canelones;* ☎ *4332 8831;* m *099 336782;* e *bodegabartora@adinet.com.uy*) Just north of Juanicó, this winery welcomes visits by appointment.

Vinos Finos Beretta (*Camino La Renga 2443, Melilla;* ☎ *2322 7503;* e *turismo@vinosfinosberetta.com, folgtberetta@montevideo.com.uy; www.vinosfinosberetta.com*) Founded in 1911, Beretta welcomes visitors by appointment, with snacks or lunch available. With three vineyards around the Melilla region of Canelones, they grow Merlot and Syrah in particular.

Buzzone y Sciutto (*Camino Guerra 6950, Punta de Rieles;* ☎ *2514 5722;* e *bys@internet.com.uy; www.bys.com.uy*) Founded in 1888, Sciutto works closely with university consultants and also grows grapes in Durazno and at Cerro Chapeu, Rivera. They produce good Tannat as well as sparkling and fortified wines; 90% of production is table wine for the demijohn market.

Bodega Gimenez Mendez (*Plaza Vidiella, Batlle y Ordóñez 165, Canelones;* ☎ *4332 0307;* e *sgonzatto@plazavidiella.com; www.gimenezmendez.com*) Produces a million litres a year of table wine, plus fine Tannats (including a fortified licor de Tannat, and the Tannat–Tannat, a blend of two wines from different vineyards made seperately), and the young and fresh Las Brujas Cabernet Sauvignon and Sauvignon Blanc.

Monte de Luz (*Ruta 23 km125, Mal Abrigo, San José;* ☎ *2369 1855;* e *contact@leda-sa.com; www.vignobles-lesgourgues.com*) The French-owned Monte de Luz is at 150m, close to the Sierras de Mahoma. Half the vineyard is planted with Tannat and the rest with Cabernet Sauvignon, Cabernet Franc and Syrah. They produce fruity young varietals and oaked Reservas. Nearby is the **Finca Piedra** (see page 176), which also produces a nice Tannat.

Traversa Vinos Finos (*Avda Pedro de Mendoza 7966, Las Piedras;* ☎ *2222 0035;* e *bodega@traversahnos.com*) and **Bodega Juan Toscanini e Hijos** (*Ruta 69 km30,*

Canelón Chico; ☎ *2368 9696;* e *info@toscaniniwines.com; www.toscaniniwines.com*) are two of Uruguay's biggest wineries, producing large quantities of table wine as well as fine wines.

FLORIDA DEPARTMENT

From Canelones, Ruta 5 continues north as a 90km/h single carriageway towards Durazno and Rivera, near km73 passing the junction of Ruta 76 west to the town of 25 de Mayo – after 10km, Ruta 5 passes **Paso Severino**, where the OSE water utility has a recreation centre at a dam that attracts over 1,000 people on sunny weekends. There are swimming pools, sports and boating facilities, barbecues, a restaurant and **accommodation** (☎ *4330 9033/5;* e *pasoseverino@ose.com.uy;* **$**) with both shared and private bathrooms. There's also a good native forest here for birdwatching. A bus runs from Florida at 10.00 on Sundays, returning at 19.30.

FLORIDA The town of Florida (pronounced *Floreeda*) is 50km north of Canelones and 100km from Montevideo, making it the last convenient stopover if you're heading towards the capital. Founded in 1809, and now a quiet provincial town of just over 30,000 inhabitants, it had its moment in the limelight when a provisional government was set up here on 14 June 1825, and the Assembly of Representatives declared Uruguay's independence on 25 August (see page 17).

Getting there and away Just north of km95, Ruta 5 crosses Ruta 56, which leads west past Parque Robaina and the Piedra Alta to the centre of town, but **buses** from Tres Cruces may continue up Ruta 5 past km97 to run south past the Piedra Alta railway station (where 0-6-0 steam locomotive No 3 is preserved) to Plaza Artigas and the bus terminal, just west of the main Plaza Asamblea.

From the terminal at Batlle y Ordóñez and Herrera, CITA runs frequent buses to Montevideo (see page 87), most calling at Canelones; Turismar has five services a day to Durazno, three of which continue to Paso de los Toros and San Gregorio de Polanco. Bruno Hermanos and CTTM also go to Durazno. Turismar has three buses a day to Punta del Este via Piriápolis, and a COOM bus leaves at 15.00 daily for Punta del Este via Minas. These buses, plus five (*3 on Sun*) with Cuidad de Florida and OPAC (Piedra Alta), go via San Ramón, where you can change for buses on Ruta 7 to Melo. OPAC also has two buses a day to Santa Lucía, although it's usually easier to go via Canelones.

Tourist information The Centro de Información Municipal is at Gutiérrez Ruiz and Saravia, at the corner of the Prado Park (☎ *4352 1738;* e *floridaturismo@adinet. com.uy; www.imf.gub.uy;* ⊕ *09.00–17.00 daily*).

🏠 **Where to stay** All listings are included on the map opposite.

🏠 **Hotel Real** Independencia 627; ☎ 4352 2498; e hotelreal@adinet.com.uy. Nothing grand, but it has nice large rooms with cable TV, AC & Wi-Fi, although rooms at the front can be noisy. **$$**

🏠 **Hotel Español** Rodó 360 & González; ☎ 4352 2262; e hotelesp@adinet.com.uy. This more economical option was built in 1926 & is in excellent condition, with a garage, Wi-Fi, rooms with cable TV & AC, but no lift. B/fast US$3 extra. **$$–$**

Å **Campsite** ☎ 4352 7395; ⊕ all year. In the Parque Robaina, east of the centre before the Ruta 5 bypass, it's in thick native forest, although the area is too busy for there to be much birdlife. **$**

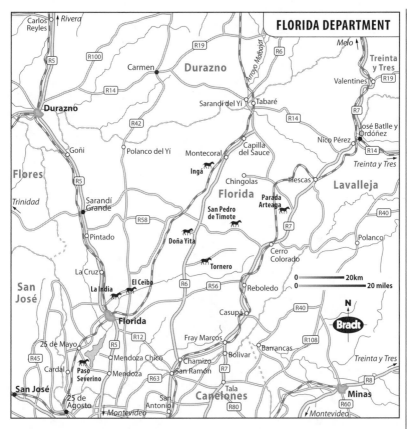

FLORIDA DEPARTMENT

Carlos Reyles | Rivera

R19 · R6 · Melo ↑

R5 · R100 · Carmen · **Durazno** · Treinta y Tres

R14 · Valentines · R19

Durazno · Sarandí del Yí · Tabaré · R7

R42 · R14 · José Batlle y Ordóñez

Goñi · Polanco del Yí · Montecoral · Capilla del Sauce · Nico Pérez · R14

Ingá · Treinta y Tres

Flores · Chingolas · Illescas · **Lavalleja**

Trinidad · R5 · Sarandí Grande · **Florida** · Parada Arteaga · R40

San Pedro de Timote · R7

R58 · Polanco

Pintado · **Doña Yita** · Cerro Colorado

La Cruz · El Ceibo · R6 · R56 · Reboledo · 0 ____ 20km / 0 ____ 20 miles

San José · La India · Tornero

Casupá · R40 · **N**

Florida · **Bradt**

R12 · Fray Marcos · R108

25 de Mayo · R5 · Barrancas

R45 · Mendoza Chico · Chamizo · Bolívar · Treinta y Tres

Cardal · Paso Severino · Mendoza · San Ramón · R7 · R8

San José · R63 · Tala · **Minas**

25 de Agosto · San Antonio · **Canelones** · R60

↓ Montevideo · R80 · ↓ Montevideo

✗ Where to eat There's a limited choice of eating places, beyond the fast-food joints on the main drag, Independencia. All listings are included on the map above.

✗ Albahaca González & Rivera; ☏ 4353 0181. Opposite Multiahorro, this serves decent & affordable pizza & empanadas. **$$**

✗ Churrasquería Pajarito Ituzaingó between Gallinal & Independencia; ⏰ 11.30–15.00, 20.30–00.30 daily. A bit of a party place, but serves good grilled meats & has AC & Wi-Fi. **$$**

✗ Club Florida Independencia 674; ☏ 4352 2074; ⏰ 10.00–midnight daily. **$$**

✗ Parador Florida Junction Ruta 5 & Ruta 56; ☏ 4352 3359. **$$**

✗ Confitería del Centro Independencia 645. Serving snacks & cakes since 1878. **$**

Shopping The cast-iron municipal market (opened in 1909) is at Fernández and Barreiro; supermarkets include MultiAhorro (*Rivera & González;* ⏰ *08.00–22.00 daily*), Ta-Ta (*Independencia 666, north of Rodó;* ⏰ *08.00–22.00 Mon–Sat, 09.00–13.00, 17.00–22.00 Sun*) and the Supermercado San Cono (*opposite the bus terminal at Herrera & Batlle, & at Fernández & Barreiro;* ⏰ *08.00–13.00, 15.00–22.00 Mon–Fri, 08.00–13.30, 15.30–22.00 Sat, 08.00–13.30, 17.00–21.00 Sun*).

The good Albanes bike shops are at Fernández and Rivera and on Plaza Artigas; bike repairs can also be done at La Magyca, Fernández 578 (⏰ *15.00–20.00 Mon–Fri*).

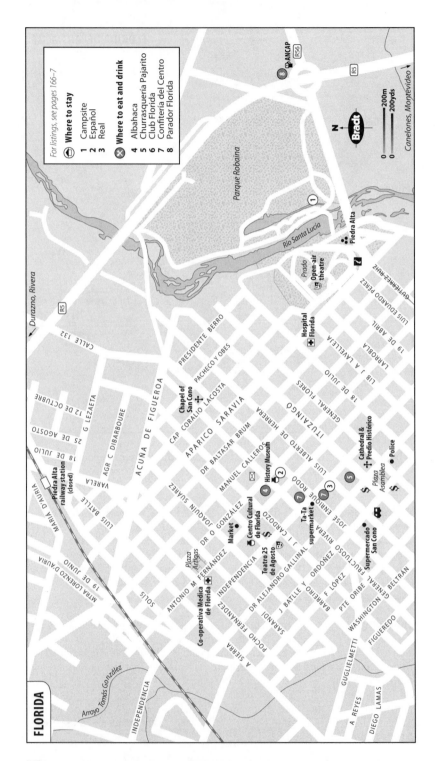

FLORIDA

For listings, see pages 166–7

Where to stay
1 Campsite
2 Español
3 Real

Where to eat and drink
4 Albahaca
5 Churrasquería Pajarito
6 Club Florida
7 Confitería del Centro
8 Parador Florida

Other practicalities

Banks There are ATMs on the northwest and southwest sides of Plaza Asamblea and on Independencia east of Cardozo, where you'll also find Cambio Real Servicios at Independencia 736 (⊕ 08.30–19.30 Mon–Fri, 08.30–13.00 Sat).

Communications The post office is in the Paseo Florida mall (*Rivera 3320 & González;* ⊕ 09.00–17.00 Mon–Fri, 08.00–12.00 Sat). Antel's *telecentros* are at Fernández 872 (⊕ 09.00–17.00 Mon–Fri, 09.00–13.00 Sat) and Independencia 749 (⊕ 07.00–23.00 Mon–Sat). There's public Wi-Fi on Plaza Asamblea and the Prado, and a good signal at a school on Fernández between Rodó and Herrera.

Emergency services The state-run Hospital Florida (✆ 4352 2109/2119) is at Baltasar Brum and Lavalleja, towards the Prado, and the Co-operativa Medica de Florida hospital (✆ 4352 5141) is at Fernández 492, on Plaza Artigas. The police (*Flores 509;* ✆ 4352 3301/2) are on the south side of Plaza Asamblea.

What to see and do Plaza Asamblea, its 'elephant's foot' araucarias busy with noisy, small, pale-green *cotorras* (parakeets), is immediately east of the bus terminal; on its east side is the cathedral of the **Virgén de los Treinta y Tres**. In the usual neoclassical style, it was built in 1887–94, although the towers were left unfinished until 1908. The interior walls were totally covered with rather uninspired paintings in 1931 when it became a cathedral. The large organ at the west end, installed in 1935, is one of the best in South America, and the bronze doors are by the sculptors José and Stelio Belloni. On the altar (dating from 1898) is a tiny spotlit statue of the Virgin to which the Treinta y Tres lowered their flag and pledged their loyalty; now the Virgén de los Treinta y Tres (a copy of Our Lady of Luján) is honoured with a festival on the second Sunday of November, including a choral festival in the cathedral.

On the north side of the cathedral is the **Predio Histórico** (*Historic Site; Ituzaingó & Gallinal*), site of the rancho of Don Basilio Fernández where the Sala de Representantes declared Uruguayan independence on 25 August 1825. Later a school, it was destroyed in 1864 in the Guerra Grande and now there is just a commemorative plaque on the site.

The **Centro Cultural de Florida** (*Barreiro 420*) houses a library and paintings of local scenes by local artists, as well as José Cuneo's easel and palette; its small historical collection, of miscellaneous portraits, uniforms and swords and a model of the Battle of Sarandí Grande, has been moved to Rivera 373 where the **museum** opened in August 2013. The **Teatro 25 de Agosto**, built as the Cine Nelson in 1945, is at Independencia 787, and the Cine Florida is at Rodó 360, just west of the Hotel Español; carnaval events are held in the open-air Teatro de Verano in the Prado.

Just northeast of the centre, the **Chapel of San Cono** (*Rodó 150 & Lacosta*), built in 1955, has a relatively modern exterior but a gaudy interior with murals of the 12th-century saint's miracles. To the rear of the altar is an amazing display of ex-voto offerings from the faithful in search of divine help, including bikes and motorbikes, many *quinceaño* dresses (worn by girls for their 15th birthday parties, when they supposedly reach adulthood) and lots of foreign banknotes, watches, rings, pearl necklaces and the like. On 3 June each year the statue of San Cono is taken in procession to the plaza and back, and up to 20,000 people come to pray for help with lotteries and gambling, Cono's speciality.

Five blocks southeast from here along Lacosta is the **Prado**, a park overlooking the Río Santa Lucía Chico (a minor branch of the main river) which was laid out in

Southern Uruguay   FLORIDA DEPARTMENT

4

1910 and last remodelled in 1981, with sculptures, exotic flora, a **summer theatre** and the Parador Piedra Alta Restaurant. At the southern end of the Prado, by the road bridge across the river to the Parque Robaina and Ruta 5, is the **Piedra Alta (High Rock)**, actually just a couple of metres high, where the Declaration of Independence was read to the people; there are lots of plaques and a monument with the text of the declaration.

Estancias

San Pedro de Timote (*Between Ruta 6 & Ruta 7;* ✆ *4310 8086–88;* m *099 614110;* e *centraldereservas@montevideo.com.uy, info@sanpedrodetimote.com; www. sanpedrodetimote.com;* **$$$$$**) Perhaps the most historic and upmarket of Uruguay's tourist estancias, Timote is in the Cuchilla Grande range 14km from Cerro Colorado – definitely a countryside hotel rather than a working ranch. It was part of the first and most important of Uruguay's Jesuit estancias, Nuestra Senora de los Desamparados (c100,000ha in area), founded in the 1740s and when the Jesuits were expelled in 1767. The present estancia, a mere 30,000ha in area, was founded in 1854; in the late 1990s a *hotel de campo* (rural hotel) was established here. Beautifully restored in colonial style, you can see the Jesuits' chapel, the library and a patio decorated with 1930s Spanish majolica tiles. There are 30 bedrooms, with open fireplaces and contemporary if rather conventional décor. You can walk in the 50ha park, swim in the outdoor heated swimming pools, take carriage rides, go fishing, visit the farmyard and above all go horse riding, although there's less scope for working with gauchos than on other estancias. You can also play soccer, volleyball, tennis, basketball, and pelota, as well as pool, table tennis, mini soccer table and other board games.

Other estancias Other tourist estancias nearby include Parada Arteaga (*Ruta 7 km142;* ✆ *4310 8086;* m *099 614110*), Estancia Tornero (*Ruta 6 km121;* ✆ *4336 4164, 4350 2169;* e *matildev@adinet.com.uy*), Estancia Doña Yita (*Ruta 6 km137;* m *099 624973;* e *estanciayita@movinet.com.uy*) and Estancia Ingá (*Ruta 6 km171½;* ✆ *4360 7138;* e *mmurgate@hotmail.com*). Closer to the town of Florida are La India (*Camino La Macana km4;* ✆ *4352 3883;* m *099 355396*), with a menagerie and archaeological collection, and Estancia El Ceibo (*15km northeast from Ruta 5 km97.4;* ✆ *4352 3393;* m *099 125761; www.elceibo.com.uy*), which offers horse riding weekends for US$300 per person.

SAN JOSÉ DEPARTMENT

Ruta 1 westbound (to Colonia) splits from Ruta 5 at a flyover junction at km7 and crosses the Río Santa Lucía (from Montevideo department to San José department) at km21, where the village of **Santiago Vásquez** lies below to the right. Traffic on Ruta 1 stops at a toll and continues westwards, but there's an older metal bridge to the right which is open to bicycles and other traffic; buses 127 and 494 from Montevideo's Baltasar Brum terminal come here too.

Santiago Vásquez was founded in 1878 around a slaughterhouse, well placed at the mouth of the river, and was also a resort for the citizens of Montevideo. It was prosperous until the 1940s but was then left isolated by new roads.

On the east side of the village is the **Parque Zoológico Lecoq** (*Avda Luis Batlle Berres km19.2;* ⊕ *09.00–18.00 Wed–Sun; US$1/car w/ends only*), a zoo which has native fauna kept in newly planted native woodland, exotic fauna kept in pretty decent conditions and organised by their continent of origin, and new aviaries with over 140 species of birds, as well as a new narrow-gauge railway, about 1km long. There are also trails into the *humedales* (wetlands) of the Río Santa Lucía, a protected ecosystem with lots of native plants and waterfowl. In fact, there are over 20,000ha of wetlands around the mouth of the Río Santa Lucía that can also be explored by boat, horse and bicycle; from the village, Silvestre Ochoa leads east to Avenida de los Deportes via an 800m wooden footbridge, alongside a *pista de regatas* (rowing lake, which also gives good views of birds), and loops right around the back of the zoo to Camino los Camalotes. It's also possible to enter from from km20 of Batlle Berres (the old main road from Paso de la Arena in Montevideo). By the River Plate a couple of kilometres west on Ruta 1, the Reserva Natural Playa Penino is another good spot for birding, with 244 species seen in the area.

The Centro de Visitantes de la Comisión de Humedales is on La Guardia s/n, opposite the Club Alemán de Remo (German Rowing Club); free walks are led by rangers on weekends and holidays. The best place to eat is nearby at the Yacht Club Uruguayo (\ *2312 1258;* ⊕ *09.00–21.00 daily*).

The Parque Municipal Parque Espinillo (*8km southwest on Camino General Basilio Muñoz from Ruta 1 km20, the exit for the complejo carcelario or prison;* ⊕ *w/ends & holidays; 1 Dec–15 Apr daily*) is the nearest **campsite** to Montevideo. There's space for 70 tents (with electric lighting and hot water), cabins, barbecues and a stony little beach. At the gate is a parador with restaurant and shop.

Along the San José coast there's a string of minor beach resorts. The Río de la Plata is muddy and semi-salty here, and the surf is poor, but the beaches are popular with local people in summer. At km32 of Ruta 1 there's a turning to **Playa Pascual**, a small beach resort with restaurants and cafés but no hotels. From Libertad, at km50, a road (Ruta 1 Vieja) heads north to Rincón de Buschental, on the Río Santa Lucía, where the Complejo Buschental (\ *4340 5068;* e *complejobuschental@gmail.com*) comprises a parador (with restaurant and rooms) and dock, with canoes to rent, as well as the Cabañas Santa Esmeralda (\ *4340 5230*). At km61 a paved road runs south for 14km to the larger beach resort of **Kiyú**, known for hang-gliding and fishing; there's camping at the Parador Chico (\ *4345 7078*) and about 1km south in Vista Mar.

At km67 there's a flyover where Ruta 3 turns north for San José, Paysandú and the litoral; continuing on Ruta 1, the **Estancia Turística Don Joaquín** (*km94½;* \ *4349 2007; www.donjoaquin.com*) offers horse riding, boating, cycling and walks in 600ha of native forest. There's a heated pool and a new spa; double rooms cost US$300, cabins cost US$125 per person, and a day's activities, with lunch and tea, costs US$80 per person.

At km96 (90 minutes from Montevideo), at the junction of Ruta 1 and Ruta 11, immediately before the boundary with Colonia department, is **Ecilda Paullier**, a small village known for cheese-making, with a couple of roadside restaurants; 17km south by an unmade road is **Boca del Cufré**, another small beach resort with accommodation at Casapuerto (m *099 332102*) and cabins and camping (\ *4340 9344*). At the mouth of the **Arroyo del Cufré**, it's a good location for fishing.

SAN JOSÉ San José (93km from Montevideo) was founded in 1783 and settled by families from the Galicia, Castille and León regions of Spain. In 1811 José Artigas's cousin Manuel Artigas was killed in the Battle of San José, when Spanish forces were defeated by those fighting for independence, and the town became known as San José de Mayo (so its citizens are known as *maragatos*). In 1828 the Asamblea Constituyente y Legislativa (see page 17) met here to draw up the new nation's constitution, adopted nationwide in July 1830. In 1856 San José became a city, and is now capital of the department and a prosperous commercial and agricultural centre with a population of around 36,000.

4

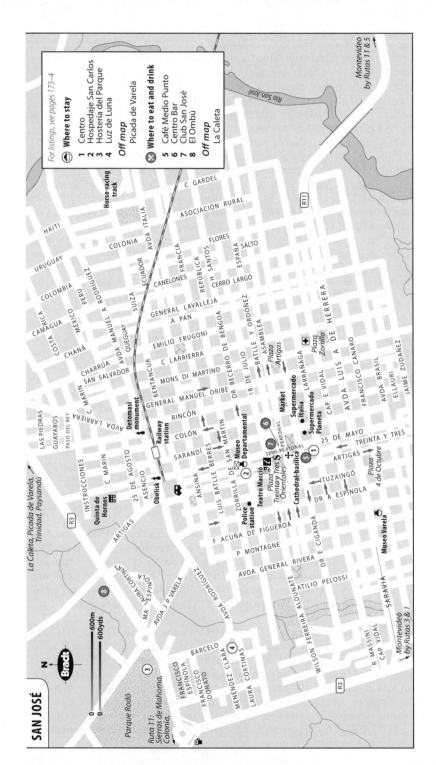

SAN JOSÉ

For listings, see pages 173–4

Where to stay
1 Centro
2 Hospedaje San Carlos
3 Hostería del Parque
4 Luz de Luna

Off map
Picada de Varela

Where to eat and drink
5 Café Medio Punto
6 Centro Bar
7 Club San José
8 El Ombú

Off map
La Caleta

Montevideo
by Rutas 11 & 5

Río San José

R11

Horse-racing track

C GARDEL

ASOCIACIÓN RURAL

HAITÍ

COLONIA

AVDA ITALIA

URUGUAY

ECUADOR

FRANCIA

FLORES

SALTO

COLOMBIA

PERÚ

SUIZA

CANELONES

REPÚBLICA

H SANTOS

ESPAÑA

CAMAGUA

MÉXICO

QUEGUAY

GENERAL LAVALLEJA

CERRO LARGO

COSTA

CHANÁ

A PAN

CHARRÚA

AVDA MANUEL A RODRÍGUEZ

EMILIO FRUGONI

C LARRIERRA

MONS DI MARTINO

DR BECERRO DE BENGOA

BATLLE Y ORDOÑEZ

SAN SALVADOR

C MARÍN

BENTANCUR

GENERAL MANUEL ORIBE

18 DE JULIO

ASAMBLEA

Plaza Zorrilla

AVDA LUIS A DE HERRERA

LAS PIEDRAS

AVDA LARRAÑAGA

Detomasi monument

RINCÓN

Plaza Artigas

FRANCISCO CANARO

GUAYABOS

PASO DEL REY

Railway station

COLÓN

LARRAÑAGA

CAP E VIDAL

AVDA BRASIL

ELLAURI

JAIME ZUDAÑEZ

INSTRUCCIONES

25 DE AGOSTO

ASENCIO

SARANDÍ

Market

Supermercado Italia

Supermercado Planeta

25 DE MAYO

Quinta de Hornos

Obelisk

ANSINA

LUIS BATLLE BERRES

ZORRILLA DE SAN MARTÍN

6

Museo Departamental

SEMI-PEATONAL

7

1

TREINTA Y TRES

ARTIGAS

Plaza 4 de Octubre

ARTIGAS

Teatro Macció

Plaza Treinta y Tres Orientales

Cathedral-basilica

ITUZAINGÓ

DR A ESPÍNOLA

Police station

2

La Caleta, Picada de Varela, Trinidad, Paysandú

R3

F ACUÑA DE FIGUEROA

P MONTAGNE

AVDA GENERAL RIVERA

DR E CIGANDA

Museo Varela

MA ESPÍNOLA

LAURA CORTINAS

AVDA J P VARELA

AVDA RODRÍGUEZ

WILSON FERREIRA ALDUNATE

ATILIO PELOSSI

SARAVIA

CAP VIDAL

R MASSINI

Montevideo by Rutas 3 & 1

R3

N

Bradt

0   600m
0   600yds

Parque Rodó

Ruta 11: Sierras de Mahoma, Colonia

3

FRANCISCO ESPÍNOLA

FRANCISCO DONATO

BARCELO

MENÉNDEZ CLARA

4

8

ARTIGAS

Getting there and away

By car Coming from Santa Lucía on Ruta 11, there's a toll near the Arroyo Santa Lucía at km81 (from Ecilda Paullier). There's a long bridge across the Río San José at km53 and then you enter San José by Avenida Herrera. Coming up from Ruta 1, Ruta 3 bypasses San José to the west, so you'll come in from the other end of Avenida Herrera.

By bus Frequent CITA buses from Montevideo (about 34 a day *directo* (via Ruta 1, where you can change to/from Colonia) and ten via Santa Lucía and Canelones; US$5.70) arrive at the terminal at Bentancur & Artigas (\ *4342 6863*); COTMI also has roughly hourly services from Montevideo. Comsa also runs roughly hourly to Santa Lucía. Buses to Montevideo pick up passengers a block north of Avenida Herrera, those via Canelones on Oribe and others on Espínola. Agencia Central (book through CITA) has five buses a day (from Montevideo) to Trinidad, three continuing to Paysandú. Three COTMI buses continue to Cardona, to the northwest, as well as two Don Pepe services as far as Mal Abrigo. To the southwest, Don Pepe runs four services (three at weekends) to Boca del Cufre.

By train Two blocks east of the terminal on Bentancur is the railway station, which now sends out just one train a day to Montevideo, except on Sundays (US$2). There are plans for a cultural centre in the station, including a railway museum and craft studio.

Tourist information
There's a tourist information centre (*Treinta y Tres 604;* \ *4342 8452;* e *turisanjose@adinet.com.uy;* ☼ *summer 09.00–18.00 daily*) on the northeastern corner of the main square, Plaza Treinta y Tres Orientales. There's also the Espacio Cultural here, with exhibitions and a craft shop, and on weekdays they can open the Teatro Macció, immediately to the west (see page 174).

Where to stay
All listings are included on the map opposite.

⌂ **Luz de Luna** Barceló 847 & Menéndez Clara; \ 4342 1708; e hoteluzdeluna@hotmail. com. Northwest of the centre, this new hotel has comfortable rooms with balconies overlooking spacious gardens. **$$$$**

⌂ **Centro** 25 de Mayo 407; \ 4342 3901; www. hcentro.com. The only accommodation in the centre is the fairly modern 3-star Centro, 2 blocks south of the plaza. It has AC rooms with hairdryers & Wi-Fi, & has parking but no lift; there's a fairly simple breakfast & a 24hr cafetería. **$$$**

⌂ **Hostería del Parque** Ruta 3 km92½; \ 4342 2339; www.hosteriadelparque.com.uy.

Just inside the Parque Rodó, on the northwestern edge of town, is this good 3-star place, with a nice magazine-strewn lobby, shaded parking, a swimming pool & AC rooms with internet access. Good buffet b/fast inc. **$$$**

⌂ **Hospedaje San Carlos** Bengeo 541; \ 4342 2604. This is the town's only cheap place & it's less than welcoming. Near the museum. **$$**

Å **Picada de Varela** 2km north, Ruta 3 km95; \ 4342 8452. There's also 'camping' on the north side of the zoo in Parque Rodó, which is intended for day use but might be usable overnight. Free.

Where to eat
As well as in town, there are other good parillas out north by Ruta 3. All listings are included on the map opposite.

In town

✗ **Café Medio Punto** Treinta y Tres 402 & Larreñaga; m 096 741598; ☼ from 10.00 Mon–

Sat (Jan–Feb from 19.30). This stylish cafetería-confitería has art hanging on the walls & organises cultural events. **$$**

4

✕ Club San José 25 de Mayo 550; ☎ 4342 6344.
Probably one of the town's best restaurants, &
certainly the most convenient, this is on the east
side of the plaza. It serves standard fare in a rather
old-school ambience. $$
✕ Centro Bar 25 de Mayo 514; ☎ 4343 0842. A
simple bar-cafeteria serving pizzas & chivitos. $

Out of town
✕ El Ombú Ruta 3 km93 & Artigas; ☎ 4342 7715.
The thatched Ombú is on the way to the Hostería
del Parque (see page 173), which itself has a good
restaurant. $$
✕ La Caleta 2km north on Ruta 3; ☎ 4343 0637.
It's worth the journey from town to this rural grill. $

Shopping The Mercado Municipal (*Asamblea 676 & Colón, east of the plaza*) is
a proper food market. It's across the road from the Supermercado Italia (⊕ *07.30–
12.30, 14.30–22.00 Mon–Fri, 07.30–13.00, 15.00–22.00 Sat, 07.30–13.00 Sun*).
There's also a Planeta a block south (*Sarandí & Ciganda; ⊕ 08.00–21.30 Mon–Sat,
08.30–13.00, 16.30–21.30 Sun*).

Other practicalities
Banks There are ATMs on the west side of Plaza Treinta y Tres Orientales and
elsewhere; to change money go to Cambio San José (*25 de Mayo 560*) on the east
side of the plaza.

Car rental Cars can be rented from Gol Rentacar (*Vidal 758;* ☎ *4342 9907;* m *099
874066;* e *golrentacar_sj@hotmail.com*). There are several 24-hour petrol stations
near the junction of Ruta 3 and Ruta 11.

Communications There should be Wi-Fi on the plaza but it is weak. The post
office (*25 de Mayo 683;* ⊕ *09.00–17.00 Mon–Fri, 09.00–12.00 Sat*) is two blocks
north of the plaza.

What to see and do The **cathedral-basilica**, on the south side of Plaza Treinta
y Tres Orientales, was built in 1857–75, in a pretty grand neoclassical style with
eight Doric columns of Carrara marble from Italy and chandeliers of Murano glass.
The marble main altar and baldacchino, also on eight Corinthian pillars, are by the
Catalan sculptor Domingo Mora; there's a grander marble altar in the chapel of
the Holy Sacrament, to the left. The modern frescoes of St Joseph in Glory in the
central dome and the reliefs of the Four Evangelists on the pendentives are by Lino
Dinetti (1951–54). On the plaza is a pyramid to the Peace of April 1872 (the end of
the Revolución de las Lanzas), designed by Juan Manuel Ferrari. Four blocks east is
Plaza Artigas, which boasts the first statue of Artigas in Uruguay, designed by the
painter Juan Manuel Blanes in 1898.
    On the north side of the plaza is the **Teatro Macció**, opened in 1912, a grand
Eclectic edifice which claims to be the second most important theatre in the
country; certainly all of Uruguay's leading actors have appeared here, as well as
singers of the stature of Carlos Gardel.
    A block to the north is the **Museo Departamental** (*Bengoa 493 & Treinta y Tres;
www.museo.ensanjose.com; ⊕ 15.00–18.00 Tue–Sun & holidays; free*), partly in a
colonial house (built in 1806) from the mirador of which Artigas directed the Battle
of San José in 1811. It has some displays on local history, some old furniture and
art, and a good art collection, including works by Torres García, Figari, Barradas,
Cúneo, Serrano and Carmelo de Arzadun, as well as some foreign works. Unusually
for Uruguay, it has a museum shop, where you can buy T-shirts and other souvenirs.
The city's other museum is the **Museo Varela** (*Varela 267, just south of Avda
Herrera;* m *094 315200;* ⊕ *10.00–12.00, 15.00–19.00 Tue–Sun; free*), a small cottage

commemorating the 'last gaucho poet', Wenceslao Varela (1908–97), with personal belongings including traditional gaucho items that he collected from his youth.

Six blocks north of the plaza, just east of the bus terminal at 25 de Mayo and Avenida Rodríguez, is a short but quite stylish **obelisk** commemorating the battle of 1811, and three blocks east, at the end of Avenida Larriera, a **monument** set up by the Aero Club del Uruguay in honour of pioneer aviator Ricardo Detomasi, who died in a crash in San José in 1915. Three blocks north of the obelisk, on the west side of Leandro Gómez, the **Quinta de Hornos** is one of the oldest houses in the city, now preserved and used mainly for weddings and other events; but the gardens and some farm buildings are worth a visit.

To the northwest of the city by the junction of Ruta 3 and Ruta 11, the Parque Rodó is a pleasant place to spend a hot afternoon, with grills and play areas, but its zoo has some of the smallest cages in any Uruguayan zoo and the animals seem to have lost the will to live. Alternatively, you can go 2km north on Ruta 3 to the Picada de Varela, where there's a summer-only parador (✆ 4342 8452) with open swimming pools and beaches on the Río San José, both very popular in hot weather.

THE SIERRAS DE MAHOMA In the northwest of San José department, on Ruta 23 towards Mercedes, the Sierras de Mahoma is a low range of hills better described as a 'sea of stone', with its exposed rocks that appear to have been beaten by a shower of meteorites into weird formations such as the Turtle, the Waterfall and the Three Brothers. The rocks are intrusive granite with some metamorphic ectinites on the edges; few cows wander up here so unusual plants flourish, including orchids, mosses, *Tillandsia* epiphytes, *Echinopsis* cacti and other specialised plants. Birds include cardinals, mockingbirds, monjitas, white woodpeckers, blue-and-yellow tanagers, pampas finches, sharp-tailed streamcreepers and masked ducks, and foxes are common.

This area has an almost iconic status for Uruguayans, partly owing to the strange aura of its unusual rocky formations, and partly because Artigas passed through here during the Exodo del Pueblo Oriental (see page 15), camping at the so-called Casa de Piedra (Stone House) formation.

On the northwestern flank of the Cuchilla de Mahoma (part of the Cuchilla Grande Septentrional or Great Northern Range), the Sierras cover an area of 20km² and rise to a maximum of just 178m above sea level, with an average of 140m. They can be explored on foot, by horse or even on a bike – you'll be quite exposed to the sun, so take water and suncream.

Getting there and away
By car The entry to the Sierras is 37km from San José at km126 of Ruta 23 (131km from Montevideo), where a track leads to the right to the Posada Sierras de Mahoma (see below). There's a gate here (🕐 *08.00–20.00 daily*) at which you'll have to pay about US$2 – except on the 25th of each month, when there's free access for pilgrims to a shrine to the Virgén del Rosario de San Nicolás. You can book a guide by calling m 099 340345.

By bus Three COTMI buses a day from San José to Cardona pass the entry, and two Don Pepe services run as far as Mal Abrigo, the village at km123.

Where to stay and eat
🏠 **Posada Sierras de Mahoma** m 099 342220; www.sierrasdemahoma.com. Meals & accommodation available & there's a paddock with goats, sheep & even a fallow deer for the delight of school groups. **$$**

Finca Piedra ☎4340 3118; www.fincapiedra.com. This French/English-owned ecotouristic estancia is much nicer & visible on the hill to the right just beyond the village of Mal Abrigo; the gate is at km125, where buses will drop you off. With 1,000ha (including 20ha planted with Tannat & other vines & now producing a very palatable Pinot Noir), horse riding (with 27 horses, mostly *criollos*) is a core activity here, both in the Sierras & helping the gauchos work with the 500 Hereford cattle & 300 Corriedale sheep. The excellent restaurant uses the estancia's own vegetables, eggs, milk & meat (beef, pork & lamb). There's a jacuzzi, outdoor swimming pool, table tennis, pool table & other games, & even a soccer pitch – the owners are keen to attract sports teams & other groups, with facilities for groups in a converted barn. Packages include 3 days of riding (30–40km/day) & 5 days riding to the River Plate (with 2 nights camping). Their Casco Viejo was actually only built c1950 & recently extended. There's a living room with an open fire, library, cable TV & internet access. Rates are US$65/100 for a standard room, US$70/110 for a superior room, or US$80/130 single/double for a deluxe room, with breakfast; FB with a daily horseride costs US$120/300 single/double in the cheapest rooms, US$220/340 in the superior rooms & US$260/420 in deluxe rooms. They have 4 cheaper rooms, aimed more at the backpacker market, at US$50 for 2 inc b/fast. **$$**

CANELONES DEPARTMENT: EAST

Following the ramblas east from Montevideo and crossing the Arroyo de Carrasco in Canelones department, you'll continue through a succession of beach resorts/ mid-range suburbs – incorporated in 1994 as the Ciudad de la Costa – including **Solymar** (Sunandsea), where the Museo del Pan (*Bread Museum; Avda Márquez Castro & Gestido km24.3; ⊕ summer 16.00–20.00 Fri–Sun & holidays; winter 10.00–18.00; US$1*) is worth a brief stop – it doesn't exactly cover all the wonderful worldwide variations of bread, but does a fair job of showing how the traditional Uruguayan loaf was produced, with old mills and ovens.

In **Pinar**, just beyond Solymar at km30½, the Proyecto Karumbé has a marine turtle breeding centre (⊕ *summer 10.00–20.00 Tue–Sun; winter 10.00–18.00 Fri–Sun & holidays; US$2*), worth a visit if you're not going to their main station in Rocha (see page 269). There are frequent buses from Montevideo's Baltasar Brum terminal (via Muñoz and Avenida Italia) to Solymar and Pinar.

Just east of Pinar the main highway to Punta del Este (the Ruta Interbalnearia), coming from Montevideo via the airport, merges with the coast road and Avenida Giannattasio, and continues towards Maldonado. There's a toll at km34, immediately east of the Arroyo Pando, then the road runs through pine forest, with resorts such as Salinas on the right. At km44 there's a turning to the right to El Águila (see page 179) and 1km later the main turning into **Atlántida**, at the junction with Ruta 11 from Canelones town (see page 143).

Continuing east, the Interbalnearia crosses the Arroyo Solís Chico at km51½ and gives access to the strip of coastal resorts known as the Costa de Oro (Gold Coast); to the right at km60 (an hour from Montevideo by direct bus) is Guazú Vira (or Guazubirá), where there's a hide for birdwatching, and where you can also see migrating southern right whales and false orcas in October and November. At km70½ is the small resort of Biarritz, where the **Posada-Restaurant Biarritz** (*Calle 6;* ☎*4378 8968;* m *099 156795;* e *biarritz@internet.com.uy; www.posadabiarritz.com. uy;* **$$$** *during summer,* **$$** *rest of the year*) is a small hotel by the sea with a classy restaurant serving meats, seafood and homemade pastas as well as Asian dishes such as Thai chicken and chop suey, with wines from Bodegas Carrau. Nearby, the beaches of Santa Lucía del Este (km68) and Jaureguiberry (km80), reached by COPSA bus 712 from Tres Cruces, can have good surf, attracting crowds from

Montevideo when conditions are right. At km80.7 the highway crosses the wide Arroyo Solís Grande and enters Maldonado department (see pages 189–242) at a toll and summer-only tourist office.

ATLÁNTIDA The main beach resort of Canelones department is somewhat misnamed, as the Río de la Plata only gives way to the Atlantic at Punta del Este. The first hotel opened here in 1913; in 1956 the great Chilean poet Pablo Neruda, returning from exile in Italy, met secretly here with his last wife Matilda Urrutia (however, the museum dedicated to him is now closed). The town does have a sizeable permanent population, and is noted for its active participation in Las Llamadas (see page 29), with a massive parade on Balet and Avenida Artigas late on the day before Shrove Tuesday, with 18 drumming comparsas.

Getting there and away Frequent **buses** (operated by Cutcsa and COPSA, from Montevideo's Baltasar Brum terminal) take about an hour to reach Atlántida, continuing east to Parque del Plata (km49) and La Floresta (km55). Local bus 7 goes as far east as Biarritz; to go further, towards Piriápolis, Punta del Este or Rocha, you should reserve through Turismo del Este, just off the rambla at Ciudad de Montevideo and Calle 1 (❀ *4372 2132; www.turismodeleste.com; ⊕ 10.00–13.00, 14.00–18.00 Mon–Sat, 10.00–16.00 Sun*) – buses pick up on the Ruta Interbalnearia at the Tienda Inglesa, but they're unlikely to stop if you don't have a reservation.

Tourist information There's a small tourist office (❀ *4372 2371; ⊕ 10.30–17.00 Sun–Thu, 11.30–16.00 Fri–Sat*) on Avenida Artigas (*Ruta 11*) just after leaving the Ruta Interbalnearia. Continuing south on Artigas for half a dozen blocks, you'll find the Church of the Sagrado Corazón (fairly modern, and attractive enough); turning right at the roundabout here, it's just over one block to the very helpful tourist information centre (*Calle Roger Balet & Calle 18;* ❀ *4372 3104/6122;* e *turismo@imcanelones.gub.uy; www.canelonesturismo.gub.uy; ⊕ 09.00–22.00 daily in season*). There's another small office at El Aguila (see page 179; ❀ *4372 8699*). Free 40-minute tours of the centre and the Edificio Planeta leave from the main tourist office (*summer 09.00 & 10.00 Fri & Sun*); see page 179 for similar tours of El Águila and the Cristo Obrero church.

Where to stay Calle 11, one block from the rambla, has been closed to traffic north of Calle 20, forming a *microcentro*, a pedestrianised block of restaurants, bars and craft stalls. The town's main hotels are immediately north and south of the pedestrianised zone; all listings are included on the map, page 178.

⌂ **Argentina** Calle 11 & 24; ❀ 4372 2414; e info@hotelargentina.com.uy, marichal@netgate. com.uy; www.atlantida.com.uy/ hotelargentina. A decent newish 3-star place with AC rooms & a covered swimming pool with hydro-massage. No Wi-Fi. **$$$$**
⌂ **Centenario** Calle 11 & 24; ❀ 4372 2451; e htl.centenario@hotmail.com; www. hotelcentenario.com.uy. Older than the Argentina, but reasonably spruced up. Has 106 AC rooms & a covered swimming pool. **$$$**

⌂ **Hostal Playa Mansa** Calle 11 between 24 & 26; ❀ 4372 4370; e playamansatlantida@hotmail. com; www.activeb.es/hostalplayamansa. A pleasant hostel in a suburban house just north of the centre, with rooms for 3–4 with bathroom & cable TV. **$$$**
⌂ **Birikina** Rambla Mansa & Argentina; ❀ 4372 8462; e fermajoyroma@yahoo.com.ar; www. atlantida.com.uy/birikina. No longer a youth hostel & does not offer shared rooms; nevertheless it's a decent budget option, especially since the introduction of free Wi-Fi. **$$**

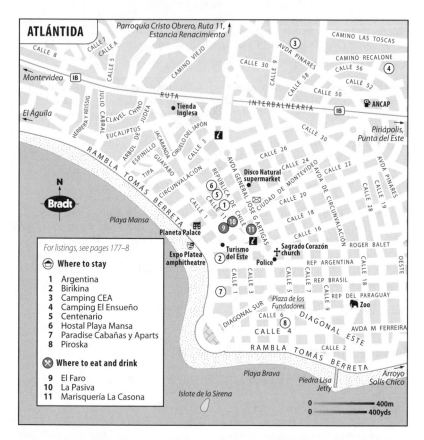

Parroquía Cristo Obrero, Ruta 11,
Estancia Renacimiento

CAMINO LAS TOSCAS

CALLE 7 · CALLE A · CALLE 8

CALLE 5

AVDA PINARES

③

CAMINO RECALONE

CALLE 30 · CALLE 9

CALLE 58 · CALLE 56 · CALLE 52 · CALLE 50

④

Montevideo · IB

JULIO CABRAL · HERRERA Y REISSIG

CAMINO VIEJO

RUTA

INTERBALNEARIA

IB

ANCAP

El Águila

CLAVEL CHINO · EUCALIPTUS · ARBOL DE JUDEA · ESPINILLO · JACARANDA · CIRUELO DEL JAPÓN · GUAYABO · TIPA

Tienda Inglesa

CALLE 30

Piriápolis, Punta del Este

RAMBLA TOMÁS BERRETA

CIRCUNVALACIÓN

CALLE 1 · CALLE 3

REPÚBLICA DE CHILE

AVDA GENERAL JOSÉ G ARTIGAS

CIUDAD DE MONTEVIDEO

CALLE 26

CALLE 24 · CALLE 22

CALLE 20

AVDA DE CIRCUNVALACIÓN

CALLE 19 · CALLE 28

AVDA PINARES

N

Bradt

Playa Mansa

Planeta Palace

Disco Natural supermarket

⑥ ⑤ ①

⑨ ⑩ ⑪

CALLE 18

CALLE 16

ROGER BALET

OESTE

For listings, see pages 177–8

Expo Platea amphitheatre

Turismo del Este ②

Sagrado Corazón church

Police

REP ARGENTINA

REP BRASIL

REP DEL PARAGUAY

CALLE 18 · CALLE 7 · CALLE 5 · CALLE 3 · CALLE 1

Where to stay

1 Argentina
2 Birikina
3 Camping CEA
4 Camping El Ensueño
5 Centenario
6 Hostal Playa Mansa
7 Paradise Cabañas y Aparts
8 Piroska

⑦

DIAGONAL SUR

CALLE 6

CALLE 4

Plaza de los Fundadores

DIAGONAL ESTE

⑧

Zoo

AVDA M FERREIRA

Where to eat and drink

9   El Faro
10 La Pasiva
11 Marisquería La Casona

RAMBLA TOMÁS BERRETA

CALLE 2

Playa Brava

Piedra Lisa Jetty

Arroyo Solís Chico

Islote de la Sirena

0 —— 400m
0 —— 400yds

🏠 **Paradise Cabañas y Aparts** Rambla Mansa, between Brasil & Paraguay; ☎ 4372 1573; e paradise@adinet.com.uy; www.paradise.com.uy. Facing the sea just south of the centre, Paradise has 'VIP' cabins & 4-person apartments with kitchens, Wi-Fi, a spa, gym & swimming pool. **$$**

🏠 **Piroska** Calle 5 between 4 & 6; ☎ 4372 8334; www.hotel-piroska.com. Near the Playa Brava, this German-owned little place has just 6 rooms & 6 apartments, for 2 or 3 people, around a lush garden; there's a restaurant & free Wi-Fi. **$$**

🏕 **Camping CEA** Antel Employees Club, Avda Pinares; ☎ 4372 4171. Nearer Ruta 11 on Avda Pinares, this a posher, more formal place, with cabañas as well as tent space. **$**

🏕 **Camping El Ensueño** ☎ 4372 3467; m 099 971871; e psiconando@hotmail.com. A friendly but slightly run-down campsite with cabins & tents under eucalyptus trees, with rough old concrete picnic tables. **$**

✗ **Where to eat and drink** There's a fair choice of restaurants, including a branch of **La Pasiva**, in the microcentro, plus two *heladerías* (ice-cream shops) – **El Faro** on Cuidad de Montevideo is the classier option. Immediately south, the **Marisquería La Casona** (*Balet & Chile;* ☎ *4372 0800/1571;* e *lacasonasrl@hotmail.com;* **$$**) is a popular fish restaurant with a large terrace. There are several pub-discos at Cuidad de Montevideo and 11, on the triangular plaza just southwest of the microcentro, such as **La Birra** and **Ilheus**.

Shopping For buying your own food, the handiest supermarket is Disco Natural (*Artigas & Calle 24;* ⊕ *08.00–23.00 daily*). There's a branch of the upmarket Tienda

Inglesa on the Interbalnearia (*at Calle 11*; ⊕ *07.00–midnight*) – the only place in town with free open Wi-Fi.

Other practicalities

Car rental Melo Rent a Car is at km46.2 Ruta Interbalnearia (📞 *4372 4455;* 📱 *098 024455;* 📧 *melorentacar@hotmail.com; www.melorentacar.com.uy).*

Communications The main post office is on Artigas south of Calle 22, but stamps are also available at Farmacía Rodríguez in the microcentro, opposite a cambio (⊕ *09.30–23.00 Mon–Sat, 10.00–22.00 Sun in season*).

What to see and do A block south of the tourist information centre is the sheltered Playa Mansa, famed for its sunsets. Just to the right is the **ExpoPlatea beachfront amphitheatre**, used for bands and other entertainments in summer. Opposite this is the Art Deco **former Hotel Planeta Palace**, built in 1937–41; now used as apartments, it's still a very striking sight, like a beached ocean liner.

From here you can see **El Águila** (*The Eagle;* ⊕ *summer 09.00–19.30; winter 09.00–18.00; free*), a 25-minute walk west (turn left off Zorrilla de San Martín on to Carlos Roxlo, and it's 300m further, just off the edge of the tourist map in the Villa Argentina area). This bizarre viewpoint over the beach was built in 1945 by local builder Juan Torres for the Neapolitan-born Natalio Michelizzi, developer of the Hotel Planeta Palace and the casino behind it. Michelizzi asked for a small room (4m square) in which to read and paint, with a niche for a statue of the Virgin; then he asked for a bigger space in which to entertain friends, and Torres produced this eagle's head (as well as a mock ship below, now washed away by the sea); a narrow corridor leads to stairs up into the head and a platform atop the beak. Tours are available hourly (*summer 10.00–19.00 daily; free*) – book through the tourist office (📞 *4372 3104*). A kilometre to the west is the gay beach known as the (ex-)Playa de la Boya.

Turning left along the rambla from Calle Roger Balet, it's five blocks to a headland where you'll find the yacht club and a viewpoint. The Rambla Tomás Berreta continues east along the shore past the Piedra Lisa jetty, known for its fishing. Just beyond this, Avenida Circunvalación leads three blocks north to the small and unexciting **zoo** (⊕ *10.00–20.00 daily; free*), which has mainly exotic species such as goats, deer, llama, guinea fowl, ostrich, peacock and golden pheasant, as well as seals and parrots.

It's also worth heading 4km north to Estacíon Atlántida (*Ruta 11 km161*), where Eladio Dieste (see page 35) built the **Parroquía Cristo Obrero** (*Church of Christ the Worker;* ⊕ *15.00–18.00 Sat*) in 1957–58, just south of the railway crossing. It's one of his best designs, its curved brick walls and roof magically meeting with a tolerance of just 5mm, while the broad façade is free-standing. Inside, hidden openings direct light to the altar and a wooden statue of Christ by Joaquín Torres Garcia's pupil Eduardo Díaz Yepes. To the right is the bell tower, with a spiral staircase of bricks cantilevered on steel rods. Free tours are organised by the Atlántida tourist office (📞 *4372 3104; summer 17.00–20.00 Wed & Sun*).

Another 4km north, at Ruta 11 km157, the **Estancia Renacimiento** (📞 *4370 2021;* 📱 *099 108597;* 📧 *cabren@netgate.com.uy; www.estanciarenacimiento.com.uy*) offers free entry all year to its 500ha, with opportunities to feed farm animals and enjoy tractor, horse and sulky rides; there's a shop and a restaurant serving solid traditional food.

Between the beachside suburbs of Parque del Plata and La Floresta is the Arroyo Solís Chico, where the riverside rambla is very popular at full moons. On the rambla at the far end of La Floresta is an open-air sculpture park by another creek, the Arroyo Sarandí. The church of the Virgén de las Flores (Virgin of the Flowers) houses a statue of the Virgin brought from Italy in 1917, the focus of fervent Marian pilgrimages.

LAVALLEJA DEPARTMENT

Named Minas, after its capital and main town, until 1927 when it was renamed after the father of Uruguayan independence, Lavalleja is the hilliest department in Uruguay and thus one of the most scenic. Although the hills are not amazingly high, they are quite steep, with some fine canyons. As Darwin said in 1832, 'The country was rather more hilly, but otherwise continued the same; an inhabitant of the pampas no doubt would have considered it as truly alpine.' Nowadays the north of the department is ranching country, with Hereford cattle, sheep and pigs, while the south is more agricultural; near Minas are some quarries and cement plants, including the most modern cement plant in the Mercosur countries.

Ruta 8 leads northeast from Montevideo to Minas; leaving the city it's a tediously slow drive, with lots of speed humps, and it's far easier to go via Carrasco airport and take the road that joins Ruta 9 1km before the small town of Pando (at km31). The suburbs end here and the going is faster, bypassing Soca and crossing the Arroyo Solís Grande to reach Solís de Mataojo, the first town in Lavalleja department, 80km from Montevideo. At km91 you can turn right on Ruta 81 for 10km to reach the Aguas Blancas dam in the Sierras del Abra de Zabaleta, where the water of the Arroyo Mataojo is used to irrigate fruit farms; nearby are a Tibetan Buddhist temple and a municipal campsite (❘ 4370 9121; ⊕ all year) with electric lighting, hot water, barbecue grills and a shop. You can fish and watch birds, as well as the wild goats that roam the hills.

The country gets hillier, with some eucalyptus plantations; the old road is still alongside the modern highway for much of the way, giving cyclists a quieter alternative. At km109½, two hours by bus from Montevideo, is a junction in the middle of the fields, with the Virgin of Verdún and accompanying radio masts on a hill to the northeast; it's about 500m right to the old Ruta 8 and the entry to the **Parque Salus**. Since 1892 Salus mineral water, filtered through the rocks of the Sierra de Coronilla, has been bottled here; the waters are supposedly protected by a mythical puma, hence the name of the spring, the Fuente del Puma. In 1936 the company also began to make Patricia beer, now Uruguay's favourite, with the same mineral water. In 2000 the Salus company was bought by the multi-national company Danone, which sold the brewery on to the equally global Inbev.

A palm-lined avenue leads to the brewery, behind which, 1.2km from the gate, is the **Parador Parque Salus** (❘ 4443 1652/3; e paradorsalus@dedicado.net.uy; www. paradorsalus.com.uy; **$$$**), a fairly upmarket **hotel** with just 14 air-conditioned rooms, cabins, a swimming pool and a good restaurant. It's another 3km along a dusty unpaved road to the bottling plant, where you should continue up to the right for 700m to the rangers' house and plant nursery (which distributes native plants free to schools and the like), opposite a viewpoint over the bottling plant. The road loops to the left to the far side of the plant, passing the Vieja Carpintería, a corrugated iron shed that now houses an interpretation centre, with information on local flora and fauna, and advice on recycling your mineral water bottles. At the end of the road, steps lead down past magnolias and *Ceiba* (*palo borracho*) trees to the Fuente del Puma, where cups are provided for you to sample the Salus mineral water that pours into the bottling plant at a rate of 200,000 litres per day.

You might be forgiven for thinking that the whole park is planted with introduced eucalyptus trees, but in fact they only cover the central 370ha of a total

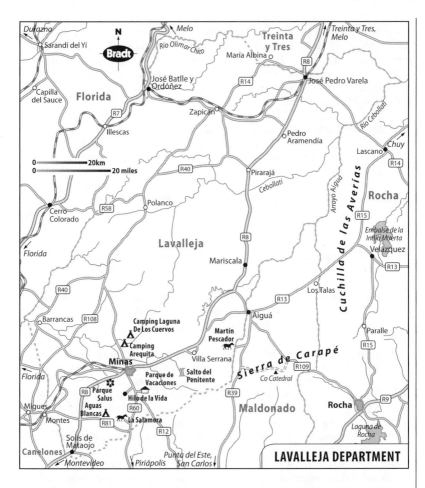

1,300ha. The rest is typical *monte serrano* (though damaged by a fire in 2004), with birds such as pava de monte (dusky-legged guan) remarkably easy to spot. As of yet there are no paths into the native area (although these are planned), but a dirt road does continue from just after the rangers' house to a disused quarry. There are open hills to the south and east, but these are likely to be planted with eucalyptus at some point.

A bus runs from the plaza in Minas via the bus terminal to the brewery every two hours (from 06.20), returning on the odd hour from 07.00 to 21.00.

Ruta 8 continues past a couple of cement plants and the turning (at km114) to Cerro de Verdón (390m; named after a pioneer called Berdom); a track leads to the statue of the Virgen de la Inmaculada Concepción (Virgin of the Immaculate Conception) on a sort of arched tripod atop the peak. Since 1901, thousands of pilgrims have come from Montevideo and further afield to worship here every 19 April. A road leads halfway up, after which there's a path lined with shrines and the Stations of the Cross. From here it's 5km down into Minas.

MINAS Minas, capital of Lavalleja department, with a population of 38,000 *minuanos* (just over half the department's total population), is a pleasant country

4

town, although it gets pretty hot, being set in a bowl of hills. Founded in 1784 as Villa Concepción de las Minas, its name refers to the gold mines along the Arroyo San Francisco. This was as far inland as Darwin came in Uruguay: 'Las Minas … is seated on a little plain, and is surrounded by low rocky mountains. It is of the usual symmetrical form; and with its white-washed church standing in the centre, had rather a pretty appearance.'

Getting there and away Regular **buses** from Montevideo (some continuing to Treinta y Tres, Melo or Río Branco – see page 87) arrive at the terminal at Treinta y Tres and Sarandí, where facilities include a tourist office (see below), as well as a baggage store (⊕ *06.00–midnight daily*). COOM also operates buses south to Punta del Este, via San Carlos or via Pan de Azúcar and Piriápolis, and one daily west to Florida. Emtur also go to Punta del Este, and Emdal/Expreso Chago have a couple of buses a day (*only 07.50 on Sunday*) to Chuy, with a few more as far as Aiguá and Lascano.

Tourist information A helpful tourist information office is located at the bus terminal (☎ *4442 9796*; e *turismo@lavalleja.gub.uy*; ⊕ *08.00–20.00 daily*).

🏠 **Where to stay** The main hotels are on the main Plaza Libertad, two blocks southeast of the terminal. There are good campsites 10km away at Arequita (see page 186). All listings are included on the map opposite.

🏠 **Hotel Verdún** 25 de Mayo 444 & Roosevelt; ☎ 4442 0910/0219; e hverdun@adinet.com.uy; www.hotelverdun.com. A nicely modernised 3-star with 25 AC rooms, a swimming pool, parking & Wi-Fi. **$$$**

🏠 **Hotel Minas** 25 de Mayo; ☎ 4442 4272; m 094 610487; e hotelminas@gmail.com; www.hotelminas.com. Opened in 2010 on the pedestrianised street just north of the plaza, this has 16 standard rooms for up to 4, & 3 larger rooms with AC; there's limited parking & Wi-Fi only in the reception area, as well as a PC. **$$**

🏠 **Hotel Plaza** Roosevelt 639 & Pérez; ☎ 4442 2328; e info@hotelplazaminas.com.uy; www. hotelplazaminas.com.uy. A modern 3-star place (although it doesn't have a lift); rooms have Wi-Fi & balconies looking over the plaza, & there's a computer at reception. **$$**

🏠 **Posada Verdún** Washington Beltrán 715; ☎ 4442 4563; e posadaverdun@hotmail.com. The cheapest option is this friendly posada 2 blocks north of the plaza, with 16 rooms with cable TV & private bathrooms. **$$**

✖ **Where to eat** All listings are included on the map opposite.

✖ **El Ombú** Treinta y Tres 457 & Pérez; ☎ 4442 2176. At the northwestern corner of the plaza is this friendly pizzería-parrillada, although it only offers café food until 21.00; it also has a good *heladería* at the rear, & Wi-Fi. **$$**

✖ **Ki-Joia** ☎ 4442 5884. Immediately south of El Ombú is this lively parrilla (known for its lamb) next to a good ice-cream shop. There are 2 other pizzería-parrilladas on the east side of the bus terminal. **$$**

✖ **Nuevo Sabor** Batlle y Ordóñez 707; ☎ 4442 1520/2418. A stylish new restaurant next to the Teatro Lavalleja with take-away & deliveries. **$$**

✖ **Confitería Irisarri** Treinta y Tres 618; ⊕ 09.00–21.00 daily. The most notable food outlet in town is this famous Belle-Époque *patissería-café* on the northeastern side of the plaza that has been serving *alfajores*, *damasquitos*, *yemas* & other sweet things since 1898 (with Art Deco additions). **$**

Shopping The Ta-Ta supermarket (⊕ *08.00–22.00 daily*) is a block north of the plaza on 18 de Julio, opposite the splendid 1931 Petrobras station.

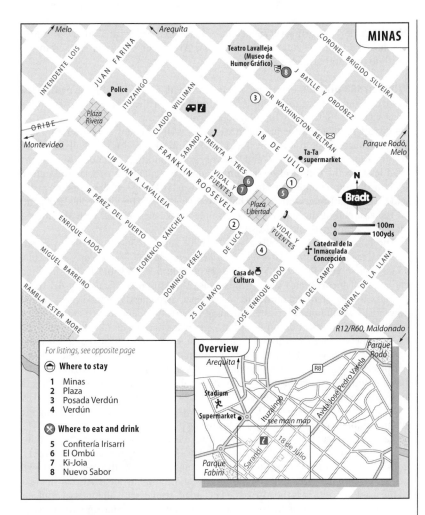

MINAS

Melo

Arequita

Teatro Lavalleja
(Museo de
Humor Gráfico)

CORONEL BRIGIDO SILVEIRA

J BATTLE Y ORDOÑEZ

INTENDENTE LOIS

JUAN FARINA

Police

ITUZAINGÓ

DR WASHINGTON BELTRÁN

Plaza
Rivera

CLAUDIO WILLIMAN

18 DE JULIO

Parque Rodó,
Melo

ORIBE

Montevideo

SARANDÍ

TREINTA Y TRES

Ta-Ta
supermarket

FRANKLIN ROOSEVELT

LIB JUAN A LAVALLEJA

VIDAL Y FUENTES

N

R PÉREZ DEL PUERTO

Plaza
Libertad

Bradt

ENRIQUE LADOS

FLORENCIO SÁNCHEZ

DE LUCA

VIDAL Y
FUENTES

0   100m
0   100yds

MIGUEL BARREIRO

Catedral de la
Inmaculada
Concepción

RAMBLA ESTER MORE

DOMINGO PÉREZ

25 DE MAYO

Casa de
Cultura

JOSÉ ENRIQUE RODÓ

DR A DEL CAMPO

GENERAL DE LA LLANA

R12/R60, Maldonado

For listings, see opposite page

🏠 **Where to stay**

1 Minas
2 Plaza
3 Posada Verdún
4 Verdún

❌ **Where to eat and drink**

5 Confitería Irisarri
6 El Ombú
7 Ki-Joia
8 Nuevo Sabor

Overview

Arequita

Stadium

Supermarket

R8

Avda José Pedro Varela

Ituzaingó

see main map

18 de Julio

Sarandí

Parque
Rodó

Parque
Fabini

Other practicalities

Banks There's an ATM on the plaza at 25 de Mayo and Treinta y Tres, and another just north at Pérez and 18 de Julio; Cambio Aguerrebere is by the bus terminal at 18 de Julio 751 and Sarandí.

Car rental Cars can be rented from Minas Rentacar (☏ 4442 0190; ⏱ 08.30–12.30, 14.30–20.00 Mon–Fri, 08.30–13.30 Sat), at the junction of Rutas 8 and 12 to the west of town.

Communications Antel has two telecentros, at Treinta y Tres and Sarandí, opposite the bus terminal, and at Treinta y Tres 589 (both ⏱ 08.00–20.00 Mon–Fri, 08.00–13.00, 16.00–20.00 Sat). The post office is at Washington Beltrán 612 and 25 de Mayo (⏱ 09.00–17.00 Mon–Fri, 09.00–12.00 Sat). There's free Wi-Fi on the main plaza; internet access is also available at Cyber Peatonal, immediately north of the plaza at 25 de Mayo and Treinta y Tres (⏱ 09.00–01.00 daily), and Cyber Pato's (Pérez 743 & Carabajal).

Healthcare The Farmacía Garmendía-Sabia is on the plaza at Treinta y Tres 630. The hospital is at Avenida Varela and Casas Araújo, on the main road from the north to the centre (✆ *4442 2355/2058*).

What to see and do Plaza Libertad is an attractive square, with fine palm trees, fountains and a statue of Lavelleja, raised in 1902 for the 77th anniversary of his great victory at Sarandí by Juan Manuel Ferrari; this was both the first equestrian statue in Uruguay and the first bronze statue cast in Uruguay. To the southeast of the plaza, across the road from the Hotel Verdún, the Jefatura de Policía (police headquarters) dates from 1897 and is in very good condition; just north of it a short road leads to the **Catedral de la Inmaculada Concepción**, a neoclassical edifice built in 1892, and modernised in 1966. It's unusual in being set back from the plaza, and surprisingly long, with a dome halfway along the nave providing plenty of light. At the east end of the south aisle is a simple neoclassical chapel with an unusual altar in a sort of Arts and Crafts style.

The house in which Lavalleja was born in about 1786 is now incorporated in the **Casa de Cultura** (*Lavalleja 572, between Rodó & 25 de Mayo;* ⊕ *07.00–19.00 Mon–Fri, 15.00–19.00 Sat, 13.00–19.00 Sun; free*), two blocks south of the cathedral. It incorporates several museums. The Museo del Gaucho y del Indio displays the usual round stones for *boleadoras*, arrowheads, lance-heads, carved cow-horns, some fine silverware and some very rusty independence-era swords, a late 19th-century poncho, and some lance pennants bearing *divisas* or mottos from the Guerra Grande. The Museo Eduardo Fabini commemorates Uruguay's leading composer (see page 27), born in Solís de Mataojo in 1882; on show are scores and various personal effects, such as a huge maté gourd and *bombilla*, his violin, pedal harmonium and two guitars, and portraits of Fabini by Manuel Espinola Gómez (a protégé who also came from Solís de Mataojo), by Alessandro Métalo Gibert and by Pedro Blanes Viale (see page 32), the last showing Fabini and a friend playing the organ outdoors. Alas, you won't hear his music playing here.

Lavalleja's birthplace, known as the Casa de Ramona de la Torre (after his mother, the only resident of Minas to follow Artigas on the Exodus of 1811), consists of a couple of rooms under a new concrete roof in the courtyard; you'll see his ceremonial sabre and some uniforms, guns and bayonets. Also at the rear of the Casa de Cultura is the Museo de la Ciudad, stuffed with all kinds of artefacts such as hats, fans, musical instruments, an Edison voice-recorder, a Victrola record player, and a chestnut-roasting trolley disguised as a steam locomotive. There are also rooms dedicated to the local writers Santiago Dossetti (1902–81) and Juan José Morosoli (1899–1957), who left school at ten, worked in a café, became a journalist and ended by writing successful novels that gave a sympathetic portrait of the lives of the people of rural Uruguay. There's also a theatre here, as well as a library and temporary exhibition spaces.

A block northeast of the Posada Verdún is the **Teatro Lavalleja** (⊕ *08.00–18.00 Mon–Fri, 16.00–18.00 Sat–Sun; free*), a striking pile by Cayetano Buigas, a Catalan Modernist of the school of Gaudí, although this is not externally obvious. The drab interior is apparently similar to the Liceu of Barcelona and the Teatro Colón in Buenos Aires; the building is being restored for its centenary in 2009. It now houses the **Museo del Humor Gráfico**, a collection of cartoons and caricatures which are quite good and varied, though not very well displayed. The star turn is Julio E Suárez (1909–65), Uruguay's most distinguished cartoonist, who created his character Peloduro in 1933 as a vehicle for political satire. In the lobby you'll also see six statues by José Belloni (see page 34) and his son Stelio.

One of the attractive features of Minas is that you can see hills at the end of the streets in all directions, and the city is also ringed by parks, which all have picnic facilities and playgrounds. The closest to the centre is the **Parque Fabini**, beside the Arroyo San Francisco by Ruta 8 to Montevideo. To the east is Parque Artigas, with a hilltop statue of Artigas by Stelio Belloni that's supposedly the largest equestrian statue in the world. Raised in 1974, it's 10m high plus a plinth of almost 8m, and consists of 150 tonnes of concrete; it's possible to drive up to the statue and viewpoint of Cerro Artigas, and city buses also come here. To the northeast, by Ruta 8 to Melo, the **Parque Rodó** is the largest of Minas's parks, with a rose garden, municipal swimming pool and zoo, which houses a motley collection of animals such as llamas, lions, tigers, monkeys, boars, foxes and goats, and birds such as vultures, eagles, caracaras, owls, jays, cardinals, hooded siskins, herons, ducks and black-necked swans. There's also a fine display of plant life. The cages are clean and spacious enough, but this is mainly a zoo for children.

Parque Rodó is the venue for the Minas y Abril festival, named after a song and held in aid of the local hospital. Over a weekend in mid-April, up to 30,000 people enjoy a combination of music, displays of clowning and of gauchos' riding skills. This is followed on 19 April by the pilgrimage to the Virgin of Verdún (see page 181); Verdún is usually reached from the north side – served by COSU buses five-times daily.

AROUND MINAS Just 3km southeast of the centre of Minas (following Roosevelt, then Bonilla), the Represa OSE is a dam built in 1934 by the OSE water utility, with a 33ha park that's popular for family picnics and for fishing (for bagre and tararira). At km347½ on Ruta 12, 8km south on the road to Maldonado, the **Parque de Vacaciones Sierra de Minas** is owned by UTE-Antel, the state electricity and telecommunications company. There's a classy **hotel** [map page 181] (✆ 4443 0000; e *parquerecepcion@ute.com.uy; www.parquedevacaciones.com.uy;* **$$$**) with 160 rooms and ten bungalows, as well as conference facilities, and the **Complejo San Francisco de las Sierras** (✆ 4442 1105; e *sanfranciscodelassierras@hotmail.com;* **$$**), which has cabins, restaurants and a spa, as well as an internet room and Wi-Fi throughout. The 523ha park is also open to day visitors (US$1), with open and covered swimming pools, other sports facilities and playgrounds, all in beautifully tended grounds; there's a plant nursery, a petting farm and horse riding. There's good birding along the Arroyo San Francisco, which also runs along the west side of Minas (past the Parque Fabini). COSU buses run here from Minas, especially at weekends and holidays, and COOM buses from Maldonado will leave you at the entrance.

Just north of the Parque de Vacaciones, turning west at km346, 6km south of Minas, the **Valle del Hilo de la Vida** (Valley of the Thread of Life), named after the stream that flows through it, is a narrow valley where over 100 circular stone towers (up to just 1.2m in height) stand on a slope, seemingly oriented to the setting sun. They may be over 1,000 years old and have not yet been excavated or investigated professionally, but there are plenty of theories about the valley's natural energies. The land is owned by a friendly couple who welcome visitors at weekends (*reserve on* m *099 663084; www.valledelhilodelavida.com; US$10*) and are keen to acquaint Uruguayans with the idea that their country has an unknown history that long pre-dates the arrival of European colonists. They plan to open rooms and a spa soon at the Parador La Madriguera, the restaurant where their 90-minute tours start.

Further south off the Pan de Azúcar road (6km northwest from km42.9 of Ruta 60), the **Posada de Campo La Salamora** [map page 181] (m *099 923997;*

Southern Uruguay   LAVALLEJA DEPARTMENT

4

e *lasalamora@gmail.com; www.lasalamora.com*) is an eco-friendly **estancia** with five comfortable en-suite rooms that offers activities such as horse riding, mountain biking and birdwatching in beautiful surroundings; they have also recently set up a bird rehabilitation centre.

One of the most popular excursions from Minas is to **Cerro Arequita** [map page 181], 10km north on the road to Santa Lucía and Polanco. There's a riverside beach below the 230m-high granite hill (painted by Blanes Viale and others), and one of the few caves in Uruguay that can be visited. A COSU bus leaves from bay 1 at the Minas terminal (three–four daily; US$1, day return US$1.25), running via the long-closed railway station before picking up the signed route along Avenida Flores. Most people get off, laden with folding seats and picnics, at the Parque Arequita, 12km (25 minutes) from Minas just before the bridge over the Arroyo Santa Lucía, where there's a riverside beach (lifeguards in summer 13.00–19.00 Tue–Sun), picnic tables, a restaurant and a small shop, as well as a campsite (see below).

About 500m before the campsite, by a small school, signs point east (right) to the Isla de Ombues (at least 500m away, although the sign reads 300m) and the **Gruta Colón (Columbus Cave).** An unpaved track leads along the flank of the hill for 800m to the Mirador Arequita restaurant (❧ *4440 2731;* e *grutaarequita@ hotmail.com; www.complejoarequita.com; $$*), a modern building set at the top of a field, looking out across the *llanura* (plain) that stretches west all the way to Colonia. You can buy tickets here for hour-long tours of the cave (⊕ *10.30–17.30 daily; US$3*), which start with a rather tedious introduction making as much as possible of what's only an averagely interesting cave, before walking up the hill and then into the cave. You'll go down metal stairs which Health and Safety officers would definitely not approve of, but you only need to be vaguely fit and mobile to visit the cave.

The cave was formed in the Cretaceous period, 144–100 million years ago (at the time of the break-up of the super-continent of Gondwana), of 300-million-year-old rocks. It was 'discovered' in 1873, although of course it had long been known by the indigenous people, who called it Araicaihuita (Water of the High Rocks of the Caves). There are two chambers, of which you'll visit the main one, 57m long, 19m wide and 9m high, and inhabited by millions of bats. There's also an unusual blind white cricket here that feeds on the bat droppings. For more information on wildlife and the environment, consult the Grupo Ecológico Arequita, which has offices in the Minas bus terminal (⊕ *07.00–13.00 Mon–Fri*) and at Domingo Pérez 570 (❧ *4442 3916*).

Halfway back to the road there's space for a few cars, and a path across a field to the foot of the Cerro. Going up into the trees, you'll come in a couple of minutes to the Sendero de los Ombues, a path around the country's second-largest *isla* (grove) of ancient and weirdly contorted ombú trees. Following a tiny path steadily up to the left, you'll come in five minutes to the limit of the trees and in a couple of minutes more reach the flattish top of the Cerro. In fact it comprises two main hills, Cerro Arequita and Cerro Arequito Chico (also known as Cerro de los Cuervos or Vulture Mountain), separated by a gully from which a steam flows into Río Santa Lucía, plus the lower Cerro de Iriarte. Nowadays you'll find cowpats up here, but in the mid 19th century access was a little harder and it served as a refuge for combatants in the Guerra Grande. Even so, there's no invasive flora here and this is a good place to study native plants. There are guided walks to the *cima* (summit) at 11.00 and 16.00 daily in summer, as well as full moon walks.

There are two **campsites** here, where you can sleep in tents or cabins. The Camping Municipal Parque Arequita [map page 181] (❧ *4440 2503, 4442 9796;*

⏱ *all year;* **$**) is divided into Zona A (*day use US$2 pp, tents US$4.50 pp*) by the bridge, and the classier Zona B (*tent pitches with electricity US$4.50 pp, 6-person cabañas with/without private bathroom, 2-person mini cabañas without bathroom;* **$**), with a swimming pool and shop. Horse riding is available from the Zona B gatehouse in summer (⏱ *15.00–21.00 Mon–Fri, 11.00–21.00 Sat–Sun; US$3/hr*); call **m** 094 463682 to ride on Sundays or holidays in winter. You can cut across the fields on foot directly from here to the cave.

Alternatively, 2km beyond the cave is Camping Laguna de los Cuervos [map page 181] (↖ *4440 2746;* ⏱ *all year; camping US$3.50/4.50 pp without/with electricity, 5-person cabañas with bathroom from US$41, 2-person cabañas with bathroom from US$36;* **$**).

Continuing northeastwards from Minas, Ruta 8 is a fast modern road through rolling country with some rocky outcrops (the old road runs parallel and is largely usable by mountain bike). Turning right at km125, an unpaved road leads 18km south to the **Parque Salto del Penitente** (↖ *4440 3096;* **m** *099 844386; www. saltodelpenitente.com;* ⏱ *09.30–19.30 daily; US$1*), where a waterfall drops 60m from the Sierra del Carapé. The falls are very dramatic after rain, but can dry up in summer, but the area has now been developed as an adventure tourism centre, with horse riding, hiking, birdwatching, bathing pools and a native plant nursery. At weekends you can try 'canopy', a 190m-long Tyrolean or zip-wire ride over the waterfall (US$7); or 'rappel', abseiling down 20–50m (US$9). The fairly new **Parador El Penitente** [map page 181] houses a restaurant specialising in lamb and wild boar (**$$$**), and there's a refuge and a simple campsite (**$**). If transport is a problem, call the owner, who may be able to pick you up in Minas in the morning.

There's also the 'panoramic' road to Parque Salto del Penitente, a much rougher 8km road starting at km139.8 (20 minutes from Minas by bus); turning left off this road after 2km, Avenida Bernasconi leads over a low pass to Villa Serrana, but it's better to continue on Ruta 8 to the main entry at km145. **Villa Serrana** (*Mountain Town; www.villaserrana.info, www.portaldevillaserrana.com.uy*) was laid out in 1945–50 by architect Julio Vilamajó (see page 35) as a new kind of settlement in harmony with nature. In a bowl between the sierras del Penitente and de Carape, with a reservoir, market gardens and orchards, he built over 100 thatched houses of local stone and wood. Many are now in a poor state – although there was a revival after the arrival of electricity. People mostly prefer to visit rather than to live here. One recent development has been the arrival of a Buddhist temple and yoga centre; the area is said to be full of natural energies. The conservation NGO Probides is working at Villa Serrana, to enhance the habitat for the many native birds.

Uruguay's first **youth hostel** (**m** *099 226911/624098;* **$**) opened here in 1958, and is still going strong – the oldest youth hostel still in operation in South America – a tiny, very simple thatched cottage which makes a great place to spend a day or two riding horses and relaxing in nature. The hostel consists of a snug lounge (with a fireplace and DVD player; there's no television reception here), one four-bed room and four two-bed rooms (one of them just a platform up a ladder), as well as sofas and mattresses on the floor; sheets and blankets are supplied. There's a kitchen, and a barbecue in the garden, but water is often in short supply; you may have to buy water from the nearby shop-bar to cook with. The garden is delightful, with epiphytic orchids hanging from the trees and hummingbirds and parkeets visiting.

The new La Casona Tourist Information Office is at km134 of Ruta 8. There's a COSU bus from Minas (*09.00 & 17.30 Tue & Thu only*) which goes into Villa Serrana and will leave you at the hostel; alternatively, any bus from Montevideo towards Melo will drop you at the junction at km145 (23km from Minas). From there a newly paved road leads across a valley – forking right past some rocky outcrops – (about 2km from the highway) to the simple, affordable **Hospedaje Familiar La Olla** (☏ *4440 2799; m *099 379113; **$$**) – and on for almost another kilometre to a police post; the youth hostel is a couple of hundred metres to the left on Calle Molle.

Just beyond the hostel an attractive house is available to rent (m *099 180970*). Where the road more or less ends you can turn right on Carobá to two **hosterías**, **La Calaguala** (☏ *4440 2955; m *099 387519*; e *lacalaguala@adinet.com; www. lacalaguala.com*; **$$$**), which also has rustic camping (with electricity and water), and *refugios* with eight–ten beds, and **La Fortaleza Hostería** (m *099 613564; (Montevideo)* ☏ *2707 1492*; **$$$**). Both have swimming pools and offer good filling food and contacts for horse riding. La Fortaleza has the best views over Villa Serrana, and also boasts a collection of hundreds of witch dolls, which might put you off your food in the otherwise charming restaurant and *salón de té*.

From the police post the main route, Avenida Vilamajó, drops steeply (past a kiosk where you can buy drinks or arrange horse riding) to the low Stewart Vargas dam. Immediately before the dam, Calle Coronilla leads left for 500m to the **Cabañas del Lago** (☏ *4442 5212; m *099 840094*; e *minadeoro@adinet.com.uy*; **$$**). Camping is allowed by the dam (although there are no toilets or water supply), and there are opportunities here for horse riding. Also at the dam is the **Villa Serrano Naturaleza Pura B&B** (m *099 380430*; e *villaserrananp@hotmail.com; www. villaserrananp.com*; **$$$**), which has two doubles and bunk rooms for four and eight (mixed and women-only), as well as offering horse riding. Continuing up the hill on the far side you'll see classic Villa Serrana houses such as the Mesón de las Cañas and then (100m to the right) the **Ventorrillo de la Buena Vista**, a thatched restaurant (☏ *4440 2109; www.ventorrillodelabuenavista.com.uy*; **$$$**) with great views across the valley and recently refurbished, which also has five rooms (**$$$**). Beyond this the road continues towards km139.8 on Ruta 8.

Continuing up Ruta 8, it's a five-minute drive from the Villa Serrana turning to the start of Ruta 13 (at km150½), leading to Aiguá and Rocha (see pages 241 and 245); it's not much further to Mariscala, where you can eat and sleep at the **Nuevo Parador El Rancho** (☏ *4449 2082*; **$$$**); at the southern end of the village. At km207 there's a toll and a very long narrow bridge over the Río Cebollati, fringed by lots of *monte nativo*. Ruta 8 continues through pretty empty cattle country to the tiny towns of Pirarajá and José Pedro Varela (*where the simple* **Hotel Patrón** *is right on the plaza at Podestá 668;* ☏ *4455 9138*; **$$**). Bypassing the centre, Ruta 8 immediately crosses into Treinta y Tres department (see page 364) at km258.

5

Eastern Uruguay

The southeastern departments of Maldonado and Rocha, along the Atlantic coast, are known for their beaches – with very developed resorts in Maldonado, above all Punta del Este, and much wilder ones to the east in Rocha – but they also have some interesting countryside. The wetlands of Rocha are internationally important bird habitats, and the highest hills in Uruguay are not far inland from Punta del Este.

MALDONADO DEPARTMENT

Entering Maldonado department at km80 of the Ruta Interbalnearia, there's a toll with a small tourist office (summer only). At km83 there's a turning to the coastal route to Piriápolis, but it's better to stick to the main highway unless you want to go via the beaches of Solís (still home to Anglo-Uruguayan descendants of British railway workers) and Bella Vista. Ruta 9 joins from the left just before the junction at km86 to the Sierra de las Ánimas (see page 199) to the north; to the south you'll see the obvious Pan de Azúcar, with a huge cross and antenna on top (see page 198). At km94.5 (75 minutes by bus from Montevideo) there's an interchange with Ruta 37, leading north to the town of Pan de Azúcar (see page 198) and south to Piriápolis.

PIRIÁPOLIS This small town has an interesting history and makes an enjoyable and genuinely Uruguayan place to enjoy the beach when Punta del Este is packed with partying Argentines.

History This area has been inhabited for close to 13,000 years, judging from arrowheads found just west of the present town at Playa Verde and Playa Hermosa; there are also traces of a Charrúa cemetery on Cerro del Toro.

The modern history of Piriápolis began in 1890 when the property developer Francisco Piria (1847–1933) established it as his own private town – he owned the roads, the utilities, the stone quarries: everything. As an alchemist (taught by a Jesuit uncle, it seems), he is supposed to have laid the town out on mystical lines, oriented to springs and water courses below the Hill of the Bull (an alchemical figure) – but it's also inspired by the French resort of Biarritz, with its promenade and Belle-Époque hotels. Piria planted large numbers of eucalyptus trees to hold the sand dunes in place, and some 200ha of vineyards, taking Uruguayan soil to France in which to bring the vines back. He promoted his wines by writing as an anonymous critic in a newspaper he happened to own, and also tried selling cognaquina, a medicinal blend of cognac and quinine. In 1897 he completed his castle (see page 197) and in 1905 the first permanent hotel; in 1913 he built a narrow-gauge railway to Pan de Azúcar, where there was a main-line station (the Interbalnearia highway came only in the 1950s). He also built a port in 1916, with ships coming direct from

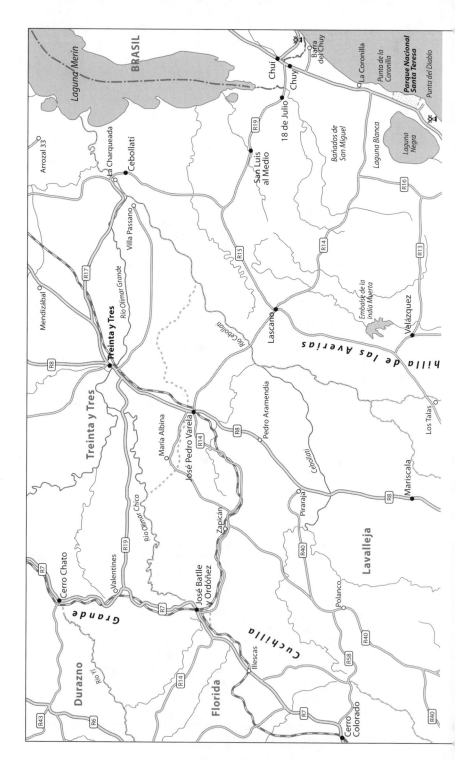

BRASIL

Laguna Merín

Arrozal 33

La Charqueada
Cebollatí

Villa Passano

Mendizábal

R17

Río Olimar Grande

Treinta y Tres

R8

Treinta y Tres

Río Olimar Chico

María Albina

José Pedro Varela

R14

R8

Pedro Aramendia

R19

Valentines

Cerro Chato

R7

Grande

Durazno

R43

R6

Río Yí

R14

José Batlle y Ordóñez

R7

Cuchilla

Zapicán

Illescas

Florida

R58

R7

Cerro Colorado

R40

Polanco

Piraraja

R40

Cebollatí

Mariscala

R8

Lavalleja

Los Talas

Velázquez

R13

R16

R14

Embalse de la India Muerta

Cuchilla de las Averías

Lascano

Río Cebollatí

R15

San Luis al Medio

R19

18 de Julio

Chui

Chuy

Barra del Chuy

La Coronilla

Punta de la Coronilla

Parque Nacional Santa Teresa

Punta del Diablo

Bañados de San Miguel

Laguna Blanca

Laguna Negra

190

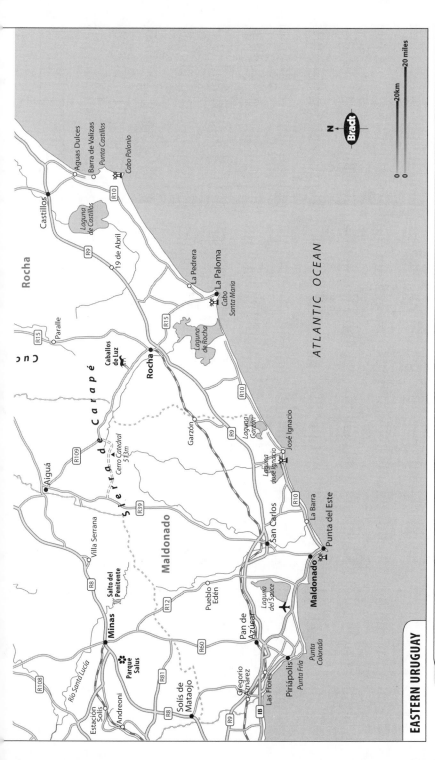

ATLANTIC OCEAN

EASTERN URUGUAY

Rocha

Maldonado

Sierra de Carapé

Cerro Catedral
513m

Castillos
Aguas Dulces
Barra de Valizas
Punta Castillos
Cabo Polonio

Laguna
de Castillos

19 de Abril

Paralle

La Pedrera
La Paloma
*Cabo
Santa María*

Laguna
de Rocha

Rocha
Caballos
de Luz

Garzón
*Laguna
Garzón*

*Laguna
de José Ignacio*
José Ignacio

La Barra
San Carlos
Punta del Este

Aiguá

Villa Serrana

Salto del
Penitente

Minas

Parque
Salus

Pueblo
Edén

Pan de
Azúcar
*Laguna
del Sauce*
Maldonado

*Punta
Colorada*

Gregorio
Aznárez
Las Flores
Piriápolis
Punta Fría

Solís de
Mataojo

Estación
Solís
Andreoni
Río Santa Lucía

N
Bradt

0   20km
0   20 miles

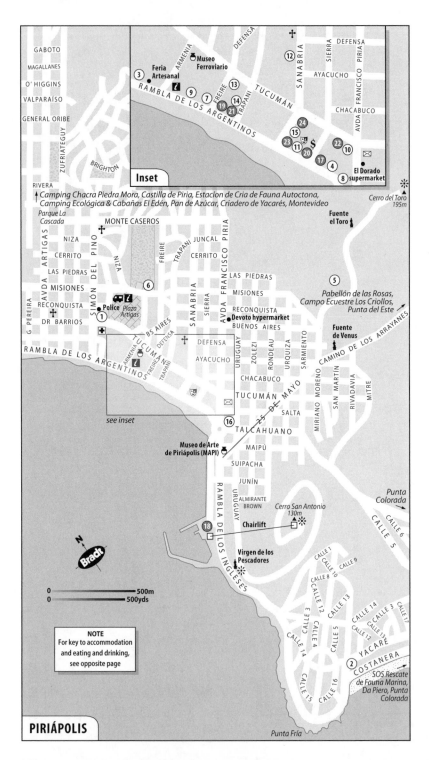

Inset

GABOTO
MAGALLANES
O'HIGGINS
VALPARAÍSO
GENERAL ORIBE
RIVERA
BRIGHTON
ZUFRIATEGUY

Feria
Artesanal

Museo
Ferroviario

RAMBLA DE LOS ARGENTINOS

ARMENIA
FREIRE
TRAPANI
TUCUMÁN
SANABRIA
DEFENSA
AYACUCHO
CHACABUCO
AVDA FRANCISCO PIRIA
SIERRA
DEFENSA

El Dorado
supermarket

Cerro del Toro
195m

Camping Chacra Piedra Mora, Castilla de Piria, Estación de Cria de Fauna Autoctona,
Camping Ecológica & Cabañas El Edén, Pan de Azúcar, Criadero de Yacarés, Montevideo

Parque La
Cascada

MONTE CASEROS

Fuente
el Toro

AVDA ARTIGAS
NIZA
CERRITO
LAS PIEDRAS
MISIONES
RECONQUISTA
DR BARRIOS
G PEREIRA
SIMÓN DEL PINO
AZUL
FREIRE
TRAPANI
JUNCAL
CERRITO
SANABRIA
SIERRA
AVDA FRANCISCO PIRIA
LAS PIEDRAS
MISIONES
RECONQUISTA
BUENOS AIRES

Police
Plaza
Artigas

Pabellón de las Rosas,
Campo Ecuestre Los Criollos,
Punta del Este

Devoto hypermarket

Fuente
de Venus

RAMBLA DE LOS ARGENTINOS

BS AIRES
TUCUMÁN
ARMENIA
DEFENSA
FREIRE
TRAPANI
URUGUAY
ZOLEZI
RONDEAU
URQUIZA
SARMIENTO
MIRIANO MORENO
SAN MARTIN
RIVADAVIA
MITRE
CAMINO DE LOS ARRAYANES

DEFENSA
AYACUCHO
CHACABUCO
TUCUMÁN
SALTA
25 DE MAYO

see inset

TALCAHUANO

Museo de Arte
de Piriápolis (MAPI)

MAIPÚ
SUIPACHA
JUNÍN
ALMIRANTE
BROWN
URUGUAY

RAMBLA DE LOS INGLESES

Punta
Colorada

Cerro San Antonio
130m
Chairlift

Virgen de los
Pescadores

CALLE 6
CALLE 5
CALLE 1
CALLE 9
CALLE 8
CALLE 10
CALLE 13
CALLE 14
CALLE 3
CALLE 17
CALLE 12
CALLE 13
CALLE 3
CALLE 5
CALLE 12
CALLE 4
YACARÉ
COSTANERA
CALLE 14
CALLE 16
CALLE 15

SOS Rescate
de Fauna Marina,
Da Piero, Punta
Colorada

N
Bradt

0   500m
0   500yds

NOTE
For key to accommodation
and eating and drinking,
see opposite page

PIRIÁPOLIS

Punta Fría

Buenos Aires, followed by a 7km-long waterfront promenade, parks, walks and other beautification. In 1929 Piria began construction of the Hotel Argentino, the largest in South America, with beds for 900 guests, and decorations by craftsmen brought from Italy. Many fine Deco hotels were also built in the next couple of decades.

However, after Piria's death in 1933 his manager quarrelled with Piria's elder son and killed him and then himself, and the surviving sons also quarrelled with their adopted sister (in fact Piria's mistress), so that most of the estate ended up in the pockets of lawyers, with the state taking over the Hotel Argentino and the port. The decaying infrastructure was finally handed over to the department of Maldonado from 1974, after which the Parque Municipal La Cascada and the Camping El Toro were laid out, followed by the opening of Piria's Castle as a museum. Nowadays Piriápolis is thriving, although it's a laid-back sort of place.

Getting there and away

By bus The bus terminal is on Niza at the end of Misiones; Buquebus and Colonia Express have offices here, selling tickets for their ferries from Montevideo and Colonia to Buenos Aires, with bus connections from Piriápolis included. In addition to the frequent Copsa and COT buses to Montevideo and Punta del Este (see page 87), COOM runs four buses a day to Minas, Turismar goes to Florida and Durazno three times daily, and Tur-Este has four departures a day to La Pedrera. Linea 100 runs to Maldonado via the airport hourly, and Linea 8 runs four times a day to Maldonado via coastal resorts such as Punta Colorada and Punta Ballena. Guscapar (\4434 9253; www.bienvenidoauruguay.com.uy) runs once or twice hourly to Pan de Azúcar (looping around town and stopping again outside the terminal ten minutes after leaving it).

To the south, at the rear of the terminal, is the large Plaza Artigas (with an unlikely Constructivist monument to the Heroes of the Uruguayan Refrigeration Industry!) and then, across Tucumán, the Hotel Argentino and the waterfront Rambla de los Argentinos, leading left/east to the main commercial area.

By boat The rambla curves southeast from the town centre to the Puerto Nuevo; there are some fishing boats working out of the harbour, together with some sailing yachts, mostly with owners in the northern hemisphere, but the Buquebus ferries no longer use the port. If you happen to arrive by yacht from abroad, you should call on Customs (*Aduana;* \ 4432 0038) and Immigration (*Migración;* \ 4432 0555) at the port, although you may be sent to Punta del Este airport.

PIRIÁPOLIS
For listings, see pages 194–6

🛏 **Where to stay**

1 Albergue Piriápolis
2 Apart-Hotel Terrazas de San Francisco
3 Argentino
4 Bakari
5 Camping El Toro
6 Camping Piriápolis FC
7 City Hotel
8 Colón
9 Escorial
10 Genovés
11 Hostería Miramar
12 Ocean
13 Rex
14 Rivadavia
15 San Sebastián
16 Tamariz

Off map
  Camping Chacra Piedra Mora

✖ **Where to eat and drink**

17 Don Quijote
18 Drakar
19 El Faro
20 La Goleta
21 La Langosta
22 Rotisería Alba Express
23 Terranova
24 Yoyo

Off map
  Trattoria Da Piero

Tourist information The tourist information centre, on the rambla just east of the Hotel Argentino (✆ *4432 5055;* ☉ *10.00–18.00 daily*) is helpful, and also has public phones and an ATM. Immediately to the west is another office run by the Liga de Fomento business association (*www.piriapolistotal.com;* ☉ *12.00–18.00 Mon–Thu, 12.00–17.00 Fri, 13.00–19.00 Sat*), in a wing of the former Hotel Piriápolis. There's also a tourist information desk in the bus terminal, along with a café, WCs and internet centre.

Bikes and rollerblades can be rented at Trapani Center (*Trapani & Tucumán;* ✆ *4432 5727*).

⌂ Where to stay The cheapest hotels, slightly further from the seafront but therefore quieter, open only for the peak season (mid-December to Easter), while those that are open for longer have a wide seasonal range in prices. There are two good campsites in Piriápolis as well as beach campsites not far to the west in Las Flores, Uruguay's oldest beach resort, with thatched cottage-style houses, and still very quiet. All listings are included on the map, page 192.

Hotels

⌂ **Apart-Hotel Terrazas de San Franciso** Rambla de los Ingleses & Rawson; ✆4432 7153; www.terrazasdesanfrancisco.com. Something a little different, this hotel has AC apartments with Wi-Fi & kitchens. It's just east of the town on the Playa San Francisco. B/fast inc. **$$$$$**

⌂ **Hotel Argentino** Rambla de los Argentinos s/n; ✆4432 2791; e reservas@argentinohotel.com; www.argentinohotel.com.uy. The town's classiest place to stay was founded by Piria as a centre for thalassotherapy (treatments with seawater); you can still have massages with seaweed extracts or bathe in the saltwater pool. There's also a casino, an international restaurant & a big traditional bar that hosts afternoon tea & a Sat night dinner-dance. Although well modernised, it still has the original lifts, staircase & stained glass, & the corridor leading to the casino is lined with historic photos & posters – well worth a look even if you're not staying here. **$$$$$**

⌂ **City Hotel** Rambla de los Argentinos & Freire; ✆4432 2522; e cityhotelpiriapolis@gmail. com; www.cityhotelpiriapolis.com. An adequate fallback option; rooms have cable TV, fan & frigobar, & they have a restaurant-cafetería-lounge on the rambla. **$$$$**

⌂ **Hotel Bakari** Rambla de los Argentinos 994 & Piria; ✆4438 1112/4; www.hotelbakari.com. An excellent new boutique hotel, with friendly service, indoor pool, jacuzzi, sauna, massage room, gym, & a comfortable microcine with a wide choice of films. Open all year. **$$$$**

⌂ **Hotel Escorial** Rambla de los Argentinos 1290; ✆4432 2537; e hotel_escorial@hotmail.com; www.

hotelescorial.com. Next to the tourist information centre is this 3-star Art Deco jewel worthy of Miami Beach that's been nicely refurbished; it has 52 en-suite rooms & a swimming pool. **$$$$**

⌂ **Hotel Genovés** Rambla de los Argentinos 1050; ✆4432 2505; www.hotelgenoves.com.uy. Has AC rooms, covered & open swimming pools, jacuzzi & Wi-Fi. **$$$$**

⌂ **Hotel Colón** Rambla de los Argentinos 950 & Piria; ✆4432 2508; e colon@adinet.com.uy; www. hotelcolonpiriapolis.com. One of the nicer small hotels, it was built in a half-timbered style by Piria in 1910; there's lovely tiling & stained glass inside. Open all year, it has an indoor swimming pool, Wi-Fi & cable TV. **$$$$–$$$**

⌂ **Hostería Miramar** Rambla de los Argentinos 1082; ✆4432 2544; e info@ hosteriamiramar.com; www.hosteriamiramar. com. On the seafront, the Miramar is open all year & boasts a panoramic solarium & beach service, & also has shaded parking & Wi-Fi, as well as the Restaurante-marisquería Don Quijote (see opposite). **$$$**

⌂ **Hotel Ocean** Sanabria 1009; ✆4432 2554; e pirocean@adinet.com.uy. An affordable 3-star that's open longer than some; rooms are spacious (although TVs are small) & there's a good big breakfast. There's a great garden & parking at the rear, but no lift. **$$$**

⌂ **Hotel Rex** Freire 968; ✆4432 2543; e correodelrex@adinet.com.uy; www.hotelrex. com.uy. A simpler, but clean & comfortable, Art Deco place that has a lift, free internet access & AC pool. **$$$**

🏠 **Hotel Rivadavia** Rambla de los Argentinos & Trápani; ☎4432 2532; e rivacol@adinet.com. uy. This seafront 2-star hotel is fairly simple (with fans rather than AC) but has undergone a stylish refurbishment & has Wi-Fi. **$$$**

🏠 **Hotel San Sebastián** Sanabria 942; ☎4432 3546. An older place, with 29 rooms with very basic old bathrooms; there's Wi-Fi & a PC in the dining room. **$$$**

🏠 **Hotel Tamariz** Salta 933; ☎4432 2509/4509; www.hoteltamariz.com. A classic Deco 3-star on a quiet side road that's been very well modernised; staff are very friendly, & the breakfast is excellent – great value for money. The restaurant may be closed outside high season. **$$$**

🏠 **Hostel Albergue Piriápolis** Simón del Pino 1106-36; ☎4432 0394/2157; e jorgepm@ hostelpiriapolis.com.uy; www.hostelpiriapolis. com.uy; closed May–Aug. A good old-style youth hostel, somewhat institutional but with plenty of space. It's definitely not a party hostel, & you'll get a good night's sleep. There are rooms with 2, 3 & 4 beds, a large patio with parrilla, laundry space, PC, kitchen, a TV room & bikes for rent. A bed costs from US$18 including breakfast (*08.30–10.30*); non-HI members pay US$5 more. **$**

Camping

🏕 **Camping Ecológico & Cabañas El Edén** Parada 19, Las Flores; ☎4438 0565; m 099 107795; e eledencamping@adinet.com.uy; www.eledencamping.com; ⏰ mid-Nov–Feb daily; Mar–May & Oct–mid-Nov w/ends. In the other direction, 80km east of Montevideo in Balneario Las Flores, this campsite charges US$4/ day for caravans/camper vans, US$10 for tents, & from US$54/70 per night (low/high for 2) to US$97–120 for 6 for cabañas. There's electricity & Wi-Fi, & Montevideo buses stop outside. Las Flores is Uruguay's oldest beach resort, with thatched cottage-style houses, & is still very quiet.

🏕 **Camping Chacra Piedra Mora** Ruta 37 km3.8; ☎4432 4057; ⏰ all year. Located towards the Pan de Azúcar, a pretty place with thatched buildings, camping, mini cabañas, swimming pool & facilities for soccer, volleyball & basketball. **$**

🏕 **Camping El Toro** In the Parque Municipal behind the Fuente de Venus; Avda 25 de Mayo; ☎4432 3454; ⏰ Dec–Mar. Attractively planted with pines & eucalyptus trees. **$**

🏕 **Camping Piriápolis FC** Opposite the bus terminal; Misiones & Niza; ☎4432 3275; e piriapolisfc@yahoo.com; ⏰ Nov–Easter. Space for 800 tents & 15 chalets. Wi-Fi. **$**

✖️ **Where to eat** There are various restaurants with pleasant waterfront terraces along the rambla between the Hotel Argentino and the Hotel Colón. All listings are included on the map, page 192.

✖️ **La Goleta** Sierra; ☎4432 8215. Good for steak & pasta, with a cheap set-lunch menu. **$$**

✖️ **La Langosta** Trápani; ☎4432 3382. A better-than-average seafood restaurant that does a fine paella. **$$**

✖️ **Restaurante-marisquería Don Quijote** Sierra; ☎4432 0347; www. donquijotepiriapolis.com; ⏰ Nov–Apr. Offers seafood including a fine paella. **$$**

✖️ **Restaurant-marisquería Drakar** ☎4432 7207; e restaurantdrakar@hotmail.com. At the north end of the port housed in a nice thatched building, with affordable fresh seafood. The snack-bar at the chairlift (see page 197) is open 24hrs in summer. **$$**

✖️ **Terranova** Sanabria; ☎4432 7879. Serving the full range of chivitos, pizzas, parrilla & a 3-course lunch menu at US$15. **$$**

✖️ **Trattoria Da Piero** ☎4432 3356; m 099 103099; e trattoriadapiero@yahoo.com. At the Playa San Francisco, this is an attractive spot specialising in fish & seafood, as well as pasta; a little further east they have their own lobster farm, raising Australian red-claw lobsters, which is interesting to visit. **$$**

✖️ **Yoyo** Sanabria & Tucumán; ☎4432 2948. A block inland, this is a stylish place that also has a pavement terrace & specialises in fish & seafood while also serving the usual range of meats, pastas & pizzas. **$$**

✖️ **The Rotisería Alba Express** Tucumán 973 & Piria; ☎4432 0218. Great for snacks - chivitos, milanesas, pasta, & huge vegetarian tartas. **$**

Afterwards, or indeed at any time, you could sample the ices at the **Heladería El Faro**, on the rambla at Freire.

Entertainment Films are shown at the **Cine Miramar** (*Rambla de los Argentinos 1124 & Sierra;* ↘*4432 0600;* ☉ *Jan–Feb nightly; rest of the year Fri–Sun*). Horseriding on the Cerro del Indio is on offer from the **Campo Ecuestre Los Criollos** (*Calle 24 (Ñacurutú);* m *099 170168;* e *jupodele@adinet.com.uy*) – take Calle Ayacucho opposite the Fuente de Venus and then the track towards Punta Colorada.

The best-known annual event is the Paella Gigante in mid-December, when 4,500 people share a paella cooked up from 300kg of rice, 100kg of vegetables, 500kg each of seafood and chicken and 200kg of pork.

Shopping There's a fairly large El Dorado supermarket on Avenida Piria at Salta, and a Devoto hypermarket four blocks north on Piria at Buenos Aires; on Saturdays there's a market on Plaza Artigas. On the Paseo de La Pasiva, just east of the Hotel Argentino, is the **Feria Artesanal craft market** (☉ *daily in summer*).

Other practicalities

Banks There are ATMs at Banco República (*Rambla 1405*) and Bandes (*Tucumán & Piria*) and at the supermarkets; to change cash go to Monex on the rambla at Sanabría.

Communications The Antel telecentro is on Barrios just east of Plaza Artigas (☉ *09.00–18.00 daily*). The post office is near the south end of Avenida Piria near Tucumán (☉ *09.00–17.00 Mon–Fri, 09.00–12.00 Sat*).

Emergency services For health problems, the *policlínica* is across the road south of the youth hostel (*Simón del Pino & Barrios;* ↘*4432 2648*), and the police station is immediately north of the hostel (*Simón del Pino & Reconquista*).

What to see and do Piriápolis has a fine sandy beach that is sheltered from the Atlantic waves, and has a gentle slope that's very safe for children. Alongside Calle Armenia, on the east side of the Hotel Argentino, the **Museo Ferroviario** (☉ *summer 17.00–21.00 daily*) is home to a goods wagon and carriage and other decaying bits of railwayana; a rusted narrow-gauge steam locomotive is outside the fence at Armenia and Tucumán and well graffitied. Across the road at the rear of the Hotel Argentino is the circular Pabellón de las Rosas (Rose Pavilion), ordered by Piria from the Eiffel company in France as a banqueting hall (now sometimes hosting art exhibitions). Walking southeast along the rambla, you'll pass the Feria Artsanal (craft market) and fine Art Deco edifices such as the Hotel Escorial (see page 194), as well as Piria's Gran Hotel Piriápolis (1905) and Hotel Colón (1910). Crossing Avenida Piria and heading inland, the Casa Lorenzo Piria, a mini castle which was the home of Piria's son, houses MAPI, the **Museo de Arte de Piriápolis** (*Avda 25 de Mayo 843;* ↘ *4432 2375;* e *museopiriapolis@hotmail.com;* ☉ *summer 18.00–21.00 daily; free*), which hosts a different art exhibition every summer (although maybe not until February). Avenida 25 de Mayo continues to the Fuente de Venus (Fountain of Venus), a pool surrounding a circular classical temple that's a copy of one at the Villa Parravicini near Milan in Italy; to the north is an attractively landscaped park (with children's playground), with a road winding up past the campsite to the Fuente del Toro. This is another fountain (of alchemical importance to Piria), with water flowing from the mouth of a life-size bronze sculpture of a bull by Antoine Bourdelle, one of Rodin's best students; it weighs three tonnes and was shipped from Paris by Piria.

To the south by the harbour, the statue of Stella Maris, also known as the Virgen de los Pescadores (Virgin of the Fishermen), was brought by Piria from Italy. The western end of Cerro San Antonio was cut away to make room for the road and port, but there is now a **chairlift** (*aerosilla*; \ *4432 5235;* ⊕ *winter 10.00–19.00 Thu–Sun & holidays; summer 10.00 till late daily; US$5)* and restaurant. Cerro San Antonio was known as Cerro de los Ingleses (Hill of the English), but after a chapel to St Anthony of Padua was built on top, together with a road in 1952, it gradually became known by its current name.

The Rambla de los Ingleses continues around Punta Fría to the Playa de los Ingleses, home to a small British colony at the start of the 20th century. At its eastern end is the rocky Punta Colorada, popular with local fishermen, on the sheltered side of which you'll find **SOS Rescate de Fauna Marina** (\ *4432 0011;* m *094 330795;* e *sos-faunamarina@adinet.com.uy; www.sosfaunamarina.com; US$5)* (see Punta del Este overview map, page 207), a rescue and rehabilitation centre for marine wildlife. Since 1993 they've been looking after sea lions, Magellanic penguins and other stranded and injured creatures, and now have four saltwater pools, other enclosures and a small shop.

If you (or your children) are interested in captive wildlife, there's also the Criadero de Yacarés (*Caiman Breeding Centre;* m *099 687136; www.yacares.org;* ⊕ *summer 10.00–sunset daily; winter Sat–Sun; US$2.50),* 600m north from km86 of the Interbalnearia, to the west of Piriápolis. Here they breed the *yacaré overo* (*Caiman latirostris*), threatened by hunting, and the *tortuga morrocoyo* (*Trachemys dorbignyi*) or Orbigny's slider, a water turtle threatened by the pet trade.

PIRIÁPOLIS TO PAN DE AZÚCAR On the other side of town, three blocks west of the Hotel Argentina, Avenida Artigas heads straight inland as Ruta 37 to Pan de Azúcar; it's eight blocks to the **Parque La Cascada**, laid out by Piria in 1899. There's a 5m cascade in old woodland on the Cañada del Puesto Viejo, and it's a pleasant creekside park with barbecues, play areas, thatched shelters, WCs and a snack-bar, and an exhibition of exotic reptiles (⊕ *09.00–22.00; US$5).* There's car parking a couple of blocks north of the entrance beyond Rivera. The road rises for 2km to a roundabout immediately beyond Piria's neoromanesque hilltop church (begun in 1914 and uncompleted by his death in 1933, it was never consecrated and is now roofless and semi-ruined) and heads into the countryside. Goscopar bus No 27 to Pan de Azúcar takes this road at least hourly.

At km4.8 the Castillo de Piria is about 300m up a tree-lined drive to the right (east). This is Piria's home, completed in 1897 by the architect Aquiles Monzani and opened to the public in 1979 as the **Museo Parque Municipal Castillo Francisco Piria** (⊕ *10.00–16.00 Tue–Sun; free).* It's somewhat fortress-like, with its Ghibeline battlements, but far too symmetrical. To the left inside the front door is a small chapel, and to the right space for temporary art shows and odds and ends such as old Bibles and a phone exchange. Upstairs, a tiled corridor gives access to seven rooms (including two bedrooms), containing mock-medieval furniture, some very average paintings and three pianos. There's a brace of Turkish shields, helmets, axes and maces, and a view to the church and the sea. It's worth a stop if you're passing, but not worth a special trip (although free recitals are held here on Fridays in January). A plaque commemorates a visit in around 1901 by the poet Julio Herrera y Reissig, whose congenital heart defect, aggravated by typhoid fever, left him unable to travel further from Montevideo than Piriápolis and Buenos Aires.

In the park you'll see a fine Canary Islands dragon tree (*Dracaena draco*), and a little glorieta (summer house). Behind the castle is a very ruined railway carriage, as well as the Pueblo Andaluz (Andalusian Town), built as a set for a television series and now in ruins.

It's another 1km north (passing a smaller castle that was the house of Piria's mistress) to the **Estación de Cria de Fauna Autoctona** (*Native Fauna Breeding Centre;* \ *4432 3468;* ⊕ *07.00–19.00 daily (Jan–Feb to 20.30); free*) (see Punta del Este overview map, page 207), also known as the Parque Municipal Cerro Pan de Azúcar, which is well worth a visit. Set up when the area was replanted with native species after a fire in 1980, a track and side-paths lead through the woodland to various enclosures housing many different kinds of birds (including ducks, egrets and other waterbirds, owls, screamers, seriemas, caracaras, vultures and dusky-legged guans) as well as slider turtles, yacarés, capybaras, wild cats, opossums, raccoons and otters, and at the end, pampas deer. You'll also see wild tegu lizards (*Lagarto overo*) lurking in the undergrowth. The circuit ends at the reptilarium, with snakes and other cold-blooded beasts; you can also turn uphill to a viewpoint and some pinturas rupestres (indigenous rock paintings). Back by the entry you can find refreshments at the Parador Drago (m *094 178136;* e *paradordrago@ adinet.com.uy*), which sells chivitos, pizzas, ice cream and other snacks; there are also picnic tables, a play area and a craft shop run by a rural women's co-operative.

You can also start here to hike up Cerro Pan de Azúcar (Sugar Loaf Mountain) (see Punta del Este overview map, page 207), the third-highest hill in Uruguay at about 390m, and probably the most popular hike in the country. Keeping left and passing the reptilarium, a track turns into a steep path, taking between 45 minutes and two hours to the top, following yellow-painted arrows, first through eucalyptus trees and then through boulders on the bare hillside.

On the summit is a 30m concrete cross that can be seen from miles around. Erected in 1938, it was designed by the sculptor Juan Zorrilla de San Martín (who had died in 1931). A spiral staircase leads up inside the main shaft to the arms, where there are miradors (fantastically graffitied inside) giving a panoramic view that's not very different from that of the base of the cross. Alarmist signs advise you not to start the climb after 18.00, and give a phone number (m *098 177418*) for rescue.

On the north side of the Cerro, 1km south from km93.8 on the Interbalneario, the Eco Parque Aventura (m *091 527845, 098 807090; www.cerropandeazucar. com*) calls itself a geo-tourist adventure park, offering canopy (zip-lining), rappel (abseiling), Kiwi balling (zorbing), slack-lining, mountain biking, hiking and birdwatching, costing from US$13 per activity. They have the longest zip-line in the Americas, about 1,200m long and with a drop of over 200m, on which you may reach a speed of 100km/h. You can also try your hand at falconry.

It's another 3km to the cloverleaf interchange with the Interbalnearia, on the far side of which is the small town of **Pan de Azúcar**, founded in 1874 and known mainly for its Museo al Aire Libre (Open Air Museum), consisting of murals dotted around town. Most are nothing special, but there is one by Carlos Páez Vilaró, painted in 1980, just east of the junction of Ruta 9 and Ruta 60, south of the centre. Many buses to Rocha pass by on Ruta 9 but will pick you up by the roadside, although there may well be standing room only; COT buses stop at Lizarza 724 and Artigas, half a block west of the plaza (near the Panadería-Confitería Bonsai), and Rutas del Sol at de Lizarza and Ituzaingo. There's an ATM on the plaza; the only accommodation is at the **Hospedaje del Calé** (*Lavalleja 608 nr de Lizarza;* \ *4434 8754;* m *098 888914; www.infopandeazucar.com.uy;* **$$**).

ECOTOURIST ESTANCIAS There are several places in the hillier country north of the Ruta Interbalnearia that offer family-friendly outdoor activities. The best known is the **Paseo Sierra de las Ánimas** (*km86 of the Interbalnearia;* m *094 419891; www. sierradelasanimas.com;* ⏰ *summer, Easter & Carnaval 09.00–sunset daily; rest of the year on w/ends depending on the weather; US$2.50*). Cars have a 600m drive in but pedestrians have a shorter path (get off the bus at the Parador Los Cardos, the nearest restaurant). A very basic campsite is available. There are walks to the Cerro de las Ánimas (formerly known as the Mirador Nacional) or to the Cañadón de los Espejos, a dramatic little gorge with pools and waterfalls, each taking three hours (round trip), or five hours as a combined circuit. The Cerro de las Ánimas is, at 501m, the second-highest peak in the country, and was much visited by the indigenous inhabitants, as well as by Artigas and by Darwin, who wrote:

> On the summit of the mountain there were several small heaps of stones, which evidently had lain there for many years. My companion assured me that they were the work of the Indians in the old time. The heaps were similar, but on a much smaller scale, to those so commonly found on the mountains of Wales.

Immediately east, the **Estancia Bellavista** (*km87 of the Interbalnearia;* ☎ *4438 0414;* m *094 382387;* e *estanciabv@adinet.com.uy; www.estanciabellavista.com.uy;* ⏰ *all year*) offers horseriding and birdwatching walks, has a hostería and salón de té, and can arrange asados for groups of up to 60.

Just west, the **Estancia El Centinela** (*6km from km87 of Ruta 9;* ☎ *4490 2262;* ⏰ *all year*) specialises in horseriding, although you can also hike and swim or canoe in the river. There's also a swimming pool outside the adobe house full of antique furniture, where the owners serve lunch and tea.

Finally, the luxury **Posada Kururu** (*6km from km82 of Ruta 9;* ☎ *2901 8821; www. kururu.com.uy;* **$$$$$**) has eight beautifully designed rooms and offers full board (with four meals including wine) and horseriding, canoeing and hiking on colonial routes such as the Camino Real. Good-quality Trek mountain bikes are available, and there's a swimming pool; television and internet are available in a separate building.

PIRIÁPOLIS TO PUNTA DEL ESTE From Pan de Azúcar the Interbalnearia (Ruta 93) swings southeast to run between the Laguna de los Cisnes (Swan Lake) and the coast; at km113.3 it passes Punta del Este's airport, crosses the Arroyo El Potrero, flowing out of the Laguna del Sauce, and at km116 reaches the Chihuahua roundabout. Immediately to the west is Playa Chihuahua, which has been Uruguay's main naturist beach (with a popular gay section at the right-hand end) since the 1960s, although it was strictly illegal then.

It's less than a kilometre on to the Solanas roundabout, with a 24-hour petrol station, supermarkets and various pizza stands and the like lining the road. Immediately to the right, Playa Solanas is shallow and sheltered, and known for the best sunsets in the area. There are often glamorous yachts anchored here in the summer, and the **Tommy Bistró Beach Club** (*km115.5; www.tommybistro.com*) is one of the coolest paradores in the area, with top-class DJs. The Playa Portezuelo area, immediately southeast, was laid out by the Catalan architect Antonio Bonet (1913–89, a disciple of Le Corbusier), who also designed several fine buildings here. The long, low former Hostería Solana del Mar and adjacent Casa Berlingieri (both built in 1946) are perhaps the best of the few Corbusieresque buildings in Uruguay, with their flat roofs and succession of arches, together with his own house, the more minimalist Casa Rinconada.

From the Portezuelo flyover, just east, Avenida Lussich runs inland to the Arboretum and Museo Lussich (see page 218), the Camping Internacional Punta Ballena (see page 209) and the Tambo Lapataia (see page 219); the Interbalnearia climbs sharply up to the Punta Ballena (Whale Point) ridge, with a viewpoint accessible by eastbound traffic and the turning south to Carlos Páez Vilaró's Casapueblo (see page 217). Dropping back to near sea level, there's a turning south to Las Grutas, caves which once housed bars and discos but since the 1990s have been protected. The tiny half-hidden beach is still very popular, with paradores such as El Chiringo offering food and drink on the beach. Soon you enter the coastal sprawl of Punta del Este, starting with new apartment blocks by the small Laguna del Diario to the north. At parada (numbered bus stop) 24, where Avenida España turns north to the older, more historic town of Maldonado, there's a tourist information office by the beach. Buses from Montevideo follow the seaside Rambla Williman for a bit longer before looping up to the Maldonado bus station, 110 minutes from the capital; otherwise follow the rambla, lined with hotels and apartment blocks, to Punta del Este, set on the low peninsula that marks the end of the Río de la Plata.

PUNTA DEL ESTE Not only Uruguay's premium beach resort but Argentina's as well (there being no decent beaches anywhere near Buenos Aires), Punta del Este is a strange mix of surfers, party animals, celebrity spotters and curious tourists wondering why the others spend their holidays in such an overpriced madhouse. In fact it's only a madhouse for about three weeks a year, covering the New Year holiday and the two following weekends, when every Argentine celebrity has to be seen at several obligatory parties here every night, with paparazzi chasing them from one to another and world-class DJs charging US$30,000. At other times, although Punta is still more expensive than other resorts along the coast, you might be able to see some reasons why it's worth it.

The heart of Punta del Este is the eponymous peninsula (an island for most of the last 20 million years) that marks the boundary between the Río de la Plata and the Atlantic Ocean, 134km east of Montevideo; just inland is the town of Maldonado, the historic capital of the department of the same name. Punta del Este now sprawls along the coast both east and west of the peninsula, with rows of modern apartment blocks lining the waterfront rambla; this heavily built-up strip ends just beyond La Barra, 10km east, which is where the best surfing and the best bars and clubs are, and where many of the hottest stars rent houses for the summer. The richest and highest-ranking celebrities mostly stay much further east, towards José Ignacio, although this is often counted as 'Punta del Este' for these purposes.

There's always a breeze, so even the hottest days are bearable, while even summer evenings may require an extra layer. The sea is warmest in February and March, but the weather is better in January.

History The peninsula and the sheltered haven on its western side were 'discovered' by Juan Díaz de Solís in 1516. There have been many shipwrecks along this coast: in 1812 the Spanish barque *El Salvador* was wrecked near what is now parada 8 of the Playa Mansa, with only 116 of the 800 on board surviving. She was carrying 500 soldiers, who would probably have allowed Spain to win the Battle of El Cerrito, near Montevideo, on New Year's Eve of 1812, and the history of Uruguay might have been rather different.

A tiny fishing settlement was established by Francisco Aguilar in 1829, followed in 1835 by salt pans set up by the American Luis Burmester for preserving beef. In

1860 a lighthouse was built on what was then known as Punta Salinas. From 1880 Antonio Lussich (1848–1928, who ran a salvage company and wrote Uruguay's first gaucho stories) and Henry Burnett (1845–1927, the British vice consul and Lloyd's insurance agent) devoted themselves to planting pine and eucalyptus trees to stabilise the sand dunes that lined this coast and made it largely unfit for settlement. By 1897 the people of Maldonado were building summer houses on the coast, initially at La Aguada, the present parada 24 of the Playa Mansa, west of Punta del Este, where a jetty had been built in 1890 (functioning until 1968). In 1907 the first hotels and a school were built on the peninsula (then known for the first time as Punta del Este), together with bathing cabins near the present port. In 1909 President Claudio Williman visited, and in 1911 mixed bathing was permitted. The resort's development really took off after World War I, with electric lighting from 1916 (only in summer until 1919), water-skiing from 1920, a church consecrated in 1922, and many new hotels and other developments. The main street, Avenida Gorlero, was laid out in 1918 and named after the first Mayor of Maldonado department (1909–13). Punta was seen as very 'fast' and liberated compared with the more traditional resorts close to Montevideo.

It was General Perón's decision in 1955 to allow Argentinians to travel abroad again that started Punta del Este's modern fame and prosperity. It soon vied with Havana as the hottest destination in the hemisphere, and has been very busy in summer ever since, its population rising to close to half a million every January. There was an annual Festival Internacional de Cine de Punta del Este from 1951 to 1958, revived in 2006; this has brought global stars such as Yves Montand, Jeanne Moreau, Anita Ekberg, Yul Brynner, Rita Hayworth, Marcelo Mastroianni, Gina Lollobrigida and more recently Antonio Banderas, while figures such as Prince Philip, Princess Diana, Sarah Ferguson, the royal families of Spain and Monaco, Pablo Neruda, Jorge Luis Borges, Rudolf Nureyev, Pamela Anderson, Simon Le Bon and Naomi Campbell (snapped nude by a paparazzo) have also passed through. In the 1960s South American summits were regularly held here. The first Queen of Punta del Este was crowned by Sacha Distel in 1967, and the second the next year by Tony Curtis.

The dictatorship of 1973–84 had little effect, the generals allowing it to carry on as a social safety valve (and they and their wives liked to come and play bridge and tennis here), but since the return of democracy it has become far more open and inclusive. The early 21st-century boom brought glitzy new developments, such as Aqua (*parada 19, Playa Brava; www.aqua.com.uy*), by Uruguayan 'starchitect' Rafael Viñoly, the penthouse of which sold for US$7.3 million, and a planned US$60 million apartment tower by Donald Trump.

Getting there and away
By air The modern airport (*PDP*; ☎ *4255 9777; www.puntadeleste.aero*), 24km west at Laguna del Sauce, has at least one flight a day from Buenos Aires, and many more at weekends in summer, as well as from Brazil and Chile.

Airline companies
✈ **Aerolíneas Argentinas** Galería Santos Dumont, Local 2, Avda Gorlero between calles 30 & 31; ☎ 4244 4343 (*call centre:* ☎ *000 405 486527;* ⏰ *09.00–21.00 Mon–Sat)*; e arpdpuy@ aerolineas.com.uy; ⏰ summer 09.00–13.00, 17.00–21.00 daily; rest of the year 10.00–13.00, 14.30–18.00 Mon–Fri, 10.00–14.00 Sat

✈ **BQB** Bus terminal, Gorlero & 32, Local 9; ⏰ 09.00–17.00 daily; Punta Shopping, Avda Roosevelt, Local 104; ⏰ mid-Dec–mid-Mar 10.00– 22.00 daily; rest of the year 11.00–20.00 (*call centre:* ☎ *130;* ⏰ *08.00–21.00 Mon–Fri, 09.00–14.00 Sat*); airport ☎ 4255 8109–12; e operaciones.pdp@ buquebus.com.uy; www.flybqb.com.uy

✈ Gol Punta del Este airport (summer only);
☎ 2606 0901−3; www.voegol.com.br

✈ Sol Punta del Este airport (summer only);
☎ 2601 2072 (*call centre:* **☎ 000 405 210053**);
www.sol.com.ar

Airport transport From the airport it's easiest to rent a car or take a taxi (around US$40), although buses do stop on the main highway half a kilometre to the south. Local buses from Maldonado to Pan de Azúcar and Piriápolis run hourly; buses to Montevideo, though faster, cost a lot more and may be reluctant to take a booking for such a short journey.

From Montevideo's Carrasco airport, it's possible to catch buses operated by CUT and COPSA to Punta del Este. Private transfers (*car for 4, US$220; minibuses for 15, US$270*) are available with Taxi Aeropuerto (**☎** *2604 0323/0188; www. taxisaeropuerto.com*), Transfers Lema (**☎** *4248 8788;* **m** *094 357375; www.transfers. com.uy*) and Remises Punta del Este (**☎** *4244 1269;* **m** *099 413045*).

Car rental is available at the airport through Avis, Budget, Hertz and Puntacar (see opposite).

By bus The bus terminal is on the site of the former railway station (which operated only from 1930 to 1983), right at the neck of the peninsula where Avenida Artigas runs into Gorlero. There are frequent buses to Montevideo (see page 87): COOM goes at 09.00 to Minas and Florida, and COT goes twice a day to Rocha, Punta del Diablo and Chuy, and offers connections via Montevideo to Colonia and (with Turil) northern Uruguay. Tur-Este's Bus de la Costa runs four times a day from Piriápolis via Punta del Este to La Pedrera. Local buses go to Piriápolis, Maldonado, San Carlos and José Ignacio. Ferry companies run buses to connect with their boats from Montevideo and Colonia to Buenos Aires, and international buses from Montevideo to Brazil call here (*contact EGA c/o El Maragato Turismo, office 7;* **☎** *4249 2380;* **e** *maragatoturismo2009@hotmail.com*). In the terminal are a café, telephone/internet office, left luggage (⊕ *09.00−23.00 daily*), exchange desk and tourism office (**☎** *4249 4042;* ⊕ *Jan−Feb 08.00−22.00 daily; out of season, generally 09.00−17.00*) − not to be confused with the Buquebus Turismo office opposite.

By sea Punta del Este is a regular stop for cruise liners (about one ship a day on average in season); there's no dock but passengers are brought ashore by boats to the port or the new teardrop-shaped double-decker La Pastora pier (open to the public at other times). This is at the Terminal de Cruceros (*parada 3, Playa Mansa, just north of the peninsula by the Conrad Resort & Casino*), which has toilets, tourist information and a waiting area for 300 passengers.

For **yachts**, there are 538 berths in the port (**☎** *4244 3787/3490;* **e** *puntadeleste@ dnh.gub.uy;* ⊕ *Apr−Sep 09.15−16.30 Mon−Fri, 10.00−16.30 Sat−Sun; Jan−Mar 09.00−17.30 daily*), with free Wi-Fi and public hot showers (*24hrs*). For immigration matters, see page 216. **Ferry companies** − for bookings from Montevideo/Colonia to Buenos Aires:

🚢 Buquebus Bus terminal, Local 9; **☎** 4248 4995; ⊕ 09.00−17.00 daily; Punta Shopping, level 1, Local 104; ⊕ mid-Dec−mid-Mar 10.00−22.00 daily; rest of the year 11.00−20.00; (*call centre:* **☎** *130;* ⊕ *08.00−21.00 Mon−Fri, 09.00−14.00 Sat*)

🚢 Colonia Express Bus terminal, c/o COPSA or El Maragato, Local 7; **☎** 4242 1975; ⊕ 04.30−23.30 daily

🚢 Seacat Colonia (Ferrylineas) Bus terminal, Local 9; **☎** 4249 3892; **e** ventas@ferrylineas.com.ar

top left　Tango is nearly as important to Uruguayans as it is to Argentines – it was born in Montevideo when the folk music of the poor Italian and Spanish immigrants blended with the rhythms of the African slaves and their descendants (JB) page 28

top right　*Carnaval* dancers finish their dazzling make-up before joining in with the world's longest carnival (S/KD) pages 110–11

left　Thousands come to the Fiesta de la Patria Gaucha in Tacuarembó dressed in *gaucho* gear to take part in riding competitions and parades (S/KD) page 349

below　The thunderous rhythms pounded out by *candombé* drummers have become an emblematic part of *carnaval* and Uruguayan culture in general (S/KD) pages 28–9

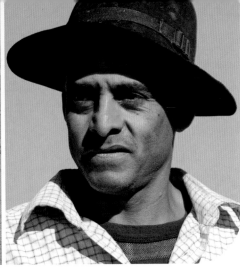

above left The vast rural plains of Uruguay's interior are largely empty aside from considerable numbers of cattle (JB) pages 333–73

above right Originating in missions created by the Jesuits, the main tasks of a *gaucho* are to plant *maté*, herd livestock and practise leatherwork (JB) page 42

left Horses are one of the most iconic images of the Uruguayan landscape, and riding is a key element of many people's visits (JB) pages 42–3

below With its rodeos, *asados* and live music, the Semana Criolla (Countryside Week) attracts hordes of people from across the country (S/KD) page 115

above left Meat is traditionally grilled on an _asado_, a grill fuelled by wood rather than coal as in Argentina (JB) page 67

above right Found in almost any craft shop, leather is the most obvious souvenir option for tourists (S/T) page 115

right Uruguay has around 270 wineries, and almost all are run privately by families (S/I) pages 149–66

below Uruguay's national drink, _maté_, is traditionally drunk from a gourd also known as a _maté_ (from the Quechua for 'cup') through a silver straw called a _bombilla_ (JB) page 70

above left   The ruins of the Calera de las Huérfanas (Lime Kiln of the Orphan Girls) just outside Carmelo was a point of study for Darwin in 1833 (SS) page 294

above right   The church of Nuestra Señora de la Candelaría near the Playa de los Ingleses is a pleasant refuge from Punta del Este's beach bustle (SS) page 217

left   This lighthouse in Colonia's old town is built on the ruins of the San Francisco Xavier convent (S/T) page 284

below   Known to English speakers as 'The Hand in the Sand', *Los Dedos* has become an iconic image of Punta del Este (S/KD) page 217

top The tiny resort of Aguas Dulces is home to an attractive jumble of bungalows as well as a nudist beach
(SS) pages 257–8

right Once his home, the fortress-like Castillo de Piria is now a museum dedicated to mystical alchemist, Francisco Piria
(SS) page 197

below The billion-dollar paper-pulp plant at Botnia, near Fray Bentos, has increased Uruguay's GDP by 1%
(JB) pages 308–9

<table>
<tr><td>top left</td><td>Found in almost any field, park or garden, the *tero* or southern lapwing (*Vanellus chilensis*) is Uruguay's national bird (NB/FLPA) page 11</td></tr>
</table>

top left   Found in almost any field, park or garden, the *tero* or southern lapwing (*Vanellus chilensis*) is Uruguay's national bird (NB/FLPA) page 11

top right   Fairly common across the wetlands, the red-breasted blackbird (*Pecho colorado grande*) is actually a meadowlark (RC/FLPA) page 11

left   The greater rhea (*Rhea americana intermedia*) is an ostrich-like bird easily visible in northern Uruguayan fields (SS) page 10

below left   The rockhopper (*Eudyptes chrysocome*) is one of two penguin species found in Uruguay (FL/FLPA) page 11

below right   The *hornero* or ovenbird (*Furnarius rufus rufus*) is emblematic because of the rounded mud nests it builds on fence-posts and trees (J&CS/FLPA) page 10

top left   The capybara (*Hydrochoeris hydrochaeris uruguayensis*) is the world's largest rodent, weighing up to 70kg (ML/FLPA) page 8

top right   The grey brocket deer (*Mazama gouazoubira*) is one of Uruguay's principal surviving large mammals (J&CS/FLPA) page 7

right   The margay (*Leopardus wiedii*) is Uruguay's largest cat (TW/FLPA) page 7

below   One of two very common species of fox in Uruguay, the crab-eating fox (*Cerdocyon thous*) is found in wooded areas (J&CS/FLPA) page 7

top   With beautiful beaches that are never too crowded, the colourful fishing village of Punta del Diablo is great place for surfing (AH) pages 263–8

left   Spot a sea lion or southern fur seal on the rocky islets at Cabo Polonio (S/JB) pages 260–3

below   With its fine sandy beach, the small but fascinating town of Piriápolis is an enjoyable and genuinely Uruguayan place to stay (MTSU) pages 189–97

Getting around

By bus Lots of local buses (some very smoky) run between Punta del Este (some running south as far as Calle 7) and Maldonado, mostly running via either Punta Shopping or Rambla Williman (Playa Mansa), Las Delicias and Avenida España. Routes 1 and 24 continue north to the small town of San Carlos (see page 239) for connections to Rocha department.

By taxi Taxis wait at various locations, eg: the bus terminal, the Conrad Resort and Casino, Gorlero and Calle 27, and by a small obelisk (☏ *4244 1123*) at the south end of Avenida Gorlero.

By car All the major companies can be found just south of the bus terminal.

🚗 **Avis** Avda Gorlero & Calle 31 (at rear of casino); ☏4244 2020; ⊕ 09.00–19.00 daily. Also at Punta del Este airport; ☏4255 9858; ⊕ 09.00–22.00 daily; www.avis.com.uy

🚗 **Brisas Rentacar** Avda Gorlero 838, Local 8; ☏4244 9698/9; m 099 409036; e eduardohomerodiaz@gmail.com; ⊕ 10.00–13.00, 14.00–18.30 Mon–Fri

🚗 **Budget** Punta del Este airport; ☏4255 9848; www.budget.com.uy; ⊕ 24hrs

🚗 **Dollar** Avda Gorlero 993; ☏4244 3444; e dollarpdp@dollar.com.uy; www.dollar.com.uy; ⊕ summer 10.00–19.00 daily; rest of the year 10.00–13.00 daily & 15.00–19.30 Mon–Sat. Also at Punta del Este airport; ☏4255 9550; 24hr m 094 434937; e dollarlaguna@dollar.com.uy

🚗 **DW Service** Bvar Artigas & Chiverta; ☏4249 1749; 24hr m 094 440812; e dwrentacar@movinet.com.uy; www.dwservice.com.uy

🚗 **Europcar** Calle 24 (El Mesana) & Calle 29; ☏4244 5018; e punta@europcar.com.uy. Also at Punta del Este airport; ☏4244 5018; www.europcar.com.uy

🚗 **Federal Car Rental** Calle 31 (Inzaurraga) & Avda Gorlero; ☏4244 9489; 24hr m 096 209427; e punta@federal.com.uy; www.federal.com.uy

🚗 **Hertz** Calle 31 (Inzaurraga) between Avda Gorlero & Calle 20; ☏4248 9775/8; 24hr m 094 413936; ⊕ 09.00–19.30 daily. Also at Punta del Este airport; ☏4255 9032; ⊕ 07.00–midnight daily. Punta Shopping, Avda Roosevelt, parada 7;

m 099 640202; ⊕ 10.00–20.00 daily (mid-Dec–mid-Mar until 22.00); e reservashertz@maderal.com.uy; www.hertzuruguay.com.uy.

🚗 **InterAutos** Calle 28 (Los Meros) near Avda Gorlero; ☏4244 6869; 24hr m 094 440420

🚗 **José Garrido** Avda Gorlero & Calle 32; ☏4248 6800; m 094 725177; e info@josegarrido.com; www.josegarrido.com

🚗 **Localiza** Calle 29 (Las Gaviotas) & Avda Gorlero, Galeria Apolo; ☏4244 9489; m 098 181010; www.localiza.com.uy; ⊕ 09.00–14.00, 17.00–21.00 daily

🚗 **Multicar** Apart-Hotel Punta del Este, Avda Gorlero 860 near Calle 28; ☏4244 3143; 24hr m 094 443868; www.redmulticar.com; ⊕ 10.00–19.00 daily; summer 09.00–21.00 daily)

🚗 **Punta Car** Bvar Artigas 101, facing the bus terminal; ☏4248 2112/9444. Also at Punta del Este airport; ☏4255 9299; e puntacar@puntacar.com.uy; www.puntacar.com.uy

🚗 **Sixt** Calle 29 (Las Gaviotas) & Gorlero, Galeria Apolo, Local 30; ☏4248 3254; ⊕ 10.00–20.00 Mon–Fri, 10.00–14.00 Sat–Sun. Also at Punta del Este airport; ☏4248 3254; www.sixt.com.uy; ⊕ 08.00–22.00 daily;

🚗 **Thrifty** Bus terminal, Local 8; ☏4249 9462; (call centre: ☏0800 8278); e puntadeleste@thrifty.com.uy; ⊕ 08.00–22.00 daily

🚗 **Win Rentacar** Avda Roosevelt, parada 13½; ☏4248 3004; www.win-rentacar.com.uy

By bicycle Bikes are available at many hotels and hostels, or in summer (*15 Dec–15 Mar 08.00–20.00 daily*) there's the Bicis Itaú scheme, with bikes that are free for an hour (three hours for customers of Itaú Bank), and then cost US$13/hour – you'll need ID and a credit card. There are two stations on the peninsula (*Rambla & Virazón, & Rambla & Calle 27*), one at parada 19 de la Brava, and one in José Ignacio. They also offer organised rides (*08.15 Tue/Thu*).

5

Otherwise they can be rented at Amalfi Sports (*Calle 24 & 27*; ⊕ *10.00–13.00, 15.00–22.00 Mon–Sat*), DW Service (*Bvar Artigas & Chiverta*; ☏ *4249 1749; 24hr* m *094 440812*; e *dwservice@movinet.com.uy; www.dwservice.com.uy*), Mariño Sport (*Calle 29 & Gorlero*; ☏ *4244 8834; 24hr* m *096 408124/7*), Rueda Cycles (*Lenzina & Bvar Artigas*; ☏ *4248 6732*) and Zap (*Calle 28 between Gorlero & Calle 24*; ☏ *4244 1899*). The main roads outside the peninsula often have parallel cycle tracks, but you'll need to pay attention to their idiosyncratic features. DW Service offers bike tours of Punta (*summer 09.00 daily*). The best bike shop for buying bikes, parts or spares is probably Trek Punta del Este (*Avda Roosevelt & Londres*; ☏ *4248 0906*; e *trekpunta@adinet.com.uy; www.trekpunta.com*; ⊕ *10.00– 20.00 Mon–Sat, 15.00–20.00 Sun, winter closed Wed*).

Orientation

Like most of the Uruguayan resorts, Punta del Este is divided into a *brava* (wild) side and a *mansa* (calm) side, with crashing surf on the brava side, facing the Atlantic to the east, and family-friendly beaches on the mansa side, on the estuary of the Plate to the west (very popular at sunset). The peninsula itself is largely rocky, although there are tiny patches of sand, and a large harbour on the west side. A dual-carriageway rambla runs along the coast in both directions, with locations along it indicated by numbered bus stops (parada) – eg: parada 11, Playa Mansa. On the peninsula itself roads have both names and numbers, eg: Avenida Gorlero is also Calle 22 (although the numbers are not always obvious). The first part of the peninsula is the main commercial area, with fairly high modern buildings, while south of the port, around the lighthouse and church, there are only older buildings with a maximum of four storeys.

Tourist information

There are various tourist information offices. Those at the bus terminal (☏ *4249 4042*), on Plaza Artigas (☏ *4244 6510*) in the centre of the peninsula, at parada 24, Playa Mansa (☏ *4223 0050*) and temporary offices at the port (☏ *4244 8685*; ⊕ *summer only*) and cruise terminal are run by the Municipio de Maldonado (☏ *4222 0847*; e *dgturismo@maldonado.gub.uy; www.maldonado.gub. uy*) and are open January–February 08.00–22.00 daily, and out of season generally 09.00–17.00. The Liga de Fomento business association has a helpful office just west of the terminal by the Playa Mansa (☏ *4244 6519*; ⊕ *summer 09.00–22.00 daily*), which also offers internet access. The national Ministry of Tourism, Uruguay Natural, also has an office (*Gorlero 942 between calles 29 & 30*; ☏ *4244 1218*; ⊕ *10.00–18.00; summer 09.00–13.00, 15.00–19.00*). Useful websites include www. vivapunta.com and www.quehacemoshoy.com.uy (What Shall We Do Today?).

Local tours Reputable tour companies include the following:

AGT Vajes y Turismo Bus terminal, Local 8; ☏ 4249 0570; e info@alvarogimenoturismo.com; www.agt.com.uy. Also & in Maldonado at Pérez del Puerto & Sarandí; ☏ 4225 0057

El Maragato Turismo Bus terminal, Local 7; ☏ 4249 2380; www.elmaragatoturismo.com. Also in Maldonado at Avda Batlle y Ordóñez & Francisco Maldonado; ☏ 4224 4775
Turismo Top ☏ 4224 9495; m 098 735805; http://turismotop.com.uy

⌂ Where to stay

There's no end of hotels in Punta del Este, of course, including some of the best and most expensive in Uruguay. They are all amazingly expensive in early January, merely expensive in February and for carnaval and Easter, and really quite affordable the rest of the year. All are open year-round unless indicated otherwise.

To do things properly, you might consider renting your own **villa** by the week or month through a company such as Terramar (*Edificio Portofino, Gorlero & Calle 17;* \ *4244 2222;* e *peninsula@terramar.com.uy; Ruta 10 km161, La Barra;* \ *4277 0707;* e *labarra@terramar.com.uy; & Saíz Martínez, José Ignacio;* \ *4486 2525;* e *joseignacio@terramar.com.uy;* **$$$$$**). There are only a few **budget** hotels on the peninsula, but there are several backpacker hostels in Punta del Este, as well as others in Maldonado (page 223), La Barra (pages 228–9) and Manantiales (pages 228–9) There are also **campsites** within each, but none too close to the centre of Punta del Este. All listings are included on the map pages 206–7.

Hotels
Luxury

⌂ **AWA** Pedragosa Sierra & San Ciro, parada 5; \ 4249 9999; www.awahotel.com. A flashy modern boutique hotel, 1.5km north of the bus terminal, this has microcinema, swimming pool, spa (e *spa@ awahotel.com*) & bistro with wine cellar (\ 4249 7777; e *reservas@life-bistro.com; www.life-bistro. com*) with live music Fri & Sat, & Mediterranean food such as sole in mustard with tabouleh, chicken risotto, rib-eye beef, ceviche & salads. **$$$$$**

⌂ **Conrad Resort & Casino** Rambla Williman, parada 4; \ 4249 1111; e *conradpe@conrad. com.uy; www.conrad.com.uy.* The huge casino parachuted in from Las Vegas to just north of the bus terminal (& operated by Vegas giant Harrah's) offers tasteless luxury in 296 rooms & 30 suites, all with terrace. **$$$$$**

⌂ **La Capilla** Viña del Mar & Valparaíso, San Rafael, parada 12, Playa Brava; \ 4248 4059; tf 0800 8101; e *capilla@punta.com.uy; www. lacapilla.com.uy.* One of Punta's more established celebrity bolt-holes, even though the Roma Amor Italian restaurant isn't world-class, rooms are not huge & there's Wi-Fi only in the lobby. The gardens, however, are big, with a sizeable outdoor pool. The bars & salón de té are open 24hrs in summer. **$$$$$**

⌂ **Las Cumbres** Ruta 12 km3.9, Las Cumbres de La Ballena; \ 4257 8689; e *hotel@cumbres.com. uy; www.cumbres.com.uy;* ⊕ Jun–Apr. Calling itself a Hotel-Art & Spa, this is fairly handy for the airport (across the Laguna del Sauce) but 4km from the nearest beach, which seems to suit many of the rich & famous. Nevertheless it promises sea views, thanks to the winding road that brings you to the *cumbre* (summit). Beautifully designed & fitted out, & frequently voted one of the best hotels in South America, it's a wonderful place to relax, with just 28 rooms & a fine restaurant – a great location for sunset cocktails. **$$$$$**

⌂ **L'Auberge** Avda del Agua & Carnoustie, Parque del Golf, parada 19, Playa Brava; \ 4248 8888; e *lauberge@laubergehotel.com; www. laubergehotel.com.* Around a fortress-like water tower, built in 1947, with a legendary tea room (⊕ *summer daily; winter Fri–Sun*) that serves truly decadent waffles with *dulce de leche*, honey or jam (Punta's high society still gathers here from 17.00), this is an elegant 5-star hotel, with rooms in the tower itself added in 1981. **$$$$$**

⌂ **Serena** Rambla Williman, parada 24, Las Delicias; \ 4223 3441; www.serenahotel.com.uy. Uniquely, this modern hotel is on the seaward side of the rambla, & has full beach service as well as a pool (with bar). With its all-white décor, it feels more like José Ignacio than Punta del Este. But it has to be said that it is actually on the wrong side of town for easy access to the hotspots of La Barra & José Ignacio. Service is very attentive, & with just 32 rooms you'll need to book early; no children. **$$$$$**

Mid-range

⌂ **Azul** Avda Gorlero 540; \ 4244 1117; e *reservas@hotelazul.com.uy; www.hotelazul. com.uy;* ⊕ Nov–Easter. This is a clean bright 3-star place with friendly staff, swimming pool & good buffet breakfast. Rooms have cable TV, AC & hairdryers. Right at the south end of the main drag, it's not as noisy as you might fear. **$$$$**

⌂ **Don Pepe** Bvar Artigas & Scasso, parada 14, Cantegril; \ 4248 0535/3555; e *info@ hoteldonpepe.com.uy; www.hoteldonpepe.com. uy;* ⊕ Oct–Mar. One of the best of the more affordable places, this has spacious gardens with an outdoor pool, plus spa, sauna, aqua-gym & jacuzzi. There's a restaurant & bar, & free Wi-Fi. **$$$$**

⌂ **San Fernando** Calle 30 (Las Focas) between 18 & 20; \ 4244 0720; e *hotelsanfernando@ hotmail.com;* ⊕ Oct–Easter. Just 3 blocks from

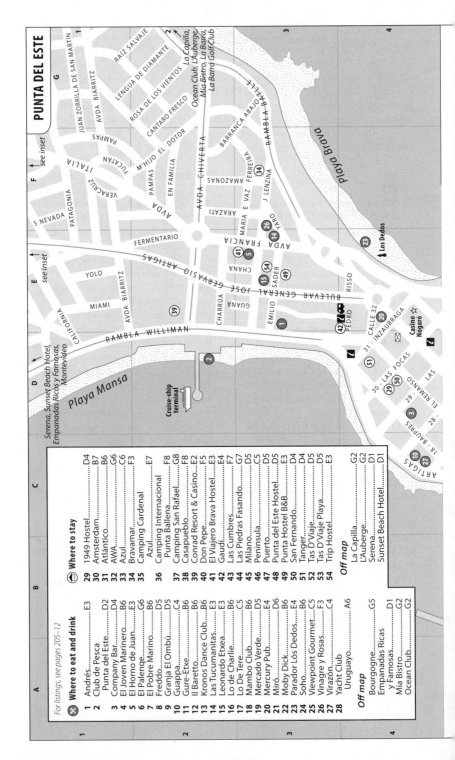

PUNTA DEL ESTE

Where to eat and drink

For listings, see pages 205–12

1 Andrés	E3
2 Club de Pesca	
Punta del Este	D2
3 Company Bar	D4
4 El Joven Marinero	B6
5 El Horno de Juan	E3
6 El Palenge	G6
7 El Pobre Marino	B6
8 Freddo	D5
9 Granja El Ombú	D5
10 Guappa	C4
11 Gure-Etxe	B6
12 Il Baretto	B6
13 Kronos Dance Club	B6
14 Las Tucumanitas	E3
15 Leonardo Etxea	E3
16 Lo de Charlie	B6
17 Lo De Tere	C5
18 Mambo Club	B6
19 Mercado Verde	D5
20 Mercury Pub	E4
21 Miró	D6
22 Moby Dick	B6
23 Parador Lós Dedos	E4
24 Soho	B6
25 Viewpoint Gourmet	C5
26 Vinagre y Rosas	F3
27 Virazón	C4
28 Yacht Club	A6

Off map

Bourgogne	G5
Empanadas Ricas	
y Famosas	D1
Mia Bistro	G2
Ocean Club	G2

Where to stay

29 1949 Hostel	D4
30 Amsterdam	B7
31 Atlántico	B6
32 AWA	G6
33 Azul	C6
34 Bravamar	F3
35 Camping Cardenal	
Azul	E7
36 Camping Internacional	
Punta Ballena	F8
37 Camping San Rafael	G8
38 Casapueblo	F8
39 Conrad Resort & Casino	E2
40 Don Pepe	F5
41 El Viajero Brava Hostel	E3
42 Gaudí	E4
43 Las Cumbres	F7
44 Las Piedras Fasando	G7
45 Milano	D5
46 Peninsula	C5
47 Puerto	D5
48 Punta del Este Hostel	D5
49 Punta Hostel B&B	E3
50 San Fernando	D4
51 Tanger	D4
52 Tas D'Viaje	D5
53 Tas D'Viaje Playa	D5
54 Trip Hostel	E3

Off map

La Capilla	G2
L'Auberge	G2
Serena	D1
Sunset Beach Hotel	D1

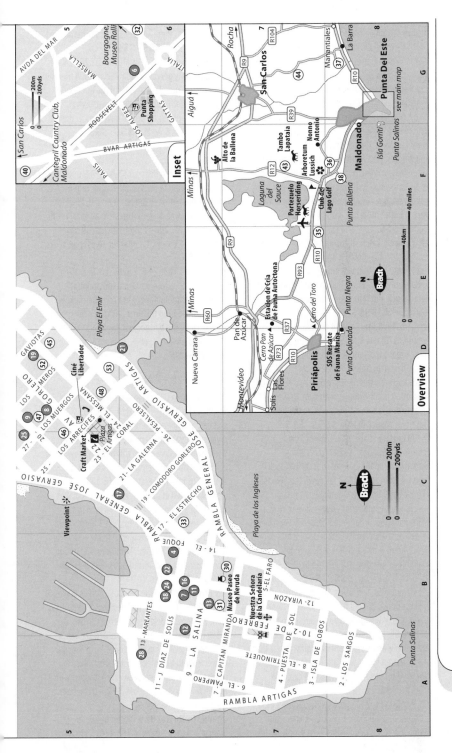

the bus terminal, this is decent & affordable, with relatively small AC standard rooms plus superior rooms, & a rooftop sun terrace. There's 1 PC with internet access & Wi-Fi. **$$$$**

⌂ **Sunset Beach Hotel** Rambla Williman & Charrúa, parada 3, Playa Mansa; ✆4248 4353; e reservas@sunsetbeach-hotel.com; www. uyhoteles.com/sunsetbeach. This fairly modern block has 38 AC rooms (only 8 with sea view) & 8 apartments, plus a fitness centre, small indoor & outdoor swimming pools, as well as beach service. Rooms are small but have cable TV, minibar & hairdryers, & some are non-smoking. There's a decent buffet breakfast, but Wi-Fi is in the lobby alone. **$$$$**

⌂ **Tanger** Calle 31 (Inzaurraga) between 18 & 20; ✆4244 1333, 0601; e tangerhotel@hotmail. com; www.hoteltanger.com; ⊕ all year. Very close to bus terminal & Playa Mansa, this is a somewhat dated block, but it has both indoor & open-air rooftop pools. **$$$$**

⌂ **Amsterdam** Calle 14 (El Foque) 759; ✆4244 4170; www.hotelamsterdampunta. com. A reasonably modern (but somewhat coach-partyish) hotel with views over the Playa de los Ingleses, this has both open-air & covered swimming pools & sauna with gym, as well as bikes to rent. There's Wi-Fi & a PC in the lobby. Closed for a week in May. **$$$$–$$$**

⌂ **Atlántico** Calle 10 & Calle 7 (2 de Febrero & Miranda); ✆4244 0229; www. hotelatlanticopuntadeleste.com. Just a block from the lighthouse (& as far down the peninsula as buses go), this is a remarkably affordable new boutique hotel that's open all year, with a swimming pool & bar in the garden & apartments as well as stylish rooms with a clean white décor throughout, & nice touches such as movies available on pendrives. Bikes can be rented for US$5/hr, US$15/day. **$$$$–$$$**

⌂ **Bravamar** Lenzina & Amazonas, parada 2, Playa Brava; ✆4248 0559; e hotelbravamar@ gmail.com; www.hotelespuntadeleste.com. Not far from the bus terminal (but on the mainland side), this is an attractive brick & glass 3-star that's bigger than it looks, with affordable pleasant rooms with both AC & fans, Wi-Fi & cable TV. **$$$$–$$$**

⌂ **Peninsula** Avda Gorlero 761; ✆4244 1533; e hotpenin@yahoo.com; ⊕ Oct–Easter. This 3-storey 3-star is good value, with simple AC rooms

with cable TV; there are 2 PCs & Wi-Fi offering free internet access. **$$$$–$$$**

⌂ **Puerto** Calle 27 (Los Muergos) 626; ✆4244 0332; e olmosgervasio@adinet.com.uy. A friendly little family-run place, this is simple but clean & great value (although breakfast costs extra). Some rooms are without TV, but all have fans, & there's internet access & Wi-Fi. **$$$$–$$$**

Budget

⌂ **Gaudí** Pedro Risso s/n; ✆4249 4116; e info@ hotelgaudi.com.uy; www.hotelgaudi.com.uy. A friendly place next to the bus terminal. Ideal for late arrivals & early departures; ⊕ all year. 1st-flr rooms have AC, 2nd-flr rooms do not; all have cable TV. There's a PC for internet access plus Wi-Fi. **$$$$–$$**

⌂ **Milano** Calle 24 880 between 28 & 29; ✆4244 0039; e reservas@hotelmilanopunta. com; www.hotelmilanopunta.com. Remarkably stylish considering the price, although the rooms (& especially the bathrooms) are small. Friendly staff, good breakfast, Wi-Fi, parking & bikes for rent. **$$$–$$**

Hostels

⌂ **El Viajero Brava Beach Hostel** Francia south of Charrúa; ✆4248 0331; e info@ elviajerobravabeach.com; www. elviajerobravabeach.com. Opened in 2009 by the successful El Viajero chain, this bright yellow block is 3 blocks from the terminal & has dorms & private rooms plus internet, & surfboard & bike rental. **$$**

⌂ **1949 Hostel** Las Focas & Baupres (calles 30 & 18); ✆4244 0719; e info@hostel1949. com; www.1949hostel.com. Just 3 blocks from the terminal, this is cramped & lively – sleep is not guaranteed. Kitchen, bar, lockers & 30mins' free internet (or unlimited but slow Wi-Fi) are included. **$**

⌂ **Punta del Este Hostel** Los Arrecifes (Calle 25) 544; ✆4244 1632; e puntadelestehostel@hotmail. com; www.puntadelestehostel.com; ⊕ Dec–Apr; b/fast 09.00–11.00. Just off Plaza Artigas, Punta del Este's official HI hostel is a once-pleasant villa converted into a cramped hostel, with mixed & single-sex dorms. There's free internet access with 2 PCs & Wi-Fi, as well as lockers, TV & a DVD player, a kitchen & board games. **$**

⌂ **Punta Hostel B&B** Sader between Francia & Artigas, parada 2; ✆4248 3316; www.

puntahostel.com. Just 100m from the terminal (& 50m from the beach), this small bungalow has beds for US$18–30 in dorms for 4, 6 and 10. They also have bikes, Wi-Fi, & a garden bar. B/fast inc. **$**

🏠 **Tas D'Viaje** Calle 24 between 28 & 29; ☏4244 8789; www.tasdviaje.com. A smallish house with a nice little roof terrace & garden (with hammocks & bar), 4 10-bed AC mixed & women-only dorms & an AC private double with private bathroom. There's a kitchen, 2 PCs, Wi-Fi, & decent bikes & skateboards for rent. They also have the **Tas D'Viaje Playa**, just south of the Miró Restaurant at Calle 26 & 27 (☏*4244 5734*; e *playa@tasdvieje.com;* ⊙ *summer only*), slightly scruffier but fine for the surfer crowd. **$**

🏠 **Trip Hostel** Sader between Francia & Artigas, parada 2; ☏4248 8181; www.thetriphostel.com. Opposite the Punta Hostel, & much hipper, this has a private double (en suite) & mixed & women-only dorms with shared bathrooms. There's a deck with BBQ & bar, & bikes can be rented. **$**

Camping

⛺ **Camping Cardenal Azul** Ruta Interbalnearia km117½, Sauce de Portezuelo; ☏4257 8178. One of 2 campsites located west of Punta del Este. **$**

⛺ **Camping Internacional Punta Ballena** Camino Lussich km2, Portezuelo; ☏4257 8902; www.campingpuntaballena.com; ⊙ all year. US$10–13 per tent, motorhome US$10–15, cabañas from US$70–92 for 4 people to US$92–120 for 8 people. West of Punta del Este. **$**

⛺ **Camping San Rafael** 1km west on Camino Saravia, or a similar distance north from parada 29; ☏4248 6715; www.campingsanrafael.com. uy; ⊙ Nov–15 Mar & Easter. On the Punta side of the bridge at La Barra. US$12.50 for 2 with tent, 4-person cabañas with private bathroom US$100. **$**

🍴 **Where to eat** Fish is the thing here, especially *brótola* (Brazilian codling), which you'll find on many menus. The reliable La Pasiva chain, serving excellent chivitos (steak sandwiches), is here too. There are also paradores (beachside diners), which are local institutions, especially for sunset drinks and snacks. Thanks to the mismanagement of the Argentine economy, many decent restaurants have had to close in the last couple of years, alas. All listings are included on the map, pages 206–7.

🍴 **Bourgogne** Avda del Mar & Pedragosa Sierra, on border of El Bosque & Brava beach zones; ☏4248 2007; e bourgogn@adinet.com.uy; www. labourgogne.com.uy; ⊙ Dec–Easter lunch & dinner daily, Easter–Nov closed Mon–Wed. An elegant French restaurant that also serves superb beef in classic Uruguayan style; some consider this the best restaurant in South America. It's also one of the most expensive. Their patisserie is a slightly cheaper option for delicious almond croissants, pains au chocolat & breads. **$$$$$**

🍴 **Club de Pesca Punta del Este** Parada 3, Playa Mansa; ☏4248 5060; ⊙ all year to 01.00 (to 01.30 Fri–Sun). Next to the cruise jetty, this serves the best fish in town (try the *merluza*), as well as snacks, sandwiches, salads, omelettes, steaks, & pastas with a good range of sauce options. The waterside deck more than compensates for the plastic furniture. **$$$$**

🍴 **El Joven Marinero** Calle 11 (Solís) 739 between calles 12 & 14; ☏4244 3565; e eljovenmarinero@hotmail.com; http://

eljovenmarino.com; ⊙ summer 12.00–15.00, 19.00–02.00 daily; rest of the year weekends only. Run for 25 years by the Marrero family, this friendly, unstuffy place serves the Uruguayan Riviera's best paella & grilled fish (such as *corvina* & *brótola*), as well as fine *mejillones a la provenzal* (Provençal mussels) & *chipirones a la plancha* (small squid), as well as pastas. It's not cheap, but portions are huge & can be shared. **$$$$$**

🍴 **Gure-Etxe** Calles 9 (La Salina) & 12 (Virazón); ☏4244 6858/7235; www.gureetxe.com.uy. A nice uncomplicated place specialising in Basque fish & shellfish dishes, as well as steaks & omelettes. **$$$$$**

🍴 **Lo de Charlie** Calle 12 (Virazón) 819 between calles 9 & 11; ☏4244 4183; ⊙ summer lunch & dinner Wed–Mon; rest of the year 19.00–midnight Thu–Sat, 12.00–16.00 Sat–Sun. One of Punta's most renowned (& priciest) restaurants, Charlie's Place is a little bistro with an open kitchen. It's in a small house where you can eat on the front veranda or indoors in a room brightly decorated by

Carlos Páez Vilaró. It specialises in Mediterranean food, especially seafood, such as paella, sautéed chipirones with caramelised onion, fish such as brótola with polenta or stingray with a saffron sauce, as well as ravioli & other pastas, with good desserts such as tiramisu to follow. $$$$$
✕ **Lo de Tere** Rambla Artigas & Calle 21; ☏4244 0492; www.lodetere.com; ☉ lunch from 12.00, dinner from 19.30. A local favourite since 1993, & still perhaps the best place in town, serving the best local ingredients with a French (& Basque) twist, & great service. There are attractive AC rooms & a terrace with a view of Isla Gorriti. It's pricey, & many of the dishes need 20–30mins' preparation time. The menu may include starters (US$10–20) such as soup, shrimp risotto, crab ravioli or octopus carpaccio; & mains such as chicken breast in honey salsa with a julienne of endive, spinach & carrot (US$24), swordfish (US$32), Basque txipirones (US$33), salmon with quinoa & a salsa of yoghurt & ciboulette (US$36), rack of lamb (US$48), or steak (US$52). $$$$$
✕ **Andrés** Edificio Vanguardia, Parada 1, Playa Mansa; ☏4248 1804; www.restaurantandres. com.uy; ☉ Dec–Feb daily lunch & dinner 18.00–midnight; Mar–Nov lunch Sat–Sun, dinner Thu–Sat. Looking out across the rambla, excellent steaks & grilled meats, fish & soufflés are served at very reasonable prices. $$$$
✕ **El Palenque** Avda Roosevelt, parada 6; ☏4249 4257/60; www.elpalenque.com.uy; ☉ 20.00–23.30 Tue, 12.00–16.00, 20.00–23.00 Wed–Sun, closed Aug. Facing the Punta Shopping mall, this is an offshoot of the parrilla restaurant in Montevideo's Mercado del Puerto, & is reputed to serve the best red meat in town. It also serves fish & seafood, including paella especial with chicken, goat & rabbit. It's big, noisy & a bit pricey. $$$$
✕ **Guappa** Rambla Artigas between calles 27 & 28; ☏4244 0951; www.guappa.com.uy; ☉ 09.00–02.00 daily. With a restaurant (with AC & Wi-Fi) on the inland side of the rambla & a terrace on the other side looking out to Isla Gorriti, this is known for its shellfish. It delivers other good solid dishes, eg: *kassler* (pork chops smoked, then grilled), salads, as well as the usual pasta, meats, fish & chivitos, coffees & snacks. You pay for the setting, but it's not excessive. $$$$
✕ **Il Baretto** Calle 9 & 10, Altos del Puerto; ☏4244 5565; m 095 808099; www. ilbarettopunta.com; ☉ 12.00–16.00, 20.00–

midnight Thu–Mon (summer daily). An excellent Italian restaurant, with a large terrace & garden, serving fine pasta, meat & fish &, of course, gourmet pizza, plus fine desserts. There's a lunch menu (US$30), & dinner costs 30% less before 21.00, out of season. $$$$
✕ **Leonardo Etxea** Lenzina just east of Bvar Artigas, parada 2, Playa Brava; ☏4249 3723; e leoetxea@gmail.com; ☉ 12.00–15.30, 18.00–midnight daily. 'Leonardo's House' is a traditional Basque restaurant, in a quiet location just north of the bus terminal. Grilled seafood is the speciality, with pastas as an alternative. $$$$
✕ **Mia Bistro** Parada 19 Brava; ☏4249 7035; www.miabistropuntadeleste.com; ☉ summer 09.00–14.00 daily; winter Thu–Sat & holidays. On the Acqua beach, near L'Auberge, this is a stylish place for lunchtime wraps with an Asian flavour, chivitos & sushi with caipirinhas. $$$$
✕ **Vinagre y Rosas** Lenzina near Francia; ☏4249 8839; e vinagrayrosaspunta@hotmail. com. A stylish restaurant-cafeteria with a terrace that's best for snacks such as sandwiches, tartas, empanadas, meat or vegetarian chivitos in pita bread, as well as breakfast (*from 10.00*), pasta (US$11–15), pizzetas (US$7), fish (US$13–17) & grilled meats (US$11–20). $$$$
✕ **Virazón** Rambla Artigas & Calle 18 (Baupres); ☏4244 3924; www.virazon.com.uy; ☉ daily. With a terrace by the Playa Mansa just north of the port, this is a great place for fish, including good sushi & sashimi; also late breakfast, coffees, salads & excellent chivitos. $$$$
✕ **Yacht Club Uruguayo** Rambla Artigas & Calle 8; ☏4244 1056; e yacht@adinet.com. uy; ☉ 11.00–16.00 & from 20.00 daily. Not to be confused with the Yacht Club de Punta del Este, in the port, this is a local institution, run by the Idiarte family for 15 years. The fish is good, especially the paella, but salads are unexciting; prices are fair for the quality & location. $$$$
✕ **El Pobre Marino** Calle 12 (Virazón) & Calle 11 (Solís); ☏4244 3306; ☉ till 01.00+. This *rotisería-marisquería*, serving a wide range of fish, seafood, grilled meats & pastas, is far less trendy & overpriced than those by the port immediately to the north, & has friendly, relaxed service. Take-aways available. $$$
✕ **Granja El Ombú** Calle 27 (Los Muergos) 626; ☏4244 4692; e olmosgervasio@adinet.com.uy. An unpretentious & very affordable parrilla, serving

the usual grilled meats as well as fish (eg; brótola) & spinach crêpes. $$$

✗ **Miró** Rambla Artigas & Calle 27, Playa El Emir; ☎ 4244 9380; e diegormiro@hotmail.com; ⏲ from 10.00 daily. A lively Resto–Music–Bar serving breakfast, sandwiches, the usual pizza, pasta, fish & steak, plus stir-fries & sushi, all at reasonable prices. Big screens show music & pop videos (not too loud) during the day & after midnight there's dancing to 'pop-house', disco, Latino hits & oldies. $$$

✗ **Viewpoint Gourmet** Calles 20 & 27, Edificio Walmer, 3rd & 4th Flrs; ☎ 4244 8015; www. viewpointgourmet.com; ⏲ 10.00–midnight daily. A very trendy place in a modern glass block with a terrace, where most people eat gourmet sandwiches, salads & desserts, although full meals are available. Across the road on the Paseo Calle 20 the Viewpoint Coffee & Wine Bar (☎ 4244 8016; ⏲ 08.00–21.00 Thu–Tue) is more casual. $$$

✗ **El Horno de Juan** Lenzina just west of Francia; ☎ 4249 2772; ⏲ from 18.00 daily in season. Simple but effective, serving good affordable pizzas (with figazza or faina) in a cheery ambience. $$

✗ **Empanadas Ricas y Famosas** Pedragosa Sierra & San Francisco, parada 5, Playa Mansa; ☎ 4249 4066; ⏲ 10.00–02.00 daily. Founded as a grocery in 1946, this is now famous for its 26 varieties of excellent empanadas; you can also call for free deliveries. $

✗ **Las Tucumanitas** Avda Francia between Lenzina & Yaro, parada 2, Playa Brava; ☎ 4249 7388. Authentic Argentine empanadas for food on the run, as well as other Andean dishes such as locros & humitas. $

🍴 **Freddo** Gorlero & Calle 27 (Los Muergos); also Calle 20 (El Remanso) between 29 & 30; & calles 24 & 25 (Plaza Artigas); www. freddouruguay.com; ⏲ summer only. An Argentine chain selling the best ice cream in town; long queues all evening. $$

🍴 **Mercado Verde** Calle 24 (El Mesana) south of 28 (Los Meros); ☎ 4244 7165; www. mercadoverde.com.uy; ⏲ 10.00–21.30 Mon–Sat (all year 10.00–14.00 Sun). Pricey, but this is the only place in town to find vegetarian/vegan sandwiches, organic vegetables, local olive oils & honeys, & all sorts of super-foods as well as salads, juices & licuados. $$

Nightlife The bars and nightclubs of Punta del Este set the musical fashions of the season for Brazil and Argentina as well as Uruguay, and CDs are in great demand. The epicentre is La Barra (see page 230), with famed venues such as Buddha Bar and Tequila; you can get there by bus or taxi, but it's also quick and easy for girls in particular to hitch a ride – being Uruguay, there's no great risk.

Note that in January people (Argentines in particular) have a nap when it gets dark and eat around midnight. Bars and clubs only get really lively around 04.00, and it'll be broad daylight when many people head home. By March things are much quieter, with little happening except at weekends (although Easter is again a lively time).

One key element in Punta's revival was the 1997 opening of the Conrad Resort and Casino (see page 205), largely to cater for Brazilians, who are unable to gamble at home. A huge chunk of Las Vegas has been parachuted in to Punta; you expect to see Elvis impersonators, Céline Dion and Californian college kids, or perhaps a software developers' convention. Being Uruguay, however, you get the Copacabana Show (US$25), the Conrad Dolls shaking it all about, Julio or Enrique Iglesias, fashion shows and book readings. In fact, from April to December the Conrad provides locals with a remarkable range of cultural events (and decent restaurants) when the town is otherwise dead. There's a mural by Carlos Páez Vilaró at the top of the escalators from the southern entry.

There's also the Casino Nogaró (*Avda Gorlero 996 & Calle 31;* ☎ *4244 1918; www. nogarobymantra.com*), a more straightforward wallet-emptying operation, with 200 slot machines, three blackjack tables, four punto banco tables and six roulette tables. There are also slots in the Punta Shopping mall (*Locales 234/5*).

♀ **Company Bar** Calle 29 (Las Gaviotas) between calles 18 & 20; ☎4244 0130; e companybar@ netgate.com.uy; ☺ summer daily from brunch time (serving very average pasta, fish, meat & snacks); rest of the year from midnight Fri–Sat. There's live music here daily in summer, plus Wi-Fi & a smokers' terrace.

♀ **Kronos Dance Club** Below the Hotel Aquarium, calles 9 (La Salina) & 10 (2 de Febrero); m 099 154529; e kronosdance@hotmail.com; www.kronosdance.com; ☺ summer nightly; winter at w/ends

♀ **Mambo Club** Rambla Artigas between calles 10 & 12; ☎4244 8956; m 098 075738; ☺ mid-Dec– end Feb. Well-established nightclub with nightly dinner shows with live music & dancers; also hosts events such as Miss Universe Uruguay. Food & service are acceptable, drinks very overpriced.

♀ **Mercury Pub** Gorlero 1045 & Calle 32; ☺ nightly, but only really lively at weekends (winter Sat only). A small gay dance bar. Staff & clientele are friendly, but there are some men there who'll cost more than the price of a drink.

♀ **Moby Dick** Rambla Artigas 650; ☎4244 1240; www.mobydick.com.uy; ☺ all year. One of the longer-lasting bars on the all-night party strip of the rambla by the port.

♀ **Ocean Club** Barrio San Rafael, parada 12, Playa Brava; ☎4248 4869; www.oceanclub.com.uy. In a modern 1-storey building, a series of large rooms with teak floors & large chandeliers serve as one of the hottest upmarket dance clubs of the moment. There are themed (ie: sponsored) events with top DJs throughout the summer, & the beachside patio hosts afternoon lounge sessions.

♀ **Parador Los Dedos** Parada 1, Playa Brava; ☎4249 7289. Just north of the Hand in the Sand (see page 217), this is a restaurant–pub serving sandwiches, salads, fish & shellfish, as well as cakes, coffes, licuados & harder drinks, then turning up the salsa from 23.00.

♀ **Soho** Rambla Artigas; ☎4244 7315; www. sohopuntadeleste.com. At the port, this is a long-established dance bar that also serves good food (especially sushi) & cocktails.

Entertainment There's one cinema in downtown Punta del Este: the **Ciné Libertador** (*Avda Gorlero & Calle 25, on north side of Plaza Artigas;* ☎*4244 4437;* ☺ *out of season Fri–Sun only*), and the **Life** multiplex (☎*4249 2196; www.lifecinemas. com.uy;* ☺ *all year*) in the Punta Shopping mall [207 G6].

The Orquesta Municipal de Maldonado performs open-air evening concerts in many locations in January and February. There's always plenty going on at the **Conrad** [207 E2] (*www.conrad.com.uy*) and **Nogaró** (*www.nogarobymantra.com*) casinos, and other venues include the Teatro Sala Cantegril (*Salt Lake & Avda Litman, near parada 16 Avda Roosevelt;* ☎*4222 3242*) and Arcobaleno Convention Centre (*Parada 16, Playa Mansa;* ☎*4222 4822*).

Events At weekends in January in particular there's a constant succession of glitzy events in Punta del Este, including Harley-Davidson motorcycle rallies, sailing regattas and motor racing (which closes part of the Playa Brava rambla). The Punta del Este International Jazz Festival (*www.festival.com.uy*) takes place in early/mid-January, a big carnival parade usually in late February and the Festival Internacional de Cine de Punta del Este film festival (*www.cinepunta.com*) in March or April. The free Punta Rock festival takes place in San Carlos on the first weekend of March. On the last weekend of October, the Punta del Este Food and Wine Festival (*www. puntafoodandwine.com*) features dinners hosted by leading chefs, with a grand finale on the plaza at Garzón. The Que Hacemos Hoy (What Shall We Do Today?) website (*www.quehacemoshoy.com.uy*) is a good source of further information.

Shopping There's a surprising variety of designer stores on Calle 20 (El Remanso) [206 D4] and the intersecting Calle 29 (Las Gaviotas), including Louis Vuitton, Tommy Hilfiger, Gap and Banana Republic. **Magma** (*Calle 20 between calles 27 & 28;* ☎ *4244 1273*) sells Argentine clothing lines such as Jazmín Chebar, Rhapsodía and

María Vásquez. There's also the self-described 'Design District' on Avenida Italia, including a Versace outlet. For crafty souvenirs and the authentic beach boho-chic look, try street markets such as the one on Plaza Artigas, or boutiques in La Barra.

For upmarket craftwork, go to **HechoAca** [207 E2] (*Galeria Comercial, Hotel Conrad;* \ *4248 6168*) or **Manos del Uruguay** [206 D4] (*Gorlero between calles 30 & 31;* \ *4244 1953*). For leatherware, go to **Pecarí** [206 C5] (*calles 20 & 27;* \ *4244 7357; www.pecari.com.uy*). The best place for art is La Barra, where there are many galleries (see pages 230–1).

An Uruguayan speciality is amethyst and agate, from the northern border region; the place to buy this is **Van Der Brüin** [206 C5] (*at the junction of calles 20 & 27;* \ *4244 3434; www.vanderbruin.com.uy*).

Punta Shopping [207 G6] (*Avda Roosevelt, parada 7, east of Bvar Artigas, between Punta del Este & Maldonado; www.puntashopping.com.uy*), near the Cantegril Country Club, is a rather futurist mall, designed by Carlos Ott, with shops (⏲ *10.00–22.00 daily, until 23.00 Fri–Sat*), a Tienda Inglesa supermarket (⏲ *08.00–22.00, until 23.00 Fri–Sat*), a *plaza de comidas* or food court and the Life multiplex cinema (see opposite).

Other supermarkets include **Devoto** (*Avda Roosevelt, parada 11, & Brasil, Barrio Cantegril*), **Disco** [206 C6] (*Avda Gorlero & Calle 17; Avda Italia, parada 5 & Pedregosa Sierra*) and **El Dorado** [206 B6] (*Calle 9 (La Salina) & Calle 12;* [206 D4] *Gorlero 630 & Calle 29 (Las Gaviotas);* [207 E2] *Avda Francia & Charrúa*).

For good Uruguayan wines, try **Grand Cru** (*Torre Amadeus, Avda Roosevelt, parada 7;* \ *4249 8980; www.grandcru.com.uy*) or **Vinos del Mundo** (*opposite Punta Shopping at Los Alpes & Bvar Artigas, parada 7;* \ *4249 9897;* m *094 120302; www.vinosdelmundo.com.uy;* ⏲ *10.00–21.00 Mon–Fri*).

There's a surprising number of **bookshops** along Gorlero (clearly not all the bodies lying on the beaches have switched their brains off), notably Libros Libros (*just south of Calle 29/Las Gaviotas*).

Activities

Watersports Naturally Punta del Este is ideal for just about any watersport, from swimming to kite-surfing, parasailing and water-skiing, but the most popular and the easiest to try for yourself is probably surfing, practised all along the Playa Brava (the beach facing the Atlantic) and the coast to the east of Punta del Este. The real centre of surfing in the region is La Barra (see page 226). You can rent boards from many shops, as well as these schools:

Escuela de Surf AA Parada 29, Playa Brava; m 094 070465; e surfearesunprivilegio@gmail. com; www.escueladesurfaaa.blogspot.com
Escuela de Surf H2O Parada 30, Playa Brava; m 099 687554; e escueladesurfh2o@yahoo.com. es; ⏲ summer 09.00–19.30 daily
Escuela de Surf La Olla Playa La Olla, parada 3, La Brava; m 099 905549; e escuelasurf@hotmail. com, juanmalek@hotmail.com

Escuela de Surf Los Dedos Playa Los Dedos, La Brava; m 099 337688/548172; e surflosdedos@ gmail.com; www.surflosdedos.blogspot.co.uk; ⏲ summer 10.00–19.00 daily
Sun Valley Surf Chalet Baraka, parada 3, Playa Brava; \ 4248 1388; www.sunvalleysurf.com; ⏲ all year 11.00–17.00 daily; Playa El Emir, Calle 28 (Los Meros) near the Rambla; \ 4244 86 22
Zorba Parada 5, Playa Brava; m 099 903090; e escuelazorba@gmail.com; ⏲ 09.00–19.30 daily

Lessons cost around US$35, or US$110 for five days. A local speciality is Flesh wetsuits, hand-cut in Punta del Este (*Avda Gorlero & Calle 25;* \ *4244 3703; www. fleshwetsuits.com*).

Windsurfing Windsurfing is possible on Laguna del Diaro (*Rambla Williman, parada 40*) at the western entry to Punta del Este – contact Shaka's Windsurf (m *099 816600;* e *shakaswindsurf@hotmail.com; www.shakas-windsurf.es.tl*).

Scuba diving There's good scuba diving on over 50 wrecks near Punta del Este and off the Isla de Lobos; operators include Punta Divers (m *099 171098;* e *puntadivers@hotmail.com; www.puntadivers.com*), Club de los Balleneros (*west of Punta Ballena, from km129.5 of the Interbalnearia;* m *094 401878*) and Mariano Boyadjian (🕿 *4225 2971;* m *099 276372;* e *buceo@punta.com.uy*).

Fishing Fishing is very popular, as all along the Uruguayan coast, with anglers on the beaches and boats leaving from the port. The very detailed Mapa de Pesca Deportiva should be available at the Club de Pesca Punta del Este (*Parada 3, Playa Mansa*) and also tourist offices. *Burriqueta, pescadilla* and *lisa* are present all year; from September to March/April there are also *corvina blanca, corvina negra, lenguado* and *cazón* (a small shark).

Beach activities If you plan to stick to the beach, remember that there's no topless sunbathing here (but no-one seems unhappy with this). Watch out for jellyfish (*medusas*), particularly Portuguese men-of-war, which appear occasionally when prolonged dry weather reduces the flow of water from the Río de la Plata. **Beach volleyball** happens on the Playa Mansa at paradas 7, 9 and 10.

Golf Golf clubs include the **Cantegril Country Club del Uruguay** (*Avda San Pablo s/n;* 🕿 *4248 2121/6;* e *golfccc@adinet.com.uy; www.cantegril.org.uy*), founded in 1947; the **Club del Lago Golf** [207 F7] (*Ruta Interbalnearia km116.5;* 🕿 *4257 8423/4; www.lagogolf.com*), a testing American-style course opened in 1983 with a five-star resort; and the **La Barra Golf Club** (*Ruta 104 km2.5, Camino al Golf, Manantiales;* 🕿 *4277 4440; www.labarragolfclub.com*), opened in 1994 with computerised watering.

Horseriding Horseriding, both along the beaches and inland, is very popular, as is polo. **Portezuelo Horseriding** [207 F7] (*Interbalnearia km116, Laguna del Sauce;* m *097 371619*) offers riding on the Portezuelo beach, west of Punta, including sunset rides. **Huellas** (m *099 295030/615094; www.huellascabalgatas.com*) offers full-moon rides on the beach, and longer rides, eg: from La Pedrera to the Laguna de Castillos with a local historian (around US$50/day including bed and breakfast). Riding clubs include the Club Hípico Burnett (*Parque Burnett, Calle Tauro s/n, Camino a la Laguna, parada 32½, Playa Mansa;* 🕿 *4223 7292; www.hipicoburnett.com;* ⊕ *summer 09.30–18.30 daily; rest of the year Tue–Sun*) and the Club Hípico Cantegril (*Avda Aparicio Saravia & Tacuarembó;* 🕿 *4222 0560;* e *hipico@cantegrilcountryclubpe.com; www.cantegrilcountryclubpe.com;* ⊕ *Tue–Sun*).

Spectator sports The main venue for **polo** is the Medellín Country Club (*Ruta 10 km176, La Boya;* 🕿 *4277 4520;* m *099 903011; www.medellinpoloclub.com.ar;* ⊕ *early Dec–Feb*), with six fields in a 1,500ha estate near José Ignacio.

In early January in particular there are lots of sporting events, such as the Punta Sevens **rugby** tournament (*www.7punta.com*), the most prestigious in South America (though it's actually in Maldonado); the San Fernando **10K run** from Maldonado to the peninsula; **polo** at the Medellín Country Club; **pro-am golf** and the International Classic Sport Car **rally**.

Other practicalities

Banks In summer banks are all open around 15.00–20.00, and the rest of the year 13.00–17.00 or 18.00. There are plenty of ATMs, especially along Gorlero.

$ **Banco Comercial** Avda Gorlero 705 & Calle 23; ☎4244 1801/4; Avda Roosevelt, parada 14, Local 8–9; ☎4248 8412

$ **BBVA** Avda Gorlero 630 between calles 19 & 21; ☎4244 4060

$ **BROU** Avda Gorlero & Calle 25; ☎4244 1930; Punta Shopping, Local 249B; ☎4249 8445

$ **Centro de Atención VISA** Calle 24 & 27; ☎2902 2200; ⏰ 12.00–20.00 Mon–Fri

$ **Citibank** Avda Gorlero & Calle 21; ☎4244 4841/0881

$ **HSBC** Avda Gorlero & Calle 28; ☎2915 1010

$ **Itaú** Avda Gorlero 644 & Calle 21; ☎4244 5556/6902; Avda Paris 21 between Roosevelt & Rambla Artigas; ☎4249 3366

$ **Santander** Avda Gorlero & Calle 25; ☎4244 4050; Avda Roosevelt, parada 11; ☎4249 1887/8

$ **UBS** Edificio Biarritz, Avda Gorlero & Calle 27; ☎4244 2582

Exchange offices

$ **Aeromar** Avda Gorlero 965 & Calle 31; ☎4248 2565; ⏰ 10.00–18.00 Mon–Sat

$ **Brimar Cambios** Calle 31 610 & Avda Gorlero; ☎4248 3472/3

$ **Cambio 18** Avda Gorlero 953 & Calle 30; ☎4244 6474; Avda Gorlero 998 & Calle 31; ☎4244 1918; Avda Gorlero & Calle 25; ☎4244 8835

$ **Cambio Aspen** Avda Gorlero & Calle 28; ☎4244 6979; Avda Gorlero & Calle 29; ☎4244 8809

$ **Cambio Nelson** Bus terminal; ☎4248 4744; ⏰ 08.30–22.00 daily

$ **Cambio Uruguay** Francia & Yara, parada 2, Playa Brava; ☎4249 7458; ⏰ from 09.00 daily

$ **Gales** Avda Gorlero & Calle 29; ☎4244 6571

$ **Indumex** Punta Shopping, Local 228; ☎4249 2079; & Local 213; ☎4249 7458

Communications The post office [206 D4] (*Avda Gorlero 1035;* ☎ *4249 3691;* ⏰ *10.00–17.00 Mon–Fri, 09.00–12.00 Sat*) is just south of the bus terminal. Antel has telecentros on Plaza Artigas at the junction of calles 24 and 25 (⏰ *09.00–23.00 daily*) and at Pedragosa Sierra and Francia, north of the Conrad. There's free Wi-Fi at a school on the south side of Plaza Artigas; internet/phone centres are at Avenida Gorlero 815, Avenida Gorlero 811 and Calle 27, and on the north side of Plaza Artigas.

For courier service, go to DHL Express [206 C5] (*Edificio El Monarca, Local 5, Avda Gorlero & Calle 21;* ☎ *4244 1725, 2604 1331; www.dhl.com.uy;* ⏰ *09.30–17.30 Mon–Fri*).

Crime, safety and police Punta del Este is largely crime-free, which no doubt helps visitors from Buenos Aires and Brazil to relax. The occasional high-profile burglary is usually (rightly or wrongly) blamed on Argentine gangs following their targets from Buenos Aires.

Useful telephone numbers

Police ☎911 or 4222 4401/2; at the port; ☎4244 1971

Fire ☎104

Marine rescue ☎1767

Health The nearest public hospital is in Maldonado (*Continuación Ventura Alegre;* ☎ *4222 5889/90*). There are plenty of farmacías in Punta, especially along Avenida Gorlero [206 D5].

✚ **Campus** Avda Gorlero 920 near Calle 29; ☎4244 4444

✚ **Farmashop** Avda Roosevelt, parada 10; ☎4248 6927

✚ **Font** Edificio Vanguardia, Rambla Williman, parada 1.5; ☎4248 2923

✚ **Ituzaingó** Avda Gorlero & Calle 19; ☎42 44 1819

✚ **La Pastora** Avda Francia & Lensina; ☎ 4248 3132
✚ **Las Delicias** Avda España, parada 27; ☎ 4222 5966

✚ **María Amelia** Avda Gorlero 685; ☎ 4244 3082
✚ **Menafra** Calle 28 near Calle 20; ☎ 4244 6888
✚ **San Roque** Punta Shopping, Local 239–41; ☎ 4249 2236/38

Immigration For immigration issues, the Inspectoría de Migración is at Ventura Alegre 272 and Sarandí in Maldonado (☎ *152 1906/7, 4223 7624*; e *dnm-maldonadooficina@minterior.gub.uy*) and at the airport (☎ *4255 9137*; e *i13laguna@ dnm.minterior.gub.uy*).

What to see and do Being a beach resort, there's not much to see here other than beaches and their occupants; the one museum is of interest mainly as a temple to bad taste. One unusual feature of beaches along this coast is whale-watching towers, allowing tourists to view migrating right whales from March to October; the whales rest on the mansa side of the Punta for a week or two.

To the west of the peninsula, the Playa Mansa is largely patronised by Uruguayan families, while the Playa Brava, to the east, is popular with Argentines. Some hotels attempt to stake out private beaches but by law all Uruguayan beaches are open to all. On the west side of the peninsula itself, a wooden boardwalk leads north from the bus terminal to the cruise ship terminal (near the Conrad Resort and Casino), and is being extended further north to parada 5. There's also, rather bizarrely, a totem pole just north of the Liga de Fomento tourist office, west of the bus terminal, as well as a sculpture by Pablo Atchugarry.

The broad promenade continues around the peninsula, busy with power-walkers and flanked by the busy Rambla Artigas. At the west end of Calle 23 (El Coral) are two ship's anchors and a short boardwalk leading to a *glorieta* (viewing pavilion), where you may spot cormorants, oystercatchers and miscellaneous wading birds. Immediately south is the port, which has three or four working fishing areas, where sea lions wait in the water for fish guts or lie hauled out. There are plenty of fish restaurants here, mostly fairly downmarket although one or two are pretty good. On the inland side of the rambla are some very lively all-night bars. You'll see some pretty fancy motor yachts here in high season.

Nearby, the **Museo Paseo de Neruda** [206 B6] (*Calle 12 (Virazón) 794 near Calle 9*; ☎ *4248 4826*; e *pneruda@adinet.org.uy*; ⊕ 19.30–22.00 *Thu–Sun; voluntary donation*) is open for guided tours of a collection of manuscripts, books, personal objects and photos of the great Chilean poet Pablo Neruda, who lived in Atlántida in the early 1950s. There are also films, readings and other events.

Beyond the port in the Altos del Puerto quarter, buildings are restricted to a maximum of four storeys to avoid blocking the lighthouse, and this area has the feel of a quiet suburb, with few striking or modern houses. Rusty walkways lead to tiny islets on the rocky west side of the headland, where you'll see more waders and other birds. Jogging around the headland is popular, past the Plazoleta Gran Bretaña at its southern tip, with a helipad and the rusty anchor of HMS *Ajax*, commemorating the Battle of the Plate. This point, known as **Punta Salinas** [206 A8], is the southernmost point of Uruguay and marks the northern end of the imaginary line from Punta Rasa (Argentina) drawn in 1857 to mark the end of the Río de la Plata (River Plate). At the highest point, a couple of blocks inland, the **lighthouse** (*faro*) stands on a grassy plaza; originally raised in 1858 on the Isla de Lobos (see page 220), it was moved here in 1860 and rebuilt in 1923. The light, 44m above sea level, has a range of 11 nautical miles. It's possible to climb the 25m-high tower, but it depends on whether the personnel are free.

Also on the plaza is the church of **Nuestra Señora de la Candelaría** [206 B7] (Our Lady of Candlemas); built in 1909–11 and rebuilt in 1942–50, it's not unattractive and a pleasant refuge on a hot day. To the east is the **Playa de los Ingleses** [206 B7] (British Beach), not really much of a beach, and beyond the rocky Punta del Vapór (with an image of Nuestra Señora de la Candelaría) the Playa El Emir (the Emir's Beach – named after Emin Arslan, an exiled Turkish noble, who built a house here in 1920). It's one of the country's busiest surfing spots, with powerful left- and right-hand waves, and sheltered from winds from the southwest. Just inland is **Plaza Artigas** [206 C5], where the statue of the father of the country seems to be leaning backwards, kept upright only by the weight of his nose. Lots of parakeets live in the palms on the plaza, which is being re-landscaped; on its northern and eastern sides are the modern structures of the Feria Artesanal or craft market, busy with shoppers until late at night (☼ *winter 12.00–20.00; summer until 02.00*), and on its south side a school has exhibitions of local artists in summer.

The main commercial zone of Avenida Gorlero runs from Plaza Artigas to the Paseo de las Américas, with the bus terminal to the left and the start of the Playa Brava to the right. The emblematic former ANCAP station (*Avda Gorlero 946 & Calle 30*) is to be the city's cultural centre, and currently houses the Espacio Cultural Gastronómico, with tasting and sales of local olive oil, wine and goat's cheese. At the start of the Playa Brava you'll see the striking concrete sculpture of the **Dedos** (Fingers), known to English-speakers as 'The Hand in the Sand', created in 1981 by the Chilean Mario Irrarazabal. It's become an iconic image of Punta del Este, but on the grassy road islands there are half a dozen other steel or concrete sculptures (by Gyula Kosice, Enio Iomo, Hernán Jugiari, Edgard Negret, Francisco Matos and Waltercio Matos), which are always overlooked. Immediately beyond is Playa La Olla, with good surf (up to 2m high) that can start to break 200m offshore. The Rambla Lorenzo Batlle Pacheco continues along the Playa Brava, with some striking apartment blocks on the inland side, and some older villas surviving between them. Beyond parada 10, the upmarket Barrio San Rafael (named after a Spanish frigate, wrecked here in 1765) was laid out by Giovanni Veltroni and is a shameless mix of thatched cottages, mock-Tudor houses and Modernist white cubes.

A kilometre or so inland (about 15 minutes' walk from the nearest buses on Avenida Roosevelt, or half an hour from the Conrad), the **Museo Ralli** (*Los Arrayanes & Los Platanos, Barrio Beverley Hills;* ☎ *4248 3476; www.museoralli.com. uy;* ☼ *Jan–Feb 17.00–21.00 Tue–Sun; Mar/Easter 14.00–18.00 Tue–Sun; Apr–May & Oct–Dec 14.00–18.00 Sat–Sun; Jun–Sep closed; free*) is the perfect art museum for the kind of town that thinks Salvador Dalí is a great artist. It's a temple to bad art (mainly Surrealism and excessive Realism), although there's no doubt that plenty of money has been spent on the huge collection. There's a Modigliani in the sculpture patio, as well as *Eve* by the Colombian Fernando Botero.

AROUND PUNTA DEL ESTE

Casapueblo [207 F8] (*Punta Ballena;* ☎ *4257 8041/8611; www.clubhotelcasapueblo. com;* **$$$–$$**) Some 11km west of Punta del Este, Casapueblo is one of the area's compulsory sights thanks to its cultural importance, its visual impact and stunning setting, and the sundowner drinks and snacks you can have here. As a hotel, however, it's overpriced and just too eccentric and awkward. It's a huge house-sculpture that the artist Carlos Páez Vi100aró began with his own hands in 1960 (when there were no roads and no electricity here), around a shack he was then living in. It grew into a studio, then a house that could accommodate friends (with a room sometimes added for a particular guest), and then a sizeable hotel and a monument to his self-importance. Influenced in a relatively shallow way by Picasso and Matisse (you'll see the ubiquitous photo of him with Picasso), he's as much a great publicist as a great artist. Visitors have included Lech Wałęsa, Placido Domingo, Bo Derek and Astor Piazzolla.The whitewashed concrete structure climbing up the cliffside was partly inspired by the mud nests of Uruguay's *horneros* (ovenbirds) but has overtones of Mykonos, Gaudí's Barcelona, Hundertwasser's Vienna and Malian mud mosques. In the words of CPV, 'I call it my habitable sculpture … the result of my personal war against the right angle.' Staying in one of the 70 different rooms, small and sunny and with stunning views out over the bay, still feels like staying in a guestroom at a friend's beach cottage, although the dark, twisting, tunnel-like passages undermine this effect somewhat, as do the poor breakfast and service.

Virtually at the end of the Ruta Panorámica, a 2.5km scenic loop road built in 1978 along the crest of Punta Ballena, it's easiest to come by car or on a tour from Punta del Este. The Linea 8 bus between Piriápolis and Punta del Este comes this way just four times a day. The **Museo–Taller de Casapueblo** (❧ *4257 8041; www. carlospaezvilaro.com;* ⊕ *10.00–17.00 or sunset daily; US\$7*) displays and sells prints and original pieces by CPV. Entering at the top of the building, you can take a tiny old lift down to level –9, where there's a terrace bar by an open-air swimming pool. There's no entry fee, but as you arrive you'll have to pay a minimum US\$5 towards drinks and snacks, which are not at all overpriced, though service can be slow (*snack-bar* ⊕ *10.00–23.00 daily, restaurant* ⊕ *08.30–11.00, 12.30–15.30 & 20.30–23.00 daily*). The terrace is a great spot to enjoy the best sunsets in the area, as is the viewpoint at the end of the Ruta Panorámica. Overnight guests also have use of a covered pool with hydromassage, sauna, solarium and gym.

Arboretum Lussich [207 F7] (❧ *4257 8077;* e *arboretumlussich@maldonado. gub.uy; www.arboretumlussich.com.uy;* ⊕ *mid-Dec–Easter 10.00–19.30 daily; rest of the year 10.00–17.00 daily; free*) The Arboretum Lussich has the biggest collection of trees in Uruguay, although most of the 400 foreign and 70 native species are unlabelled. From the Portezuelo flyover (15km from Punta del Este, at km120 of the Interbalnearia), reached by Linea 21 midibuses heading for Solanas and Piriápolis (15 minutes from Maldonado terminal, 30 minutes from Punta), it's 300m uphill on the road north towards Lapataia.The Ballena (Whale) ridge was first settled in 1755. In 1896 Antonio Lussich (see page 201) bought 1,800ha, continuing his self-imposed task of planting trees to stabilise the coastal sand dunes (and bringing birds to populate the new woodland), and building himself a house on the ridge. He first planted native tamarisks, eucalyptus, pines and locust trees to provide windbreaks, then araucaria, oak, cypress, cedar, walnut, maple, lime, fir, birch, cork oak, camphor, magnolia and many others, as well as cacti and bamboos.

In 1979, 182ha were handed over to the departmental government to be opened to the public, with another 10ha added in 1990. The entrance is at the top of the ridge, with a small museum in Lussich's house to the left (there's a smaller area also open to the public across the road to the right). There are photos of Lussich and his family, and of the early years of forestation, a few of the books he wrote, and upstairs a collection of tiles, similar to that of the Museo del Azulejo in Montevideo (see page 138) but more spacious. There are a few Catalan tiles from the 18th and early 19th centuries, but most are from Desvres in northern France.

Continuing past the house, a track leads north to a *glorieta* (viewpoint) on the first hilltop, and continues to a watchtower (marked *prohibido subir*, but there's nothing to actually stop you climbing up); you'll have to return the same way.

It's worth continuing along the road for 3km to **Nonno Antonio** (*Camino Lussich & Paseo Marrero;* ☏ *4224 1664; www.nonnoantonio.com.uy*), which produces perhaps the best cheeses in Uruguay, including mascarpone, Gorgonzola and reblochon. Having been a near-secret for some years, they have just recently opened a shop at the dairy.

Tambo Lapataia [207 F7] (*Camino Lussich, 4km from Ruta Interbalnearia km128 (parada 45);* ☏ *4222 0000, 4223 6288; www.lapataiapuntadeleste.com;* ⊕ *summer 12.00–21.30 daily; rest of the year until 20.00; free*) Tambo Lapataia, also known as Estancia El Sociego, is a very popular tourist estancia, a dairy farm where children can pet and bottle-feed young farm animals and then enjoy pancakes with the farm's wonderful *dulce de leche*, and other dairy products. There are free guided tours, including to the cheese and dulce de leche plants, as well as tours in open carts. Horseriding is available, and you can walk on four trails; 113 species of bird have been recorded so far on the 45ha property, and there's also a native plant nursery. There's live jazz daily at 'pancake hour' (late afternoon), and one of the country's leading jazz festivals, the Punta del Este International Jazz Festival (see page 212), is held here in early/mid-January, in an open-air amphitheatre. The property is owned by Princess Laetitia d'Arenberg, who was born in 1941 in Lebanon (to a Belgian father and French mother) and came to Uruguay at the age of ten; she's been very successful in business: for instance owning the Mitsubishi franchise.

Alto de la Ballena [207 F6] (*Ruta 12 km16.4, Maldonado;* m *094 410328; www. altodelaballena.com*) One of Uruguay's most impressive newer wineries is Alto de la Ballena, which certainly indicates that Maldonado has a promising future as a winemaking region. Álvaro Lorenzo and his wife Paula Pivel were high-flying MBAs (he was also a member of Congress from 2004 to 2010) but decided to follow their passion and create a boutique winery. Their research identified southeastern Uruguay as ideal for dry wines, with sea breezes and temperatures of 30°C when it's 35° or 40° in Canelones and the interior. They planted 10ha from 2001 on, and began making wine using equipment at other wineries; since 2008 they've had their own winery and the results are even better than before. They're producing 55,000 bottles a year, and aim to increase that to 70,000, exporting 20,000 soon.

Almost half the area is planted with Merlot, with Tannat, Cabernet Franc and half a hectare each of Syrah and Viognier. They make a unique and very successful Reserva of Tannat (85–90%) and Viognier, and also blend up to 20% Viognier with their Syrah. The spicy, plummy Merlot Reserva is excellent too, spending a year in French oak; having identified Merlot as the best grape for the area, this became something like a flagship product for them (and is still popular with local restaurants), but they now make better wines, eg: the Tannat–Viognier Reserva, and the new Cetus Syrah, very elegant and without the big fruit attack of Australian Shiraz. They have a beautifully rounded Cabernet Franc Reserva, and are working on Merlot–Cabernet Franc blends.

The entry-level line includes a clean, well-balanced Viognier, a Tannat–Merlot–Cabernet Franc blend (with half the Merlot aged in French oak, but still a young wine overall with lots of tannin) and a rosé (60% Cabernet Franc, 40% Merlot, so like a light red wine).Turning south off Ruta 9 at km127 on to Ruta 12 (from Minas to Maldonado), the vineyard is 16km from the sea, with iron-rich soil of oxidated grey granite with schist and quartz. Some of their land is too rocky to plant, but it's a haven for wildlife (with lots of field flickers) and has great views out across the

Laguna del Sauce. Tastings are in a tasting room in the newly extended winery, or on a hilltop deck, where 90-minute visits tend to stretch to two hours or more as people relax in hammocks to enjoy the breeze and the vista.

A dirt track leads about 500m from Ruta 9 (west of km128) to the vineyards and the hilltop tasting room, with stunning views. Small groups come mainly from Punta del Este's hotels, and can buy Reserva wines (which sell for US$50–80 in Punta's restaurants) for US$25 a bottle; there's an extra charge for a selection of wonderful cheeses from Nonno Antonio (see page 219).

A visit here can be combined with birdwatching and visits to local **olive oil producers** (a new industry and not yet as organised as the wineries) such as Oliva Sana (*Ruta 39 km50;* ↘ *4410 2855;* m *098 592829; www.olivasana.com*), Finca José Ignacio (*Ruta 9 km156;* ↘ *2712 2979; www.o33.com.uy*) or Finca Babieca (*north of San Carlos; www.fincababieca.com.uy*); there's also the Punta Lobos olive oil shop on the west side of Plaza Artigas in Maldonado (⊕ *15.00–20.00 Mon–Sat*).

Isla Gorriti and Isla de Lobos

Just 1.5km offshore, and reached by frequent boats from the port, Isla Gorriti [207 F8] is known for its beautiful sandy beaches (used for fashion and glamour shoots) and for fishing. In 1531 a cross was raised, below which captains left messages for other ships; pirates and other mariners used it as a haven for many years. Originally known as Isla Maldonado, it was renamed after Captain Francisco Gorriti, imprisoned in 1771–73 for refusing to pay his share of the expenses of a war against the indigenous peoples. Fortified by the Spaniards, it was bombarded by the British navy in 1806; ironically HMS *Agamemnon* (the ship on which Nelson wooed Lady Hamilton, and which fought at Trafalgar in 1805) was wrecked just northeast of the island in 1809 and is now a popular dive site. In 1827 Brazilian troops dug in on Isla Gorriti and the peninsula, but soon left for Montevideo. In 1832 the *Adventure*, accompanying the *Beagle*, was repaired on the beach.

Planted with pines in the mid 20th century, its trees are now lit up at night. Two kilometres long and 1km across, the island has two beaches, Playa Honda to the west and Puerto Jardín to the northeast. So many people bring get-away-from-it-all picnics here that it's actually very crowded in high season. You can see the ruins of the Spanish battery of Santa Ana, and at the southern tip of the island the *faroleta* (little lighthouse). Boats (US$15 round trip) leave every half-hour from 08.00 to 19.00, returning from 10.15 to 19.00.

It's 12km further (*2hr round trip; US$80*) to Isla de Lobos, named after the 'marine wolves' (ie: sea lions) which live here, and when you arrive you can't actually land. Said to be the world's biggest sea lion reserve, introduced species such as rabbits have been eliminated and landing is allowed only with a special permit; nevertheless the boat trip is well worth making. The sea lions breed here and come into the harbour of Punta del Este in search of fish scraps; they're also happy to approach boats. There's a total of around 200,000 sea lions and southern fur seals here, plus elephant seals in winter. It's also easy to see two species of petrels from the boats, and possibly albatrosses, especially after stormy weather.

A lighthouse was built here in 1857–58, but was moved to Punta del Este in 1860 so as not to disturb the sea lions, which were 'harvested' commercially. However, there were still so many wrecks here and on the rocks offshore that the present lighthouse was built in 1907. At 59m above the ground (and 66m above sea level), it's the highest lighthouse in the Americas. It was built this high in order that the light would only be seen at sea and not on the island, again to avoid disturbing the sea lions.

Boat operators, who also offer fishing for shark and other fish, include:

✦ Calypso Charters Rambla Artigas & Calle 21; ☎ 4244 6152; m 094 443600; www.calypso.com.uy

✦ Dimar Tours Local 1A, Puerto Punta del Este; ☎ 4244 4750; m 094 410899; www.dimartours.com.uy

✦ Samoa ☎ 4244 6166/8955; www.crucerosamoa.com

MALDONADO [207 F8] The name of the town (and the department) is thought to be based on *mar de ao*, Guaraní for 'sea lion', rather than for Francisco Maldonado, who was supposedly sent by Cabot to explore inland in 1527 and never returned. In 1755 Joaquín de Viana founded the town, which soon became the second city of Uruguay. The town's inhabitants are known as *fernandinos* after Ferdinand VI, King of Spain when the town was founded (and the cathedral was dedicated to San Fernando). In 1806 Maldonado was captured by the British, who left in early 1807 to take Montevideo. In June 1810 a *cabildo abierto* (open council) was the first to support the *primer cabildo* established in Buenos Aires on 25 May 1810. The Brazilians again captured the town in 1827; Lavelleja failed to drive them out but they too soon marched on to Montevideo.

In July 1832 the *Beagle* arrived with Charles Darwin, who spent ten weeks in the area, travelling inland as far as Aiguá and Minas, collecting what he called 'all my treasures from Maldonado' and beginning to formulate the ideas that were to lead to his theory of evolution. He wrote:

> I stayed ten weeks at Maldonado, in which time a nearly perfect collection of the animals, birds, and reptiles, was procured ... It is a most quiet, forlorn, little town; built, as is universally the case in these countries, with the streets running at right angle to each other, and having in the middle a large plaza or square, which, from its size, renders the scantiness of the population more evident. It possesses scarcely any trade; the exports being confined to a few hides and living cattle. The inhabitants are chiefly landowners, together with a few shopkeepers and the necessary tradesmen, such as blacksmiths and carpenters, who do nearly all the business for a circuit of fifty miles round. The town is separated from the river by a band of sand-hillocks, about a mile broad; it is surrounded, on all other sides, by an open slightly undulating country, covered by one uniform layer of fine green turf, on which countless herds of cattle, sheep, and horses graze. There is very little land cultivated even close to the town. A few hedges, made of cacti and agave, mark out where some wheat or Indian corn has been planted.

Bizarrely, on Darwin's 200th birthday, 12 February 2009, a volunteer at the Cambridge Zoology Museum rediscovered a tinamou egg that he had collected in Maldonado – it was damaged because he packed it in too small a box, but it is the only surviving egg that he collected.

Now Maldonado is part of the sprawling Punta del Este conurbation, but still has its own small-town character and some relaxing places to eat and sleep.

Getting there and away

By bus Buses arrive at the terminal on Avenida Roosevelt and Sarandí, seven blocks south of the plaza; virtually every bus to and from Punta del Este calls here, and there are a few extra services north to Treinta y Tres (with EmTur, via San Carlos and Aiguá). Lots of local buses link Maldonado and Punta del Este, mostly running via either Punta Shopping or Avenida España, Las Delicias and Rambla

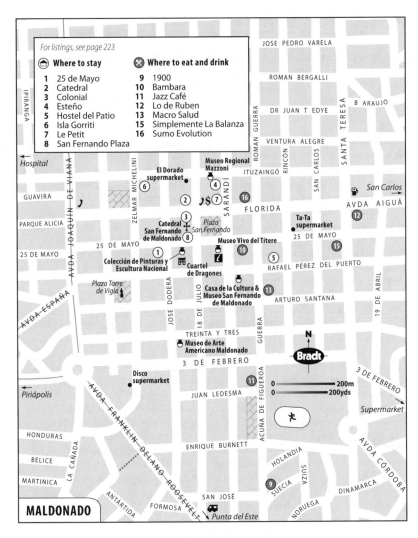

For listings, see page 223

Where to stay

1 25 de Mayo
2 Catedral
3 Colonial
4 Esteño
5 Hostel del Patio
6 Isla Gorriti
7 Le Petit
8 San Fernando Plaza

Where to eat and drink

9 1900
10 Bambara
11 Jazz Café
12 Lo de Ruben
13 Macro Salud
15 Simplemente La Balanza
16 Sumo Evolution

MALDONADO

Williman (Playa Mansa); some continue north to the small town of San Carlos (see page 239) for connections to Rocha department. Northbound, these run up Dodera, a block west of the plaza; southbound, they use Rincón, two blocks east of the plaza (stopping almost at the Hostel del Patio). Linea 20 buses go from the terminal past the airport to Pan de Azúcar; Linea 55 runs every couple of hours to La Barra, Manantiales and Barrio Buenos Aires without entering Punta del Este.

Local bus timetables are displayed in the IMM Informes window, and there is a left luggage counter (⊕ 06.15–20.30 daily). Tickets for Colonia Express services to Buenos Aires can be booked at the COPSA desk (⊕ 04.30–23.30 daily).

Tourist information The tourist information office is in the Paseo San Francisco on the south side of the plaza (☏ 4222 3333; e informes@maldonado.gub.uy; www. maldonado.gub.uy; ⊕ summer 08.00–20.00 daily; rest of the year 09.15–14.45 Mon–Fri).

Where to stay There's a very limited range of hotels in Maldonado, open all year and not oriented solely to holidaymakers. All listings shown are included on the map opposite.

San Fernando Plaza Hotel 25 de Mayo 810 & 18 de Julio; ☎4224 2410; www.sfplazahotel. com. This is the best place in town, a nicely refurbished 4-star on the plaza. It's nicer inside than out, with attractive public areas, especially the bright, well-lit breakfast room. Rooms aren't huge but have AC, flat-screen TV, minibar & Wi-Fi, & there's a lift. Good, big b/fast inc. **$$$**

Hotel Colonial 18 de Julio 841 & Florida; ☎4222 3346; www.colonialhotel.com.uy. Decent 2-star place on the plaza, with Wi-Fi. **$$$–$$**

Hotel 25 de Mayo 25 de Mayo 851 & Dodera; ☎4222 0573. Nice simple 1-star hotel. **$$**

Hotel Catedral Florida 830 & 18 de Julio; ☎4224 2513; www.hotelcatedral.com.uy. Bright red 2-star place half a block west of the plaza. **$$**

Hotel Esteño Sarandí 881; ☎4222 5222. On the pedestrianised street, this 2-star place has 30 relatively quiet rooms. **$$**

Hotel Isla Gorriti Michelini 884, just south of Izutaingo; ☎4224 5218. Simple 1-star hotel with rooms around a patio. **$$**

Hotel Le Petit Upstairs in Galería Marco de los Reyes, Sarandí & Florida; ☎4222 3044. Has AC rooms with cable TV; there's Wi-Fi, but they don't take credit cards. **$$**

Hostel del Patio Rafael Pérez del Puerto 678 & Roman Guerra; ☎4222 1052; e hosteldelpatio@ gmail.com; www.hosteldelpatio.com. The best backpackers' hostel in the area – far nicer than those in Punta del Este – del Patio's reception is in an antiques shop & there are spacious rooms upstairs around a 3-sided patio. Also has a kitchen, dining room, lounge with cable TV & PC (& Wi-Fi throughout). There are shared rooms for up to 8 people with large individual lockers (US$15) & private rooms for 2 (US$40). Good b/fast inc (*09.00–12.30*). **$**

Where to eat All listings are included on the map opposite.

1900 Acuña de Figueroa & Suiza; ☎4224 7775; e 1900@adinet.com.uy. Near the bus terminal (with easy on-street parking), this is a good parrilla, with a salad bar, in a pleasant, modern, AC setting. It also offers jazz & cocktails. **$$$**

Bambara 25 de Mayo 711 (just west of Román Guerra); ☎4222 1724; ⏱ 11.30–16.00, 19.30– 00.30 daily. This cafeteria-parrilla, whose owner spent 4 years in London, offers great value with no cover charge, huge portions & low prices. There's good meat, fish & pasta, a rear patio & Wi-Fi. **$$$**

Lo de Ruben Santa Teresa 846 & Avda Aiguá; ☎4222 3059; www.loderuben.com.uy; ⏱ 12.00– 17.00, 20.00–04.00 daily. You may have to wait for a table at this local institution, which serves grilled meats swiftly & exactly as you requested them. You can also order grilled vegetables & provolone cheese, pasta or fish, all at very reasonable prices. There are only basic salads, but desserts are good, & you can bring your own wine for US$5. **$$$**

Simplemente La Balanza 25 de Mayo & Santa Teresa; ☎4225 3909. A cheap & homely parrilla, although the service can be variable. **$$**

Sumo Evolution Sarandí & Florida; ☎ 4222 3959. This youth-oriented place serves chivitos, *milanesas*, burgers, pizza & pasta. It's a bit chain-like but has AC. On the northeastern corner of the plaza, it's a great spot for people-watching. **$$**

Jazz Café Ledesma between Acuña de Figueroa & Sarandí; ☎4223 3042; www.jazzcafe. com.uy; ⏱ 08.00–19.00 Mon–Fri. A lively modern place with jazz videos, Wi-Fi & good coffees, wines, snacks & cakes. **$$**

Macro Salud Guerra 736, south of Pérez del Puerto; ☎4222 2695; ⏱ 08.00–21.30 Mon–Sat. A friendly little health-food café, selling cooked meals by weight as well as diabetic desserts & products for coeliacs. **$$**

Entertainment The **theatre** at the Casa de la Cultura (*Pérez del Puerto & Guerra;* ☎ *4223 09898;* e *dgcultura@maldonado.gub.uy;* ⏱ *summer 08.00–14.00 daily; rest of the year 10.00–16.00*) stages plays, music, dance, comedy and other events. The **Club de Teatro Fernandino** (*25 de Mayo 828;* ☎*4223 0599*), opposite the **Cuartel**

5

de **Dragones**, is a small theatre that puts on good plays year-round. There are also concerts and exhibitions at the **Azotea de Haedo** (*Bvar Artigas & Mercedes;* \ *4222 3288;* ⏰ *10.00–16.00 daily*), the little summer house of President Haedo.

Shopping Isabel Fonseca wrote in the *Sunday Times* that 'the city of Maldonado is one of the great ironmongery capitals of the world … a wholesalers' paradise, with a large shop that sells only hinges, and an enormous emporium called Todo Goma, or Everything Rubber'. Todo Goma is at Florida 670, if you need it, and there are plenty of supermarkets in the centre of Maldonado, including El Dorado (*between 18 de Julio & Dodera*), immediately north of the plaza (the branch at 25 de Mayo & Román Guerra, half a block east of the plaza, deals in home furnishings and the like), Ta-Ta (*25 de Mayo & Rincón*), two blocks east of the plaza, Disco (*Avda Roosevelt & Michelini*) and Macro Mercado (*Bvar Artigas & 3 de Febrero*).

Other practicalities
Banks There are ATMs at Banco República (*Florida 774;* ⏰ *summer 15.00–20.00 Mon–Fri; rest of the year 09.45–14.45 Mon–Fri*), on the north side of the plaza, and on Sarandí a block south of the plaza. You can also change money at Cambios Bacacay (*Florida 758 & Sarandí, & just west of the plaza at Florida 803 & 18 de Julio*), Cambio Nelson (*25 de Mayo & San Carlos*) and Cambios Maiorano (*Dodera & Florida*).

Car rental DW Service, on Avenida Chiossi between Tailandia and Roosevelt (\ *4224 3155/3332*), rents cars, bikes and scooters, and organises transfers.

Communications The main post office is at 18 de Julio 965 (⏰ *09.00–17.00 Mon–Fri, 09.00–12.00 Sat*). Antel's main call centre (*Florida & Avda Joaquín de Viana;* ⏰ *09.00–19.00 daily*) is four blocks west of the plaza; there's a more convenient call centre but with shorter hours on the north side of the plaza (⏰ *09.00–18.00 Mon–Fri (summer until 23.00), 09.00–13.00 Sat*). There's free Wi-Fi on the plaza, although it's not a great signal; Ciber Plaza is in the Plaza Café, below the Hotel Colonial.

Consulates There's a British consulate at the Chalet El Arenal (*Salt Lake & Tenerife, Cantegril;* m *094 236236;* e *Andrew.Beare-honcon@fconet.fco.gov.uk*). The Argentine consulate is on the east side of the plaza at Sarandí 822 (\ *4224 3966, 4222 1195;* m *094 918237;* ⏰ *10.00–12.00, 15.00–18.30 Mon–Fri*).

Emergency services The police are at 25 de Mayo 95 (\ *4222 4401; www. policiamaldonado.gub.uy*). There are two hospitals (Continuación Ventura Alegre, \ *4222 5889/90*; Avda Roosevelt and Avda España, \ *4222 2860*).

What to see and do The town's central plaza is modern, with very little shade, but there are some attractive colonial buildings around it. On the west side of the plaza, the **Cathedral of San Fernando** (⏰ *07.00–12.00, 16.00–20.00 daily*), built between 1801 and 1895, is a plain neoclassical structure. However, it has a grand altar by Antonio Veiga (born in Vigo, Spain, in 1845), completed after eight years' labour in 1872; it was taken to Buenos Aires to be displayed at the Continental Exposition of 1882, where it won two awards but then was held by Customs in Montevideo. In 1890 it was sold to the state to pay storage costs, and was given to Maldonado. Veiga himself installed it in 1894, and in 1896 the Baroque Virgin of Santander (from the *Ciudad de Santander*, wrecked off the Isla de Lobos) was added. The effect is not overwhelming as it's not overloaded with gold.

Off the southwestern corner of the plaza, the **Cuartel de Dragones** (barracks of the Blandengues Dragoons, 1774–97) houses the Museo Didáctico Artiguista (⊕ *10.00–18.00 daily; free*), commemorating Artigas's joining the regiment of Blandengues here in 1797. Entering from the south (*Pérez de Puerto, west of 18 de Julio*), the first room has material on Artigas, and the second has busts of the Liberators of the Americas (13 of them, including George Washington), a model of the barracks and prints of independence-era uniforms. In the southeastern corner are toilets and the chapel, housing only a basic altar and crucifix.

On the north side of the barracks (with entries both from the barracks and from 25 de Mayo) is the excellent **Colección de Pinturas y Escultura Nacional** (*Collection of Uruguayan Paintings and Sculptures;* ⊕ *10.15–18.00 Wed–Sun (in summer to 21.45 Tue–Sat); free*). This houses many sculptural studies by José Belloni (1882–1965), including ones for Montevideo monuments such as *La Diligencia* (The Stagecoach, in the Prado), the Rodó monument (in Parque Rodó) and a funerary monument for the Gorlero family (in the Central Cemetery). They're impressive, but they seem of Rodin's age rather than the mid 20th century. The Argentine cement heiress Amalia Lacroze de Fortabat has given substantial donations, including self-portraits by José Cúneo and a painting by Pedro Blanes Viale. In the other wing are sketches by Antonio Pena (1894–1947) and José Luis Zorrilla de San Martín, as well as a bust of his father Juan Zorrilla de San Martín, and another Pedro Blanes Viale painting, of the Cerro de Arequita. There are also good sketches and models by Federico Moller de Berg (1900–91) for sculptures of Artigas and of Victory, works by Edmundo Prati and Rafael Barradas, and a case of commemorative medals.

On the south side of the plaza is the **Museo Vivo del Títere** (*Puppet Museum; Paseo San Fernando, 25 de Mayo & Sarandí;* ⊕ *10.00–16.00 Wed–Sun; free*) – follow the mosaic line upstairs to the museum door. This displays puppets from around the world, including an Italian Pinocchio, Czech and Romanian puppets, one of Gardel from Uruguay, and Turkish, Burmese and Javanese shadow puppets. There are also 8th-century Toltec and pre-Inca dolls, and German porcelain, as well as puppets made by classes here in winter (when occasional shows are staged).

A block south of the plaza, in the same building as the **Casa de la Cultura**, the **Museo San Fernando de Maldonado** (*Sarandí & Pérez del Puerto;* ⊕ *15.00–21.00 daily; free*) consists of two rooms used for temporary shows of contemporary art, and it's a pleasant setting with very nice patios.

A block north of the plaza, the **Museo Regional Mazzoni** (*Ituzaingó 789, east of 18 de Julio;* ☎ *4222 1107;* ⊕ *summer 10.15–21.45 Tue–Sat, 14.00–21.45 Sun; Apr–Nov 10.15–17.45 Tue–Sun; free*) is housed in an atmospheric late 18th-century house with 12 rooms and two exuberantly vegetated internal patios. The home of Professor Francisco Mazzoni (1883–1978), it houses an entertainingly diverse collection, with lots of dark wood furniture and glass-fronted cabinets containing, for instance, Masonic regalia and voting urns, guns, family photos and portraits, a few sad stuffed animals and the usual indigenous stone weapons (bolas and rompacabezas). In the room dedicated to Henry Burnett (see page 201) you'll see his telescope and certificates from Lloyd's and from King George V, the latter conferring the Order of the British Empire on him. There's the odd Páez Vilaró painting, Blanes's painting smock and boots, and a pretty average collection of woodblock prints and other art. Beyond the garden is a room with temporary exhibits of art or photography.

Two blocks west of the barracks is the well-tended **Plaza Torre del Vigía**, surrounded by suburban bungalows and centred on the Torre del Vigía (Watchtower), built in 1801 to watch for ships at sea. Just to the southeast, the

5

red-painted house of Henry Burnett now houses the **Museo de Arte Americano Maldonado** (*Treinta y Tres 823 & Dodera;* ⊕ *summer 18.00–22.00 daily; free*), founded in 1973 by Jorge Páez Vilaró (1922–98; brother of Carlos) to house his collections of pre-Columbian and contemporary Latin American art. Temporary exhibitions are also staged here, as well as concerts in the lush gardens.

To the east of town, buses pass the Cachimba del Rey (Royal Well), a not particularly attractive monument on 3 de Febrero just east of Bulevar Artigas; it was the town's main source of water from its foundation until around 1873.

LA BARRA AND MANANTIALES As opposed to the rather sterile strips of mega-villas to either side, La Barra seems like a real seaside resort, with lots of bars, shops and streetlife. It was never a fishing village, but developed as a resort for the people of San Carlos, the first hotels appearing in the 1920s. Nowadays this is the resort of choice for hip fashionistas (above all at New Year), with the best bars in the Punta del Este area, playing the coolest tunes, and the best displays of surfer dudes and bikini babes on the beaches. It's the St Tropez to Punta's Cannes. On a Saturday morning in summer it's totally gridlocked with cruising cars and motorbikes.

Getting there and away A ferry crossed the Arroyo Maldonado from 1912 until 1936, when a wooden bridge was built; in 1963 Lionel Viera designed the famous *puente ondulado* (undulating bridge) now named after him. Something like a pair of giant speed humps, this was simply the cheapest way to span the river, but it has become the iconic image of La Barra (inspiring a poem by Neruda). An identical bridge was built alongside in 1999, providing two lanes in each direction, and the original bridge was rebuilt in 2005–10.

There are regular **midibuses** (*routes 14 & 22; every 20mins until midnight*) to La Barra from Punta del Este's terminal, although if late they may just drive through rather than pulling into a bay. There's also a **cycle** track along the rambla of the Playa Brava.

Orientation and tourist information Continuing due north from the bridge you reach the excellent Museo del Mar (see page 232). The main Ruta 10 turns sharply right, past the striking, modern Edificios Delamar (by far the tallest buildings here) to a brief one-way section of road past the ANCAP station and a few shops. Then the road swings left at a summer-only **tourist information office** (*Calle Los Ensueños;* ⊕ *09.00–21.00 daily; Jan–Feb until 22.00*), staffed by helpful students, and follows the coast, lined with bars, restaurants and art galleries. This soon ends at Playa Montoya, perhaps Punta's most stylish beach. From here a dual carriageway and parallel cycle track continue east for a kilometre or so to Manantiales, where high-ranking Argentine politicians and others rent houses.

Entering Manantiales you have Bikini Beach on your right, aptly described as 'less a fleshpot than a fleshcauldron'. There's also plenty of silicon on view here, it must be said. It's also a surfing beach, known for its consistent waves; the surfers have the beach to themselves in the mornings, and it only really becomes a social scene after about 16.00, when the Buddha Bar's DJ starts to crank out tunes.

🏠 **Where to stay** Most of La Barra's and Manantiales's summer residents rent houses. There are several backpackers' hostels and some luxury hotels, but nothing in the middle market. Two of Punta del Este's campsites are just across the bridge (see page 209). All listings are included on the map opposite.

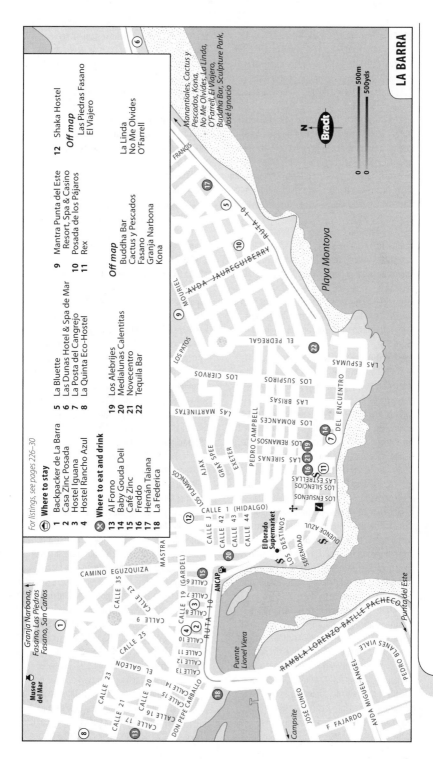

For listings, see pages 226–30

Where to stay
1 Backpacker de La Barra
2 Casa Zinc Posada
3 Hostel Iguana
4 Hostel Rancho Azul
5 La Bluette
6 Las Dunas Hotel & Spa de Mar
7 La Posta del Cangrejo
8 La Quinta Eco-Hostel
9 Mantra Punta del Este Resort, Spa & Casino
10 Posada de los Pájaros
11 Rex
12 Shaka Hostel

Off map
Las Piedras Fasano
El Viajero

Where to eat and drink
13 Al Forno
14 Baby Gouda Deli
15 Café Zinc
16 Freddo
17 Hernán Taiana
18 La Federica
19 Los Alebrijes
20 Medialunas Calentitas
21 Novecentro
22 Tequila Bar

Off map
Buddha Bar
Cactus y Pescados
Fasano
Granja Narbona
Kona

La Linda
No Me Olvides
O'Farrell

Manantiales, Cactus y Pescados, Kona, No Me Olvides, La Linda, O'Farrell, El Viajero, Buddha Bar, Sculpture Park, José Ignacio

LA BARRA

N

0   500m
0   500yds

Bradt

Playa Montoya

FRANCIS

RUTA 10

AVDA JAUREGUIBERRY

MOURIEL

LOS PATOS

LOS CIERVOS

LOS SUSPIROS

LAS BRISAS

LAS MARTINETAS

LOS ROMANCES

EL PEDREGAL

LAS ESPUMAS

DEL ENCUENTRO

PEDRO CAMPBELL

LOS REMANSOS

LAS SIRENAS

LAS ESTRELLAS

LOS SILENCIOS

LOS ENSUENOS

EXETER

GRAF SPEE

AJAX

LOS FLAMENCOS

CALLE J

CALLE 1 (HIDALGO)
CALLE 42
CALLE 43
CALLE 44

El Dorado Supermarket

DESTINOS

SERENIDAD

DUENDE AZUL

CAMINO EGUZQUIZA

MASTRA

CALLE 35

CALLE 23

CALLE 9

CALLE 25

CALLE 19 (GARDEL)
CALLE 6
CALLE 7
CALLE 8

RUTA 10

CALLE 10

CALLE 11

CALLE 13
CALLE 12
CALLE 15
CALLE 14

CALLE 21

EL GALEÓN

CALLE 20

CALLE 23

CALLE 17
CALLE 16

DON PEPE CARBALLO

ANCAP

Museo del Mar

Granja Narbona, Fasano, Las Piedras Fasano, San Carlos

Puente Lionel Viera

RAMBLA LORENZO BATLLE PACHECO

JOSÉ CUNEO

F FAJARDO

PEDRO BLANES VIALE

AVDA MIGUEL ANGEL

Campsite

Punta del Este

⌂ **Casa Zinc Posada** Calle 9, parada 40; ☎4277 3003; m 099 620066; www.casazinc.com. A very stylish little boho-chic place using salvaged materials; there's no swimming pool or restaurant, but breakfast is served till mid-afternoon! Service is superb. **$$$$$**

⌂ **La Bluette** Ruta 10, parada 49, Manantiales; ☎4277 0947; www.hotellabluette.com. One of the most exclusive hotels in Punta del Este, very affordable Mar–Sep but remarkably pricey in high season. It's a 2-storey ochre colonial-style building that's more like a home than a chic boutique hotel. Each room is individually designed, with private terrace. **$$$$$**

⌂ **La Posta del Cangrejo** Los Remansos & Ruta 10, La Barra; ☎4277 0021; www.lapostadelcangrejo.com; ⊕ all year. With just 30 rooms, an outdoor pool & a good French restaurant looking out across the Playa de la Barra (& patronised by the likes of George Bush Snr & Julio Iglesias), this has a sort of country-house style, with soft sofas & softly spoken welcoming staff. **$$$$$**

⌂ **Las Dunas Hotel & Spa de Mar** Ruta 10 km163½, Manantiales; ☎4277 1211; e lasdunas@adinet.com.uy; www.lasdunas.com.uy. Glitzy, very expensive spa & resort near Bikini Beach, with 72 rooms, each with glazed terrace & ocean view. There's an AC pool with a glass roof as well as an outdoor pool & paddling pool, plus gym, spa, sauna, hydromassage & tennis courts. It's actually quite quiet & not too tacky. **$$$$$**

⌂ **Las Piedras Fasano** Camino Egusquiza & Paso del Barranco; ☎4267 0000; e puntadeleste@fasano.com.br; www.laspiedrasfasano.com. The ultra-trendy Brazilian Fasano group opened their first property in Uruguay in 2011, with 32 pillbox-like bungalows set in 480ha of rolling pasture. Just 5km from the beaches of La Barra, it has a 9-hole golf course, spa, cocktail bar, 2 fine restaurants & even a VIP programme for dogs. **$$$$$**

⌂ **Mantra Punta del Este Resort, Spa & Casino** Ante Millat, Ruta 10 km162, parada 48, Montoya; ☎4277 1000; www.mantraresort.com. The only rival to the Conrad, with a luxury spa & casino, not to mention cinema, boutique shops, art gallery, restaurants & wine bar. Modelled on a Mediterranean village, sprawling down a hillside, Mantra is divided in 2 parts, the lively Plaza (open to outsiders) with restaurants, bars & casino, & the quieter hotel area, with 100 minimalist

white rooms. The Zafferano restaurant serves innovative Mediterranean cuisine, & you can also eat at the more casual Indigo Grill with salad bar, pizza & parrilla, or the poolside La Piscina café. Most local buses run up Avda Jaureguiberry & turn around just east of the Mantra; guests can use golf-carts to reach the hotel's section of the Playa Mantra, with attentive service. Catamarans, jet-skis, fishing & whale-watching are all available. **$$$$$**

⌂ **Posada de los Pájaros** Calles 10 & 5, parada 48.1, Montoya; ☎4277 2181; www.posadadelospajaros.com.uy. Modern villa in the white-cube style with sweeping lawns & a swimming pool, this boutique place has just 16 rooms & impeccable service; it's open all year. **$$$$$**

⌂ **La Quinta Eco-Hostel** Calles 19 & 24; ☎4277 2424; m 095 460990; www.laquintaecohostel.com; ⊕ Nov–Apr. Just south of the Museo del Mar, this reasonably green place has 4-, 6- & 8-bed mixed dorms (with fans, lockers, & bed linen included), an 8-bed female dorm, a private double & a private 4–5-bed room, as well as a restaurant (using their own produce), a swimming pool with wet bar, beach volleyball & soccer pitches, & free PCs & Wi-Fi throughout. Extra services include laundry, rental of bikes & beach umbrellas, etc, & transfers. **$$**

⌂ **Backpacker de La Barra** Calle 9, just north of Calle 29, La Barra; ☎4277 2272; e backpacker@vivapunta.com; www.backpackerdelabarra.com. Calle 9, a very nice residential street that quickly becomes rural, leads north from parada 40 (Galería del Paseo), just east of the bridge, to the hostel about 1km from the main road. Very bright & multi-coloured, this is the original budget option here (though prices nearly double in the first half of Jan) & you'll need to book. Open only for pre-booked groups Mar–Nov. It's a nice place, with lots of greenery & a swimming pool. Standard dorms have 8 beds (US$19–29), & there are 4-bed rooms for US$10 pp extra, plus private doubles (**$$$**) & quads. There's a kitchen, BBQ, TV/DVD, 2 computers & Wi-Fi; bikes can be rented. **$$–$**

⌂ **El Viajero** Ruta 10 km164.5, Manantiales; ☎4277 4427; www.elviajerohostels.com; ⊕ Nov–Apr. On the edge of the woods just 500m from Bikini Beach, this is a slightly Casapuebloesque white house with swimming pool, open-air bar & BBQ, & terraced gardens. Indoors there's a kitchen,

TV room, Wi-Fi, mixed & women-only dorms, & double & triple rooms. It's aimed at international travellers, with an emphasis on surfing in the daytime (lessons available) & hitting the bars & clubs at night. Bikes are available for rental, & horseriding can be arranged. **$**

🏠 **Hostel Iguana** Calle 8 & Ruta 10; 📞 4277 2947; m 099 106458; www.iguanadelabarra.com; ⏰ all year. In a solid thatched house with a bar in the garden, there are 5 rooms (for 4, 6, 8 & 12), all with private bathrooms & Wi-Fi; bikes & surfboards can be rented, & surfing lessons are available. **$**

🏠 **Hostel Rancho Azul** Calle 10 (Domingo Arena) & Ruta 10; m 099 602763; www. ranchoazul.hostel.com. A pale (Cambridge) blue single-story house with a veranda all around & a lovely garden with swimming pool; there are rooms for 2, 4, 10 & 12, & free PC & Wi-Fi. **$**

🏠 **Shaka Hostel** Hidalgo between Gardel & Mastra; 📞 4277 2348; www.shakahostel.com. A nice little family-run hostel in a white adobe-style house with garden & asado; there's a kitchen, the usual free Wi-Fi, & rooms with fans. **$**

✗ **Where to eat** La Barra has some excellent and very pricey restaurants. If you want chivitos, empanadas or other snacks, head for the area near the ANCAP filling station. All listings are included on the map, page 227.

✗ **Cactus y Pescados** 1er bajada a Playa Bikini (1st road leading down to the beach), Manantiales; 📞 4277 4782. A popular Mediterranean-style restaurant (serving the usual range of grilled meats, fish, pasta & pizza), not too overpriced for the excellent location – it claims the region's best sunsets; there's Wi-Fi. **$$$$$**

✗ **O'Farrell** Ruta 10 km164.5 (Plaza 19 de Abril), Manantiales; 📞 4277 4331; www. ofarrellrestaurant.com; ⏰ Dec–Feb 20.00–00.30 daily; Easter & holiday w/ends 13.00–16.30, 20.00–midnight Sat–Sun, then w/ends from 20.00. On the road to the Viajero hostel, though catering to a different market, this offshoot of a Buenos Aires restaurant is one of the best in the area, & very expensive. It offers a modern Mediterranean cuisine with seasonal ingredients & a Mallmannesque (see page 242) emphasis on wood fires, smoking & a large clay oven. Fresh fish is a staple, or try the rack of lamb (*costillar de cordero*) with a Malbec sauce; there's also a tasting menu with matching wines. It's in a stylish modern house with sofas, director's chairs & other cool furnishings, & a summer garden. From the bar there's a nice vista towards the beach, but the interior rooms are shady & without much of a view. Service is excellent, & there's a very long wine list, quite a few by the glass (they also work as wine merchants). **$$$$$**

✗ **Al Forno** Calles 17 & 20, La Barra; 📞 4277 2775; m 099 375566; http://federicoamandola. com; ⏰ Oct–Apr 12.00–16.00, 20.00–midnight daily. Perhaps the most imaginative cooking in the area, inspired by Francis Mallmann (see page 242),

for instance in their use of cast-iron boxes. Dishes such as wagyu beef, king crab lasagne, brótola, salmon ravioli or porcini risotto cost cUS$15–30. **$$$$**

✗ **Fasano** Camino Cerro Egusquiza & Paso del Barranco; 📞 4267 0000; www.laspiedrasfasano. com. A clifftop restaurant at the luxury resort (see page 228) offering fine Italian dining (booking required); there's also Las Piedras, an informal Italian trattoria, but still not cheap. **$$$$**

✗ **Granja Narbona** Camino del Golf; 📞 4410 2999; www.narbona.com.uy; ⏰ 11.00–16.00, 19.00–23.00 daily. A foodie haven on a century-old estancia that serves fine cheeses, wines & other products from the Narbona winery near Carmelo (see page 295), & their own vegetables & salads. Enjoy starters such as seafood fritters & mains such as sautéed fish in a caper-butter sauce, spinach & ricotta ravioli, steak or rack of lamb with onion focaccia. There's also a wine bar, art gallery & deli. **$$$$**

✗ **Baby Gouda Deli** Ruta 10 km160.9 & Los Romances, La Barra; 📞 4277 1874; www. babygouda.com.uy; ⏰ summer 11.00–02.30 daily. One of the hippest places to see & be seen, & the food's good too. The open kitchen produces a wide range of salads, sandwiches & wraps, pasta & desserts, to be eaten indoors or on the terrace looking out over the beach. There's Wi-Fi, & sometimes belly-dancing in the evening. **$$$$–$$**

✗ **No Me Olvides** Ruta 10 km164, Manantiales; 📞 4277 5531. A simple pizza-parrilla with a large wood-fired oven, wooden seats, wooden tables.

The pizzas are good & affordable, as are the mojitos. $$$$–$$

✘ **Los Alebrijes** Ruta 10 km161, La Barra; 4277 3519; m 097 473611; www.alebrijes-restaurant.com; ⏰ 12.00–02.00 daily. A gourmet Mexican restaurant that uses the local tradition of grilled meats in its own way. $$$

✘ **Rex** Ruta 10 km161, La Barra; 4277 1504; www.rexpuntadeleste.com; 24hrs daily. A diner, serving the best chivitos in the area since 1996. $$$

🍴 **Freddo** Ruta 10 & Las Sirenas, km161, La Barra; 4277 0120; www.freddouruguay.com; ⏰ Dec–Easter 10.00–04.00 daily; rest of the year 12.00–01.00 Fri–Sun. An Argentine chain selling the best ice cream in town. $$

Nightlife

🍸 **Buddha Bar** Bikini Beach, Parada 49; ⏰ Nov–Mar from 11.00. Covered beach bar that serves fine sushi & cocktails. A DJ cranks out the coolest music on the coast from about 16.00 but the party only really gets going towards midnight, when celebrity supermodels such as Naomi Campbell & Gisele Bundchen may pass through. More realistically, you may find a sponsored fashion event or glamour shoot.

🍸 **Café Zinc** Ruta 10 & Calle 6, La Barra; 4277 0626; e casazinctrading@gmail.com; ⏰ 10.30–19.00 (until 18.00 Wed, until 20.00 Fri–Sat). In a corrugated iron shed with lots of antique junk for sale, the quite stylish café seems a bit of an afterthought, but it does have Wi-Fi.

🍸 **Kona** Ruta 10 km164, Manantiales. A cool resto-bar, serving wraps, bocatas, tapas, salads & licuados, as well as 'music & onda' (with DJs & videos), this claims to be Punta's best chill-out lounge.

🍴 **La Linda** 18 de Julio & Montevideo, Manantiales; 4277 5224; www.lalinda.com. uy; ⏰ 08.00–02.00 daily. A bakery & café serving the best breakfast & breads in the area, as well as lunch, dinner & all-day pizzas, empanadas & foccacias from their wood-fired oven. They grow all their fruit & veg themselves organically. $$

🍴 **Medialunas Calentitas** Ruta 10, Palmas de La Barra, La Barra; 4277 2347; www. medialunascalentitas.com; ⏰ summer 24hrs. The original branch of the 'Hot Croissants' chain (now also in Montevideo & Punta del Este), selling croissants with & without fillings (such as *dulce de leche*), cakes, empanadas, milkshakes & coffees. There's live music in the late afternoon in summer, & you can eat at picnic tables outside. $

🍸 **La Federica** Sobre el arroyo, La Barra; 4277 2698. A simple bar in a lovely location by the river, immediately northwest of the bridge.

🍸 **Novecento** Ruta 10 & Las Sirenas, La Barra; 4277 2363; ⏰ Dec–Feb 20.30–02.00 daily. A large & lively bar-café that's very trendy in season, with a covered terrace right in the heart of La Barra. There's food ($$$$), such as fish, shellfish & pasta, but it's not recommended, except for the desserts.

🍸 **Tequila Bar** Ruta 10 & Calle 15; 4277 1922; m 098 950960; ⏰ Dec–Mar from 22.30 daily. Season after season, this is the hottest dance club in Uruguay, perhaps because of a strict door policy that allows only the best lookers in. Once in, you'll find a small lounge with just 1 floor & cosy booths, & not much action until about 03.00. Music including vintage electronica & Latin & global beats. Cocktails can cost US$30, & there's a minimum age of 23 for men, 21 for women.

Shopping For practical purchases such as food your best bet is the El Dorado supermarket (*Ruta 10 near Calle Los Destinos*). There are smaller supermercados on Ruta 10 in Manantiales and on Calle 7 in La Barra.

For fun stuff, there's an array of **boutiques** including in La Barra Daniel Curto (leather and suede), Diablito (CDs, surfer clothes and trainers), Lanas del Este (knitted sweaters), Kosiuko (trendy clothing, belts, shorts, purses for men and women, and vintage denim; http://kosiuko.com) and No Se (eclectic art, antiques and home accessories), and, in Manantiales, Kallalith (jewellery), Manga Rosada (reversible embroidered Brazilian bikinis), Piramide (sequinned and embroidered bags and sandals) and Velas de La Ballena (perfumed candles).

This is also the best place in Uruguay to buy **art and photographs**, with many cool contemporary art galleries. The Gallery Nights event involves all the galleries opening from 20.00 to midnight every Friday night in January, with a free bus shuttle between them. Between the ANCAP petrol station and the tourist information centre, the Paseo Real de la Barra is a small group of galleries, including the black and white photographer Roberto Fernández Ibañez (*Local 23;* \ *4277 2297; www. robertofernandez.com.uy*). At the other end of La Barra near Playa Montoya, the Galería Sur (*parada 46, La Barra;* \ *4277 2014; www.galeriasur.com.uy;* ⊕ *Dec–Mar 10.00–midnight daily*) is a modern space selling works by Torres García, Gurvich, Figari, Barradas and Blanes Viale, as well as the Brazilian Portinari, the Chilean Matta and a range of contemporary artists. It takes its name from the Escuela del Sur, inspired by Torres García's comment, 'Nuestro Norte es el Sur' (Our North is the South), turning a map of Latin America upside down. Other galleries in La Barra include Atelier Carlos Musse (*Ruta 10 opposite the ANCAP station;* m *094 443389; www.carlosmusse.com*); Grupo Taller Jones-Vicente (*Ruta 10 km160.5;* m *094 454157; www.grupojonesvicente.com*); and Atelier José Etchepareborda (*Duende Azul & Ruta 10 km160.5;* \ *4277 1974; www.etchepareborda.com*). Taller Elina Damiani (*Ruta 10 & Los Silencios;* \ *4277 2103; www.elinadamiani.com*) shows the rather naïf works (sailing ships, birds, cats, fruit and the like) of this self-taught Uruguayan. Nearby are Adrián Martínez Bojko (*Calle de Las Estrellas;* \ *4277 2697; www.martinezbojko.com*), Oscar Rocha Atelier (*Calle 27 & Las Sirenas;* \ *4277 1970*) and the Atelier Aguiló-Abal (*calles 4 & 1, Atajo de la Barra;* \ *4277 2855; www.arteuy.com.uy/aa/ee.htm*). The Lasarte Gallery (*Ruta 10 & Las Espumas, parada 46;* \ *4277 1112; www.mercedeslasarte.com*) shows the excellent post-Impressionist/Expressionist works of Mercedes Lasarte.

In Manantiales there's the Galería del Paseo – Arte Contemporáneo (*Ruta 10 & 18 de Julio, km164;* \ *4277 5860; www.galeriadelpaseo.com*) and the Atelier Marizú Terza (*Calle Pan de Azúcar;* \ *4277 5240*).

Activities Surf shops include Sun Valley Surf (*Ruta 10 km160, Complejo Koby VIII, Local 1;* \ *4277 2451*), next to Baby Gouda. For surfing lessons, ask here or call Bagus School (*Posta del Cangrejo;* m *099 262943;* e *alfonso_fermin@hotmail.com*).

Other practicalities

Banks There are ATMs in La Barra at the El Dorado supermarket (km160), at Ruta 10 and Duende Azul, and at the casino in the Mantra Resort. There's a branch of the Banco República (⊕ *15.00–20.00 Mon–Fri*) north of the ANCAP petrol station, which will exchange cash, as will Cambio Maiorano (*Ruta 10 & Duende Azul;* \ *4277 1080*), opposite the tourist information office, and Cambio Aspen (*Ruta 10 & Las Sirenas, km161*).

Car rental You can rent a car at La Barra Rentacar (\ *4277 2511*) just west of the tourist information centre, and the Dollar agency in an estate agency nearby at La Serenidad or Punta Car (*Ruta 10 just east of Los Suspiros;* \ *4277 2194*).

Communications For phone and internet services there are locutorios on Ruta 10 just west of Baby Gouda, opposite the El Dorado supermarket and by the tourist information centre at Calle Los Ensueños.

Laundry Opposite the El Dorado supermarket is the Lavadero La Barra (⊕ *09.00–21.00 Mon–Sat*).

Taxis For a taxi call Taxi La Barra or Taxi Manantiales (both \ *4277 1122*).

5

What to see and do Other than the beach life, the bridge, the shops and the art galleries, the main sight is the large and very interesting **Museo del Mar** (*Museum of the Sea;* \ *4277 1817;* e *museodelmar@gmail.com; www.museodelmar.com.uy;* ⊕ *summer 10.30–20.00 daily; rest of the year 10.30–17.00 Mon–Thu, 10.30–19.00 Fri–Sun; US$5*), 1km north of the bridge on Calle El Galeón and easily spotted by the large blue shark in front. Opened in 1995, this has grown to fill a warehouse-scale building, with lots of whale skeletons (up to 15m in length) as well as a 6m manta ray and a 2.6m moonfish, lots of insects and stuffed birds (all found dead of largely natural causes) and a bathing machine. There's not a lot on actual ships (other than a room for the kids on pirates) but there's lots of material on wildlife and on the social history of Uruguay's beach resorts. The music is good too, and the staff are very helpful.

Another option is the **Fundación Pablo Atchugarry** (*Ruta 104 km4.5, El Chorro, Manantiales;* \ *4277 5563; www.fundacionpabloatchugarry.org;* ⊕ *summer 11.00–23.00 daily; free*), displaying the amazingly delicate abstract marble sculptures of Pablo Atchugarry, as well as temporary exhibitions which may feature locally big names such as Octavio Podestá, and free concerts in January. A 15ha park displays a variety of modern sculptures in metal, concrete, marble and other materials. It's signposted 'Parque de Esculturas' from Ruta 10 km165.

EAST OF MANANTIALES Ruta 10 continues along the coast east of Manantiales, via **Punta Piedras**, where the virtually empty beach that stretches from here east to José Ignacio is overlooked by houses worth US$1.5 million. It costs about US$100,000 to rent the best ones for the month of January – no problem for the likes of supermodels Naomi Campbell, Eva Herzigova and Valeria Mazza, Argentine tycoon Eduardo Constantini or Prince Albert of Monaco. The architectural style is consistently Modernist – cool white cubes with great expanses of glass, in contrast to the catholic mix of styles in Punta and La Barra. In 2008 Michael Caine's daughter Natasha and her husband created the Villalagos gated development, with 13 *chacras* or plots (of close to 5ha, each with villa and infinity pool) surrounded by lakes and woods, which won a RIBA award in 2010. There are many more chacra developments along the coast to the east, with prices rising spectacularly in the early years of the century before global recession pushed them down.

There are also small *balnearios* (beach resorts) such as Balneario El Chorro and Balneario Buenos Aires (where most local buses turn around), where you'll see signs for houses to rent at far lower rates than the luxury villas. Beyond km168 the developed strip (with a lot of speed humps) gives way to dunes and pine trees, with the Pueblo San Vicente to the left at km170, a planned development begun in 1959 and revived in 2002. At km174.5 there's the surprising sight of ANCAP oil tanks on the left and a buoy for discharging tankers a couple of kilometres offshore.

At km180 (30km from Punta del Este) the road crosses a bridge over the outflow from the Laguna José Ignacio, where you may see flamingos and remarkable numbers of crabs. At km183 it reaches a petrol station and roundabout with José Ignacio 2km to the right; the road to the left leads to Pueblo Garzón (see page 241) and Ruta 9, while Ruta 10 continues for 7km (newly paved) to **Laguna Garzón**. This passes the vaguely medieval gate towers of the Laguna Escondida development at km184½, then at km185.1 the modern greeny-blue shark metal sculpture marking the turning to the Posada Azul Marino (see page 236) and the very cool Marismo and Namm restaurants (see page 237), hidden in the forest. The road ends at km190½ at the slipway to the free ferry (⊕ *08.00–12.00, 14.00–18.00 daily*), a raft on a cable (moved by a boat tied alongside with an outdoor motor) that

Seemingly a larger-than-life force of nature, the sculptor Pablo Atchugarry dominates the artistic life of the Punta del Este area. Born in Montevideo in 1954, he now divides his time between Italy (near the quarry his beloved white marble comes from) and Manantiales, just east of Punta.

A few kilometres north of Manantiales is the Pablo Atchugarry Foundation (see opposite) where his burly figure, covered in white dust, can often be seen; in addition to his sculptures, around an artificial lake, this is a venue for outdoor concerts and other artistic events. His dream is to forge a connection between art and nature, and also, like many of his wealthy patrons, to bring people closer to the land and culture of Uruguay. Hence his distinctive white marble columns can be seen in many of the plazas and hotels of the greater Punta del Este area.

He is also planning a new art and tourism project near Garzón and collaborations with Carlos Ott, for instance the circular ARTower project in Punta del Este, where his vision will be as important as the architect's.

can take cars and small vans across the mouth of the lagoon. There are remains of an unfinished bridge here, and an odd circular bridge (by Rafael Viñoly) is about to be built, causing property prices on the far side of the lagoon (a currently isolated part of Rocha department) to soar. Here on the west bank are a windsurfing school (see page 238) with a small café, and a few huts selling drinks, snacks and fresh fish. On the east side is the new Laguna Garzón Lodge, with 12 rooms on rafts and the Garzuana Restaurant on stilts (☏ 4486 2526; ⊕ 20.30–01.00). There are flamingos, herons, ducks, swans and other waterbirds to be seen on the lagoon.

JOSÉ IGNACIO The small fishing village of José Ignacio has recently been transformed into one of the world's most chic and exclusive holiday destinations, with boutique hotels (and absolutely no budget accommodation), superb restaurants and an array of stunning modern houses. In summer the traffic jams are mad, but from March to November this is still a remarkably peaceful fishing village. The sandy roads, empty beaches, hand-painted wooden signs and boho-chic style are key to its success, studiously avoiding the Miami Beach-style high-rise development of Punta del Este.

The first couple of weeks of January are fairly manic, with parties sponsored by brands such as Lacoste and Chivas Regal, with catering by Francis Mallmann (see page 242) and music by the likes of Brazilian singer Bebel Gilberto, in beachfront tents or at the La Huella Restaurant. Otherwise there's a 02.00 curfew and there are no discos – it's not far to the clubs of La Barra. It's a great place to let your children loose to roam and make friends with other kids.

In any case this is a place of great and subtle beauty, set on a rocky headland with the usual brava and mansa sides, and the quintessential lighthouse on the point. Set between two lagoons totalling 4,000ha, this is a paradise for birdwatchers (even the streets are named after birds), and from March to October southern right whales are easily seen from the point. Horseriding, cycling and walking are ideal ways of getting into nature here.

The village is named after a José Ignacio who built a slaughterhouse on the headland, an easy location for rounding up cattle. The lighthouse was built in 1877 and in 1917 the first streets were laid out as a small fishing village grew up.

The coastal Ruta 10 only reached José Ignacio when the outlet from Laguna José Ignacio was bridged in the 1980s; until then access was by a dirt road from Ruta 9, well to the north. This direct link to Punta del Este and La Barra transformed José Ignacio, unleashing a property speculation boom that is set to be repeated to the east when the Laguna Garzón Bridge is built. This is merely the latest phase of a process that began when the Carrasco Bridge, just east of Montevideo, was built in 1951. First a few high-society families from Montevideo and Buenos Aires built summer homes here, but it was only in the 1990s that Argentine television star Mirtha Legrand, Latina pop star Shakira (and then boyfriend Antonio de la Rúa, son of a former Argentine president) and British writer Martin Amis and his Uruguayan wife Isabel Fonseca began to give the village a wider reputation. It was only in 2006 that luxury style magazines began to tout José Ignacio as the coolest place in the world to go for the southern summer. It's usually compared to the Hamptons on Long Island (the summer refuge for the rich and famous of New York).

Now many people worry about runaway development along the coast, although upmarket projects such as Laguna Escondida (227 lots with houses by Carlos Ott, being built just east of José Ignacio by Cuban-American tycoon Jorge Pérez, the man who turned Miami around) and Bahía Vik (immediately west of the roundabout on Ruta 10) will not immediately lead to high-rise sprawl. The global recession has however led to the suspension of other projects such as Barrancas de San Ignacio, a 98ha development by the Laguna José Ignacio.

Getting there and away From Montevideo COPSA and COT each run three **buses** a day to José Ignacio in summer (US$8), all calling at Montevideo airport, Maldonado and Punta del Este too. It's often more convenient just to take the next bus to Punta del Este and change there for the local *micro* (bus) 14 which runs 13 times a day from bay 2 to José Ignacio, taking about 50 minutes. There are also nine modern Machado buses a day from San Carlos via La Barra. The four daily Tur-Este buses from Piriápolis and Punta del Este to La Pedrera run via José Ignacio and the newly paved link to Ruta 9.

Orientation and tourist information Buses terminate on Los Teros, by the police office on the south side of the wide grassy plaza. At the plaza's northwestern corner is a tourist information centre that is open late into the evening in January but cannot be relied on otherwise. There's limited information online at www.jose-ignacio.com.uy.

To the west, Los Teros leads to a slipway on the Playa Mansa where a few fishing boats usually lie drawn up below a small shrine; to the east it leads to the lighthouse, where good boardwalks lead to the beach and nearby craft stalls. The faro (lighthouse), built in 1877, is 25m high (32m above sea level, with a range of 14 nautical miles), with 122 spiralling steps, but is not usually open to visitors. Along the shoreline you'll see granite boulders, small cacti, salt-resistant waxy-leaved plants and hummingbirds.

A sign at the entrance to the village reads 'The only thing that moves fast here is the wind', and there is a speed limit of 25km/h throughout the village.

Where to stay There's no campsite and just one backpacker hostel in the neighbourhood, but you may see a few *alquilo* signs ('for rent'), for houses and cabins to rent, by the main road to the west. All listings are included on the map opposite.

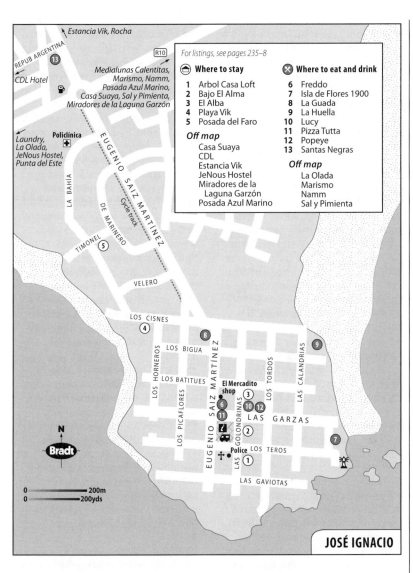

For listings, see pages 235–8

⌂ Where to stay

1 Arbol Casa Loft
2 Bajo El Alma
3 El Alba
4 Playa Vik
5 Posada del Faro

Off map
 Casa Suaya
 CDL
 Estancia Vik
 JeNous Hostel
 Miradores de la
  Laguna Garzón
 Posada Azul Marino

✖ Where to eat and drink

6 Freddo
7 Isla de Flores 1900
8 La Guada
9 La Huella
10 Lucy
11 Pizza Tutta
12 Popeye
13 Santas Negras

Off map
 La Olada
 Marismo
 Namm
 Sal y Pimienta

JOSÉ IGNACIO

⌂ **Arbol Casa Loft** Los Teros, just east of the plaza; ☎4486 2278; bookings Buenos Aires ☎+54 11 4803 1113; e arbol@curiocitytravel.com; ⊕ all year. Expensively simple & elegantly rustic, this discreet assemblage of white cubes includes 1 loft, 4 suites & an apartment (with open-air shower). All rooms are spacious, with heated floors, flat-screen TV, CD players, Wi-Fi, minibar & electronic safe, handmade candles & flowers. A swimming pool is tucked away in the beautifully manicured subtropical garden; there's also an honesty bar & games room with pool table. The friendly staff can arrange cars, tours, massages or horseriding. **$$$$$**

⌂ **Casa Suaya** Ruta 10, km186.5; ☎4486 2750; Buenos Aires ☎+54 11 4771 1667; e info@ casasuaya.com; www.casasuaya.com. Aimed at those who want luxury, seclusion & an empty beach, this was created in the dunes 3.5km east of the village by the Argentine-American restaurateur Adolfo Suaya, who founded the Gaucho Grill, the Lodge & Geisha House in Los Angeles. The stone-walled suites are furnished fairly minimally but are cosy with open fireplace, kitchenette & balcony

235

giving views of the ocean & of fantastic clear night skies. They come with cable TV, Wi-Fi & own-label toiletries. Bicycles are available, & horseriding can be arranged nearby. New blocks are being added, & the excellent Sal y Pimienta restaurant (see opposite). which opens on to an infinity pool, has been joined by a new bar-restaurant. $$$$$

🏠 **Estancia Vik** Camino Eugenio Saiz Martínez, km8; m 094 605212; www.estanciavik.com; ⏲ Oct–Apr. Set on a hilltop with huge views, on a 4,000ha estate offering fantastic birdwatching & horseriding, the Estancia is a delightful maze of patios & buildings in various authentic rural styles; each bedroom is by a different Uruguayan artist, & the central living room is dominated by a 3.5m-high white marble piece by Pablo Atchugarry & a ceiling mural by Clever Lara, a bird's-eye view of the Uruguayan landscape. A superb breakfast is included, together with unlimited horseriding; you can also take polo lessons if you want. $$$$$

🏠 **Miradores de la Laguna Garzón** Ruta 10 km188.5; m 093 861000; www. miradoreslagunagarzon.com.uy. This exquisite *hotel boutique de campo* has just 4 suites in a classic-style brick estancia house, & a restaurant for guests only. $$$$$

🏠 **Playa Vik** Los Cisnes & Los Horneros; m 094 605212; www.playavik.com. The Norwegian-Uruguayan businessman Alex Vik has created a pair of superb boutique hotels in & near José Ignacio, both packed with works by South American artists (& with huge rock crystals from Artigas). In the centre of the village, Playa was designed by Carlos Ott & consists of 6 linked 'houses', glass-walled & with sea-grass roofs, & a titanium-clad building aptly dubbed 'Sculpture', with massive oxidised-bronze doors by Pablo Atchugarry & a swimming pool cantilevered out to the west. Inside are artworks by Carlos Musso, Marcelo Legrand, Carlos Páez Vilaró, & the 19th-century painter Juan Manuel Blanes, as well as non-Uruguayans such as Zaha Hadid, Anselm Kiefer & James Turrell. There's a fine restaurant, & activities such as horseriding at Estancia Vik are included. $$$$$

🏠 **Posada Azul Marino** 300m north from Ruta 10 km185.1; ☎ 4486 2363; www.azulmarino.

com.uy. Established as a relaxed & unpretentious private home offering B&B accommodation, it's on the same road as the ultra-chic Naam & Marismo restaurants, but you'll almost certainly need a car to go anywhere else. It's a classy Modernist house with 6 doubles & 3 suites (for up to 4), all with private deck or balcony (the best suite has a 40m^2 terrace with hot tub), sharing 4 common rooms with TV & DVD player, & a bar-restaurant. There's free Wi-Fi & a swimming pool. $$$$$

🏠 **Posada del Faro** Calle de la Bahía & Timonel; ☎ 4486 2110; www.posadadelfaro. com; ⏲ all year. A delightful boutique hotel with Mediterranean hacienda-style rooms looking out over a small swimming pool (with in-pool bar, underwater stools & floating candles) to the Playa Mansa &, far in the distance, the towers of Punta del Este. The 12 rooms are individually designed but essentially all white, & TV-free (but with Wi-Fi). Service is excellent but unobtrusive, not disturbing the peace & tranquillity. Breakfast is provided (*from 09.00*) & dinner in winter (when guests would otherwise have to drive to Punta). $$$$$

🏠 **Bajo El Alma** Golondrinas & Garzas, just east of the plaza; ☎ 4486 2098. A couple of rooms to rent on a B&B basis, with a small kitchenette. $$$$

🏠 **CDL** República Argentina between Delfines & Focas; m 094 422598; www.cdljoseignacio.com; ⏲ all year. Set in a stunning Zen-style garden just west of the Ruta 10 roundabout, the Container Design Lofts are indeed based on 4 old shipping containers totally transformed into retro-styled self-catering apartments, each with AC & balcony. There's a jacuzzi, BBQ & free Wi-Fi, kayaks & bikes. $$$$

🏠 **El Alba** Los Batitues, west of Las Golondrinas; ☎ 4486 2088. 3 rooms to rent, with a deck & BBQ; perfectly comfortable, but the closest you can get to a budget option in José Ignacio itself. $$$$

🏠 **Jenous Hostel** Ruta 10 km181; ☎ 4486 2275; http://jenoushostel.com. 3 blocks inland from the main road & half a block to the left in La Juanita, 2km west of the Ruta 10 roundabout, this is the only hostel in the area, with female & mixed dorms & an apartment for up to 4 people. $$

✕ **Where to eat** Fish is the thing here, of course, but a local seaweed is a speciality, cooked mainly in omelettes (*omeletta de algas*). Cooking with clay ovens and open fires is the current trend with local chefs. Beachside *paradores* serve slow-motion lunches through the afternoon, and dinner in the coolest places doesn't get going before 22.00. With a reservation and a very full wallet, it's well worth the expedition from here to Pueblo Garzón (see page 241). All listings are included on the map, page 235.

✖ **Isla de Flores 1900** ☎4486 2009; www. isladeflores1900.com; ⊕ mid-Dec–mid-Mar 12.00–16.00, 20.30–midnight daily. Just north of the lighthouse, this is the summer site of one of Montevideo's finest restaurants, serving casual lunches such as sandwiches, salads, grilled seafood & pasta, & more formal & original dinners of grilled meats, seafood & vegetable platters. $$$$$
✖ **La Olada** Balneario La Jacinta; ☎4486 2745; ⊕ summer from 20.30 daily. In the very non-touristy village 2km west (enter at km181.5 on Avda Hectór Soria, take 2nd right), this is a real find, the restaurant that opens first every season & stays open longest, & serves remarkably fine food in what seems to be the chef's front room & porch. The wooden furnishings, candles & earth oven give a deceptively bohemian feel. Typical meals include sweetbreads with provolone cheese followed by lamb (from the family farm) with ratatouille, homemade pasta or seaweed risotto, with a dulce de leche flan to finish. $$$$$
✖ **Sal y Pimienta** Ruta 10 km185.5; ☎4486 2751; www.casasuaya.com; ⊕ 09.00–01.00 daily. The restaurant of the Casa Suaya hotel, this serves Mediterranean-style cuisine with fish, chicken, lamb & beef cooked in the wood-fired oven or grilled. Specialities include *corvina negra* (sea bass) baked with glazed onions, *chipirones* (small squid) & squid with sweet pepper. The style is very relaxed, with some poolside tables & some in a thatched hut, lit by torches & the pool's underwater lighting. $$$$$
✖ **Marismo** Ruta 10 km185.1; ☎4486 2273; ⊕ mid-Dec–Feb from 22.00 daily. Turning off the Laguna Garzón road at the sign for the Posada Azul Marino, you'll head into the forest for a few hundred yards until someone with a torch waves you in to a car park. This ultra-chic restaurant is totally al fresco, with candles on wooden tables around a bonfire. The menu is short but delicious, with tender slow-braised lamb shank a speciality. It's not too expensive, but credit cards are not accepted. $$$$$
✖ **Namm** 700m from Ruta 10 km185.1; ☎4486 2526; ⊕ mid-Dec–Feb from 22.00 daily. In a wooden hut in the forest, near Marismo,

the equally trendy Namm (run by the owner of Montevideo's Café Misterio) serves sushi, grilled meats & fusion cuisine, in a magical atmosphere with lanterns & soft cushions. No credit cards. $$$$$
✖ **La Huella** Los Cisnes, Playa Brava; ☎4486 2279; www.paradorlahuella.com; ⊕ lunch Fri–Sun (from 1 Dec daily); dinner mid-Dec–Mar. Great food in a wonderful setting, & *the* place to eat (& people-watch) in José Ignacio – it's best to reserve, although there will be a queue all afternoon. It's a beachfront parador that seems casual but is actually very precisely run, with a simple menu of grilled or stewed fish, squid, langoustines, mussels, sushi or pizza. There's a good choice of vegetarian dishes such as polenta & spinach with blue cheese. The bar is well stocked, & there's good music with a suitably relaxed vibe. You can come for a leisurely lunch or coffee in your swimsuit, sip *clericó* at sunset, wrapped in a blanket on a deckchair, or enjoy a candlelit dinner. $$$$
✖ **Lucy** Garzas & Golondrinas; ☎4486 2090; www.lucy.com.uy; ⊕ 09.00–midnight daily. Not as cool as La Huella or Marismo but it's just off the plaza & the food is outstanding. Starting with organic breads, pastries & jams, the menu continues with a variety of fish, shellfish & meat dishes, with a good range of teas & cakes in the afternoon. $$$
✖ **Popeye** Tordos & Garzas; ⊕ Dec–Easter. A friendly diner that serves good chivitos as well as seafood paella, pasta, gnocchi & seaweed ravioli. $$$
✖ **Santas Negras** Camino Saiz Martínez & Los Lobos ☎4486 2409. In a very stylish new shop north of the Ruta 10 roundabout there's also a cool little bar for cocktails & tapas. $$$
🍴 **La Guada** Saiz Martínez & Los Bigua ☎4486 2558. A wine shop & deli-café, open from breakfast to dinner for deli sandwiches, salads & other light meals. $$
🍴 **Medialunas Calentitas** Ruta 10 km183.5; www.medialunascalentitas.com. Local branch of the Montevideo chain, for croissants with & without fillings (such as dulce de leche), cakes, empanadas, milkshakes & coffees. $$

✖ **Pizza Tutta** Plaza; ☎ 4486 2924; ⊕ 12.00–02.00 daily. Right in the heart of the village, this is a popular meeting spot, serving crusty pizza, fish sandwiches & chivitos; also for take-away/delivery. $$

🍴 **Freddo** Las Garzas & Sainz Martínez; www.freddouruguay.com. Local branch of the Argentine chain, serving the best ice cream in town. $

Shopping Upmarket boutiques include El Canuto (*Los Cisnes & Los Horneros, Playa Mansa;* ☎ *4486 2028*), including sundresses by Uruguayan designers, soft woollen ponchos and shoes, and Takkai (*Plaza;* ☎ *4486 2515; www.takkai.com.ar*) for beachwear and costume jewellery. Next to La Huella, Sentido (*Los Cisnes & El Océano;* ☎ *4486 2749; www.sentidojoseignacio.com;* ⊕ *11.00–midnight daily*) has a wide range of textiles, furnishings, scents, candles and stationery.

For art, the best places are Galería Los Caracoles (*Saiz Martínez & Los Biguá;* ☎ *4486 2408; www.galerialoscaracoles.com*), and Galería de las Misiones (*Las Garzas;* ☎ *4486 2645; www.galeriamisiones.com;* ⊕ *10.00–18.00 Mon–Fri*).

For basic foodstuffs there's El Mercadito (*Saiz Martínez, immediately north of the plaza*), with a farmacía alongside. Nearby, facing the tourist information office, the Almacen El Palmar sells cheeses and cold meats, and also has a bar-salón de té. There's also the Carnicería Manolo (*north end of Las Golondrinas*).

Vinos del Mundo (*Saiz Martínez & Los Biguá;* ☎ *4486 2558; www.vinosdelmundo. com.uy;* ⊕ *09.00–23.00 daily*) sells wines and olive oils and also has a deli-café for coffees and wine by the glass.

Activities

Surfing Surfing is the main sport here, with ideal conditions when the *pampero* is blowing from the southwest, when waves can reach 2m; for lessons call **m** 099 106707.

At Laguna Garzón, 7km east, Laura Moñino, sub-champion (ie: runner-up) at the South American windsurfing championships, offers windsurfing and kite-surfing lessons – contact Laura Kite and Windsurf (☎ *4486 2060;* **m** *094 420704;* **e** *laumonino@hotmail.com; www.kiteywindsurflaura.com*).

Water-skiing Water-skiing is banned on the lagunas but a 700m-long artificial lake has been created 9km north of José Ignacio on Camino Sainz Martínez (leading to Ruta 9) at Lassarena Club de Ski (**m** *099 265483;* **e** *info@lassarena.com; www.lassarena.com*).

Horseriding Horseriding is very popular, with various operations along Ruta 10 east of José Ignacio – first is Cabalgatas (*entre el Campo y el Mar, 600m north;* **m** *099 956262*), then the recommended Haras Godiva (*km183½;* ☎ *4480 6112;* **m** *099 100057; www.harasgodiva.com*).

Other practicalities

Healthcare For healthcare, there's a policlínica (⊕ *10.00–11.55 Mon–Fri*) to the west of Sainz Martínez, just south of the Ruta 10 roundabout.

Laundry and communications There's a laundry and internet place on Calle Albatros in the Balneario La Jacinta (*inland from Ruta 10 km181.5;* ☎ *4486 2421*).

Taxis Taxis wait on the plaza (☎ *4486 2173;* **m** *099 815643*), or for a remise call ☎ *4486 2225*.

SAN CARLOS Immediately south of Ruta 9, the unassuming little town of San Carlos was founded in 1763 by Viceroy Pedro de Ceballos (1715–78), first Viceroy of the River Plate in 1776, and largely settled by Portuguese families. Famous *carolinos* include Colonel Leonardo Oliveira (who captured the Fortaleza de Santa Teresa from Brazil in 1826), Father Antonio Vidal (president in 1880–82 and 1886) and Mariano Soler (1846–1908, the first Archbishop of Montevideo). With a population of 25,000, it's now the main agricultural centre of Maldonado department, and is also known for artesanal brick-making by the roadside. It's a cheap place to spend the night if you want to experience authentic small-town Uruguay rather than the madness of Punta del Este. It also has a good zoo, as well as a poor museum.

Getting there and away

By bus Codesa buses run from Punta del Este and (usually) Maldonado to San Carlos every 15 minutes through the day, and every 30 minutes in the evening. These leave you near the terminal, where you can connect with buses from Montevideo to Rocha. COT's two daily buses from Punta del Este to Rocha also call here. Machado Turismo have nine buses a day to José Ignacio, and COOM and EmTur run north to Minas and Treinta y Tres four times a day. The bus terminal is on Avenida Rodó a block west of the main north–south road, Avenida Jacinto Alvariza; a block to the north, this passes the secondary Plaza 19 de Abril, with the main Plaza Artigas six blocks further east along 18 de Julio; there is free Wi-Fi and toilets and a cafeteria at the terminal.

By car San Carlos is 15km and 20 minutes north of Maldonado, following Ruta 39 (dual-carriage for most of the way) through attractive open country and wetlands. It's just south of km138 of Ruta 9.

🏠 Where to stay   There are only a few places to stay, all pretty cheap ($).

🏠 **Hospedaje Carlitos** Avda Rodó 1158; ☏4266 9545; e hospedajecarlitosop@hotmail.com. The simplest place to stay is this clean & friendly establishment on the north side of the terminal, which has quiet rooms with fan or AC & shared or private bathrooms. No breakfast but a microwave & hot water are available, as well as free Wi-Fi.

🏠 **Hospedaje El Mago** Avda Ceberio, opposite the bus terminal; ☏4266 0606. This new establishment has AC en-suite rooms with Wi-Fi, cable TV, parking & breakfast.

🏠 **Hospedaje Terminal** Avda Rodó 1115; ☏4266 8011. On the south side of the bus terminal, this decent place has rooms with private bath & cable TV, or with shared Wi-Fi, but no breakfast.

🏠 **Hospedaje Uruguay** 25 de Agosto 1053 & Alvariza, 3 blocks north of the terminal; ☏4266 9463. Slightly better rooms are on offer here, with bathroom, cable TV & breakfast.

✕ Where to eat   There are not many places to eat, but the **Plaza Café** restaurant-pizzería (☏4266 2767; $) on the northwestern corner of Plaza Artigas is acceptable, and the **Pizzería Don Luis** at Alvariza 1138 and Basilio Araujo (☏4266 0193; $$) are worth the walk north for pizza, milanesas and good cheer. At Alvariza and Ituzaingo the **Pizzeria El Rancho** (☏4266 7191; $$) serves decent pizza and chivitos, although it's more a take-away/delivery operation.

Shopping   The most convenient supermarkets are Ta-Ta (*Calle 738 & 18 de Julio, a block east of Plaza 19 de Abril;* ⊕ *08.00–22.00 daily*) and El Dorado (*25 de Agosto & Sarandí, & Avda Ceberio & Rincón*).

Other practicalities

Banks There's are ATMs at the Banco República (*18 de Julio 651 & Oliveira, on the east side of Plaza Artigas*) and at the Petrobras station (*Avda Alvariza 1180 & Basilio Araujo*).

Communications A weak Wi-Fi signal is available on the southwest corner of Plaza Artigas. The post office is in a farmacía by the Punta del Este bus stop, immediately east of the bus terminal. Antel's telecentro (⊕ *09.00–18.00 daily*) is at 18 de Julio and Soler, midway between the two plazas.

Emergency services The San Carlos hospital (*Avda Ceberio 519 & 4 de Octubre;* ✆ *4266 9127*) is southwest of the centre. The police are at 18 de Julio 802 and Juan de Díos Curbelo, two blocks west of Plaza Artigas.

What to see and do On the west side of Plaza Artigas you'll find the Church of San Carlos Borromeo (1792–1801), with a simple colonial-style façade and plain white brickwork inside. Next to it is a radio station in an Art Deco former cinema. On the southeastern corner of the plaza, by a cannon, La Garita is a tiny turret, a replica of one at the Fortaleza de Santa Teresa in Rocha, erected in 1953 to commemorate Leonardo Oliveira and other carolinos who fought for independence. On the northeastern corner of Plaza Artigas, the Teatro Sociedad Unión (*http://sociedaduniondesancarlos.blogspot.co.uk*), built in 1929 and one of the finest in the area, is now being refurbished.

Three blocks east of the plaza is the riverside Teatro Municipal de Verano, the open-air theatre where carnaval shows are held in the second half of February. A footbridge leads across to the Parque Municipal Cayetano Silva, named after the son of a black slave (1868–1920) who moved to Argentina and became famous there for composing the army's 'March of San Lorenzo'. The Festival Criollo, on the last weekend of January, brings lots of gauchos here. Continuing through the park brings you to the stadium and the **Parque Medina Zoo** on Camino Eguzquiza (⊕ *to sunset Tue–Sun; free*). There's also a road bridge (leading to Ruta 9) a block to the north; about half a kilometre to the east of the bridge a road leads south to the stadium, the zoo and 12km away, La Barra.

The zoo is quite large and well kept, but a bit old-fashioned. In an area of 14ha (once the Medina family estate) it houses around 600 animals of 48 species, mainly native and African (including lions and various monkeys). South American animals include llamas, pumas, foxes, boar (introduced for hunting), *carpinchos* (capybaras), *guazuvirá* (grey brocket deer), birds including vultures, parrots, jays, rheas and flamingos, and snakes. There's also a large grassy area with picnic tables, barbecues and drinking water, as well as a souvenir kiosk.

A block south from the east side of Plaza Artigas is the **Museo Histórico Regional** (*Reyles & Oliveira;* ⊕ *10.00–19.00 Tue–Sat, 13.00–19.00 Sun; summer 10.00–19.00 Tue–Sat; free*), with a small collection of indigenous and pioneer oddments; there are also temporary art shows. Built in 1782, this was the Spanish commander's house.

CERRO CATEDRAL The highest point in Uruguay is Cerro Catedral (513.7m), although the Cerro de las Ánimas, at 509m, was thought to be the highest until 1973. An almost traffic-free dirt road passes within a couple of hundred metres of the summit, making it an easy hike, with some excellent birdwatching along the way.

Just north of San Carlos, main roads meet at a roundabout at km138 of Ruta 9 (Montevideo–Chuy) and km20 of Ruta 39 (Punta del Este–Aiguá). Continuing northwards on Ruta 39, the scenery gets rockier, with lots of *chirca* scrub, as the road winds up to km56 and then down. Three EmTur buses a day (Maldonado–Treinta y Tres) come this way and will set you down at km67.5, by a radio mast to the west and a dirt road to the east signposted to Villa El Cordillera and La Laguna. Hiking east from here, you'll drop a bit to a broad valley, with a ridge of almost equally high tops ahead – it's easy to see why it took so long to identify Cerro Catedral as the highest point. This is all open farmland at first, with some eucalyptus trees and agaves, as well as horneros, flickers, teros, doves, swallows and vultures. After an hour you'll drop and swing right at the gate of Establecimiento Villa del Cordillera. After crossing a creek you'll climb again to the entry to the **Estancia Lagunas del Catedral** (m *094 4410408; www.lagunasdelcatedral.com*), 6km to the left, after about 40 minutes (8km from the road). It's possible to stay here (by reservation), a different experience from most tourist estancias in the flatlands. Horseriding and guided walks are available, and there's a stream with cascades and five pools and plenty of birdlife, as well as margay cats and vampire bats. Day visits are possible as well as overnight stays; bunkrooms (for visiting students) may be available, as well as double rooms (*US$280 with FB*). There's also a small winery (using grapes grown near Atlántida) – the Aripuca licor de Tannat is very tasty. Another 15 minutes on the dirt road brings you up on to a plateau with pools of water and big views back to the west. There are cattle here as well as teros, kestrels and other birds. In another 20 minutes (about 2½ hours from the road) you'll come to a sign reading 'Cerro Catedral', with an obvious small pile of stones where you can climb the fence to the right, or squeeze through. It takes a couple of minutes to reach the highest point in Uruguay, where a survey point bears its former name, Cerro Cordillera. There's a small outcrop on the flank of the summit that looks vaguely like cathedral spires.

It's tempting to explore along the ridge north and south, but when you're ready to continue the dirt road drops into a valley with much more birdlife, including tijeretas (fork-tailed flycatchers) and other flycatchers and tyrants, field flickers, teros, doves, partridge and brown-and-yellow marshbirds. After 40 minutes you'll pass a farm and will then need to turn left at a junction, bringing you in about half an hour to the unpaved Ruta 109 from Rocha to Aiguá. There are no buses on this road, and not much traffic, but you should get a ride eventually. Alternatively, walk back from Cerro Catedral to Ruta 39.

AIGUÁ Aiguá is a small town, bypassed by Ruta 8 between Minas and Treinta y Tres; 2km from the town at Ruta 39 km90, the Stella Maris farm (☏ *4440 6127;* ⌚ *all year;* **$$$**) offers agroturismo, guided walks, horseriding, cart-rides and farm activities. There's simple accommodation for six, or day visits are possible. Just south in the Sierra del Caracol, a couple of kilometres west from km74 of Ruta 39 (from Aiguá to Punta del Este), the welcoming **Cabaña Martín Pescador** (☏ *4440 6020;* m *098 623201; www.mpescador.com*) has nine rooms (*US$80 for 2 with HB*) and offers activities such as horseriding, birdwatching, cycling and helping out on the farm.

PUEBLO GARZÓN The town of Garzón, 42km north of José Ignacio and 70km from Punta del Este (about an hour and US$80 by taxi), was founded in 1892 by Fermín de León, at a ford on the road to Rocha where governor Vicente Garzón had a ranch. It had a population of over 2,000 until the granite quarries and railway closed in the 1960s, when it fell to around 200. Since then it has looked like a classic western ghost town (without the tumbleweed rolling down the main street), although there is more work nowadays, with wineries, olive oil and forestry plantations.

The station is still there, along with the church, school and town hall on the plaza with its old palm trees, but on a corner of the plaza the 140-year-old red-brick general store is now a five-star boutique hotel with just five rooms, and perhaps the country's most prestigious restaurant.

The Argentine star chef Francis Mallmann (born Francisco, to a Uruguayan mother), who owns the prestigious Restaurant 1884 (Mendoza, Argentina), Patagonia Sur (Buenos Aires) and Patagonia West (Westhampton, New York), created a restaurant called Los Negros in José Ignacio back in 1977, when it really was known only to those far ahead of the trends. It became legendary, partly because of the cast-iron boxes which he used as both cooking utensils and serving dishes. As José Ignacio filled up and became, to Mallmann's mind, more affluent, crowded and less interesting, he began looking for somewhere new to set up a small luxury guesthouse, and at the start of the century moved to Garzón, which he describes as *el Uruguay de adentro*, authentic backcountry Uruguay. Since then the village has become very desirable indeed, with houses that would cost US$10,000 selling for US$80,000 to wealthy Argentines and British showbusiness figures such as the Rolling Stones' tailor and Helmut Newton's agent.

Where to stay and eat

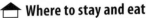

Hotel & Restaurant Garzón 11km north from Ruta 9 km175; ☎ 4410 2811; e info@ restaurantegarzon.com; www.restaurantegarzon. com. The hotel has just 5 smallish rooms, with boho-rustic décor, lots of cushions on the floor, oversized candelabras & claw-foot bathtubs. They also have free Wi-Fi & slightly thin walls, & there's an attractive patio, garden & swimming pool. But all that really counts is the food, & the jaw-dropping room rates (*dbl US$780*) do include FB (breakfast, lunch, tea & dinner, including wines from Finca Anita in Mendoza) as well as laundry, bikes, horseriding & sulky rides. The cooking is bold & simple, based on the traditional *inferniello* (little hell) technique of cooking between 2 wood fires on iron griddles that are also used to serve the food at the table. There's also a wood-fired oven for baking pizza, breads & desserts. Mallmann's best-known dishes include chicken in a salt crust, lamb in a mustard-&-thyme crust, duck breast with Malbec sauce & potatoes, endives & tomatoes, & grilled steak with chimichurri sauce (olive oil, parsley, oregano & garlic), along with corn humitas, baked peaches with Iberian ham & hazelnut, leeks vinaigrette with eggs & anchovies, & pears

in Tannat sauce. You can also dip into poetry books & magazines in Spanish, English, French & Portuguese. Mallmann gives free cookery classes for local children, & 90% of the staff are from the village. $$$$$

Casa Anna ☎ UK +44 20 7351 7778; www. casaannagarzon.com. Next door to the Hotel & Restaurant Garzón & home of the owner of a Mayfair, London, art gallery, Casa Anna is a traditionally styled house with an acre of exquisite gardens, an observatory & a pool house that becomes a cinema. Riding, birdwatching, yoga & massage are also available. There are 5 double rooms (*from US$480 B&B*) & a 4-bed room. $$$$$

✕ Lucifer m 099 255249; http:// restaurantlucifer.com; ⏰ Dec–Mar every evening. Just beyond the school on Camino a la Estación Custiel is this casual restaurant where Mallmann's pupil Lucía Soria produces simple but equally inspired dishes from local produce. You'll eat in the rear courtyard, warmed by an open fire & glimpsing the semi-open kitchen. Dinner costs about US$60. $$$$$

ROCHA DEPARTMENT

Ruta 9 continues east from San Carlos in pleasant park-like country with lots of trees. At km143½ Ruta 104 leads south to Manantiales (see page 226), and at km160.8

Argentina's richest man, hydrocarbons tycoon Alejandro Bulgheroni, has bought a huge swathe of land immediately west of Pueblo Garzón with amazingly ambitious plans for producing wine and olive oil. Uruguay's wine industry has been trapped in its boutique niche, with no producer big enough to sell to foreign supermarkets rather than specialist retailers – but the situation is set to change. Bodega Garzón's output should be both good enough and plentiful enough to break out when its huge new winery starts production in 2014.

It cost around US$35 million and is built to the highest levels of sustainability, with grass roofs, natural light and wind power; with 60ha of Tannat, Albariño and Petit Manseng plus smaller quantities of Gamaret, Marsellan, Calvadoc, Cabernet Franc, Merlot, Petit Verdot, Pinot Noir, Pinot Gris, Viognier and Sauvignon Blanc, and Alberto Antonini (father of the Super-Tuscan blend) as consultant, there's huge potential.

Their Tannat is intense but floral with surprisingly soft tannins, aged for 18 months in oak giving structure and elegance; the Tannat–Merlot blend is rounded and plummy with an underpinning of velvety tannins. On the white side, the Albariño is already superb, tart and fruity with a fine dry finish, the Viognier is smooth and dry, also after 18 months in oak, and the Sauvignon Blanc is lovely, with fresh citrus and melon flavours. They're also terrific value, with varietals selling for US$12 and reservas for US$24.

There are also 60ha planted with olives, mainly Arbequina (fruity and bittersweet, and vaguely equivalent to the Merlot grape) and Coratina (spicey and vaguely equivalent to Tannat), as well as Barnea, Picul and other varieties. The olives are washed and homogenised for a maximum of one hour then centrifuged to produce just 13 litres of oil from 100kg of olives; the different varieties are blended only at the end of the process and the oil is only bottled on demand – it remains extra-virgin (with less than 0.2% acidity) for two years once in the bottle, or for three months once opened. You can buy a Coratina monovarietal oil (the most intense), bivarietal (not too strong, and good with pastas and salads) and trivarietal (stronger and oilier, for fish and seafood) as well as Corte Italiano (a blend of Frantoio and Leccino that's fruity and fresh, good with grilled meats); half-litre bottles sell for US$10. Garzón olive oil has been judged the sixth best in the world and the best outside Europe.

The high-tech olive oil plant has a beautiful tasting area (opened by President Mujica in 2011), the starting point for two-hour tours (⌕ 4224 4040; m 091 392687; www.colinasdegarzon.com; tours Tue–Sat; US$60) that include a short film on the olive's origins in the Middle East, then a gallery with short videos and windows that then slide open to show the production process, and a tasting of three oils, three wines, olives, almonds, cheese and breads, also produced here and for sale locally. Tours of the winery will be available too (⌕ 4224 1759; www.bodegagarzon.com), and a wine bar will also open soon. The whole site is landscaped around a lake where you may see carpinchos and ñandues.

Other tours feature cycling, horseriding, hot-air balloon, a barbecue, the Sunset Experience (*summer on Fri*), the Picnic Experience (*11.00 Tue–Sat*) and the Harvest Experience (*end Mar–Jun 10.30 Tue–Sat*).

Camino Saiz Martínez heads south to José Ignacio (see page 233). At km175 a police post and school mark the turning north to Pueblo Garzón (see page 241), and 2km further east the highway crosses the Arroyo Garzón into Rocha department, with a toll post just beyond. At km187 a dirt road leads south to the isolated stretch of Ruta 10 between lagunas Garzón and Rocha (which offers fantastic birdwatching), and at km205 another road leads 5km south to the *zona de playa y pesca* (beach and fishing zone) and the *puerto de las botes* (boat harbour) on the north shore of Laguna de Rocha. At km206 (68km from the San Carlos junction, one hour by bus) is a large roundabout, with a tourist information office and parador, where buses turn left into the town of Rocha, capital of the department of the same name; with your own vehicle you can turn left earlier, on Herrera or Kennedy.

Rocha is one of Uruguay's most attractive departments, with its long, empty coastline, windswept sandy beaches separated by rocky points, inland lagoons – formed when the sea rose at the end of the last ice age – with plentiful birdlife, and rolling interior dotted with butia palms. This is the area that Prince Charles particularly asked to see on his 1999 visit to Uruguay. The largest grove of ombú trees in the country grows beside the Laguna de Castillos (reached from km267 of Ruta 10 or km261.5 of Ruta 9).

From around 4,000 years ago, around 800 large mounds known as *cerritos* (up to 40m in diameter and 7m in height) were constructed in the coastal area – not, as was assumed, burial mounds, but the sites of villages created as the climate changed and marshlands dried out. The border with Brazil moved to and fro across this area in the 18th and 19th centuries, with many skirmishes and raids, delaying settlement and development; now it is largely occupied with cattle ranching. In the 1940s future resorts were designated along its 180km Atlantic coast and divided into lots on paper, but no money was forthcoming to build anything. Then some totally unplanned settlements, such as Aguas Dulces and Cabo Polonio, appeared, with cabins being built on public land without permission, and no services whatsoever – not even road access in the case of Cabo Polonio. In 1990 the department began to regulate these developments, in order to boost tourism but without losing what makes the department special. Property speculation is moving along the coast from Punta del Este and José Ignacio into Rocha, anticipating the building of the bridge at Laguna Garzón. Some huge private houses are being built here, notably one of 2,300m² by Microsoft vice president Ralf Harteneck.

In 1976 the **Bañados del Este** (Eastern Wetlands) Biosphere Reserve was designated by UNESCO, encompassing various existing nature reserves and historic monuments including the Santa Teresa and San Miguel forts, Cabo Polonio and lagunas Rocha and Garzón (12,500km² in total, in five departments). This also became a Ramsar wetlands reserve in 1982, but there are not enough environmental controls on development, particularly given the increase in rice farming. Habitats include seashore, dunes, lagoons, inland marshes, palm swamps, grassland, gallery forest and hilly bosque serrano, supporting at least 75% of the bird species found in Uruguay; in Rocha you can easily see 60 or more species in a day. These include austral migrants that breed in Patagonia and then move north, Nearctic migrants, especially shorebirds, that winter here (in the southern summer) and Neotropic migrants that breed here and fly north for the winter. The brackish coastal lagoons are South America's most important coastal site for American golden plover, while grasslands provide breeding habitat for several threatened capuchino seedeaters (*Sporophila* spp). In addition 60% of Uruguay's mammal species are found here, including carpincho (capybara), paca, otter, guazu-birá and pampas deer, and marine mammals such as sea lions and cetaceans.

The non-profit body **Probides** (*Programa de Conservación de la Biodiversidad y Desarrollo Sustentable en los Bañados del Este; Ruta 9 km205, Rocha;* \ *4472 5005/8021;* e *probides@probides.org.uy; www.probides.org.uy*) produced the management plan for the Bañados del Este in 2000 and now manages the Laguna de Rocha, working closely with local fishing communities.

ROCHA The town of Rocha was founded in 1793, basically by accident: a group of settlers from Asturias in northern Spain were heading for Patagonia, but their ship was forced to put in to Maldonado. It was named after the Argentine Luis Rocha, who issued permits for the slaughter of cattle here at the time. Now it's a typical quiet market town with a population of 26,000 (of a total of 70,000 in the department). It calls itself the Uruguayan capital of maté and hosts the Fiesta Nacional del Maté in early December, with gauchos and carts riding into Plaza Independencia at midday on Sunday with sprigs of the medicinal herb. This follows the Semana de Rocha, in the second week of November, featuring music and crafts events and of course a fair.

Getting there and away The **bus** companies COT, Cynsa and Rutas del Sol all have offices on the southwestern side of Plaza Independencia, where taxis (\ *4472 7870*) also wait. All bus services from Montevideo to Chuy and La Paloma (see page 87) call here, as well as COT's two daily buses from Punta del Este to Chuy and local services to La Paloma and La Pedrera. COT, Cynsa/Nuñez and Rutas del Sol all have between eight and 14 services a day from Montevideo (most calling at Pan de Azúcar and San Carlos), most continuing either to La Paloma or to Punta del Diablo and Chuy. Some go on from La Paloma to La Pedrera and a few call at Cabo Polonio, Valizas, Aguas Dulces and Castillos.

The local company Cotec/Tur-Este, at Graña and 25 de Mayo, a block behind the Hotel Arrarte, runs ten times daily to La Paloma and La Pedrera, twice daily to Treinta y Tres and to Maldonado/Piriápolis, and once daily to Cebollati (*Mon–Sat*) and Lascana (*Tue–Sun*).

Orientation and tourist information The departmental tourism office (*junction of Ruta 9 & Ruta 15;* \ *4472 9728/3100;* e *info@turismorocha.gub.uy; www.turismorocha.gub.uy;* ⏰ *10.00–20.00 Mon–Fri, 10.00–18.00 Sat–Sun*) is on the southeastern edge of town. From here José Batlle y Ordóñez leads northwest into the town, continuing as Ruta 109 to Aiguá; turning left on 25 de Agosto it's four blocks to Plaza Independencia, the leafy central square.

The tourism office is now distributing digital multi-media cards loaded with information about tourist destinations, hotels and restaurants. The information can be viewed and downloaded by simply zapping the card's QR code with a smartphone or by entering the card number at www.rochauy.com.

Where to stay There are just a few fairly simple but central places to stay. All listings are included on the map, page 247.

🏠 **Hotel Trocadero** 25 de Agosto & 18 de Julio; \ 4472 2267. Just east of the plaza, this 1970s-style 3-star has some AC rooms (US$10 extra). **$$$**

🏠 **Hotel Arrarte** Ramírez 118 & 25 de Mayo; \ 4472 6756/4597; e arrarte@hotmail.com. On the southwest side of the plaza, this nice old-style place is traditional & not tatty; there's also parking. Buffet b/fast inc. **$$**

🏠 **Hostel de Acá** Artigas 136A; m 098 604706; www.facebook.com/hosteldeaca. A new hostel with shared & private rooms, kitchen & Wi-Fi; if no-one is in send a text & you should soon be let in. **$**

🛏 **Hotel Municipal** 19 de Abril 87; ☎ 4472 2404. Just southeast of the plaza, this quiet & very friendly 2-star hotel has clean simple rooms, some with cable TV. Decent b/fast inc (*07.00–10.00*). **$**

✗ **Where to eat** Likewise, the choice of restaurants is limited, but all are on or close to Plaza Independencia. Near the bus offices on the southwestern side of the plaza, the **City Café** (**$$**) is a bar-café which serves a basic range of steaks, pastas and the like; the air conditioning is chilly, there's a terrace with bus fumes, or there's a salón comedor upstairs with a more peaceful atmosphere, but it'll probably be open at lunchtime only. The **Club Social de Rocha** on the north side of the plaza is an attractive Art Deco building that now houses Fono Pizza (☎ 4472 9012; **$$**), with a wood oven and good ice creams. There are some tiny but enjoyable cafés on Paseo Vaz Mendosa, the refurbished alley on the southeastern side of the plaza, and the Féola ice-cream shop on J P Ramírez just south of the plaza. Just northeast of the plaza on 25 de Agosto, Chivits' Centro serves chivitos, pizza and parrilla; there's also a nice little bakery just off the plaza on 25 de Mayo.

Shopping For food shopping, the Los Jardines supermarket is opposite the Intendencia at Artigas 169 & Rodó (⊕ *08.00–22.00 daily; summer 07.00–23.00*), and Ta-Ta is at Artigas 221 & Sanz y Sancho (⊕ *08.00–22.00 daily*).

Other practicalities

Banks Banco República and Banco Comercial have ATMs on the eastern corner of the plaza. Cambio Nelson (⊕ *08.00–20.00*) is on the southeast corner of the plaza.

Bike repair Bike and motorbike parts are available at **Bike Center**, east of the plaza at 25 de Mayo 129A (m *098 257300*), as well as at Ciclo-Moto Repuestos (*Ramírez & Zorrilla de San Martín*) and Rubén Cano (*Artigas 150 & Rodó*).

Car rental Cars can be rented from Rent a Car Ganesha at 18 de Julio 286 (☎ *4472 3209*; m *099 579336*; e *mbianco2006@msn.com*).

Communications Antel's call centre is nearby (*19 de Abril 116 near Artigas; ⊕ 09.00–19.00 Mon–Sat*). The post office is east of the plaza (*18 de Julio 2085 north of 19 de Abril; ⊕ 09.00–17.00 Mon–Fri, 08.00–12.00 Sat*).

Emergency services The public hospital (☎ *4472 2608*) is on Avenida Martínez at Treinta y Tres, to the left off Ruta 109 towards Aiguá. For less urgent matters you can go to the Policlínico del Este at Artigas 254 (☎ *4472 8373–7*).

What to see and do On the northwestern side of the plaza is the church of **Nuestra Señora de los Remedios**, founded in 1794, remodelled in 1956 and now pretty unattractive, with a very plain neoclassical interior and a spotlit Virgin and Child above the altar. At the southwestern corner of the plaza are the single-storey Belle-Époque **Teatro 25 de Mayo** (1910; reopened in 2007) and the Art Deco-style Primero Agosto cinema (currently closed). Going northeast from the plaza on 25 de Agosto you'll see two Constructivist **murals by Joaquín Torres García** in front of the Teacher Training Centre (25 de Agosto 131), then the ornate **Società Italiana di Mutuo Soccorso** (*Italian Mutual Aid Society; Treinta y Tres 1985*). A block further, beyond the duller Sociedad Española de Socorros Mutos (*Spanish Mutual Aid Society; 25 de Agosto 149*), is the fairly missable **Museo Regional**

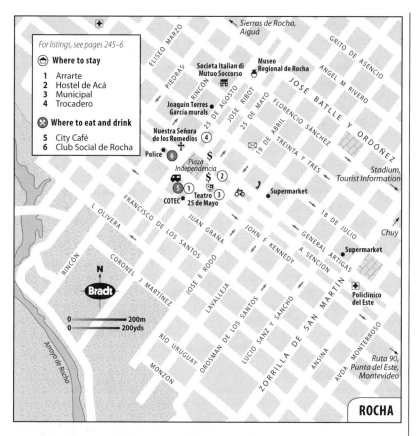

Where to stay
1 Arrarte
2 Hostel de Acá
3 Municipal
4 Trocadero

Where to eat and drink
5 City Café
6 Club Social de Rocha

Sierras de Rocha, Aiguá

ELISEO MARZO
PIEDRAS
GRITO DE ASENCIO
Societa Italian di Mutuo Soccorso
RINCÓN
Museo Regional de Rocha
ANGEL M RIVERO
25 DE AGOSTO
JOSÉ RIBOT
JOSÉ BATLLE Y ORDÓÑEZ
25 DE MAYO
FLORENCIO SÁNCHEZ
Joaquín Torres García murals
19 DE ABRIL
18 DE TREINTA Y TRES
Nuestra Señora de los Remedios
Police
Plaza Independencia
Stadium, Tourist Information
Teatro 25 de Mayo
COTEC
Supermarket
18 DE JULIO
Chuy
FRANCISCO DE LOS SANTOS
JUAN GRAÑA
JOHN F KENNEDY
GENERAL ARTIGAS
A SENCIÓN
L OLIVERA
Supermarket
RINCÓN
CORONEL J MARTÍNEZ
JOSÉ E RODÓ
LAVALLEJA
Policlínico del Este
N
Bradt
JOSÉ E RODÓ
LUCIO SANZ Y SANCHO
0 ——— 200m
0 ——— 200yds
RÍO URUGUAY
OROSMAN DE LOS SANTOS
ZORRILLA DE SAN MARTÍN
ANSINA
AVDA MONTERROSO
Ruta 90, Punta del Este, Montevideo
MONZÓN
Arroyo de Rocha

ROCHA

de Rocha (*25 de Agosto 162 & Sánchez;* ⊕ *08.00–13.45 Mon–Fri; free*). Its old-fashioned displays feature ancient bones, bolas and rompacabezas, material on local children's author Constancio Vigil, the landing of a flying boat on the Laguna de Rocha in 1945 by Lionel de Marmier (inaugurating the Paris–Buenos Aires service), and a local man who served in the French Foreign Legion in World War II. The end room contains swords, uniforms, harnesses and a carriage for taking prisoners from court to jail.

Films and other events take place at the Centro Cultural María Élida Marquizo (*18 de Julio & 19 de Abril;* \4472 0889; *http://centroculturalmem.blogspot.co.uk*).

CABALLOS DE LUZ The Sierras de Rocha, north of Rocha, are small but rugged, and home to various 'alternative' tourism outfits. Perhaps the best is **Caballos de Luz** (m *099 400446;* e *caballosdeluz@gmail.com; www.caballosdeluz.com*), a horseriding operation with just three guest rooms and shared vegetarian meals (using their own produce except in high summer). Longer multi-day rides are their passion but there's far more demand for half-day rides on their fine, professionally cared-for horses. There's limited wind and solar power (no Wi-Fi or television), composting toilets and bathing in lovely pools in the all-year river. Heading north on Ruta 109, turn right after 10km on Camino Sierras de Rocha (signposted Parador-Camping Sierras de Rocha) and then right again after 3.5km through an unmarked gate (after one signed Piedra Verde).

The **Parador Sierras de Rocha** (✆ *4470 2122;* m *099 402061/861010;* e *paradorsierradelosrocha@hotmail.com;* **$$**) has simple accommodation and good food dominated by grilled meats; trails lead to waterfalls and rock pools. On the same road, the **Posada de las Estrellas** (m *098 040596, 099 399619;* e *posadaestrellas@gmail.com; http://laposadadelasestrellas.com;* **$$$**) is a thatched house with two en-suite rooms and three split-level apartments, plus a tipi.

LA PALOMA From the junction of Ruta 9 and Ruta 15, on the southeastern edge of Rocha, it's 28km to La Paloma, the most developed beach resort in Rocha and one of the most popular with the surfing community. A lighthouse was built on the rocky headland known as the Cabo Santa María in 1874, followed by a port at the start of the 20th century. In 1936 the Sociedad Cabo Santa María was set up, led by Nicolás Solari (a prosperous merchant in Salto), to construct a new resort, designed by Carlos Gómez Gavazzo (1904–87), who had worked in Le Corbusier's office in Paris. It's a very pleasant low-rise development, but there are few actual Corbusieresque buildings; in fact there are a lot of thatched houses.

The port (north of the resort, protected from the Atlantic by a long mole) is one of the Uruguayan navy's main bases, and is now being expanded for exports of iron ore. This will take ships with a draught of up to 24m, double what's possible in Montevideo. However, it may seriously compromise the country's fastest-growing centre of tourism. For the last couple of years, La Paloma has been totally packed out with school leavers and students for the first two weeks of January – it's said that up to 20,000 young people come here, ten or 12 to a house, although they don't seem to sleep much, with all-night parties everywhere.

Getting there and away

By bus There are reasonably frequent local buses between Rocha and La Paloma (many going on to La Pedrera) with COTEC and RochaTur, as well as through services from Montevideo (see page 87), and one or two from Chuy, with Rutas del Sol, Cynsa and COT. Rutas del Sol also runs six buses a day along Ruta 10 to La Pedrera, Cabo Polonio and Valizas, and Tur-Este runs four buses a day to Piriápolis via Punta del Este. Bus companies are in the terminal. For tickets to Buenos Aires, Buquebus (*Avda Solarí & Antares;* ☉ *09.00–13.00, 17.30–20.30 Mon–Sat, 10.00– 12.00, 18.00–21.00 Sun*) is in the only tall building in town.

By taxi There are various taxi co-ops, all at the bus terminal: Central de Taxis (✆ *4479 6710*), Taxi Costa Azul (✆ *4479 8064;* m *099 389024*), Taxi 24 Hours (✆ *4479 8152;* m *099 953231*) and Radio Taxi (✆ *4479 8664;* m *099 279625*). There's also Rentacar del Faro (m *099 333033*).

By boat The port office (✆ *4479 6043;* e *dnhpalom@adinet.com.uy*) is open mid-March to mid-December 09.00–16.00 Monday–Saturday; summer 09.00–17.00 Monday–Friday, 08.00–16.00 Saturday–Sunday.

Orientation and tourist information Ruta 15 crosses Ruta 10 5km north of La Paloma, and 2.5km further on passes La Aguada, site of the most popular student campsite. After another 2km through pine woods you suddenly arrive at La Paloma's bus terminal, separated from the resort by a row of trees; there's a tourist information desk here (m *099 398903;* ☉ *09.00–17.00 daily*) and a bank of lockers (from US$3 for a small one for four hours to US$37 for a large one for five days). Walking ahead (southwest) you emerge on Avenida Paloma by the police

station. Turn left towards the centre; just beyond the Hostel Ibirapitá (on the right) and craft market (on the left) are a roundabout and petrol station, with the main tourist information centre (✆ *4479 6088;* m *098 258205;* e *ligalaploma@adinet.com. uy; www.ligalapaloma.com.uy, www.lapaloma.net, www.lapalomadigital.com.uy;* ⊕ *summer 09.00–midnight daily*) on the traffic island.

🏠 **Where to stay** There are quite a few mid-range hotels spread around the rather suburban area west of the centre. Most young people who flock here in January stay in the campsites and cabañas just north of La Paloma, but there are a couple of hostels. There are also alquilo signs around the resort, advertising houses and cabins for rent. All listings are included on the map, page 250.

Hotels
🏠 **UY Proa Sur** Avda Solari & Del Faro; ✆ 4479 6860; www.uyhoteles.com/proasur; ⊕ all year. New, well located & pretty luxurious, with a small heated swimming pool, sauna, gym & a good breakfast. Rooms are simple, uncluttered & not huge. **$$$$$–$$$**

🏠 **Bahía** Avda del Navío & Avda del Sol; ✆ 4479 6029; www.elbahia.com.uy; ⊕ all year. Just off the main drag, this 3-star place is a classic 1936 edifice but well modernised, with clean, bright rooms, cable TV, Wi-Fi & a decent restaurant. There are double & triple rooms plus superior rooms with balconies & better bathrooms. **$$$$**

🏠 **Portobello** Tres Marías near Foque, Playa Anaconda; ✆ 4479 6159; www.hotelportobello. com.uy; ⊕ mid-Dec–Feb. In a quiet area 2km west of the centre, on Playa Anaconda (aka Playa Los Botes or Solarí), this has 46 rooms for up to 4 people, all opening on to the sea & garden. Sports facilities & bicycles are available. **$$$$**

🏠 **Zen Boutique Apart Hotel** Calle Botavara, Playa Anaconda; ✆ 4479 6090; www.zenlapaloma. com. A lovely new place a mile or so west of the centre, with a huge pool & 16 suites all with kitchenette & balcony with beach view & BBQ. Green touches include free bikes, solar hot water & whale-watching (*Jul–Oct*). **$$$$**

🏠 **Cabo Santa María** Avda Solari between Sirio & Titania; ✆ 4479 6004; www.cabosantamaria. com; ⊕ all year. Once the grandest hotel here, built in 1980 to house a casino (now only slot machines; ⊕ *summer daily; rest of the year from 20.00 w/ends*), this is a rambling pile of a place near the lighthouse, 1km from the bus terminal. Rates include buffet breakfast in summer & continental breakfast the rest of the year. At the rear of the hotel there are apartments & bungalows with kitchenettes. **$$$**

🏠 **Perla del Este** Adonis between Apolo & Júpiter; ✆ 4479 6078; e hotelperladeleste@adinet. com.uy; www.destinorocha.com/perla. By the sea just north of the lighthouse, this 3-star place looks like a rather run-down apartment block, but is open when most others in the area are closed. Cable TV, shaded parking. Buffet b/fast inc. **$$$**

🏠 **Tirrenia** Avda de Navío between Leo & Piscis; ✆ 4479 6230; http://htirrenia.com. A smallish 3-star (nicer inside than out) with 7 rooms with fan & 7 with AC, as well as apartments for up to 7 people, all with Wi-Fi, cable TV & frigobar. Free umbrellas & deck chairs available on the beach. **$$$**

🏠 **Yerutí** Grulla near Aries, La Balconada; ✆ 4479 6235; m 099 635707; e yaruti@adinet. com.uy; www.hotelyeruti.com. An attractive Modernist building with a balcony all around the upper floor, this has 22 rooms with cable TV & fans; service is excellent. **$$$**

🏠 **Palma de Mallorca** Parada 11, La Aguada; ✆ 4479 6739; www.hotelpalmademallorca.com. uy; ⊕ Nov–Mar. About 3km north of La Paloma (with a local bus every couple of hours), on one of the main surfing beaches, this resort-style place has an indoor pool, beach service, children's games room, video room, tennis courts & bikes, & offers a fine buffet breakfast, as well as free coffee 24hrs/ day. However, it's a bit run-down & overpriced. **$$**

🏠 **Viola** Avda Solari near Antares; ✆ 4479 6020; www.hotelviola.com.uy. On the main drag close to the tourist information centre, this is friendly, clean & simple, with AC or fans in rooms, Wi-Fi & PCs with internet access. There's also a decent restaurant serving seafood & pasta. **$$**

Hostels
🏠 **Hostel Ibirapitá** Avda Paloma s/n; ✆ 4479 9303; m 099 960869; e hostelibirapita@hotmail.

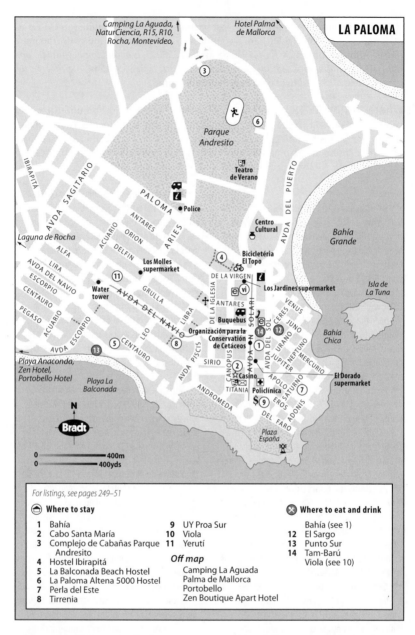

LA PALOMA

Camping La Aguada, NaturCiencia, R15, R10, Rocha, Montevideo,

Hotel Palma de Mallorca

Parque Andresito

Teatro de Verano

PALOMA

● Police

Centro Cultural

Bahía Grande

IBIRAPITÁ

AVDA SAGITARIO

ANTARES

ARIES

ACUARIO ORION

Laguna de Rocha

ALFA

DELFIN

LIRA

AVDA DEL NAVIO

ESCORPIO

CENTAURO

ACUARIO

PEGASO

ESCORPIO

Los Molles supermarket

Water tower

AVDA DEL NAVIO

GRULLA

DE LA VIRGEN

Bicicletería El Topo

Los Jardines supermarket

Isla de La Tuna

Bahía Chica

AVDA DEL PUERTO

LIBRA

DE LA IGLESIA

ANTARES

LEO

Buquebus

Organización para la Conservación de Cetáceos

AVDA SOLARI

VENUS

CERES JUNO

URANO

NEPTUNO

MERCURIO

AVDA DEL SOL

JUPITER

APOLO

SATURNO

EROS

ADONIS

El Dorado supermarket

Playa Anaconda, Zen Hotel, Portobello Hotel

AVDA ESCORPIO

CENTAURO

PISCIS

SIRIO

ANDROMEDA

TITANIA

Casino

Policlínica

Playa La Balconada

N

Bradt

0 ———— 400m
0 ———— 400yds

DEL FARO

Plaza España

For listings, see pages 249–51

🛏 **Where to stay**

1 Bahía
2 Cabo Santa María
3 Complejo de Cabañas Parque Andresito
4 Hostel Ibirapitá
5 La Balconada Beach Hostel
6 La Paloma Altena 5000 Hostel
7 Perla del Este
8 Tirrenia
9 UY Proa Sur
10 Viola
11 Yerutí

Off map
  Camping La Aguada
  Palma de Mallorca
  Portobello
  Zen Boutique Apart Hotel

✖ **Where to eat and drink**

   Bahía (see 1)
12 El Sargo
13 Punto Sur
14 Tam-Barú
   Viola (see 10)

com; www.hostelibirapita.com; ⏰ all year. Just 5mins from the bus terminal & the beach, this friendly place has rooms around 2 interior patios behind the shopfront-style reception, where new arrivals are given a Google Map tour of the area. There are men-only, women-only & mixed rooms with 4–10 beds, & rooms for couples. A kitchen is

available, as well as a PC, Wi-Fi, cable TV, laundry service, bike rental & surfing lessons. Fairly poor b/fast inc (*09.00–11.00*). **$**

🛏 **La Balconada Beach Hostel** Playa La Balconada at rear of Punto Sur restaurant; ☎ 4479 6273; www.labalconadahostel.com; ⏰ all year. Cooler & more stylish than the other hostels, this is virtually on La Balconada Beach, 10–15mins' walk or free taxi from the terminal. It has shared rooms for 4 & 6, plus en-suite doubles, with kitchen, internet access (Wi-Fi & a PC) & open-air bar. Cash only. B/fast inc. **$**

🏠 **La Paloma Altena 5000 Hostel** Parque Municipal Andresito; ☎ 4479 6396; e lapaloma@ hosteluruguay.org; www.lapalomahostel.com; ☉ Nov–Apr. A small thatched place on the east side of Parque Andresito, with male, female & mixed dorms, this is the cheapest hostel in La Paloma; it's also the least clean & has the largest dorms (11 or 17 beds). A kitchen is available, as well as internet access. Continental b/fast inc. **$**

Camping

🏕 **Complejo de Cabañas Parque Andresito** Ruta 15 km1.5; ☎ 4479 6081; e complejoandresito@adinet.com.uy. In the woods between the terminal & the port, there are 3 sizes of cute thatched cabañas, all with cable TV (☉ *all year*). On the west side is the *zona de camping*, with pretty basic facilities (☉ *Dec–Mar*). There's Wi-Fi at reception only. **$$–$**

🏕 **Camping La Aguada** Ruta 15 km2.5; ☎ 4479 9293; e complejolaaguada@hotmail.com; ☉ all year. With tent space & cabañas, this is packed with students in high season & probably not a lot of sleeping takes place. Buses stop outside, & there are BBQ, electrical sockets & a laundry. **$**

✗ **Where to eat** There are family-style restaurants along Avenida Solari, and a Paseo Gastronómico with food stalls from the ANCAP petrol station to the Centro Cultural. All listings are included on the map opposite.

✗ **Bahía** Avda del Navío & Avda del Sol; ☎ 4479 9411; www.elbahia.com.uy. A long-standing restaurant serving a standard range of fish, steaks, chicken & pasta, as well as some salads. **$$$**

✗ **Punto Sur** Playa La Balconada; ☎ 4479 9462; ☉ Dec–Easter. You pay for the ideal beachfront location, but service is good & food is well presented; the menu is limited but this is the perfect spot for a bit of seafood at sunset. **$$$**

✗ **El Sargo** Mercurio & Ceres; ☎ 4479 7922. Across the road from the Bahía, this is a lively pizza & fish restaurant that's excellent value. **$$**

✗ **Viola** Avda Solari near Antares; ☎ 4479 6020. At the top of the main street, this has a good choice of fresh fish, as well as pasta & gnocchi. **$$**

🍨 **Tam-Barú** Avda del Navío & Avda Solari. Excellent ice cream. **$$**

Entertainment and nightlife La Paloma, and La Aguada in particular, has changed rapidly from a family-oriented resort to one dominated by youth, at least in the first half of January. Now up to 8,000 people a night head for the discos (US$10) in the woods between the port and La Aguada. These get going around midnight and close only at 08.00, when the party continues with dancing to car stereos for another hour or two. The best disco is said to be Pogo, followed by Arachanes and Hippie. A row of carritos opposite the discos sells hot dogs from 07.30. The noise and disruption may oblige the discos to be moved north to the junction of Ruta 10 and Ruta 15.

Some of the bar-restaurants listed above have live bands in summer and stay open late; other bars are along Avenida Solarí and Calle de la Virgen.

The Cine La Paloma (☎ *4479 7022; ☉ Dec–Mar; US$7*) is just south of the casino.

Shopping There are two supermarkets on Avenida Solarí: Los Jardines (☉ *summer 08.00–23.30 daily*) at the roundabout at its north end, and El Dorado (☉ *08.00–21.30 Mon–Thu, 08.00–22.00 Fri–Sat, 08.30–21.00 Sun*) at Sirio, opposite the casino. To the west at Delfín and Aries (south of the terminal) the Los Molles supermarket (☉ *summer 07.30–23.30 daily*) is also pretty good. Just south of the Hostel Ibirapitá, Pastas Oggi (Avda Paloma; ☉ *summer daily; rest of the year 09.30–13.00 Sat, 09.00–14.00 Sun*) sells ready-made meals (largely pasta) to heat up in your cabaña. A good bakery is Don Dante at the north end of del Iglesia.

Activities Surfing is the main sport here, with beaches that face south and east on either side of the headland. To the south, the Los Botes or Anaconda beach often has waves up to 150m long and 2m high; to the east the La Aguada beach is 7km long (stretching to La Pedrera) but gets crowded in summer as it's popular with Brazilian surfers. Surf shops are on Avenida Solarí, including Peteco Surf Shop (m *099 626726;* e *petecosurf@adinet.com.uy*), south of Sirio, and Surfshop (*junction of Avda Solarí & Avda del Navío*). The H2O Surf School (m *099 687554, 098 938373; www.h2Oescueladesurf.com.uy*) is at Solari and Titania and the Escuela de Surfing La Paloma (m *099 173078; www.surfinglapaloma.com*) is at Playa Los Botes.

Just west of the lighthouse, Playa La Balconada has particularly clear water and is popular with **swimmers**. To the east, **canoes** can be rented in the sheltered and very attractive Bahía Chica. Tiny Isla de la Tuna can be reached by swimming for about 20m.

Other practicalities

Banks Banco República (*Avda Solari & Titania*), with an ATM, is handily placed opposite the casino. Two exchange offices are Cambio Nelson (*Avda Solarí south of Antares;* ⊕ *Jan–Feb 08.00–22.00 daily; rest of the year 09.00–20.00 Mon–Sat*) and Cambio Maiorano (*Avda Solarí & Avda Del Navío;* ⊕ *09.00–19.00 Mon–Sat, 09.00–13.00 Sun*).

Bike hire The **Bicicletería El Topo** is on Calle de la Virgen just west of Avenida Solarí (✆*4479 7081*); there's also the Taller de Bicicletas (⊕ *09.00–13.00, 15.00–19.00*), a very basic shed opposite the police station on Avenida Paloma, near the terminal.

Communications The post office (⊕ *11.30–17.00 Mon–Fri*) is next to the casino. The Antel telecentro, which has free Wi-Fi, is on Avenida Solarí north of Avenida del Navío (⊕ *09.00–19.00 daily*). There's an internet café by the Hotel Viola on Avenida Solarí, and Cyber del Navío and the Barahona Cafetería-Cyber, both on Avenida El Navío east of Avenida Solarí.

Emergency services There's a 24-hour pharmacy just southwest of this junction, and a policlínica (✆ *4479 8928*) on Avenida Solarí between Sirio and Titania. And on the subject of health issues, there are plenty of dropped kerbs for wheelchairs here, thanks to Rotary. The police are on Avenida Paloma near the bus terminal (✆*4479 6017/6058*).

What to see and do Between March and October migrating southern right whales rest along Uruguay's Atlantic coast, on their way to and from breeding around Patagonia, and they may come within 200m of the shore. There's a whale observation platform in Costa Azul, immediately north of La Aguada, but they can also be seen from Cabo Santa María by the lighthouse.

In the central reservation of Avenida Solarí just south of Avenida del Navío, the skeleton of a southern right whale sits at the rear of a municipal building (⊕ *09.00–14.00 Mon–Fri*) that is the contact point for the **Organización para la Conservación de Cetáceos** (*Organisation for the Conservation of Cetaceans;* m *099 124144; www.ballenafranca.org*). Some of their excellent (Spanish-language) posters are on display in the windows. In early October each year the OCC organises the Semana de la Ballena Franca Austral (Southern Right Whale Week), including the National Day of the Whale, with many activities for schoolchildren in particular, here and in Piriápolis, Punta del Este and elsewhere.

It's well worth taking a trip to the **Laguna de Rocha**, an hour's walk west along the beach (10km by road), where you can almost see the only black-necked swans in Uruguay (up to 15,000 of them), as well as flamingos, and a total of 220 recorded bird species, as well as mammals such as nutria, carpincho, foxes and otters. Covering 72km^2, this is semi-fresh water, with an outlet to the sea opening in winter. Travel agencies can arrange for fishermen to take you out in boats. In any case you can see plenty of birds around the port, including green-barred woodpeckers, great grebes, Neotropic cormorants, kelp gulls and oystercatchers.

At the southern end of Avenida Solarí is the faro or **lighthouse** of Cabo Santa María (☉ *summer 08.00–sunset daily; rest of the year w/end & holiday afternoons; US$1*), opened in 1874 after the first attempt to build a tower ended in 1872 in a collapse that killed 15 workers. It's nicely set up, with red and green navigation lights beside the path from the gate to the door, and, on the beach to the south, hourposts that work as a sundial with the lighthouse as the gnomon.

The church at the west end of Antares is bare and barn-like, but a cool refuge on a hot day; mass is said at 19.00 'almost every day'.

NaturCiencia (*Ruta 15 km7.2, heading towards Rocha;* ✆ *4470 9065;* e *naturciencia@adinet.com.uy;* ☉ *Dec–Apr 11.00–20.00 daily; May–Nov 11.00–18.00 w/ends & school holidays; US$2.20*) is a *museo de ciencias interactivo* (interactive science museum). In addition to walk-in kaleidoscopes, trick mirrors and other fun stuff including magnetic black sand, there's a collection of skulls of over 100 mammals and birds, an olive ridley turtle shell and various strange plants. There are also disabled toilets, a play area and a souvenir shop.

LA PEDRERA From km6 of Ruta 15, north of La Paloma, Ruta 10 runs west to Laguna de Rocha and east for 7km to La Pedrera, La Paloma's more bohemian little sister. The name means 'stony place' and it feels rather Cornish, especially when the wind is blowing and the surf is rolling. It's currently very popular with the arty crowd, with new cafés, boutique hotels and architect-designed houses appearing, but it's hardly José Ignacio as yet, and there's still plenty of wildlife, including woodpeckers and tegu lizards crossing the sandy roads. Surfing is great here, but only for those with experience; on the south side of the village, Playa del Barco (Boat Beach) has deep water and consistent breaks up to 2m high, but the rusty bow of a cargo ship that sank in 1977 lies half-buried in the sand. Immediately below the cliffs at the end of Avenida Principal and to the northeast, El Desplayado (The Beachless) has perfect waves up to 2m high that run for up to 200m.

Getting there and away, and orientation Some Rocha–La Paloma **buses**, some starting in Montevideo (see page 87), make the ten-minute detour to La Pedrera, leaving you in the centre by the **OSE water tower**; six a day continue along Ruta 10 to Cabo Polonio, Valizas and Castillos. In high season local buses run hourly between La Paloma and La Pedrera. From here Avenida Principal leads southeast to finish at the cliff-top rambla. It's jammed solid with cars in January in the daytime, but closed to traffic in evenings from the water tower to one block from the sea; the first block east from the water tower is lined with craft stalls. Turning left (north) here brings you down to the beach, where new white-cube houses are appearing. You can loop back to the water tower; turning right, you'll swing around to some wood and metal sculptures just south of Avenida Principal.

For bus tickets, **COT** (✆ *4479 2164;* ☉ *10.00–18.00 daily*) is on Avenida Principal just east of the water tower, and **Cynsa** (☉ *13.00–17.00 daily*) and Rutas del Sol (✆ *4479 2425*) are on the same road close to the junction with Ruta 10.

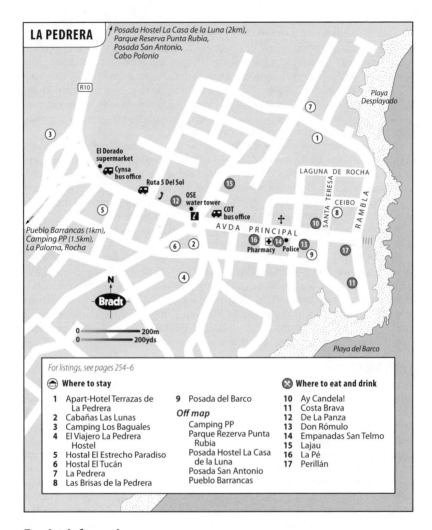

LA PEDRERA

↑ Posada Hostel La Casa de la Luna (2km),
Parque Reserva Punta Rubia,
Posada San Antonio,
Cabo Polonio

R10

Playa
Desplayado

El Dorado
supermarket
Cynsa
bus office
Ruta 5 Del Sol
OSE
water tower
COT
bus office

LAGUNA DE ROCHA

SANTA TERESA

CEIBO

RAMBLA

Pueblo Barrancas (1km),
Camping PP (1.5km),
La Paloma, Rocha

AVDA PRINCIPAL

Pharmacy Police

N

Bradt

0 ———— 200m
0 ———— 200yds

Playa del Barco

For listings, see pages 254–6

🛏 **Where to stay**

1 Apart-Hotel Terrazas de
   La Pedrera
2 Cabañas Las Lunas
3 Camping Los Baguales
4 El Viajero La Pedrera
   Hostel
5 Hostal El Estrecho Paradiso
6 Hostal El Tucán
7 La Pedrera
8 Las Brisas de la Pedrera

9 Posada del Barco
Off map
   Camping PP
   Parque Rezerva Punta
   Rubia
   Posada Hostel La Casa
   de la Luna
   Posada San Antonio
   Pueblo Barrancas

✖ **Where to eat and drink**

10 Ay Candela!
11 Costa Brava
12 De La Panza
13 Don Rómulo
14 Empanadas San Telmo
15 Lajau
16 La Pé
17 Perillán

Tourist information There's a tourist information office at the water tower (m *099 398847; www.lapedrera.com.uy;* ⊕ *10.00–21.30*), with toilets (⊕ *10.00–midnight in summer*).

🏠 **Where to stay** There's not a lot of budget accommodation here, other than campsites (located off Ruta 10 between La Aguada and La Pedrera) and hostels. All listings are included on the map above.

🏠 **Las Brisas de La Pedrera** Ceibo & Sta Teresa; ☏4479 2265; m 099 804656; e brisasreserve@ gmail.com; www.brisasdelapedrera.com; ⊕ Oct–Apr. Built in the early 20th century, this was refurbished & reopened in 2009 as a delightful boutique hotel filled with vintage 20th-century furniture. A block from the rambla & from Avda

Principal, it has 14 rooms with no phones or TVs, & an excellent breakfast. Green touches include supplying cold filtered water at night rather than plastic bottles. **$$$$$**

🏠 **Hotel La Pedrera** Camino del Indio & Costanera; ☏4479 2001; e hpedrera@adinet. com.uy; www.hotelesderocha.com; ⊕ mid-Aug–

254

mid-Jul. A 4-star hotel incorporating a seawater thermal spa (with indoor & outdoor pools), this is not the most stylish or up-to-date (there's only limited internet access), but rooms do have AC as well as cable TV. **$$$$$–$$$$**

🏠 **Posada San Antonio** Ruta 10 km234; 📞4470 9143; m 095 209334; www.sanantonio.com.uy. This boutique guesthouse, 6km east of La Pedrera, was originally a carpentry workshop lost in a forestry plantation; now it has 4 split-level rooms (2 with sea view), a good little restaurant, & a swimming pool in a round cattle tank. **$$$$$–$$$$**

🏠 **Apart-Hotel Terrazas de La Pedrera** Costanera; 📞4479 2102/2197; www.terrazasdelapedrera.com; ⏰ all year. Opened in 1999, this is an upmarket place where apartments have kitchenette, balcony, satellite TV & Wi-Fi; there are also several PCs downstairs as well as an open-air swimming pool, a pool table & a telescope for watching the sea. **$$$$**

🏠 **Hotel Posada del Barco** Santa Teresa; 📞4479 2028/2257; e posadadelbarco@adinet.com.uy; www.hotelesderocha.com; ⏰ all year. With a terrace facing the Playa del Barco, this friendly, arty place has a cafetería, salón de té & restaurant serving good seafood & lamb. **$$$$–$$**

🏠 **Parque Reserva Punta Rubia** Between Calle Chuy (km229) & Avda de las Maravillas (km230); m 099 616682; www.parquereserva.com.uy. This nature reserve, just east of the La Pedrera junction on Ruta 10, is home to native & farm animals & exotic birds & a great setting for horseriding & a canopy zip-line circuit. There's also accommodation in wooden cabins, with a swimming pool but without TV or internet, for total tranquillity. **$$$$–$$**

🏠 **El Viajero La Pedrera Hostel** 📞4479 2252; www.elviajerolapedrera.com; ⏰ Dec–Apr. In a quiet location 500m from the beach & 150m from Avda Principal. There are men-only & women-only dorms plus private doubles with bathroom & balcony, as well as a kitchen, BBQ, a wooden porch & garden with hammocks, free internet access, & bike & surfboard rental; surfing lessons can also be arranged. **$$$–$$**

🏠 **Cabañas Las Lunas** 📞4479 209; m 099 692882; e laslunaslapedrera@hotmail.com; ⏰ all year. In a tranquil location a block south of the water tower, there are 4 thatched cabins here for up to 6 people, with cable TV & BBQ. **$$**

🏠 **Hostal El Estrecho Paradiso** Golondrina 📞4479 2026; m 098 299844; e elestrechoparadiso@yahoo.com; www.hostalestrechoparadiso.com; ⏰ Christmas–Mar. Entering La Pedrera from Ruta 10 & taking the first right turn (opposite the supermarket), it's half a block to this stylish new hostel with kitchen, laundry, Wi-Fi & some disabled facilities. Shared dorms (4 beds) cost US$27 pp, private doubles US$64. **$$**

🏠 **Hostal El Tucán** 📞4479 2978; m 094 298019; www.lapedre.com. 1 block south of the water tower, this is an immaculate white modern house with small, clean rooms & a microwave but no real kitchen, & no breakfast. There's a pleasant garden with sunbeds. **$$**

🏠 **Posada Hostel La Casa de la Luna** Ruta 10 km230; 📞4470 2857; m 094 602271; e recepcion@lacasadelaluna.com.uy; www.lacasadelaluna.com.uy; ⏰ Dec–Mar. At Punta Rubia, 2km east of La Pedrera, this is the most stylish place to stay here, & one of the greenest. They'll pick you up from the bus & also run you down to the bars in La Paloma. There's a kitchen & BBQs, laundry facilities, cable TV & internet access. Bikes, books & DVDs are available, as are kite-surfing lessons (see page 256). You can also hike to the Cárcavas Milenarias, eroded rock formations full of fossils. Beds from US$16 (*US$37 for carnaval*) in 10-person dorms, US$24 (*US$43*) in 4-bed rooms, US$48 (*US$65*) in doubles; fully equipped tents are available for US$24 for 2. B/fast inc. **$**

🏕 **Camping Los Baguales** At the La Pedrera junction, km228.5; m 098 376954, 099 390567. **$**

🏕 **Camping PP** km226.5; 📞4479 2069; m 096 206464, 099 128545; www.campingpp.com.uy; ⏰ all year. 500m from the beach & 2km from La Pedrera. The campside has has shaded tent spaces, carpicabañas (tent-cabins), picnic tables, BBQs, electric sockets, soccer & volleyball pitches, restaurant, bar, shop & TV room. **$**

🏕 **Pueblo Barrancas** km227.5; 📞4479 2236; m 097 438404; www.pueblobarrancas.com; ⏰ all year. There's even 'glamping' 15mins' walk west along the beach. This *super-tranquilo* camp on a virtually private stretch of beach, offers yurts on wooden platforms hidden in the woods behind the dunes. Costs are US$80–180 for 2, US$190 for 4 inc b/fast, as well as 'military tents' costing US$80–180 for 2, & 3 cabañas costing US$110–260 for 2. **$**

✕ Where to eat Along Avenida Principal there are a couple of panadería-confiterías where locals gather early in the morning – opposite the church, **Empanadas San Telmo** serves tasty snacks – and there are a couple of ice-cream shops and some snack-bars. All listings are included on the map, page 254.

✕ La Pé Avda Principal, Posada El Torbellino; ☎ 4479 2122; m 094 408955; ⏰ Dec–Easter. In a walled garden 3 blocks from the rambla (with very few tables indoors), this is one of the best restaurants here, with a wide-ranging menu based on seafood, including sole, paella or langoustines in a sort of teriyaki sauce, as well as *buñuelos de algas* (seaweed balls), a vegetable tower or *jamón crudo*. Desserts are excellent, & there's a good wine list as well as house wine by the jug. $$$$$

✕ Perillán Avda Principal & Rambla; m 096 227683, 091 048949; ⏰ Nov–Easter. The cliff-top location is fantastic at lunchtime, while in the evening there's music, low lighting & a great atmosphere. The menu focuses on seafood, with a grilled fish of the day, brótola & shellfish risotto, all fresh & well presented. $$$$$

✕ Lajau Santa Teresa & Laguna de Rocha; m 099 922091; e lajaulapedrera@gmail.com; ⏰ 13.00–16.00, 21.00–01.00 daily. This friendly place serves a menu based on the seafood available on the day, perhaps shellfish tapas, grilled squid, fresh fish or pasta. $$$$

✕ Costa Brava Rambla; ☎ 4479 2051. A simple but decent seafood restaurant almost on the headland, with a view over miles of beach to the north & east. $$$

✕ De La Panza Avda Principal 418; ☎ 4479 2121; m 098 824314. In a nice older house near the water tower, this is known for its focaccia but also serves pasta, ravioli, fine salads & other dishes such as curried chicken, as well as exquisite desserts; excellent service too. $$$

✕ Don Rómulo Avda Principal & Palmares de Rocha; ☎ 4479 2820; e donromulo08@adinet.com. uy, marcoarrospide@hotmail.com; ⏰ noon–late daily in high season, Thu–Sun low. Friendly place that specialises in homemade pasta, especially ravioli, such as boar with butía sauce, or aubergine & tomato, as well as other pastas, gnocchi & pizza. Great salads are made from their own garden produce. $$$

✕ Ay Candela! Avda Principal & Santa Teresa; m 098 554007; e carolinaruda@gmail.com; ⏰ all year. Just a shack in a large garden, but it produces superb crêpes as well as pizza & seafood. $$

Events With so many cool kids and crazy artists here, there are quite a few interesting festivals: Vox y Pop on the first weekend of January, the Festival de Cortometrajes (*Short Film Festival*; ☎ 2708 2174; www.lapedrerashortfilmfestival. com) on the second weekend of January, a Jazz Festival at Easter and the biggest and best Desfile de Carnaval (Carnival Parade) on the Uruguayan coast. This was very popular but totally unorganised until 2012, when a teenager was killed by a drunken driver, but is now controlled by police and the Intendencia.

Activities For **surfing** lessons, contact the Escuela de Surf La Pedrera (m *099 744783*), who charge US$30 for a lesson or US$120 for five classes or three days. The Posada Hostel La Casa de la Luna (see page 255) offers kite-surfing courses.

Other practicalities The El Dorado supermarket is at the junction with Ruta 10. There is no bank here, but there's now an ATM near the bus offices, as well as the Locutorio Movistar (⏰ *11.00–14.00, 17.00–22.00 daily in season*), with PCs and Wi-Fi as well as phones. There's a police office (☎ *4479 2030*) opposite the little church on Avenida Principal.

CASTILLOS In the 30-odd kilometres between La Pedrera and Cabo Polonio ten balnearios were designated in the 1940s, but none was developed beyond a few houses at Punta Rubia and Oceanía del Polonio. This stretch of Ruta 10 is recently paved and now sees a few Rutas del Sol buses from Rocha to Chuy. At km255 a sign with a Chaplin-like tramp figure marks the dirt road that leads a couple of kilometres to the **Posada Buscavida** (✆ *4470 5207*; **$$$$**), an amazingly isolated boutique resort with ten rustic rooms, a fine restaurant/clubhouse and a beach bar.

Virtually all traffic takes Ruta 9 east from Rocha, passing a turning at km220.5 which leads south to the **Estancia Turística El Charabón** (✆ *4470 2403*; m *099 127345*; e *gsbarbaro@elcharabon.com*; *www.elcharabon.com*; ☼ *all year*; **$$$$$**), a 950ha working farm with around 650 Hereford cattle, 500 Hampshire Down sheep and 30 horses. Horseriding is the main activity here, including working with the cattle or a day ride to La Pedrera for a gallop along the beach. There's good birdwatching, or you can just enjoy the tranquillity and the big views over the surrounding plains. There's a swimming pool, Wi-Fi and satellite television. There are nine air-conditioned rooms (*US$500*), and rates include four excellent meals each day and guided rides.

Ruta 9 continues through 19 de Abril (km235, with fuel, food and drink) and passes the Parque Eólica Loma Alta, 16 wind turbines on a hill to the north; this was Uruguay's first wind farm, opening in 2008. Loma Alta has been known for its herd of Polled Hereford cattle, and is now diversifying into olive-growing. From around km246 you'll see the Laguna de Castillos to the south, with sand dunes beyond.

At km260 there's a small tourist information centre at the turning into the sleepy little single-storey town of **Castillos**, where you may have to change buses to reach Cabo Polonio or Valizas. With barely 7,000 inhabitants, it's still the third-largest town in Rocha. Rutas del Sol, COT and COTEC share an office at Ferrer 1201 and 18 de Julio, on the northwest corner of Plaza Artigas, where taxis wait. There's not much shade on the plaza, but there is a weak Wi-Fi signal (which works inside the bus office), a statue of Artigas (raised in 1966) and on the west side a modern church with some murals inside. It's two blocks east to the Banco República (*Ferrer & Pintos*), with an ATM, and another block to the Cynsa bus office (*Ferrer 1404*).

 Where to stay and eat

Castillos

🏠 **Hotel A Mi Gente** Lavalleja 1235, between Ferrer & 19 de Abril, east of the plaza; ✆ 4475 7273; m 099 871929; www.hotelamigente.com. uy. **$$$**

🏠 **Hostal La Vieja** González 1226 & 19 de Abril; m 098 242571, 099 875041; e hostellavieja.uruguay@gmail.com; http://

hostallaviejaturismouruguay.blogspot.co.uk. This new hostel has AC rooms, parking & Wi-Fi. **$**

✕ **La Strada** 19 de Abril 1375 & Pintos; ✆ 4475 7717; ☼ 12.00–16.00, 20.00–24.00 Thu–Sun. Not a place for a quick chivito, but for shrimp risotto, fish of the day with polenta, lamb or spaghetti with chicken pesto, all well done & very affordable. **$$$**

AGUAS DULCES Turning right just south of Castillos at km261.5, it's 10km to the **Estancia Guardia del Monte** (✆ *4470 5180, 4475 9064*; e *guardiam@adinet.com. uy*; *www.guardiadelmonte.com*; **$$$$$**), one of the most attractive and historic ranches that's open for visitors. Named after an old Spanish guardpost, the single-storey colonial house dates from 1785 and has a dining room like a *pulpería* or rural shop-bar, and in the kitchen a massive Danish cooking range salvaged from a shipwreck in 1884 and still in use. It's just 250m from the Laguna de Castillos, and you can swim, canoe or fish, as well as riding horses through the shallows and across the plains dotted with palms. You may see black-necked swans, spoonbills, egrets, herons or ducks, and can also visit the fascinating Monte de Ombúes (see page 263). The 1,000ha spread is a working ranch, with just a few rooms for guests (prices include some activities); however, day visits are possible, including a slap-up lunch (starting with a taste of *licor de butia* or butia palm syrup).

From the southeastern exit from Castillos (km265), Ruta 16 runs south to the coast. You'll see plenty of palm trees, but largely on the road verges because cows eat the young shoots elsewhere. It's hard to believe that in colonial times the *palmares de Rocha* grew too thick and close for people to get through. Turning left after 9.5km (km277.5 of Ruta 10, 50km east of La Pedrera) it's a couple of kilometres more to the tiny settlement of **Aguas Dulces**, a very laid-back resort with an unplanned jumble of bungalows close together, and a nudist beach (Playa La Sirena, about 2km east). Most visitors stay in rented houses and cabins, enjoying seafood and butia palm fruit, but there are various other options. Midway between the junction and the beach are the **Camping Aguas Dulces** (✆ *4470 5874;* **$**) and the **Aguas Dulces Resort Club** (✆ *4475 2235;* m *099 875699; http://aguasdulcesresortclub.com;* **$$$**), an attractively landscaped development of cabañas around a large swimming pool, with a bar (and pool table) and a parrilla restaurant. The cabañas have a full kitchen, cable television, indoor fireplace and a porch with outdoor barbecue; breakfasts and transfers are available.

Buses turn around just short of the beach and stop about 200m inland on the main Avenida Los Palafitos, before returning to the main road. Two blocks south of Avenida Los Palafitos on the rambla is the **Complejo Los Arinos** (*Cachimba y Faroles;* ✆ *4475 2161;* m *099 872504; www.complejoarinos.com;* **$$**), with six apartments and a restaurant. The **Hostel Vaimaca** (*Cachimba y Faroles;* m *091 311431, 098 042938;* e *cochongo2012@hotmail.com;* **$**) is a simple thatched hut on the beach at the north end of the rambla.

Other accommodation and eating options can be found on the excellent website www.aguasdulces.com.uy. There's a tourism office at the entry to Aguas Dulces and another where Avenida Los Palafitos meets the rambla (m *098 591662;* ☉ *summer 10.00–13.30, 17.30–19.30 daily*).

The best place to eat is Doña Tota (*Avda Palafitos & Rambla*), which is known for its pasta (canelones and sorrentinos) and *buñuelos de algas* (seaweed fritters), as well as good licuados. Frog's, on the rambla just south of Avenida Palafitos (m *098 698865; www.frogsrestoran.com*) is a lively place for fish, milanesas and snacks.

BARRA DE VALIZAS

From Aguas Dulces buses head west on another isolated section of Ruta 10 for 5km to km272, the start of a dirt road leading 4km south to Barra de Valizas, a similarly bohemian resort to Aguas Dulces, with stunning empty beaches that stretch for ever. Most buses continue on Ruta 10 to the Arroyo de Valizas (km267; for boats to the Monte de Ombúes; see page 263) and the Cabo Polonio terminal at km264 (see page 260) and then return to enter Barra de Valizas. Buses stop on Calle Rutas del Sol, immediately south of the main Calle Veiga, and just west of the centre of the village, with thatched wooden shacks serving as bars, food stores and rental cabins; there are plenty of hippies here, selling the usual beads and jewellery, as well as families in summer. In the evenings people hang out, playing guitars and singing by candlelight; many houses have no electricity and there are no street lights (and thus great night skies). However, in 2009 there were protests at plans to install street lights. Many of the shops and cafés open only for the summer season, but houses can be rented very cheaply so there are various alternative types here through the winter. There are plenty of free-range animals, and everyone seems to have a dog or three.

The main road, Calle Aladino Veiga, ends by the beach at the Plazoleta Fragata Leopoldina Rosa (named after a ship wrecked here in 1842), from where sandy tracks lead left to Aguas Dulces (6km along the beach) and right past a pond to the Arroyo Valizas. Between this stream and Cabo Polonio lie 40km² of sand dunes, the last significant remnants of the dunes that lined the whole of this coast from over 4,000 years ago until pines and other trees were planted from the end of the 19th century. They abut the granite Cerro Buena Vista (50m high), which marked the end of the Spanish–Portuguese border from 1750 to 1777; in 1752 a boundary stone was placed at the foot of the hill and can still be seen. Valizas is also associated with the French pirate (really more of a leather smuggler) Etienne Moreau, who bought the hides of stolen cattle from indigenous inhabitants from 1717 until he was shot in a skirmish with government troops here in 1720.

Tourist information Local tourist information is available from the **iLocal** mini museum (\ *4475 4033;* e *ilocal@adinet.com.uy;* ⏰ *high season*) on Artigas Da Costa, just south of Plazoleta Fragata Leopoldina Rosa. The museum is a collection of fossils and indigenous objects picked up in the dunes and elsewhere over the last few decades. You'll also find some information online at www.portaldevalizas. com.uy.

Where to stay Most people stay in rented houses or cabins – you'll see hand-painted alquilo signs, or you can ask at iLocal (see above) or in the shops. In peak season you should book something in advance through Casas en Valizas (m *099 103607;* e *casasenvalizas@gmail.com; www.casasenvalizas.com/alquiler*). Most cabañas consist of just a bedroom, sitting room and kitchenette, with a water pump and often no electricity, for US$40–60 a week in season; in winter a house can cost under US$100 a month.

It's possible to **camp** at La Comarca de Valizas or in the centre of the village, either in a yard with about 50 tentfuls of people sharing one toilet or in any other yard where you make friends with people renting a cabaña.

Posada Valizas Tomas Cambre 19; \ 4475 4067; www.posadavalizas.com. Just south of the Rutas del Sol bus office, this highly recommended guesthouse has just 6 rooms (2 with private bathroom), a sitting room with games & books & a delightful garden with deckchairs – it's all simple but very comfortable. **$$$$–$$$**

La Comarca de Valizas Halfway to Ruta 10, 1.8km from Barra de Valizas; m 099 177004/893668; e lacomarcadevalizas@gmail. com; www.lacomarcadevalizas.com.uy; ⏰ all year. An estancia house, built in 1900 & opened in 2006 as a *posada de campo* or country inn with camping (US$10 pp). With its large bedrooms it's ideal for families who want to let their children run free. The living room has a fireplace made of granite slabs & a wooden door from a wrecked ship; the former *pulpería* (rural shop) is now the dining room, serving largely their own organic products.

On relatively high ground, with native trees such as ombúes, it has good views of the sea, dunes & lagoon. Horseriding is available, as well as free transfers (every 2hrs) to the beach. **$$$–$$**

Posada Eireté \ 4475 4011; m 099 296600; e mariabelosoeirete@hotmail.com; http://posadaeiretevalizas.webs.com. The nicest place in the village, Eireté is run by an artist. It's composed of thatched cottages with 6 shared rooms combining rustic charm & modern comforts (including internet access), & organic food from local producers (the restaurant is open to all). **$$**

Hostel Valizas Aladino Veiga at Plazoleta Valizas; \ 4475 4045; m 094 925782; e hostelvalizas@hotmail.com; ⏰ all year. This bright & friendly hostel has shared rooms for 4, 6 & 8 & en-suite doubles. There's a patio with hammocks, Wi-Fi, a kitchen & snack-bar. B/fast inc. **$**

Where to eat There's excellent food at **Punto G** (*G Spot;* ⏰ *Dec–Feb*), a charming café by the small lagoon a block southwest from the main street, all with fresh local fruits and no artificial colorants, including homemade ice cream (with flavours such as butia, mburucuya, pitanga, dulce de leche, lemon and mint, and honey orange and ginger), cakes and desserts, toasted sandwiches, smoothies, coffees and teas. **Proa** (❧ *4475 4981; www.laproa.com.uy*), on the beach directly east from the end of Aladino Veiga, serves good fish, shellfish, milanesas and salads. Quite a few other places serve local seafood (such as crab empanadas), beer, milanesas and pizzas.

Activities Cabalgatas Valiceros, on Calle Tomás Cambre at the west end of the village (m *099 574685;* e *cabalgatasvaliceras@gmail.com; www.cabalgatasvaliceras. com.uy*), has a reputation as one of the best **horseriding** outfits around, offering excursions for anything between 90 minutes and ten hours. (In neighbouring resorts such as La Paloma you'll still see horses kept tied up under a tree (with luck) to just take tourists for an hour's ride on the beach.) Senderos Valiceros (*Aladino Veiga 294 & Pepe;* m *098 804946;* e *senderosvaliceros@gmail.com; www.senderosvaliceros.com*) offer hiking, bird and whale-watching, cycling, canoeing and kite-surfing.

Other practicalities There are almost no services here, and certainly no ATMs or anywhere to exchange money – the nearest ATMs are in Castillos and at the entry to Cabo Polonio.

CABO POLONIO Cabo Polonio – named after Joseph Polloni, captain of the *Nuestra Señora del Rosario*, wrecked here in 1753 (and not after a ship called the *Polonio*) – is one of the most alluring destinations in Uruguay for backpackers and others in search of isolation and tranquillity. It's a headland much like Punta del Este, La Paloma and José Ignacio, with brava and mansa sides; the Playa Sur (or Playa La Ensenada) offers surfers a great variety of waves, thanks to its constantly moving sandbanks, and the Playa de la Calavera (Beach of the Skull, to the northeast – so called because of the cattle slaughtered here by the indigenous people) is the only beach on the whole coast which faces east and northeast. The beaches are always virtually empty, and to the southwest you can walk all the way to La Pedrera, seeing little more than a few shanties and shipwrecks.The area has been inhabited for 14,000 years; in the 19th century (and until 1991) sea lions were hunted for their skins, and in the 1940s, when there was a brief fashion for hunting sharks for the vitamin A found in their livers, a few fishermen's shacks were constructed. This has been a *monumento natural* within the Bañados del Este Biosphere Reserve since 1976. In 2009 it was declared a national park and a 'protected cultural landscape', with hunting, mining and other damaging activities prohibited and tourism more tightly regulated. The legendary squatter settlement here – a collection of shacks and cabins that have sprung up on the point near the lighthouse – will not be removed or interfered with, but a modern reception centre has been built at the main road, with a ticket desk for jeep access (see opposite), a tourist information desk (m *099 094617;* ⊙ *09.00–19.00 daily*), ATM, Wi-Fi and Environmental Information Area (with an aerial photo on the floor showing the natural limit of the dunes, north of Ruta 10). Community-based non-profit organsations are now involved with planning issues and collecting rubbish. The government is taking a very restrained approach to tourism, realising that while mega-complexes like Punta del Este have their place, there's a need for diversity, and places like this are sought out by many. Cabo Polonio is developing in any case, and what was until recently a fishing village with a few hippies in summer shacks, and no fresh water or electricity (except for the lighthouse), is now a permanent settlement (population 88) with half-decent accommodation and seafood restaurants, many with generators or solar panels. Mobile phones now work in places, and some businesses even take Visa. The scene is a bit druggy in summer, but most people are just getting high on the isolation and natural beauty of the endless beaches of perfect sand.

There's been considerable over-grazing, and you'll still find cows in the unlikeliest places, looking for scraps of grass among the dunes which are the natural habitat of snakes, rodents and burrowing owls. Sea lions (*lobo marino de un pelo*) and fur seals (*lobo fino de dos pelos*) breed on the three rocky islets about a kilometre off the point, spending a lot of time on the point as well – do not get too close, as they can be aggressive. Pups are born between November and February; it's quite normal to find dead seal pups on the beach after storms, as there's less shelter on these islands than, for instance, on Isla de Lobos. You may also see right whales (July–November) and the odd orca or elephant seal. There are also otters, whales, dolphins, at least seven species of crabs, plus mussels, sea anemones, sponges, starfish, Darwin's toad, sea slugs, over 40 species of seaweed, and birds up to the size of petrels and albatrosses – although the most common birds are southern lapwings, semi-palmated plovers, gulls and oystercatchers.

Information is available online at www.cabopolonio.com.

Getting there and away

By 4x4 Cabo Polonio has no road access. The main way in is on 4x4 trucks which shuttle along a sandy track from the new Terminal Puerto de Polonio at km264½ on Ruta 10. Buses come here from Rocha via either Castillos or La Pedrera, and there's shaded car-parking (*US$6 day/US$9 overnight*). Until recently there was just one beat-up truck that made the journey when its owner saw fit; now there's a fleet of trucks with double-deck seating on the back, with a ticket desk (US$9 return) and regular departures (the minimum service leaves the Cabo on the hour and the terminal on the half-hour). The 7km journey takes about 30 minutes of slow rocking and rolling, on a wide track through pine trees and then following the coast for the last kilometre or so. This hurdle filters out most day trippers, although in fact it's perfectly easy to come for the day if you have accommodation elsewhere.

Across Ruta 10 from the terminal is the Refugio de Fauna Laguna Castillos, where a viewing platform has been provided with aid from the British Embassy; there's no information, but the Monte de Ombúes is visible in the distance across the damp meadows.

On foot or horseback From the Plazoleta Fragata Leopoldina Rosa in Barra de Valizas, a sandy track leads to the right for about half a kilometre past a pond, reaching the beach at the Arroyo Valizas, where a boat is usually waiting to ferry you across to the south side of the river (US$1). The arroyo is not deep but it's wide and fairly fast, and wouldn't be easy to wade.

Once across, it's about 7km to Cabo Polonio by the direct route across the dunes, or 9km if you follow the coast around Punta Castillos Grande. Taking the direct route, you should head up the highest dune, for the views as much as anything – inland you'll see a couple of shacks and scrubbier land with rock outcrops and some cows, while to the south is the rocky headland. Dunes stretch ahead for about 3km – head southwest as well as you can, and keep just to the left of the forest when you see it on a ridge ahead. Passing through the trees you'll come at once to a nice grassy place with views to the lighthouse of Cabo Polonio and the rocky islets and reefs to the east. Going down towards Cabo Polonio, you'll soon find a faint 4x4 track, ending up on the beach which is usually good firm going. It takes about two hours to hike from the Arroyo Valizas to the Cabo Polonio Hostel. A few also hike in from the terminal, which is hard work in loose sand, and definitely not recommended with a bike – you'll push all the way and still get punctures.

If you don't fancy the hike, you can do it on horseback – contact A Caballo a Polonio (✆ *4470 5386;* m *099 635441;* e *elparaiso@cabopolonio.com*), based at the Estancia Turística El Paraíso (*Ruta 10 km274.5;* ✆ *4470 5266*), where there's a child-friendly collection of turkeys, peacocks, Asian pheasants, carpinchos and boars. You can drive several hundred metres beyond the terminal and park for free if you're riding with them. From Barra de Valizas, Cabalgatas Valiceras (*Tomás Cambre;* m *099 574685;* e *cabalgatasvaliceras@gmail.com; www.cabalgatasvaliceras. com.uy*) will take you to the Cabo in 2½ hours.

🏠 Where to stay
There are other hostels, mostly only open in summer, and huts for rent.

🏠 **Hostería La Perla del Cabo** Playa de la Calavera; ✆ 4470 5125; m 099 921037; www. laperladelcabo.net; ⏲ all year. Near the point, this has tiny en-suite rooms, some with sea views, others just with skylights, & a decent candlelit restaurant. There's a generator & hot water, Wi-Fi & a new spa with reiki & mud treatments. B/fast inc. **$$$$**

🏠 **Posada Mariemar** ✆ 4470 5164/5241; m 099 875260; e mariemar@cabopolonio.com; ⏲ all year. A very normal-looking place near the point that doesn't altogether fit in here, but open for 40 years, with 6 comfortable rooms (all with bathroom & hot shower, & Wi-Fi soon) & its own generator, good restaurant & waterfront terrace. B/fast inc. **$$$$**

🏠 **Posada de las Noctilucas** m 095 310330; e posadadelasnoctilucas@cabopolonio.com. On the beach between the truck turnaround & the lighthouse, there are 3 doubles with sea view & 5 shared rooms, with solar hot water, solar LED lights & even internet access, as well as a restaurant offering fish, pizza & pasta. On the beach there's also a bar with deckchairs & a fire at night. **$$$**

🏠 **Hostal del Cabo** Playa de la Calavera; ✆ 4682 4900; m 099 307870/355378; e hostaldelcabo@cabopolonio.com; www. hostaldelcabo.com.uy; ⏲ mid-Dec–Feb & Easter. Small orange A-frame with shared rooms with 4 & 6 beds, 3 bathrooms, kitchen & electric lighting. B/fast inc. **$$**

🏠 **Hostel Lo de Marcelo** m 099 146139; e lodemarcelocabopolonio@gmail.com; ⏲ all year. Right at the turnaround point for the trucks,

this has 2- & 4-bed rooms with a kitchen & solar hot water & electricity. **$$**

🏠 **Posada de los Corvinos** Playa de la Calavera; m 098 565966; e vientodobien@ gmail.com; ⏲ all year. A pink house 300m from the centre of the settlement, this is a lovingly maintained Zen oasis of greenery, both botanical & ecological. It has 4 doubles (1 with private bathroom) & 1 shared room with 5 beds (& individual lockers), kitchen & living room with wood stoves (as well as solar power). There's a shared bathroom as well as an outdoor shower with solar-heated water. Books, games & guitars can be borrowed, & there's a kitchen. It also houses the community's library (⏲ 10.00–12.00 daily), depending largely on donated books. B/fast inc. **$$**

🏠 **Posada Santa Maradona** m 099 922371; e posadasantamaradona@yahoo.com.ar. Where the 'road' enters the settlement, there's a double & 2 4-bed rooms here, but on hot summer nights they're just as likely to take everyone off to sleep in the dunes or the forest. A kitchen is available, but at weekends there's usually a shared meal of roast lamb or pasta with their homemade bread. **$$**

🏠 **Cabo Polonio Hostel** Playa de la Calavera; m 099 000305/445943; e cabopoloniohostel@ hotmail.com; www.cabopoloniohostel.com. A 3-room wooden shack that's better inside than it seems outside, simply furnished & quite comfortable. The Argentine owner Alfredo is a trained chef who may cook up superb fresh fish by candlelight. There are 4-bed dorms & a double room, with LED lighs & a gas-powered hot shower. B/fast inc. **$$–$**

✗ Where to eat
There's no gourmet cooking here but the fish is as fresh as could be, and you can also enjoy the local speciality of *buñuelos de algas* (seaweed fritters).

✘ **Hostería La Perla** Playa de la Calavera; ⊕ all year. Near the point, with a wooden terrace that's almost in the sea, this is a nice friendly spot for seafood & good simple salads, with desserts such as pancakes with dulce de leche. $$$$

✘ **Posada Mariemar** Right on the point, a good restaurant that looks too decent for Cabo Polonio, serving fresh fish, scampi, meats & *buñuelos de algas*. $$$$

✘ **Duendes** By the road out (& opposite the main food shop, the Almacén Templao, which is open all year), this serves a huge salad of brown rice with tuna, fruit & egg, meat or vegetarian tarts, or fish & chicken; there's often live music from 23.00. $$$

✘ **La Golosa** m 094 778388; e lagolosa@ cabopolonio.com. On the main track towards the point, this restaurant-tearoom-café serves good food in the garden or the more hippyish interior (no shoes). The menu includes hummus, tabouleh, stir-fried vegetables, empanadas, crêpes, pizza & *feijao golosa* (Brazilian black beans). $$$

✘ **Arco Iris** Right at the truck turnaround, this is recommended both for its tarts & for crafts. $$

✘ **Lo de Dani** m 099 875584. Just towards the point from the truck turnaround, this serves decent paella, shellfish, fish, buñuelos de algas & pastas. $$

What to see and do The lighthouse, built in 1881–84, is 26m high (40m above sea level) (⊕ *10.00–13.00, 15.00–20.30; US$1*).

There are lifeguards on the first couple of hundred metres of each beach; surfing (best in spring and autumn) can be arranged with Chonga Surf School at the very basic Rancho de Chonga surfers' lodge (m *099 150933*) or Escuela de Surf Cabo Polonio (*Playa Sur*; m *099 026837, 095 788164*; e *poloniosurf@poloniosurf.com*).

Through the posadas and hostels it's possible to arrange horseriding (*about US$90/ day*), along the beach, through dunes and to the wetlands of the Arroyo Valizas. There are also boats which will take you out for half an hour to watch the sea lions. Walks with local guides (anything from 90 minutes to six hours) can be arranged through Senderos Cabo Polonio (m *091 340201; www.senderoscabopolonio.com*) – the walk along La Calavera beach to Cerro de la Buena Vista and back is best early in the morning or at sunset.

Monte de Ombúes At km267 of Ruta 10, 3km east of the start of the trail to Cabo Polonio, boats leave from the bridge over the Arroyo Valizas to the Laguna de Castillos and, on its east shore, the Monte de Ombúes (ombú forest). On the hour-long boat ride you'll see plenty of birds such as ducks, cormorants, gulls, herons, ibis, storks, kingfishers and teros, and perhaps even wood-rails, coscoroba swans, southern screamers or flamingos.

Ombúes grow along a 25km stretch of the lakeshore, but the main grove consists of about 100 of these odd trees with their stumpy trunks and seemingly random branches. In fact it's unclear whether the ombú is actually a tree or an overgrown bush – in addition to its weird shape, it has soft flaky wood that falls apart like a croissant, so that it gradually becomes hollow inside. This makes it hard to calculate their age by the normal technique of counting rings, but it seems that many of these trees are 500 – possibly as much as 800 – years old. It also means that they are not strong and can easily be blown over by a storm – hence their development in groves.

Laguna de Castillos, including the Monte de Ombúes, is one of the best-run areas within the biosphere reserve, with a very active ranger (☏ *4470 5191*) and a popular junior rangers' programme (Pequeños Guardaparques Castillos). The area is closed from March to December.

PUNTA DEL DIABLO From Castillos Ruta 9 continues northeast through an area of small estancias where you'll see *ñandues* (rheas) roaming. At km273 the

Camping and Parador El Cocal (↖ *4470 5832; www.elcocal.com.uy; US$7 pp*) is on a delightfully remote beach. At km280.5 a dirt road leads a couple of kilometres to the right to **Dunas La Esmeralda** (*www.dunasesmeralda.com*), a very isolated spot with plans for major development; there's accommodation at **Cabañas del Sol** (↖ *4470 5005; www.cabasol.com; $$*), with cabins for two or four people, with or without kitchen; and **Cabañas El Pinar de la Esmeralda** (m *093 713820; www. elpinarapart.com.ar;* ⊕ *all year; $$*); and camping at **La Esmeralda Resort** (m *099 618602;* ⊕ *Dec–Easter*) and **Camping y Cabañas Oasis de Paz** (↖ *4470 5364*). You can **eat** at the **Restaurant Du Chef** at the Cabañas del Sol, the **Parador Dunas** or **Bar y Sandwich La Especial**.

After passing through low flat country beside the Laguna Negra (17,500ha), at km298 (91km from Rocha) you'll come to the turning to Punta del Diablo, a more upmarket and international version of Barra de Valizas. A paved road leads south for 4km to this colourful fishing village that over the summer months becomes a funky surfers' resort, although its sandy beaches are never too crowded.

There are good fish restaurants and bars in the village, and the beaches are beautiful in both directions. The east-facing Playa del Rivero (or Playa Pescadores) has waves up to 2m in height, and easy surfing when the wind is from the southwest. Beyond the Punta del Rivero, to the northeast, the Playa Grande continues for miles, past the Parque Nacional Santa Teresa. The Playa de la Viuda faces south-southeast and has powerful multi-peak waves, forming large barrels in the shallow shoals. This is less developed (with even fewer street signs), but affluent Argentines and Brazilians are now building modernistic new houses similar to those in José Ignacio. But there's none of the chacra development that is so big there, and only a couple of real-estate agents. The roads are all sand, some impassable, and there are lots of happy free-range dogs looking to adopt you for a few hours.

At the south end of the Playa Pescadores, where fishermen unload their boats and stalls sell fresh fish, a path leads east past a craft market on to the rocky point, with sea anemones in rock pools. There's no lighthouse here, but there's a small light with a very naff statue of Artigas and the text of his letter to Bolívar about respecting the Uruguayan flag.

For further information and accommodation see the excellent website www.portaldeldiablo.com.uy.

Getting there and away Most **buses** heading for Chuy (some from Punta del Este, as well as Montevideo, and a couple via Cabo Polonio; see page 87) drive 2km down the access road to drop passengers off at a new terminal, from where minibuses cover the remaining 2km to the centre (m *099 875119; every 30mins; US$1.25*).

Tourist information There's a tourist information desk at the bus terminal (↖ *4472 3100;* m *099 298847;* ⊕ *08.00–21.00 daily in summer*), toilets and a snack-bar. There's also a tourist information shack (⊕ *summer 14.00–18.00 daily*) at San Martín and Baldomir, in the heart of the resort.

⌂ **Where to stay** The listings below are less liable than others to be closed out of season. Most South American visitors stay in cabañas, which are easily available on the spot (*about US$40–60 for 2 or 3, US$70+ for 6*); look for alquila ('for rent') signs. You can also try the two-storey thatched cabins listed below. About two dozen **hostels** have sprung up in the last few years, mostly catering for the all-night party crowd. All listings are included on the map, page 266.

Hotels

⌂ **La Viuda del Diablo** San Martín, Playa de la Viuda; m 099 681138; www.laviudadeldiablo. com. The chic new place to stay in the dunes west of the point, & run by an Argentine interior designer, the 'Devil's Widow' is a posada-resto & beach-bar with 9 rooms with jacuzzi & floor-to-ceiling windows. There's an excellent little restaurant (with good vegetarian options) & service is faultless. **$$$$$**

⌂ **Aquarella** Calles 5 & 12; ☎ 4477 2400; m 094 510000; e aquarella.puntadeldiablo@ gmail.com; www.hotelaquarella.com; ⊕ all year. A 5-star apart-hotel with AC apartments, with cable TV & Wi-Fi, as well as a spa-jacuzzi, swimming pool & bar, & a restaurant that offers some of the finest dining in town. **$$$$**

⌂ **Hostal del Diablo** Avda Central; ☎ 4477 2667; www.hostaldeldiablo.com; ⊕ all year. An attractive 2-storey thatched building around a garden, with 16 en-suite doubles, a 10-person cabaña, swimming pool & TV lounge. **$$$$**

⌂ **Hostería del Pescador** Bvar Santa Teresa km2; ☎ 4477 2017; m 098 772704; e hosteriadelpescador2012@hotmail.com. An attractive place in a fairly tranquil location with 16 rooms for up to 6, & restaurant, swimming pool & pool table. **$$$$**

⌂ **Nativos Posada** Santa Teresa 215; ☎ 4477 2161; m 099 641394; www.nativos.com.uy. In a delightful & spacious garden close to the centre, this welcoming & exquisitely designed new place has double & quadruple rooms plus en-suite dorms, & a fine restaurant serving fish, lamb, boar or ñandú, seasonal vegetable dishes & tapas. **$$$$**

Cabañas

⌂ **Cabañas Amanacer** Next to Cabañas Los Apaches on Baldomir; ☎ 4477 2138; m 099 867000

⌂ **Cabañas Bien al Este** Playa la Viuda; ☎ 4477 2102; m 099 849062; www.bienaleste.com.uy; ⊕ all year. **$$**

⌂ **Cabañas Del Rey** Bvar Santa Teresa west of Miramar; ☎ 4477 2025. With an attractive paddling pool & minigolf. **$$**

⌂ **Cabañas Los Apaches** San Martín; ☎ 4477 2040; e losapaches10@gmail.com. **$$**

⌂ **Vilasar de Mar** calles 9 & 8; ☎ 4477 2641; m 099 475061; e agrestepuntadeldiablo@hotmail. com. Gay-friendly cabañas 80m from the sea. **$$**

Hostels

⌂ **El Diablo Tranquilo** Avda Central, north of Tonino (Calle 12); ☎ 4477 2647; www. eldiablotranquilo.com; ⊕ all year. For many foreign travellers, visiting Punta del Diablo is synonymous with staying in this beautifully designed boutique hostel, which has become a destination in itself thanks to its American owners. Opened in 2007, it's built around a large thatched hall with sofas & an open fireplace in the reception area downstairs. On the mezzanine level there are computers, a foosball table & a somewhat cramped kitchen. Accommodation is in mixed or women-only dorms, private rooms for 1, 2 or 4, or 2 suites with private bathroom (& bathrobes), fireplace & balcony with hammock. There are also 28 newly added beds at the beachfront pub (see page 267) including 4 penthouses. The helpful staff can arrange hiking or horseriding along the beach & into the Santa Teresa National Park, or surfboard rental (*US$15/hr, US$20/day, wetsuit US$10/15*) or lessons (*US$15/hr*). **$$$**

⌂ **Hostel El Nagual** Bvar Santa Teresa km1; ☎ 4477 2009; m 099 824164; e hostelelnagual@ gmail.com; www.hostelelnagual.com; ⊕ mid-Dec–Easter. On the main road, 1km from the terminal towards the village, this is one of the original & more basic hostels here, with rooms with 2, 3, 4 & 6 beds, 4 clean bathrooms & a kitchen. There's a thatched common room with cable TV & Wi-Fi inside & hammocks in the large garden, where there's also room for a few tents, as well as a couple of cabañas. Simple b/fast inc. **$$**

⌂ **Que Puedo Hacer Por Ti?** San Martín & Playa La Viuda; ☎ 4477 2552; m 093 824138; www.quepuedohacerporti.net. A new boutique hostel in a striking modern house with 2 swimming pools & AC rooms with jacuzzis; however the service may not always be up to scratch. **$$**

⌂ **Bitácora Hostel** Avda Central & Calle 24; m 095 897090/100; www.bitacorabar.com/index. php/hostel. The ultimate party hostel, under the same ownership as Punta del Diablo's leading disco; it has dorms for 6, 8, 10 & 12 people, a garden with swimming pool & open-air bar, plus kitchen & resto-bar. **$**

⌂ **Hostel de la Viuda** San Luis & Nueva Granada; ☎ 4477 2690; m 098 193136; e hosteldelaviuda@yahoo.com.ar; www. hosteldelaviuda.com. In a solid 2-storey modern

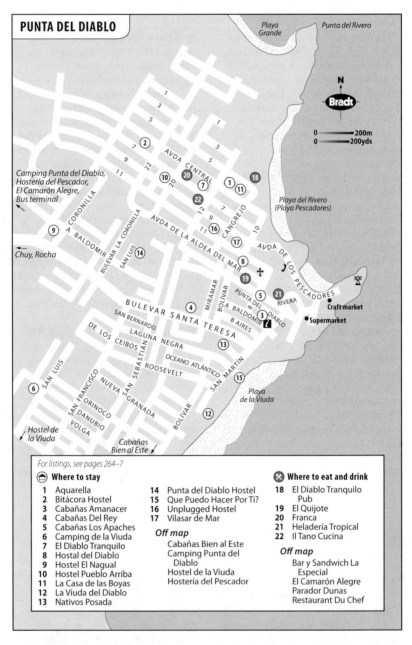

PUNTA DEL DIABLO

Playa Grande

Punta del Rivero

N

Bradt

0 ——— 200m
0 ——— 200yds

Camping Punta del Diablo,
Hostería del Pescador,
El Camarón Alegre,
Bus terminal

Playa del Rivero
(Playa Pescadores)

Chuy, Rocha

AVDA CENTRAL

CANGREJO

AVDA DE LA ALDEA DEL MAR

AVDA DE LOS PESCADORES

RIVERA

CORONILLA

A BALDOMIR

BULEVAR LA CORONILLA

SAN LUIS

MIRAMAR

BOLIVAR

PUNTA DEL DIABLO

A BALDOMIR

B AIRES

Craft market

Supermarket

BULEVAR SANTA TERESA

SAN BERNARDO

DE LOS CEIBOS

LAGUNA NEGRA

OCEANO ATLÁNTICO

ROOSEVELT

SAN SEBASTIÁN

SAN MARTÍN

BOLIVAR

SAN LUIS

SAN FRANCISCO

NUEVA SAGRANADA

SAN DANUBIO

VOLGA

ORINOCO

Playa
de la Viuda

Hostel de
la Viuda

Cabañas
Bien al Este

For listings, see pages 264–7

⌂ **Where to stay**

1	Aquarella
2	Bitácora Hostel
3	Cabañas Amanacer
4	Cabañas Del Rey
5	Cabañas Los Apaches
6	Camping de la Viuda
7	El Diablo Tranquilo
8	Hostal del Diablo
9	Hostel El Nagual
10	Hostel Pueblo Arriba
11	La Casa de las Boyas
12	La Viuda del Diablo
13	Nativos Posada
14	Punta del Diablo Hostel
15	Que Puedo Hacer Por Ti?
16	Unplugged Hostel
17	Vilasar de Mar

Off map

Cabañas Bien al Este
Camping Punta del Diablo
Hostel de la Viuda
Hostería del Pescador

✕ **Where to eat and drink**

18	El Diablo Tranquilo Pub
19	El Quijote
20	Franca
21	Heladería Tropical
22	Il Tano Cucina

Off map

Bar y Sandwich La Especial
El Camarón Alegre
Parador Dunas
Restaurant Du Chef

house with a large garden with hammocks &
swimming pool, there are comfortable doubles &
dorms for up to 6; it's 10mins' walk from the beach
with bikes available & a transfer van. **$**

⌂ **Hostel Pueblo Arriba** Calles 9 (La Coronilla)
& 20; ☎ 4477 2279; m 098 874766/869851; www.

puebloarriba.com. Attractive thatched buildings in
a wooden stockade, with a lively bar; dorm beds &
private rooms. **$**

⌂ **La Casa de las Boyas** Calle 5 (Las Corvinas),
Playa del Rivero; ☎ 4477 2074; m 099 661218;
e arembare@adinet.com.uy; www.

lacasadelasboyas.com. An attractive hostel on wooden piles with a big deck, a bar-restaurant, & a selection of art & archaeological remains; there's a very good breakfast. **$**

🏠 **Punta del Diablo Hostel** Sarandi & Ciudad de Rocha; 📞4477 2655; www. puntadeldiablohostel.com; ⏱ mid-Dec–mid-Apr. This HI-affiliated hostel has shared dorms & camping space, kitchen, TV lounge, free internet & free use of bicycles. **$**

🏠 **Unplugged Hostel Punta del Diablo** Calle 9 between 10 & 12; 📞4277 2048; www. unpluggedhostel.com/puntadeldiablo. A rather anonymous place in single-storey wooden huts, but the basics are there – kitchen, free Wi-Fi & towel & bike rental – & it's just 200m from the beach. Hi members pay just US$16–20 for a dorm bed (non-members US$20–44), including breakfast. **$**

Camping

⛺ **Camping de la Viuda** 📞4477 2228; www. campingdelaviuda.com; ⏱ all year. On the edge of the village (take Danubio to the right from San Francisco) this is smaller than the Camping Punta del Diablo, & decently managed, with free Wi-Fi throughout & a mini market (⏱ *mid-Dec–Feb*). Camping from US$10 pp; also 4-person cabins. **$$**

⛺ **Camping Punta del Diablo** Bvar Santa Teresa km2.5; 📞4477 2060; e campingpuntadeldiablo@yahoo.com.ar; www. portaldeldiablo.com.uy/camping; ⏱ all year. A pleasant wooded site with 175 pitches & cabañas, electricity, BBQ, bar, restaurant, laundry & shop, huge swimming pool, & hourly shuttles to the village. In season it can become a crowded tent city. **$**

✕ Where to eat
There are quite a few lively little fish shacks and empanada stands near the fishing harbour and craft market. All listings are included on the map opposite.

✕ **El Camarón Alegre** Ruta 9 km298; 📞4477 2263/2055; e camaronalegre@hotmail.com; www.portaldeldiablo.com.uy/elcamaronalegre; ⏱ all year. This ordinary pink house, about 80m from the Punta del Diablo junction with Ruta 9, is a temple to Slow Food & regional Rochense cuisine. Specialities include *sirí* (crab), *centolla* (king crab), seaweed ravioli, shellfish salad, paella, *gatuzo* (a small shark), sole, *jabalí* (boar) & the always excellent 'Elizabeth's choice'. Desserts include *chajá* (see page 69), apple pancakes with a caramel sauce or a sublime butía mousse. Service is friendly & enthusiastic & prices are very reasonable. **$$$$$**

✕ **El Diablo Tranquilo Pub** Calles 5 & 10; ⏱ from 12.00 daily. On the beach a couple of blocks from their hostel, this stylish place serves excellent food & is also a great place for an afternoon drink, an evening pub session or a full-moon party. Dishes include salads, grilled fish of the day, grilled meats & pasta, with crumble or cheesecake to follow. They have good Uruguayan wines &, amazingly, 3 types of draught Mastra beer from Uruguay's original craft brewery. **$$$$**

✕ **Franca** calles 20 & 7; 📞4477 2619; www. franca.com.uy. One of the best restaurants here, with lots of fish dishes (including risotto & pasta) as well as main-course salads & steak. **$$$$**

✕ **El Quijote** Aldea del Mar & Calle 8 (Belgrano); 📞4477 2258; m 099 392633. A reliable & fairly formal parrilla, also serving pizza. **$$$**

✕ **Il Tano Cucina** Paseo del Rivero, calles 9 & 12; 📞4477 2538; m 096 589389. Quite a way from the centre but well worth seeking out for fine Italian food (the chef-patron spends 8 months of the year there), mainly pasta & fish, as well as the usual grilled meats. **$$$**

🍦 **Heladería Tropical** Rivera. An ice-cream shop right at the centre of the action. **$**

Other practicalities
In practical terms, the centre of Punta del Diablo is San Martín, the end of the asphalt access road. There's a police office here and a couple of supermarkets (La Barca and El Vasco; both closed in winter); there are also a couple of supermarkets a kilometre out on Bulevar Santa Teresa. In high season you'll find a couple of internet places dotted around, as well as restaurants, cafés and bakeries. The only ATM is at the upmarket new Paseo del Rivero shops at calles 9 and 12.

Surfboards can be rented just below the craft market. Surfing lessons (*about US$25/hr*) and horseriding can be arranged through your accommodation, as well as birdwatching by Laguna Negra and volunteering at the Karumbé Project in La Coronilla (see page 269). A rental car can be useful, or you can take a taxi one-way for visiting the Parque Nacional Santa Teresa and walk back. Alternatively you can borrow bikes or hike or ride horses along the beach.

PARQUE NACIONAL SANTA TERESA At km302 of Ruta 9 a cloverleaf junction gives access to Laguna Negra to the west and the Parque Nacional Santa Teresa to the east. The national park is based around the historic Fortaleza Santa Teresa, although the entry to the fort is further north at km306. Between the volcanic Cerro Rivera (at the southern end of the national park) and Cerro Verde (at the northern end) is an area of native parkland with plenty of palm trees and native birds. It's dotted with campgrounds and is very popular in summer, especially with Brazilians. It's well set up and maintained, with some good boardwalks and birdwatching miradores.

Tourist information Buses pull off at km302 and stop at some new wooden ticket offices on the old road 100m south of Ruta 9; from here an avenue of palms leads to a junction with the so-called Capatacia to the left, where some colonial buildings house the park visitor centre (⊕ *08.00–12.00, 14.00–18.00 daily; free*) and a new environmental information centre with multi-media displays (⊕ *14.00–20.00 daily*), as well as a shop, a restaurant, an ATM and Antel phone office and, nearby, a 19th-century hothouse, the *invernaculo* (⊕ *08.00–19.00 daily*), amid formal gardens and pools.

Where to stay Camping Santa Teresa (✆ *4477 2101;* e *cabanas.santateresa@hotmail.com; www.sepae.webnode.es;* ⊕ *early Dec–Easter;* $) has spaces for 2,500 tents and 1,200 caravans, as well as 18 cabañas; electricity and barbecues are provided, and it's all very cheap and full of young people. In fact the park and campsite are managed by the army, who are friendly but not always the most efficient at telling you where to pitch your tent. Choose your site with care: La Moza, at the northern end of the park, is full of partying surfers in summer, while Cerro Chato is quieter. A tent for four costs US$18–45 (for a minimum of three nights), and there's hostel accommodation from US$14 per person.

Activities Surfing is very popular (especially with Brazilians at Mardi Gras). Playa del Barco and Pesqueros de Playa Grande are good. Playa La Moza, to the north is one of the best in Uruguay, with right-hand waves 500m long from about 300m off the beach. There's a beach-bar here, the only one in the area, where you can also rent surfboards. Playa Cerro Chato, near the centre of the park, is partly sheltered from the wind, and always busy with campers from the nearby site.

What to see and do From the Capatacia, tracks lead to the camping sites, east to the Playa del Barco and north to the fort via the *pajarera* (aviary), which houses various colourful birds and also monkeys and rabbits. There are ducks in a nearby pond, where you might also see an otter. Elsewhere in the park you may see axis deer (*Axis axis*), introduced from south Asia, as well as both candelabra and prickly pear cacti, plentiful cotorras, swallows, field flickers, armadillos and semi-wild cattle. Ñandues (rheas) can wander in to the campsites, and whale-watching is possible in season on the coast.

From the junction at km302 a road also leads west to Potrerillo de Santa Teresa, on the north shore of Laguna Negra, where there's a **biological station** run by Probides (*Programa de Conservación de la Biodiversidad y Desarrollo Sustentable en los Humedales del Este;* \ *4470 6028, 4472 5005; www.probides.org.uy*), with an exhibition including indigenous relics. You can take tours in 4x4 vehicles and boats, to see birds, carpinchos and the cerritos or mounds left by the indigenous people.

Fortaleza Santa Teresa (⊕ *10.00–19.00 daily; US$1*) Construction of the Fortaleza Santa Teresa was begun in 1762 (on St Teresa's Day, 15 October) by the Portuguese Colonel Tomás Luis Osorno. It was captured by Ceballos in 1763 and completed by the Spaniards. In 1826 it was definitively captured from Brazil by Colonel Leonardo Olivera (1793–1863), and was held by the Blancos during the Guerra Grande. It was very run-down by 1919 when President Baltasar Brum visited, and was restored in 1927–31.

Opposite the entry to the fort is the Posta del Viajero restaurant, and a small cemetery. Inside the fort's buildings you'll see lots of mainly 18th-century uniforms (mostly in prints), guns and pikes, and the forge and kitchen. In the sacristy are ceramic medicine jars, healthcare being part of the chaplain's role; there's also a Bible with onionskin pages. Some cannons dating from 1813 stand on the ramparts, from where there's a view over Laguna Negra.

Getting there and away Buses will tend to assume you want the Capatacia, but you can ask to be dropped at km306, where the fort is visible about 1km east, turning right at the first junction. To the left, the road continues to a statue of Colonel Oliveira and a national park gate, from where pedestrians can continue to the Punta de la Moza beach and campsite, at the northern end of the park. It's tempting to walk to the park's southern part from Punta del Diablo, but it's not easy to know where to turn inland from the beach – it's easier to take a bus to the fort (heading towards Chuy) and walk the 6km back to Punta del Diablo.

LA CORONILLA Ruta 9 passes the Aduana La Coronilla (where there's no real Customs check, but there is a birdwatching hide just north) at km311 and the new four-star **Hotel Parque Oceanico** (*www.hotelparqueoceanico.com.uy*; **$$$$$**) at km312.5. It crosses the Canal Andreoni, built to irrigate the rice plantations in the interior, just before km314 where a tourist information office (m *099 466132;* ⊕ *10.00–18.00 daily*) stands at the entry to **La Coronilla**. This is a small beach resort that's known for its fishing and is of interest to tourists mainly because of the **Marine Turtle Centre**, run by a group called Karumbé (*Avda Giannattasio km30.5 & Roma, Montevideo;* m *098 614201, 099 917811;* e *karumbemail@gmail.com; www.karumbe.org*), which welcomes volunteers to help with its work of protecting marine turtles (the green turtle, *Chelonia mydas*; loggerhead turtle, *Caretta caretta*; olive ridley turtle, *Lepidochelys olivacea*; and leatherback turtle, *Dermochelys coriacea*).

Cerro Verde, just south on the edge of the Parque Nacional Santa Teresa, is an important feeding area for juvenile green turtles, many of which die after being caught in fishing nets. Cerro Verde became Uruguay's first Coastal-Marine Protected Area in 2007 (covering 1,700ha on land and over 7,000ha offshore), and is part of the Sistema Nacional de Areas Protegidas (SNAP), the new national system of protected areas. There are also various dolphins, sharks, seabirds and sea lions here, as well as migrating right whales in season. Karumbé ('turtle' in Guaraní) works with local fishing people and holds many public events including

5

turtle festivals and turtle camps, when children help with tagging and rehabilitation of stranded turtles. The Karumbé field station is on the beach in La Coronilla (⊕ *Jan–Apr 10.00–19.00 daily*), and volunteers are welcome to help with cooking and cleaning, as well as caring for turtles, monitoring the local fishing industry and working with researchers.

Buses enter on the main street, Leopoldo Fernández, where there are COT and Rutas del Sol ticket offices as well as a police station and policlínica.

The **Hotel Las Maravillas** is at Fernández and Escudo del Mar (✆ *4476 2089*; m *099 469630*; **$$$**) and other hotels, including the **Costas del Mar** (✆ *4474 2781*; **$$$**) and Rivamare (✆ *4476 2986*; e *hotalrivamare@hotmail.com*), are on the beach about half a kilometre north. Information on accommodation is available online at www.lacoronilla.com.uy. For **Camping La Coronilla** (✆ *4474 1611, 4476 2608*; ⊕ *mid-Dec–Easter*; **$**), turn off Ruta 9 at km314.5; it has plenty of space, with electric lighting, barbecues and a shop.

CHUY Ruta 9 continues northeastwards through more park-like country, passing the turning to Barra del Chuy (see page 273) at km331 and reaching the Aduana Chuy at km336, where the main road swings right to bypass the town and proceed directly into Brazil. Buses take this then swing left on to Samuel Priliac, into the centre of the little border town of Chuy, 2km north and 340km from Montevideo (five hours by bus). The Uruguayan and Brazilian border posts are respectively 2km and 3km from the actual border, and people can move freely in the area between them, including Chuy and its Brazilian twin, Chuí. Buses will stop at Customs (Aduana) for you to have your passport stamped, but only if you ask – otherwise you'll have to hike back. There's a **tourist information** office there (✆ *4474 4599*; e *citchuy@mintur.gub.uy*; ⊕ *09.00–17.00 daily*), and another very helpful one (with WCs) on the plaza (*Artigas & Arachanes*; ✆ *4474 3627*; e *infochuy@turismorocha.gub.uy*; ⊕ *all year 09.00–21.00 daily*).The centre is tiny, soon giving way to unpaved residential roads. There's no bus terminal, with bus companies using their offices near the plaza, which is between Oliveira and Artigas a block south of Avenida Internacional, the wide boulevard that runs along the border (technically Avenida Brasil on the Uruguayan side and Avenida Uruguay on the Brazilian side). This area is dominated by 'free shops', ie: duty-free stores, as well as a **casino** (⊕ *14.00–01.00 Tue–Thu, 14.00–02.00 Fri–Sat*) on the Uruguayan side. Prices in the free shops are posted in US dollars, but you can pay in Uruguayan or Brazilian currency, and can of course import the goods freely into either country.

Getting there and away Cynsa/Nuñez, Rutas del Sol and COT are all on the block of Oliveira between the plaza and the border; each sends half a dozen **buses** a day to Montevideo (see page 87) as well as some to La Paloma and Punta del Este. Some buses also call at Barra del Chuy. Expreso Chago (*Avda Brasil at San Miguel, near Hotel Internacional*) has slower services to Montevideo via Lascana, Aiguá and Ruta 8.

Into Brazil Ruta 9 passes around the east side of Chuy, becoming BR-471 in Brazil. You'll need to clear Uruguayan Immigration and Customs at the Aduana, 2km short of town, and the Brazilian equivalent at the Policía Federal post nearly 3km towards Pelotas. Buses will stop as long as you ask, and the procedures don't take long. If you're on an international bus (with EGA or TTL – see pages 54–6) it'll all be taken care of without your needing to leave the bus.

In Chuí, Brazil (or Brasil as it's written locally, of course), there are more hotels, but they cost more than in Uruguay. The Rodoviario (bus terminal) is at Ruas Venezuela and Chile, two blocks from the border at Laguna de los Patos (a block to the right (east) from Avenida Argentina, the continuation of Artigas). Buses run from Chuí to Pelotas (*5 daily, US$15, 4hrs*), Rio Grande (*07.00 & 15.30 daily; US$12; 5hrs*), Porto Alegre (*12.00 Mon–Sat; 23.00 Sun–Fri; US$33–40; 7¾hrs*) and Florianópolis (*01.30 Sun; 20.30 Sun–Fri; US$60; 14hrs*).

Where to stay There's not a great choice of hotels (though there are others on the Brazilian side and in the beach resort of Barra del Chuy; see page 273); see www.chuynet.com/guia/hoteles.htm for information.

Hotel Alerces Laguna de Castillos 578, just off Artigas; 4474 2260; e alerces@adinet.com. uy. A motel-style place with rooms that are not huge but are light & clean. Use of swimming pool & PC or Wi-Fi included. Breakfast costs extra. **$$$**

Hotel Internacional Avda Brasil 679; 4474 2153/2055; e hotel@adinet.com.uy. Simple but central; some rooms have AC, & there's Wi-Fi & a good breakfast. **$$$**

Nuevo Hotel Plaza On the plaza at Artigas & Arachanes; 4474 2309; e hotelplaza@hotmail. com; www.hotelplaza.chuynet.com. The best hotel in town, a relatively grand 3-star. There's also the El Mesón del Plaza restaurant (see below). **$$$**

Etnico Hostel Laguna Negra 299; 4474 2281; m 099 980141; www.etnicohostel.com.uy. A bright & lively hostel in a modern house with dorms, family rooms, doubles & singles, all en suite, plus parking & kitchen. B/fast inc. **$$**

Hospedaje Atlántico Oliveira 211, 150m south of the plaza; 4474 2575; m 099 877015. US$40 for basic room with no window & shared bathroom; some rooms are en suite with external windows & TVs. No breakfast or Wi-Fi, but it's friendly & adequate. **$**

Where to eat There are several pizza-parrilla restaurants near the plaza, including **Javier** (*on the plaza at Arachanes*; **$$**), **Jésus** (*Brasil 630 & Oliveira*) and **Las Leños** (*Artigas 113, between the plaza & the border;* ⊕ *10.00–02.00 daily*; **$$**), which is the liveliest of the three and also serves sweet pizzas, with dulce de leche or chocolate. The restaurant-cafetería **El Mesón del Plaza** (**$$$**) at the Nuevo Hotel Plaza is a bit quieter and more formal, although it hits no gastronomic heights.

Shopping The El Dorado supermarket (⊕ *08.30–22.30 daily*) is on the south side of the plaza next to El Mesón del Plaza. There are lots of 'free shops' (duty-free outlets) on the Uruguayan side of the border, and Hiper- and Supermercados on the Brazilian side.

Activities There's a **bike shop** at Artigas 175, on the southeastern corner of the plaza, and bikes can be rented at the Fortín de San Miguel (m *094 453943, 099 121720*) (see page 272).

Other practicalities

Banks The Banco República (with ATM) is at Artigas & Ventura, on the east side of the plaza; exchange offices include Gales (*Avda Brasil & Artigas;* ⊕ *08.30–18.00 Mon–Fri, 08.30–12.00 Sat*), Cambios Nelson (*Avda Brasil 611 & Olivera*) and Cambio 3 (*Artigas 120*).

Communications The Antel office (⊕ *09.00–19.00 Mon–Sat, 09.00–17.00 Sun*), which has free Wi-Fi, is on Priliac just west of Artigas; the post office is a block and a half further south, in an obscure shopfront on Artigas (⊕ *09.00–15.00 Mon–Fri, 08.00–13.00 Sat*). There's free public Wi-Fi on the plaza.

Immigration and consulate There is a Brazilian consulate (*Tito Fernández 147 & Laguna Merín;* \ *4474 2049;* e *chubrcg@internet.com.uy;* ⊕ *08.30–12.30 Mon–Fri*) and an office of the Inspectoría de Migración (Aduana) (*Ruta 9 km336;* \ *4474 2072;* e *i08chuy@dnm.minterior.gub.uy*).

What to see and do
Fortín de San Miguel (⊕ *summer 10.00–19.00 daily; rest of the year Fri–Sun; US$1*) Chuy's only attraction (other than duty-free shopping) is the Fortín de San Miguel, an 18th-century fort 6.5km west on Ruta 19. Construction was begun by the Spanish in 1734 and completed by the Portuguese in 1737 to observe Spanish military movements, rather than as a major defensive site. Smaller (and more attractive) than Santa Teresa (see page 269), it was built of compacted stone rather than masonry. It was already in ruins when captured by the Spanish in 1763; by 1927 it was in a very bad state but was then very well restored and became a monumento nacional in 1937. In 2010 the surrounding 1,500ha of native forest became part of the SNAP system of nature reserves.

The fort is managed jointly by the army and Probides, and is in very good condition. You can walk around the Vaubanesque ramparts, with cannons and viewpoints, as well as the original toilets (not in use), on the outside wall. The buildings inside are labelled with their original functions but now house mannequins in military uniforms, as well as 18th-century kitchen equipment and so on. There are toilets opposite the gate.

Nearby are the Campo Santo (cemetery) and barn-like buildings housing the Museo Criollo (Rural Museum) and Museo Indígena (Museum of Indigenous Life). The former is mainly a surprisingly varied collection of carts and carriages (note the high cart for getting through floods), while the latter displays arrowheads, mortars, bolas, rompecabezas, ornolitos and other examples of worked stoneware, as well as a model of a *toldo* (leather shelter), and preserved insects.

A signed path leads from the road a few hundred metres to the Guardia Perdida (Lost Guardpost), a tiny sentry post in a partially walled-in gap under a rock – not very interesting in itself, but the path leads on in good native woodland to a field and the road from the museum to the low wooded hill of Cerro Picudo. In addition to palms, cacti and other native flora, there are birds including cotorras, jays and raptors.

On the main road towards 18 de Julio is the Fortín de San Miguel **hotel** (\ *4474 6607; www.elfortin.com;* **$$$**), a delightful spot to get away from it all but with few luxuries other than the swimming pool.

Getting there and away Occasional **buses** run from Chuy to 18 de Julio, not far beyond the fort. If you're driving or cycling, turn left at the border on to Avenida Internacional, which looks like a dual carriageway but is two separate roads: Avenida Brasil on the Uruguayan side and Avenida Uruguay on the Brazilian side. Only the Uruguayan road continues, with border markers on the right separating it from huge rice paddies on the Brazilian side. At km8 (from Ruta 9; about 6km from the town) the road crosses the Arroyo San Miguel on two longish bridges, at the far end of which is a highways maintenance depot. Behind this, bizarrely, is a *mirador de aves* (birdwatching hide) looking over the wetlands – only about 50m from the road but a good place to bring children. There is a good photographic guide to the birds of the area, with Spanish, English and scientific names.

Just west beyond a Customs (Aduana) checkpoint, an asphalt road leads up through attractive native trees and loops right around the back of the fort; on foot it's easier to walk up to the left as soon as you see the fort. What seems to be a moat is actually just a pool with a drawbridge over it.

Barra del Chuy Returning 6km towards Montevideo, an unpaved road turns south at km331 and runs through rice paddies for 7km to the beach resort of Barra del Chuy. It's a rather exposed beach which can yield good surfing. Just before the centre of this very scattered settlement is the **Complejo Turístico Chuy** (↘ *4474 9425/8113;* e *turchuy@adinet.com.uy; www.complejoturisticochuy.com;* ⊕ *all year;* **$$$$**), with a Parque de Aguas (thermal pools), large campsite, 14 cabañas and a hostel. The **Hostal del Camping** (**$$$**) is a fine big wooden building, built in 2000, with rooms for two, three and four plus family suites (all with private bathroom), with a television room and wood-burning stove. The bungalows and cabins are in a quiet area, away from the campsite but near enough to the pools; they cost from US$85 for four in the low season, and some duplex cabañas have air conditioning. The campsite (**$**) has 150 pitches, with electricity and barbecues.

About 100m to the east along the main access road, the Complejo Los Orozco (↘ *4474 9047;* m *099 231905;* e *orozco8@adinet.com.uy; www.losorozco.com;* **$$**) has cabañas and bungalows (**$$**); they also offer free Wi-Fi.

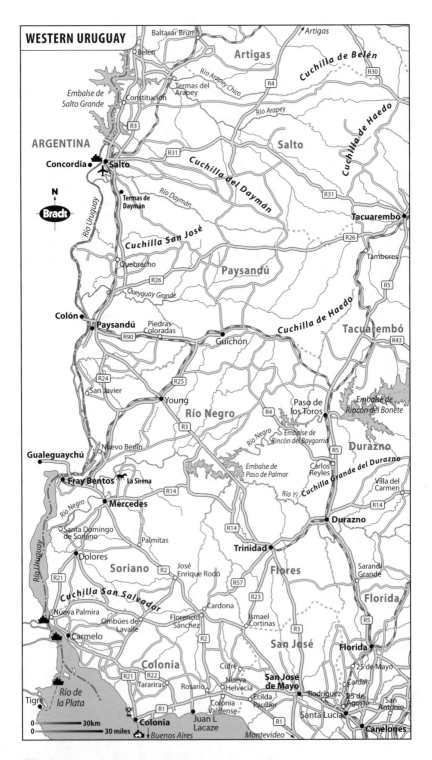

Baltasár Brum

Artigas

Belén

Artigas

Cuchilla de Belén

R4

R30

Embalse de
Salto Grande

Termas del
Arapey

Río Arapey Chico

Constitución

Río Arapey

R3

Salto

Cuchilla de Haedo

ARGENTINA

R31

Concordia

Salto

Cuchilla del Daymán

R31

Tacuarembó

Termas de
Daymán

Río Daymán

Bradt

Río Uruguay

R26

Cuchilla San José

Tambores

Quebracho

Paysandú

R26

R5

Queyguay Grande

Colón

Cuchilla de Haedo

Tacuarembó

Paysandú

Piedras
Coloradas

R43

R90

Guichón

R24

R25

San Javier

Young

Paso de
los Toros

Embalse de
Rincón del Bonete

Río Negro

R4

R3

Río Negro

Embalse de
Rincón del Baygorria

Durazno

Gualeguaychú

Nuevo Berlín

R5

Carlos
Reyles

Fray Bentos

La Sirena

Embalse de
Paso de Palmar

Cuchilla Grande del Durazno

Villa del
Carmen

R14

Mercedes

Río Negro

Río Yí

R14

Santa Domingo
de Soriano

Palmitas

R14

Durazno

Dolores

Soriano

R2

José
Enrique Rodó

Trinidad

Flores

Sarandí
Grande

Río Uruguay

R21

Cuchilla San Salvador

R57

R23

Florida

Nueva Palmira

Ombúes de
Lavalle

Florencio
Sánchez

Cardona

Ismael
Cortinas

R3

R5

Carmelo

R2

San José

Florida

Colonia

R21

R22

Cufré

25 de Mayo

Tarariras

Rosario

Nueva
Helvecia

San José
de Mayo

Cardal

Tigre

Río de
la Plata

Ecilda
Paullier

25 de
Agosto

San
Antonio

Colonia
Valdense

Rodríguez

R1

Santa Lucía

0   30km

Colonia

Juan L
Lacaze

R1

0   30 miles

Buenos Aires

Montevideo

Canelones

6

Western Uruguay

Some 2½ hours' drive west of Montevideo, across the rich dairylands of San José and Colonia departments, and an hour by ferry from Buenos Aires, the town of Colonia is a magnet for tourists. Beyond here the border follows the Río Uruguay northwards past the towns of Fray Bentos, Paysandú and Salto to the border with Brazil. This litoral is a prosperous area, with forestry, soya and citrus plantations expanding fast, but there are also large areas of wetlands that are home to a wide variety of birds and other wildlife. This area also produces some of the world's most beautiful sunsets. Beyond Paysandú is Uruguay's hot-springs district, with lots of spas providing enjoyable stopovers year-round.

COLONIA DEPARTMENT

Buses from Montevideo's Tres Cruces terminal have a smooth run on Ruta 1, now largely dual-carriageway, past Santiago Vásquez (see page 170) and the turning to San José (see page 171). Beyond Ecilda Paullier there's a toll at km107 as the highway enters Colonia department after 1½ hours.

NUEVA HELVECIA AND COLONIA VALDENSE
These two towns were settled between 1858 and 1862 by Swiss colonists, who were given free land and cows; after World War II there was an influx of Germans (the evil Dr Mengele lived in Argentina but visited Nueva Helvecia for eight days in 1958 to marry his brother's widow). They are known for their (frankly rather bland) cheeses; there's the odd antique shop and Swiss-themed restaurant, but both villages look rather like American suburbs, with comfortable bungalows on wide lawns. A Swiss-style portal has been erected over the main road into Nueva Helvecia, but the water tower (just north of the main crossroads, after the La Estrella supermarket and before Helados Helvecia, an excellent homemade ice-cream shop) is more amusing, and more Swiss. Colonia Valdense holds a cheese festival in mid-November and Nueva Helvecia (also known as Colonia Suiza) holds a Bierfest in mid-December.

Tourist information is available in Colonia Valdense at the Centro Artesanos Ciudad Jardín (✆ 4558 8412). Banco Santander has an ATM in Colonia Valdense, where there's also an internet café next to the Agencia Turil bus office.

Getting there and away Buses from Montevideo heading for Ruta 2 and Mercedes turn at km118 to Nueva Helvecia, 5km to the north. Most buses for Colonia detour through Colonia Valdense, just south of Ruta 1 at km121.

Where to stay

🏠 **Hotel Nirvana** Avda Batlle y Ordóñez, Nueva Helvetica; m 095 544081. A pretty comfortable spa hotel just south of the centre. **$$$$$**

🏠 **Estancia La Vigna** ✆4558 9234; e infolavigna@gmail.com; www.lavigna.com.uy. Just east of Colonia Valdense, at km120 of Ruta 51 (the road to Playa Fomento), this estancia was built in neorenaissance style in 1880 by Italian-born winemakers; it has 5 rooms furnished with rustic antiques & ceramics made on site. It's a beautiful & tranquil spot where you can get involved in organic farming, sheep shearing & other gaucho activities. **$$$$**

🏠 **Estancia Indare** ✆4550 7063/7000; www. estanciaindare.com; ⏰ 07.30–18.30 daily (summer to 20.30). Continuing west on Ruta 1, at km123.5 you can turn south for 14km to this estancia at the mouth of the Río Rosario. The narrow-gauge railway that once brought stone & sand to the dock for shipping to Buenos Aires has been restored; rides behind a steam locomotive built in 1900 are available on weekends & holidays, when there are also guided visits to the ship yards, carpentry shops & the residential area, with shops, schools, a cinema, bar & restaurant. Accommodation is also available here all year. **$$$**

🏠 **Granja Hotel Suizo** Federico Fischer 355; ✆4554 4002; e granjahotelsuizo@adinet.com.uy; www.hotelsuizonuevahelvecia.com. Founded in 1872, offers a swimming pool & Swiss food. **$$$**

🏠 **Hotel del Prado** Erwin Holdel; ✆4554 4169; e hotprado@adinet.com.uy; www. hoteldelprado.info. Housed in a former brewery converted to a hotel back in 1896, with double & triple rooms & also hostel accommodation (US$20 inc b/fast). **$$**

🏠 **El Galope** Camino Concordia; m 099 105985; e m_zubieta@hotmail.com; www.elgalope. com.uy; ⏰ all year. This delightful hostel is 6km east of Nueva Helvecia & 2km north of Ruta 1 (from the Balneario Santa Regina crossroads at km114.5 head inland for 2km on an unpaved road, then about 400m left on asphalt). It's a nice low adobe-style building with 5 double rooms sharing bathrooms & a little paddling pool. Their focus is on horseriding, although you have to pay by the ride (US$25–35), unlike on the all-inclusive estancias. Their horses are young but very well trained (although you will need to master the correct gaucho technique!) – most tourist places just have older slower horses. There's a sauna in winter, but no Wi-Fi or TV; an excellent breakfast is included, & the communal lunch & dinner are optional, with drinks available. Otherwise the kitchen is available from noon to 18.00. You can also rent bikes to visit Nueva Helvecia or Victoria's goat farm. 2-bed dorms cost US$25 pp & private rooms cost US$35/45 pp; HI discounts are available only via www.hihostels.com. **$**

🏕 **Blancarena (White Sand) campsite** ✆4587 2110; ⏰ Dec–Easter. The road from km123.5 leads to this campsite. **$**

🏕 **Campamento Artigas YMCA campsite** A bus passes 3 times a day (more in term time), going from Nueva Helvecia to the Balneario Santa Regina. The campsite is situated on a quiet shady beach & it rents out canoes for paddling on the river. **$**

COLONIA Colonia del Sacramento was founded in 1680 by Manuel Lobo, Governor of Rio de Janeiro, to be a Portuguese rival to Buenos Aires, directly across the River Plate. Fought over by Spain and Portugal for almost a century (changing hands seven times between 1680 and 1778), it was known as *la manzana de la discordia* (the apple of discord). In 1763 it was also attacked by the British, whose ship the *Lord Clive* was sunk and her officers hung in the plaza. In 1750 Colonia was awarded to Spain, but Portuguese settlers resisted the handover until the Spanish captured the town in 1777, ratified by the Treaty of San Ildefonso in 1778.

In 1807 the British again tried to capture Colonia. In 1818 the Portuguese seized it from pro-independence Artiguistas, and in 1826 a squadron under Admiral Guillermo (William) Brown drove off what were now Brazilian ships and bombarded the town but was unable to capture it. Until 1828, when the Brazilians left, this was a centre for smuggling (backed by the British) into Buenos Aires. In 1836 its population was just 762, plus 166 in Real de San Carlos. Colonia continued to be in the wars, being bombarded by an Argentine squadron in 1842, captured by Garibaldi and an Anglo–French force in 1845, and taken again by Oribe and the Blancos in 1848.

Darwin visited in 1833, describing:

> a fine grass country, but which is very poorly stocked with cattle or inhabitants ... The town is ... strongly fortified, but both fortifications and town suffered much from the Brazilian war. It is very ancient, and from the irregularity of the streets and the surrounding groves of old orange trees and peaches had a pretty appearance.

After the Guerra Grande, Colonia was at last free to develop as a port and regional centre, with frequent ferries from Buenos Aires. The opening of bridges across the Río Uruguay at Paysandú (1975) and Fray Bentos (1976) removed a lot of the freight that had passed through Colonia. In compensation the government began a programme to restore Colonia's historic buildings, culminating in the old town being added to UNESCO's World Heritage List in 1995.

Today, there are many boutique hotels and chic restaurants in old Portuguese houses, and many houses are owned by Argentines. The restoration work has been well done, and regulations about not altering façades have been strictly observed. Tourism is the main industry, but there's a nice sideline as a location for filming adverts and historical movies. Colonia is famed as an unspoilt and tranquil historic town; it's certainly quiet but isn't nearly as picturesque as your average French or Italian village, or as Paraty in Brazil. Nevertheless, it is very busy at weekends, and restaurants are crowded and expensive.

Getting there and away

By bus The bus terminal (*Avda Roosevelt & Manuel Lobo*) is immediately north of the port, just east of the old town. It houses a tourist information desk, ATM and exchange office, car rental and a phone/internet office; you can also leave your luggage (⊕ *09.00–22.00; from US$0.75/1hr to US$5/24hrs*). Buses to Montevideo (with COT and Turil) are frequent enough (see page 87) that if you arrive from Buenos Aires and go to the terminal in the morning, you'll have no problem booking a bus for the afternoon; there's no need to call ahead from Argentina. Many of these buses connect to Rosario and Nueva Helvecia, and Compañía Omnibus Colonia (*www.omnibuscolonia.com.uy*) also runs frequent local buses there and elsewhere. Nossar go to Trinidad and Durazno (three daily), Berrutti to Carmelo and Nuevo Palmira (*13 daily, w/end 4–6 daily*), a couple continuing to Mercedes, and Chadre all the way up the litoral route to Mercedes, Fray Bentos, Paysandú, Salto and Bella Unión (*05.40 & 14.30 daily*).

By road From Montevideo, Ruta 1 has now been dualled as far as Ruta 22, just short of Colonia; then you'll pass the so-called international airport (used by private planes from Argentina) and cross the river into Colonia, 177km from Montevideo.

By boat A new **ferry** terminal opened in 2009, with ATMs, toilets and a basic snack-bar. There are tourist information offices by the exit for cars (east of the bus terminal) and by the pedestrian exit (to the west at Calle Méndez). Luggage can be stored at the port (free with a ticket to or from Buenos Aires). The ferry companies all have ticket offices at the port: Buquebus (✆ *4522 2950/3030*), Colonia Express (✆ *4522 9676; ⊕ 1hr 45mins before each departure to 30min afterwards*) and Seacat Colonia (✆ *4522 2919; ⊕ 07.30–19.00 Mon–Sat*). Colonias Express are

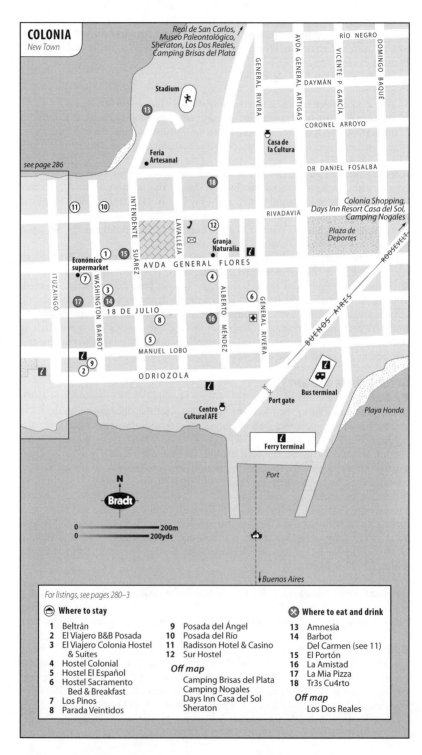

COLONIA
New Town

Real de San Carlos,
Museo Paleontológico,
Sheraton, Los Dos Reales,
Camping Brisas del Plata

RÍO NEGRO

AVDA GENERAL ARTIGAS

GENERAL RIVERA

VICENTE P GARCÍA

DOMINGO BAQUÉ

DAYMÁN

CORONEL ARROYO

Stadium

Casa de
la Cultura

see page 286

Feria
Artesanal

DR DANIEL FOSALBA

Colonia Shopping,
Days Inn Resort Casa del Sol,
Camping Nogales

RIVADAVIA

Plaza de
Deportes

INTENDENTE SUAREZ

LAVALLEJA

Granja
Naturalia

Económico
supermarket

AVDA GENERAL FLORES

ROOSEVELT

ITUZAINGÓ

WASHINGTON BARBOT

18 DE JULIO

ALBERTO MENDEZ

GENERAL RIVERA

BUENOS AIRES

MANUEL LOBO

ODRIOZOLA

Bus terminal

Playa Honda

Port gate

Centro
Cultural AFE

Ferry terminal

N

Port

Bradt

0 ——— 200m
0 ——— 200yds

Buenos Aires

For listings, see pages 280–3

Where to stay

1 Beltrán
2 El Viajero B&B Posada
3 El Viajero Colonia Hostel
   & Suites
4 Hostel Colonial
5 Hostel El Español
6 Hostel Sacramento
   Bed & Breakfast
7 Los Pinos
8 Parada Veintidos

9 Posada del Ángel
10 Posada del Río
11 Radisson Hotel & Casino
12 Sur Hostel

Off map

Camping Brisas del Plata
Camping Nogales
Days Inn Casa del Sol
Sheraton

Where to eat and drink

13 Amnesia
14 Barbot
   Del Carmen (see 11)
15 El Portón
16 La Amistad
17 La Mia Pizza
18 Tr3s Cu4rto

Off map

Los Dos Reales

also in the bus terminal (✆ *4522 9677/8;* ⏲ *10.00–19.00 Mon–Fri, 10.00–16.00 Sat, 10.00–12.00 Sun).*
Arriving by **yacht**, the port administration (✆ *4522 4225/8715;* ⏲ *08.00–18.00; summer to 20.00),* with WCs and showers (*08.00–20.00; summer to 22.00).*

Getting around The cobbled streets of the centre are largely car-free; most locals ride scooters, but visitors can rent golf-carts if they don't want to walk or cycle. Local buses run up and down Avenida Flores: bus A (every 15 minutes to 14.30 then every 30 minutes, also at weekends) continues via Artigas to Real de San Carlos (see page 288), 5km north around the bay, which was built 100 years ago as a tourism development and still boasts a few hotels and museums. There's also an hourly bus to the Los Nogales campsite (see page 281). The new hop-on–hop-off Bus Turístico Colonia, operated by Buquebus (✆ *130; www.busturistico.com.uy; US$25*) leaves every 30 minutes from the southern end of Ituzaingó and goes along the coast as far as Real de San Carlos and back.

Car rental Dune buggies and golf carts are a local speciality, available from Moto Rent, Punta Car and Thrifty.

🚗 **Avis** Bus terminal; ✆ 4522 9842; e avis@avis. com.uy; www.avis.com

🚗 **Budget** Bus terminal; ✆ 4522 9841; e budget@budget.com.uy; www.budget.com.uy

🚗 **Dollar** Rivera 128 near 18 de Julio; ✆ 4522 9805, 24hr m 099 224557; e dollar.colonia@ adinet.com.uy; www.dollar.com.uy

🚗 **Europcar** Avda Artigas 154 & 18 de Julio; ✆ 4522 8454; m 098 500922, 24hr m 096 222828; e reservas@europcar.com.uy; www.europcar. com.uy

🚗 **Hertz** Bus terminal; ✆ 4522 9851; m 094 415243/528768; www.hertz.com; ⏲ 09.00–19.00 daily

🚗 **Mariño Sport Rent a Car** Florida 419; ✆ 4523 0073/0608; e colonia@mariniosport.com; www.mariniosport.com

🚗 **Moto Rent** Ceballos 223; also Manuel Lobo 505 & Rivera; ✆ 4522 2266/9665; www.motorent. com.uy. For motorbikes & dune buggies.

🚗 **Multicar** Manuel Lobo 505 & Rivera; ✆ 4522 4893; m 094 447500; e colonia@redmulticar.com; www.redmulticar.com

🚗 **Prado Rentacar** Odriozola 415; ✆ 4522 7375; m 094 576099; www.pradorentacar.com

🚗 **Punta Car** 18 de Julio 496 & Rivera; m 094 619858; Florida s/n; ✆ 4522 2353, m 099 609643, 098 522522; www.puntacar.com.uy

🚗 **Rentacar Daymán** Manuel Lobo 319; ✆ 4522 6285/1285; m 099 522278; www. rentacardayman.com

🚗 **Thrifty** Ferry terminal; ✆ 4522 1936; 24hr m 095 606033; Flores 172 (also bikes); ✆ 4522 2939 (*call centre: 0800 8278; 08.00–22.00 daily*); e colonia@thrifty.com.uy;

🚗 **UruCar** Ferry terminal; ✆ 4522 8889

🚗 **Viaggio Rentacar** Avda Roosevelt & Rivera, opposite bus terminal; ✆ 4522 2614/2929; 24hr m 098 655325

Tourist information The most convenient tourist office is the **Centro de Informes del Barrio Histórico** (*Portón de Campo, Manuel Lobo 224;* ✆ *4522 8506;* ⏲ *09.00–19.00 daily*), run by the Corporación Turistica Departamental de Colonia; there are also free WCs here. One-hour **guided walks** of the historic centre (*11.00 & 15.00 daily; US$7.50 in Spanish, US$10 other languages – book ahead*) leave from here when it's dry. Colonia department's **tourist office** is at Rivera and Flores (✆ *4522 6141/3700; e turismo@colonia.gub.uy; www.colonianet.com;* ⏲ *08.00–19.00 Mon–Fri, 10.00–18.00 Sat–Sun),* together with the **Cámara Hotelera y Turística de Colonia** (✆ *4522 7302; e camhotel@adinet.com.uy; www.hotelesencolonia.com*), which has information on hotels including availability. The national tourist office is at the port (✆ *4522 4897).* The new **Experiencia Uruguay** complex (also known as BIT – the Centro de Bienvenida, Interpretación y Turismo del Uruguay), just west of the port at Odriozola 434 and Méndez (↪ *4522 1072; www.bitcolonia.com;* ⊕ *09.00–19.00 daily*) houses a tourist information desk, shop, café-restaurant, lockers, an audio-visual area (*charging US$3.50 for an 11min 'experience'*) and five interactive screens (giving detailed information on history and society, culture, sport, current affairs and Colonia).

🏠 Where to stay
As well as the hotels, there are plenty of **hostels**, most busy with international backpackers all year round. All listings are included on one of the two city maps, pages 278 and 286.

Hotels

🏠 **Hotel Sheraton** Continuación de la Rambla de Las Américas s/n, 7km north beyond Real de San Carlos; ↪ 4523 2021; e reservas.colonia@ sheraton.com; www.sheraton.com/colonia. Calling itself a 'golf & spa resort', a good base for those who like predictable 5-star megahotels. In addition to the golf course, it's right on the beach. The Sendero Arenisca leads in 50m to a pool with waterbirds. **$$$$$**

🏠 **Radisson Hotel & Casino** Washington Barbot 283; ↪ 4523 0460; www.radissoncolonia. com. Behind a very cool & unobtrusive modern exterior, this has indoor & outdoor swimming pools, jacuzzi, sauna & gym; the 60 rooms have AC & Wi-Fi. **$$$$$**

🏠 **Days Inn Resort Casa del Sol** Ruta 1 km170; ↪ 4522 6383; www.daysinncasadelsol. com. Much nicer than you might expect, with sizeable AC rooms, gym, indoor & outdoor pools & a restaurant-parrilla. It's by the highway 5km towards Montevideo (bikes are available). **$$$$**

🏠 **Hotel Beltrán** Flores 311; ↪ 4522 6260; www.hotelbeltran.com. A classy place, dating from 1873 (making it the country's second hotel) but now thoroughly modern, with AC & Wi-Fi in all rooms, & a fine restaurant. **$$$$**

🏠 **Hotel La Misión** Misiones de los Tapes 171; ↪ 4522 6767; e lamision@adinet.com.uy; www. lamisionhotel.com. A very stylish place right in the heart of the historic district, in a refurbished 19th-century house with lots of exposed stonework; AC rooms, Wi-Fi, & good buffet breakfast. **$$$$**

🏠 **Posada del Ángel** Washington Barbot 59; ↪ 4522 4602; www.posadadelangel.net. In a lovely older house & garden near the harbour, this has 11 rooms with AC throughout, swimming pool, sauna & gym. **$$$$**

🏠 **Posada del Gobernador** 18 de Julio 205; ↪ 4522 3018; e posadadelgobernador@adinet.

com.uy; http://delgobernador.com. A classy 4-star with just 15 AC rooms, swimming pool & 'ancient reading lounge'. **$$$$**

🏠 **Posada del Virrey** España 217; ↪ 4522 2223; www.posadadelvirrey.com. Right in the World Heritage district, this beautifully restored historic house has AC rooms for 2, 3 or 4 as well as suites with jacuzzi. There's free internet access & Wi-Fi in the public areas of the hotel. **$$$$**

🏠 **Posada Don Antonio** Ituzaingó 232; ↪ 4522 5344; www.posadadonantonio.com. One of the larger central hotels, with 37 rooms & spacious gardens with outdoor swimming pool, this is a nice blend of historical & modern, with AC & Wi-Fi. **$$$$**

🏠 **Posada Manuel de Lobo** Ituzaingó 160 & 18 de Julio; ↪ 4522 2463; www.posadamanuelelobo. com. In the former Hotel Oriental, a large 19th-century colonial house with patio & garage, this has AC rooms & a suite with jacuzzi. **$$$$**

🏠 **Posada Plaza Mayor** Del Comercio 111; ↪ 4522 3193; e hmayor@adinet.com.uy; www. posadaplazamayor.com. A boutique 4-star in the heart of the historic district, combining an 18th-century Portuguese rancho & a mansion built in 1860, with flower-bedecked patio & a famous fountain by local ceramicist Ariel Chape. 12 historic rooms on the ground floor, 3 new ones upstairs with sea views. All have AC & cable TV, but there's Wi-Fi only in the cafetería, lobby & business centre. **$$$$**

🏠 **El Capullo** 18 de Julio 219; ↪ 4523 0135; www.elcapullo.com. Classy British/American-owned place which has been beautifully refurbished for style & sustainablility, with a sky-lit hallway running the length of the building to the lovely gardens, swimming pool & bar. There's a great breakfast of local foods & their own bread, free Wi-Fi & PCs plus iPod docks in all rooms, & decent Trek bikes for rent (US$3/hr, US$10/day). **$$$**

🛌 **Parada Veintidos** 18 de Julio 374; 📞4522 4613; 📱 099 857383; 📧 paradaveintidos@ hotmail.com; www.paradaveintidos.com. In a nice mid-20th-century house with river views from the terrace, this B&B has doubles plus family suites for 4 or 5 & also offers tango classes. **$$$**

🛌 **Posada del Río** Washington Barbot 258; 📞4522 3002; 📧 hdelrio@adinet.com.uy; www. posadadelrio.com.uy. A nice family-style 2-star place around a patio, with AC, cable TV & a filling breakfast included (**$$**). Half a block to the south at Rivadavia 288, the same owners have the **Hostel & Suites del Río** (📞*4523 2870; 📧 hosteldelrio@gmail.com; www.guiacolonia.com. uy/hostelsuitesdelrio/hotel.htm*), a modern block with en-suite dorms (**$**) & suites (**$$$**), all AC & with breakfast & Wi-Fi throughout.

🛌 **Hotel Los Pinos** Washington Barbot 191; 📞4523 1470; 📧 lospinoscoloniahotel@adinet. com.uy; www.lospinoscoloniahotel.com.uy. Very good value, just a block from the World Heritage district. AC, free Wi-Fi & a snack-bar, but no credit cards. **$$**

Hostels

🛌 **El Viajero Colonia Hostel & Suites** Washington Barbot 164; 📞4522 2683; www.coloniahostel.com. The liveliest & most stylish of Colonia's HI hostels, this nicely refurbished house has AC rooms, kitchen & BBQ, free internet access with PCs & Wi-Fi, & bikes for rent (*US$7/day;* **$**). Nearer the port is the **El Viajero B&B Posada** at Odriozola 269 (📞*4522 8645;* 📧 *infobb@viajerocolonia.com; www.elviajerobb.com*), which has private en-suite rooms for up to 4 (*dbls from US$60 winter/US$100 summer*). **$$**

🛌 **Hostel Colonial** Flores 440; 📞4523 0347; 📧 hostelling_colonial@hotmail.com. There's nothing colonial about this building between the casino & La Pasiva – it looks like a 1980s shopfront but inside is a pleasant patio with rooms around it for up to 9 (mixed & women-only), as well as private rooms, all with shared bathrooms, free Wi-Fi & PCs, kitchen, BBQ & TV/DVD lounge. HI

members pay 15% less & have breakfast included. Bikes are available free, but are mostly broken; horse riding can also be arranged. **$$–$**

🛌 **Hostel El Español** Manuel Lobo 377 between Suárez & Lavalleja; 📞4523 0759; 📧 elespaniol@ adinet.com.uy; www.hostelelespaniol.com. A homely brick single-storey house dating from the 19th century, this has dorms with en-suite bathrooms for 8 & 10 (*US$13*), dorms for 6 & 8 with shared bathroom (*US$12*), doubles with/without bathroom (*US$32/38*). Breakfast, linen & towels included. There's a kitchen, BBQ & TV/DVD room, as well as free internet & bikes. **$**

🛌 **Hostel Sacramento Bed & Breakfast** 18 de Julio 487 & Rivera; 📞4522 5752; 📧 sacramentohostel@gmail.com; www. hostelsacramento.com. A nicely refurbished 19th-century house, all rooms are AC & breakfast & Wi-Fi are included; there's also a kitchen. Dorm beds cost US$16–18 & private rooms US$25–27.50 pp. **$**

🛌 **Sur Hostel** Rivadavia 448; 📞4522 0553; 📧 surhostel@gmail.com; www.surhostel.com. A 2-storey apartment block, with its entrance on Méndez, this also has a backyard with BBQ; dorm beds cost from US$14 winter/US$17 summer, doubles are US$50 all year, with breakfast & Wi-Fi included. **$**

Camping

⛺ **Camping Brisas del Plata** 📞4520 2207; ⊕ Dec–Easter. Another option, 6km west on a dirt road from San Pedro, itself 11km north of Colonia on Ruta 21 at km189. It's pretty simple but popular with lovers of fishing. You can go kayaking & horseriding with **Parque Brisas del Plata Turismo Aventura** (📞*4520 2207;* 📧 pbpturismo@gmail.com; www.facebook.com/ pbpturismoaventura.erramuspe). **$**

⛺ **Camping Nogales** Parque Ferrando, Ruta 1 km175.5; 📱 098 171008, 099 565616; 📧 campinglosnogales.colonia@gmail.com. This is a new campsite, a pleasant wooded site 2km east, with parrilla grills, restaurant & shop, play area & Wi-Fi; it's reached by the hourly bus to El General via Los Nogales (not via Ruta 1). **$**

✖ **Where to eat** All listings are included on one of the two city maps, pages 278 and 286.

✖ **La Casa de Jorge Páez Vilaró** Misiones de los Tapes 65; 📞4522 9211. An art gallery & restaurant

opposite the Viceroy's house, this nice colonial-style building displays the modern paintings of Carlos Páez Vilaró's less famous brother. The restaurant serves well-presented steak, fish & pasta, as well as crêpes, indoors & in a nice garden; there's also Wi-Fi. $$$$$

✗ **Lola** Santa Rita s/n; \4523 2738. At the Club de Yachting y Pesca, with a rooftop restaurant & a harbourside terrace (giving great sunset views), this is one of the nicest places in town to eat fish, although it also serves steak & homemade pastas such as *raviolones de surubí* and *sorrentinos de calabaza*. $$$$$

✗ **Mesón de la Plaza** Vasconcelos 153; \4522 4807; e mplaza@adinet.com.uy; www.mesondelaplaza.com; ⏰ 12.00–15.00, 20.00–23.30 Mon–Fri (until 01.00 Sat–Sun). Opposite the Casa del Gobierno on Plaza Manuel Lobo, this is perhaps Colonia's finest restaurant. In a beautifully restored house, with a patio & 2 fine rooms on either side, you can choose from a long, classy menu including salmon, fondue, lamb ragout, ravioli in squid ink & typically Uruguayan desserts. The wine list & service are also excellent. $$$$$

✗ **Casa Grande** Misiones de los Tapes 143, opposite the Plaza Menor; \4522 8371; e casagrande.colonia@gmail.com; www.restocasagrande.com.uy; ⏰ 10.00–midnight daily. This has one of the nicest terraces for daytime drinks & snacks, & serves reasonably decent lunches & dinners, though at a price that reflects the location. It's a fairly traditional menu with good steak & homemade pasta. $$$$

✗ **Del Carmen** Washington Barbot 283; \4523 0460; ⏰ 07.00–midnight daily. The restaurant/lounge bar of the Radisson Hotel, this is a quiet & refined setting for fairly pricey food & drink. $$$$

✗ **El Drugstore** Vasconcelos 179 & Portugal; \4522 5241; e eldrugstore@yahoo.com; ⏰ 12.00–01.00 daily. Facing the church, this is the funkiest place to eat in town, with lots of vegetarian & Japanese choices; the interior is attractive & the pavement seating is pleasant too. No credit cards. $$$$

✗ **La Florida** Odriozola 215, Portón del Campo; m 094 293036; www.restoranlaflorida.com. A charming little place, if you happen to find it open, with eccentric owners offering a small diverse menu of *cocina de autor* – it's expensive but worth it. $$$$

✗ **La Mia Pizza** 18 de Julio 267; \4522 2882; http://lamiapizzabarriosur.amawebs.com. A very

decent but totally non-touristy place, run by the Barrio Sur sports club. $$$$

✗ **Pulpería de los Faroles** Misiones de los Tapes 101 & Comercio; \4523 0271; e pulperiadelosfaroles@hotmail.com; ⏰ 12.00–midnight daily. An attractive place with its brick-lined interior or seating outside on the plaza, this serves simple food, cooked well, including fish & pasta as well as good salads & interesting vegetarian options (eg: pumpkin fritters). Desserts include great meringues. Sometimes there's live music, & prices are not unreasonable for the location. $$$$

✗ **El Portón** Flores 333; \4522 5318; e parrilladelporton@hotmail.com. A simple, cheerful parrilla with semi-industrial décor that's a good place to feed a family, with chivitos, pizza, pasta & fish as well as grilled meats, all very affordable. $$$

✗ **El Torreón** Flores 19; \4522 0823. Below a fairly ugly modern tower, the waterfront terrace is the place to drink *clericó* & eat anything from chivitos to pasta, paella or ice cream. $$$

✗ **La Bodeguita** Comercio 167; \4522 5329; ⏰ from 19.30 Tue–Sun, from 12.00 Sat–Sun. A hip place serving great chivitos or pizza, including vegetarian options, & *faina*. There's outdoor seating & it's all cheap. $$

✗ **Los Dos Reales** Dr Carlos Martínez 96; \4223 0694. The best place to eat in Real de San Carlos (other than the Sheraton), serving homemade pastas (try the pumpkin ravioli), parrilla & snacks in a nice old house, well restored, not far beyond the bullring. $$$

✗ **Mercosur** Flores 252 & Ituzaingó; \4522 4200; ⏰ from 09.00 daily. An uncomplicated, touristy place that serves good chivitos & Uruguayan approximations of Swiss cuisine such as polenta, *agnolotti* (stuffed pasta), *tortilla a la suiza* (a sort of omeletty version of *rösti* with cheese & onion) or cheese fondue. $$$

✗ **Patrimonio** San José 111; \4522 4254. A modern lounge bar & restaurant with standard parrilla & grilled fish, as well as vegetarian dishes, on a pleasant terrace with Wi-Fi. $$$

✗ **Viejo Barrio** Vasconcellos 169; \4522 5399; ⏰ 12.00–15.00, 20.00–midnight Thu–Tue. Facing the church, this serves simple, traditional food – steak, fish & pastas – at very reasonable prices. The waiter is a bit mad but highly entertaining. $$$

✖ **La Amistad** 18 de Julio 448 & Méndez; m 9454 1596. Near the port, this non-touristy place serves good chivitos, vegetarian pasta, pizza & fish at half the price you'd pay in the historic district. **$$**

🍺 **Lentas Maravillas** Santa Rita 61; ☎4522 0636; e lentasmaravillas@gmail.com; ⏰ 14.00–19.30 Thu–Tue. This café's beautiful harbourside garden is the perfect place for afternoon tea or coffee & cakes; they also serve good sandwiches. **$$**

🍺 **El Cali** Paseo San Miguel 91. Just inside the old city gate, this sells the best ice cream in town, as well as pizzas. **$**

🍺 **Ganache** Calle Real 178 & Portugal; ⏰ to 23.00 Thu–Tue, 02.00 Sat (with live music). The best place for barista coffee (espresso US$3) as well as vegetarian sandwiches; there's a terrace with Wi-Fi too. Also on Calle Real, Moscato Café is another good coffee option, also with frappucino, lemonades, beer & wine, & empanadas, tartas, salads & sandwiches; again, there's a nice terrace with Wi-Fi. **$**

Nightlife

☆ **Amnesia** Suárez s/n. A lively disco in the rowing club that also hosts live bands.

🍷 **Barbot** Washington Barbot 160; ☎4522 7268; m 096 099069; www.facebook.com/barbotcerveceria. A new homebrew pub next to the El Viajero hostel, serving 6 tasty beers from lager to porter via Burton bitter, plus Mexican food.

🍷 **Matamala** Ituzaingó 222; ☎4522 0548; e quechanguita@hotmail.com; ⏰ winter from 20.00 Thu–Sun; summer from 11.00 daily. A very cool bar (really only worth visiting late at night) offering tapas & good music.

☆ **Tr3s/Cu4rto** Méndez 295 & Fosalba; ☎4522 9664; www.trescuarto.com. The best nightclub in town (from midnight), & also home to an arts collective.

Entertainment The **Centro Cultural Bastión del Carmen** (*Rivadavia 223;* ☎*4522 7201;* ⏰ *10.30–21.00 Tue–Sun*) puts on art exhibitions and theatre performances. There are also exhibitions at the cultural centre of the **Argentine consulate** (*18 de Julio 428;* ⏰ *13.00–18.00 Mon–Fri*) and the **Casa de la Cultura** (*Rivera 346 & Arroyo*).

Shopping For craft shopping, the **Feria Artesanal** is on Fosalba at Suárez, with permanent stalls provided by the municipality; for more expensive items, including clothing, try the Paseo del Sol (*Comercio & de la Playa*), Plaza Menor and Almacen La Carlota (*Calle Real*) and Santolina (*San Antonio 138*). For leather goods, look for Casacuero (*Paseo del Sol, Comercio 158;* ☎ *4522 8997;* e *casacuero@movinet. com.uy*), and for knitwear Manos del Uruguay (*Flores 100 & Real;* ☎ *4522 1793;* e *malvon_colonia@yahoo.com*).

The most convenient supermarket is Económico (*Flores 1730 near Washington Barbot;* ⏰ *08.30–22.00 Mon–Sat, 09.00–13.30, 17.30–22.00 Sun*). For wines and cheeses from Nueva Helvecia head for Granja Naturalia (*Flores 437, opposite Hostel Colonial;* ⏰ *08.00–20.00 Mon–Fri*). There's also the Colonia Shopping Mall (*www.coloniashopping.com.uy*) at Roosevelt 458, not far northeast of the centre, also home to a Ta-Ta supermarket and Cinema Movie & Fun (☎ *4522 0541; www. cinemacolonia.com*).

Activities Colonia's best **beach** is said to be the Playa Ferrando, 1km east of the port, a pleasant site with woods along the shore, and a restaurant. There are also beaches along Avenida Costanera, north of central Colonia, with bars and paradores, but they're less attractive with the road alongside.

One of the best of Uruguay's few **golf** courses is at the Sheraton Golf and Spa Resort, on the north side of Real de San Carlos (*Continuación de la Rambla de Las Américas s/n;* ☎ *4522 9000*).

Other practicalities

Banks There are ATMs along Flores, and at the port and bus terminal. Shops and restaurants will accept Argentine pesos, US dollars and, often, Brazilian reals and euros. Exchange offices include Cambio Colonia (*at the port; & Flores 401 & Lavalleja;* ⊕ *09.00–18.00 Mon–Fri, 09.00–13.00, 15.00–18.00 Sat, 10.00–13.00 Sun*); Cambio Nelson (*at the bus terminal;* ⊕ *08.00–20.00 daily*); Cambio Varlix (*De La Peña 168;* ⊕ *10.00–20.00 Mon–Fri, 10.00–21.00 Sat, 09.00–20.00 Sun; & at the port;* ⊕ *03.00–04.30, 09.00–20.30 Mon–Sat, 09.00–21.30 Sun*); and Cambio Dromer (*Flores 350 & Suárez;* ⊕ *10.00–18.00 Mon–Fri, 10.00–17.00 Sat*).

Communications The post office faces the plaza at Lavelleja 226 (⊕ *10.00–16.00 Mon–Fri, 09.00–12.00 Sat*). Antel's telecentro is at Rivadavia 404 and Lavalleja (⊕ *09.00–18.00 Mon–Sat*), Flores 172 (⊕ *09.00–20.00 Sun–Thu, 09.00–21.00 Fri–Sat*). There's also a combined post office and telecentro at the port (*Local 12;* ⊕ *09.00–17.00 daily*). There's free public Wi-Fi on Plaza 25 de Agosto.

Emergency services The public hospital is near the terminal at 18 de Julio 462 (*just east of Méndez;* ☏ *4522 2994/2945*). To contact the police call ☏ 109 (emergency) or 4522 3348; the Policía Turística are very visible patrolling the historic district.

Immigration and consulate For visa issues, the Inspectoría de Migración is at 18 de Julio 428 (☏ *4522 2126/6105;* e *dnm-colonia@minterior.gub.uy*). The Argentine consulate is at Flores 209 (☏ *4522 2093/2086;* e *conccolo@adinet.com.uy;* ⊕ *13.00–18.00 Mon–Fri*).

What to see and do From the port and bus terminal, Florida leads west past the former railway station and turntable (across the tracks from the Experiencia Uruguay tourist office, with ramped access, is the former locomotive roundhouse, now a cultural centre); just before reaching the old city wall, turn right to the Centro de Informes del Barrio Histórico (see page 279). Immediately west of this is the **Portón de Campo** (Country Gate), built in 1745 by the Portuguese and rebuilt in 1968–71 (bronze nails in the wall mark the level above which it is a reconstruction). Continuing into the walled town (and the UNESCO World Heritage district), the Plaza Mayor (or Plaza 25 de Mayo) opens in front of you, a long square planted with *palo borracho* (drunken stick, actually the silk floss tree), figs, palms, cycads, jasmine and bougainvillea, with cotorras and swallows flying about. To the left the **Calle de los Suspiros** is the most photographed street in Uruguay, a short traffic-free lane leading down to the Plate that is essentially unchanged from the 18th century, with its cobbles and central drain, and single-storey cottages on either side. It's named 'Street of Sighs' perhaps because convicted criminals were taken to the beach to be executed, or perhaps because of the brothels that lined the street.

Just beyond this on the south side of the Plaza Mayor is the best of Colonia's museums, the Museo Portugués, in an 18th-century Portuguese house, and at the western end of the plaza are other museums, the Casa Nacarello, the ruined **Casa del Virrey** and the Museo Municipal. To the left are the **ruins of the convent of San Francisco Xavier**, built in 1683 and burnt down in 1793; the **faro** (lighthouse; US$1) was built on its ruins in 1855–57. At 27m it's higher than the Faro Punta Brava in Montevideo, but the stairs are better. You can just make out the towers of Buenos Aires on the horizon, to the left of the leftmost islet (with a navigation light on it).

From the faro head west on San Pedro to the headland, where you can still see traces of the Bastión de San Pedro de Alcántara, built in 1723. Following the shore north (with sandy patches between rocky points and reeds) you'll come to the former Bastión de Santa Rita (1736) at the end of Avenida General Flores, the main street. To the north is the yacht club and the long jetty of the marina, and two blocks to the east an older jetty built in 1866 which reopened in 2001.

Going a few blocks up Flores and then south on Vasconcelos, you'll come to the **Basilica del Sanctísimo Sacramento** (Basilica of the Holy Sacrament), the oldest in Uruguay, built in 1680, rebuilt in 1695–99 and 1808–10 and destroyed in 1823. As Darwin put it:

> The church is a curious ruin; it was used as a powder magazine and was struck by lightning in one of the ten thousand storms of the Río Plata. Two thirds of the building was blown away to the very foundation, and the rest stands a shattered and curious monument of the united powers of lightning and gunpowder.

It was rebuilt between 1836 and 1842 and restored between 1957 and 1995, although with its plain white exterior and interior it's not especially attractive.

On the south side of the church is the Plaza Manuel Lobo, an attractive park at the heart of what was the Portuguese fort. The **Casa del Gobernador** (Governor's House), ruined by the Spanish in 1777, was excavated in 1990–93 (some of the finds are on display in the Archivo Regional) and the foundations have been restored, with walkways through and over them and interpretative signs (in Spanish only).

To the north of Flores at Ceballos 236 is the **Acuario** (*Aquarium; Ceballos 236; www.acuario.com.uy;* ⏲ *16.00–20.00 Wed–Mon (summer until 21.00); US\$2*). This houses a tank with 12 glass windows through which you can see mainly indigenous fish. There's also an interactive centre for schoolchildren.

At the north end of Ceballos by the harbour, the Bastión del Carmen, built in 1722–48, marked the northern end of the city wall. It was demolished in 1859 but its foundations are still visible near the 38m-high chimney of a soap factory, built in 1880, that went bankrupt when its owners lost a lawsuit with an Argentine company. Now it houses the Teatro y Centro Cultural Bastión del Carmen (see page 283), with an attractive waterside garden and sculpture.

Museums The town's main museums are managed collectively, with a combined ticket (*US\$2.50;* ☎ *4522 5609; http://museoscolonia.blogspot.com*) available only at the Museo Municipal and valid for all of them for a week. All are open at weekends (and Easter Week), closing on different weekdays. The Naval Museum, the Museum of Shipwrecks and Treasure and the Railway Museum are not part of this system – see pages 287 and 288.

Archivo Regional (*Misiones de los Tapes 115;* ⏲ *11.15–16.30 Mon–Fri*) A Portuguese house built by 1750, this houses the Regional Archives (including some mid-19th-century watercolours) and archaeological finds from the excavation of the Casa del Gobernador, including bottle shards, ceramics and bones.

Museo Casa Nacarello (*Comercio 67;* ⏲ *11.15–16.30 Fri–Wed*) This little Portuguese rancho, bright red on the outside and whitewashed inside, was restored in 1993. Three rooms are equipped with simple furnishings (some replicas) from the period when it was built (c1790), and you can also see the kitchen.

Museo del Azulejo (*Museum of Decorative Tiles; Misiones de los Tapes 104;* ⏲ *11.15–16.30 Fri–Wed*) There's not a lot to see in the three rooms of this very

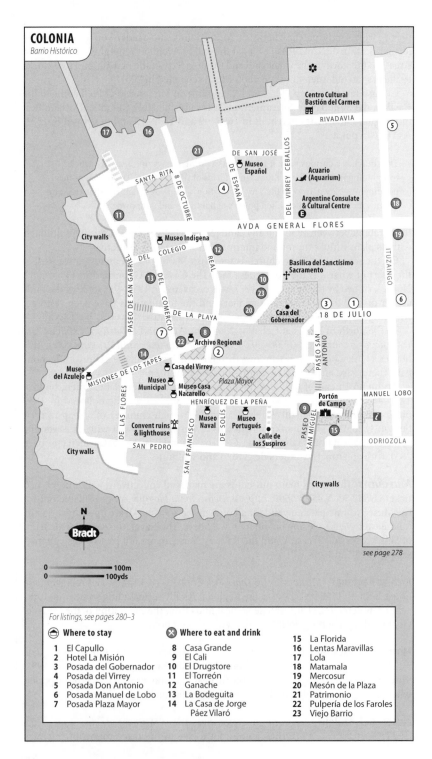

COLONIA
Barrio Histórico

Centro Cultural
Bastión del Carmen

RIVADAVIA

⑤

DE SAN JOSÉ

Museo
Español

④

DE ESPAÑA

SANTA RITA

8 DE OCTUBRE

㉑

DEL VIRREY CEBALLOS

Acuario
(Aquarium)

Argentine Consulate
& Cultural Centre
Ⓔ

⑱

AVDA GENERAL FLORES

⑪

City walls

Museo Indígena

DEL COLEGIO

⑫

REAL

⑲

ITUZAINGÓ

Basílica del Sanctísimo
Sacramento

PASEO DE SAN GABRIEL

⑬

DEL COMERCIO

⑩

⑥

DE LA PLAYA

㉓

18 DE JULIO

③ ①

⑳

Casa del
Gobernador

⑦

㉒ ⑧ Archivo Regional

②

PASEO SAN ANTONIO

⑭

MISIONES DE LOS TAPES

Casa del Virrey

Museo
del Azulejo

Museo
Municipal

Museo Casa
Nacarello

Plaza Mayor

MANUEL LOBO

DE LAS FLORES

HENRÍQUEZ DE LA PEÑA

Portón
de Campo

Ⓘ

Convent ruins
& lighthouse

Museo
Naval

Museo
Portugués

⑨

PASEO SAN MIGUEL

⑮

ODRIOZOLA

SAN PEDRO

SAN FRANCISCO

DE SOLIS

Calle de
los Suspiros

City walls

City walls

N

Bradt

0 ——— 100m
0 ——— 100yds

see page 278

For listings, see pages 280–3

⊖ Where to stay

1 El Capullo
2 Hotel La Misión
3 Posada del Gobernador
4 Posada del Virrey
5 Posada Don Antonio
6 Posada Manuel de Lobo
7 Posada Plaza Mayor

✖ Where to eat and drink

8 Casa Grande
9 El Cali
10 El Drugstore
11 El Torreón
12 Ganache
13 La Bodeguita
14 La Casa de Jorge
　 Páez Vilaró

15 La Florida
16 Lentas Maravillas
17 Lola
18 Matamala
19 Mercosur
20 Mesón de la Plaza
21 Patrimonio
22 Pulpería de los Faroles
23 Viejo Barrio

modest Portuguese house from the mid 18th century. Restored in 1987, it houses a small collection of tiles that belonged to Jorge Páez Vilaró, mostly the standard ones from Desvres in northern France (see page 138), as well as some very early Uruguayan tiles, dating from 1840.

Museo Español (*Spanish Museum; San José 152;* ⊕ *11.15–16.30 Tue–Sun*) This museum, built as the Casa de Don Juan de Águila in 1720 and rebuilt in 1840 in neoclassical style, presents life in the Spanish colonial period, with basketry, ceramics and costumes; there are also modern paintings by Jorge Páez Vilaró.

Museo Indígena (*Museum of Indigenous Life; Comercio & Flores;* ⊕ *11.15–16.30 Fri–Wed; guided visits 13.30 & 16.00 Sat–Sun*) Upstairs in this townhouse is a private collection of Charrúa grinding stones, arrowheads (a few from Chubut in Argentina), ceramics and some miscellaneous minerals and fossils.

Museo Municipal (*Municipal Museum; Comercio 77;* ⊕ *11.15–16.30 Wed–Mon*) Built in 1795 and rebuilt in 1835 with a simple neoclassical façade, the so-called Casa Almirante Brown (although it never in fact belonged to Admiral Brown, the father of the Argentine navy) was the town's original museum, opening in 1951. Outside are three rusty cannons, and in the first room a few indigenous ceramics, bolas and rompacabezas. The second room has some fascinating material on the Real de San Carlos development (fliers for bullfights, banderillas, stirrups and crockery) and the third is a former kitchen with pots and also models of ships. The fourth and fifth rooms house furniture, a clavichord and harp, fans, guns and a very detailed timeline (in Spanish) of national and local history until 1931, including the arrival of the railway in 1901 and the first bus from Montevideo in 1925 (with six passengers, taking at least ten hours). Upstairs there's more furniture, a palaeontology room with a huge Glyptodon shell and a fine Lestodon skeleton, and a room of stuffed birds and butterflies. There's usually no access to the garden, with a whale skeleton, a statue of Brown and some models of prehistoric beasts.

Museo Naval (*De La Peña & De San Francisco;* ⊕ *11.15–16.30 Thu–Sun; US$0.50*) Opened in 2009, this focuses on the strategic importance of the sea to Colonia and the naval battles that determined its history.

Museo Portugués (*De la Peña 180;* ⊕ *11.15–16.30 Thu–Tue*) Built for the Ríos family in about 1720, this was opened as a museum in 1977, incorporating an annexe built by the Spanish in 1792. Reorganised by the Gulbenkian Foundation in 1997, it is now the best presented of Colonia's museums, with replicas of furniture, Chinese porcelain, tableware, uniforms, azulejo tiles and portraits of Portuguese monarchs of the period, as well as real guns. Downstairs are rooms on the Portuguese Discoveries, with excellent reproduction maps of the voyages to Africa and Asia, and a room on slavery, abolished in 1813 in the United Provinces (including Uruguay) and only in 1888 in Brazil.

Museo Paleontológico (*Roger Balet, Real de San Carlos;* ⊕ *11.15–16.45 Thu–Sun, by reservation on* ☎ *4523 0952*) A formerly private collection of megafauna remains, many found in the sea off Colonia, such as Glyptodon shells, a Megatherium femur and a two-million-year-old armadillo shell, as well as some rocks and indigenous artefacts.

Real de San Carlos Avenida Costanera leads 5km north around the bay to Real de San Carlos, a tourism development built in 1910 by the Argentine immigrant Nicolás Mihanovich. Sadly his hotel and casino lost its business when the Argentine government levied punitive taxes on ferries. The *hipódromo* (horseracing track, opened only in 1942) survives, facing the *frontón* (pelota courts), but everything is very run-down. The **Plaza de Toros** (bullring), at the inland end of Avenida Mihanovich, is fenced off; it closed down when Uruguay banned bullfighting in 1912. On its north side is the **Museo del Ferrocarril** (\ *4522 1496; www. recrearlahistoria.com;* ⊕ *10.00–18.00 Wed–Mon, to 20.00 Sat–Sun & holidays; US$1*) with five old railway carriages and a reproduction signal-box and loco-shed, as well as a café which sometimes puts on art shows and jazz. To the southeast of the bullring, Río del la Plata leads to the Museo Paleontológico (see page 287) and the **Museo de Naufragios y Tesoros** (*Museum of Shipwrecks and Treasure; Roger Balet & Calle de los Argentinos;* m *9445 5133;* e *museonaufragios@hotmail.com;* ⊕ *10.00–17.00 Wed–Mon; US$1*), fun for kids with a replica 18th-century pirate ship and a pirate cave, but also with material rescued by divers from the wreck of the Spanish frigate *Nuestra Señora de Loreto*, which sank off Montevideo in 1792. The next project is to explore the British ship *Lord Clive*, sunk off Colonia in 1763 (see page 276).

Bus A runs every 15 minutes from Flores to Real de San Carlos, but it's more pleasant to cycle along the *costanera* (waterfront esplanade)

Excursions Just east of Colonia, **Bodega Bernardi** (*Ruta 1 km171.5 Laguna de los Patos;* \ *4522 4752; www.bodegabernardi.com;* ⊕ *late Dec–late Mar 09.00–12.00, 15.00–19.00 Mon–Sat; rest of the year 09.00–12.00, 14.00–17.30 Mon–Sat; free*) is known for its grappas but does make wines too. Founded in 1892 and still run by the same family, they have been open for guided visits and tastings since 2000 and are now a very popular destination.

At the small settlement of San Pedro (*Ruta 21 km189, 11km north of Colonia*) you can turn west to the Camping Brisas del Plata (see page 281) or east for 5km to the **Estancia Los Tres Botones** (\ *4520 2163;* m *099 522868;* e *los3botones@adinet. com.; www.los3botones.com*), where you can take horse-and-cart rides, learn about farm work and then of course tuck into the product of that work. A little further, 3km west from km192, **Villa Celina** (\ *4520 2486;* m *099 769098;* e *villacelina@ adinet.com.uy; www.villacelinaturismorural.com.uy*) is similar, with visits to the *tambo* (dairy), and cheeses and jams for sale.

After km193 a sign points left to the site of the battlefield of San Pedro, where British and Spanish forces fought in 1807. Discovered by chance in 2005, this is the only undisturbed Napoleonic battlefield in South America, yielding lots of buttons and bullets for archaeologists. It was a minor victory for the British, outnumbered but armed with modern Baker rifles. In 2007 a small monument was set up to commemorate the battle's bicentenary, but there's nothing else to see.

At km197.5 an asphalt road leads west to the **Parque Nacional Anchorena** (*www.parqueanchorena.gub.uy; tours: 10.00 & 14.30 Thu–Sun; US$1.50*), the former estate of the Argentine Aarón de Anchorena (1877–1965), given to him by his mother on condition he gave up flying. He left the half-timbered house (built in 1911) and a park of 1,370ha to be the holiday home of the President of Uruguay; it's been used for meetings with the likes of presidents Lula and George W Bush, but is open to the public at other times. Beyond the visitor centre is a small lake, a chapel and a 75m-high tower built in 1927 by Anchorena in honour of Sebastián Gabato (Cabot), who may have landed here in 1527, from which you can see as far as Buenos Aires when conditions are clear. There are attractive gardens and a park with axis deer and wild boar introduced by Anchorena. Tours from Colonia are operated by Colonia Escondida Minitur (♦ 4520 2030; m 093 724893; www. coloniaescondida.com). After the junction with Ruta 22 (from Montevideo), you come into more rolling country; passing the small settlement of Paso de la Horqueta and a bridge over the Río San Juan, a road leads west from km213.5 for 7km to **Los Cerros de San Juan**, Uruguay's oldest vineyard. It was founded in 1854 by the Lahusen family from Germany, who established a cattle ranch and general farm as well as the winery. It became a self-contained community of 900 people, with two schools, a bakery, laundry and shops. This continues today to a certain extent, the farm supplying bread and meat to the restaurant, which doubles as a tasting room. It's all been lovingly restored; tours are available Monday–Saturday but must be booked in advance (♦ 2481 7200; www.loscerrosdesanjuan.com.uy/english/cerros. htm; ⊕ 08.00–17.00 Mon–Fri). An asado lunch can be provided.

This was the first Uruguayan winery to plant Cabernet Sauvignon (in 1971) and has now released an organic Cabernet Sauvignon. Other grapes are Merlot, Tannat, Tempranillo, Pinot Noir, Riesling, Sauvignon Blanc, Chardonnay and Gewürztraminer. They have four main lines, from the cheap San Juan Fiesta (introduced in 1975) and the San Juan Crianza table wines to the oaked reserve wines of Cuna de Piedra and Maderos lines; there's also the fortified Soleado wine.

From km223 of Ruta 21 (47km from Colonia), it's 10km west to **Conchillas**, a hidden jewel that's largely as it was a century ago. The British firm C H Walker & Co Ltd established a quarry here in 1887, to provide sand and stone for the construction of a modern port in Buenos Aires, and built a company town as well. After 1911 David Evans, a former ship's cook, settled here and built up a big import–export business. There are streets of identical stone houses, as well as warehouses, a hotel (closed), a former Anglican church and a cemetery. Puerto Conchillas (and a beach) are 7km further south. Now a National Monument, it's a quiet place where old men drink maté and ancient cachila cars sit by the kerb, still in daily use. However the world's largest paper pulp mill is to open nearby at Punta Pereira early in 2014, and the new Ruta 55 has been built just to the south to keep traffic out of the old town.

A local bus meets passengers from Colonia–Carmelo buses on Ruta 21. A tourist information office and a small museum can be found in the Casa de Cultura on Calle David Evans.

CARMELO Carmelo prides itself on being the only town founded by Artigas, on 12 February 1816, although he simply granted land to allow a nearby settlement to move from a rather swampy site. In fact its recorded history goes back to c1611 when Hernandarias (Hernando Arias de Saavedra, Governor of Asunción) landed cattle near the mouth of the Arroyo de Vacas; the first settlers arrived from Buenos Aires in 1708. Now the second-largest town in Colonia department, with a population of 22,000, it's a quiet place that serves as a port for ferries from Argentina and offers a couple of delightful places to stay nearby. There are some historic relics and a couple of wineries to visit.

Getting there and away
By road Ruta 22 is the link between Ruta 1, from Montevideo, and Ruta 21, from Colonia. In addition to direct buses to Montevideo (see page 87), there are services to Colonia with Berrutti (*also to Mercedes at 06.00 & 13.00 Mon–Sat*), and Chadre's two litoral services, all the way to Bella Unión via Mercedes, Fray Bentos, Paysandú and Salto. The Agencia Central (Chadre/Sabelin) bus office is on

the south side of Plaza Independencia at 18 de Julio 411 (✎ *4542 2987;* ⏱ *03.00–04.00, 06.00–23.30 daily*); Berrutti is two blocks south at Uruguay 337 (✎*4542 2504;* e *berruttiturismo@adinet.com.uy; www.berruttiturismo.com*). Intertür are just west of Plaza Independencia at 18 de Julio and Zorrilla de San Martín (✎*4542 3411*), with five services a day (four on Sundays) to Montevideo and to Dolores and Mercedes.

Just east of the port, Ruta 21 crosses the Arroyo de Las Vacas (at km252.6) on a picturesque swing bridge (Puente Giratorio), the first in the country and still (occasionally) hand-cranked; 88m long, it was built in Germany and assembled in 1912 by Juan Smith. There's also an old Grafton crane from Bedford (England) at the ferry port.

By boat Small but modern ferries (pedestrians only), operated by Cacciola Viajes (see pages 53–4 and 85), sail here twice daily from Tigre, north of Buenos Aires, arriving at a small terminal on the Rambla de los Constituyentes, in the centre of town. It's a pleasant trip through the Paraná Delta, full of birdlife. From Carmelo there are minibus connections to Colonia and Montevideo. Tickets to Tigre can be bought from Cacciola at Calle del Puerto 263 (✎ *4542 7551*), across the road from the terminal; if you're taking the one at 04.00 the security guard will probably let you wait in the terminal from around midnight.

The busy yacht harbour (✎*4542 2058;* e *dnhcarmelo@adinet.com.uy*) has showers (⏱ *08.00–22.00/midnight*).

Getting around Plaza Independencia is the place to look for taxis. Cars and golf-carts can be rented from Thrifty (*19 de Abril 239;* ✎ *4542 7073; (call centre:* ✎*0800 8278);* ⏱ *08.00–22.00 daily*), just north of the swing bridge. Urucar is at 19 de Abril 143 and Solis (✎*4542 2008;* m *098 542542;* e *info@urucar.com.uy*) and cars can also be rented at the Cacciola ticket office (m *094 106907*). DW Service is at Uruguay 286 (✎*4542 7346; 24hr* m *094 440812;* e *dwservice@movinet.com.uy; www.dwservice.com.uy*).

Tourist information There's a tourist information kiosk on the northwestern corner of Plaza Independencia (⏱ *09.30–17.00 daily*). Two local groups co-ordinate tours of wineries and other attractions: Bon Vivre (*Roosevelt & 19 de Abril;* m *099 692545;* e *bonvivrecarmelo@gmail.com*) and El Paseo del Vino (*www.elpaseodelvino.com*).

Where to stay As well as in town, there are a few places just outside Carmelo which deserve to be mentioned separately. All listings are included on the map opposite.

In town

⌂ **Los Muelles** Wilson Ferreira Aldunate 219; ✎4542 5485; e www.losmuelles.com. A new boutique hotel on a quiet little street just west of the port, this has 11 smallish rooms (with big beds) & a mini apartment, each featuring a different artist; there's plenty of humour (look out for the elephant beneath the stairs). **$$$$**

⌂ **Hotel-Casino Carmelo** Avda Rodó s/n; ✎4542 2314/33; e airemar@adinet.com.uy; www.hotelcasinocarmelo.com. A 4-storey block in the beach area with 2 swimming pools, this has 85 rooms for up to 5 (all with cable TV & Wi-Fi) plus AC suites. **$$$**

⌂ **Hotel Playa Seré** Tabaré 2671; ✎4542 6202; m 098 143914; e airemar@adinet.com.uy, hotelplayasere@hotmail.com. Next to the casino, this is a spiffy ranch-style single-storey place, with swimming pool, AC & free Wi-Fi throughout. **$$$**

⌂ **Hotel Timabe** 19 de Abril 140 & Solís; ✎5401 4725; e timabe@adinet.com.uy; www.ciudadcarmelo.com/timabe. A fairly new & decent

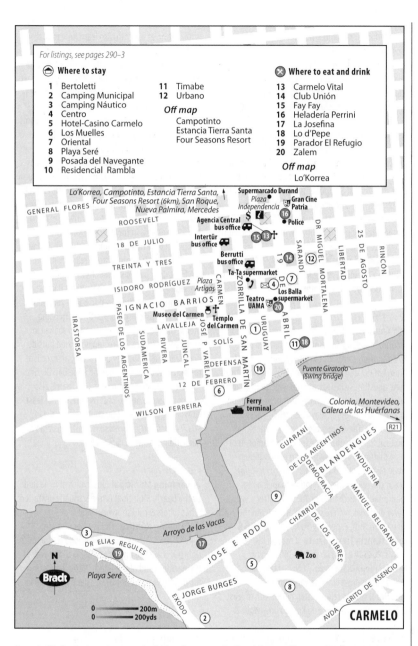

For listings, see pages 290–3

⊜ **Where to stay**

1	Bertoletti	11	Timabe
2	Camping Municipal	12	Urbano
3	Camping Náutico		
4	Centro		***Off map***
5	Hotel-Casino Carmelo		Campotinto
6	Los Muelles		Estancia Tierra Santa
7	Oriental		Four Seasons Resort
8	Playa Seré		
9	Posada del Navegante		
10	Residencial Rambla		

❌ **Where to eat and drink**

13	Carmelo Vital
14	Club Unión
15	Fay Fay
16	Heladería Perrini
17	La Josefina
18	Lo d'Pepe
19	Parador El Refugio
20	Zalem

Off map

Lo'Korrea

CARMELO

3-star behind a single-storey neocolonial façade; rooms have AC & cable TV, & there's Wi-Fi, parking & a *hidromasaje* pool. **$$$**

🏠 **Hotel Urbano** Sarandí 308; ✆4542 2224; www.hotelurbanocarmelo.com. The most modern place in the centre, a bit minimalist in style, with services including free internet access. **$$$**

🏠 **Hotel Centro** Uruguay 370; ✆4542 4488; e hotelcentro@ciudadcarmelo.com; www. ciudadcarmelo.com/hotelcentro. Calling itself a 3-star hotel, this has dated but adequate rooms, plus a honeymoon suite with jacuzzi. **$$**

🏠 **Hotel Posada del Navegante** Avda Rodó 383; ✆4542 3973; m 099 362281;

e posadadelnavegante@hotmail.com; www.
posadadelnavegante.com. Near the yacht club &
casino & 200m from the Playa Seré, this attractive
place has just 8 AC rooms with private bathroom,
cable TV, Wi-Fi & a decent breakfast. **$$**
🏠 **Hotel-Residencial Rambla** Uruguay &
12 de Febrero; 4542 2390/2638;
e carmeloramblahotel@adinet.com.uy; www.
ciudadcarmelo.com/ramblahotel. Nicely located
by the river, this has tired but affordable rooms in
various categories, from *económico*, standard (with
AC), *preferencial* & superior (with AC & balcony) to
suites with AC, balcony & kitchenette. **$$**
🏠 **Hotel Bertoletti** Uruguay 171; 4542 2030.
Dated but cheap & functional, with 25 rooms with
private bathrooms. **$**
🏠 **Hotel Oriental** 19 de Abril 284; 4542
2404. An adequate *hospedaje*-type place, although
rooms do have private bathrooms. **$**

Further afield
🏠 **Campotinto** Camino de los Peregrinos, San
Roque; 4542 7744; e info@campotinto.com;
www.posadacampotinto.com. A kilometre east
from km257 of Ruta 21 just north of Carmelo, this
new guesthouse is dedicated to wine tourism, with
a 'museum vineyard' displaying varieties of grape
planted in traditional ways (as well as gazebos
for picnics). There are 4 big rooms (1 wheelchair-
accessible) & a safari-style luxury 'glamping' tent
on a platform, plus a swimming pool & Italian-
style restaurant (⏰ *to guests & lunch Fri–Sun*).
It's at the rear of the San Roque chapel, a big
pilgrimage church built in 1869–70 after a yellow
fever outbreak, where services are held on the 16th
of each month, especially 16 August. **$$$$$**
🏠 **Estancia Tierra Santa** Costa de las
Vacas; 4540 2331; m 099 543607; www.
estanciatierrasanta.com; ⏰ Nov–May. This
American-owned working ranch makes a
delightful spot to relax, watch birds (with at least
50 resident species) or ride Karen's fine *criollo* &

Arabian horses. You can also learn how to make
herbal medicines & skin & bodycare products,
with plants grown organically on the estancia or
found wild. The Tuscan-style farmhouse, with parts
dating from 1830, has been lovingly restored & a
guest wing added, with a veranda giving on to 3
beautifully decorated rooms with huge bathrooms
& Wi-Fi (but no TV). From US$385, including 2
superb meals & lots of drinks. **$$$$$**
🏠 **Four Seasons Resort** 7km northwest at
Ruta 21 km262; 4542 9000; e reservations.bue@
fourseasons.com; www.fourseasons.com/carmelo.
This is a one-off, a truly luxurious resort that flies
guests in from Buenos Aires in a private plane &
has little interest in travellers passing through
Carmelo. Furnished with southeast Asian antiques,
including a 12th-century stone relief from Java
& a front door commissioned from Balinese
woodcarvers, it feels something like a Bariloche
mountain chalet transposed to Bali – very odd!
The luxury is astonishing, starting with being
met at the grass airstrip with a towel soaked in
eucalyptus essence. There's an unheated outside
pool & an indoor infinity pool & spa, an excellent
restaurant & a hookah-themed wine bar. Duplex
suites & bungalows, from US$265. There's also
what's meant to be the best (& perhaps the least
crowded) golf course in South America (4542
9047; e golf.uru@fourseasons.com), plus polo &
horse riding facilities. **$$$$$**

Camping
🏕 **Camping Municipal** Just south of Avda Rodó
by the beach, Municipal is free & usually unstaffed;
it has toilets & cold showers.
🏕 **Camping Náutico** Dr Elías Regules s/n;
4542 2058. Across the swing bridge to the south,
right/west at once on Avda Rodó, & all the way to
the northern end of the beach, Náutico is mainly
for visiting yachties but there's plenty of space for
others. **$**

✕ **Where to eat** All listings are included on the map, page 291.

✕ **Fay Fay** 18 de Julio 324; 4542 4827. A
standard parrilla, also serving pasta, pizza, & a
menu of the day, with seating outside for people-
watching on Plaza Independencia. **$$$**
✕ **La Josefina** Avda Rodó; 4542 2506. At the
yacht club, with a great view across the river & a

very varied menu including *malfati de espinaca*
(spinach dumplings), Mexican & wok dishes, & a
chivito al plato for 2. **$$$**
✕ **Club Unión** 19 de Abril 330; 4542 2079.
A classic small-town club restaurant, serving
traditional dishes in a traditional way. **$$**

✗ **Lo d'Pepe** 19 de Abril & Solís. A nice new parrilla in a historic building liked to the Hotel Timabé, its main claim to fame is that the president, 'Pepe' Mujica, & his wife pop in for lunch when holidaying here. $$

✗ **Lo' Korrea** Colonia Estrella (past the San Roque chapel & right at the Almacen de la Capilla); ⏱ only Sat night & for Sun lunch. This very simple traditional place is very popular for it's all-you-can-eat buffet of ravioli & chicken. $$

✗ **Parador El Refugio** Elias Regules; ☎ 4542 2325/4070; e elrefugiocarmelo@gmail.com; ⏱ winter w/ends only (with heating). This large-ish thatched building is a beachfront institution, especially at sunset; it serves basic parrilla, pizza, burgers, milanesas & the like. $$

⏛ **Carmelo Vital – Dietetica Integral** 18 de Julio 366; ☎ 4542 6504; ⏱ 09.30–14.00, 19.00–22.00 Mon–Sat. Next to the church, serving healthy salads, breads, sugar-free ice cream & the like. $

⏛ **Heladería Perrini** 19 de Abril 440, on Plaza Independencia. The best ice cream. $

⏛ **Zalem** 19 de Abril 225; ☎ 4542 5735; ⏱ 20.30–03.00 Tue–Sun. A bar-pizzeria with a pool table. $

Shopping Supermarkets include Durand (*Flores & 19 de Abril;* ⏱ *08.30–12.15, 15.30–21.00 Mon–Fri, 08.30–12.30, 16.30–21.00 Sat*); Ta-Ta (*Zorrilla de San Martín 278 & Isidoro Rodríguez;* ⏱ *08.00–22.00 daily*); and Los Balla (*Uruguay 224;* ⏱ *08.00–midnight Mon-Sat, 09.00–midnight Sun*).

At Zorrilla de San Martin 373 (☎ *4542 2749;* m *098 162634; www.escultorjosecastro. com;* ⏱ *10.00–12.00, 15.00–19.00 Tue-Sun*) the sculptor **José Castro** sells his excellent and quirky woodcarvings, in a wide range of techniques and styles; arriving from Spain at 17, he made fine furniture until turning to sculpture over the last two decades.

Other practicalities

Banks ATMs can be found on the west side of Plaza Independencia; you can also exchange money at Cambio Lerga (*19 de Abril 300 & Rodríguez;* ⏱ *08.00–12.00, 13.00–18.00 Mon–Fri*) and at EuroCred Cambio, on the southwestern corner of the plaza (*Uruguay 400;* ⏱ *08.30–19.30 Mon–Fri, 08.30–13.00 Sat*).

Cinema The Teatro UAMA at Uruguay 220 was built in 1928 and was recently refurbished; it functions mainly as a cinema and is surprisingly big, with three U-shaped galleries. Just north of the plaza at 19 de Abril 462, the Gran Cine Patria is another striking Deco edifice.

Communications The post office is at Uruguay 360 (⏱ *09.00–15.00 Mon–Fri*). Antel's phone centre is at Barrios 349 and Uruguay (⏱ *09.00–18.00 Mon–Fri, 10.00–18.00 Sat*). There's internet access at Ciber Station (*19 de Abril 110;* ☎ *4542 6843*) and Carmelo Digital, north of the plaza at 19 de Abril. There's public Wi-Fi on the north side of the plaza.

Emergency services The police station is on the east side of Plaza Independencia. The main hospital sits across the north end of Uruguay on Bulevar Artigas. The Inspectoría de Migración is at Solís 378 (☎ *4542 2461/2433;* e *dnm-carmelo@ minterior.gub.uy*).

What to see and do Five blocks north of the ferry terminal on the south side of Plaza Artigas (where a statue of Artigas was unveiled on the centenary of the town's foundation in 1916), the **Museo del Carmen** (*Ignacio Barrios 208 & José Pedro Varela;* ⏱ *summer 10.00–12.00 Mon–Fri; winter 15.00–17.00 Mon–Fri, usually closed in Jan; free*) is a pretty amateurish museum of local history. It was built in

6

1847 as a school, alongside the **Templo del Carmen**, the town's main church (built 1830). On the livelier Plaza Independencia, the parish church seems unfinished but has a fine interior in contrasting pastel colours. Three blocks south down 19 de Abril is the famous swing bridge (see page 290); on its south side is a memorial to Atilio François (1922–2007), the town's greatest sporting hero, known as El León de Carmelo, who won the Vuelta Ciclista del Uruguay three years running in 1946–48 and came fourth at the 1948 Olympics in London.

Turning right immediately south of the bridge, Avenida Rodó leads past the rowing and yacht clubs, with yacht moorings along a 600m stretch of the river, to the Playa Seré beach, with restaurants and bars. Just south of Avenida Rodó are the casino and a small zoo, with goats, peacocks and so on.

AROUND CARMELO Ruta 21 leads south towards Colonia; turning left after 13km on to Camino Teniente Juan de San Martín, it's 4km to the ruins of the **Calera de las Huérfanas** (Lime Kiln of the Orphan Girls), built as a Jesuit mission in 1740, with the lime kiln added in 1744. Established by the Colegio de Belén in Buenos Aires, it was administered by Juan de San Martín, future father of the Liberator of Argentina, Chile and Peru, José de San Martín, after the Jesuits were expelled from the Spanish Empire in 1767. In 1777 the Sisters of Charity moved here from Buenos Aires, setting up a home for orphaned girls. In 1833 Darwin visited the quarry to study the rocks, and then passed through the 'straggling thatched town' of Arroyo Las Vacas (now Carmelo) to stay the night with an American who ran a lime kiln at Puente Camacho, just beyond Carmelo. Continuing beyond the Calera and turning left after 2km, it takes about 40 minutes by bike to reach Estancia Tierra Santo. There's not a lot left to see other than the roofless remains of the red-brick chapel, but it's an evocative site with plenty of birdlife.

Also on Camino Teniente Juan de San Martín is the **Bodega Zubizarreta** (⚲ 4542 3080; e mzubiza@adinet.com.uy; www.vinoszubizarreta.com.uy; ⏱ 08.00–11.00, 13.30–16.30 daily), which offers wine tasting without advance reservations.

Uruguay's largest vineyard by area is 2.2km east of central Carmelo: **Viñedos Irurtia** (Avda Paraguay; ⚲ 4542 2323/3355; e turismo@irurtia.com.uy; www.irurtia. com.uy) was founded in 1913 and was run from 1954 to 2010 by Dante Irurtia, a legendary figure in the development of New World wines, although his children (the fourth generation) have now taken over. Carmelo has an ideal microclimate for wine-growing because of the warm water flowing out of the Río Uruguay, with warm days and cool nights, plus well-balanced and drained soils. Growing a wide variety of French grapes including Tannat, Syrah, Marsellan and Viognier, as well as Gewurztraminer, they produce a lot of bulk wine plus fine wines, including the Reserva del Virrey Malbec, a unique example of Malbec in Uruguay. A year after Dante's death the new Km.0 Río de la Plata single-parcel line was launched, celebrating Irurtia's location at the head of the Río de la Plata; there are seven Reserva varieties and Tannat, Pinot Noir and Viognier oaked Gran Reservas. There's also a late harvest Botrytis Gewurztraminer, a sparkling Pinot Noir champenoise and grappas, from Pinot Noir, Tannat and Gewurztraminer grapes. You can also see goats, kept for cheese-making, and *ñandues* (rheas), kept for meat. **Tastings** are held in the fine brick cellars (⏱ tours 11.00 & 15.00 daily; free, or US$18 for a plate of cheeses & breads or for premium wines). They also have some fine old Model A Ford trucks which will be used to take tourists to the vineyard and to the quarries which supplied much of the granite used to build the port of Buenos Aires.

In the Colonia Estrella area, just north, at the end of the asphalt just beyond the Campotinto guesthouse (which also makes its own very drinkable Tannat), the

Almacen de la Capilla (✆ *4542 7316;* m *099 544255;* e *almacendelacapilla@adinet. com.uy*) was founded around 1900 and has a 12ha vineyard including 120-year-old Moscatel vines (for table grapes) and possibly the oldest Tannat vines still in production in Uruguay: about 100 years old. Their Bodega Cordano wine is largely for the local market (in five-litre carafes) but it's worth seeing the very authentic shop/bar (selling excellent local jams etc, as well as wine) and the lovely tasting cellar below a trapdoor.

The excellent **El Legado** (*The Legacy;* m *098 307193, 099 111493;* e *bodegalegado@adinet.com.uy; www.facebook.com/ellegadobodegaboutique*) has remained deliberately small-scale, with a tiny winery tucked under a lean-to, but using the latest techniques (such as vertical planting) and with a true feeling for the wine. They grow Tannat and Syrah, macerated for 24 hours then warmed and pressed again, and c70% oaked; visits are generally by reservation and cost US$30 (US$50 with lunch).

To the northwest on Ruta 21, beyond a birdwatching hide (on the left) and the Four Seasons Resort (see page 292), the **Puente Camacho** (or Castells) crosses the Arroyo de las Víboras (Stream of Vipers) near the original site of Carmelo. Built in 1858 with five stone arches, it was Uruguay's first toll bridge. To the left are the Puerto Camacho marina, the Posada Camacho hotel and the stylish but casual Basta Pedro pizzeria-cafeteria (✆ *4542 9258;* e *bastapedro@puertocarmelo.com*), all part of the same property development as the Four Seasons and very popular with affluent Argentines who come across by speedboat from Tigre. At km264 the Estancia Narbona is the oldest unaltered building in Uruguay (although the chapel is largely ruined), built in 1732–38 by Juan de Narbona, a Buenos Aires builder, and later named after his son-in-law and heir Francisco Martín Camacho. Four kilometres further on, the **Finca & Granja Narbona** (✆ *4540 4778; www.narbona. com.uy;* **$$$$**) produces wines and cheeses and offers very comfortable rooms with a swimming pool, gym and an amazing breakfast. Next to the hotel is the new winery, inspired by the Estancia Narbona chapel; having started replanting their vineyards in 1990 (with Sauvignon Blanc, Viognier, Petit Verdot, Pinot Noir, Syrah, Tempranillo and Tannat), they now produce 80,000 bottles a year (with star consultant Michel Rolland) and started exporting in 2012. Their new Sauvignon Blanc is more French than New World in style, floral on the nose and with very good acidity and complexity. Their only rosé is a Tannat that is macerated for just two hours and then kept in oak for four months; it's excellent with fish such as salmon. The Pinot Noir is made from two different clones, vinified separately and blended only at the end of the process; it's light and fresh and goes well with chicken or even fish. Their excellent 100% Tannat Roble spends a year in oak and has lots of complex tannins; the top-of-the-range Luz de Luna Tannat is ideal with rack of lamb and cream sauces. All need time to open up but are worth the wait – the Pinot Noir in particular is wonderful on the nose.

Across the lovely garden is a good restaurant specialising in pasta (as well as beef and salmon); free transfers are provided from the Four Seasons Resort. There's also a shop here selling their wines, as well as sparkling champenoise, grappa and *grappamiel* (with honey), olive oil, and their own jams, cheeses and yoghurts. At the marina, La Lechería is more of a deli, selling their full range of Narbona products.

Just upstream of the mouth of the Río Uruguay, **Nueva Palmira** (founded in 1831) is a small port being expanded as an outlet for paper pulp, Brazilian iron ore and Bolivian soya. There's not much to see beyond the Museo Municipal (*Lucas Roselli 1130*) and Punta Gorda (where Darwin took some important rock samples in 1833), just south, where the Río Uruguay becomes the Río de la Plata.

There not much reason to come here, unless you arrive by boat. Currently Líneas Delta Argentinas sail once daily from Tigre to Nuevo Palmira, leaving early in the morning and returning from Uruguay in the afternoon, with connecting buses to and from Colonia (see pages 53–4). Regular bus services between Colonia and Mercedes are provided by Berrutti (*Artigas 1130;* ↖ *4544 6181;* e *berruttiturismo@adinet.com.uy; www.berruttiturismo.com*). Chadre has a couple of services a day from Montevideo via Colonia that continue north to Mercedes, Fray Bentos, Paysandú, Salto and Bella Unión. The best place to stay is the Posada Al Natural (↖ *4544 8881; www.alnatural. com.uy;* **$$$$**), just south at Laguna Solís, Punta Gorda; it has beautifully minimalist chalets around a swimming pool. There's also the Posada del Cabo (*Varela & Artigas;* ↖ *4544 7810;* e *delcabo@adinet.com.uy;* **$$$**), Mi Posada (*on the rambla at Estados Unidos & Lavalleja;* ↖ *4544 7161; www.mipueblo.com.uy;* **$$$**), the one-star Hotel Centro (*Artigas 822;* ↖ *4544 6807;* **$$**) and the Camping Náutico Las Higueritas (↖ *4544 6368;* **$**) at the newly refurbished yacht harbour (*Dársena Higueritas;* ↖ *4544 6516;* e *dnhnp@adinet.com.uy*), which has showers (☉ *07.00–18.00/22.00 daily*). The tourist information office is also at the Darsena Higueritas (↖ *4544 7637*), along with the Inspectoría de Migración (↖ *4544 6553;* e *dnm-nuevapalmira@minterior.gub.uy*). There are ATMs, and you can change money at Cambio Lerga (*Artigas 1028*) and Cambio Nelson (*Artigas 953*).

SORIANO DEPARTMENT

Soriano is one of Uruguay's most historic departments, where the first European settlement, the Jesuit mission of Santo Domingo de Soriano, was founded in 1624 on Isla Vizcaino. This was soon shifted to the mainland, eventually moving four times before settling on the site of the present Villa Soriano. Artigas triggered the movement for independence from Spain with the Grito de Asencio (27 February 1811), 11km south of Mercedes, and the capture of Mercedes and Santo Domingo de Soriano (also known as Villa Soriano) the next day. The department also played a major role in the Cruzada Libertadora (Crusade of Liberation), starting on 19 April 1825 when Lavalleja and Oribe crossed the Río Uruguay and landed at the Playa de la Agraciada. A couple of days later they met Rivera at Monzón, agreeing to overcome their rivalry to unite against Brazil.

Nowadays Soriano is a prosperous agricultural region. Its northern boundary is the Río Negro, which flows right across the country and into the Río Uruguay just below Villa Soriano. Both rivers are known for their fine sandy beaches, their islands and backwaters, and the many opportunities they give for boating and camping. There are plenty of large and tasty fish such as *dorado, boga, tararira, bagre, pejerrey, surubí* and *mojarra*. There are also wild boar and deer in sizeable numbers, having been introduced to Anchorena and then escaped.

Ruta 2 runs from Montevideo to Mercedes, passing through the farming towns of Cardona and José Enrique Rodó. Coming from Colonia and Nueva Palmira on Ruta 21 you'll pass a turning to **Playa de la Agraciada** soon after entering Soriano. The beach is still popular, and a small pyramid marks the spot where the 33 Orientales landed in 1825. Juan Manuel Blanes stayed at a nearby estancia (or ranch) while working on his painting of the landing. Berrutti buses come here from Nueva Palmira at 12.00 and 19.00 on Monday, Wednesday and Friday; there's a parador and campsite (☉ *all year*).

DOLORES At km321 on Ruta 21, midway between Nueva Palmira and the departmental capital of Mercedes, this small town is the heart of Uruguay's wheat-

and soya-growing belt. It's the jumping-off point for the even smaller and quieter Villa Soriano, Uruguay's oldest settlement, although there's little to see in either. Dolores itself (Nuestra Señora de los Dolores del Espinillo in full) was only finally moved to this site on the Río San Salvador in 1801, having failed to establish itself in several other locations.

The riverside rambla is the town's best feature, with thick gallery forest on the far side, and nice parks to left and right of the six blocks that constitute the waterfront; Plaza Constitución and the business centre are over 1km south.

Getting there and away, and getting around Bus offices are on the plaza: Agencia Central (*Chadre/Sabelin; Ascencio 1756 & Vasquez;* ☏*4534 2700;* ⊕ *08.00–23.30*) go to Montevideo, and twice daily from Colonia to Mercedes, Fray Bentos, Paysandú, Salto and Bella Unión. Intertür (*Artigas & Asencio*) go to Montevideo and Mercedes. Berrutti (*Asencio 1671;* ☏ *4534 4179*) serve Carmelo and Colonia. An ancient bus shuttles occasionally from the plaza to the rambla, going north on Puig and returning south on 18 de Julio.

Tourist information Tourist information is available at the library (☏*4534 5016;* e *turismo.dolores@soriano.gub.uy;* ⊕ *07.30–13.30 Mon–Fri*) at Rico Puppo and Puig, where you'll also find the Almacen de Artesanos craft centre (⊕ *08.00–14.00, 15.00–18.30 Mon–Fri*).

🏠 Where to stay and eat

🏠 **Hostal del Espinillo** Redruello 1032; ☏4534 5077/5576; www.hostaldelespinillo.com.uy. This new hotel is the best place in town, with spacious riverside gardens & swimming pool. **$$$**

🏠 **Hotel Argón** Varela 1600 & Sotura; ☏4534 5590/2; e hotelargon@adinet.com.uy; www. hotelargon.com.uy. A block southeast from the church, this mid-20th-century building has been done up with AC rooms of various sizes behind a black glass façade. Dinner is available. B/fast inc. **$$**

🏠 **Hotel Dolores** Puig 1693 & Schuster; ☏4534 3235; e hoteldolores@adinet.com.uy. A friendly place which has rooms with cable TV & Wi-Fi around a nice courtyard; rooms with AC cost substantially more, & breakfast is extra. **$$–$**

🛖 **Campsite** On the shady Península Timoteo Ramospe, immediately to the west on the rambla; ☏4534 2703. Hot showers, BBQs, a cafeteria-bar, swimming & a boat-launch. **$**

✗ **Asociación La Agropecuaría** South side of the main plaza; ☏4534 4742. More or less the only place to eat – very decent. **$$**

Shopping There are supermarkets on the west side of the plaza and at Puig and Vásquez, two blocks south.

Other practicalities

Banks There's an ATM opposite Intertür on the south side of the plaza, and Cambio Iberia (*Asencio 1606*) is on the west side of the plaza.

Communications There's free Wi-Fi on Plaza Artigas (between Puig and Asencio, three blocks from the river, not on the main Plaza Constitución), as well as a British-style green letter box made in Montevideo in 1897. The post office is at Varela 1402 (⊕ *09.00–15.00 Mon–Fri, 09.00–12.00 Sat*).

What to see and do On Plaza Constitución is José Zorrilla de San Martín's *Monumento a la Libertad*. On the east side of the plaza is the neoclassical church **Nuestra Señora de Dolores (Our Lady of Sorrows)**, its red-brick exterior never finished. To the north on the corner of the plaza is the Torre de Reloj (clock tower), built in 1904 because the church tower was not ready to hold the clock as planned. It's also worth noting the Templo Evangélico Valdense (Waldensian Protestant church), built in 1934 at Vásquez and Varela. On the other side of town, a block from the river at Grito de Asencio and Alimundi, is the **Museum of Regional History and Agriculture** (*Museo Histórico Regional y de Agricultura;* ☉ *14.00–18.00 Sat–Sun; free*), with a wide-ranging collection of indigenous ceramics, hand axes, spear and arrow points, glyptodont shells, a megatherium jaw, rifles, soda bottles, a threshing machine as well as an anchor and rigging, and various paintings; just to the west on Plaza Italia, before the tiny port, are an old steam crane and a statue of Garibaldi by Edmondo Prati (1957).

The town's big event is the Fiesta de la Primavera (Spring Festival) on the second weekend of October, when thousands of people come to see the town decked out in spring flowers, as well as the usual procession and dances.

VILLA SORIANO The sleepy village of Santo Domingo de Soriano, known as Villa Soriano, is the successor to the first European settlement in Uruguay, founded in 1624 by the Jesuits on Isla Vizcaino, as a mission to the Chaná natives, and moved here in 1708.

There are no buses on the direct Ruta 95 from Mercedes to Villa Soriano; instead buses from Mercedes to Dolores drop passengers at a junction 3km north of Dolores (km323), where they are soon collected by a rattletrap bus from Dolores to Villa Soriano, about 20km northwest.

At the entrance to the village there's a massive timbó tree (a couple of centuries old), where the road splits into the only two asphalted streets, Lavalleja and Cabildo, leading through the village to the long wooden jetty on the Río Negro. Plaza Artigas sits between them, three blocks before the river, with the **Capilla de Santo Domingo**, built in 1797, on its south side; inside is an articulated wooden Christ made by a Chaná craftsman.

A block south of the chapel, the brightly painted Casa de las Máscaras (*Cabildo & Ituzaingó*) is almost hidden by ceramic masks hanging from nails; these were made of sand and cement by the late 'Don Paco' Juan Artega, and are good for amusing children. Almost opposite is the Casa de Marfetán, built in 1805 and housing the **historical museum** (☉ *11.00–17.00 daily; free*). Around a patio with an old cistern are rooms displaying a ragtag collection of Mylodon (giant sloth) bones, glyptodon (giant armadillo) bones and shell, indigenous arrowheads, bolas and ceramics, 19th-century lamps and a carriage, rusty guns and bayonets, and lots of really bad paintings of historical scenes. At the rear through the office are coins and banknotes, ancient adding machines and moveable type. It's really not worth the detour, although the Artigas family history could be interesting: in 1790, when he was 26, the father of the nation married his first wife Isabel Sánchez (aged 30, from Villa Soriano), who was descended from a Chaná *cacique*. Their four children were born at the Solar de Artigas, two blocks east of the museum (although two soon died). In 1811 Spanish ships shelled Villa Soriano, trying to capture Artigas (who was then in Mercedes) and were driven off by local heroes.

Along Cabildo are various very tatty 19th-century houses, including the Aduana (Customs; in the former Hotel Olivera) opposite the jetty, the Casa de Alessio opposite the museum, and the Casa de Galarza, once home of a Colorado leader. Opposite this is a small park, at the rear of the museum, where two thatched cabins constitute the municipal motel. If you want to stay here you'll have to contact the Junta Local (*Cabildo, facing the plaza;* ☏ *4530 4144*), and bring your own food; you should also ask before putting up a tent here. There are also lots of houses to rent (alquila) in the village.

There's no beach or other obvious holiday attractions, but Uruguayans, including ex-President Tabaré Vásquez, do enjoy fishing here for dorado, boga, tararira and bagre. It's also known for birdwatching, with wetlands and gallery forest – start with the riverside road to the right from the jetty (to the Parque Municipal La Islita), or go west on Asencio from the Casa de Alessio.

MERCEDES The capital of Soriano department, Mercedes was founded in 1788 and is now a city of around 40,000 with an attractive setting on the Río Negro, with over 2km of waterfront gardens and promenades that are astonishingly lively until midnight. It is also home to one of the best art galleries in the interior of Uruguay and is known for its Belle-Époque buildings.

Mercedes has a lively carnival, known for the drag queens (*travestis*) who come from all over Uruguay, and one of Uruguay's best jazz festivals, Jazz a la Calle (*www. jazzalacalle.com*), in the second week of January, with free gigs on street corners and in the historic area known as Manzana Veinte (Block Twenty).

Getting there and away Ruta 2 from Montevideo skirts the east side of town on its way to Fray Bentos and the international bridge to Argentina. There's a busy modern **bus terminal** at Don Bosco 734 between Artigas and Colón, 13 blocks south of the river (nine uphill blocks from Plaza Independencia). Converted from an army barracks, it houses exchange, phone and post offices and free WCs (but no left luggage or Wi-Fi), and has a shopping centre attached.

All the bus companies are here: Agencia Central (✆ *4532 1717;* e *mercedes@ agenciacentral.com.uy*), Berrutti (✆ *4532 5033*), CAUVI/Intertür (✆ *4532 2046*) and CUT/Bus de la Carrera and ETA (✆ *4532 3766*). Agencia Central has eight departures a day to Montevideo (*6 on Sat & 5 on Sun*), and two from Montevideo and Colonia to Paysandú, Salto and Bella Unión. CUT has a dozen departures a day to Fray Bentos and five to Montevideo, as well as one (*06.30 Mon–Sat*) to Gualeguaychú in Argentina; Cauvi runs to Buenos Aires at 00.45 daily. Intertür has seven services to Dolores (*3 on Sun*) and three to Represa Palmar (*13.30 Mon–Sat, 19.00 Mon–Fri, 21.15 daily*). CUT has two buses a week (*00.40 Mon & Fri*) to Rivera via Trinidad, Durazno and Tacuarembó, and ETA has two (*00.40 Wed & Sun*) as far as Trinidad and Durazno.

Tourist information The tourism office (*Detomasi 415, just east of 19 de Abril;* ✆ *4532 2733/2201; www.soriano.gub.uy;* ⊕ *09.00–17.00 Mon–Fri*) is in Manzana Veinte, facing the Isla del Puerto.

🏠 **Where to stay** All listings are included on the map, page 301.

🏠 **Gran Hotel Brisas del Hum** Artigas 209; ✆4532 9794; e info.mercedes@granh.com; www. granh.com. On the plaza, this is the most modern & stylish hotel in town, with swimming pool, sauna & gym, parking in the courtyard, & AC rooms with cable TV, minibar. There are data sockets in the bedrooms but the only Wi-Fi is in the public areas downstairs. A good breakfast is served in the Don Peperone chain restaurant next to reception. **$$$$**

🏠 **Mercedes Rambla Hotel** Avda Asencio 728; ✆4533 0696; e mrh@adinet.com.uy. The best in town until the Brisas del Hum appeared, this is still very nice, with a trim garden, although staff could be friendlier. There are 25 suites with AC, but Wi-Fi only in public areas. **$$$$**

🏠 **Hotel Colón** Colón 169; ✆4532 4720/1; e hotelcolon@adinet.com.uy. A fine Belle-Époque frontage with 40 rooms behind, this has AC rooms, a good breakfast, & a PC in the lobby. **$$$**

➤ **Hotel ITO** Haedo 184; ☎4532 4919. A pleasant family hotel with some unwarranted pretensions, but decent rooms with private bathroom, cable TV & frigobar. B/fast US$4 extra. **$$**

➤ **Hospedaje-Cafetería Mercedes** Sánchez 614; ☎4532 3804. Excellent value, simple but friendly, with rooms with either private or shared bathroom. **$**

➤ **Hotel del Litoral** Haedo 262; ☎4532 4872; m 099 165201. In a nice older house, this has large rooms all with AC & cable TV, a garden with BBQ, & a PC in the lobby. **$**

➤ **Hotel Mercedes** Giménez 659; ☎4532 3204. A simple place that's pretty fair value, with rooms with TV & shared or private bathrooms; no breakfast. **$**

➤ **Club de Remeros** Rowing Club; Rambla de la Rivera 949 & Gomensoro; ☎4532 2227;

e remeros@adinet.com.uy. The only hostel-style accommodation. Aimed at sports groups but may be available. They have 6-bed rooms with shared bathrooms. **$**

Å **Camping del Hum** (Hum meaning the Río Negro) On the Isla del Puerto; Avda República Argentina; contact the tourism office, ☎4532 2733; ⏱ mid-Dec–Easter. Reached by a narrow bridge with manually operated traffic lights from the rambla just west of the centre, with a beach, a bar-restaurant & picnic tables. Simple. **$**

Å **Club Pescadores Biguá** Ruta 2 km281; ☎4532 1779; e contacto@clubbigua.com. A fishing club at the north end of the bridge across the Río Negro, with shaded beachfront plots & no fewer than 52 grills with tables & benches, as well as a shop. **$**

✗ Where to eat
All listings are included on the map opposite.

✗ **Club de Remeros Mercedes** Rambla de la Rivera 949 & Gomensoro; ☎4532 1520/2534; e remeros@adinet.com.uy. At the city's rowing club (also offering tennis, table tennis & basketball); you can eat well in the restaurant or on the excellent riverfront terrace. **$$**

✗ **Parador Martiniano** Rambla Costanera & 18 de Julio; ⏱ 12.00–15.30, 20.30–00.30 Tue–Sun (until 01.00 Fri–Sat). A nice thatched place by the river that serves parrilla, pastas & snacks, & is a great spot for a sunset drink. **$$**

✗ **Café de la Onda** Colón 194; ⏱ 18.30–midnight or later. Just off Plaza Independencia, this is a lively new pub that serves burgers, chivitos, etc. **$$**

✗ **Café del Sol** Rambla de la Rivera. A terrace bar by the river, serving a good range of parrilla, chivitos, fish (plancha or milanesa) or pizza. **$$**

✗ **Potenza resto-bar** Artigas 426; ☎4532 8893. A bar-pizzeria-chivitería that's lively & cheap. **$**

⊑ **Don Diego** Artigas 707. A handy little panadería on the east side of the bus terminal, for carry-on snacks. **$**

⊑ **Sajuba** Plaza Artigas & Don Bosco. Just outside the bus terminal, this is a stylish little café-heladería for classy ice creams & treats; it also has Wi-Fi. **$**

⊑ **Topo Gigio** Colón 222. On the west side of Plaza Independencia, & also in the bus terminal, this serves superb ice cream. **$**

Entertainment The Casa de Cultura, in the former Masonic Temple (1885), shows some interesting films; the municipal Teatro 28 de Febrero (at 28 de Febrero and Ferreira Aldunate; a superb building dating from 1938) has recently been refurbished but the Cine Rex (at the rear of the Gran Hotel Brisas del Hum) is closed.

Shopping The main supermarket downtown is Ta-Ta (*Artigas & Rodó;* ⏱ *08.00–22.00 daily*). Casa Puerta (*Ituzaingó & Ferreira Aldunate;* ⏱ *08.30–12.00, 14.30–19.00 Mon–Fri, 08.00–12.00, 16.00–19.00 Sat*) is a classy crafts shop diagonally opposite the Casa de la Cultura.

Other practicalities

Banks There are ATMs at the bus terminal and around Plaza Independencia; you can also change money at Cambio Maiorano (*Colón 255 near Plaza Independencia;*

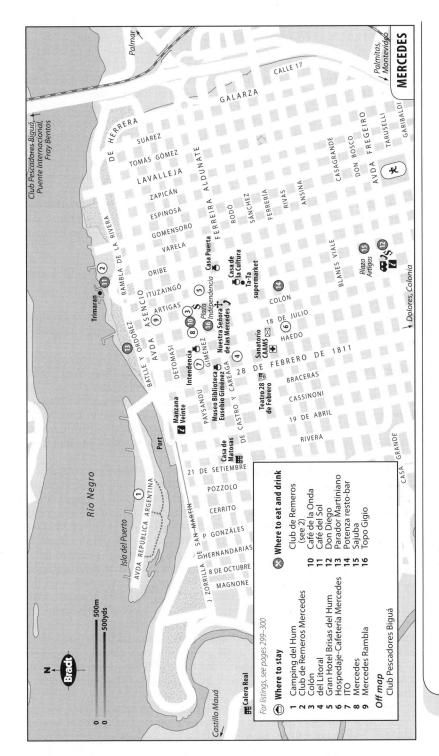

CALLE 17

GALARZA

DE HERRERA

SUÁREZ

TOMÁS GÓMEZ

LAVALLEJA

ZAPICÁN

ESPINOSA

GOMENSORO

VARELA

ORIBE

ITUZAINGÓ

ARTIGAS

FERREIRA ALDUNATE

Casa Puerta

Casa de
la Cultura

Ta-Ta
supermarket

RODÓ

SÁNCHEZ

RIVAS

ANSINA

FERRERIA

CASAGRANDE

DON BOSCO

AVDA FREGEIRO

TARUSELLI

GARIBALDI

BLANES VIALE

Plaza
Artigas

Palmitas,
Montevideo

Palmar

Club Pescadores Biguá,
Puente Internacional,
Fray Bentos

RAMBLA DE LA RIVERA

Trimarán

DETOMASI

PAYSANDÚ

Manzana
Veinte

Museo Biblioteca
Eusebio Giménez

Intendencia

Nuestra Señora
de las Mercedes

Plaza
Independencia

GIMÉNEZ

28 DE CASTRO Y CAREAGA

Teatro 28
de Febrero

COLÓN

18 DE JULIO

HAEDO

Sanatorio
CAAMS

DE FEBRERO DE 1811

BRACERAS

CASSINONI

19 DE ABRIL

RIVERA

Dolores, Colonia

CASA GRANDE

Casa de
Matosas

21 DE SETIEMBRE

POZZOLO

CERRITO

P GONZÁLES

DHERNANDARIAS

8 DE OCTUBRE

MAGNONE

J ZORRILLA SAN MARTÍN

AVDA REPÚBLICA ARGENTINA

Isla del Puerto

Port

Río Negro

Castillo Maud

Calera Real

For listings, see pages 299–300

(i) Where to stay
1 Camping del Hum
2 Club de Remeros Mercedes
3 Colon
4 del Litoral
5 Gran Hotel Brisas del Hum
6 Hospedaje-Cafetería Mercedes
7 ITO
8 Mercedes
9 Mercedes Rambla

Off map
Club Pescadores Biguá

✗ Where to eat and drink
Club de Remeros
(see 2)
10 Café de la Onda
11 Café del Sol
12 Don Diego
13 Parador Martiniano
14 Potenza resto-bar
15 Sajuba
16 Topo Gigio

500m
500yds

N

Bradt

⊕ *08.30–19.00 Mon–Fri, 08.30–12.30 Sat*) and Cambio Fagalde (*Giménez 709, on the north side of Plaza Independencia;* ⊕ *08.30–18.30 Mon–Fri, 08.30–12.30 Sat*).

Car rental Cars can be rented from Avis (*c/o Jetmar, Colón 260;* ☎ *4532 4794;* m *098 170015*), Hertz (*c/o GeoTour, on Plaza Independencia at Giménez 703;* ☎ *4532 8281;* e *geotour@adinet.com.uy*), Mariño Sport Rent a Car (*c/o Adventour, Artigas 100 & Detomasi;* ☎ *4532 0863;* m *098 426187; www.mariniosport.com*), Multicar (*Tomás Gómez 363;* ☎ *4532 5324;* m *095 535421; www.redmulticar.com*) or Rentacar Daymán (*Rodó 1033;* ☎ *4532 4612;* m *099 734638; www.rentacardayman.com*).

Communications There are post offices at Rodó 650 and 18 de Julio (⊕ *09.00–12.00, 12.30–16.00 Mon–Fri*), and at the bus terminal. There's free Wi-Fi on Plaza Independencia but it's unreliable. There's no Wi-Fi yet at the terminal. Antel has call centres at Ferreira Aldunate 681 (⊕ *09.00–20.00 Mon–Sat, 10.00–18.00 Sun*) and Ferreira Aldunate 730 (⊕ *09.00–20.00 Mon–Fri, 09.00–13.00 Sat*) and the terminal (⊕ *09.00–22.00 Mon–Fri, 09.00–13.00, 18.00–22.00 Sat–Sun*).

Emergency services The Sanatorio CAAMS (*Sánchez 621 & Haedo;* ☎ *4532 2313*) has an emergency clinic.

Immigration For visa issues, the Inspectoría de Migración is at 18 de Julio and Ferreira Aldunate (☎ *4532 2528;* e *dnm-mercedes@minterior.gub.uy;* ⊕ *summer 08.00–14.00; winter 12.00–18.00 Mon–Fri*).

What to see and do The centrepiece of Plaza Independencia, three blocks south of the rambla, is the fine monument of the Gaucho de Asencio (1942) by José Luis Zorrilla de San Martín. On the south side of the plaza the cathedral of **Nuestra Señora de las Mercedes (Our Lady of Mercies)** was consecrated in 1868 on the site of the first church, established in 1788 by Padre Manuel de Castro y Careaga. It's neoclassical, with a fairly striking façade and a relatively simple interior except for the gilded wooden altar, carved in Buenos Aires.

In the foyer of the **Intendencia** (*Giménez & 18 de Julio*) the *antropolito*, almost 6.5kg and 48cm long, is the only human figure carved by indigenous people yet found in Uruguay (although it may be from near Florianopolis in Brazil). Three blocks west of the plaza, the **Museo Biblioteca Eusebio Giménez** (*Giménez & 28 de Febrero;* ⊕ *Jan–Feb 07.30–13.30 Mon–Sat; rest of the year 12.30–18.30 Mon–Fri; free*) houses one of the best art collections outside Montevideo. Eusebio Giménez (1850–1933) was born on this site but his parents were forced to move to Argentina on account of their politics, and he grew up to be the dean of Buenos Aires's notaries, leaving money in his will for a library and an art gallery here. The ground floor opened in 1935 and the rest in 1945, and Education Minister Victor Haedo (born in Mercedes) donated paintings. There are lots of kitsch sculptures in the ground-floor foyer, leading to spacious galleries upstairs. There are a few European paintings, most notably the *Dead Christ* by Martin da Udine (also known as Pellegrino da San Daniele; 1467–1547), probably the only Renaissance painting in Uruguay. It's lovely, and has an interesting frame with ivory insets. There's also a neoclassical portrait of a lady by José de Madrazo (1781–1859), court painter of King Fernando VII of Spain.

There are many Uruguayan paintings, including four very different ones by Pedro Blanes Viale (born in 1878 in Mercedes, near the Casa de Cultura at Ferreira Aldunate & Artigas), a Romantic work of 1898, two portraits, and a very Fauvist painting from 1924, two years before his death. There are also charming sketches on newspaper of cats and snakes. Four of the five main exponents of Planismo (see page 32) are displayed here – Rafael Barradas, Pedro Figari, José Cúneo and Carlos Federico Sáez (born in Mercedes in 1878).

Four blocks west, the **Casa de Matosas** (1934–36) and adjacent Panadería Matosas (*Careaga 337 & Rivera*) are locally famed for their Gaudiesque decoration, though it's more riotous and less tasteful than Gaudí.

The waterfront Rambla de la Rivera continues west past the bridge to the Isla del Puerto, to the former port (where some old rail lines are still visible), now redeveloped for yachts, with three new pontoons. There's a wash-block across the road near the Surubí Club, a very friendly fishing club in what was the town's first permanent school. This is the historic **Manzana Veinte**, including the house in which Garibaldi lived in the 1840s. Avenida Asencio continues west by the water to the more open Parque Guernika, dotted with eucalyptus trees and a few picnic tables, east of the Arroyo Dacá. A new road (unsurfaced) loops around by the stream to join the west end of Careaga at the Puente Dacá (Bridge over the Dacá). On the far side of the bridge are the ruins of the **Calera Real** (Royal Lime Kiln), built by the Jesuits in 1722; the small building with a tin roof is actually their chapel, with four large kilns to the south by the stream. This is the oldest industrial site in Uruguay, and there's talk of creating a Museum of Industry.

Camino Tuya continues from the Calera Real to the **Castillo Mauá** (⊕ 07.00– 21.00 daily; free), a kilometre or so west, which was built in 1857–62 by the Brazilian Baron Mauá (born Irineu Evangelista de Sousa; 1813–89), a self-made banking and railway magnate who played a huge role in Brazil's development but eventually overreached himself and went bankrupt in 1875.

The estate is open to the public and the 3ha park is a favourite place for weekend strolls and picnics. There's a small zoo, to the right just inside the entry, with goats and a few interesting birds. A winery was established here in 1892, but the property was taken over by the Intendencia (departmental government) of Soriano in 1961 and remains municipally owned, producing 450,000 litres of table wine in 2008, as well as olive oil and sheep's cheese. Vinos Mauá (⊕ 07.00–14.30 Mon–Fri, 07.00– 11.00 Sat) is on the left-hand side of the castle-like main building. To the right is the Museo Paleontológico Alejandro Berro (⊕ 11.00–17.00 daily; free), which has one of the country's best collections of bones and shells of extinct megafauna such as mastodons, megatherium, lestodon, glassotherium and 25 species of glyptodon, as well as a dinosaur egg. It's larger and more didactic than the Colonia museum but in dated 1980s displays, with much of the collection in store. They hope to post a digital catalogue online and perhaps even to expand upstairs in the largely empty castle, although there's also talk of building a modern hotel to the rear.

Boating is naturally very popular; motorboats shuttle across to the Playa Los Arrayanes, on the north shore of the river, and many people go across by canoe too. The **trimaran** *Capitán Dinamita V* (c/o Geo Tour, Giménez 701; ☏ 4532 8281; m 099 531254), which can land at any beach, carries 28 passengers on plastic seats and has a simple bar with music. The Intendencia has built a modern catamaran, *Soriano 1*, which will carry groups of up to 50; moving at up to 80km/h, it can reach Villa Soriano in under an hour and continue to Dolores, with passengers returning by bus. In addition to charters, there are regular scheduled trip at weekends; contact the tourism office for details.

EAST OF MERCEDES Heading east from Mercedes on Ruta 14, beyond the interchange with Ruta 2, it's 4km to a left turning to the **Estancia La Sirena** (☏ 4530

2271; m 099 102130; www.lasirena.com.uy), a delightful, historic ranch 10km to the north, near the river. Founded in the mid 18th century, the house was a virtual fortress in the lawless 1820s. It was sold to Bernardino Rivadavia, who had been first President of Argentina but then went into exile, who built the current house (in 1830) but soon sold it. Now the house is surrounded by huge eucalypti full of cotorra nests, with views west as far as Fray Bentos. Near the river is gallery forest with algarrobo trees over 800 years old, and lots of birdlife (129 species in all).

The wonderfully hospitable Bruce family created one of the first tourist estancias in Uruguay, while also raising Hereford cattle and collecting tennis cups. There are two bedrooms in the main house with the kitchen and dining room, and six new rooms in a converted barn, with fans but no air conditioning or television. It can seem like being sucked into an endless family holiday, with horse riding in the morning, followed by lunch and a siesta, then boating on the Río Negro, then perhaps sundowners on a sandbank and an asado. With luck Lucía will get out her guitar and teach you the gaucho version of 'Blue Moon'. Water-skiing is available, and they hope to offer two-day canoe trips from the Palmar dam and four-day horseback trips. Day rides are included, for US$120 per person full board (on a double basis).

Continuing east on Ruta 14, at km33.5 there's a turning to **Villa Darwin**, about 30km north. Darwin stayed for a few days on an estancia just to the north, studying the geology of the cliffs by the Río Negro; he also acquired the skull of a toxodon (an extinct giant armadillo). There's a small granite obelisk to him overlooking the river, but there's a movement to return the village to its earlier name of Sacachispas ('striking sparks', a gaucho term for knife-fighting).

Turning left on to Ruta 55, it's 15km to **El Palmar** (72km from Mercedes), a village built for workers at the Represa Constitución, one of the biggest hydro-electric dams on the Río Negro (opened in 1980). You can take a dull tour, but it's far more popular for fishing (for dorado), boating and swimming. The simple Camping del Palmar (\ *4532 1611; US$3 pp*) is at km14, at the southern end of the village. Going through the village (dotted with sculptures made of recycled metal at summer camps) to a headland on the lake, you'll find the Complejo del Palmar, incorporating the **Hotel Municipal** (\ *4530 2156; from US$40 dbl, including breakfast but without AC;* **$$**) with a swimming pool and simple rooms that are excellent value, and large tegu lizards in the garden. It's not exactly scenic, but very restful. Down the dirt road to the former ferry below the sluices, there's good fishing downstream and *monte nativo* woodland with plenty of birdlife. There's another campsite 45km away on the south side of the lake, at the Parque Bartolomé Hidalgo on Ruta 3.

RÍO NEGRO DEPARTMENT

Named after Uruguay's main river, Río Negro was part of Paysandú department until 1880. It's known for the wetlands and islands along the Río Uruguay, the border with Argentina, and its international bridge is the main route into Uruguay for Argentine tourists, with Buenos Aires just 270km away.

FRAY BENTOS To Uruguayans, Fray Bentos is known largely for its international bridge to Argentina and the blockades that kept it closed as a result of Argentine dislike of the Botnia paper pulp mill, close to Fray Bentos. To the British, however, Fray Bentos is synonymous with corned beef, and happily the *El Anglo* meat-packing plant has reopened as an industrial heritage museum.

Deep water and woodland attracted wood-cutters and charcoal-burners, plus José Hargain, an Argentine merchant who opened a shop and bar, and the British entrepreneur Richard Bannister Hughes, who set up a meat-salting business in 1859. Established as Villa Independencia in 1857, the town was renamed in 1900 after Friar Benedict, a 17th-century hermit who lived in a cave at Bahía Caracoles, about 20km downstream. After the meat plant closed in 1979 there followed a period of stagnation, but now it's a city of over 23,000 *triperos*, with new prosperity from the Botnia mill (see the box on pages 308–9).

The great Argentine writer Jorge Luis Borges, who always loved Uruguay, had relatives in Fray Bentos and even claimed to have been conceived there. The title character of the wonderful *Funes the Memorious* was from Fray Bentos, and he mentioned the town in *El Aleph* too.

Getting there and away, and getting around

By bus The bus service from Mercedes, just 35 minutes away, is frankly very poor, with only about a dozen buses a day, many in the evening, and fewer at weekends. From Montevideo there are ten buses a day, taking 4½ hours. The main bus company is CUT, with offices on the Plaza Constitución (*Avda 25 de Mayo 2263;* ☏ *4562 7598;* ⊕ *08.00–12.00, 14.00–18.00 Mon–Fri, 09.00–12.00 Sat*) and the bus terminal (*Avda 18 de Julio & Varela;* ☏ *4562 2618*). Chadre (Agencia Central) also runs to Montevideo, in addition to its twice-daily litoral service from Colonia to Paysandú, Salto and Bella Unión. The local companies Plama (m *096 808221*) and Jota Ese (*JS;* ☏ *4562 9644*) run to Young and Paysandú via San Javier and Nuevo Berlin. CUT has two buses a week (leaving at midnight Sunday and Thursday) to Rivera via Trinidad, Durazno and Tacuarembó, and ETA has two (*midnight Tue & Mon*) as far as Trinidad and Durazno.

Services to Argentina are run by ETA to Gualeguaychú (*07.00 Mon–Sat*), Cauvi to Buenos Aires (*01.00 daily*), and Bus de la Carrera to Buenos Aires (*02.00 daily*).

By car Leaving Mercedes, the Ruta 2 bridge (shared with a disused railway) crosses the Río Negro into Río Negro department. There's a turning left to the Los Arrayanes beach at the north end (km281), then a toll, and at km286 a monument on the site of the Battle of Rincón in 1825, the first clash in the war for independence from Brazil. Buses turn left at km301.8, from where it's 9km to Fray Bentos, or 7km continuing on Ruta 2 to the international bridge and Argentina. From the ANCAP station at km308 there are speed humps until the road splits into Avenida 18 de Julio (the main street, inbound) and Avenida Rincón (outbound). The bus terminal is between these two roads at Varela, from where it's four blocks to Plaza Artigas and five more to the main Plaza Constitución, between 25 de Mayo and Treinta y Tres Orientales and four blocks short of the river. A faster route in is the Carretera Puente-Puerto, a bypass (with parallel cycle track) leading from near km306 of Ruta 2 to the port and former train station immediately north of the centre.

The 5.4km-long Puente Internacional (International Bridge) Libertador General José de San Martín, 9km east of the town, opened in 1976. It usually carries 5,000 lorries per month and a third of the tourists entering Uruguay. It was blockaded by Argentine protestors against the Botnia paper pulp plant, just west of its southern end, from 2006 to 2010.

Car rental
🚗 **Avis** Avda 18 de Julio 1227 & 25 de Mayo; ☏ 4562 0322; 24hr m 098 170004; e fraybentos@ avis.com.uy; ⊕ 09.00–12.00, 14.00–19.00 Mon–Fri, 09.00–13.00 Sat

🚗 **Dollar** Rincón 1198 & 25 de Mayo; ☎ 4562 8300; e dollarfb@adinet.com.uy

🚗 **Hertz** Treinta y Tres Orientales 3162; 24hr ☎ 4562 7770; m 099 481111; e hertzfraybentos@maderal.com.uy; ⊕ 09.00–13.00, 15.00–19.00 Mon–Fri, 09.00–13.00 Sat

🚗 **Multicar** Zorrilla 1483; ☎ 4562 3316; m 099 563362/137103; e faviopolaskiarcioni@hotmail.com; www.redmulticar.com; ⊕ 08.30–13.00, 16.00–19.00 Mon–Fri, 09.30–13.00 Sat

Tourist information There's a tourist information office (☎ *4522 8369*) at the bus terminal, and a new kiosk on Plaza Artigas, between the terminal and the city centre at 18 de Julio and Instrucciones, although it's not often open. The departmental Dirección de Turismo is at 18 de Julio and 25 de Mayo (☎ *4562 2233*; e *turismo@rionegro.gub.uy*; ⊕ *09.00–18.00 Mon–Fri, 09.00–15.00 Sat*).

🏠 **Where to stay** There are a variety of reasonably central hotels as well as campsites on either side of the town and at the beach resort of Las Cañas, 8km south of town. All listings are included on the map opposite.

Hotels

🏠 **Gran Hotel Fray Bentos** Paraguay 3272 & 18 de Julio; ☎ 4562 0566; e info.fraybentos@granh.com; www.granh.com. The best hotel in town, with modern AC rooms with cable TV & internet access (& Wi-Fi in the public areas), plus swimming pool, gym & sauna; the restaurant is less good. **$$$**

🏠 **La Posada del Frayle Bentos** 25 de Mayo 3434; ☎ 4562 8541/2; e pfrayle1@adinet.com.uy. On the lovely Plaza José Hargain, this is an attractively restored colonial house with patio & fountain, pool table & swimming pool in a tiny garden. Rooms have AC, fans & cable TV; bikes are available. **$$$**

🏠 **Plaza Hotel** 18 de Julio & 25 de Mayo; ☎ 4562 2363/3815; e plazahotelfraybentos@hotmail.com. On the plaza, with a casino, this can be a bit noisy but is a decent mid-range place with a good breakfast. Rooms have AC, fans & cable TV; bikes are available. **$$$**

🏠 **Parador Playa Ubici** Continuación Ferreira Aldunate; ☎ 4562 4915; www.paradorplayaubici.com.uy. Simple rooms at a nice family-type place (ie: with lots of kids running around) 3km east of town, with a restaurant & view to Botnia & the international bridge. **$$**

🏠 **Alojamiento Los Primos** Rincón 1228; ☎ 4562 4126/8607; m 099 560514; e nrosas@

internet.com.uy. Just south of the plaza, this has AC rooms mainly to let by the week. **$**

🏠 **Hotel 25 de Mayo** 25 de Mayo & Lavalleja; ☎ 4562 2586/8536; e hotel25demayo@adinet.com.uy. Also on the lovely Plaza José Hargain, this is simpler & not as friendly as the Posada del Frayle Bentos, but also has AC rooms around a nice patio with Wi-Fi. **$**

🏠 **Nuevo Hotel Colonial** 25 de Mayo 3293 & Zorrilla; ☎ 4562 2260. A fine budget option with large rooms (with fans) round a patio; a decent breakfast costs US$4 extra. **$**

Camping

🏕 **Camping Club de Remeros** Rambla Rodó; ☎ 4562 2236; m 099 274347; ⊕ all year. Small but central site at the rowing club, with spaces for just 20 tents & 10 motorhomes. **$**

🏕 **Club Atlético Anglo** Rambla Cuervo s/n; ☎ 4562 2787; ⊕ all year. By the bay on the road out to El Anglo, this newly restored site has basic facilities. **$**

🏕 **Playa Ubici** Continuación Ferreira Aldunate; ☎ 4562 4915; ⊕ all year. At the parador of the same name, 3km east of town (1km from km311 of the Carretera Puente-Puerto), this isn't the most convenient site but has a nice waterfront setting, with views of the Botnia plant & the international bridge. **$**

✗ **Where to eat** All listings are included on the map opposite.

✗ **El Muelle** Club Remeros, Rambla Costanera; ☎ 4562 2873. The rowing club has a friendly, simple bar-restaurant. **$$**

✗ **Medio Mundo** 25 de Mayo 3311 & Zorrilla; ☎ 4562 8533; ⊕ Wed–Mon. A very decent new place for pizza, chivitos, milanesas, burgers, pasta & desserts; Wi-Fi available. **$$**

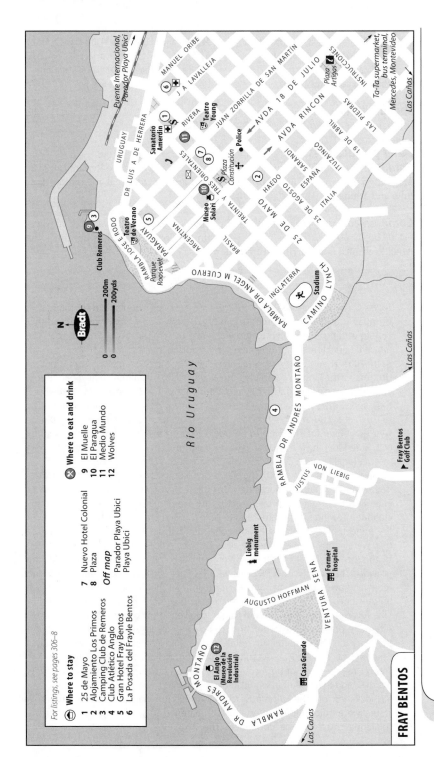

For listings, see pages 306–8

⊙ Where to stay
1 25 de Mayo
2 Alojamiento Los Primos
3 Camping Club de Remeros
4 Club Atlético Anglo
5 Gran Hotel Fray Bentos
6 La Posada del Frayle Bentos
7 Nuevo Hotel Colonial
8 Plaza

Off map
  Parador Playa Ubici
  Playa Ubici

⊗ Where to eat and drink
9 El Muelle
10 El Paragua
11 Medio Mundo
12 Wolves

FRAY BENTOS

✕ Wolves Parque Industrial Municipal, Barrio Anglo; ☏4562 3604; ⏱ 09.00–14.30 Tue–Sun. A nice little place in the former staff club at El Anglo for lunches of homemade pasta. $$

✕ El Paragua 18 de Julio 1110 & Brasil;☏4562 6165; m 099 563453; ⏱ from breakfast onwards. This is a decent enough cafeteria-confitería for coffees, cakes, chivitos & the like. $

Shopping The most convenient supermarket is Ta-Ta (*Avda 18 de Julio 1625, between Young & Beaulieu;* ⏱ *08.00–22.00 daily*).

Other practicalities

Banks There are ATMs around Plaza Constitución and at Banco República (*25 de Mayo 3375 & Lavalleja*), and Cambio Nelson is near the terminal at Avenida 18 de Julio and Young (⏱ *08.00–20.00 Mon–Sat*).

Communications The post office is at Treinta y Tres 3271 (⏱ *08.30–17.00 Mon–Fri, 08.00–12.00 Sat*). There's free Wi-Fi from the library in the bus terminal. The Antel telecentro is at Zorrilla and Treinta y Tres (⏱ *09.00–20.00 Mon–Sat*).

BOTNIA

Towards the end of the 20th century large areas of woodland were planted in Uruguay with the aim of producing biofuels. However, when it was noticed that certain varieties of eucalyptus grow at a rate of 1cm per day (3.5m per year) the multi-national forestry companies quickly took an interest.

In 2003 a subsidiary of Shell sold 80,000ha of eucalyptus plantations in Uruguay to the Finnish company Botnia, which began planning a new paper pulp plant in the area. Although they apparently looked in Argentina and elsewhere, they soon settled on a site outside Fray Bentos, near the international bridge to Gualeguaychú in Argentina's Entre Ríos province, from where pulp would be sent downriver for shipping to Europe. In December 2005, a World Bank study concluded that the factory would have no harmful effects and a year later the WB's International Finance Corporation approved a US$170 million loan.

Opened in November 2007, the billion-dollar Botnia plant uses the latest chlorine-free technology and produces no measurable pollution. However, the citizens of Entre Ríos, the Argentine province across the river, familiar only with their own filthy chlorine-spewing plants, refused to believe this and protested vehemently against the project, blockading the international bridge from November 2006 (although they were happy to take bribes to allow certain vehicles to cross). This was backed by the then Governor of Entre Ríos, Jorge Busti, an old-style Peronist caudillo who provided the *asambleístas* (pickets) with facilities such as toilets and a television room, and even paid them a wage – rumour has it that he had bought land which he presumed Botnia could be persuaded to buy for their plant, and decided to take revenge when they refused to get involved in his corrupt dealings. In 2006 Argentine president Néstor Kirchner came to a rally in Gualeguaychú to support the blockade, the day after Argentina filed a formal complaint at the International Court of Justice in The Hague, claiming that Uruguay had ignored the Uruguay River Treaty's requirement for both countries to consult on any project that could affect the river, and that pollution would affect Argentina.

Blockades on the crossings to Paysandú and Salto, in other Argentine states, were quickly lifted after courts threatened to send in the army; but the Gualeguaychú blockade continued. The Argentine government, now led by

Emergency services The Sanatorio Amerdin is at Rivera and 25 de Mayo; the police station is at 18 de Julio and 25 de Agosto.

Immigration and consulate The Inspectoría de Migración is at 18 de Julio 1225 (✆ 4562 2302; e *dnm-fraybentos@minterior.gub.uy*; ⏰ *08.00–14.00 Mon–Fri*) and at the international bridge (✆ 4562 2687). There's an Argentine consulate at Treinta y Tres 3237 (✆ 4562 3510; e *consarfb@adinet.com.uy*; ⏰ *08.00–13.00 Mon–Fri; winter 13.00–17.00*).

What to see and do The cast-iron *kiosco* (bandstand) in the centre of Plaza Constitución, raised in 1902, is a copy of one at the Crystal Place in London and has become a symbol of the town. The grand building (receiving a much-needed refurb) on the east side of the plaza is the Junta (local council), while the lovely neoclassical building on the north side, built in 1879 as a Mutual Aid Society for immigrants, is the **Museo Solari** (⏰ *Mar–Dec 08.00–14.00, 16.00–22.00 Mon–Fri, 18.00–22.00 Sat–Sun; Jan–Feb 08.00–14.00, 18.00–midnight Mon–Fri, 18.00–midnight Sat–Sun; free*).

Néstor's wife Cristina Fernández de Kirchner, gradually distanced itself from this kind of vigilante action as an instrument of foreign policy, but still felt unable to actually reopen the bridge. Tourism in Entre Ríos was badly hit by the blockade and the state's new governor, Sergio Urribarri, also wanted to end the blockade but seemed powerless. By January 2009, even Néstor Kirchner was calling for the blockade to be lifted, denying that he'd ever supported it. This was not enough for Uruguay, which blocked Kirchner's appointment as chair of Unasur, the Union of South American Nations, to Argentine fury.

Since the plant opened in late 2007, environmental monitoring (including by the World Bank) has shown no evidence of pollution, but the so-called Asamblea Ambiental de Gualeguaychú (Environmental Assembly of Gualeguaychú) has refused to accept this evidence. The Uruguayan government has been firm in its support for Botnia; the protestors thought they would soon bring Uruguay's tourist industry to its knees, but their compatriots continued to flock to Punta del Este and elsewhere.

In April 2010, the International Court of Justice ruled in favour of Uruguay (although with some sops to Argentina); new presidents José Mujica of Uruguay and Cristina Fernández de Kirchner of Argentina met several times and in June the bridge blockade was finally lifted. In July the presidents agreed to create the binational Comisión Administradora del Río Uruguay to monitor pollution.

Argentines claim that Uruguay has simply sold out to big business, as Botnia and its suppliers are responsible for increasing Uruguay's GDP by 1% and its workforce by 1½% (or 12,000 new jobs); Botnia has also created some useful nature reserves near the Río Uruguay. The Uruguayan government is unrepentant, and is keen to see another pulp plant built near Conchillas (see page 289), proposed by the Spanish Grupo Ence; in 2009 this was taken over by Stora Enso of Finland and Arauco of Chile, who confirmed plans for a US$2 billion plant. This should create around 3,000 jobs and boost GDP by another 2%. Stora Enso and Arauco also became Uruguay's largest private landowners, with 250,000ha of eucalyptus plantations.

Free visits to the UPM (Botnia) plant can be arranged on ✆ 4562 7710, including a bus transfer from Plaza Constitución in Fray Bentos.

6

Luis Solari, born in Fray Bentos in 1918, studied art in Montevideo and Paris, lived mainly in the US from 1967 to 1988, and died in Montevideo in 1993. His style is generally naïve, with fantastical subjects, often with animal heads or masks. There are also temporary shows here. The Banco Comercial, on the west side of the plaza, is a less grand neoclassical pile, as is the church to the south, which has a pleasant interior with a low coffered ceiling. A block northeast of the plaza at 25 de Mayo and Zorrilla de San Martín, the splendid eclectic **Teatro Young** (1912) is where Juan Zorrilla de San Martín gave his last public speech in 1931. Local artists exhibit at La Proa (⊕ *14.00–19.00 Mon–Sat*), on the north side of Plaza Hargain, thick with trees, and at the Casa de las Artes at Brasil and España (⊕ *07.00–20.30 daily*).

Avenida 18 de Julio and parallel streets end at Paraguay, beyond which is a small park around an open-air theatre, facing over the riverside rambla, with the former train station and port to the right. To the left, the attractive Rambla Cuervo leads west to the Barrio Anglo, the residential area laid out in 1887 for the Liebig plant's managers. Justus von Liebig leads up to the **Fray Bentos Golf Club** (❨ *4562 2427;* e *dalgorta@adinet.com.uy, ainovales@jetmar.com.uy*), the oldest golf club in Uruguay. The nine-hole course, among old native trees, was designed by Dr Alister MacKenzie in 1928 and has now been beautifully restored for use by Botnia's expatriate managers. The little clubhouse, built to mark King George VI's coronation in 1937, is a period piece, with plaques recording the sporting feats of the mainly Scottish staff of El Anglo. The Río Negro Tennis Club is also here.

The rambla leads to a monument by a palo borracho tree which is a reproduction of the Liebig stand at the 1885 Food Fair in Paris, and the gate of El Anglo, now the **Museo de la Revolución Industrial** (*Museum of the Industrial Revolution;* ❨ *4562 3690; https://sites.google.com/site/fraybentosmuseoanglo, www.rionegro.gub. uy/web/rio-negro/sistema-patrimonial-industrial-anglo;* ⊕ *09.30–19.00 Mon–Fri, 09.30–13.00, 15.00–19.00 Sat–Sun; US$1.50*). A guided tour (*10.00 & 15.00 daily, English available Mon–Fri; US$2.50*) is essential if you want to see the parts of the site not yet fully open to the public. There's parking by the jetty, now disused but with two cranes built in Rodley, near Leeds, still standing at its end. To the left is the *cámara fría* (cold store), a massive concrete block with the word ANGLO still visible, painted across its face. This was more or less the last part of the complex to be built, in 1921–23 and 1926; 400m long by 100m wide, with 70km of ammonia gas coolant pipes, it could hold 18,000 tonnes of frozen meat. Like modern Uruguayan wineries, the process was designed to be gravity-aided, with the *corrales* and slaughterhouse at the highest point and the carcasses finally rolling into the cold store hanging on hooks on an open-air overhead conveyor.

Cattle were killed by a hammer to the head, then slid into the *matadero* or *plaza de faena*, where they were hooked on to the conveyor belt and systematically skinned, gutted and deprived of each internal organ in turn until the bare carcasses rolled into the cold store. For many the most interesting part of the visit is the *sala de maquinas* or machine hall (1922), with huge boilers, turbines and generators produced in places like Derby and Stoke-on-Trent, as well as ammonia compressors from Bradford and a gantry crane from Loughborough. This machine hall is visible from the museum hall through a window which may become the entry to a walkway. Outside there's also a Merryweather fire pump, all scarlet paint and shining brass, built in 1893.

You enter and pay in the offices, with a central hall that once rang with the clatter of the typewriters that still sit on the ranks of clerks' desks. Below, the main hall of the museum has some excellent displays, all in Spanish, on both technology and social history, including early posters and packaging. There's also a chemical laboratory full of flasks and retorts; on the same site is the LATU lab, testing outflows from the Botnia plant – it would be very appropriate if a viewing gallery could allow visitors to see this too, as part of the museum's search for contemporary relevance. Also on the site is the Museo de los Puentes (or the Museo Puentes de

EL ANGLO

It was Justus von Liebig (1803–73), the 'father of organic chemistry', who invented concentrated meat extract around 1840, but with 32kg of meat needed for 1kg of extract, it was too expensive to produce in Europe. George Christian Giebert, a German engineer working on railways in Uruguay, spotted the potential for using the meat of cattle raised for leather. In 1865 he sent his first 800kg of extract to Europe and followed it to London in search of investment. The same year the Liebig Extract of Meat Company (Lemco) was formed in London with British and Belgian capital, and in 1866 a plant was set up in Fray Bentos. This was one of the first companies to use modern marketing techniques, and by 1875 the plant was producing 5,000 tonnes of extract per year.

A cheaper meat extract called Oxo was introduced in 1899 (Bovril, with added flavourings, was produced from the 1870s in Argentina). In 1887, once canning technology had advanced, the Liebig company started to produce corned beef and then canned tongues and steak-and-kidney pies. Immigrants from over 60 countries flooded here, with over 25,000 people having worked at the plant since 1863. In 1883 the first electric lighting in Uruguay was installed here (using coal imported from Britain!).

The plant's record year was 1890, when 208,890 animals were killed (and almost half of Britain's meat came from the southern hemisphere). In subsequent years the plant's products were used by Henry Morton Stanley, Captain Scott, Florence Nightingale, Alcock and Brown, and on the British Everest expeditions (and by the first men on the moon, according to Jules Verne), and were crucial to the British war effort of 1914–18. (One of the early British tanks was code-named Fray Bentos because its crew were 'meat in a can'.)

Big changes came with refrigeration, and major expansions of the factory in 1921–23 and 1926–29. However, the company overreached itself and in 1924 was sold to the British firm Vesteys, after which the plant came to be known as El Anglo. It was the British who discovered a market for 'every part of the cow but the moo', including hooves, hair, bones, even bile stones (for the French perfume industry) and dried blood (for fertiliser). At its peak the plant processed 2,000 or more cows a day as well as 6,000 lambs, pigs and turkeys. It played a big role in World War II, with fruit and vegetables being canned as well as meat (16 million tins of corned beef were exported in 1943, with an animal processed every five minutes).

Fray Bentos had fewer links with North America, feeding the military only in the Korean War. After this there was no investment, plus terrible floods in 1959, and the plant's fortunes declined. Its famous pies have been made in Britain since 1958, and British entry into the Common Market meant the end of special trading links with Uruguay. The plant was given to the Uruguayan government in 1971; it closed in 1979, reopening as a museum in 2005. Meanwhile, corned beef is again being produced in Fray Bentos, by the Brazilian company Marfrig, although rights to the Fray Bentos brand are owned by Unilever.

6

Integración y Innovación – the Bridges of Integration and Innovation Museum), a tribute to Ponce Delgado, the local engineer who built the international bridge and two others in the area; however, there are not enough staff to open it.

The road continues on around El Anglo; heading back into the Barrio Anglo you'll soon come to the **Casa Grande** (Manager's House, built in 1868), where Robert Baden-Powell spent a night in 1909. It has a spectacular garden and opens for tours at noon on Tuesday, Thursday and Sunday. An asphalt road to the right continues downriver to a viewpoint and the *Aduana vieja* (old Customs post), which is in fact a small cottage. There are lots of loose horses and cattle which, rather bizarrely, can be seen wandering into El Anglo itself. There's good birdwatching here, with both monte nativo and eucalyptus trees. The road eventually continues to the beach resort of Las Cañas, but this is best reached by the main road.

Las Cañas From the centre of Fray Bentos, Camino Batlle runs past the new Barrio Botnia (with modern homes for Botnia's executives) and continues southwest for 8km to the beach resort of Las Cañas. Normally a quiet little place, during summer weekends it can have a temporary population of 10,000 or more, many coming from Argentina to enjoy its safe beach.

Getting there and away, and tourist information A **bus** comes here from Fray Bentos (*09.30 & 15.30 Fri–Sun, returning 12.00 & 20.00, also 22.00 Sat–Sun; US$1.50*). There are two entrances to the resort, with an information booth at each.

🏠 Where to stay and eat

🏠 **Bungalows Sol y Luna** Calle 8/de los Boyeros; ☎4562 3872. One block inland. **$$**

🏠 **Hotel Sol de Las Cañas** Calle 1/de los Crespines; ☎4562 7433/2124; e leonsol@adinet. com.uy. Just inside the campsite's northern entrance is this very attractive option. Thatched with AC rooms, each with both double & single beds, & cable TV. **$$**

🏠 **Posada del Barranco** ☎4562 7109; www. delbarranco.com. A good place to sleep near the beach in the central area.**$$**

🏠 **Posada del Naranjo** ☎4562 6285; e pnaranjo@adinet.com.uy; ⊕ all year. Has nice thatched cabañas & is another good place to sleep near the beach in the central area. **$$**

🏠 **Motel Municipal** At the northern end of the campsite, just south of Calle 7; ☎4562 2224. Very simple bungalows, next to the Parador El Entorno – a decent restaurant. **$**

⛺ **Camping Las Cañas** ☎4562 2224/2148; e lascanas@adinet.com.uy; ⊕ 15 Dec–15 Mar & Easter. Has space for 2,000 tents, mostly at the southern end of the resort. To the north are the Playa El Paraíso and the El Paraíso sector of the campsite, much quieter than the main site, in a very natural setting with lots of native trees right down to the beach. There's a shop & showers here, as well as a natural amphitheatre. Swinging left, there are a few blocks of thatched bungalows & posadas, & then (beyond the jetty & Restaurant Punta Bahía) the large area of native woodland that comprises the main campsite. There are shops, parador restaurants, craft stalls & a polyclinic. **$**

⛺ **Camping Los Pescadores** (Fishermen's Beach) At the far southern end. A remote campsite where you can indeed buy fish from the fishermen. **$**

FRAY BENTOS TO PAYSANDÚ Within Río Negro department, the litoral of the Río Uruguay north of Fray Bentos is largely undeveloped wetlands and gallery forest, with plenty of large riverine islands, an area famed for its hunting and fishing but more recently known to birdwatchers and other nature lovers. There are also amazing sunsets. An area of 17,496ha has been designated the **Parque Nacional Esteros de Farrapos y Islas del Río Uruguay** (Backwaters of Farrapos and Islands of the River Uruguay National Park) – and a Ramsar site since 2004 – and is home to at least 159 species of birds, as well as reptiles (14 species), amphibians (16 species), mammals (60 species, including perhaps the very occasional visit by a puma or maned wolf) and many insect and butterfly species.

From km287½ on Ruta 2 an unpaved short cut heads north to Ruta 24 towards Paysandú. (Buses turn north just short of km298, at the Parador La Víbora, an excellent thatched restaurant at the junction of Ruta 24 and a road north to M'Bopicuá, where there's a wildlife reserve, breeding bird species threatened by trafficking.) Heading up Ruta 24, at km9 is the junction with the short cut from Mercedes, and at km17 a pond where you'll often see spoonbills.

Nuevo Berlín
At km20½ of Ruta 24 there's a junction to Nuevo Berlín, 9½km west. The village was founded in 1875 by German settlers invited to work on the Estancia Nueva Melhem, just to the north, the birthplace of modern farming in the Plate region. It now has around 3,000 inhabitants.

Turning left as you enter, you'll pass the policlínica and police station to reach the Playa El Sauzal by the jetty, *Prefectura* (harbourmaster), Aduana (Customs) and the Parador El Sauzal restaurant (m *099 111659*). Also here is the Moteles Municipales, four very simple and clean rooms for four people each; contact the Junta Local (*18 de Julio & Treinta y Tres;* ✎ *4568 2049;* ⏲ *08.00–14.00;* $) about this or about camping here. A better place to stay, facing the river three blocks to the right, is the **Posada Don Sebastián** (✎ *4568 2281;* m *096 277113;* $$–$), with rooms for up to eight people with private bathrooms, television, fridge and fan; there's a parrilla, or meals can be provided, including breakfast (not included in the cost).

The best starting point for boat trips into the islands of the national park (*about US$30*) is the Junta Local (✎ *4568 2049*). The Festival desde la Costa is held usually on the third weekend of January, with folklore and other acts.

Plama and Jota Ese rural buses from Fray Bentos to the farming town of Young run via Nuevo Berlín. A minibus meets some Mercedes–Fray Bentos–Paysandú buses at km20½ to shuttle passengers into Nuevo Berlín.

Young
Ruta 24 continues north, reaching the Tres Bocas junction at km54, an hour by bus from either Mercedes or Paysandú. There's an ANCAP service station here with shop, coffee machine and hot water for maté, but no restaurant. Ruta 25 leads 27km east to Young (pronounced 'Jung'), centre of one of the country's richest agricultural districts, now also known for its polo players, especially the Stirling family. Some of the surrounding villages, including Colonía Ombú, 12km southeast on Ruta 3, are German-speaking Mennonite colonies, their culture reinforced by German television and radio received by satellite or internet. Claldy (*Compañia Lactea Agropecuaria Lecheros de Young; www.claldy.com.uy*), on the outskirts of Young at km311, is one of the country's leading dairy co-ops.

There are several adequate **hotels**, including the Casa Nuestra (*Ruta 3 immediately north of Ruta 25: Montevideo & Rincón;* ✎ *4567 2371;* $$). Five blocks further east on Ruta 20 (18 de Julio) is the town centre, with a 2-6-0 steam locomotive preserved on a plinth opposite the former station, the church, a cinema and a supermarket. At the Junta Local (✎ *4567 4125*) you can ask for tourist information. There's a campsite 20km southeast (*Ruta 3 & Paso de las Piedras;* ✎ *4567 3031/2744;* $), where there's a kilometre-long riverside beach, hot showers, barbecues, restaurant, café and shop, as well as cabañas with private bathrooms.

On Ruta 3, Young sees a dozen buses a day between Montevideo and Paysandú, as well as local buses to Fray Bentos.

San Javier Continuing up Ruta 24 from Tres Bocas, it's 11km to the crossroads at Tres Quintos (km65), with the scattered Mennonite settlement of Gartental to the right and San Javier 13km to the left (west) on the Río Uruguay. Settled by Russians of the rather odd New Israel sect in 1913, this village of around 2,000 people is now the main jumping-off point for ecotourism in the national park.

The New Israel sect believed in the existence of a living God, who was declared in 1891 to be Vasili Lubkov (1869–1937). It spread across much of southern Russia, attracting official persecution. In 1912 representatives of the Batlle y Ordóñez administration visited Russia to encourage emigration, and the next year two ships brought Lubkov and 580 followers to Montevideo, and on 27 July 1913 to Puerto Viejo, 5km north of San Javier. By 1914 the community numbered about 2,000, living largely in isolation from Uruguayan society and with all property handed over to Lubkov, who enforced tight control. In 1926 Lubkov made the mistake of returning to Russia, where he was imprisoned in Siberia (and finally shot under Stalin in 1937). He was succeeded here by Andres Poiarkov, then Miron Gayvoronsky, and the community gradually opened up. Uruguay's military government burnt all the Russian books they could find and arrested some of the community. Today about 85% of the population is of Russian origin.

There are also Mennonite communities nearby, who came from East Prussia after 1948 (fleeing from the Russians, ironically), and about 100 Russian Old Believers, 3km north in Colonia Ofir, who came from Brazil in the 1960s.

As you enter the village on Artigas, the Sala Cultural Pobeda ('Victory' in Russian) is on the right just before the main crossroads with Calle Lubkov. The small Museo de los Inmigrantes is here, with interesting photos and documents of the Russian community; however, it may move to the former Cooperativa shop, just across Lubkov. Next to the Cooperativa on Artigas is the Galpón de Piedra (Stone Store), built without cement in 1914 when each family brought two cartloads of stone; it's now the national park's visitor centre (✎ 4569 2652). Alongside is the community's flour and oil mill, built in similar style to the *galpón* but enlarged in concrete in 1945, and now abandoned.

Beyond this is an area of parkland by the Río Uruguay, with a slipway and jetty. Turning left at the Prefectura on the Paseo de los Inmigrantes, you'll see two tombs to the left under a large eucalyptus tree. These belong to Natalia Gregorivna Lubkova, Lubkov's wife, and Maxim Lavrentievich Shevchenko, the group's 'apostle'.

Following the Paseo to the end of Lubkov and turning left you'll come at once to the Casa Blanca, built in 1860 as the *casco* (main house) of the Estancia Montserrat. This was where the Lubkovs and Shevchenko lived, and it is being restored to house the **Museo de la Diáspora Rusa** (*Museum of the Russian Diaspora*; ⊕ w/ends only; free), with Lubkov's office and desk, an icon and furniture left by Princess Ekaterina Romanova (who lived in Montevideo until her death at 92 in 2007), and various pictures and documents (not only about the community in San Javier).

A block inland from the Casa Blanca, on 18 de Julio south of Artigas, the **Sabrania** ('Assembly' in Russian) is the very simple, white worship hall (with 'Novi Izrael' in Cyrillic on the front wall). Built after Lubkov's departure (until then the community had met in the Casa Blanca), it's open on Sunday afternoons, when older members of the community meet to sing the old hymns – there's no spiritual leader now and the community seems very much in tune with secular Uruguay. A block north beyond Artigas on Plaza Libertad are the large *matrioshka* dolls that appear in almost every picture of San Javier.

To the south of San Javier there are riverside cliffs and gallery forest with wetlands to the east, then another line of cliff and forest – it's ideal for exploring by horse, but you can also walk (in about three hours, if you're busy watching birds) along the river to the Arroyo Farrapos. Watch out for the spiky acacias near the start; unfortunately cows are still being grazed on islands in the national park, spreading acacia seeds there. It's also possible to take a boat, the *Manuelita II*: ask at the Junta Local (\ *4569 2108*) or Prefectura.

The only **accommodation** in San Javier is at the Comedor La Estrella on Lubkov (there are also some basic options in Puerto Viejo; see below). The only place to eat is the Centro Bar, also known as **Elsa's** (*Artigas & 18 de Julio;* ⊕ *from 07.00 daily*), which serves basic pizza. There's also a bakery (*Lubkov & Colón*) where you can buy Russian *pirogis*. Right at the other end of the village, La Casita Mujer Rural (*Lubkov & 18 de Julio*) is a women's co-op that sells great jams and craftwork. Diagonally opposite the *matrioshkas* at the northwestern corner of Plaza Libertad are the Junta Local (\ *4569 2018/77*), post office, Antel call centre and the Maxim Gorki cultural centre. The Banco República, opposite the Museo de los Inmigrantes on Artigas, doesn't have an ATM but will give advances on Visa cards.

The Fiesta del Girasol, on the Saturday before Easter, celebrates the introduction of the sunflower (for cooking oil) in 1913. The anniversary of Lubkov's release from prison is celebrated on 31 May. On 27 July, the anniversary of the Russians' arrival at Puerto Viejo, there's a huge feast with 2,000 lamb shashlik kebabs cooked, with honey-flavoured *kvaas* to drink.

Buses between Mercedes and Paysandú run up Ruta 24, most going via Fray Bentos and a few via San Javier. The Sabelin bus company has an office by the Casa Blanca (⊕ *07.30–11.30, 15.30–19.30 Mon–Sat*).

Puerto Viejo Heading north, Calle Lubkov becomes Camino Vladimir Roslik (in honour of the last victim of the dictatorship). Taking two left turns you'll come to Puerto Viejo, where the Russians first landed. In the village there's a memorial, some old millstones and a jetty, and an attractive, busy campsite (\ *4569 2146;* ⊕ *Dec–Apr*), with 280 sites spread over 5ha. The Resto-Pub Zona Zero (\ *4569 2235*) runs the **Moteles Municipales ($$)**, six simple cabañas on a terrace with four beds, bathroom, fridge and AC. There's a noisy Saturday night dance in Puerto Viejo, which goes on until 05.00 in summer; you might not get much sleep.

The road to Puerto Viejo is asphalted, but there's no bus. You can take a taxi from San Javier, or follow the footpath along the river for about 2km from calles Fray Bentos and Colonia Ofir.

PAYSANDÚ DEPARTMENT

You can return to Ruta 24 either via Tres Quintos, or by continuing north past Puerto Viejo to km81½; another 2km north you'll leave Río Negro and enter Paysandú department across the long Arroyo Negro Bridge, with birdwatching possible in *monte espinilla* (spiney woodland) on the north side.

At km86.5 you can turn right to **Estancia La Paz** (\ *4720 2272;* m *099 721513;* e *awyaux@adinet.com.uy; www.estancialapaz.com.uy;* **$$$$**), 5km to the east on a dirt road that leads to km336 of Ruta 3. This was one of the first tourist estancias, and is still one of the best. It was founded in 1856 by Richard Bannister Hughes, owner of a meat-salting business at the future Fray Bentos, who introduced Durham cattle and wire-fencing. In 1956 it was bought by the Belgian Pierre Wyaux, whose daughter still runs the estate. You'll pass a Protestant church built by Hughes in 1873, based on one in Liverpool, with lovely Arts and Crafts-style stained-glass. The main house, built in 1863, has been lovingly restored, and has a swimming pool, tennis court and spa with jacuzzi and sauna. The ten guest rooms are not huge but are nice, with air conditioning, heating and Wi-Fi. Activities include riding, hunting, canoeing on the Río Uruguay and star-watching; gourmet tourism is also a feature, with fine local food and a shop selling their own preserves and pecans. A room for two costs US$113 including breakfast, but watch out for extra charges.

PAYSANDÚ Uruguay's second-largest city, with around 115,222 *sanduceros*, Paysandú is a river port and a centre of the meat-processing industry (together with leather and wool). Founded in 1749, the city was bombarded in 1845 by Garibaldi's squadron of British, French and Uruguayan ships and captured in 1846 by Rivera. The Third Defence of Paysandú came in 1864–65 when General Leandro Gómez heroically resisted Brazilian forces, who shelled the city from land and river; when they finally captured it after a 33-day siege the city centre was in ruins. With industrial development came international immigration, and the city still has Swiss, Belgian, German, Russian and Ukrainian communities. There are some worthwhile museums in Paysandú, as well as practical services.

Getting there and away
By bus The bus terminal is six blocks south of the main Plaza Constitución at Zorrilla de San Martín & Artigas. There are a least a dozen buses a day from Montevideo to Paysandú, by three routes. Sabelin offers three services via Trinidad (Ruta 3 – the fastest option) plus three Magic semi-cama services, and five via Mercedes (Ruta 2), as well as two via Colonia, Dolores and Fray Bentos, which continue to Salto and Bella Unión. Copay has four a day (via Trinidad) and Cynsa/Nuñez has two a day.

From Mercedes Chadre runs four services to Paysandú, but from Fray Bentos there are just two a day with Chadre plus an early-morning service with Plama via Nuevo Berlín and Young. There are also five buses a day (*2 on Sun*) run by Vittori between Young and Paysandú. There are six buses a day between Paysandú and Guichón, four a day (*2 on Sun*) continuing to Tacuarembó.

To the north, Agencia Central runs seven buses a day to Salto (two continuing to Bella Unión), Alonso runs four (via Guichón), and Nuñez and Quebracho two each. Copay has two buses a day to Tacuarembó, one (*at 04.00*) continuing to Rivera except on Sundays. Copay also run two or three international buses to Concepción del Uruguay and Colón, both in Argentina, where they usually just fail to make proper connections to Rosario, Córdoba, Paraná and Santa Fe. Flecha Bus has two buses a day to Colón and one (at midnight) to Buenos Aires. There's also a bus run by the Brazilian company Ouro e Prata (*www.viacaoouroeprata.com.br*) on Friday afternoons to Sao Gabriel and Porto Alegre, returning on Sundays.

By car Coming from the south, Ruta 24 and Ruta 3 meet at km94 and km355 respectively. Ruta 3 bypasses Paysandú to the east and at km370 crosses Ruta 90 (from Guichón), which leads west to the city centre as, successively, avenidas Italia, Argentina, España, 18 de Julio and Brasil.

Getting around Plaza Constitución, at the end of Avenida España, marks the centre of the city, from where Zorrilla de San Martín leads to the large bus terminal, six blocks south. The port is at the west end of Avenida Brasil, to the north of which parks and beaches are being developed into an increasingly attractive recreational zone, with the Artigas bridge to Colón in Argentina at its northern end. Note that there's a Bulevar Artigas running north–south and a Calle Artigas running east–west. Attendants charge for car parking in the city centre (*12.00–18.00 Mon–Fri*).

Car rental

🚗 **Avis** Leandro Gómez 1087 bis & 19 de Abril; 📞 4723 2037; 24hr m 098 170006; e paysandu@ avis.com.uy; ⏰ 09.00–12.30, 14.30–19.00 Mon– Fri, 09.00–13.00 Sat

🚗 **Dollar** Leandro Gómez 1118; 📞 4722 5004; e gonzapu@adinet.com.uy

🚗 **Multicar** Leandro Gómez 1325, between Varela & Mauá; 📞 4724 0464; m 095 722276; www.redmulticar.com; ⏰ 09.00–19.00 Mon–Fri, 09.00–13.00 Sat

Bike hire A good bike shop is Milton Wynants Sport Bike (*Sarandí 952 & Pereda*), run by a silver medallist in the 2000 Olympics.

Tourist information The Oficina de Turismo (*Avda 18 de Julio 1226 bis;* 📞 *4722 6220;* e *turismo@paysandu.gub.uy;* ⏰ *07.00–19.00 Mon–Fri, 09.00–19.00 Sat, Sun & holidays*) is on the south side of Plaza Constitución, on the site of the city's first church. There's another office (*Avda de los Iracundos;* 📞 *4722 9235;* e *plandelacosta@ paysandu.gub.uy;* ⏰ *08.30–21.30 daily (until 14.00 24 & 31 Dec), closed 25 Dec & 1 Jan*) to the north near the beach, between the Museo de la Tradición and the amphitheatre, and a summer-only office at the bus terminal.

🏠 **Where to stay** All listings are included on the map, page 318.

Hotels

🏠 **El Jardín** Montevideo 1085 between Uruguay & Charrúas; 📞 4722 3745; e reservas@hoteljardin. com. Opened in 2008, this nicely converted house has 9 AC rooms with flat-screen TV, Wi-Fi (& a PC), attractive garden & good buffet breakfast. **$$$$**

🏠 **Gran Hotel de Paysandú** 19 de Abril 958; 📞 4723 2295, 4722 0525; www.ghpaysandu.com. A 1970s block recently refurbished throughout as a very good business-class hotel; there's free Wi-Fi throughout, as well as free national phone calls. **$$$**

🏠 **Hotel Casagrande** Florida 1221; 📞 4722 4994; www.hotelcasagrande.com.uy. On the north side of Plaza Constitución, this is a modern house built into a Deco house & very attractively fitted out; there's Wi-Fi, a good breakfast & the Brutto Taverna resto-pub. **$$$**

🏠 **Hotel La Castellana** km6.5 Ruta 90; 📞 4723 8773; www.hotellacastellana.com. About 8km east of town & near Ruta 3, this is a delightful retreat, with gardens & swimming pool, except when there's a wedding or some other party at the *centro de eventos* – check first at weekends. **$$$**

🏠 **Mykonos** 18 de Julio 768; 📞 4722 8201; m 099 727743; e mykonos@adinet.com.uy. A rather slick & chilly 3-star place with 26 rooms with AC, cable TV, hairdryer, frigobar & safe, as well as 2 suites. Business room & Wi-Fi. Buffet b/fast inc. **$$$**

🏠 **Hotel La Posada** Varela 566 & Solís; 📞 4722 7879; e laposada@adinet.com.uy; www. hotellaposada.com.uy. A nice enough 2-star hotel, which is listed in places as an HI-affiliated hostel, but it is definitely not. Handy for the bus terminal. PC & Wi-Fi. Buffet b/fast inc. **$$**

🏠 **Hotel Papiros** Brasil 323; 📞 4724 0100; www.hotelpapiros.com. Opened in 2012, this is a nicely adapted Deco house with all comforts, including a swimming pool in the garden. **$$**

🏠 **La Casona del Centro** Zorrilla de San Martín 975, Plaza Constitución; 📞 4722 2998; m 095 242868; e lacasonadelcentro@paysandu.com. Family home in a great location, with bunks fitted into bedrooms, some huge, with private bathroom, AC & cable TV. **$$**

🏠 **Lobato** Leandro Gómez 1415; 📞 4722 2241; e hotellobato@adinet.com.uy; www.hotellobato. com.uy. A very decent, modern 2-star place with AC rooms & Wi-Fi; no credit cards. **$$**

🏠 **Nuevo Hotel Rafaela** Avda 18 de Julio 1181; 📞 4722 4216; e hotelrafaela@hotmail.com. A bit tired but adequate & reasonable value, with AC rooms & Wi-Fi. **$$**

🏠 **Plaza** Leandro Gómez 1211; 📞 4723 3545; www.hotelplaza.com.uy. A block south of Plaza Constitución, this is a good mid-range hotel with AC rooms, Wi-Fi, laundry & garage. **$$**

🏠 **Hotel de Paris** Leandro Gómez 1008 & Treinta y Tres; 📞 4722 3774. A grand 19th-century

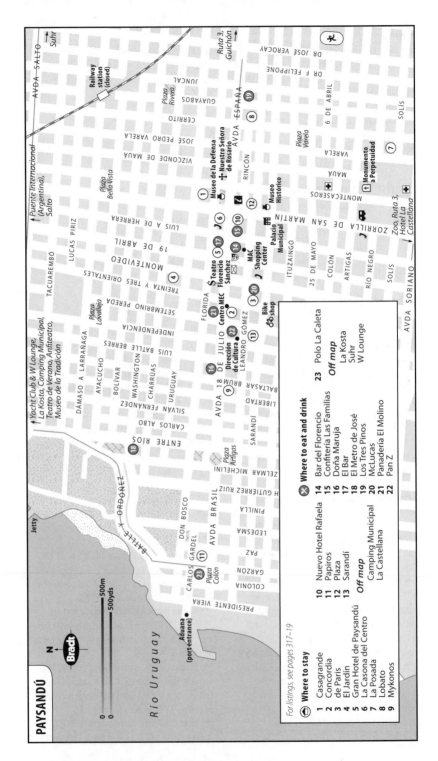

PAYSANDÚ

N

Bradt

500m
500yds

Río Uruguay

Jetty

Aduana
(port entrance)

Railway
station
(closed)

Puente Internacional
(Argentina),
Salto

Suhr

AVDA SALTO

Ruta 3,
Guichón

Yacht Club & W Lounge,
La Kosta, Camping Municipal,
Teatro de Verano, Anfiteatro,
Museo de la Tradición

Zoo, Ruta 3,
Hotel La
Castellana

For listings, see pages 317–19

Where to stay

1 Casagrande
2 Concordia
3 de Paris
4 El Jardin
5 Gran Hotel de Paysandú
6 La Casona del Centro
7 La Posada
8 Lobato
9 Mykonos
10 Nuevo Hotel Rafaela
11 Papiros
12 Plaza
13 Sarandi
Off map
  Camping Municipal
  La Castellana

Where to eat and drink

14 Bar del Florencio
15 Confiteria Las Familias
16 Doña Maruja
17 El Bar
18 El Metro de José
19 Los Tres Pinos
20 McLucas
21 Panaderia El Molino
22 Pan Z
23 Polo La Caleta
Off map
  La Kosta
  Suhr
  W Lounge

building which seems to have had only minor refurbishment since, this is a basic place in a good but noisy location; there's Wi-Fi but no breakfast. Cash only. **$$–$**

🏠 **Concordia** Avda 18 de Julio 984; 📞4722 2417; e nuevohotelconcordia@hotmail.com. An old-style 1-star hotel, with a choice of simple rooms with or without private bathroom, all with cable TV & some with AC & Wi-fi; no breakfast. **$**

🏠 **Sarandí** Sarandí 931; 📞4722 3465. Behind the black glass front lies a simple little hotel, some

rooms with AC, some with fan, all with bathroom & cable TV. **$**

Camping

🏕 **Camping Municipal** In the Parque Guyunusa, north of the yacht club at the west end of Henderson. It's very simple, without showers, & is always open for day use & BBQs. Electricity is provided only from 22.00 Fri to 02.00 Mon. To camp, contact the tourism office. **$**

✗ Where to eat and drink   All listings are included on the map opposite.

✗ **Los Tres Pinos** Avda España 1474 & Guayabos; 📞4724 1211; e lostrespinos@adinet.com.uy; www.lostrespinos.com.uy; ⊕ 11.30–15.00 & from 19.00 Mon–Sat, 11.30–15.00 Sun. A versatile place serving parrilla, pasta (& *ñoquis*), fish & seafood; the dish of the day costs US$5.50, & lunch menus start at US$12. There's Wi-Fi, & a terrace. **$$$**

✗ **Doña Maruja** 18 de Julio 833; 📞4724 1711; e marujaresto@adinet.com.uy; ⊕ 12.00–15.00, 20.00–midnight Mon–Fri, until 01.30 Sat, 12.00–15.00 Sun. Attractive place with bare-brick walls & good service, offering parrilla, pasta, fish, omelettes & a good range of salads, this is a friendly, efficient place with reasonable prices & a decent wine list; AC rooms & patio terrace. **$$**

✗ **Pan Z** 18 de Julio 950 & Pereda; 📞4722 9551; e pizzeriapanz@adinet.com.uy; ⊕ 12.00–15.00 & from 20.00 daily. A cheerful & affordable place for pizza, pasta, parrilla & chivitos, with a streetside terrace; it looks like a fast-food joint but is actually a cut above that. **$$**

✗ **Confitería Las Familias** 18 de Julio 1152 & Herrera; 📞4722 2181; e paysandu@postrechaja. com; www.postrechaja.com; ⊕ 09.00–13.00,

16.30–20.00 daily. The home of Paysandú's famous *chajá* dessert. You can also get vegetarian snacks here as well as burgers & hot dogs. **$**

✗ **El Metro de José** Entre Ríos 1139 & Washington; 📞4723 5038; e elmetro@adinet.com. uy; ⊕ from 19.00 daily. A cheery spot for pizza (by the metre), parrilla, pastas, chivitos & snacks; follow it with an ice cream across the road. **$**

✗ **McLucas** Leandro Gómez 1050 & Montevideo; 📞4722 9610; ⊕ 20.00–23.30 daily. A take-away with over 20 types of empanada, horno or frito, take-away or eat in, all excellent (most US$2). **$**

🍴 **Panadería El Molino** 18 de Julio & Pereda; ⊕ 06.30–23.30. A bakery & cafetería with a wide range of breads, cakes & sandwiches, as well as light meals & ice cream. Also a smaller branch at Gómez & Montevideo. **$**

🍸 **Bar del Florencio** 19 de Abril 930. The bar of the fantastic Teatro Florencio Sánchez, this still has its ornate 1870s décor (currently being restored). **$$**

🍸 **El Bar** Herrera 955, 1 block west of Plaza Constitución; 📞4723 7809; e elbaresotracosa@ adinet.com.uy. Cafeteria-type bar with plenty of atmosphere & live music at weekends; good spot for breakfast & for drinks throughout the day. **$$**

Nightlife   There's a group of lively disco-pubs in the run-down area near the port on Plaza Colón (reached by bus 101 Barrio Obrero), and also to the north by the beaches.

🍸 **La Kosta** Avda Costanera s/n, north of Avda Salto. A stylish & trendy music bar opposite the yacht club.

🍸 **Polo La Caleta** Avda Brasil 259 & Avda de los Deportistas; www.pololacaleta.com. A dark green disco pub, alongside the bright blue La Guapa music bar.

🍸 **Suhr** Avda Wilson Ferreira Aldunate 2103; www.suhr.com.uy; ⊕ Apr–Dec. A lively pub that serves pizzas & snacks.

🍸 **W Lounge** Baldomero Vidal; m 095 134436. At the yacht club, this is a trendy club hosting DJs & live acts; there's also the Veleros restaurant here.

Entertainment There's a wide range of cultural activities throughout the year at the **Teatro de Verano** (Summer Theatre) and **Anfiteatro** (Amphitheatre), both of them by the Balneario Municipal (municipal beach); the **Teatro Florencio Sánchez** (*currently closed for refurbishment; 19 de Abril between Leandro Gómez & Avda 18 de Julio*); the **Centro MEC** (*Leandro Gomez & 33 Orientales;* ✆ *4724 3845; www. cmecpaysandu@gmail.com;* ◷ *11.00–17.00 Mon–Fri*); and the tatty **Dirección de Cultura** (*Leandro Gómez 852 & Berres;* ✆ *4722 2398*). The city's main festival, held at Easter, is the **Semana de la Cerveza** (Week of Beer), which has been running for 48 years and continues strongly despite the closure of the Norteña brewery.

Shopping The **MAC Shopping Center** (with the Cine Shopping) is on Avenida 18 de Julio between Herrera, Leandro Gómez and 19 de Abril; the SuperStar Centro supermarket at the rear (*Herrera & Giménez*) is better than the Ta-Ta at the front. There's a huge Ta-Ta hypermarket at Argentina 1680 east of Avenida Artigas (◷ *08.00–22.00 daily*). The Mercado de Artesanos (craft market) is in the refurbished Mercado Municipal (1941) at Sarandí and Montevideo (◷ *08.30–12.30, 16.00–20.00 Mon–Sat, 09.00–13.00 Sun*), and the Sol craft shop (*Leandro Gómez 659*) is just east of Plaza Artigas.

Other practicalities

Banks There are plenty of banks and ATMs around the intersection of 18 de Julio and Montevideo, and elsewhere; you can change money at Cambio Bacacay (*18 de Julio 1039;* ◷ *08.30–18.30 Mon–Fri, 08.30–12.30 Sat*) or Cambilex Herrera (*18 de Julio 928; 08.30–21.00 Mon–Fri, 08.30–20.00 Sat, 09.00–13.00 Sun*).

Communications The post office is at 18 de Julio 1052 and Montevideo (◷ *09.00–17.00 Mon–Fri, 08.00–12.00 Sat*). Antel's telecentro is opposite the terminal at Zorrilla de San Martín 645 (◷ *06.30–23.30 Mon–Thu, 06.30–23.00 Fri–Sat, 07.00–23.00 Sun*). There's a very weak Wi-Fi signal on Plaza Constitución and a much better one on Plaza Artigas, as well as at the MAC Shopping Center (see above). There are cyber centres at España 1376 and Gómez 1193 between Herrera and Zorrilla de San Martín.

Emergency services The hospital (*Avda Soriano & Montecaseros;* ✆ *4722 4836*) is near the bus terminal, and the Sanatorio Modele is at Montecaseros and Colón. Police headquarters are at Leandro Gómez 1039 (✆ *4722 6471*), facing the Argentine consulate (*Leandro Gómez 1034;* ✆ *4722 2253;* e *cpays@adinet.com.uy;* ◷ *10.00–13.00 Mon–Fri*); there's a more convenient police station on the north side of the Palacio Municipal at Zorrilla de San Martín 873.

Immigration The Inspectoría de Migración is at Independencia 961, between 18 de Julio and Florida (✆ *4722 4997;* e *dnm-paysandu@minterior.gub.uy;* ◷ *summer 08.00–14.00 daily; winter 12.00–18.00 daily*) and at the international bridge (✆ *4722 5105*).

What to see and do On the east side of Plaza Constitución, the **Cathedral of Nuestra Señora de Rosario** was begun in 1860, destroyed in the siege of 1864, inaugurated in 1873 and completed in 1879; it's in a pretty grand neoclassical style, with frescoes over the ceiling and elsewhere, and a large altar which was burnt in 1882 and made again by the same Argentine woodcarver. There's an unusual attractive little stained-glass lantern on top of the dome. The organ above the entry was built in 1906 and restored in 1997. In front of the cathedral sits a bell cast in 1689 at one of the Jesuit missions to the north of Paysandú and donated by Fructuoso Rivera to commemorate his capture of the city. In the centre of the plaza is a statue of Leandro Gómez, the brave (and suicidal) defender of Paysandú, above the underground **Museo de la Defensa** (*Museum of the Defence*; ⊕ *09.00–16.00 Tue– Sat, 11.00–16.00 Sun; free*), housing his ashes; both here and in the cathedral there are historic photos, eg: of the cathedral after the siege, and the bodies of Gómez and companions after their execution, as well as guns, shells and cannonballs.

Two blocks south of the plaza, the grand neobaroque (almost Plateresque) **Palacio Municipal** stands nearly opposite the **Museo Histórico** (*History Museum; Zorrilla de San Martín 874;* ⊕ *09.00–16.00 Tue–Sat, 11.00–16.00 Sun; free*) in the so-called Casa del Espíritu. Built in 1890 as a girls' orphanage, it became a museum in 1989. With some captions in English and a file with information in Braille, it covers local history in a broad sweep from the arrival of humans around 10,000 years ago (leaving rough stones and arrowheads) to the 19th century. Also on display are a large well-made Guaraní burial urn from the Arroyo Negro sands, the first map of Paysandú (1749), copies of English watercolours of Paysandú (1846) and a good model of the city centre after its capture in 1865 by Brazil, together with photos, a flag, cannonballs and rusty swords. Another room displays Lavalleja's pistol, and 19th-century items such as a theodolite, a typewriter, an organ and bedroom furniture.

Two blocks west, the **Teatro Florencio Sánchez** (*19 de Abril between Leandro Gómez & Avda 18 de Julio*), built in 1876 (and being refurbished in 2012–13), is Uruguay's oldest theatre outside Montevideo. Behind a 20th-century façade, it has an auditorium with three galleries, red plush seats and fine plasterwork; you should be able to look inside as long as it's not in use.

Eight blocks west along Avenida 18 de Julio, Plaza Artigas has attractive trees on its southern half, but only flagpoles on its sun-baked northern half. It's another five blocks to Plaza Colón, heart of a run-down area with some disco-pubs. Immediately beyond is the Aduana (Customs) gate, which you can go through to visit the port. Here are rail-mounted Belgian cranes, and picnic tables with benches. About 700m north, beyond former railway sheds and the Playa Park (Park Beach), are a long jetty, now closed off, and an obelisk with municipal-toilet tiling at its base that commemorates Artigas's joining the struggle for independence in 1811. Just beyond this is the yacht club, a nice little port with a smaller antique crane, and the campsite; the start of the Balneario Municipal (Municipal Beach) is marked by craft stalls, the Teatro de Verano and the bigger, more modern Anfiteatro.

Immediately north of the Anfiteatro is the **Museo de la Tradición** (*Museum of Tradition;* ⊕ *08.00–12.45, 16.00–20.45 daily except Christmas & New Year; free*), with displays of archaeology, weapons (including Swiss target-shooting rifles), a school and a model of a *pulpería* (rural shop). There's also good material on gaucho culture, the chajá dessert, the Norteña brewery (now closed) and other local industries, and Los Iracundos (a Beatlesesque sextet from Paysandú who became 'the most famous band in Hispanic America', making their début at the Teatro Florencio Sánchez in 1961). It's nicely landscaped, with lots of labelled native trees and plants, and there are modern sculptures in the park immediately north.

The cemetery, east of the bus terminal, is now known as the **Monumento a Perpetuidad** (*Monument to Perpetuity; Montecaseros between Artigas & Soriano;* ⊕ *09.00–16.00 Tue–Sat, 11.00–16.00 Sun except Christmas & New Year; free*), worth a look for its dozen or so seriously ornate mausoleums (since 1881). Continuing south on Montecaseros past the hospital and five longish blocks further, beyond

Avenida Paraguay, the Parque Municipal houses the **zoo** (⊕ *summer 07.00–21.00 daily; winter 08.00–18.00; free*), with 82 species of animals and birds, including lions, monkeys, wild boars, peccaries, capybaras, caymans, otters, turtles, ducks, geese, pheasants, herons, parrots and vultures. Bus 109 comes here from Plaza Constitución via the east side of the bus terminal.

GUICHÓN AND THE RINCÓN DE PÉREZ The main town in eastern Paysandú department is **Guichón**, 89km east of the capital on Ruta 90. Founded in 1907, it's a small agricultural centre of about 5,000 residents. Birdwatchers will be interested in the Rincón de Pérez, and the hot baths at Almirón round the day off very nicely.

The town lies to the north of a roundabout on Ruta 90, with the plaza two blocks to the east of the main road, Artigas. Restaurante Guayabos is on the plaza. On a hill directly off the roundabout at the southern end of town, the **Alqimía spa** (❨ *4742 2206;* e *alqimiaspa@gmail.com*; **$$$**), opened in 2009, has comfortable accommodation for ten in four rooms, all feng-shuied and with air conditioning; television and internet access are available in the dining area. An American breakfast includes juice from their own orange and lemon trees; there's a parrilla for asados, or a cook can come in. There are two pools (with a ramp and hoist), hydrotherapy (both medical and for relaxation), massage, reiki, treatments with mud or hot stones, as well as horse riding and boar-hunting. It's one of the few places in Uruguay that is genuinely wheelchair-accessible, and very pleasant anyway. Just west at km85.5, **La Arisca** (❨ *4742 2144;* m *099 727667*; **$$**) has nice cabañas for up to nine (with kitchen, television and fan) and farm-style rooms; meals can be arranged, as can boar-hunting.

The **Termas de Almirón** (*Ruta 90 km82.5;* ❨ *4740 2203/2891;* e *termas.almiron@paysandu.gub.uy; www.termasalmiron.com, www.almirontermal.com*) are the country's only saltwater hot springs (and can be very crowded in summer), with the good modern Centro Termal including open-air and indoor pools (⊕ *07.00–00.30 & 07.00–23.00 respectively, all year; US$3 entry to the complex*). Accommodation includes camping (⊕ *all year; US$5 pp*) in the trees by the stream, where you might see otters, and excellent one- and two-storey cabañas (*from US$40 for 4, US$50 for 6*). New luxury hotels are under construction.

Artigas continues north as a dirt road – nominally Ruta 4 – crossing the Arroyo Santana at km392, where there's a beach with free camping (toilets but no water except from the arroyo), and the Río Queguay Grande at km402 (Paso Andrés Pérez), where you can also camp (with dry-composting toilets). There's an interpretative nature trail on the south side just before the old bridge.

A kilometre to the north, a road turns left (west) to Colonia Juan Gutierrez. It's about 20 minutes' drive to the Rincón de Pérez, in the forested fork between the Río Queguay Grande and the Río Chico, where there's an unmarked path through a field to the right to the Cueva de Tigre, a cave inhabited by vampire bats. It's another 500m or so to the entrance to the **Reserva Ecológica Rincón de Pérez**, the largest area of native woodland left in Uruguay, where you'll find birdwatching hides and trails of about a kilometre in length. There's little infrastructure and no rangers here; to make the most of a visit you should contact Guichón's Junta Local (*Penza & 18 de Julio, a block east of Artigas;* ❨ *4742 2225*) for one of the guides who have been trained as part of a sustainable-tourism project. Danny at the Junta Local can also put you in touch with the Club Queguay Canoas to organise a canoe trip down the Río Queguay. In January there's a mass descent of the river by hundreds of canoeists, from the Paso Andrés Pérez.

NORTH OF PAYSANDÚ Heading north from Paysandú on Ruta 3, you'll pass a big interchange at km375, with a road west to the bridge to Colón (Argentina); 19km north of the interchange there's a toll and a bridge over the Río Queguay, and just north at km395.5 **Puerto Peñasco** (m 098 048181; e *momosway@adinet.com.uy, momosway@hotmail.com*), with cabañas (*US$50 pp, inc b/fast*) and camping (*US$5 pp*) by the river. Ruta 26 turns east to Tacuarembó at km404, then Ruta 3 crosses the Arroyo Guaviyú at km431, with the **Termas de Guaviyú** (🛪 *4754 2323;* e *guaviyu@ paysandu.gub.uy; www.termasguaviyu.com;* ◉ *all year; US$4*) on the left. This, like the Termas de Almirón, is run by the department, keeping prices moderate, although it's not the most modern of resorts. There are seven pools, with a covered complex at the north end and open pools to the south. In the centre are bungalows (**$$**) and to the south by the river a large campsite (🛪 *4750 4049;* ◉ *all year; US$5 pp;* **$$**). Bikes and pedalos can be rented and there's a call centre and a butcher's shop to supply all those barbecues.

Across the main road at km432 is the excellent **Complejo Villaggio** (🛪 *4755 2041; www.termasvillaggio.com;* **$$$$**), with indoor and outdoor pools, a hotel (**$$$**) and bungalows (*US$117–150, b/fast inc*).

From km453.2 a road leads west to the **Parque Histórico Meseta de Artigas**, where a 37m granite column bearing a bust of Artigas, 45m above the river, was raised in 1899 to mark the place where the first independent Uruguayan government was declared in 1815.

At km473.5 there's a turning to the left to the **Hotel Termal Los Naranjos** (🛪 *4736 9999; www.losnaranjos.com.uy;* **$$$**), the best in the Daymán area, with open pools amidst fields of orange trees, and horseriding available. From km475 Camino Tierras Coloradas leads back southeast for 13km to the **Termas de San Nicanor** (🛪 *4730 2209*), where a former estancia is now the centre of one of the smaller and quieter hot-spring resorts, with two pools (slightly hotter than others, up to 40°C), four lakes (12–75ha), cabañas and camping. It's delightfully remote, but not well managed.

At km477 Ruta 3 crosses a long bridge over the Río Daymán (with good gallery forest for birding to the west) and into Salto department. Just before the bridge is the Paraíso Natural Daymán campsite – see the Termas de Daymán, page 330.

SALTO DEPARTMENT

SALTO Slightly smaller than Paysandú by most counts, Salto (at km487, under two hours from Paysandú) is also a port shipping meat, leather and, more recently, citrus fruit down the Río Uruguay. It also trades with Argentina via the highway and railway across the Salto Grande dam, just to the north. For tourists it's a transport hub, and the centre of the thermal spas of the region.

It was founded here, in 1756, because of the *salto* (waterfall or rapid) blocking navigation just upstream. In 1811 Artigas led the Exodo del Pueblo Oriental (Exodus of the Eastern People), crossing the Río Uruguay here with perhaps 10,000 soldiers and civilians into what is now Argentina. Development took off after 1830, and from 1860 considerable numbers of European immigrants arrived, as did the railway. The first Tannat grapes in Uruguay were planted here (see page 156), and by 1900 there were perhaps 100 vineyards around the city. Between 1880 and 1894 General Teófilo Córdoba ran the city, building the theatre, hospital, racecourse and other monuments. It's the birthplace of both Luis Suárez (see box, pages 38–9) and Edinson Cavani – two of the three best-known Uruguayan soccer players worldwide at the moment.

Getting there and away

By air BQB (*Brasil 819;* ⬚*4733 8919/8651; www.flybqb.com;* ⊕ *09.00–12.30, 14.30–19.00 Mon–Fri, 08.30–12.30 Sat*) has flights from Montevideo at 13.00 on Monday, Wednesday, Friday and Saturday, returning at 14.30, with bus connections to and from Punta del Este. Tickets can also be booked at the Salto Shopping Terminal (⊕ *10.00–19.00 Mon–Fri, 10.00–14.00 Sat*). The airport is 6km south, reached by a shuttle bus from the Hotel Salto Casino.

By bus Buses arrive at the modern Terminal Salto about 1km east of the centre (*Avda Blandengues/Ruta 3 & Avda Batlle*), which has a *depósito de equipaje* (baggage store; ⊕ *04.30–midnight*) and incorporates the Salto Shopping mall, with cinemas, restaurants, Wi-Fi, ATMs and an exchange office. Agencia Central (Chadre/Sabelin) has a booking office on Uruguay 711, just east of Sarandí (⬚ *4733 1717;* e *salto@agenciacentral.com.uy;* ⊕ *09.00–20.30 Mon–Fri, 09.00–13.00 Sat*). Nuñez has a ticket office at Uruguay 932 (⬚ *4733 5581*).

You can find bus schedules at www.saltoshopping.com.uy: from Montevideo Agencia Central runs six buses a day (four direct on Ruta 3 and two via Durazno) and Cynsa/Nuñez runs three (via Trinidad); El Norteño also has day and overnight services to Salto and Bella Unión. Two Agencia Central services run via Colonia, Mercedes, Fray Bentos and Paysandú, and continue to Bella Unión. From Paysandú Agencia Central runs seven buses a day, Alonso runs four (*via Guichón; 2 on Sun*), and Nuñez and Quebracho two each.

Heading north, Cotabu runs two services a day via Bella Unión (Rutas 3 and 30) to Artigas; Jote Ele (ie: JL) has two to Artigas via Rutas 31 and 4, and COA (c/o Agencia Central) has three (*2 on Sun*) by this route. Agencia Central has a departure to Tacuarembó and Rivera at 03.00 on Mondays and Fridays only. Flecha Bus runs two buses a day to Concordia (Argentina), with connections to Buenos Aires and elsewhere, Chadre and Cottur have three more buses a day to Concordia, and COIT runs direct from Salto to Buenos Aires (23.00 Tuesday–Thursday, Saturday–Sunday).

By car Arriving from the south on Ruta 3, the built-up area starts at the Puerta de la Sabidurea (Gate of Wisdom; km483½), where there's a monument and some industrial buildings by Eladio Dieste to the right. Four blocks south of the bus terminal, in the northeastern part of the city, Calle Uruguay leads to the central Plaza Artigas, ten blocks west, continuing another seven blocks to Plaza Treinta y Tres and two more to the river. Heading north and to the interior, Ruta 3 is 6km east of the city centre.

By ferry Pedestrians can also go to and from Concordia in Argentina by *lancha* (*ferry; from Concordia 08.35, 12.00, 15.00 & 18.30 Mon–Sat (& Argentine holidays), returning about 45mins later*). Tickets (*US$5.50*) are sold from a basic shack at the entry to the port, at the west end of Brasil, or contact San Cristóbal srl at Blanes 440 (⬚ *4733 2461*); bikes travel free.

Getting around Note that north–south streets have different names on either side of Calle Uruguay.

By bus Salto has quite a dense bus network; buses 1 and 7, heading east on Brasil, run from the centre to the terminal.

By car There are charges for parking in the city centre (*09.00–11.00, 14.00–18.00 Mon–Fri*). Cars can be rented from:

🚗 **Maxicar** Paraguay 764; ☏ 4733 5554; m 099 435454; www.maxicarsalto.com; ⏱ 08.00–22.00 daily

🚗 **Rentacar Daymán** Amorim 368; ☏ 4734 0863, 4733 4892; m 099 731188; e rentacar@ adinet.com.uy; www.rentacardayman.com; ⏱ 08.00–22.00 daily. Also Brasil & Blandengues, 2 blocks from the terminal; ☏ 4734 1003; m 099 731188

🚗 **Salto Rentacar** Lavalleja 151; ☏ 4733 5666; m 098 647470; e saltorentacar@adinet.com.uy; http://saltorentacar.com

🚗 **Thrifty** Avda Blandengues 520, outside the bus terminal; ☏ 4734 0051; e salto@thrifty.com.uy (*call centre:* ☏ 0800 8278; ⏱ 08.00–22.00 daily)

Tourist information There's a tourist information stand (⏱ 06.30–18.30 daily) at the Terminal Salto. The main tourism office (*Uruguay 1052;* ☏ 4732 5194, 4733 4096; e turismo@salto.gub.uy; ⏱ 08.00–20.00 Mon–Sat) is understaffed and usually busy taking bookings for the Arapey hot-springs resort.

🏠 **Where to stay** As well as hotels, camping is available at the Termas de Daymán, 9km south (see page 330). All listings are included on the map, page 326.

🏠 **Salto Hotel & Casino** 25 de Agosto 5; ☏ 4733 7037; www.saltohotelcasino.com. Very slick place on Plaza Artigas, incorporating a casino, the La Botica restaurant & La Recova cafeteria, bar, solarium & gym & swimming pool deck. **$$$$**

🏠 **Casa Ambrosoni** ☏ 4730 2002; m 099 680232; www.casaambrosoni.com. Built in 1876, this casona (the main house of the estancia) in San Antonio, 15km north of Salto, has lots of period fittings & is a fine base for rural tourism. There are 20 comfortable rooms, with a historic lift, a swimming pool in subtropical gardens, horses & other sports facilities. **$$$**

🏠 **Gran Hotel Concordia** Uruguay 749; ☏ 4733 2735; www.granhotelconcordia.com.uy. A historic place, opened in 1865, with delightful cool patios, this was refurbished in 2009. The room in which Gardel stayed in 1912 is preserved as a museum, or maybe a shrine. **$$$**

🏠 **Gran Hotel Uruguay** Brasil 891; ☏ 4733 5197; e hoteluru@adinet.com.uy; www. hoteluruguay.com. A 1960s block with 40 AC rooms, this is very decent & friendly. Rooms have flat-screen TVs & there's Wi-Fi & parking. **$$$**

🏠 **Hotel Danaly** Agraciada 2060; ☏ 4733 5784, 4732 5680. The only hotel near the bus terminal, a decent budget place with fan or AC as well as cable TV, BBQ & a garage. **$$**

🏠 **Hotel Eldorado** Sarandí 20; ☏ 4732 5042; www.eldoradosalto.com, www.hoteleldorado. com.uy. A good & friendly business/tourist-class place. Rooms have AC, cable TV, Wi-Fi or ADSL. There's a PC for internet access, 24hr bar & good buffet breakfast. **$$**

🏠 **Hotel Español** Brasil 822/826; ☏ 4733 4048, 4732 5400; www.hotelespanolsalto.com. Not quite as nice as the adjacent Gran Hotel Uruguay, this has slightly dark rooms with AC & cable TV. There's parking & internet access. B/fast inc. **$$**

🏠 **Hotel Los Cedros** Uruguay 657; ☏ 4733 3984/5; www.loscedros.com.uy. A decent but dated place with 70 rooms, with AC, cable TV & free Wi-Fi. There's a buffet breakfast & a garage. **$$**

🏠 **Hostal del Jardín** Colón 47 between Artigas & Uruguay; ☏ 4732 4274, 4733 2325; e hostalj@ adinet.com.uy; http://hostaldeljardin.es.tl. A nice enough little place, though not quite the boutique it wants to be, with AC, cable TV & very soft mattresses, & a lovely garden. **$$–$**

🏠 **Hotel Tia** Brasil 566; ☏ 4732 6574; m 095 103210; e hana-murad@hotmail.com; www. hoteltia.com.uy. Excellent value, this rambling place (definitely not disabled-friendly, with steps all over the place) has regular rooms with cable TV & private bathroom, & bigger AC ones in a 3rd-floor extension. There's a Wi-Fi signal only on the balcony (with swings). **$$–$**

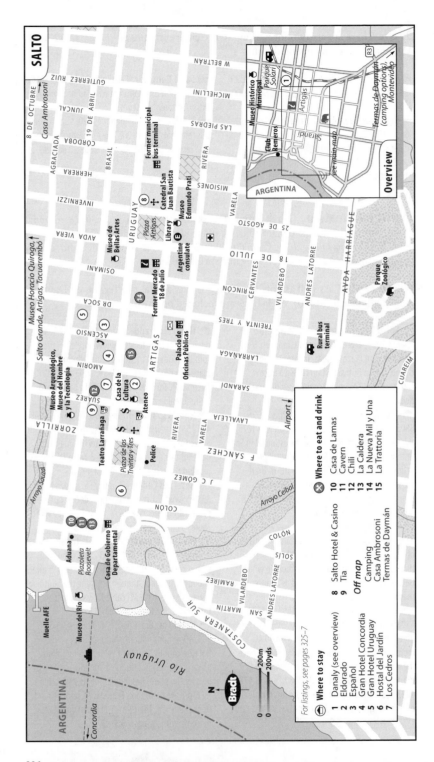

SALTO

Overview

ARGENTINA

Museo Histórico Municipal
Parque Solari
Artigas
Club Remeros
Termas de Daymán (camping options), Montevideo
see main map

Museo Horacio Quiroga, Artigas, Tacuarembó
Salto Grande, Artigas, Tacuarembó

Casa Ambrosoni

8 DE OCTUBRE
GUTIERREZ RUIZ
JUNCAL
19 DE ABRIL
CÓRDOBA
AGRACIADA
HERRERA
BRASIL
IZZINNERI
INVERNIZZI
AVDA VIERA
OSIMANI
DR SOCA
ASCENSIO
AMORÍN
SUÁREZ
ZORRILLA

W BELTRÁN
MICHELLINI
LAS PIEDRAS
RIVERA
MISIONES
VARELA
25 DE AGOSTO
18 DE JULIO
CERVANTES
RINCÓN
TREINTA Y TRES
LARRAÑAGA
SARANDÍ
LAVALLEJA

Former municipal bus terminal
Catedral San Juan Bautista
Museo Edmundo Prati
Plaza Artigas
Library
Argentine consulate
Museo de Bellas Artes
Former Mercado 18 de Julio
Museo Arqueológico, Museo del Hombre y la Tecnología
Casa de la Cultura
Ateneo
Teatro Larrañaga
Plaza de los Treinta y Tres
Police
Palacio de Oficinas Públicas
Rural bus terminal
Parque Zoológico

AVDA HARRIAGUE
CUAREIM
ANDRES LATORRE
VILARDEBÓ
F SÁNCHEZ
J C GÓMEZ
RIVERA
VARELA
Airport ↓

URUGUAY
ARTIGAS

Arroyo Ceibal
Arroyo Sauzal
Río Uruguay

Aduana
Plazoleta Roosevelt
Casa de Gobierno Departamental
Muelle AFE
Museo del Río
COSTANERA SUR
COLÓN
SOLÍS
RAMÍREZ
VILARDEBÓ
ANDRES LATORRE
SAN MARTÍN

ARGENTINA
Concordia

0   200m
0   200yds

N

Bradt

For listings, see pages 325–7

Where to stay

1 Danaly (see overview)
2 Eldorado
3 Español
4 Gran Hotel Concordia
5 Gran Hotel Uruguay
6 Hostal del Jardín
7 Los Cedros
8 Salto Hotel & Casino
9 Tía

Off map
Camping
Casa Ambrosoni
Termas de Daymán

Where to eat and drink

10 Casa de Lamas
11 Cavern
12 Chili
13 La Caldera
14 La Nueva Mil y Una
15 La Trattoria

✖ Where to eat All listings are included on the map opposite.

✖ Casa de Lamas Chiazzaro 20 & Purificación; ☎4732 9376. In a historic house near the port, this is fairly classy, with the usual meat & pasta options & a relatively good range of vegetarian dishes; there's outdoor seating too. $$$

✖ La Caldera Uruguay 235; ☎4732 4648. A pleasant, rustic-styled place with seating indoors & out & a varied menu including parrillada, pasta & tasty desserts, & a good wine list. $$$

✖ La Trattoria Uruguay 754; ☎4733 6660; ⏰ 09.00–01.00 daily. In the historic building of the Club Uruguay (with an internal balcony & murals painted in 1945), this serves a good & very affordable range of chivitos, burgers, other meats & fish, pastas, pizzas, salads, sandwiches, omelettes & coffees; there's Wi-Fi too. $$$

✖ La Nueva Mil y Una Uruguay 906; ☎4732 6331. Hardly 1,001 options, but a decent choice of pizzas, chivitos, salads & other fast foods; with AC. $$

✖ Chili Suárez 24; ☎4732 3314; ⏰ 11.00–13.30, 19.30–midnight Mon–Sat, lunchtime only Sun. A choice of 27 empanadas, 17 pizzas, quiche & salads – & yet the vegetarian choice is pretty standard. $

♀Cavern Brasil 204 & Chiazzaro; ☎4734 2013. A busy bar with occasional live music & food such as tapas. $

Entertainment In Salto Shopping at the bus terminal, **Cine Shopping** (☎ 4734 0757) has 3D and normal 2D screens. There might be something on at the **Casa de la Cultura** at Lavalleja 48, south of Uruguay.

Shopping There's a big MultiAhorro supermarket in the **Terminal Shopping**, and the Super Salto and El Revoltijo supermarkets on Uruguay west of Plaza Artigas. There's a big general market on Sunday mornings (food, clothes, jewellery and so on) on the Plaza Deportivo, on the way to the terminal. For genuine gaucho gear (as well as handbags and lampshades), go to the Talabartaria La Criolla (*Artigas 1005, just east of Rincón*) or Calzado Pampero (*Ascensio 397 & 8 de Octubre*).

Other practicalities

Banks There are plenty of ATMs on Uruguay between Lavalleja and Plaza Treinta y Tres, and outside the bus terminal, where there's also the Indumex exchange office (*Local 12;* ⏰ *10.00–21.00 daily*). There are also exchange offices in the centre, such as Cambilex at Uruguay 547 and 934 (*both* ⏰ *08.00–20.00 Mon–Fri, 08.00–13.00 Sat*) and Cambio Salto Grande at Uruguay & Suárez (⏰ *08.30–19.00 Mon–Fri, 08.00–12.30 Sat*).

Communications The main post office is on Artigas west of Treinta y Tres (⏰ *09.00–17.00 Mon–Fri, 08.00–13.00 Sat*), with postal services in various farmacías (including on the northeastern corner of Plaza Treinta y Tres) and in Salto Shopping at the terminal. Antel has two call centres (*Asencio 55;* ⏰ *09.00–20.00 Mon–Sat, 10.00–19.00 Sun; Blandengues 255, 2 blocks south of the terminal;* ⏰ *08.00–22.30 Mon–Fri, 09.00–13.00, 17.30–22.30 Sat–Sun*). There's public Wi-Fi on Plaza Artigas, and a weak signal on Plaza Treinta y Tres. There are cyber centres at Agraciada 1823 (*facing the Plaza Deportivo*) and 25 de Agosto 26 (*Plaza Artigas*).

Emergency services The hospital (*18 de Julio 351 & Varela;* ☎ *4733 2944*) is just south of Plaza Artigas, and the Centro Medical Salto is at Artigas 931 (☎*4733 1000; www.smqs.com.uy*). Police headquarters are at Artigas 450 (☎ *4732 7031*) on the south side of Plaza Treinta y Tres, and there's a police station on 19 de Abril between Juncal and Gutierrez Ruiz.

Immigration and consulate The Inspectoría de Migración is at Artigas 450 (📞 *4733 2860;* e *dnm-salto@minterior.gub.uy;* ⏱ *summer 08.00–14.00; winter 12.00–18.00*) and at the Salto Grande dam (📞 *4732 6199*). The Argentine consulate is on the south side of Plaza Artigas (*Artigas 1162;* 📞 *4733 2931;* e *consar_salto@yahoo.com.ar;* ⏱ *09.00–14.00 Mon–Fri*).

What to see and do The central plazas Artigas and Treinta y Tres feel a bit strange – spacious, nicely laid out but a bit dead. Unusually for Uruguay, the focus of business life is along the main drag, Calle Uruguay, rather than on a plaza, making the city feel more European than many, with attractive streets with cafés and shops to explore.

Two blocks east of Plaza Artigas, on Bortagaray (Córdoba) between Uruguay and Artigas, is one of Eladio Dieste's best-known works, the former municipal bus terminal (1973–74), now the Agencia Central parcels depot, with its striking curved brick vaults, held by just a thin layer of concrete (see page 35). There are quite a few examples of Dieste's work in Salto, including another bus station, the Terminal Rural (*Latorre & Larrañaga*), a water tower and a boat shed at the Club Remeros (*Costanera Norte & Agraciada*).

On the east side of Plaza Artigas the **Catedral San Juan Bautista** (Cathedral of St John the Baptist), built in 1897, is large and impressive, with a neoclassical façade, fine marble columns with classical capitals indoors, and a neorenaissance ceiling. On the south side of the plaza, the library (⏱ *summer 07.30–12.15 Mon–Sat; winter 08.00–18.00 Mon–Fri*) houses the **Museo Edmundo Prati**, with works by the sculptor and others (the great equestrian statue of Artigas in the centre of the plaza is by Prati). Immediately behind the western side of the plaza the Mercado 18 de Julio is a fairly standard cast-iron market hall, built in 1868, that now houses temporary art and photography exhibitions. On its south side (*Paseo España 75*) is the Saltoko Euskaldunen Taldea (Salto Basque Group), which hosts social and cultural events for the local Basque community.

To the north of the former market is the tourism office and, across the road, the **Museo des Bellas Artes (Art Museum)**, properly the Museo María Irene Olarreaga Gallino (*Uruguay 1067;* ⏱ *16.00–21.00 Tue–Sat, 17.00–20.00 Sun; free*). In this ornate Belle-Époque mansion is one of the largest and best art collections outside Montevideo, with a gaucho by Blanes, *Los Ombúes* by Carlos Roberto Rúfalo (1880–1975), a roomful of fine Cúneos (including two of the port of Salto), works by Rafael Barrada, Petrona Viera and Pedro Figari, and a maquette by José Belloni. Another room is given over to Carmelo de Arzadun (1888–1968), a pretty good painter from Salto. At the rear, the Sala Carmelo de Arzadun is actually a modern extension for temporary exhibitions, leading to the garden. On the stairs are more paintings by local artists and the Hungarian-born José Cziffery; upstairs, in addition to the original bathroom (with something like a stand-up jacuzzi) there's more contemporary work, by artists such as María Freira, Manuel Pailós, Bruno Widmann, Eduardo Sarlós (fine ink and gouache drawings) and Alfredo Ghierra. There's a room of work by Eriberto Prati, born in Paysandú and not very interesting.

Four blocks west along Uruguay and immediately north at Suárez 39 is the **Teatro Larrannaga** (⏱ *16.00–21.00 Mon–Sat; free*), designed by British engineer Robert Wilkinson and opened in 1882, a grand neoclassical theatre with superb acoustics. It reopened in 2010 after restoration; the original seats survive in the galleries, but not the stalls. Just across the road to the north, the former Mercado Central, built in 1909, now houses the **Museo del Hombre y la Tecnología** (Museum of Man and Technology; *Brasil 511;* ⏱ *16.00–21.00 Tue–Sun; free*). Apart from images of

Gutenberg, Galileo and Leonardo, this is probably not what you'd expect, focusing on local history, from the development of the cattle industry and gaucho culture in the Jesuit missions, with an intact pulpería and a later Art Nouveau confitería, followed by citrus presses, typewriters, sewing machines and a battered 1980 model of the Salto Grande dam. There are some 10,000-year-old shaped stones from the Cultura Tangarupaense (Tangarupa culture), some later ceramics and the 2,000-year-old skeleton of a hunter from Salto Grande. Hidden in a shed at the rear (*19 de Abril & Zorrilla*) is a 2-4-0T steam locomotive. The rather limited **Museo de Arqueología and Ciencias Naturales** (*Museum of Archaeology and Natural Sciences; same hours; free*) is downstairs, with a separate entry to the west. Here you'll see petroglyphs from north of the Río Negro and pictographs to the south, ceramics from 2,500 years ago, and bits of megafauna killed by hunters 9,500 years ago, such as sabre-toothed tiger (smilodon), mylodon, hippidion, pampatherium and the hippo-like toxodon.

A block north and a block west, the Arroyo Sauzal leads to the Río Uruguay, past the former station of the Ferrocarril del Noroeste (Northwestern Railway) (1886, also by Robert Wilkinson) at Delgado and 19 de Abril, and opposite it Aplas (the Asociación de Artistas Plásticos Salto), in a tatty former goods shed where there are occasional exhibitions. From here you can follow 19 de Abril parallel to the stream for three blocks to the *costanera* (waterfront road) and the Río Uruguay; the **Muelle AFE** (railway jetty) is closed but is to be refurbished as a public pier. To the left (south) is the Aduana (Customs; now the Prefectura), a fine pile built in 1829, and on its south side the shady little Plazoleta Roosevelt, laid out in 1946 around a fountain donated in 1930 by the Brazilian Embassy. These look out on to the old port, with the Resguardo del Puerto (port offices) now housing the **Museo del Río** (*Museum of the River;* ⊕ *14.00–18.00 Thu–Sun, in theory*); the city's only private museum, when it's open you can see photos, tickets, uniforms, flags and pieces from sunken ships.

From south of the Plazoleta, Calle Uruguay leads east past the **Casa de Gobierno Departamental** (*Uruguay 202*), an attractive single-storey mansion, and the Intendencia Municipal (*Uruguay & Gómez*), built in 1887. This looks over Plaza Treinta y Tres, a spacious square with palm trees and a fountain, remodelled in 1999, with the Salesians' Church of Nuestra Señora del Carmen on its east side. Built in 1855, this has an ornate façade and a simple cream-coloured neoclassical interior housing a statue of the Virgin by a Guaraní woodcarver. Its bells (one dating from 1686) were brought from the Jesuit missions in 1832. On the south side of the plaza is the modern police headquarters, with the neoclassical portico of the former *jefatura* (1862) still standing in front.

Immediately east of the plaza at Artigas 529 is the **Ateneo** (1895), with a 250-seat theatre, and a block further on, at Artigas 651, the Sociedad Italiana (1884). Another two blocks east, the **Palacio de Oficinas Públicas** (*Palace of Public Offices; Artigas & Treinta y Tres*) is a grand block designed in 1925 by Veltroni, with a tower that is one of the city's main landmarks.

From here it's six blocks south on Treinta y Tres to Dieste's rural bus terminal (see opposite) and, just east at the south end of Rincón, the **Parque Zoológico** (⊕ *10.00–19.00 daily; free*), one of Uruguay's best zoos. Between 2003 and 2005 it built new pens for lions, tigers and jaguars, and also has boars, foxes, peccaries, llamas, ñandues, emus, zebras, monkeys, deer, parrots, various raptors (including vultures which can fly in and out of open pens), caymans, snakes and turtles. One of Uruguay's four breeding herds of *venado de campo* (pampas deer) is here. There's also a summer theatre in the park.

6

Three blocks north of the bus terminal is the **Parque Solari** (*Avda Blandengues*), an attractive and well-maintained place for a stroll; laid out in the late 19th century in Romantic style, it has a replica of the *Toilet of Venus* (the original Greek sculpture is in the Vatican Museum) on an islet. Immediately to the north across Avenida Amorin (opposite a 24-hour ANCAP station), the Chalet la Casona, formerly owned by the family of the novelist Enrique Amorim (1900–60), houses the **Museo Histórico Municipal** (*Municipal History Museum;* ⊕ *13.00–18.00 Tue–Sun; free*). Remodelled in 2009, it's a rural-style house with a large garden and carts in a shed; it has three rooms with historical relics, and a so-called Cultural Factory, for events and school groups. To the rear, Amorim's home, the Chalet Las Nubes (*Avda Amorim & Avda Artigas; not open to the public*), was built to plans by Le Corbusier.

Five blocks west is the **Museo Horacio Quiroga** (⊕ *14.00–19.00 Tue–Sun; free*), home of another local author (1879–1937), displaying first editions, personal objects and his bicycle; it also has lovely palm-shaded gardens. Quiroga's birthplace at Uruguay 860 is marked by a plaque.

The riverside costaneras are very popular for recreation. To the south the Costanera Sur passes fine villas, monuments to Quiroga and Lorca, two former *saladeros* (meat-salting plants), an altar where Pope John Paul II celebrated mass and, at Arenitas Blancas, 5km south, a fine hilltop viewpoint. The Costanera Norte passes the old railway jetty and the rowing club, founded in 1915, with its roof by Dieste (see page 35). The road is lined with beaches for 3km to the Parador Ayuí, a restaurant at the site where Artigas crossed the river in 1811. On weekend evenings the Bus de la Costa runs hourly from Salto Shopping to the Costanera Norte via Artigas, returning on Brasil (*16.00–23.00, US$0.50*).

AROUND SALTO

Termas de Daymán (*www.termasdayman.com*) It's 9km south on Ruta 3 to the Termas de Daymán, the largest and liveliest of all the hot baths in Uruguay, with families and busloads of youngsters pouring in on summer weekends. This has the hottest water of the Uruguayan springs (up to 44°C, from the Aquifer Guaraní, 2km down), and in most of the ten pools of the Spa Termal (⊕ *07.00–23.00 daily; US$4*) it's frankly too hot to swim much; there's also sauna, hydromassage and lockers. There's cooler water immediately north at the Acuamanía water park (☎ *4736 9222/9815; www.acuamania.com;* ⊕ *mid-Sep–Apr 10.30–18.30 daily (w/ends to 19.30), except 23–25 Dec, 29–31 Dec; US$6.50, 3 days US$9*), with slides up to 70m long, pool basketball and other games, and minigolf; the Kamikaze is a very popular closed-tube toboggan that reaches speeds of up to 60km/h. The waters are meant to be good for rheumatic, neurological and musculoskeletal disorders, and for stress. There's also the Brisas del Agua Clara Parque Termal on the Rambla Circunvalación (☎ *4736 9057;* ⊕ *08.00–22.00 Mon–Thu, 08.00–23.00 Fri–Sun and daily in summer; US$5*), recently renovated and now the most modern complex here, with hot and cold showers and hydromassage, Wi-Fi and the Entre Amigos resto-pub.

The baths are owned by Salto department and are surrounded by a great range of hotels (with 3,000 beds) and campsites; there's also a riverside park by the Río Daymán, immediately to the south (*with a lifeguard 09.00–21.00 Fri–Sun & holidays*). The 'Termas' bus (*hourly 06.30–22.30, returning 07.00–23.00; US$0.70*) runs from the port and along Brasil to Ruta 3 (a couple of blocks south of the terminal). There's a new coach stop with tourist information, ATM and toilets just south of the entry roundabout.

Where to stay The hotels are immediately to the east of the entry to the baths. Their high season is at carnaval, March–May and September–October, while the pools are busy with day visitors in summer. There's camping at the Posta del Daymán (see below) and at the cheaper and quieter Paraíso Natural Daymán, 500m south across the bridge at km476.7 of Ruta 3 (⚲ 4736 9987; m 099 741587; www. paraisonaturaldayman.com).

🏠 **Posada del Siglo XIX** Los Sauces & Los Molles, Barrio Jardines, just north of the resort (behind the school just east of km478.5); ⚲4736 9955; e psxix01@adinet.com.uy; www. posadasigloxix.com.uy. There's nothing 19th-century about this place but it's classy enough, with swimming pools in lovely spacious gardens; internet access is available only in the reception area & the best rooms. **$$$$$–$$$**

🏠 **La Posta del Daymán** ⚲4736 9801; www. lapostadeldayman.com. The only hotel west of the road, on a spacious site north of the baths, there's a 3-star hotel (AC, with thermal water in the showers), *hostal* (simple rooms, though still with private bathrooms & Wi-Fi) & a big campsite (*US$7 pp*), with an excellent restaurant (🕐 *from 07.00 daily*) with parrilla, pasta, fish & snacks, & choice of terrace or AC room. **$$$$–$$$**

🏠 **Apart Hotel Aguasol** ⚲4736 9155; www. aguasol.com.uy. The nearest hotel to the river, at the south end of the resort, this is a good, fairly modern place with its own covered thermal pool & jacuzzi, gym, bikes, table tennis & a pool table, as well as Wi-Fi & parking. **$$$**

🏠 **Apart-Hotel del Pasaje** ⚲4736 9661; m 098 932932; e hoteldelpasaje@gmail.com; www.hoteldelpasaje.com.uy. Facing the Acuamanía entrance, 18 new rooms have been added to the 19 apartments & 4 cabañas, as well as a cafetería. Room rates include breakfast; apartments & cabañas come with BBQ instead. All have AC, cable TV, Wi-Fi & access to bikes & an indoor swimming pool. **$$$**

🏠 **Hotel Aguas Calientes** ⚲4736 9840; e aguascalientes@adinet.com.uy; www. hotelaguascalientesdayman.com.uy. A decent,

modern place with no swimming pool but rooms with AC, cable TV, Wi-Fi & continental breakfast. **$$$**

🏠 **Bungalows Archi** Jacaranda; ⚲4736 9959; e b.archi@adinet.com.uy; www.archi.com.uy. Motel-style suites each have a double & single bed, kitchenette with microwave, AC, cable TV & parrilla. **$$**

🏠 **Hostal Canela** ⚲4736 9121; e hcanela@ adinet.com.uy; www.termasdayman.com/canela. HI-affiliated youth hostel a little way north of the resort (turn east at km478.6, then at once north on Los Sauces), a bungalow with 7 rooms (for 2–5), swimming pool & kitchen. **$$**

🏠 **Hotel Casablanca** ⚲4736 9325; e casablancaxcaret@adinet.com.uy; www. casablanca-xcaret.com.uy. Friendly but slightly drab, this has rooms with AC, cable TV, & thermal water in the rooms & swimming pool. **$$**

🏠 **Hotel Géminis** Calle Timbó s/n; ⚲4736 9108; www.geminishotel.com.ar. An apart-hotel at the south end of the resort, this has apartments for 2–7, with kitchenette & microwave, cable TV & parking. Breakfast is available. **$$**

🏠 **Solar del Acuario** Rambla de Circunvalación; ⚲4736 9206; http://solardelacuario.com. Out towards Ruta 3, this is a comfortable 4-star place with big rooms, but it's not particularly grand & its prices are much the same as lesser establishments. **$$**

🏠 **Termal Daymán de Caute-Antel** km378, Ruta 3 ⚲4736 9960/9995; e termal@cauteantel. com.uy; www.termaldayman.com.uy. A nice modern place with swimming pool & suites with AC & jacuzzi or 4/6-person cabañas with kitchenette & microwave. **$$–$**

✗ Where to eat

✗ **El Rancho** Ruta 3, km488.3, just north of the Termas del Daymán roundabout; ⚲4736 9942. An authentic *espeto corrido* or Brazilian-style parrillada, with waiters carving grilled meat from skewers at your table. **$$**

✗ **La Posta del Daymán** ⚲4736 9901; www. lapostadeldayman.com. To the north of the baths,

this hotel has one of the classiest restaurants here, with AC rooms & open-air seating; they serve the usual mix of grilled meats, fish & pasta. **$$**

✗ **El Fogón de Mandinga** Jacaranda & Avda Paysandú; m 099 716098. A cheery & family-friendly parrilla. **$**

Salto Grande At Salto Grande, 15km north of Salto and reached by a free bus service, are Uruguay's largest dam, hot baths, another water park and an isolated hotel. The 4ha Parque Acuático (⊕ *10.00–20.00 daily; US$8*) has three large pools, artificial waves and slides including the 73m-long Black Hole.

The **Represa Binacional de Salto Grande** (Salto Grande Binational dam) was built in 1974–79 (with 14 Russian-supplied turbines of 135,000kW each). When the 78km² lake is full, it can supply over half of Uruguay's consumption (with a similar amount generated on the Argentine side); even so, a 300kW solar plant is also being installed here, with Japanese government aid. You can take a guided visit (\ *4732 6131;* e *rrppmi@saltogrande.org; www.saltogrande.org;* ⊕ *08.00–17.00 daily except 1 Jan, 1 May, 24 & 25 Dec; free*). These are also possible on the Argentine side, on a more limited schedule; take the signposted road to Relaciones Publicas from just south of the Prefectura and the roundabout (at about km508) for the road over the dam.

On a headland just south of the water park and 2km from the road, the **Hotel Horacio Quiroga** (\ *4733 4411; www.hotelhoracioquiroga.com; $$$$$–$$$$*) is an unassuming low, red-brick hotel that used to house army officers guarding the dam; it's adequate but still a bit institutional and not a destination in itself. It now has its own hot pool, sporting facilities, Wi-Fi, 80 air-conditioned rooms and a decent restaurant. With 218ha to explore, you can take a bike or a golf-cart, or arrange horse riding.

The green Trans 19 bus runs several times a day from Salto, picking up outside the bus terminal and opposite the Parque Solari, passing the turnings to the dam and the hotel, and after 15 minutes reaching the Parque Acuático. The hotel operates its own free transfers from a *sala VIP* in Salto (*Avda Blandengues, immediately south of the bus terminal*).

Termas de Arapey The most upmarket and exclusive of the thermal resorts is the Termas del Arapey (\ *4768 2005/6 ;* tf *0800 8498; www.arapeythermal.com.uy*), reached by an asphalt road which leads 19km east from km548 of Ruta 3. Daily buses are operated by Hernández (\ *4733 1717*) (*07.30 from the terminal; US$5*) and Argentur (*Uruguay 892 & Soca, Salto;* \ *4732 9931; Termas del Arapey;* \ *4768 2028*) (*US$6, US$10 return*) from the Termas de Daymán (*11.45*) and Salto (*12.00, from south of the terminal on Avenida Batlle; returning 19.30 daily*). Argentur can also arrange private remise transfers. A daily Chadre bus from Salto to Bella Unión also runs via Arapey.

There's accommodation in the **Hotel Municipal Termas del Arapey** (\ *4733 4096, 4732 5194; www.arapeynandubay.com*), which offers bungalows (**$$$**) and so-called *moteles* (**$$**). This is the only resort in Uruguay that offers all-inclusive stays all year round, with rates including four buffet meals a day (including *merienda* or high tea). There are two **restaurants**, the better being the Restaurante Paradise (\ *4768 2441; www.restauranteparadise.com; $$$*), open every day of the year for buffet breakfast and à la carte lunch and dinner. There are six thermal pools and over 200 rooms, plus gyms, a business centre and an Ana Aslan anti-ageing clinic.

There's a large **campsite** (\ *4733 4096;* ⊕ *all year; $*), to the right of the entry, situated beside the Río Arapey, charging US$9/12 per tent plus US$3.50–6 per person.

One enjoyable option is boating and fishing on the Río Arapey with Barcos del Este (\ *4432 6665;* m *091 411111;* e *barcosdeleste@gmail.com*).

7

The Interior

Away from the coast and the Río Uruguay, the interior of Uruguay – Artigas, Rivera, Tacuarembó, Durazno, Flores, Treinta y Tres and Cerro Largo departments, plus eastern parts of Río Negro, Paysandú and Salto (otherwise covered in *Chapter 6*) – is largely empty, aside from considerable numbers of cattle. This is gaucho country; passing through, perhaps on a bus towards the Brazilian frontier, you're likely to see a man in a beret, with baggy trousers tucked into leather boots, getting off at a gate in the middle of nowhere, usually with a walk of a couple of kilometres to his estancia. There are quite a few estancias that you can stay on here, offering perhaps less luxurious but more authentic accommodation than many of those to the south, with some real down-home farming experiences.

Although the soil is thin and unsuitable for growing crops, in recent years there has been increasing forestry, notably of eucalyptus for paper pulp. In addition, some vineyards have been established near Rivera, where there's also a limited amount of mining.

In the centre of the country (between Tacuarembó and Durazno departments) the artificial lake behind the Rincón del Bonete (or Gabriel Terra) dam can only be crossed in a few places, where resorts with watersports facilities have been established. At the dam, 22km east of Paso de los Toros, is the country's largest hydro-electric station, opened in 1949, with a capacity of 160MW. Other attempts (especially by the military government) to boost the region's development have had little effect, and the departments along the northern border remain the hottest and slowest-moving part of the country, where the main activity sometimes seems to be selling bootleg Brazilian DVDs.

ARTIGAS DEPARTMENT

BELLA UNIÓN Tiny Bella Unión, in the northwestern corner of the country, seems like the town the government forgot, with its awful roads and pavements and an air of suspended animation. In truth, the town was victimised under the dictatorship, for this is the birthplace of the Tupamaros urban guerrilla movement.

Raúl Sendic (1926–89) was a labour movement lawyer who founded unions for rural workers such as those working in the sugarcane plantations in the late 1950s. Vicious repression led him to believe that armed struggle was the only solution, beginning in 1963 with a break-in at a gun shop in Colonia. Sendic was captured in 1970 and survived years of torture before being released in 1985 and dying in Paris in 1989. There's a monument to him at the junction of Artigas with Ruta 3. Sugarcane workers still live today in remarkable poverty, partly the result of price volatility which leads to frequent lay-offs. As cane waste can now be used to produce alcohol for fuel, it's possible that the industry will stabilise.

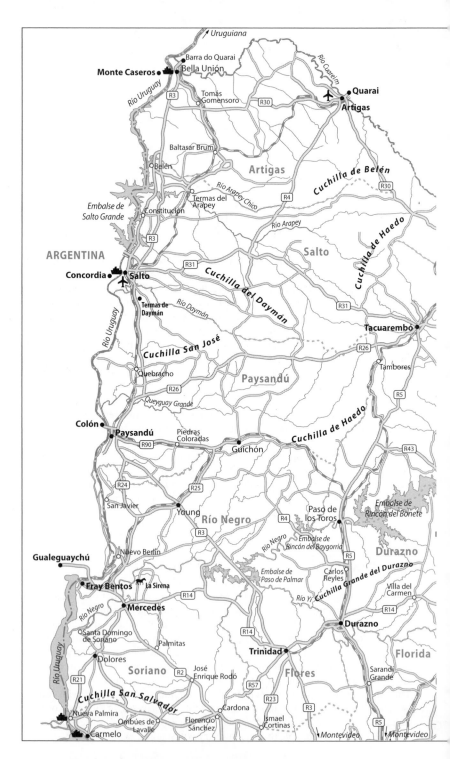

0 ━━━━━ 50km
0 ━━━━━ 50 miles

N

Bradt

Santana do
Livramento

Rivera

Cuchilla de Santa Ana

B R A S I L

Tranqueras

R27

R5

Rivera

Minas de
Corrales

Río Tacuarembó

Vichadero

Aceguá

Ansina

Tacuarembó

Cuchilla Grande

Isidoro
Noblia

Paso Centurión

R8

R7

R6   R26

Río Negro

Fraile
Muerto

Melo

Jaguarão

San Gregorio
de Polanco

Cerro Largo

R7

Río Branco

Lago Merín

R18

La Paloma

Tupambaé

❖ Quebrada
de los Cuervos

Río Tacuarí

Blanquillo

Santa Clara
de Olimar

Vergara

Laguna Merín

R6

Treinta y Tres

Cuchilla Grande

Río Yí

Cerro Chato

R8

**Treinta
y Tres**

R17

La Charqueada

BRASIL

Sarandí
del Yí

R19

Río Olimar Grande

Cebollatí

José Pedro
Varela

San Luis
Al Medio

José Batlle
y Ordóñez

R14

R6

Cebollatí

Cuchilla de las Averías

Lascano

18 De Julio

Chuí

Chuy

R7

Cerro
Colorado

R9

ATLANTIC
OCEAN

Cuchilla Grande

Bañados de
San Miguel

Lavalleja

R8

Rocha

Laguna
Negra

Punta de la
Coronilla

Founded in 1829 by Rivera and named after the meeting place of the Río Uruguay and the Río Cuareim, and of Uruguay, Brazil and Argentina, Bella Unión is home to the ALUR sugar mill and the Calvinor winery, but is of little interest except for the minor border crossings by boat to Monte Caseros in Argentina and by road (Ruta 3) to Barra do Quaraí and Uruguaiana in Brazil.

Getting there and away

By bus Buses heading north and east from Salto (see page 324) reach Ruta 3 near km481. Those to Tacuarembó continue eastwards, while those for Bella Unión head north on Ruta 3, passing the junction to the Salto Grande dam and the crossing to Argentina at km494. To the north is cattle country (with some sunflowers and sugarcane), broken by a few arroyos with gallery forest (km509, km541 and km613). It's one hour 40 minutes to Bella Unión, with a left turn just after km623 on to Artigas, leading to the central Plaza 25 de Mayo, 13 blocks west.

Bus offices are near the plaza: Chadre (*Agencia Central; Rivera;* \ *4779 2148;* e *bellaunion@agenciacentral.com.uy;* ⏰ *08.30–12.30, 16.00–22.00 Mon–Fri*) and Cotabu (*Artigas;* ⏰ *approx 06.00–08.00, 10.00–12.00, 14.00–15.00, 17.00–21.00 daily*). Chadre runs its litoral service twice daily to Colonia via Salto, Paysandú, Fray Bentos, Mercedes and Carmelo; Cotabu runs two buses a day from Salto to Artigas via Bella Unión. The local long-distance bus company is El Norteño (*Rivera 480;* \ *4779 2385*) with one or two departures to Montevideo via Salto daily, and two to Salto only.

There are occasional buses from the plaza to Barra do Quaraí, but it's usually easier to take a remise (*US$2*) and then a local bus to Uruguaiana, from where there are bus connections across southern Brazil. Entering Uruguay from Brazil, you must get your exit stamp from the Policía Federal in Uruguaiana.

By sea A small pedestrian ferry to Monte Caseros in Argentina (*09.00, 13.00 & 16.00 Mon–Fri; US$4*) leaves from the short pier at the west end of Attilio Ferrandis.

⌂ **Where to stay and eat** The only place to stay is the **Hotel Oriente** (*Rivera between Suárez & Asencio, 6 blocks east of the plaza;* \ *4779 3456; www.hotel-oriente. com.uy;* **$$**) which has air-conditioned rooms with private bathrooms or rooms with fans and shared bathroom – breakfast is extra. You can camp, with no facilities other than a bar, at Parque Rivera, the picnic area by the Río Uruguay, or 8km north at the Balneario Los Pinos, where there are better facilities, including electricity.

La Taberna (**$$**), on the southeastern corner of the plaza (north of Artigas), and **Los Amigos** (**$$**), a block east, offer pizza and grilled meats.

Shopping For food shopping, head for the Super San Jorge (*just off the plaza;* ⏰ *08.00–13.00, 15.00–23.00 Mon–Fri, 08.00–13.30, 15.00–23.00 Sat, 09.00–13.30 Sun*), or the small shop on the west side of the plaza.

Other practicalities

Banks There's an ATM at the northwestern corner of the plaza.

Communications The post office is at Rivera 800 (⏰ *09.00–14.30 Mon–Fri, 09.00–12.00 Sat*). Antel's call centre is on Rivera a block east of the plaza (⏰ *09.00–20.00 Mon–Sat, 10.00–18.00 Sun*). There's public Wi-Fi on the main plaza and at the school on its west side.

Immigration For visa issues, the Inspectoría de Migración is on the southeastern corner of the plaza (*Bianchi & Artigas*; ☏ *4779 2835*; e *dnm-bellaunion@minterior. gub.uy*; ⊕ *summer 09.00–14.30 Mon–Fri; winter 12.00–18.00 Mon–Fri*) and at the bridge to Brazil (☏ *4779 5094*).

What to see and do The grandest building in town is the Sociedad Fomento (1907–11) off the northeastern corner of the plaza. There's a small local museum and Sala de Exposiciones (*Exhibition Room; Rivera & Ferreira, diagonally opposite the post office;* ⊕ *from around 20.00*).

ARTIGAS Founded in 1852 (as Villa San Eugenio del Cuareim), the small city of Artigas (population over 40,000) is the remotest Uruguayan city from Montevideo, 612km away. It's known for heat – the summertime high temperature averages 33°C, with a recorded maximum of 42°C. In winter the average low is 7°C, but temperatures as low as –4°C have been recorded. Artigas's average rainfall is 1,235mm per year.

Artigas department is known for its semi-precious stones, including agate and amethyst, from small mines just southeast of the city, especially near the Arroyo Catalán, also important for its archaeological finds.

Getting there and away

By bus Turil has three services a day from Montevideo and Tacuarembó to Artigas (taking between seven and eight hours), and CUT (Corporación) has two a day. Jota Ele (JL) also has two buses a day from Salto to Artigas via Rutas 31 and 4, and COA has three (*2 on Sun*). Cotabu has two buses a day from Salto via the Termas de Arapey and two via Bella Unión, and there's also a Sopel bus from Bella Unión at 17.00 (except Sundays). There are no buses from Rivera to Artigas – you can either take a bus through Brazil (from Santana do Livramento to Quaraí) and then a taxi across the border, or a local bus from Rivera as far as Tranqueras and wait there for a bus from the Tacuarembó direction to Artigas. There's a baggage store on the platform by the toilets.

Traffic crosses freely between Artigas and Quaraí on the Brazilian side of the Río Cuareim (Rio Quaraí in Portuguese), but anyone going further must get their passport stamped on the Uruguayan side. Buses run along Lecueder and across the bridge, or you can take a taxi from the bus terminal or elsewhere. The Rodoviario (bus station) in Quaraí is just to the left (northwest) at the west end of the plaza, one block from the bridge. There are buses to Porto Alegre (*20.00 Sun–Fri*), Santa Maria (18.00 daily), Santana do Livramento (*7 daily*), Uruguaiana (*6 daily*), Jaguarão (*14.30 Sat*) and Rio Grande (*08.25 daily*). Brazilian and Uruguayan Immigration posts are at either end of the bridge, although you don't need to stop if you are just visiting the town.

By car The most direct route from Salto is by Ruta 31 and Ruta 4. Travelling from Bella Unión, you'll head south towards Salto, then turn left at km619 on an asphalt road that bypasses the village of Tomás Gomensoro and continues as Ruta 30 across flatter grassland to the junction with Ruta 4. There you'll turn left and follow the main road (which becomes Avenida Artigas) in to Artigas (2½ hours from Bella Unión, three hours from Salto). From the bus terminal it's three blocks northwest to the main drag, Avenida Lecueder. Immediately to the left is the main Plaza Batlle, while the international bridge, the Puente de la Concordia, is ten blocks to the right.

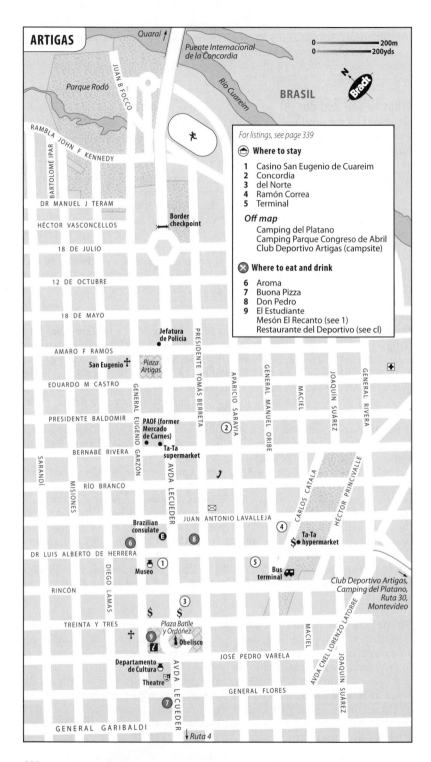

ARTIGAS

Quaraí

Puente Internacional
de la Concordia

Parque Rodó

Río Cuareim

BRASIL

0 —————— 200m
0 —————— 200yds

For listings, see page 339

Where to stay

1 Casino San Eugenio de Cuareim
2 Concordia
3 del Norte
4 Ramón Correa
5 Terminal

Off map

Camping del Platano
Camping Parque Congreso de Abril
Club Deportivo Artigas (campsite)

Where to eat and drink

6 Aroma
7 Buona Pizza
8 Don Pedro
9 El Estudiante
Mesón El Recanto (see 1)
Restaurante del Deportivo (see cl)

JUAN B FOCCO

RAMBLA JOHN F KENNEDY

BARTOLOMÉ IPAR

DR MANUEL J TERAM

HÉCTOR VASCONCELLOS

Border
checkpoint

18 DE JULIO

12 DE OCTUBRE

18 DE MAYO

Jefatura
de Policía

PRESIDENTE TOMÁS BERRETA

AMARO F RAMOS

San Eugenio

Plaza
Artigas

APARICIO SARAVIA

GENERAL MANUEL ORIBE

MACIEL

JOAQUÍN SUÁREZ

GENERAL RIVERA

EDUARDO M CASTRO

GENERAL EUGENIO GARZÓN

PRESIDENTE BALDOMIR

PAOF (former
Mercado
de Carnes)

Ta-Ta
supermarket

(2)

BERNABÉ RIVERA

SARANDÍ

MISIONES

RÍO BRANCO

AVDA LECUEDER

CARLOS CATALA

HÉCTOR PRINCIVALLE

Brazilian
consulate

JUAN ANTONIO LAVALLEJA

(4)

DR LUIS ALBERTO DE HERRERA

E

(8)

(6)

Ta-Ta
hypermarket

DIEGO LAMAS

Museo

(1)

(5)

Bus
terminal

RINCÓN

Club Deportivo Artigas,
Camping del Platano,
Ruta 30,
Montevideo

TREINTA Y TRES

(3)

$ $

Plaza Batlle
y Ordóñez

(9)

Obelisco

MACIEL

AVDA CNEL LORENZO LATORRE

JOSÉ PEDRO VARELA

Departamento
de Cultura

Theatre

AVDA LECUEDER

JOAQUÍN SUÁREZ

GENERAL FLORES

(7)

GENERAL GARIBALDI

Ruta 4

Tourist information The tourist information office is opposite the Casa de la Cultura on Plaza Batlle y Ordóñez (☏ *4772 3094; ⏱ 07.00–18.00 Mon–Fri*).

Where to stay If you don't want to stay in a hotel, there are two campsites south, off Ruta 30, by the Río Cuareim; both have small swimming pools. There's also a private site further south (see *Platano*, below). All listings are included on the map opposite.

Hotels

⌂ Hotel Casino San Eugenio de Cuareim Herrera 298 & Avda Lecueder; ☏ 4772 0710–2; www.hotelartigas.com. Modern 4-star hotel aimed at Brazilian casino-goers; the infrastructure is pretty good (apart from the dated lift) but the service may still need improving. **$$$**

⌂ Hotel del Norte Lecueder 507; ☏ 4772 2223; e hoteldelnorte@adinet.com.uy. Central & pretty nice, with patio, AC & a PC, but somewhat pricey. **$$**

⌂ Hotel Terminal Herrera 438; ☏ 4772 0599. This place looks far cheaper than it is. You'll find AC rooms with private bathroom & cable TV. **$$**

⌂ Hotel Concordia Saravia 256; ☏ 4772 2911. Large (over 50 rooms, with & without private bathrooms) & pretty comfortable for a 1-star hotel, but no breakfast. **$**

⌂ Hotel Ramón Correa Lavalleja 466 & 495; ☏ 4772 4666/2736. A cheap place 100m east of the bus terminal, with 17 rooms, some with AC; reception is in the main building on the south side of Lavalleja. **$**

Hostel

⌂ Club Deportivo Artigas Berreta & Herrera; ☏ 4772 2532. Hostel-style accommodation in the centre of town. **$**

Camping

⛺ Club Deportivo Artigas About 2km east from km133; ☏ 4772 3250. You're supposed to check in at their hostel in town first, but you won't be turned away if you don't. **$**

⛺ Camping Parque Congreso de Abril Piedra Pintada; ☏ 4772 2261. 4km southeast from km139½ by a dirt road (16km from the centre), where there's also a small menagerie. Get here via bus (*07.30 & 17.00, returning 08.15 & 17.45, 30mins later on Sun*) from the roundabout by the international bridge & continuing past the terminal. **$**

⛺ Camping del Platano Km140½; ☏ 4772 2000. Further south, this is a small private site in trees west of Ruta 30. **$**

✗ Where to eat All listings are included on the map opposite.

✗ Mesón El Recanto Herrera 298 & Avda Lecueder; ☏ 4772 0710–2. In the Hotel-Casino, this is the most upmarket restaurant in town, serving the usual range of meats, fish & pastas. **$$$**

✗ Don Pedro Berreta & Herrera; ☏ 4773 1017. This restaurant-parrillada is the most traditional & characterful place to eat, serving grilled meats, pasta, pizza & chivitos. **$$**

✗ Buona Pizza Lecueder 684 & Flores; ☏ 4773 0012; m 099 773928. A cheap & simple place for pizza (eat in or take-away). **$**

✗ El Estudiante Lecueder 517; ☏ 4773 3213. On the Plaza de Comidas (food court) of Plaza Batlle, this is basically a take-away serving pizzas, chivitos, tortillas, milanesas, salads & desserts. **$**

✗ Restaurante del Deportivo Herrera & Berreta; ☏ 4772 3015. The sports club has a decent restaurant for lunch, with a dish of the day & a tenedor libre buffet. **$**

☕ Aroma Herrera 245 & Garzón; ☏ 4772 4700; ⏱ from 10.00 Mon–Fri, 18.00 Sat–Sun. This stylish new café & yoghurt-bar (doubtless the only one in interior Uruguay) sells healthy frozen yoghurt, real coffee (& *carajillo* or Irish coffee) & hot chocolate, brownies, lemon pie, cheesecake, as well as pizza. **$**

Events The city is famed for its carnaval celebrations, the longest in Uruguay (in terms of time period, not procession length), starting with the election of the *reina del carnaval* (Carnival Queen) in early February. It's more Brazilian than other

Uruguayan carnavals, being the only one with samba 'schools' (up to a thousand strong) participating, and big ornate floats; the Carnaval de Samba lasts three nights, with two samba schools parading on each of the Saturday and Sunday before Mardi Gras, and all four on the Monday. Quaraí doesn't celebrate carnaval, so many of its population come to Artigas, where up to 20,000 spectators line Avenida Lecueder to watch the processions. Artigas itself has something of a Brazilian feel to it, with browner faces and rather Brazilian accents (and some Portuguese words, such as *churrasqueira* for a barbecue grill).

Carnaval and Lent are followed by Easter Week, marked with displays of horse riding and horse-breaking, and with traditional rural food and music. The 500 Millas del Norte cycle race, a famous series of six 105km circuits around the city and nearby, has been held here every April since 1968.

Shopping For general shopping, there's a big Ta-Ta hypermarket (⊕ *08.00– 23.00 daily*) across Herrera from the terminal, and a smaller Ta-Ta supermarket on Lecueder at Rivera (⊕ *08.30–12.30, 15.00–19.00 Mon–Fri, 08.30–12.00 Sat*). Lecueder is also lined with 'free shops', selling duty-free goods. Local specialities are amethyst and other semi-precious stones such as agate, available at shops such as Amatista (*Herrera 540;* \ *4772 1053;* m *099 772331;* e *sarnicola@hotmail.com*); you can also visit some of the mines these stones come from (see opposite). You can also buy crystals at La Casa de la Artesanía, where Lecueder becomes Rondeau just south of the centre.

Other practicalities
Banks There are ATMs on Lecueder at Herrera and at Rincón. The Cambilex exchange office is at Hererra 539, in the Ta-Ta store (⊕ *08.00–22.00 daily*).

Communications The post office is at Beretta 385 and Lavalleja (⊕ *09.00–17.00 Mon–Fri, 08.00–12.00 Sat*), and you can also buy stamps at Farmacía Melody, Lecueder 324. The Antel call centre is at Río Branco 379 (⊕ *09.00–20.00 Mon–Sat, 10.00–18.00 Sun*). There's public Wi-Fi on Plaza Batlle.

Emergency services The departmental hospital is at Castro and Rivera (\ *4772 3701–4*); emergencies can also be dealt with by Gremeda at Ansina and 18 de Julio (\ *4772 4001*), and the police headquarters is at Ramos and Lecueder (\ *109, 4772 4472*).

Immigration and consulate The Inspectoría de Migración is at 18 de Julio 29 (\ *4772 4041;* e *dnm-artigas@minterior.gub.uy*) and at the international bridge (\ *4772 8141*). The Brazilian consulate is at Lecueder 432 (\ *4772 25414;* ⊕ *09.00– 15.00 Mon–Fri*).

What to see and do The bus terminal, opened in 2001, incorporates the former railway station, in use from 1891 to 1986; in a small plaza on its south side is a preserved 2-6-0 steam locomotive, with level-crossing signs and other pieces of railway gear. In front of the terminal is an *ibirapitá* tree brought from Paraguay in 1915, a descendant of one Artigas sat under in exile. There's also a clock donated by the town's Lebanese community in 1930.

Three blocks northwest is Avenida Lecueder, named after the department's first governor. Two blocks to the left is Plaza José Batlle y Ordoñez, covering two blocks on either side of the avenue. In the centre is a stumpy **obelisk**, raised in

1930 to the glory of the heroes of the independence struggle, made of 120 tonnes of granite from Pan de Azúcar. On the west side of the plaza is the **Departamento de Cultura** (*Lecueder 606;* ✆ *4772 3094*) with a **theatre**, municipal auditorium and library at Lecueder 624, as well as the Usina Cultural Artigas or 'culture factory' (m *099 991459*). Temporary exhibitions are held here, and this is the place to ask about events – and about whether the **Museo Departamental** (*Herrera & Garzón*), with small collections of minerals, fossils, indigenous relics and stuffed animals, has reopened yet.

Three blocks northeast up Garzón, at Rivera 257, is the former **Mercado de Carnes** (Meat Market), a neoclassical structure by Giovanni Veltroni, inaugurated in 1919, refurbished in 2005 and now housing **PAOF** (Programa de Fortalecimiento de las Artes, Artesanías y Oficios), which trains young people in leatherworking, textiles and jewellery-making. There's a fine selling display of their work (including local amethysts) in the market hall (⊕ *09.00–17.00 Mon–Fri*), and a modern teaching wing.

Two blocks towards the bridge is **Plaza Artigas**, with a monument to the eponymous hero in the centre, raised in 1975 with 6,420 pieces of local agate on its base (some are now missing). On the northwestern side of the plaza is the church of **San Eugenio**, the town's original church built in 1853, an unassuming little place which is only open a couple of times a week. On the northeastern side of the plaza is the castle-like **Jefatura de Policía** (police headquarters and jail), built in 1896 and the city's most emblematic building.

At the end of Avenida Lecueder is the 750m-long Puente de la Concordia, opened in 1968. By the river below are the Paseo 7 de Septiembre and Parque Rodó, with play and sports facilities, including a mountain-bike circuit, as well as a beach, recently closed by pollution. The campsite here is closed.

You can visit several of the **mines** from which the region's gemstones come. Some 60km south of Artigas, off Ruta 30 near the Arroyo Catalán, turn right at km178 towards La Bolsa and Meneses. It's 8km to the Mina las Amatistas, well set up for visits (*book at Lecueder 367;* ✆ *4772 7833/3627*). La Limeña is an open-pit mine at km3 of the same road, and the Enzo Berardi y Andres Jacketti mine (✆ *4772 5247*) is further south at km16.

RIVERA DEPARTMENT

LUNAREJO AND LAURELES In the western corner of Rivera department, the 201km² **Parque Natural Regional Valle de Lunarejo** is one of Uruguay's newest protected areas, exciting those in the conservation and ecotourism businesses because of the rare ecosystems, relics of the mata Atlántica, lurking in its steep-sided valleys, and the way that local families are working together to create a sustainable model of rural tourism. There are pockets of subtropical vegetation here (including tree ferns, orchids and epiphytic bromeliads), hidden from the wind and with plenty of water. Various neotropic mammals (at their southern limit here) include the last known populations in Uruguay of the lesser anteater (*Tamandua tetradactyla*) and porcupine (*Coendu spinosus*), as well as one of the few Uruguayan populations of coati (*Nasua nasua*). Two new flower subspecies were found here in 2008.

Ruta 30 south of Artigas rises on to a parched grassland, crossing various streams including the Arroyo Catalán Chico at km167, with good gallery forest; there are also plenty of ñandues in this area. You'll pass the turning south to La Bolsa and the gem mines (see above), and another junction at La Charqueada, coming after 75 minutes to Masoller, where the departments of Artigas, Rivera and Salto meet. There's a memorial to the Battle of Masoller in 1904, when the rebel caudillo Aparicio Saravia was defeated and mortally wounded.

Continuing into Rivera department, you'll soon see the Balcones de Lunarejo (✆ 4650 6363) on the right at km230, offering camping, horse riding and an ecotourist guide. Then you plunge down the Bajada de Peña, the steepest hill in Uruguay, with hairpins restricted to 20km/h eastbound. The road quickly moves from windswept grassland to woodland, with eroded red hills on either side, and after 4km (km238, 90 minutes from Artigas) an unpaved road on the right leads to the Valle de Lunarejo.

The valley opens out here, with lines of hills all more or less the same height on either side. The Lunarejo road gradually swings away from the main road, coming in 1.5km to the tiny village of La Palma and, after a right-angle bend, the **Posada Lunarejo** (✆ 4650 6400; m 099 826348; *www.posadalunarejo.com*; ⊕ all year; **$$$**), a fine base for ecotourism in this area, with all meals available. A single-storey colonial-style building in an attractive rustic style, it has just three double rooms and two family rooms, and offers horse riding (*US$7.50/hr*), mountain biking (*US$2.50/hr*) and nature tours in an open 4x4 truck (*US$150*), following the Arroyo Lunarejo to its source south of La Palma. Immediately south of the posada is a *bañado* (wetland) managed as a reserve, where you may see herons, egrets, ibis, vultures or teros.

Just south of Lunarejo, in the northern fringe of Tacuarembó department, the **Quebrada Laureles** (Laurels Gorge) is similar to Lunarejo and a little remoter, best approached from the south (with no public transport; turn west from Ruta 5 at km407). There are some working estancias here preserving subtropical ecosystems in gorges which cattle can't reach, as well as about 20 waterfalls (of which perhaps five flow all year) and rock pools. The best place to stay is the **Establecimiento Vichadero** (✆ 4630 2358; m 095 225222; e *dariobichadero@gmail.com*; **$$**), run by Dario Fros, a great local guide, working with his neighbours to give access to gorges, waterfalls, swimming holes and even rope bridges (*http://quebradasdelaureles. blogspot.co.uk*). For other options contact m 099 085718; e quebradasdelaureles@ gmail.com, soniasuarez31@yahoo.com.ar. In some streambeds you may find quartz containing gems such as agate.

From the right-angle bend in the road in La Palma a track crosses a ford to reach Ruta 30 after about 2km (at km240.3). Here you can catch the occasional local bus (run by Boreal) from Masoller to Rivera via the village of Tranqueras, 11km east. The bus soon swings right on to a very slow dirt road (the former Ruta 30) to a bridge with the **Camping Municipal** (✆ 4622 3803; **$**) alongside, then on a paved dual carriageway into Tranqueras, rejoining Ruta 30 at about km254. There's no hotel, but the campsite is adequate; there are also an ATM and a Turil bus office on the plaza.

It's 12km east to km458 of Ruta 5 (from Montevideo and Tacuarembó to Rivera); turning left (north), it's 37km to the edge of Rivera, and about 5km more to the centre.

RIVERA Larger and livelier than Artigas, the city of Rivera (founded in 1867), a round 500km from Montevideo, is a more important crossing point, with the Brazilian town of Santana do Livramento immediately adjoining it (each with a population of about 100,000).

Getting there and away The Uruguayan and Brazilian Aduana (Customs) posts are 5km on either side of the actual border, and people can move freely

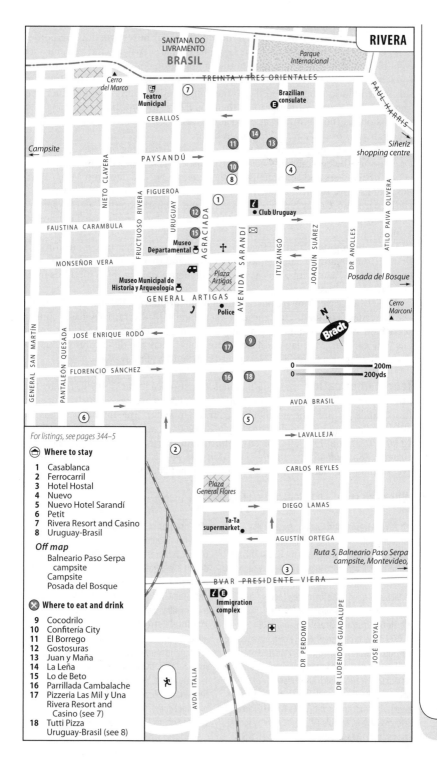

RIVERA

SANTANA DO
LIVRAMENTO
BRASIL

*Parque
Internacional*

Cerro
del Marco

TREINTA Y TRES ORIENTALES

Teatro
Municipal

Brazilian
consulate

CEBALLOS

Campsite

PAYSANDÚ

*Siñeriz
shopping centre*

NIETO CLAVERA

FRUCTUOSO RIVERA

FIGUEROA

URUGUAY

AGRACIADA

Club Uruguay

FAUSTINA CARAMBULA

Museo
Departamental

AVENIDA SARANDÍ

ITUZAINGÓ

JOAQUÍN SUÁREZ

DR ANOLLES

ATILO PAIVA OLIVERA

MONSEÑOR VERA

Plaza
Artigas

Posada del Bosque

Museo Municipal de
Historia y Arqueología

GENERAL ARTIGAS

Police

*Cerro
Marconi*

GENERAL SAN MARTIN

PANTALEÓN QUESADA

JOSÉ ENRIQUE RODÓ

FLORENCIO SÁNCHEZ

0 ————————— 200m
0 ————————— 200yds

AVDA BRASIL

LAVALLEJA

For listings, see pages 344–5

🛏 **Where to stay**

1 Casablanca
2 Ferrocarril
3 Hotel Hostal
4 Nuevo
5 Nuevo Hotel Sarandí
6 Petit
7 Rivera Resort and Casino
8 Uruguay-Brasil

Off map
  Balneario Paso Serpa
    campsite
  Campsite
  Posada del Bosque

❌ **Where to eat and drink**

9 Cocodrilo
10 Confitería City
11 El Borrego
12 Gostosuras
13 Juan y Maña
14 La Leña
15 Lo de Beto
16 Parrillada Cambalache
17 Pizzeria Las Mil y Una
   Rivera Resort and
     Casino (see 7)
18 Tutti Pizza
   Uruguay-Brasil (see 8)

CARLOS REYLES

Plaza
General Flores

DIEGO LAMAS

Ta-Ta
supermarket

AGUSTÍN ORTEGA

*Ruta 5, Balneario Paso Serpa
campsite, Montevideo,*

BVAR PRESIDENTE VIERA

Immigration
complex

DR PERDOMO

DR LUDENDOR GUADALUPE

JOSÉ ROYAL

AVDA ITALIA

in the area between them. There are no international **buses** crossing the border here; Uruguayan **buses** arrive at the terminal on Plaza Artigas, and you must go eight blocks back down Agraciada to the Immigration complex on Viera between Agraciada and Sarandí (the two main streets leading to the border). On the Brazilian side it's ten blocks from the border to the Policía Federal at Silveira Martinez and Thomas Alboronoz for Immigration, then you'll have to come back eight blocks to the Rodoviária (bus terminal) at Filho and Alves. There are three buses a day (one overnight) to Porto Alegre, taking seven hours.

From Montevideo Turil operates five buses a day (including one super cama) via Durazno and Tacuarembó, Agencia Central (Sabelin) has four a day and Nuñez five, taking between six and seven hours. Nuñez has two buses a day from Melo (*4hrs*). Posada has three services a day from Rivera to Melo and two to San Gregorio, all via Tacuarembó. Copay has two to Paysandú and Tacuarembó (*the 16.00 departure only going as far as Tacuarembó on Sun*), and one to Tacuarembó via Tambores at 17.00 daily.

There are no buses from Artigas to Rivera – you can either take a bus through Brazil (from Quaraí to Santana do Livramento) and then a taxi across the border, or an Artigas–Tacuarembó bus as far as Tranqueras, waiting there for a bus from Tacuarembó to Rivera.

A CUT bus leaves Fray Bentos at midnight on Mondays and Thursdays, running via Mercedes, Trinidad, Durazno and Tacuarambó to Rivera; ETA has a similar service on Wednesday and Sunday nights. From Salto there's an Agencia Central bus very early on Monday and Friday mornings. There are departures to Buenos Aires with Agencia Central or Nossar, at 19.00 Sunday–Friday.

Tourist information There's a national tourist office (☏ *4622 5899*), run by the Ministry of Tourism, at the Immigration complex, as well as a tourist office for Rio Grande do Sul (the neighbouring Brazilian state). The Intendencia has an office at Agraciada 570 and Artigas (☏ *4623 1960;* ⏰ *summer 07.15–13.00; winter 12.00–19.15 Mon–Fri*), and for city information there's a kiosk outside the Club Uruguay (*Sarandí 487;* ⏰ *10.00–23.00 Mon–Sat, possibly closing for lunch*). Almost everything you'd want is on the main street, Sarandí, or Plaza Artigas.

 Where to stay All listings are included on the map, page 343.

⌂ **Rivera Resort and Casino** Avda Treinta y Tres Orientales 974; ☏ 4624 1111; http://riveracasinoresort.com. Right on the border, this new casino-hotel is very popular with Brazilian visitors, & rather overpriced for most others, although the restaurant is good value for money. There's also a swimming pool, spa & solarium. **$$$$**

⌂ **Hotel Uruguay-Brasil** Sarandí 440; ☏ 4622 3068; e urubras@netgate.com.uy; www.hoteluruguaybrasil.com.uy. An adequate 3-star on the main drag with lots of pavement bars & restaurants nearby, which also means it can be noisy at night. There's a lift, free shop & parking garage, internet access with 2 PCs & a Wi-Fi area, & rooms have AC & cable TV. There's a pretty formal restaurant & a reasonable buffet breakfast. **$$$**

⌂ **Casablanca** Agraciada 479; ☏ 4622 3221; e cablanca@adinet.com.uy; www.casablanca.com.uy. A slim 5-storey 1960s block, this is a very decent 3-star hotel, with lift, Wi-Fi, meeting room & free shop. Rooms have AC & cable TV, & superior ones (same size as standard, but more modern) have minibar. **$$**

⌂ **Hotel Petit** Avda Brasil 876; ☏ 4623 4000; e petit-rivera-hotel@adinet.com.uy; www.petitriverahotel.com.uy. 4 blocks west of Avda Sarandí, this is a decent mid-range hotel with AC rooms, Wi-Fi & 2 PCs; there's also the Restaurante-Pizzería Vieja Estación (⏰ *18.00–midnight daily*), serving fish, beef, chicken, chivitos, pasta & pizza. **$$**

🏠 **Posada del Bosque** Orlando Bonilla 59, Barrio Caqueiro; ☎4622 3376; www. posadadelbosquerivera.com. Set in spacious wooded grounds 3km east of the city centre (turn north off Artigas), there are just 6 simple guest rooms (with AC, TV & Wi-Fi) & a separate building for the excellent buffet breakfast, as well as swimming pool & BBQs. **$$**

🏠 **Ferrocarril** Lavalleja 1008 & Uruguay; ☎4622 3389. A very decent little 1-star place, with an AC *comedor* (dining room) & rooms with & without cable TV & private bathroom. No breakfast. **$**

🏠 **Hotel Hostal** Viera 1181; ☎4622 2900. A cheap place on a main road opposite the hospital & close to Immigration. **$**

🏠 **Nuevo** Ituzaingó 411 & Paysandú; ☎4622 3147. This 8-storey block is a cheap but slightly tatty option very close to the border. **$**

🏠 **Nuevo Hotel Sarandí** Sarandí 777; ☎4623 3963, 4662 5296. A slightly grubby but adequate 1-star place, with rooms with private or shared bathroom. **$**

⛺ **Balneario Paso Serpa** ☎4622 3803. Further into the countryside, 17km southeast on Ruta 27. 14ha of woodland with camping, electricity, BBQ, a cantina & soccer & volleyball pitches. **$**

⛺ **Campsite** ☎4625 23083. A decent campsite 7km west on Paysandú in the Parque Gran Bretaña (a park donated in 1939 by the British ambassador, Sir Eugen Millington-Drake), where there's also a parador by a reservoir, a small zoo & motocross & car-racing circuits. **$**

✖ **Where to eat** The best restaurants are at the **Rivera Resort and Casino** ($$$) and the **Hotel Uruguay-Brasil** ($$$). **Gostosuras** (*Agraciada 490 near Carámbula; $*) is a small, homely restaurant serving homemade Brazilian-style food, salads, cakes, tea and coffee, and a buffet sold by weight. Otherwise there are quite a few pizzerias, notably **Tutti Pizza** (*Sarandí & Sánchez*), **Pizzeria Las Mil y Una** (*Sarandí 692; $$*) and the relatively classy **Parrillada Cambalache** (*Sarandí 708; ☎ 4622 0767; $$*) at the same junction. **La Leña** (*Sarandí 365 between Ceballos & Paysandú; ☎ 4623 2092; $$*) is a café-pizzeria-parrilla with a wood-fired oven. Other decent parrillas include **Lo de Beto** (*Carambula & Agraciada; ☉ from 20.00 Tue–Fri, from noon Sat–Sun; $$*), and **Juan y Maña** (*Paysandú 1151 & Ituzaingó; $$*). **El Borrego** (*Sarandí 398 & Paysandú; $*) is a decent bar-restaurant-café with cold beer, classy snacks and Wi-Fi; **Cocodrilo** (*Sarandí & Rodó; $*) is a cheery resto-pub; and the **Confitería City** (*immediately north of the Hotel Uruguay-Brasil at Sarandí 380; $*) is a fine and long-established pastry shop. All listings are included on the map, page 343.

Shopping There are Ta-Ta supermarkets south of the centre (*Sarandí 950*) and in the new Siñeriz shopping centre at Sepé 51 and Charrúa, right on the border just east of the centre (*both ☉ 08.00–22.00 daily*). There are lots of duty-free shops on Sarandí.

Other practicalities

Banks There are ATMs along Sarandi. You can change money at Indumex (*Avda Sarandi 496; ☉ 08.00–18.00 Mon–Sat*).

Communications The post office is at Sarandí 501 and Carambula (*☉ 09.00–17.00 Mon–Fri, 08.00–12.00 Sat*). Antel's call centre is at Agraciada and Artigas (*☉ 09.00–19.00 daily*). There's public Wi-Fi on both plazas, but it's too weak to be any use.

Emergency services The hospital is on Viera at the southern end of Ituzaingó (*☎ 4622 3307*); the police station is on the south side of Plaza Artigas.

Immigration and consulate The Inspectoría de Migración is four blocks from the border (*Suárez 516 between Carambula & Vera; ☎ 4622 4086; e dnm-rivera@*

minterior.gub.uy) and at the Immigration complex (✆ *4622 5254*). The Brazilian consulate is at Ceballos 1159 (✆ *4622 3278*).

What to see and do The centre of town is Plaza Artigas, with the bus terminal on its west side, the police station on the south side and the simple, white church with red marble columns on its north side. The **Museo Municipal de Historia y Arqueología** (*Municipal Museum of History & Archaeology; Artigas 1019, just south of the bus terminal; closed between Christmas & New Year; free*) has decent displays on local history and archaeology. The **Museo Departamental** (*Agraciada & Vera*) shows the works of local artists.

The Art Deco-style Club Uruguay is the most striking building on Sarandí between the plaza and the border. To the left at the Parque Internacional, marking the border, the **Teatro Municipal** (*Treinta y Tres 970*) was built as a cinema in 1977 and run by the city, then controversially privatised in 2009. Immediately beyond is the basalt **Cerro del Marco**, a viewpoint with a border marker on top.

On the slopes of the sandstone Cerro Chapeu, about 10km southeast of town, are the Carrau vineyards and ultramodern winery (see page 152). Named (in Portuguese) for its hat-like shape, this is also the site of the city's small airport. There are a couple of other new bodegas in the hills immediately west of Rivera.

TO TACUAREMBÓ Heading south from Rivera, Ruta 5 crosses a sandstone plain punctuated by plugs and mesas of volcanic basalt (for instance the striking outcrop to the west at km487½). South of the junction to Lunarejo and Artigas at km458, the road runs between mesas and limestone scarps, with lots of pine and eucalyptus plantations. At km426, Ruta 29 heads east to **Minas de Corrales**, a small town at the centre of a historic gold-mining district. The **Hotel Artigas** (*Avda Davidson;* ✆*4658 2967; www.hotelartigas.com.uy;* **$$$**) was supposedly the first in the interior of the country to have rooms with private bathrooms; now it has 15 comfortable air-conditioned rooms as well as a lovely garden and swimming pool; from here you can take a tour of the gold mines, opened in 1878 by a French company and largely closed by 1916. At the Represa Cuñapirú (Cuñapirú dam), 9km east of Ruta 5, are the remains of the first hydro-electric plant in South America, opened in 1882 and closed after flooding in 1959; the dam (314m across), buildings, turbines and a cistern for drinking water can still be seen. A ropeway ran 9km from Ruta 5 to here and also to the nearby San Gregorio gold mine, which reopened in 1997 under Canadian/Australian ownership, after being closed for over 80 years. Now massive amounts of iron ore are to be produced from the Zapucay mine south of Corrales.

The main road crosses the Río Tacuarembó into the department of the same name, with a toll at km423½ and then rolling cattle and sheep country with pine plantations and some scrubby native monte.

TACUAREMBÓ DEPARTMENT

TACUAREMBÓ The eponymous capital of Uruguay's largest department, and the largest city in the interior of the country (with a population of around 50,000), Tacuarembó also boasts the only first-division soccer team outside the Montevideo area. Its main employer is Brazilian-owned Frigorífico Tacuarembó, which ships large quantities of beef jerky to the US. Sitting in a bowl without a river to cool it, Tacuarembó is known for summer heat, with temperatures often reaching into the 40s (°C).

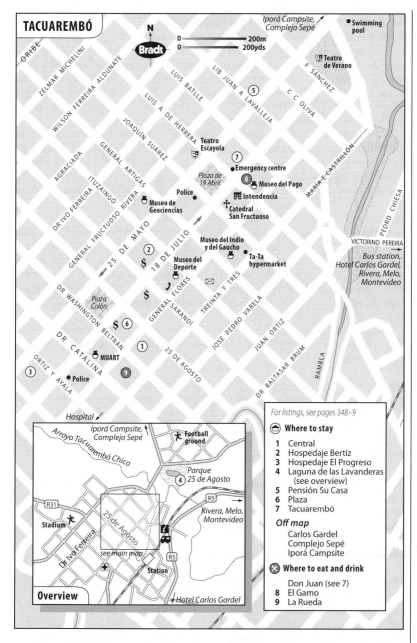

For listings, see pages 348–9

Where to stay

1 Central
2 Hospedaje Bertiz
3 Hospedaje El Progreso
4 Laguna de las Lavanderas
   (see overview)
5 Pensión Su Casa
6 Plaza
7 Tacuarembó

Off map
   Carlos Gardel
   Complejo Sepé
   Iporá Campsite

Where to eat and drink

   Don Juan (see 7)
8 El Gamo
9 La Rueda

A military post was established here in 1830 and the next year it was declared a town by General Rivera (as Villa de San Fructuoso, after his patron saint). In 1837 it became a departmental capital when Salto and Tacuarembó were split off from Paysandú. The area around the Arroyo Arerungá, west of Tacuarembó (now in Paysandú department), is known as the home of the last Charrúas, and the people of Tacuarembó have more Charrúa genes than other Uruguayans.

Getting there and away, and getting around

By bus Ruta 5 bypasses the city to the east. From the north, at km393 the first turning to the city leads past the zoo and Parque Botánico, and after km390 (one hour 30 minutes from Rivera) buses turn right (west), a couple of hundred metres west to the bus terminal. From the south, traffic turns left at km388 on to Avenida Pablo Ríos to the city centre, or continues to the turning to the bus terminal (*Avda Victorino Pereira 351*). There's Wi-Fi, a (well-hidden) left luggage store and a cafeteria at the terminal, as well as other snacky bars opposite.

Turil has five Montevideo–Rivera buses per day calling at Tacuarembó (4¾hrs) and Paso de los Toros, as well as a couple to Artigas; Nuñez has four buses daily from Montevideo to Rivera via Tacuarembó, and Sabelin/Chadre have four buses a day from Montevideo to Tacuarembó, continuing to Artigas or Rivera. Posada has five buses a day (three on Sundays) to Rivera, two a day (*1 on Sun, at 07.00*) to San Gregorio de Polanco, and three a day to Melo (*2 on Sun*). Abus also runs three services a day to San Gregorio, and Victor-Rony and Rocas have one each.

Copay-Alonso has three buses a day (*1 on Sun*) to Rivera, two (*1 on Sun*) starting from Paysandú; they also send two (*1 on Sun*) north as far as Tambores. On Tuesdays and Fridays an ETA bus from Fray Bentos to Rivera passes through at 06.00, returning to Fray Bentos at 15.00. From Salto Agencia Central has a service to Tacuarembó on Mondays and Fridays, as does Toriani on Mondays, Wednesdays and Fridays. For Buenos Aires, there are departures with Agencia Central or Nossar at 21.00 Sunday–Friday.

The parallel streets 25 de Mayo and 18 de Julio run southwest–northeast, with three plazas between them. To the northwest, about six blocks west of the terminal, is Plaza 19 de Abril.

By car Cars can be rented from Avis (*25 de Agosto 224;* \ *4632 0257;* m *098 170022;* ☉ *09.00–19.00 Mon–Fri, 09.00–13.00 Sat*), Dollar (*18 de Julio 351;* \ *4632 2203*), Multicar (*Flores 333;* \ *4632 8462;* m *095 559025; www.redmulticar.com;* ☉ *09.00–13.00, 15.00–19.00 Mon–Fri, 09.00–13.00 Sat*) and Turil (*25 de Mayo 256 & Sarandí;* \ *4632 5350*). Attendants charge for parking from 12.00 to 18.00 Monday to Friday.

Tourist information The very helpful departmental tourism office is at the west end of the bus terminal (\ *4632 7144;* e *turismo@imtacuarembo.gub.uy, turismotacuarembo@gmail.com;* ☉ *07.00–19.00 Mon–Fri, 07.00–12.00 Sat*). There's also a bus information desk (☉ *08.00–14.00 daily*).

 Where to stay All listings are included on the map, page 347.

🏠 **Hotel Tacuarembó** 18 de Julio 133, just east of the cathedral; \ 4632 2104; e htacuarembo@ yahoo.com; www.tacuarembohotel.com.uy. The best in town, this is a professionally run 3-star with 62 AC rooms, Wi-Fi & 1 PC, parking & swimming pool. **$$$**

🏠 **Hotel Carlos Gardel** Ruta 5 km387.5, on the southern outskirts; \ 4633 0301/6; e infohcg@ netgate.com.uy; www.hotelcarlosgardel.com.uy. This is aimed at tourists in buses & cars, with a live tango show & parrilla, as well as swimming pool,

disabled room & business centre. Bedrooms have internet access. **$$$–$**

🏠 **Hotel Central** Flores 300 & Beltrán; \ 4632 2841. Friendly, affordable & indeed central (rooms facing the street can be noisy at weekends), this has spacious rooms with private bathroom & cable TV, & decent breakfast but no other meals. **$$**

🏠 **Hotel Plaza** 25 de Agosto 247, just off Plaza Colón; \ 4632 7988; e hotelplaza@hotmail.com. A nice friendly place with AC rooms with cable TV, & internet access in the foyer. **$$**

Hospedaje Bertiz Ituzaingó 211 between 25 de Mayo & 18 de Julio; ☎4632 3324. A nice period house with cheap but decent rooms & a woodburning stove. **$**

Hospedaje El Progreso 25 de Mayo 358; ☎4632 0789. This friendly, simple place has rooms with private or shared bathroom, & a kitchen & nice patio. **$**

Pensión Su Casa 25 de Mayo & Lavalleja; ☎4633 1349. The closest accommodation to the bus terminal, simple rooms in a nice period house with kitchen & patio. **$**

Complejo Sepé Avda Gutiérrez, 7km north of the centre (no bus); ☎4632 9144; e sepeiporatbo@ hotmail.com; www.complejosepe.com. A new complex with 8 AC cabañas for 4 people each, with Wi-Fi. **$**

Iporá campsite Avda Gutiérrez Ruiz, 7km north of the centre (no bus); ☎4632 2612; ⏲ early Dec–Easter. Has a parador restaurant & an open-air swimming pool. **$**

Laguna de las Lavanderos Camping is also possible here, northeast of the centre, where there's an attractive lake, BBQs, a basic wash-block (& a better one at the northeast end that may be locked up). **$**

✗ Where to eat The Hotel Tacuarembó's restaurant **Don Juan** (**$$$**) is the best in town. Otherwise **La Rueda** (*Washington Beltrán 251 near Flores;* ☎*4632 2453;* **$$**) serves good traditional food (grilled meats, pasta, salads and snacks) at reasonable prices. **El Gamo** is a nice café-bar on the corner of the plaza (*18 de Julio & Herrera;* ☎*4632 3844;* **$**), with a US$5 lunch menu, plus snacks, salads, pasta and pizza. All listings are included on the map, page 347.

Events The **Fiesta de la Patria Gaucha** (Festival of the Gaucho Country), held at the Laguna de las Lavanderas in the first or second week of March, is one of the biggest of its kind in South America, with thousands of country folk coming from far and wide (including Brazil and Argentina), all in gaucho garb and many with their horses. There are parades, riding competitions, lasso, boladera and other contests, and huge parrillas producing a steady supply of grilled meats. In the evenings there's music and dancing, and traditional gaucho poetry recitals.

Since 2008 the **Fiesta Gardeliana** has been held in December at the Laguna de las Lavanderas, with lots of tango music as well as a Model T Ford rally.

Shopping There's a Ta-Ta hypermarket at Suárez 259 & Treinta y Tres (⏲ *08.00–23.00 daily*).

Other practicalities

Banks There are banks with ATMs at the junction of Sarandí and 18 de Julio, on the south side of Plaza Colón, and at the Ta-Ta supermarket. Money can be changed at Mas Cambio (*18 de Julio 252;* ⏲ *08.30–12.00, 13.00–18.00 Mon–Fri, 08.30–12.00 Sat*).

Communications The post office is at Izutaingó 262 (⏲ *09.00–17.00 Mon–Fri, 08.00–12.00 Sat*); Antel's call centre is at Sarandí 242 (⏲ *09.00–17.00 Mon–Fri, 09.00–13.00 Sat*). The school at 18 de Julio and Artigas has a decent Wi-Fi signal, and the El Cyber Azul internet centre is next to the theatre on the plaza (*25 de Mayo 169;* ⏲ *10.00–midnight Mon–Sat, 12.00–midnight Sun*).

Emergency services There is an emergency centre on Plaza 19 de Abril (*18 de Julio & Herrera;* ☎*4632 4000*), and the police station is directly across the plaza at Suárez 221 (☎ *4632 4136*); there's also a combined police and fire station at 18 de Julio 338 and Catalina. The hospital is southwest of the centre at Treinta y Tres 444 (☎ *4632 2955*).

What to see and do On the southeastern side of Plaza 19 de Abril, next to the small **Cathedral of San Fructuoso** (1899–1917), the nicely restored **Intendencia** (1911) has an unusual neoromanesque façade and a blue and yellow tiled steeple, but a plain interior. The tower was added in 1930 and in 1960 it became a cathedral. Four blocks southwest is Plaza Colón, and six blocks further (out of the city centre) is Plaza Rivera. Another five blocks southwest down 18 de Julio is the Cementerio Municipal, where the ornate Escayola and Escobar family tombs have been declared historic monuments.

The **Teatro Escayola** (*25 de Mayo 163*) was built in 1888–91 by Carlos Gardel's supposed father (see box below), with Carrara marble from Italy and a French grand piano; Gardel himself performed there in 1930. It closed in 1956, but in 2008 a campaign was started for the city to take over the building, now very run-down, and restore it to its former glory; it is now used for occasional concerts. There is a summer theatre at the northeastern end of 18 de Julio, at the site where Artigas camped with his troops in 1813. Beyond this, 25 de Mayo crosses a bridge to the Parque de las Lavanderas (formally Parque 25 de Agosto), around the attractive Laguna de las Lavanderas (Laundrywomen's Lagoon), with waterbirds on floating islands, and teenagers hanging out drinking maté. It's about 6km further along Avenida Gutiérrez Ruiz to the Balneario Iporá ('clear water' in Guaraní), a leafy resort with an artificial lake, Olympic-sized swimming pool and campsite.

One notable feature of Tacuarembó is its *centros de barrios* on the outskirts of town, architecturally striking focal points for each quarter, which include health or sport centres.

GARDEL, THE URUGUAYAN TANGO LEGEND?

When Carlos Gardel was asked about his place of birth, he used to reply, 'I was born in Buenos Aires, Argentina, at the age of two and a half years'.

One thing that is certain is that Gardel was not born in Argentina, despite being as solidly Argentine an icon as Maradona or Evita. Most written sources, including a birth certificate, indicate that he was born in Toulouse, France, in either 1887 or 1890, the illegitimate child of Berthe Gardès, who took him to Venezuela and then to Argentina. However, some Uruguayans, especially in Tacuarembó department, claim forcefully that he was born there, the illegitimate son of Tacuarembó landowner Carlos Escayola with his wife's 13-year-old sister (who may in fact have been his daughter by his wife's mother!), and that he sent the child away with Berthe Gardès. In Argentina she worked as a washerwoman and brought Carlos up in the Abasto district of Buenos Aires. Gardel was certainly a regular visitor to Uruguay, including a trip to Tacuarembó in 1915 to convalesce after being shot in a bar, supposedly by Che Guevara's father.

Gardel may have encouraged the confusion about his origins in order to cover up the shadier aspects of his youth (there's speculation that he served time in prison), to avoid conscription into the French army during World War I, or to spare his mother the shame of an illegitimate child. In any case there is now a commission in Tacuarembó dedicated to proving Gardel's Uruguayan origins (in 2004 an Argentine court refused it permission to take a DNA sample from Gardel's remains). The museum in Valle Edén (see opposite) displays a copy of another birth certificate indicating that he was born in Tacuarembó, as do his application for Argentina citizenship in 1923 and the passport found on his body after his death in a plane crash in Colombia in 1935.

There are various museums, none of great interest. The **Museo del Indio y del Gaucho** (*Museum of the Indian & the Gaucho; Artigas & Flores;* ⊕ *10.00–17.00 Tue–Sat; free*) has large but dull collections of bolas, rompacebezas, ceramics, bows and lots of arrowheads, silver stirrups, gourds, bridles, carved cow-horns, lassos, pistols and swords, and one fine set of harness. The **Museo de Geociencias** (*Geoscience Museum; Artigas 191;* ⊕ *10.00–17.00 Tue–Fri, 13.00–17.00 Sat, closed Christmas to New Year; free*) displays amethyst and other local rocks and minerals, as well as a dateline of the earth's geological history.

There's also the **Museo de Artes Plásticas de Tacuarembó (MUART)** (*18 de Julio 302 & Washington Beltrán*), the **Museo del Deporte** (*Sport Museum; Ituzaingó 241*) and the **Museo Memoria del Pago** (*Herrera 250 & Flores*), a historic museum of town and country, with old carts, tools and ceramic vessels, etc, on display – all are open 10.00–17.00 Tuesday–Saturday.

VALLE EDÉN Leaving Tacuarembó to the southwest, Ruta 26 runs through fairly empty hill country with lots of native *monte*. Just beyond km208 (at the west end of the Arroyo Tambores bridge, 23km from Tacuarembó), an asphalt road lined with bamboo turns southwest to Valle Edén (pronounced 'bashay ayden'). Named Valley of Eden by the British engineers who built a railway here in 1890, this has similar flora to Laureles and Lunarejo to the north (see page 341), with subtropical characteristics, but is less well preserved.

Nowadays the area is best known as the supposed birthplace of tango legend Carlos Gardel, although this is naturally disputed by his legions of Argentine fans (see box opposite). There's a good museum totally dedicated to proving that Gardel was born here.

Getting there and away From Tacuarembó's **bus** terminal, Calebus runs to Tambores, just beyond Valle Edén, three times daily; the 11.45 bus brings you right to the museum, returning at about 13.15, while the 06.30 and 18.00 buses leave you at the turning at km208, from where it's 500m to Camping El Mago (see below). A pedestrian exit leads to the road by a suspension footbridge (built in 1928), from where it's 500m to a police station. Here the road swings right and brings you in 300m to the museum, opposite the Posada Valle Edén at the end of the asphalt.

🏠 **Where to stay**

🏠 **Posada Valle Edén** Opposite the museum; ☏4630 2345; m 099 800100; e posadavalleeden@gmail.com; www.posadavalleeden.com.uy; ⊕ all year. This makes a pleasant stopover, in a house built of red stones in the late 19th century. There's a double & a triple room, 2 cabañas with kitchen & BBQ (*US$52 for 4*), & 17 dorm beds (*US$13*). Breakfast is extra, but all meals are available, as well as preserves & liqueurs (from local fruits), mountain bikes, horses & a nature guide. **$$**

⚑ **Camping El Mago** (aka Camping Valle Edén) ☏4632 2275; ⊕ early Dec–Easter. There's an open field with wash-blocks, then sites in native wood (with lots of epiphytic plants, as well as picnic tables & parrillas) along the Arroyo Jabonería (named after the *arbol del jabón* or soap tree, *Quillaja brasiliensis*). There are small fish in the river & various birds including *chajá* (southern screamer, *Chauna torquata*), whose squawk you'll easily identify. **$**

What to see and do

Museo Carlos Gardel (⊕ *09.30–18.30 daily; US$2*) The museum is in a former *pulpería* (rural shop/bar) once frequented by Gardel, in a spacious, nicely laid-out and maintained garden. It's delightfully cool inside, with a soundtrack of the man himself singing, interesting period photos and documents dedicated to proving his local origins. There's also a hall with a couple of horse carriages on display. Immediately below the museum is the former railway station (the line is still used by freight trains), where a couple of ancient and very decayed railcars are slowly being refurbished.

Gardel was, according to many Uruguayans, born 12km further up the valley at the Estancia Santa Blanca; an unpaved road continues through native woodland (with plenty of birds) between low hills.

Estancia Panagea (m *099 836149*; e *panagea@adinet.com.uy*; **$$$**) An hour north of Tacuarembó, Estancia Panagea is a working ranch offering hostel-style accommodation and a unique experience of rural Uruguayan life, very different from that of the traditional tourist estancias. Run by an Uruguayan veterinarian and his Swiss wife, globetrotters who settled here to farm as naturally and organically as possible, there's no television, phone or internet access, limited hot water and no mains electricity, although a generator is cranked up most evenings to show one of their 1,900 films. Juan and Susanne run the farm with just one gaucho and his wife, the cook, saddling up at 07.00 to bring cattle and sheep in for pregnancy testing, vaccination, tick removal or a myriad other reasons, returning for lunch and a siesta before riding out for another few hours. Guests are free to accompany them (you'll be kitted out in authentic gaucho garb) or to relax, play badminton or volleyball, walk, swim (in a creek 1km away), fish or birdwatch.

Accommodation is in the farmhouse (four double and two triple rooms), with simple and plentiful homestyle gaucho food, often barbecued meat or casseroles (vegetarians are well fed too, with advance notice); there's also plenty of wine (not included). For US$60 a night per person you get three meals plus snacks, fruit, tea and coffee, and plenty of horse riding (with ad hoc lessons as required). They'll meet you at the Tacuarembó bus terminal on Tuesday, Thursday or Saturday at 11.00 or 18.00, with as much notice as possible, and return you there. Spring and autumn are the best times to come here.

PASO DE LOS TOROS Continuing south from Tacuarembó, Ruta 5 follows a remarkably un-straight line across flat grassland, where you'll see cows, sheep, ñandues (see page 10) and cattle egrets. At km252, 138km (1½ hours by bus) from Tacuarembó (and exactly midway between Montevideo and Rivera), the town of Paso de los Toros (Pass of the Bulls) stands at the north side of the bridge below the Rincón del Bonete dam. Founded in 1903 and rebuilt by the army after the construction of the dam and bridge, it's known as the birthplace of the writer Mario Benedetti (1920–2009), and of the Paso de los Toros brand of soft drinks (originally a tonic water concocted by Rómulo Mangini for British railway workers, later expanded to include soft drinks, and now produced by PepsiCo). The plant (*Mangini 329, on the west side of the railway just south of 18 de Julio*) now houses the Reserva Acuario, opened in 2008 with 37 species of local freshwater fish in tanks.

Getting there and away
By bus Most buses from Rivera and Artigas to Montevideo bypass the town and will drop you off at the Esso station at the north end of the bridge. Otherwise buses stop at offices just southwest of Plaza Artigas: Nuñez and Cynsa (*Sarandí & Barreto*), opposite the former train station, Turil (*Hotel Sayonara*) at the same junction, CUT (*Sarandí, southwest of Bvar Artigas*) and CTTM (*18 de Julio 729*).

Orientation Ruta 5 bypasses the town to the east, meeting Bulevar Artigas at a statue of a bull at the north end of the bridge. Artigas leads a couple of hundred metres northwest to Plaza Artigas, with a neogothic church on its north side. From here 18 de Julio leads west beyond the railway. The town centre (with shops and restaurants but no hotels) consists of the two blocks beyond the level crossing.

Where to stay and eat
The **Hotel Sayonara** (*Sarandí 302 & Barreto;* \ *4664 2535;* m *099 864194;* **$$**) is a very decent one-star hotel with a restaurant/bar; across the way at Sarandí 301 are the **Cabañas Gallos Blancos** (\ *4660 4760;* **$$**) and **La Posta del Hum** (m *098 632389;* **$$**). At the dam, 22km upstream, is the more upmarket **Hotel Rincón del Bonete** (\ *4664 2087, 4660 4875;* **$$$**). By the northern approach to the bridge, the **Camping El Sauce** (*Herrera & Artigas;* \ *4664 3503;* ⊕ *Dec–Easter;* **$**) is pretty good, with eight cabins, a parador (to the east of the bridge) and a small beach.

The restaurant **Lo de Claudia** (*Club Social, Artigas 598;* **$$$**) is pretty formal, serving parrilla and pizza, as does the **El Edén** (*18 de Julio & Mangini;* **$$$**). The **Pinguï** (*18 de Julio & Puyol;* **$$**) is a pizzeria-heladería, so you can follow your pizza with their own ice cream; it also has new rooms upstairs.

Other practicalities
Antel has a call centre (*Mangini 357 just south of 18 de Julio;* ⊕ *09.00–21.00 daily*), and there's free public Wi-Fi on Plaza Artigas.

What to see and do
South across the Río Negro is the village of Centenario, with a picnic area by the river to the east; a hot springs resort is planned here. Ruta 5 continues south through rolling cattle country, passing a military air base and crossing a high-ish bridge at km186 to enter Durazno, 66km from Paso de los Toros (50 minutes by bus).

Las Cañadas
One of the most authentic working estancias that you can stay on is Las Cañadas (**$$$$$**), 36km north of Paso de los Toros. Owned by descendants of the families that founded Fray Bentos and first shipped frozen beef to Europe, and then largely invented rural tourism in Uruguay, the historic *casco* (main house) has been lovingly preserved, with family portraits (including one president), leather chairs, wooden furniture and welcoming fires. It's a sprawling, low house with verandas on three sides, looking over rose and herb beds and across miles of rolling ranchland. There is a small swimming pool, and a wood-fired oven and grill where gauchos tend an asado fit to feed an army. Alternatively there's an open-plan room with low cupboards dividing a kitchen from the dining area, where huge meals of hearty traditional fare are served up four times a day, including *merienda* or high tea.

As a working farm (mainly raising Hereford cattle), the main activity is horse riding, either going with the gauchos to bring in cattle or just riding the placid criollo horses to the village or a swimming hole, with armadillos, hares, skunks and ñandues to see along the way.

There's no air conditioning or television, but US$335 for two nights is great value for unlimited riding and the experience of living the traditional rural life. Book through Cecilia Regules Viajes (see page 48; *www.ceciliaregulesviajes.com*).

SAN GREGORIO DE POLANCO
At the eastern end of the Rincón del Bonete lake, where Ruta 43 crosses the Río Negro by a ferry, San Gregorio de Polanco is a peaceful little town known for fishing and for its 'living museum' of streetside murals, mainly north of the central Plaza Constitución. It has 15km of sandy freshwater beaches, with lakeside camping and plenty of other cheap accommodation. There's also a free Festival of Gospel Music on the first weekend of January, and the Los Años

Dorados (Golden Years) festival the last weekend of November, when groups of pensioners from all over Uruguay put on shows, whist drives (*truco*) and other entertainments.

Getting there and away There's a surprisingly good **bus** service, with CTTM, Bruno Hermanos and Turismar all running two or three times a day to Montevideo via Paso de los Toros and Durazno, Posada going twice a day to Tacuarembó and Rivera, and Abus (*3 times a day*) and a couple of other services as far as Tacuarembó. By **car**, take Ruta 5 to km307, then Ruta 43 east for 59km.

Where to stay and eat

🏠 **Apart-Hotel La Casona** Varela 162; ✆4369 4038. **$$**

🏠 **Los Médanos** Avda Mollo; ✆4369 4013/4074. The only real hotel is by the river, which has a decent restaurant, & horses for rent. **$$**

🏠 **Hostal Mustafa** Dr Yamandu Gamba 88; ✆4369 4049. A block from the plaza, the hostel is run by an Iranian exile & his Uruguayan wife; it has 6 attractive rooms, a garden & swimming pool, & service is great except that breakfast costs extra. **$**

🏠 **Hostel San Gregorio** Artigas 177; ✆4369 4292; e hostelsangregorio@gmail.com; www. hostelsangregorio.com. A nice old building with a

central patio – there's 1 shared mixed-sex dorm for 8, & 10 doubles with & without private bathrooms, plus kitchen, Wi-Fi & bike rental. **$**

🏠 **Bungalows Artimir** ✆4369 4228; m 099 830649; www.artimir.com.uy. **$**

🏠 **Bungalows Lugarcito** Leandro Gómez; ✆4369 4710; m 099 700443; www.lugarcito. com. **$**

🏠 **Cabañas de Carlín** Puertos de Palos; ✆4369 4006; www.cabaniascarlin.com. **$**

⛺ **Campsite** At the western end of the main street, Av Mollo. **$**

DURAZNO DEPARTMENT

DURAZNO San Pedro de Durazno was founded at a ford across the Yí River in 1821 by the then Colonel Fructuoso Rivera, and it became his base, giving him fervent support. Many of its residents came from San Francisco de Borja del Yí (or San Borja del Yí), 10km east of Durazno on the border between the present departments of Durazno and Florida, the last mission settlement of the Guaraní people. In 1833 the 8,000 so-called Guaraní-misioneros, who had accompanied Rivera from the former Jesuit missions in what is now Brazil, were settled here. The settlement was disbanded in 1843 by the government of Manuel Oribe, and in 1862 the remaining inhabitants (the last pure indigenous Uruguayans) were forcibly moved to the towns of Florida and Durazno, where they became assimilated into the existing population. Many women and children became slaves on estancias, where their genes survive to this day.

Much livelier than the towns to the north of the Río Negro, Durazno now has over 33,000 inhabitants and is known for various festivals, notably Pilsen Rock (see page 29) and a big folklore festival in February.

Getting there and away, and getting around

By bus Buses arrive at the terminal, southwest of the centre near Ruta 14 on the Avenida de Circunvalación (ring road). Tourist information is available here, and also at the zoo (by Ruta 5, arriving from the south); bus times are available at http://durazno1.tripod.com/omnibussalen.html. The local bus company is Nossar, operating both city buses and at least eight services a day from Montevideo to Durazno (*around 2½hrs*), four continuing to Paso de los Toros, and six from Carmen and Sarandí del Yí. There's a surprisingly poor service to nearby Trinidad,

For listings, see pages 356–7

Where to stay

1 Alojamiento Teresita
2 Central
3 Hospedaje del Centro
4 Hotel del Country
5 Hotel Durazno

Off map

33 Orientales Campsite
Chacra El Recreo
Hotel Santa Cristina

Where to eat and drink

6 Don Armando
7 La Farola
8 Pastelería La Catalana

Off map

La Perdiz (see Hotel Santa Cristina)

Campamento Artiguista
33 Orientales Campsite
JULIÁN LAGUNA
18 DE MAYO
Plaza Artigas
ANSINA
APARICIO SARAVIA
JUAN BAUTISTA DE LEÓN
AVDA TELEMACO B MORALES
GENERAL LEANDRO GÓMEZ
MAESTRA PETRONA TUBORAS
BRIG GENERAL JUAN A LAVALLEJA
LARRAÑAGA
DR BALTASAR BRUM
La Familia supermarket
5
Plaza Sarandí
Supermercado 18
GENERAL JOSÉ ARTIGAS
8
7
19 DE ABRIL
DR LUIS A DE HERRERA
JOSE PEDRO VARELA
JOSE BATLLE Y ORDÓÑEZ
DR EMILIO PENZA
DE SAN MARTIN
18 DE JULIO
3 Ta-Ta supermarket
Police
BRIG GENERAL FRUCTUOSO RIVERA
Tacuarembó, Rivera
R5
PEDRO LARRIQUE
BATALLA DE CERRITO
MISIONES DE SARANDI
BATALLA DE PIEDRAS
DR JUAN ZORRILLA DE SAN MARTIN
Museo de Arte
Casa de Rivera
Plaza Independencia
JULIO CESAR ZAGNOLI
BRIG GENERAL MANUEL ORIBE
2
San Pedro
ARROSPIDE
4
N
Bradt
0 200m
0 200yds
EUSEBIO PIRIZ
WILSON FERREIRA ALDUNATE
4 DE OCTUBRE DE 1828
GALARZA
MUÑOZ
1
25 DE AGOSTO
RUBINO
MORQUIO
NOGUEIRA
MARTIN SALABERRY
6
R14, Trinidad
JOSÉ GÓMEZ
DR ALCIDES BURGUES
Museo de las Charrúas (under construction)
LATORRE
GALLINAL
R5
WASHINGTON
JOSE DE SAN MARTIN
JOAQUIN SUAREZ
Rail station (closed)
Zoológico Municipal, Parque de la Hispanidad, Chacra El Recreo, Hotel Santa Cristina, Montevideo

DURAZNO

with just five Nossar buses a day (*4 at weekends*), three continung to Colonia. There are also services on Friday (*17.00*) and Sunday (*19.00*) to Cerro Chato, for connections towards Melo. Nossar has a service to Buenos Aires overnight on Mondays, Wednesdays and Fridays.

Turismar also runs ten daily buses from Montevideo, and five from Punta del Este and Piriápolis; Nuñez, Turil and Agencia Central (Sabelin/Chadre) each operate three or four daily buses from Montevideo to Florida and Durazno, continuing to Paso de los Toros, Tacuarembó and Artigas or Rivera. In addition two of Agencia Central's Montevideo–Salto services run via Durazno each day. Bruno Hermanos and CTTM offer slightly less luxurious services via Durazno to Sarandí Grande, Florida, Carmen, Paso de los Toros and San Gregorio de Polanco. From Fray Bentos and Mercedes CUT/ETA run on Tuesdays to Fridays to Rivera via Trinidad, Durazno and Tacuarembó, returning the same afternoon.

There's a big fountain outside the terminal and a modern tourist office, and just to the south three domes like the indigenous people's tents which will eventually house the small Museum of the Charrúas (see page 358). From the terminal, Oribe leads northeast for nine blocks to Plaza Independencia. A block further on, you can turn left on to 18 de Julio, the main shopping street, known as the Microcentro. This leads in three blocks to Plaza Sarandí, from where 19 de Abril leads northeast towards the river and bridges.

By car Cars can be rented from Multicar (*Wilson Ferreira Aldunate 481;* \ *4362 4502;* m *095 885764; www.redmulticar.com;* ⏱ *08.00–12.00, 14.00–18.00 Mon–Fri, 08.00–12.00 Sat*).

Tourist information The main tourist office is on the Paseo de los Artesanos on Plaza Sarandí (*Artigas & Herrera;* \ *4362 0176;* e *turindur@gmail.com; www. durazno.gub.uy;* ⏱ *09.00–20.00 Mon–Fri*); there's also one opposite the terminal (\ *4362 1601;* ⏱ *13.15–18.00 Mon–Fri*).

 Where to stay All listings are included on the map, page 355.

🏠 **Hotel Santa Cristina** Ruta 5 km178; \4362 2525; www.hotelsantacristina.com.uy. A couple of kilometres south of the Parque de la Hispanidad, this is a fairly soulless 4-star, but it does have fine gardens & an excellent restaurant. **$$$$**

🏠 **Hotel Central** Oribe 699; \4362 0305; e hotelcentral@adinet.com.uy; www.hotelcentral. com.uy. A very nice modern place with wall hangings & arty photos in reception, as well as free Wi-Fi & 2 PCs, & AC rooms with cable TV. **$$$**

🏠 **Hotel del Country** Batalla de las Piedras 284; \4362 2724; www.hoteldelcountry.com. Just southwest of the centre, this has spacious gardens with a swimming pool with slides & hydro-gym, as well as tennis, soccer & volleyball facilities; there's a good restaurant & 24hr snack-bar. **$$$**

🏠 **Hotel Durazno** Herrera 937 & Brum; \4362 2040/2371; e hoteldur@adinet.com.uy; www.hoteldurazno.com.uy. Rooms at this decent

& affordable place range from económico (no window but fan & good bathroom) to standard, superior & suites; there's cable TV & Wi-Fi plus 2 PCs in the breakfast room (which offers a decent if limited buffet). **$$**

🏠 **Alojamiento Teresita** Rubino 724 & Ferreira Aldunate; \4362 2186. Probably the cheapest option in town. **$**

🏠 **Chacra El Recreo** Ruta 5 km180.5; \4362 8888/4444; m 098 723529; e elrecreo@adinet. com.uy; www.chacraelrecreo.com. Just south of the Parque de la Hispanidad, 2km from town, this is a fairly tranquil spot with bungalows with terrace & kitchen. **$**

🏠 **Hospedaje del Centro** Zorrilla 808 & Rivera; \4362 0672. Quite a large & decent economy option, with kitchen. **$**

Λ **33 Orientales Campsite** Playa El Sauzal, by the river at the eastern end of Penza; \4362 4500;

e imdservices@adinet.com.uy; ☾ Dec–Apr. A large, shady campsite, hectic on summer weekends but much quieter at night. There's a *parador* *municipal* (restaurant), set on Corbusieresque columns, & decent wash-blocks. **$**

✖ Where to eat Perhaps the nicest restaurant in the centre is **La Farola** (*18 de Julio 412, on the southwest side of Plaza Sarandí*; **$$**), with a good range of vegetarian and meat pizzas, milanesas and other standard dishes; there's pavement seating and Wi-Fi. At the Hotel Santa Cristina, 3km south, **La Perdiz** (☏ *4362 1745*; **$$$$**) is an outpost of the fine Basque restaurant in Montevideo (see page 101). North across the road from the bus terminal, **Don Armando** (**$$**) is a friendly parrilla. **Pastelería La Catalana** (*Artigas 533*; **$**) sells classy pastries and cakes. All these are included on the map, page 355.

Shopping Supermarkets include Ta-Ta (*18 de Julio 580 between Oribe & Zorrilla de San Martín*; ☾ *08.00–21.00 Mon–Sat, 08.30–21.00 Sun*), La Familia (*Brum & 19 de Abril*; ☾ *08.00–12.45, 14.30–21.30 Mon–Fri, 08.00–15.00, 15.30–21.30 Sat, 08.30–13.00 Sun*) and Supermercado 18 (*southeast side of Plaza Sarandí*; ☾ *08.00–12.30, 14.30–22.00 Mon–Fri, 08.00–12.30, 15.00–22.00 Sat, 08.30–12.30 Sun*).

For crafts, try the Paseo de los Artesanos, by the tourist office on the north side of Plaza Sarandí (☾ *09.00–12.30 Mon–Sat, 19.30–22.30 Wed–Fri, 20.30–midnight Sat–Sun*); Talabartería Baldenegro (*Oribe 602 & Zagnoli*) and El Gauchito (*19 de Abril 948 & Brum*) sell leather saddles, harnesses and handbags.

Other practicalities

Banks There are ATMs at Oribe & 18 de Julio, Artigas & Herrera, and on 18 de Julio near Herrera on Plaza Sarandí.

Communications The post office is at Rivera 428, northwest of Herrera (☾ *09.00–17.00 Mon–Fri, 09.00–12.00 Sat*). Antel has a telecentro at Rivera 564 & Zorrilla (☾ *09.00–19.00 daily*). There's public Wi-Fi on Plaza Independencia, and an internet place on Rivera between Piria and Ferreira Aldunate.

What to see and do In the centre of Plaza Independencia is the Monumento a Cristóbal Colón, raised in 1892 to mark the 400th anniversary of Columbus's 'discovery' of the Americas. Atop the column is a stone globe containing a time capsule, opened in 1992 and again, if all goes to plan, in 2092. On the southwestern side of the plaza, the **Church of San Pedro** was built soon after the town was founded in 1821, and rebuilt in 1890–98, with a new façade added in the 1920s. Burnt out in 1967, it was rebuilt with a striking modern red-brick interior by Eladio Dieste, with a dramatic light-well at the east end. Inaugurated in 1971, it was declared a national monument in 1997. In 1975 Dieste also built a gymnasium six blocks northeast at the end of Zorrilla de San Martín.

On the northwestern side of the plaza at Oribe 775, the **Casa de Rivera** was built in 1835 for Rivera (whose bust is across the road on the plaza) as the Comandancia General de Campaña, and he took the oath of office for his second presidency here in 1838. It became the effective seat of government until 1842 but had been split up by the end of the 19th century. The **Museo Casa de Rivera** (☾ *09.00–16.00 Tue–Fri, 16.00–22.00 Sat–Sun; free*), opened in 1992, is very good, with lots of old photos and printed matter, though all in Spanish. Room 1 has a well laid-out display of indigenous stone tools, bolas and arrowheads (some at least 11,000 years old), as well as a dinosaur egg and a lestodon bone. Antonio Taddei, born in Durazno, was the founder of Uruguayan archaeology, so the items displayed are not just from Durazno but include, for instance, ceramics from Isla Vizcaino. Room 2 is about Rivera (whose father owned land between the Río Yí and the Río Negro), with a few swords and bayonets, and (depending on the rotation of the displays) paintings by the English artist Francis Vincent. You can see Rivera's office at the eastern end of the building, and go down into the big, echoing *aljibe* (cistern) at the bottom of which various items, now displayed in the museum, were found in 2004–05.

The Casa de los Reyles, just northeast of the Casa de Rivera at Uribe 805, was bought by General Carlos Genaro Reyles, a pioneer of Uruguayan cattle ranching, who gave the building its present form. It has been a school since 1913. On the north side of Plaza Independencia, Rivera 631 was home to Lavalleja in 1826–28, then to Rivera's 'friend' Ramona Fernández; it became the Jefatura de Policia at the end of the 19th century, with a new façade and an extra storey added in 1909–10, and is in very good condition.

Two blocks northwest of the Casa Rivera, the **Museo de Arte** (*Penza 719; west of Batlle y Ordóñez;* ⊕ *08.00–14.00 Mon–Fri; free*) is in the former home and office of Dr Emilio Penza Spinelli (a local doctor), a single-storey white building with a rooftop balustrade and a belvedere tower, built in the 1870s. It housed a school from 1921 to 1944 and a teacher-training college to 1981, and was restored in 2000 to house the town's art gallery. Two rooms display the rough-cut wooden sculptures of Claudio Silveira Silva (1935–2007), who moved to Durazno in the early 1960s and continued to visit after moving to Barcelona in 1978; there's also a room for temporary shows. There are some strikingly modern houses in Durazno, for instance three blocks further along Penza at Rubino. A little further, on the far side of the terminal, the new Museo de los Charrúas will preserve the memory of the area's indigenous inhabitants.

Following Ruta 5 (or the parallel cycle track) south for a couple of kilometres, you'll come to the **Zoológico Municipal** (*zoo; just south of km182;* ⊕ *daily; free*), modernised in 2008–09 with larger enclosures, a walk-in aviary and better visitor facilities. It houses 140 species of animals including lions, tigers, a dromedary, a hippo and a brown bear, as well as smaller mammals such as monkeys, deer, llamas, capybaras and anteaters, and birds such as toucans, storks, flamingos, ducks, egrets, southern screamers, black swans, ñandues and peacocks, mostly free to fly in and out. Well-tended gardens include palms and Brazilian araucaria trees. The most striking addition is a 120m-long wooden bridge south to the Parque de la Hispanidad, with a viewing platform overlooking lakes where many wild birds come to pass the night.

The **Parque de la Hispanidad** (*just south of km181;* ⊕ *07.00–21.00 daily; free*) is a spacious park planted with both Spanish and native trees and other flora. A large stage, built in 2000 in front of a lake, is used for festivals such as **Pilsen Rock**, the country's main rock festival (October) and the **Festival Nacional del Folclore** (early February), featuring guitar songs and vernacular poetry, as well as displays of gaucho skills (the Encuentro Gaucho). There's a new cafeteria building here, as well as the small Nueva Luna parrilla at the zoo gates.

On the other side of town, Calle Penza (known for a short stretch as Avenida Morales) leads northeast to the Playa El Sauzal, the town's main beach, where half the town seems to set up camp on hot summer days. The **Movida Tropical Uruguaya** (Uruguayan Tropical Festival) is held here on the first weekend of January, with around 20 bands playing vaguely Caribbean music, especially ska.

It is possible to continue on the beach and a path through the scrub to the left to the imposing long steel railway viaduct built by British engineers in 1879. Cotorras live in huge communal nests in the eucalyptus trees along Avenida Winston Churchill, which leads under the viaduct and on to the wooden Puente Sumersible (Submersible Bridge, also known as the Puente Viejo, although it was only built in 1903).

On the far side of the bridge is the **Campamento Artiguista**, a sandy area with trees and plaques reproducing the letters and proclamations that Artigas wrote here in January 1813, after crossing the river on his return from the Exodo del Pueblo Oriental (see page 15). There's plenty of native forest along the river, with good birdwatching, both here and in the other direction where Ruta 5 crosses the Yí; canoeing is also popular.

FLORES DEPARTMENT

TRINIDAD Trinidad, 192km from Montevideo on Ruta 3 to Paysandú (another 188km northwest), and 40km (25 minutes) west of Durazno on Ruta 14, is not quite as nice as Durazno but it's quieter and makes a pleasant stopover, and has a fine zoo. Founded in 1804, it's the capital of Flores, one of the few departments not named after its main city. It's built on a tight grid pattern around Plaza Constitución, but through traffic on Ruta 3 skirts around its southern and western flanks.

Getting there and away, and getting around

By bus There's no bus terminal. Bus offices include Nossar (*Ubeda, just east of the plaza;* 🖀 *4364 3786*), Agencia Central (*for Chadre & ETA; Berro 603 & Herrera, a block south of the plaza;* 🖀 *4364 2129/2460;* e *trinidad@agenciacentral.com.uy*), Nuñez (*Ramírez between Treinta y Tres & Berro;* 🖀 *4364 8930*) and Copay (*Puig & Ubeda;* 🖀 *4364 2653*). From Montevideo, 2½ hours away, Agencia Central has seven services a day calling at Trinidad (five Sabelin services to Salto (two via Guichón), and two Chadre services via Ruta 5), and Nossar has four; Copay has four services a day to Paysandú via Trinidad and Young, and Nuñez has two to Paysandú and Salto by the same route. El Norteño's overnight service from Montevideo to Salto and Bella Unión also calls at Trinidad.

Nossar operates five (*4 at w/ends*) from Durazno, three continuing to Colonia.

A CUT bus leaves Fray Bentos at midnight on Mondays and Thursdays, running via Mercedes, Trinidad, Durazno and Tacuarambó to Rivera; ETA has a similar service on Wednesday and Sunday nights. Nossar has an overnight service from Buenos Aires on Sundays, Tuesdays and Thursdays.

By car Cars can be rented from Gol Rentacar (*Batlle y Ordóñez & Avda Brasil;* m *099 874066*).

Tourist information Tourist information is half a block east of the plaza at Santísima Trinidad 520 (🖀 *4364 2210; www.imflores.gub.uy;* ⏱ *08.00–14.00 Mon–Fri*).

 Where to stay All listings are included on the map, page 360.

🏠 **Gran Hotel Flores** Herrera 612 & Fray Ubeda; 🖀 4364 2654/2458; www.granhotelflores. com.uy. A modern tower with free Wi-Fi & dataports in all rooms, AC, lift & outdoor swimming pool. **$$$–$$**
🏠 **Hotel Trinidad** Santísima Trinidad 663 & Ramírez; 🖀 4364 2307. In a less attractive house

but with nicer rooms, some AC; shared or private bathrooms. **$$**
🏠 **Hotel Potenza** Santísima Trinidad 643; 🖀 4364 2068. In a nice old house with cool patio & ancient leatherette armchairs, very clean & adequate. Rooms with shared or private bathrooms, AC or fan, & Wi-Fi. **$**

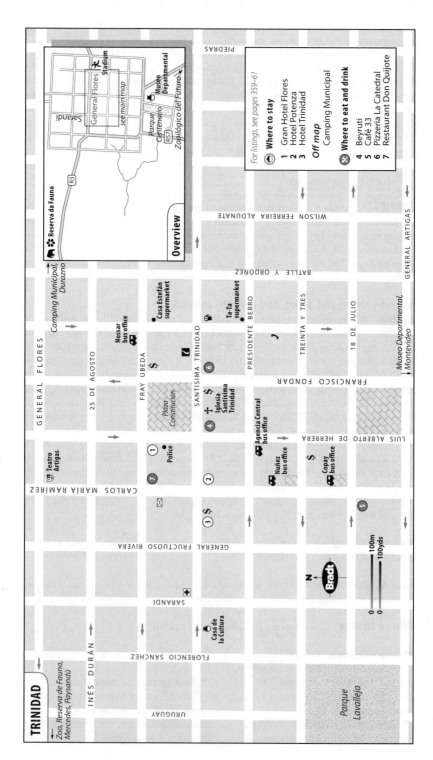

TRINIDAD

Zoo, Reserva de Fauna, Mercedes, Paysandú

Overview

Reserva da Fauna

Camping Municipal, Durazno

Stadium

General Flores

Sarandí

see main map

Museo Departmental

Parque Centenario

Zoológico del Futuro

PIEDRAS

For listings, see pages 359–61

Where to stay
1 Gran Hotel Flores
2 Hotel Potenza
3 Hotel Trinidad

Off map
Camping Municipal

Where to eat and drink
4 Beyruti
5 Café 33
6 Pizzeria La Catedral
7 Restaurant Don Quijote

WILSON FERREIRA ALDUNATE

GENERAL ARTIGAS

BATLLE Y ORDOÑEZ

GENERAL FLORES

Camping Municipal, Durazno

25 DE AGOSTO

Nossar bus office

Casa Estefán supermarket

FRAY UBEDA

SANTISIMA TRINIDAD

PRESIDENTE BERRO

Ta-Ta supermarket

TREINTA Y TRES

18 DE JULIO

Museo Departmental, Montevideo

Plaza Constitución

Iglesia Santisima Trinidad

FRANCISCO FONDAR

Teatro Artigas

Police

Agencia Central bus office

LUIS ALBERTO DE HERRERA

Nuñez bus office

Copay bus office

CARLOS MARIA RAMIREZ

GENERAL FRUCTUOSO RIVERA

SARANDI

Casa de la Cultura

FLORENCIO SANCHEZ

INÉS DURÁN

URUGUAY

Parque Lavalleja

N

Bradt

100m
100yds
0
0

▲ **Camping Municipal** Balneario Don Ricardo, 8km east on Ruta 14 (reached by buses to Durazno); ☎4364 2009. A simple place at a creekside bathing spot. No charge.

✖ Where to eat All listings are included on the map opposite.

✖ **Restaurant Don Quijote** Gran Hotel Flores. Serves the best food in town. $$$

✖ **Beyruti Restaurant** Santísima Triniday & Fondar – next to the church on the south side of the plaza. It offers the usual meat/pasta menu, but no pizza & there's certainly no falafel! $$

✖ **Pizzeria La Catedral** Fondar 655; ⊕ 11.00–17.00, 19.00–late Mon–Sat, 19.00–late Sun. Serves pizza & has live music on Fri. $$

✖ **Café 33** Ramírez & Treinta y Tres. A pleasant restaurant-parrilla. $$

Shopping
There are two supermarkets a block east of the plaza: Casa Estefán (*Puig & Ubeda;* ⊕ *08.00–13.00, 14.00–22.00 Mon–Sat, 08.00–13.00 Sun*) and Ta-Ta (*Berro 474;* ⊕ *08.00–22.00 daily*).

Other practicalities

Banks There are ATMs on the southeastern and northeastern corners of the plaza and at Herrera & Treinta y Tres. Exchange offices include Cambilex at Ramírez & Santísima Trinidad (⊕ *09.00–19.00 Mon–Fri, 09.00–12.30 Sat*) and Cambio Galimir at Fondar 694 & Treinta y Tres.

Communications The post office is a block west of the plaza (*Ramírez 620;* ⊕ *09.00–17.00 Mon–Fri, 08.00–12.00 Sat*). There's free Wi-Fi on Plaza Constitución, and at the Gran Hotel Flores.

Emergency services Comeflo (*the Co-operativa Medica de Flores;* ☎ *4364 2228*) has an emergency clinic on Sarandí just north of Santísima Trinidad; the main hospital is south on Batlle y Ordóñez (☎ 4364 2985/4555).

What to see and do The centre of town is Plaza Constitución, with a fountain and the usual statue of Artigas in the centre; on its west side is the Jefatura de Policía (police headquarters), built in 1885 and expanded in 1911, and on the northeastern corner is a fine Deco theatre. On its south side are the Intendencia Municipal (Departmental Government), opened in 1916, and the church of **Santísima Trinidad** (1863), a heavy neoclassical building with a surprisingly grand interior, with very solid columns, a coffered roof, a small baldacchino and a marble altar. The altarpiece is an oil painting of the Holy Trinity, the only painting by the sculptor José Luis Zorrilla de San Martín (1940).

Eleven blocks south on the edge of town is the **Parque Centenario**, a drab spread of gravel and eucalyptus trees opened in 1930 for the centenary of the swearing of Uruguay's constitution. Here are the municipal stadium and facilities for tennis, pelota, volleyball, basketball and other sports, as well as a children's play area, barbecues, tables and toilets. The road around the park is actually a cycle-racing track, with banked corners. To the east, the former train station (1916) now houses the **Museo Departamental** (*southern end of Alfredo Puig;* ⊕ *Oct–Jan 13.00–20.00 Tue—Sun; Feb–Sep 09.00–19.00 Tue–Sun; free*), which has polished displays on the area's prehistory (see *Around Trinidad*, page 362) and on local history, with rotating exhibitions on themes such as local railways or schooling.

The **Reserva de Fauna y Flora Dr Rodolfo Tálice** (⊕ *till sunset Tue–Sun; free*) is one of the best zoos in the country. It is approximately 3km west on Ruta 3, with an excellent cycle track, with benches and lighting, running alongside the main road to the entry at km193½. Spread across 65ha around a large lake, it is home to more than 600 animals of over 90 species, including charming free-range *maras* (Patagonian hares) wandering over the lawns, otters, alligators, tiny Brazilian titi monkeys, a puma and a jaguar (both asleep for much of the day), *coatis* (members of the racoon family) and Raza Fernandina cattle (a Hereford/Angus cross). Birds include peacocks (including an albino one), flamingos, cotorras, black ibis, southern screamers, spoonbills and giant wood-rail. There's also a *reptilario* (which includes a selection of spiders), a sculpture park with a fair variety of pieces all jumbled together with no context, a children's play area, picnic tables, a cafeteria serving simple pizzas, milanesas and the like, and across the road the better restaurant-parrilla El Portal.

It's also worth mentioning the **Zoológico del Futuro** (*junction of Ruta 3 & Ruta 23, 5km south of Trinidad*), a collection of sculptures by local artist Martín Arregui. The iron cut-outs of native animals, weapons and symbols such as sun, moon and star allude to the threats to wildlife from hunting and other human activities.

AROUND TRINIDAD The Trinidad area has been inhabited for 13,000 years, and is known for its *pinturas rupestres* (rock art), pictographs carved around 2,000 years ago. The largest collection of these is at **Chamangá**, in the southeast of the department (between Ruta 57 and the Arroyo Maciel), usually found in triangular groups of three, mostly facing northwest. They consist of lines and zigzags scored into the rock with a hard stone, and of outlined hands and other shapes in a reddish paint. Chamangá is part of SNAP, the new national system of protected areas, and can be visited by arrangement with the Comisión Departamental de Patrimonio (✎ 4364 3982/4863). Trinidad's Casa de la Cultura (*Santísima Trinidad & Sarandí*) has a pictograph from Chamangá in its patio.

Almost 50km north of Trinidad Ruta 3 crosses into Río Negro by two bridges over the artificial Lago Palmar, just north of the tiny village of **Andresito**. Between the bridges the new **Parque Bartolomé Hidalgo** is a very popular area for swimming and watersports, fishing, camping and picnicking. There's a parador with cabañas at the south end of the bridge, and a campsite in Andresito village. A casino and hotel are planned here. In January the Andresito Le Canta Al País (Andresito Sings to the Country) festival is held by the bridge, with folk singers from across the continent.

There are several excellent tourist estancias across the department. One of the most authentic gaucho experiences is at **San Martín del Yí** (*42km north of Trinidad, 24km from Ruta 3 km207;* ✎ *4360 4023;* e *sanmartindelyi@hotmail.com; www.sanmartindelyi. com.uy;* **$$$$**), east of Andresito. At the heart of the 1,830ha ranch is an L-shaped house built in 1850, with comfortably rustic rooms, and lashings of filling criollo food. You're welcome to work with the gauchos, looking after the 1,000-plus sheep and 800 cattle, or you can relax by the Yí, paddle a canoe or watch the plentiful native wildlife, including parakeets, armadillos and ñandues. Others include **La Estiria** (*north of Trinidad at Ruta 3 km209.3;* ✎ *4360 4136;* m *099 607789; www.laestiria.com;* **$$$$**); **La Amorosa** (*Camino a La Aviación, 15km northeast of Trinidad; www.gauchosruraltour. com;* **$$$$**); and **El Silencio** (*1.8km from Ruta 14 km166;* ✎ *4360 2270, 4362 2104;* e *silencio@adinet.com.uy; www.estancia-el-silencio.com;* **$$**).

TREINTA Y TRES DEPARTMENT

TREINTA Y TRES Ruta 8 from Montevideo and Minas runs through rolling cattle country into the northeast of Uruguay, the emptiest and most isolated area of the

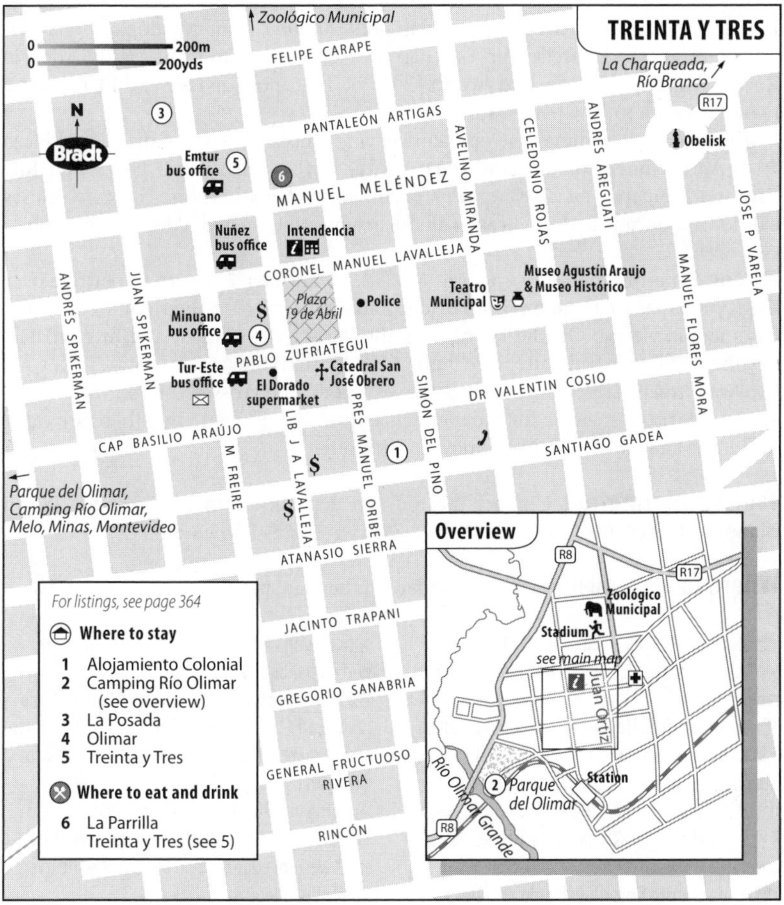
TREINTA Y TRES
Zoológico Municipal
0 200m
0 200yds
La Charqueada, Río Branco
R17
N
Bradt
Obelisk
FELIPE CARAPE
PANTALEÓN ARTIGAS
MANUEL MELÉNDEZ
CORONEL MANUEL LAVALLEJA
PABLO ZUFRIATEGUI
DR VALENTIN COSIO
CAP BASILIO ARAÚJO
SANTIAGO GADEA
ATANASIO SIERRA
JACINTO TRAPANI
GREGORIO SANABRIA
GENERAL FRUCTUOSO RIVERA
RINCÓN
AVELINO MIRANDA
CELEDONIO ROJAS
ANDRES AREGUATI
JOSE P VARELA
MANUEL FLORES MORA
ANDRÉS SPIKERMAN
JUAN SPIKERMAN
M FREIRE
LIB J A LAVALLEJA
PRES MANUEL ORIBE
SIMÓN DEL PINO
Emtur bus office
Nuñez bus office
Intendencia
Minuano bus office
Tur-Este bus office
Plaza 19 de Abril
Police
El Dorado supermarket
Catedral San José Obrero
Teatro Municipal
Museo Agustín Araujo & Museo Histórico
Parque del Olimar, Camping Río Olimar, Melo, Minas, Montevideo
For listings, see page 364
Where to stay
1 Alojamiento Colonial
2 Camping Río Olimar (see overview)
3 La Posada
4 Olimar
5 Treinta y Tres
Where to eat and drink
6 La Parrilla Treinta y Tres (see 5)
Overview
R8
R17
Zoológico Municipal
Stadium
see main map
Juan Ortiz
Station
Parque del Olimar
Río Olimar Grande
R8

country. This region was in theory ceded to Portugal by the Treaty of Madrid in 1750, but continued to be administered from Buenos Aires. The city of Treinta y Tres (Thirty-three) was founded in 1853 at a ford over the Río Olimar and became capital of the new department of the same name in 1884. The railway arrived in 1911, since when the city has grown as an agricultural centre, with rice a major product (in the east of the department) along with cattle and sheep. Of the department's population of almost 50,000, more than half live in the city. The huge Aratiri open-cast mining project near Ruta 7 west of Treinta y Tres will produce magnetite (iron ore), to be transported to the port of La Paloma.

Getting there and away

By bus From Montevideo Nuñez runs at least six regular services (*taking close to 5hrs*) and two *directos* (*taking 4hrs*) via Minas to Treinta y Tres, two continuing to Río Branco (*almost 2hrs further*); Rutas del Plata runs three services a day to Treinta y Tres and Río Branco; and Tur-Este runs four a day (*2 on Sun*) from Montevideo, and seven (*4 on Sun*) on to Río Branco. Expreso Río Branco has five services a day (just one on Sundays) to Río Branco. Expreso Minuano runs two a day (*1 on Sun*) from Montevideo to Treinta y Tres. From Melo there are five services a day with Nuñez.

EmTur has four services a day (*taking 3hrs 20mins*) from Maldonado, via San Carlos, Aiguá and Varela. Tur-Este has two services a day from Maldonado via Rocha, Aiguá and Varela; and two to Chuy via Lascano. Tur-Este and El Tala send two buses each to La Charqueada.

There's no bus terminal, the operators having offices just west of the central Plaza 19 de Abril: Nuñez (*Manuel Lavalleja & Freire*), EmTur (*Meléndez & Freire*) and Tur-Este and Minuano (*on Zufriategui between Juan Antonio Lavalleja & Freire*). Buses east to Charqueada and Río Branco all call at a bus stop on Meléndez west of Oribe.

By car Entering the department at km258, it's another 27km to the bridge over the Río Olimar (with an old road bridge and a rail bridge to the right – one of the city's iconic views). On the far bank is the Parque del Olimar, and immediately beyond you'll turn right after a 24-hour ANCAP station to enter the city, with wide two-way streets named after each of the 33 heroes who crossed the Río Uruguay in 1825 to start the struggle for independence from Brazil – note that there are three Lavallejas and two Spikermans (next to each other!).

Tourist information Contact the tourism department in the Intendencia, on Manuel Lavalleja west of Oribe (☏ *4452 2911;* ⊕ *12.15–17.45 Mon–Fri*).

Where to stay All listings are included on the map, page 363.

🏠 **Hotel La Posada** Freire 1564;☏4452 1107; www.hotellaposada33.com. A fairly modern mid-range hotel with AC rooms, PC, Wi-Fi & parking. **$$**

🏠 **Treinta y Tres Hotel** Juan Antonio Lavalleja 1534;☏4452 2325/35; e tythotel@adinet.com.uy; http://treintaytreshotel.com. The best in town, a dated 3-star place with 1 floor being refurbished to 4-star standard; there's a garage, Wi-Fi, AC rooms & a restaurant (*closed for most of Jan*). **$$**

🏠 **Alojamiento Colonial** Simón del Pino 1310 & Gadea;☏4453 0954. A cheap but very decent

option, with AC rooms with private bath, cable, Wi-Fi & parking. **$**

🏠 **Hotel Olimar** On the plaza at Juan Antonio Lavalleja 1414;☏4452 2115. The cheapest in town, an adequate 1-star place whose interior does not live up to its Art Deco façade. **$**

🏕 **Camping Río Olimar** Intendencia Municipal;☏4452 2108/2456; ⊕ all year. On the southwestern edge of town by Ruta 8 & the river; simple but adequate facilities. **$**

Where to eat All listings are included on the map, page 363.

✖ **La Parrilla** Juan Antonio Lavalleja & Meléndez;☏4452 0704; ⊕ summer 11.30–14.45, 20.30–01.00 (to 01.30 Sat); winter 11.30–14.45, 19.45–00.15 (to 01.30 Sat). A decent parrilla-pizza restaurant. **$$**

✖ **Treinta y Tres Hotel** Juan Antonio Lavalleja 1534;☏4452 2325/35. The best in town, although the menu is pretty standard. **$$**

Events The Festival del Olimar is a folk festival held in the Parque Río Olimar at Easter each year, with leading Uruguayan singers, as well as dancing, crafts and traditional foods. Also at Easter, the Treinta y Tres-La Charqueada Regatta is a waterborne procession (not a race) down the Olimar, mainly in kayaks and canoes. There are also various cross-country adventure sports events for 4x4 vehicles, mountain bikes and so on.

Shopping The main supermarket is El Dorado, on Araujo between Freire and J A Lavelleja (⊕ *08.00–22.30 daily*).

Other practicalities

Banks There's an ATM on the west side of the plaza and others three to five blocks south on Juan Antonio Lavalleja. Cambio Iberia is at J A Lavalleja 1262, just north of Atanasio Sierra.

Communications The post office is at Freire 1370 (⊕ *09.00–17.00 Mon–Fri, 09.00–12.00 Sat*). Antel's telecentro is at Miranda 1322 and Gadea (⊕ *09.00–19.00 daily*), and there's public Wi-Fi on Plaza 19 de Abril.

Emergency services The hospital is at Rodó 1831 and Zufriategui (✆ *4452 2002*) and police headquarters are on the east side of the plaza (*Oribe 1439;* ✆ *4452 2148*).

What to see and do The centre of town is characterised by wide, leafy two-way streets and single-storey houses. At its heart is **Plaza 19 de Abril** (the date of the landing of the 33 Orientales at Playa Agraciada), so well planted with trees that you can hardly see the surrounding buildings. In its centre is a monument to the 33 in black, white and pink marble (not wearing well) and the mausoleum of Juan Rosas, the last of them to die. On the north side of the plaza the Intendencia Municipal is a single-storey spread built in Eclectic style in the 1920s. On the east side of the plaza, the attractive Jefatura de Policía (police headquarters) was built in 1890. On the south side is the cathedral of **San José Obrero (St Joseph the Worker)**, built in 1871. It now has a modern red-brick façade and a simple neoclassical interior with a flat end instead of an apse below the dome, and a big, pink-marble Baroque altar.

Two blocks east of the plaza is the **Teatro Municipal** (with a very attractive Art Deco interior) and on its east side the **Casa de Cultura**, refurbished in 2009, which houses the **Museo Agustín Araujo** (*Zufriategui 1272 between Miranda & Rojas;* ⊕ *Mar–Dec 13.00–18.30 Mon–Fri, 16.30–19.30 Sat–Sun; Feb 08.00–12.00 Mon–Fri; closed Jan; free*). Its art collection includes works by Juan Manuel Blanes, Blanes Viale, Joaquín Torres García, Rafael Barradas, Luis Solari and others, including the German Carla Witte who lived here near the end of her life. Upstairs, the **Museo Histórico** (same details) has finds from the indigenous *cerritos* (raised mounds) of the department, documents and objects from the early years of the town, and an archive of black and white photos, many taken from the air.

Two blocks north and two blocks east, an **obelisk** (*Meléndez & Flores Mora*) rises 45m above a traffic island; raised in 1954, it's a memorial to the city's founders, with a bronze nymph at its base symbolising the Río Olimar. Nearby is the church of Cruz Alta, dating from 1868. At the western end of Meléndez, just off Ruta 8, is the Plaza de las Américas, with an arch over the road set up for Artigas's bicentenary. Nearby at the western entry to the city (*Ruta 8 & Fructuoso del Puerto*) there's a monument by José Belloni to the 'boy hero' Dionisio Díaz, who in 1929 rescued his 11-month-old sister from their murderous uncle (who had gone mad); he carried her for 7km to get help, but she died in the car on the way to the hospital.

At the northern end of Juan Antonio Lavalleja, 12 blocks from the plaza, the **Zoológico Municipal** (⊕ *08.00–18.00 Tue–Sun; free*) houses mainly native species, including coatí, grassland fox, hurón (similar to a weasel), carpincho, racoon, otter, Geoffrey's cat, birds such as southern screamer, dusky-legged guan, stork, falcon and eagle, as well as alligator, a puma (more or less vanished from Uruguay) and axis deer (introduced from south Asia). There's also an aquarium and a serpentarium.

QUEBRADA DE LOS CUERVOS The Quebrada de los Cuervos is the largest canyon in Uruguay, with subtropical forest at its bottom and many species of birds and flowers otherwise found mainly in Brazil. Cut into the Cuchilla Grande range by the Arroyo Yerbal Chico, the canyon reaches a depth of 175m. The area has been well protected for years, with excellent paths and signage, and in 2008 it became a national park and the first protected landscape in the Sistema Nacional de Areas Protegidas or National Protected Area System (SNAP).

The name means 'Gorge of the Crows' but refers to vultures, all three Uruguayan species of which breed on its cliffs. There are three main ecosystems: *monte de quebrada* (ravine forest), *matorral serrano* (mountain heathland) and *pradera* (grassland) and 131 plant species (over 70% of the native plant species in Uruguay), with 87 trees and shrubs (including palms and cacti), 22 ferns, lianas, creepers, green and pink lichen, and 138 species of birds (with a toucan seen for the first time in 2008), about 20 amphibians, 30 reptiles and mammals such as Geoffrey's cat, margay cat, hurón, racoon, foxes, *guazuvirá* (grey brocket deer) and armadillo.

Getting there and away, and getting around The park is 45km north of Treinta y Tres, 24km west on a dirt road from km306.5 of Ruta 8. There's no public transport so you'll have to take a **remise** if you don't have your own wheels. From the north, a dirt road leads 33km from km328 of Ruta 8. From the visitor centre (⊕ *09.00–18.00 daily; US$1*) there's a 3km *sendero de interpretación* (interpretive path), with a viewpoint over the gorge after 800m (at the end of a wooden boardwalk), and other resting points.

Where to stay and eat There's a **parador** with barbecues 2km away, near the crystalline blue Laguna Redonda and a waterfall: the **Camping Quebrada de los Cuervos** (⚫ *4450 2394;* m *099 853954;* ⊕ *all year; 6 cabins for 6; $*). At km14 of the road to the Quebrada de los Cuervos is the Cañada del Brujo, where an old school is now a simple but very friendly **hostel** (⚫ *4452 2837;* m *099 297448;* e *vlatrilla33@gmail.com; also has cabañas; $*). Hiking and horseriding can be organised and bikes can be rented; meals are available and there's a kitchen to fix your own meals.

RÍO CEBOLLATÍ From Treinta y Tres, Meléndez continues east as Ruta 17 (there's also a northern bypass from Ruta 8), reaching the small river port of **La Charqueada** (also known as Pueblo General Enrique Martínez) after 61km. Tur-Este and El Tala run up to four buses daily on this route. Founded in the 18th century, it takes its name from *charque* (jerky), the dried beef once made here.

Swinging right at the plaza, Ruta 17 ends at a free car-ferry that crosses the Río Cebollatí to a beach in Rocha department, 7km from the village of **Cebollatí** (reached by buses from Rocha). By the ferry slip is the Subprefectura, where you can enquire about boats down the river, usually either a five-person launch or the 25-passenger *Dr Antiga*, which takes two hours for the 25km trip to Laguna Merín. Canoeing and kayaking are also popular, upstream and downstream from La Charqueada. There are massive oxbow bends, and impenetrable gallery forest (really an extension of Brazil's mata Atlántica or coastal rainforest), especially on the Rocha bank, with good birdwatching. Sport fishing is of far more interest to most visitors; possibilities include patí, boga, tararira, bagre, surubí and sábalo.

To the left of the ferry slip, the riverside Coronel Machado leads to the **Cabañas Municipales** (⚫ *4459 2256; $*), with 20 cabins with kitchenette and bathroom. There's also the free **Camping Municipal** (⚫ *4459 2204;* ⊕ *all year*), with hot showers, electric lighting and barbecues. Meals are available at the parador municipal.

From La Charqueada Ruta 91 runs north for 40km to **Vergara** (40km), 55km from Treinta y Tres on Ruta 18 to Río Branco. It's little more than a village, but is home to a modern Museo Antropólogico (*Museum of Anthropology; Joaquín Suárez 1301 & Uturbey*). The eastern half of the department, now dominated by rice-farming, was home to a sizeable indigenous population, who left many *cerritos* (raised mounds) and village sites. The museum displays finds from these and also covers European colonisation and more recent history.

CERRO LARGO DEPARTMENT

From Treinta y Tres, Ruta 8 heads north, parallel to the Arroyo Yerbal, past the turnings to the Quebrada de los Cuervos (km306.5 and km328), and from km317 enters hillier country with rocky outcrops; at km346 you enter Cerro Largo (Long Hill) department. The first settlement in the department of Cerro Largo, in the northeastern corner of the country, is Arbolito (km362), just south of which is a memorial to a civil-war battle in 1897. At km375 the road crosses the Río Tacuarí, where there's a beach and wild camping. You'll start to see candelabra cacti, as well as groves of eucalyptus.

The border crossing with Brazil is at Aceguá, 60km north of Melo (the Uruguayan and Brazilian towns share the name). The Treaty of Aceguá in 1904 brought the last Uruguayan civil war to an end.

MELO Melo, capital of Cerro Largo department, was founded in three stages – first in 1791 as a military post known as the Guardía Vieja (Old Guardpost), near farms 5km south of the present city; then as the Guardía Nueva, on the site of the present cemetery, south of the centre; and finally in 1795 when Agustín de la Rosa laid out the present town on the orders of Viceroy Pedro Melo. Being close to the Brazilian border, it was captured by the Portuguese in 1801, 1811 and 1816, before becoming capital of Cerro Largo (one of the original six Uruguayan departments, cut down in 1837 and 1884).

This area has always been a stronghold of the Blancos (Partido Nacional), the main plaza being named as far back as 1845 after Manuel Oribe, Uruguay's second president and first Blanco president (it's now Plaza Constitución). General Aparico Saravia, the last of the great Blanco caudillos, lived at the Estancia El Cordobés (in the southwesternmost corner of the department), virtually the country's second seat of government from 1897 to 1903. Uruguay's first president, Fructuoso Rivera, died here in 1854. Juana Fernández Morales, later Juana de Ibarbourou, poet and novelist (see page 30), was born in Melo in 1892, and Wilson Ferreira Aldunate (1919–88), the Blanco leader who was the leading opponent of the dictatorship, grew up here.

Melo is now a city of close to 50,000 inhabitants, its prosperity based on trade with Brazil and on agriculture – largely cattle, for the PUL meat-packing plant and the Coleme dairy co-operative, but with rice increasingly important. It's still an old-fashioned, low-rise city, with a subtropical climate and a noticeably more Afro-Uruguayan population than most towns to the south. Pope John Paul II visited in 1988, the context of the 2007 film *El Baño del Papa* (The Pope's Toilet).

Getting there and away, and getting around

By bus At about km392 Ruta 8 enters Melo (396km from Montevideo), buses continue to the modern terminal on Lestido between 18 de Julio and Treinta y Tres, nine blocks north of the central Plaza Constitución; there's a cafeteria upstairs but no ATM or Wi-Fi. The bus information office (✆ 4642 2571) is hidden away upstairs, and there's no specific tourist information office.

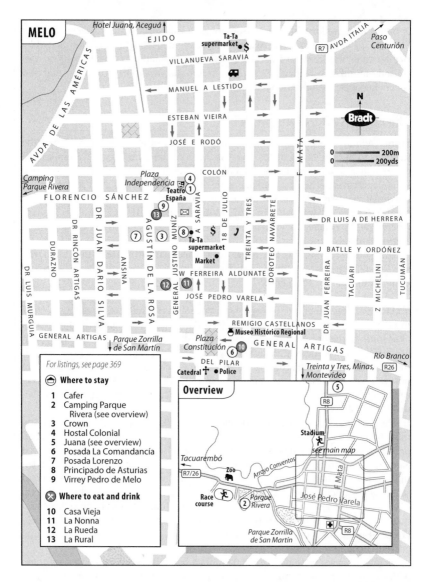

MELO

Hotel Juana, Aceguá
EJIDO
Ta-Ta supermarket
Paso Centurión
R7 AVDA ITALIA
VILLANUEVA SARAVIA
AVDA DE LAS AMÉRICAS
MANUEL A LESTIDO
ESTEBAN VIEIRA
N
JOSÉ E RODÓ
Bradt
F MATA
0   200m
0   200yds
Camping Parque Rivera
Plaza Independencia
COLÓN
FLORENCIO SÁNCHEZ
Teatro España
DR JUAN DARIO
DR RINCON ARTIGAS
DURAZNO
AGUSTÍN DE LA ROSA
ANSINA
GENERAL JUSTINO MUNIZ
A SARAVIA
18 DE JULIO
TREINTA Y TRES
DOROTEO NAVARRETE
DR LUIS A DE HERRERA
J BATLLE Y ORDÓÑEZ
Ta-Ta supermarket
Market
DR LUIS MURGUIA
SILVA
DE LA ROSA
W FERREIRA ALDUNATE
JOSÉ PEDRO VARELA
DR JUAN FERREIRA
TACUARI
Z MICHELINI
TUCUMÁN
REMIGIO CASTELLANOS
Museo Histórico Regional
GENERAL ARTIGAS
Parque Zorrilla de San Martín
Plaza Constitución
GENERAL   ARTIGAS
Río Branco
DEL PILAR
Catedral ✝ ● Police
Treinta y Tres, Minas, Montevideo
R26

For listings, see page 369

🛏 **Where to stay**

1 Cafer
2 Camping Parque
   Rivera (see overview)
3 Crown
4 Hostal Colonial
5 Juana (see overview)
6 Posada La Comandancía
7 Posada Lorenzo
8 Principado de Asturias
9 Virrey Pedro de Melo

✖ **Where to eat and drink**

10 Casa Vieja
11 La Nonna
12 La Rueda
13 La Rural

Overview

R8
Stadium
see main map
Tacuarembó
Arroyo Conventos
Zoo
R7/26
F Mata
José Pedro Varela
Race course
Parque Rivera
Parque Zorrilla de San Martín
R8

Direct traffic from Montevideo can also take Ruta 7, entering Melo from the west, although this bypasses intermediate towns such as Minas and Treinta y Tres. Ruta 7 and Ruta 8 cross in Melo, Ruta 7 going northeast to a dead end at Paso Centurión while Ruta 8 heads north to the Brazilian border.

From Montevideo, Nuñez has five daily services to Melo by Ruta 8 (*via Minas and Treinta y Tres, taking 5 to 6hrs*), and two by Ruta 7 (*via Cerro Chato, taking close to 6hrs*); Turismar (Turil/Posada) has three a day by Ruta 7, and EGA has four (*2 on Sun*) by Ruta 8. From Rivera, Nuñez has a daily service (*except Sun*) via Vichadero (*4hrs*), and Posada has two a day via Tacuarembó and Ansina. From the Brazilian border at Aceguá Decatur has three daily buses (*only at 08.00 on Sun*), La Flota has three and Unitur and Nuñez each have one daily.

From Río Branco, Nuñez has four buses a day, Turil has three, La Flota has four and Rutas del Plata has one (some of these starting at Lago Merín). Decatur/COTA runs five services (*3 on Sun*) from Río Branco and Lago Merín. Ómnibus Vidal leaves Melo (on the street to the east of the terminal) for Paso Centurión at 08.00 on Monday, Wednesday and Friday only, returning at 10.00.

By car Cars can be rented from Multicar (*Francisco Mata 570 near Varela;* \ *4642 4860;* m *095 885766; www.redmulticar.com;* ☉ *09.00–19.00 Mon–Fri, 09.00–13.00 Sat*). Note that there is a charge for parking in the city centre from 09.00 to 18.00 Monday to Friday, 09.00 to 13.00 Saturday.

🏠 **Where to stay** As well as hotels, **camping** is available in the Parque Rivera on Ruta 7 across the Arroyo Conventos bridge west of the city centre. All listings are included on the map opposite.

🏠 **Crown** Batlle y Ordoñez 609 & Agustín de la Rosa; \ 4642 2261; e hotelcrownmelo@adinet. com.uy; www.hotelcrown.com.uy. Comfortable & friendly 3-star hotel with 54 rooms & 4 suites, all with AC, cable TV & Wi-Fi. $$$

🏠 **Hotel Juana** Ruta 8 km402; \ 4642 5262; www.hoteljuana.com.uy. This minimalist 4-star is in a very tranquil location 2km north of town, & has a decent restaurant too. $$$

🏠 **Posada La Comandancía** 18 de Julio 408; \ 4643 0392/3; www.posadalacomandancia.com. On the east side of Plaza Constitución, the house was built in the 1880s & has been beautifully converted with very modern staircases & a swimming pool in the patio. Staff are very helpful, & there are 18 AC rooms with a safe, Wi-Fi & cable TV. $$$

🏠 **Virrey Pedro de Melo** Muniz 727; \ 4642 2673; www.hotelvirreypedrodemelo.com. Decent 3-star hotel with AC rooms with cable TV, as well

as Wi-Fi, PC & a restaurant; but rooms facing Plaza Independencia can be very noisy. $$$–$$

🏠 **Hotel Cafer** Sánchez 689 & Saravia; \ 4642 6565; e hotelcafer@adinet.com.uy. In a modern block, this central 2-star place has AC rooms both en suite & with a private bathroom across the corridor; there's Wi-Fi & a PC. $$

🏠 **Posada Lorenzo** Batlle y Ordoñez 593 & de la Rosa; m 095 785621. A decent mid-range place with en-suite rooms, Wi-Fi, & use of kitchen & BBQ. $$

🏠 **Hotel Principado de Asturias** Herrera 668 & Muniz, 5 blocks south of the terminal; \ 4642 2064; e jorgeg1975@yahoo.com.ar. A spotless 2-star in a period house; all rooms have private bathroom & cable TV, as well as a garage & BBQ, & there's Wi-Fi & a PC. $$–$

🏠 **Hostal Colonial** Sarandí 771 & Sánchez; \ 4643 2108. A simple place with rooms with AC & private or shared bathrooms, & Wi-Fi. $

✗ **Where to eat** At Treinta y Tres 400 and Del Pilar a café sells cooked food by weight, mainly to take out; it's all cheap and there are lots of vegetarian options such as tortilla or Russian salad. There are also various ice-cream and empanada outlets on Saravia and Lestido just west of the terminal, and two very modern kiosk cafés on the northern corners of Plaza Constitución. Melo seems to specialise in coffee-shops, such as La Nonna, below. All listings are included on the map opposite.

✗ **Casa Vieja** 18 de Julio & Artigas. Good pizza. $$

✗ **La Nonna** Wilson Ferreira Aldunate & Muniz. Serve breakfasts, pastries & sandwiches (inc *bauru*, a sort of Brazilian chivito); it has a terrace & Wi-Fi. $$

✗ **La Rueda** Varela & Muniz. A good parrillada. $$

✗ **La Rural** Muniz & Herrera. Looks like a stylish café but really is a parrilla-restaurant, serving steak & fish such as salmon & lenguado. $$

Shopping The market is at 18 de Julio and Batlle y Ordóñez. The Ta-Ta supermarket has two branches, immediately north of the terminal (☉ *08.00–22.00* *daily*) and in the centre at Saravia 665, south of Herrera (⏱ *08.00–21.00 Mon–Sat*); there's also El Dorado at Herrera and Muniz (⏱ *08.00–23.00 Mon–Sat*). Near the bus terminal is the Casa del Artesano (*Lestido 739*). The Casa de la Mujer Rural (*18 de Julio & Aldunate*) is a café/shop, but there's not much for sale.

Other practicalities

Banks There are ATMs at Saravia 599 and 699, on the north side of the terminal, and on 18 de Julio, leading south to the city centre. Cambio Central is at Saravia 676 and immediately west of the Ta-Ta supermarket on the north side of the bus terminal.

Communications The post office is at Herrera 667 (⏱ *09.00–17.00 Mon–Fri, 08.00–12.00 Sat*); Antel's call centre is at 18 de Julio 696 and Herrera (⏱ *09.00–18.00 Mon–Fri, 09.00–13.00 Sat*). There's public Wi-Fi on Plaza Constitución; Travesuras Cyber is at Treinta y Tres 950 and Lestido, diagonally opposite the bus terminal.

Emergency services The police headquarters are immediately east of the cathedral at Del Pilar 718 (📞 *4642 2421/2, 4642 2018*). The hospital is at Doroteo Navarrete and Suárez (📞 *4642 1002/2480*).

Immigration The Inspectoría de Migración is at Rodó 661 (📞 *4642 2437, 152 1912;* e *dnm-melo@minterior.gub.uy*).

What to see and do Plaza Constitución, nine blocks south of the terminal, is the city's central square, an attractive space with big trees and open space around the central monument to José Gervasio Artigas. On its south side stands the **cathedral**, clean and quiet, with light colours. It was built in 1857–76 in a simple neoclassical style, the aisles added in the 20th century in exactly the same style. The apse seems to have been added in the 1970s, with an unusual arrangement of wooden slats and marble. Across Saravia immediately west of the cathedral is a tatty but very fine palace, south of the Club Unión – a less impressive Belle-Époque pile.

On the east side of Plaza Constitución, the **Museo Histórico Regional** (*Regional Historical Museum; Artigas;* ⏱ *10.00–16.00 Tue–Sun; free*) displays mementos of the local caudillo, General Aparico Saravia (1856–1904), who led revolts against the government in 1894–97 and ran a virtual parallel government from his estancia of El Cordobés. He led uprisings again in 1903 and in 1904, and was mortally wounded at the Battle of Masoller. There are lots of pistols and rifles, his carriage and safe, and even his branding iron. Upstairs are fossils, prehistoric arrowheads, boleadoras and grinding stones, and ceramics from the Jesuit missions in the west of the country, as well as some works by local amateur artists. You'll also see the rocking chair, hat, fan and prayer book of the poet Juana de Ibarbourou (see page 30), whose birthplace, a perfectly normal single-storey house two blocks south at Treinta y Tres 317, is not open to visitors.

The city's other main square is Plaza Independencia, southwest of the terminal. On the east side the single-storey, Belle-Époque Asociación Española de Socorros Mutuos (*Muñiz 770*), built in 1914, houses the **Teatro España**.

The Arroyo Conventos flows along the city's western side, with two riverside parks. There's a summer theatre in the Parque Zorrilla de San Martín, southwest of Plaza Constitución, while the Parque Rivera, on the far side of the Ruta 7 bridge, at the western end of Florencio Sánchez, includes a campsite, a parador and play areas. At its entrance is a replica of the house of Bartolomé Silva, where Fructuoso

Rivera died on his way from Rio de Janeiro to join the ruling triumvirate. On the other side of Ruta 7 is a small **zoo**, with some native species plus tigers, lions, a black bear, llamas, monkeys and axis deer.

PASO CENTURIÓN From Melo, Ruta 7 continues northeast for about 50km to Paso Centurión, where it ends at the Río Yaguarón. A tiny portion of Brazil's mata Atlántica (coastal rainforest) has crossed the river into Uruguay here. There are butiá palms, creepers, ferns and bromeliads, animals such as anteaters, armadillos, porcupine, agoutí, margay cat, guazubirá, capybara and – a recent discovery in Uruguay – *cuica de agua* (water opossum; *Chironectes minimus*). The 120 species of birds include yellow-headed vulture, plush-crested jay, anhinga, saffron-cowled blackbird and rarities such as the reddish-bellied parakeet (or Azara's conure; *Pyrrhura frontalis chiripepe*), common or grey potoo (*urutaú; Nyctibius griseus*) and brushland tinamou (*perdiz montaráz; Nothoprocta cinerascens*).

First settled in 1778, this was a crossing point for cattle exports to Brazil, and the old Customs house and a military hospital can still be seen. Ómnibus Vidal leaves Melo at 08.00 on Monday, Wednesday and Friday only, returning at 10.00 – so unless you come by car or bike you'll have to bring a tent and stay at least two nights.

RÍO BRANCO Ruta 26 heads east from Melo towards the border town of Río Branco, after 13km passing the former **Posta del Chuy**, a stone coaching inn *(pulpería y posta de diligencias)* where two French Basques built a 85m-long toll bridge over the Arroyo Chuy del Tacuarí in 1855. Tolls were collected until 1917 and the posta is now open as the Museo del Gaucho, del Campo y de la Frontera (Museum of the Gaucho, the Countryside and the Frontier).

The Guardía Arredondo military post was built in 1792 near the present bridge, but in 1801 the Portuguese moved to the north side of the Río Yaguarón, leaving a settlement known as Pueblo Arredondo. By 1854 a new town known as Villa Artigas had appeared a couple of kilometres south, in 1912 renamed after the Barão (Baron) de Rio Branco (1845–1912), the Brazilian diplomat who guaranteed Brazil's frontiers and was responsible for the so-called free womb law of 1871, which ensured that a slave's children would henceforth be born free. Today it's a quiet and unexciting town of around 13,000.

Getting there and away, and getting around The road joins Ruta 18 from Treinta y Tres and Montevideo, and after just over an hour (km85) reaches the *paso frontera* (border post) at the western edge of Río Branco. Buses from Melo stop if required for immigration purposes, continuing via Arredondo and Plaza Artigas in the town centre, turning around near the international bridge and returning to the centre. Empresa Moreira runs a local bus roughly hourly from the *paso frontera* to the plaza and the bridge. It's just over 3km to the plaza, if you should decide to walk.

The Barón de Mauá international bridge, opened in 1930, was at the time the longest bridge in South America (until the Paysandú–Colón bridge opened). It's 2,112m long, although the main span is only a couple of hundred metres; most of it is actually the approach ramp on the Uruguayan side, carrying both a road and a railway; there's a shorter ramp from Artigas in Pueblo Arredondo. There's no bus service across the border so you'll have to walk or take a taxi (*US$5 from Plaza Artigas to the Policía Federal*).

Nuñez operates two services daily from Montevideo, Minas and Treinta y Tres to Río Branco (*at least 6hrs*), and four from Melo (*one continuing to Lago Merín except on Sun*); Rutas del Plata has three services a day from Montevideo. Turil has three buses a day from Melo, La Flota has four and Rutas del Plata has one. Decatur/COTA runs five services (*3 on Sun*) from Melo to Río Branco and Lago Merín; and La Flota runs two a day from Melo to Río Branco, one continuing to Lago Merín.

🏠 **Where to stay and eat** The only place to stay (other than the Excalibur 'love-hotel' on the Lago Merín road) is the **Hotel Status** (*Artigas & Rivera, 2 blocks south of the bridge;* ☏ *4675 2264;* **$$**), simple but decent enough. There are far more options in the attractive Brazilian town of Jaguarão, with cheap hotels near the bridge and better ones on the plaza, three blocks to the right.

There are **parrillas** on Artigas near the bridge and hotel. A block north of the plaza are the **Restaurant-Pizzeria La Campana** (*Arredondo & El Fanal;* **$$**) and a **pizzeria-churrasquería** (*Arredondo & Ferreiro;* **$$**). Six blocks south near the Nuñez bus office is the good **Panadería-Confitería Esmeralda** (*Arredondo & Arismendi;* **$**).

Shopping There are a few duty-free shops near the bridge.

Other practicalities

Banks There is an ATM at the Banco República, Artigas 301.

Communications The post office is at Arredondo 963 (⏲ *10.00–16.00 Mon–Fri, 08.00–13.00 Sat*). Antel's call centre is at the southwestern corner of the plaza (*Gundin 881;* ⏲ *09.00–18.00 daily*). There's a Wi-Fi signal on the plaza but it's a bit weak.

Immigration and consulate There are Inspectoría de Migración offices at the paso frontera (☏ *4675 2638;* e *dnm-riobranco@minterior.gub.uy*) and at the bridge (☏ *4675 2068*), and a Brazilian vice-consulate a block south of the plaza (*10 de Junio 379;* ☏ *4675 2003*). On the Brazilian side, you'll have to get your entry stamp at the Policía Federal (*1572 Rua Júlio de Castilhos;* ⏲ *24hrs*), west from the lovely Rua X de Novembro. The *rodoviaria* (bus station) is on the plaza, with three daily services to Porto Alegre (*6hrs; US$35*) and seven daily to Pelotas (*5 on Sun*).

LAGO MERÍN Laguna Merín is the second-largest lake in South America after Lake Titicaca, covering an area of about 3,800km². On its northern shore, 21km from Río Branco, is the beach resort of Lago Merín.

Founded in 1937, Lago Merín has always received many visitors from Brazil, and now sees around 15,000 on summer weekends. Some 60% of its houses are owned by Brazilians, many from the city of Pelotas. It's a simple resort, mainly attracting families, although it does have the usual hippies selling jewellery. The beach is sandy and slopes very gently, and the lake is not tidal, making it very safe for children. It has a maximum depth of 7m and often has a consistent breeze, making it popular with windsurfers and kite-surfers. There's also good fishing, notably for tararira.

The main festival is the Reina del Lago (*Queen of the Lake; www.reinadellago. com*), over a weekend in the middle of January.

There is a police post near the Municipal Camping (*calles 18 & 23*).

Getting there and away, and getting around Buses run seven times daily (*3 on Sun*) from Melo via Río Branco, the last returning at 19.00. They run between huge rice fields (with lots of termite mounds) and enter on Calle 18, reaching the beach at km21 (where there are toilets and a policlínica) and turning right to terminate four blocks south. **Bikes** can be rented by the policlínica at the end of Calle 18.

🏠 Where to stay Most visitors stay in rented cabañas.

🏠 **Hostería Alcalá** 4 blocks south of Calle 18, on the rambla between calles 2 & 4; ☎ 4679 8893. A long-established hotel-parador with simple rooms & filling meals. **$$**

🏠 **Hotel Laguna Merín** Calles 18 & 11; ☎ 4679 8033; e hotellagunamerin@hotmail.com; www. hotellagunamerin.net. The best place to stay, this nice 3-star place has a swimming pool indoors & 1 outdoors under a sunroof, plus Wi-Fi, gym & a good restaurant. **$$**

🏠 **Rincón del Lago** Calles 18 & 13; ☎ 4679 8804. Has nice apartments & cabañas, with AC & cable TV, & a parrilla. **$$**

🏠 **Asini** Calle 1; ☎ 4645 1511. The parador municipal, alongside the casino. **$**

🏕 **Camping Municipal** 2 blocks along from the Rincón del Lago; ⊕ all year. A simple, friendly campsite with hot showers. The Cabañas Municipales is on the other side of Calle 23. **$**

✕ Where to eat There are shops and bars at the end of Calle 18, and a pizzería-cervecería with pool hall just to the north. There are no fancy restaurants at all, except in the hotel.

It's worth mentioning the **Laguna Lodge**, run by Lake Merin Outfitters (m *099 085531 (May–Sep); USA* tf *+1 800 420 8707;* e *lakemerin@terra.com.br; http:// lakemerin.net*), which aims to create an American-style duck-hunting atmosphere, complete with 05.00 starts and evenings with an open fire, satellite television, Wi-Fi and hearty meals. They have various duck blinds 15–25 minutes away by 4x4 truck.

Appendix 1

LANGUAGE

PRONOUNS

I	*yo*	they	*ellos*
you (singular informal)	*vos*	they (feminine only)	*ellas*
you (singular formal)	*usted*	me/myself	*me*
you (plural)	*ustedes*	you/yourself	*te*
he/it	*él*	us/ourselves	*nos*
she/it	*ella*	you (plural)/ yourselves	*os*
it	*ello*	them/themselves	*les/se*
we	*nosotros*	them/themselves (feminine only)	*las/se*
we (feminine only)	*nosotras*		

NUMBERS

0	*cero*	19	*diez y nueve*
1	*uno/una* (m/f)	20	*veinte*
2	*dos*	21	*veinte y uno*
3	*tres*	22	*veinte dos*
4	*cuatro*	30	*treinta*
5	*cinco*	40	*cuarenta*
6	*seis*	50	*cincuenta*
7	*siete*	60	*sesenta*
8	*ocho*	70	*setenta*
9	*nueve*	80	*ochenta*
10	*diez*	90	*noventa*
11	*once*	100	*cien*
12	*doce*	101	*ciento y uno*
13	*trece*	200	*doscientos*
14	*catorce*	1,000	*mil*
15	*quince*	10,000	*diez mil*
16	*diez y seis*	100,000	*cien mil*
17	*diez y siete*	1,000,000	*un millón*
18	*diez y ocho*		

DATES

January	*Enero*	July	*Julio*
February	*Febrero*	August	*Agosto*
March	*Marzo*	September	*Septiembre*
April	*Abril*	October	*Octubre*
May	*Mayo*	November	*Noviembre*
June	*Junio*	December	*Deciembre*

DAYS

Sunday	*Domingo*	Thursday	*Jueves*
Monday	*Lunes*	Friday	*Viernes*
Tuesday	*Martes*	Saturday	*Sabado*
Wednesday	*Miercoles*		

TIME

today	*hoy*	last night	*anoche*
yesterday	*ayer*	week	*semana*
tomorrow	*mañana*	month	*mes*
morning	*la mañana*	year	*año*
tomorrow morning	*mañana por la mañana*	Good day/ good morning	*Buenos días*
afternoon	*la tarde*	Good afternoon	*Buenas tardes*
evening/night	*la noche*	Good night	*Buenas noches*

The 24-hour clock is used, so for '7pm' you can say either *son las diez y nueve* or *son las siete de la noche.*

What time is it?	*¿Qué hora es?*	12.00 (noon)	*mediodía*
01.00/ 02.00	*Es la una/Son las dos*	24.00 (midnight)	*medianoche*

BASIC VOCABULARY

Hello	*hola*	You're welcome	*de nada*
Glad to meet you	*mucho gusto*	Sorry	*lo siento*
Goodbye	*adiós*	Excuse me	*disculpe*
Good/well/very well	*bueno/bien/muy bien*	Of course	*claro*
Yes/no	*sí/no*	Open/closed	*abierto/cerrado*
Please/thank you	*por favor/gracias*	Large/small	*grande/pequeño*

Directions and transport

here/there	*aquí/ahí*	near/corner	*casi/esquina*
left/right	*izquierda/derecha*	bus stop	*parada*
north/south	*norte/sur*	bus station	*terminal*
east/west	*este/oeste*	airport	*aeropuerto*
northwest/	*noroeste*	ferry	*barca*
southeast	*sureste*	jetty	*muele*
straight ahead	*derecha/adelante*	return ticket	*pasaje ida-y-vuelta*
block	*cuadra*	Is there a bus to … ?	*Hay omnibus hasta … ?*
corner	*esquina*	I want to go to …	*Quiero ir a…*
street/avenue	*calle/avenida*	I want to get off at …	*Quiero bajar a …*
road/path	*camino/sendero*	Stop, please!	*¡Parada, por favor!*
unnumbered	*sin numero (s/n)*		

Accommodation

Do you have a room?		¿Hay un cuarto?	
What does it cost?		¿Cuánto cuesta?	
Do you have anything cheaper?		¿Hay algo más barato?	
with private bathroom		con baño privado	
with shared bathroom		con baño compartido	

too much	*demasiado*	double	*matrimonial*
expensive	*caro*	air conditioned	*aire acondicionado*
cheap	*barato, económico*	shower	*ducha*
single	*sencillo*	towel	*toalla*
twin	*doble*	toilet paper	*papel higiénico*

Food and drink (See pages 67–71 for some dishes)

bread	*pan*	wine/beer	*vino/cerveza*
butter	*manteca*	juice/milk	*jugo/leche*
(without) meat	*(sin) carne*	tea/coffee	*té/cafe*
fish	*pescado*	knife/fork/spoon	*cuchillo/tenedor/*
potatoes	*patatas*		*cuchara*
vegetables	*legumbres*	Enjoy your meal	*Buen provecha*
fruit	*fruta*	The bill, please	*La cuenta, por favor*
water	*agua*		

Questions

Where?	*¿Dónde?*	When?	*¿Cuándo?*
Who?	*¿Quién?*	Why?	*¿Por qué?*
What?	*¿Cómo?*	How?	*¿Cómo?*

Typical Uruguayan words and phrases

a las ordenes	at your service	*bárbaro*	fantastic
¿Yo que se?	What do I know?	*rambla*	waterfront
Que le pase bien	Farewell		promenade
¿Entonces, que pasa?	So, what's up?	*balastro*	dirt road
¿Que cosa?	What?	*glorieta*	viewpoint
¡Que calor!	It's so hot!		(not *mirador*)
Jaja	Yes yes		

Note that the word for government is often spelt *gubierno*, not *gobierno* as elsewhere – so the internet domain is .gub.uy not .gob.uy. The country to the north is spelt Brasil not Brazil (where Uruguay is spelt Uruguai, and its capital Montevidéu). The neighbour further to the north is called Estados Unidos (not Los Estados Unidos), and its people *americanos* (not *norteamericanos*).

Appendix 1 LANGUAGE

A1

Appendix 2

FURTHER INFORMATION
BOOKS
General

Delgardo, Mario *Boliches Montevideanos* Banda Oriental, Montevideo, 2006. A beautifully produced photographic guide to the most traditional, and significant pubs and bar-restaurants of Montevideo.

de Villiers, Greg and Vásquez, Juan *Guia de Bodegas y Vinos del Uruguay* Planeta, Montevideo, 2012. A remarkably complete bilingual guide to 33 (of course) Uruguayan wineries, with fine photographs.

Jermyn, Leslie *Uruguay (Cultures of the World)* Marshall Cavendish, Tarrytown, NY, 1999. Produced for school geography classes, this is a slim but well-illustrated volume covering the country's geography, people, politics, economy and culture (including art, sports and food).

Lanza, Eduardo, Larrimbe, Miguel and Michelini, Margarita *Vinos y Bodegas de Uruguay* Montevideo, Fin de Siglo 2005. An attractive guide to the history of Uruguay's vineyards, focusing on their transformation from the late 1980s.

Morrison, Marion *Uruguay* (Enchantment of the World series) Scholastic, New York, 3rd ed, 2005. Aimed at younger schoolchildren, this is full of photos and entertaining boxes, as well as hints for further research.

Remedi, Gustavo (trans) Ferlazzo, Amy *Carnival Theater: Uruguay's Popular Performers and National Culture* University of Minnesota Press, Minneapolis, 2004. An academic investigation of the complex roots of Uruguay's popular culture.

Shields, Charles J *Uruguay (Discovering South America series)* Broomall, PA, Mason Crest, 2nd edn 2009. A brief introduction for schoolchildren to the geography, history and culture of Uruguay, with extras such as recipes and project ideas.

Darwin

Aydon, Cyril *Charles Darwin* Constable & Robinson, 2002. A balanced account, placing Darwin in his social and economic context.

Browne, Janet *Charles Darwin: Voyaging* Princeton UP/Cape, 1996 and *The Power of Place* Princeton UP/Cape, 2003. This two-volume biography is the most detailed and up to date available.

Darwin, Charles *The Voyage of the Beagle* 1839; paperback editions by Penguin and Wordsworth Classics, UK, and NAL-Dutton, USA. Perhaps 'the greatest travel book ever'. Also *The Autobiography of Charles Darwin* Oxford UP/Dover, 1983; *The Origin of Species* 1859; paperback editions by Penguin, OUP World's Classics and Random House Modern Library; *The Descent of Man* Prometheus, US.

Keynes, Richard *Fossils, Finches and Fuegians: Charles Darwin's Adventures and Discoveries on the Beagle* HarperCollins, 2003. By Darwin's great-grandson.

Moorehead, Alan *Darwin and the Beagle* Hamish Hamilton, 1969/Penguin, 1971.

Ralling, Christopher (ed) *The Voyage of Charles Darwin* BBC, 1978.

Stott, Rebecca *Darwin and the Barnacle* Norton, 2003.

Thomson, Keith *HMS Beagle: The Story of Darwin's Ship* Norton, 1995. The remains of the *Beagle* have since been found.

Wertenbaker, Timberlake *After Darwin* Faber, 1999. Perhaps her best play.

History

Caviedes, César *The Southern Cone: Realities of the Authoritarian State* Rowman & Allanheld, Totowa, NJ, 1984. A comparative study of the military dictatorships of Chile, Argentina, Uruguay and Brazil of the 1970s and 1980s.

Gillespie, Charles *Negotiating Democracy: Politicians and Generals in Uruguay* Cambridge University Press 1991. An academic, but still fascinating, account of the negotiations behind the return to democracy in the late 1980s.

Labrousse, Alain *Les Tupamaros: des armes aux urnes* (1962–2009) Editions du Rocher, Paris, 2009. Only in French, but one of the best and most up-to-date accounts of the Uruguayan left's transition from a guerrilla campaign to forming the current legitimate government.

Parrado, Nando *Miracle in the Andes* Random House, 2006. The true story of the Uruguayan rugby club whose plane crashed in the Andes in 1972; after waiting for two months (and eating the flesh of their dead companions), Parrado and a companion made a ten-day journey to find help, and 16 of the 45 were rescued alive. Also told in:

Read, Piers Paul *Alive: The Story of the Andes Survivors* HarperCollins, 2002. Also a film.

Street, John *Artigas and the Emancipation of Uruguay* Cambridge University Press 1959, paperback 2008.

Vanger, Milton *Batlle y Ordóñez of Uruguay: The Creator of His Times, 1902–1907* Harvard UP, 1963; also *José Batlle y Ordóñez of Uruguay: The Model Country, 1907–1915*; and *José Batlle y Ordóñez of Uruguay: The Determined Visionary, 1915–1917*. An academic trilogy giving a detailed account of the creation of modern Uruguay as South America's first welfare state.

Weinstein, Martin *Uruguay: Democracy at the Crossroad* Westview Press, Boulder, CO, 1988. An academic view of Uruguayan politics, at a time when its economy was stagnant and the restoration of democracy incomplete. Also *Uruguay: The Politics of Failure* (Greenwood Press, Westport, CT, 1975), on the reasons why military dictatorship was able to supplant a democratic welfare state.

Literature

Boyd, William *Any Human Heart* Hamish Hamilton, 2002. The journals of the fictional writer Logan Gonzago Mountstuart, born in 1906 in Montevideo, whose mediocre life brought him into contact with many of the 20th century's most colourful characters; this is a substantial multi-layered novel (complete with footnotes and index) that soon moves beyond the confines of Uruguay.

Dumas, Alexandre père *Montevideo, ou une nouvelle Troie* Napoléon Chaix et Cie, Paris, 1850; Amis d'Alexandre Dumas, Le Port-Marly Yvelines, 2007. A very unusual book by the prolific novelist, a non-fiction account of the struggle for independence of the Banda Oriental between 1810 and 1848, this has not been translated from French; however, parts were recycled in his *Mémoires de Garibaldi* (1861).

Fonseca, Isabel *Attachment* Random House/Chatto 2008, paperback Vintage 2009. About an American–British couple taking a sabbatical in the tropics, this novel is partly rooted in her life in Uruguay with Martin Amis.

Hudson, William Henry *The Purple Land* University of Wisconsin, Madison, 2002. First published in 1885, this was described by Borges as 'the best work of gaucho literature'; its English hero gradually casts off his Victorian stuffiness and comes to love the freedom and indeed chaos of the New World.

Travels

Green, Toby *Saddled with Darwin* Phoenix, 1999. Following Darwin's trail on horseback through Uruguay, Argentina and Chile, this is an entertaining but serious account by a talented young writer, combining accounts of Darwin's legacy and of contemporary rural life.

Wangford, Hank *Lost Cowboys* Indigo, 1996. In the country-singing gynaecologist's inimitable style, this is a funny and very informative pilgrimage through Latin America in search of the Hispanic origins of the cowboys; 40 of 300-plus pages are on Uruguay, where he found an unspoilt heartland of gaucho tradition.

Wildlife

Achaval, Federico and Olmos, Alejandro *Anfibios y Reptiles del Uruguay* Biophoto, Montevideo, 3rd edn 2007. A photographic guide to Uruguay's 66 reptile species and 48 amphibians.

Achaval, Mario Clara and Olmos, Alejandro *Mamíferos de la República Oriental del Uruguay* Facultad de Ciencias, Montevideo, 2nd edn 2007. A Spanish-language guide to Uruguay's mammals.

Aisenberg, Anita and Toscano, Carlos *Guía de Aracnidos del Uruguay* Ediciones de la Fuga, Montevideo, 2010. Excellent guide to the spiders of Uruguay.

Arballo, Eduardo and Cravino, Jorge *Aves del Uruguay: Volume 1 Manual Ornitológico* Editorial Hemisferio Sur SRL, Montevideo, 1999. With a second volume due, these weighty Spanish-language volumes will be the most detailed account of Uruguay's birds.

Azpiroz, Adrián B *Aves de las Pampas y Campos de Argentina, Brasil & Uruguay* Varios, Montevideo, 2012. A bilingual photographic identification guide to over 500 species of birds.

Azpiroz, Adrián B *Aves del Uruguay – Lista e Introducción a su Biología y Conservación* 2nd edn 2003. Spanish-language list of 435 species of Uruguayan birds, with information on conservation issues.

Brito, Ana Helena and Llano, Liliana *Bromelias del Uruguay* Librería Linardi y Risso, Montevideo, 2008. A Spanish-language guide to Uruguay's bromeliads (pineapple-like plants, many epiphytic).

Geymonat, Giancarlo and Lombardi, Raul *Fauna y Flora de las Bosques del Uruguay* Varios, Montevideo, 2012. Excellent integrated field guide to Uruguay's native woodland, including a selection of lichen and ferns.

Lahitte, B and Hurell, J A *Trees of the Río de la Plata* LOLA, Buenos Aires, 1999. In Spanish and English; fully illustrated.

Maneyro, Raúl and Carreira, Santiago *Guía de Anfibios del Uruguay* Ediciones de la Fuga, Montevideo, 2010. Excellent guide to the amphibians of Uruguay (also some reptiles).

Menafra, R, Rodríguez-Gallego, L, Scarabino, F, and Conde, D (eds) *Bases para la Conservación y el Manejo de la Costa Uruguaya* Vida Silvestre, Montevideo, 2006. This large book on Uruguay's coastal biology costs less than US$20, owing to funding by the US Fish and Wildlife Service; it consists of 63 academic papers by local scientists, covering not just the biology of the coastal zone but also geology, paleontology and archaeology.

Muñoz, J, Ross, P, and Cracco, P *Flora Indígena del Uruguay – Arboles y Arbustos Ornamentales* Editorial Hemisferio Sur SRL, Montevideo, 1994. A Spanish-language guide to Uruguay's native trees and shrubs.

Narosky, Tito and Yzurieta, Dario *Birds of Argentina and Uruguay: A Field Guide* Vasquez
Mazzini Editores. Buenos Aires, 15th edn 2003. The classic field guide to Uruguay's
birds, available through www.wildlifebooks.com in the UK.

Rocha, Gabriel *Aves del Uruguay: El País de los pájaros pintados* Ediciones de la Banda
Oriental, Montevideo, 2004. In three volumes, this is a beautifully presented guide (in
Spanish) to Uruguay's birds; the third volume includes information on ecotourism and
birdwatching locales.

Wheatley, Nigel *Where to Watch Birds in South America* Princeton UP, 1995.

Health

Wilson-Howarth, Dr Jane, and Ellis, Dr Matthew *Your Child Abroad: A Travel Health
Guide* Bradt Travel Guides, 2005.

Wilson-Howarth, Dr Jane *The Essential Guide to Travel Health* Cadogan, 2009.

WEBSITES

Communications
www.antel.com.uy
www.correo.com.uy

Conservation and NGOs
www.anong.org.uy
www.avesuruguay.org.uy
www.karumbe.org
www.retosalsur.org
http://vidasilvestre.org.uy

Gay issues
http://uruguaydiverso.blogspot.com

Health
www.fitfortravel.scot.nhs.uk
www.istm.org
www.nathnac.org/ds/c_pages/country_
page_uy.htm
wwwnc.cdc.gov/travel
www.netdoctor.co.uk/travel

Horse riding and estancias
www.aru.com.uy
www.turismoruraluy.com

Immigration
www.dnm.minterior.gub.uy

Sport
www.auf.org.uy
www.aug.com.uy
www.oceanmind.net
www.olasyvientos.com
www.paipo.com.uy
www.uru.org.uy
www.wannasurf.com/spot/South_America/
Uruguay/

Tourism
www.turismo.gub.uy
www.uruguaynatural.com

Travel
www.afe.com.uy
www.buquebus.com
www.flybqb.com.uy
www.montevideo.gub.uy/aplicacion/como-ir
www.trescruces.com.uy

Wine
www.bodegasdeluruguay.com
www.thewine-traveler.com
www.uruguaywinetours.com

Index

Entries in **bold** indicate main entries; those in *italics* indicate maps

accommodation 66–7
Aceguá 367, 368
Admiral Graf Spee, the **80–1**, 121, 131, 142
Agraciada, Playa de la 16, 296
agriculture 4, 14–15, 24
Aguas Blancas 180
Aguas Corrientes 148
Aguas Dulces 257–8
Almirón, Termas de 322
Anchorena, Parque Nacional 288
Ánimas, Cerro de las, & Sierra de las **199**, 240
Aparicio, Timoteo 18
Arapey, Termas de 332
architecture 34–6
Arden Quin, Carmelo 33–4
Arequita, Cerro 7, 41, **186–7**
art 32–4
Artigas, department 333–41
Artigas, José Gervasio 15, **16–17**, 124, 125, 171, 174, 175, 225, 289, 296, 298, 323, 350, 359
Artigas, town 337–41, *338*
Astori, Danilo 21, 22
at a glance 2
Atchugarry, Pablo 34, 232–3
Atlántida 177–80, *178*

background Information 3–43
Bañados del Este Biosphere Reserve 10, 244–5
Barra de Valizas 258–60
Barra del Chuy 273
Barradas, Rafael 32
Batlle Berres, Luis 19
Batlle y Ordóñez, José 19
Batlle, Jorge 20
Bella Unión 333–7
Belloni, José **34**, 126, 128, 129, 131, 184, 225, 365
Belloni, Stelio **34**, 169, 184, 185
Benedetti, Mario 31, 352
Berro, Bernardo 18
Biarritz 176
  see also Villa Biarritz, Montevideo

birds 10–12, 244, 371
Blancos 18–19, 20, 367
Blanes, Juan Manuel 32, 129, 135, 140, 141, 174, 236, 296, 365
Blanes Viale, Pedro 32, 129, 140, 184, 225, 302, 365
Boca del Cufré 171
books 378–81
bookshops 116–17
Bordaberry, Juan María 20
Bordaberry, Pedro 22
Borges, Jorge Luis **31**, 79, 96, 107, 201, 305, 380
Botnia pulp mill 23, 305, **308–9**, 310, 312
Brum, Baltasar 19, 269
budgeting 62
buses from Montevideo 86–8
buying a property 75–6

Caballos de Luz 247
Cabo Polonio 260–3
Cabot *see* Gaboto
Cabrera, Germán 34
cachilas and Cherys 63
candombé 28–9, 110–11, 131
Canelones department: east 164, 176–80
Canelones department: west 143–64
Canelones, town 143–6, *146*
car rental 64, 90
Carmelo 289–94, *291*
Carmelo, around 294–6
Carnaval (carnival) 110–11, 134, 299, 339–40
casinos 24, 112, 212
Castillo Mauá 303
Castillos 256–7
Castillos, Laguna de 7, 244, 257, 263
Cebollatí 366
Cerro Catedral 3, 240–1
Cerro Largo, department 367–73
Cerro Verde 269
Cerros de San Juan 289
cetaceans 10, 252
Chamangá 362
charities *see* travelling positively
Charrúa, the 13, 18, 347, 356, 358

Chuy 270–3
cinema 36–7
climate 5, 83
climate change 5, 13
Colonia (del Sacramento, town) 13, 14,
    276–89, *278, 286*
    activities 283
    entertainment 283
    excursions 288–9
    getting around 279
    getting there and away 277–9
    history 276–7
    nightlife 283
    other practicalities 284
    Real de San Carlos 288
    shopping 283
    tourist information 279–80
    what to see and do 284–8
    where to eat 281–3
    where to stay 280–1
Colonia, department 275–96
Colonia Suiza 69, 275
Colonia Valdense 275–6
Colorados 18, 20, 22
communications 73–4
Conchillas 289
conservation 6, 11, **12**, 76
crafts 72, 115
crime 59, 119–20
cruises 24, 48, 85, 202
Cuchilla Grande 3, 170, 366
cultural and business etiquette 75
culture 26–43
Cúneo, José **32–3**, 169, 328
cycling *see* getting around

Darwin, Charles 7, 8, 14, 22, 42, 81, 180, 182,
    199, 221, 277, 285, 294, 295, 304, 378–9,
    380
Daymán, Termas de 330–1
Dieste, Eladio 35, 124, 133, 151, 179, 324,
    328, 330, 357,
disabled travellers 60
Dolores 296–8
Drexler, Jorge 27–8
drinks 70–1
Durazno, department 354–9
Durazno, town 18, 29, 35, 354– 9, *355*

Eastern Uruguay 189–273, *190–1*
eating and drinking 67–71
Ecilda Paullier 171, 275
economy 23–5
El Anglo 310–11
El Palmar 304
embassies and consulates, Uruguayan 49–51
embassies in Montevideo 48–9
estancia tourism 43, 45, 47, 48, 60, 170, 199,
    241, 257, 276, 303–4, 315–16, 352, 353

estancias in Florida department 170
Esteros de Farrapos *see* Parque Nacional
    Esteros de Farrapos y Islas del Río
    Uruguay

Fabini, Eduardo 27, 184
fauna 7–12
festivals 29, 71–2
Figari, Pedro 32, 136
fish 9
flora 5–7
Flores, department 359–62
Flores, Venancio 18, 36
Florida, department 166–70, *167*
Florida, town 166–70, *168*
Fonseca, Gonzalo 31, 33
Fonseca, Isabel **31–2**, 224, 234
football *see* soccer
forestry 5
Fray Bentos 19, 31, **304–11**, *307*, 311
Frente Amplio 20, 22
further information 378–81

Gaboto, Sebastían 13, 221, 288
Galeano, Eduardo 31, 106
Gardel, Carlos 28, 106, 107, 133, 147, 325,
    350, 351–2
Garibaldi, Giuseppe 136, 277, 303, 316
Garzón *see* Pueblo Garzón
Garzón, Colinas de 243
gauchos **42–3**, 72, 138, 175, 184, 333, 349,
    351, 362, 380
gay and lesbian travellers 60
geography 3–4
geology 3–4
getting around 63–6
    by bicycle 65–6
    by bus 65
    by car 63–4
    by train 64, 88
getting there and away 51–6
    by air 51–2
    by bus 54–6
    by ferry 52–4
golf **41–2**, 118, 214, 283, 292, 310
government and politics 22–3
Graf Spee see *Admiral Graf Spee*
Grito de Asencio 15, 296
Guaraní Aquifer 4, 330
Guardia del Monte, *estancia* 257
Guaviyú, Termas de 323
Guerra Grande 18
Guichón 322
Gurvich, José 33, 136

health 56–9
Hernández, Felisberto 30
Herrera y Obes, Julio 30, 136
Herrera y Reissig, Julio 30, 197

Hidalgo, Bartolomé 29
highlights 45
hiking 41
Hilo de la Vida, Valle del 185
history 12–22
horseracing 114
horseriding & horseback trips 42–3, 47, 214,
  238, 247, 260, 262
  see also estancia tourism
hot springs see thermal resorts
hygiene, food and water 57

Ibarbourou, Juana de 30, 62, 367, 370
Iemanjá 26
Iguazú Falls 55
Instrucciones del Año XIII 15
Interior, The 333–73, 334–5
internet 74

José Ignacio 41, 233–8, 235

Karumbé 76, 176, 269–70
Kiyú 171

La Barra 40, 200, 226–32, 227
La Charqueada 362, 364, 366
La Coronilla 269–70
La Floresta 179–80
La Paloma 41, 248–53, 250
La Paz, estancia 315–16
La Pedrera 253–6, 254
La Sirena, estancia 303–4

Lacalle, Luis Alberto 20, 22
Lago Merín 366, 372–3
Laguna Merín 372
language 26, 375–7
Larrañaga, Dámaso Antonio 62, 123, 130
Larrañaga, Jorge 22
Las Cañas 312
Las Cañadas, estancia 353
Las Llamadas 29, 110–11
Las Piedras 15, 143
Lavalleja, department 180–8, 181
Lavalleja, Juan Antonio 16–18, 92, 124, 184,
  296, 358
literature 29–32, 379–80
Lubkov, Vasili 314, 315
Lunarejo 341–2
Lussich, Antonio 6, 201, 218

M'Bopicuá 313
Mahoma, Sierras de 175–6
Maldonado, department 6, 12, 13, 66,
  189–242
Maldonado, town 14, 15, 221–6, 222
Mallmann, Francis 233, 240, 242
mammals 7–8
Manantiales 226–32

maps 61
  list of v
mata Atlántica 6, 341, 366, 371
maté 58, 70, 71, 245
Mauá, Baron 303
media 74
Melo 14, 36, 367–71, 368
Mercedes 299–303, 301
Mercosur 20, 21, 23, 64, 83
Meseta de Artigas, Parque Histórico 323
milonga 28–9
Minas 14, 180–5, 183
Minas de Corrales 346
money and budgeting 61–2, 137
Monte de Ombúes 263
Montevideo 79–142, 78 [overview], 94–5
  [centre], 109 [Buceo], 122 [Ciudad Vieja
  & Centro]
  Al Pie de la Muralla 124
  Avenida 18 de Julio 91, 126
  banks 118–19
  Barrio Sur 25, 29, 91, 103, 107–8, 110, 119,
    131–2
  bars 106–8
  bookshops 116–17
  Cabildo 124, 137
  car rental 90
  Carrasco (suburb) 91, 93, 96, 97, 98, 101,
    112, 133–4
  casinos 112
  cathedral 120, 123
  Centro 125–7
  cinemas 114
  city tour 121–34
  Ciudad Vieja 121–5
  communications 119
  Cordón 127–8
  crime, safety and police 119–20
  cultural centres 113
  Eastern Suburbs 131–4
  El Cerro 119, 131
  embassies 48–9
  entertainment 108–15
  festivals 114–15
  gay Montevideo 112
  getting around 88–91
  getting there and away 83–8
  health 120
  history 79–83
  markets 115, 116
  money and exchange 118–19
  museums 134–42
  music 108–14
  nightlife 108–14
  North to the Prado 128–31
  orientation 91–2
  other practicalities 118–20
  Pocitos 91, 96, 97, 99–100, 103, 108,
    132–3